COMPUTER SCIENCE

C S FRENCH, BSc.(Hons), M.Sc., Grad.Cert.Ed.,
AFIMA, FBCS, C.Eng.

*Carl French currently works in the financial sector of the
computer industry where, in recent years, he has been
involved in the design and implementation of a number of
large database systems. He was previously employed as a
Principal Lecturer in Computer Science at The Hatfield
Polytechnic following several years' experience of
teaching on a wide variety of computer courses.*

4th Edition

DP PUBLICATIONS LTD
Aldine Place
142/144 Uxbridge Road
Shepherds Bush Green
London W12 8AW

1992

Acknowledgements

I wish to thank the following:

Messrs EC Oliver and RJ Chapman for permission to use material from their book *Data Processing*.

Mr JA Moffat, Mr IP Page, Mr DW Bale and Mr P Harrison, all of whom read and checked earlier editions at various times and who made numerous helpful comments and suggestions.

Mr P Ashurst and Mr B Dickson who helped with the corrections for the reprint of the 3rd Edition and who gave further helpful comments and suggestions at the time when the 4th Edition was being planned.

Apple Computers UK Ltd, CalComp Ltd, Compaq Computer Ltd, IBM UK Ltd, Philips, Rediffusion Computers Ltd, Sun Microsystems Ltd and Toshiba for permission to reproduce photographs of their products. (Separate acknowledgements are given with each of the photographs.)

Mr J Beasley for permission to reproduce sample outputs from the Spider and Bezlib graphics package.

The Associated Examining Board (AEB), The British Computer Society (BCS), The University of Cambridge Local Examination Syndicate (Cambridge), The Joint Metriculation Board (JMB), The University of London Entrance and School Examination Council (London), The University of Oxford Delegacy of Local Examination (OLE) and The Welsh Joint Education Committee (Welsh) for permission to reproduce past examination questions.

A CIP catalogue record for this book is available from the British Library

First Edition 1980
Second Edition 1984
Third Edition 1989
Fourth Edition 1992
Reprinted 1993

ISBN 1 873981 19 8
Copyright CS French © 1992

Printed in the UK by
The Guernsey Press Co Ltd,
Guernsey, Channel Islands

Preface

AIMS OF THE MANUAL

1. The primary aim of this manual is to provide a simplified approach to the understanding of Computer Science, which is the study of computers and how they are used. The manual assumes a minimum of prior knowledge which enables the early chapters in the text to be used to introduce or reappraise basic methods and ideas according to the reader's needs.

2. The text is intended to suit a number of courses including those leading to these examinations:

    a. GCE 'A' Level Computer Science. Many questions set within the text are taken from examination papers set by the various boards.

    b. BCS Part 1. The manual should serve as a general introductory text. Some questions set within the text are taken from past examination papers.

    c. First year University and Polytechnic examinations in Computer Science.

    d. Computer Options in BTEC, Higher National Courses.

    e. City and Guilds examination in computing and information processing.

    f. IDPM parts I and II.

    g. BTEC National and Higher National awards in Computer Studies.

APPROACH

3. The manual has been designed for use in independent study or as a text to be used in conjunction with tuition at school, college, etc. The manual can be used to good effect both as a course text and for revision. It is recommended that readers have their own copies.

ORGANISATION OF CHAPTERS WITHIN PARTS

4. The text is organised into Parts. Each Part either deals with a particular area of Computer Science or with an aspect of computer applications. Each Part starts with a summary of what the chapters within it contain. The Part introduction also gives examination specific study guidance to the reader based upon the contents of current syllabuses and the recent trends in examinations.

END OF CHAPTER

5. At the end of chapters is found:

    a. Summary of chapter.

    b. Points to note. These are used for purposes of emphasis or clarification.

    c. Questions. (See below)

    d. Glossary Checklist. This provides a list of key terms covered in the chapter. The reader is urged to use each list as a final check that he or she could explain the terms in an examination. These checklists can also be used as a revision aid.

QUESTIONS

6. In order to satisfy a variety of uses; as an instructional manual, course text book, revision text, etc., the following types of questions have been included:

    a. Student self-test questions at the end of each chapter. These questions enable the reader to test his or her understanding of the material covered. The reader is advised to attempt all these questions. Answers are provided in appendix 1.

    b. Questions without answers at the end of most chapters. These are mostly questions appropriate for use as homework exercises but also include questions that do not require answers. Teachers and Lecturers who adopt the book as a course text may obtain a copy of answers to these questions free of charge if they send a written request to the publishers using school or college headed stationery.

    c. Revision test questions at the end of the text. Answers are given in appendix 2.

APPENDICES

7. Use has been made of appendices and the reader should note carefully the purpose of each.

    a. Appendix 1 contains answers to the Student self-test questions set at the end of each chapter and contains answers to revision test questions too.

b. Appendix 2 contains answers to revision test questions.

c. Appendix 3 contains details that have been excluded from the text in the interests of clarity.

d. Appendix 4 contains notes on projects, course work and other study. The reader may benefit from reading this appendix before attempting the first project or piece of course work.

HOW TO USE THE MANUAL

8. Students are advised to read the manual chapter by chapter since subsequent work often builds on topics covered earlier.

9. The layout of the chapters has been standardised so as to present information in a simple form that is easy to assimilate. However, in some chapters the emphasis is on principles or applications while other chapters emphasise methods and procedures. These differences reflect the fact that students will be expected to answer examination questions that require both written answers and problem solving. The study of methods and procedures should be combined with practical course work whenever possible.

10. Students are advised to attempt questions as they come to them, and to check their answers in the appendix before reading further.

11. A minimum of prior mathematical knowledge is assumed.

NOTATION AND TERMINOLOGY

12. This manual aims to cover all terminology covered by the syllabuses listed earlier and their examinations. The use of terminology is consistent with the more widely accepted definitions and, in particular, it is consistent with the booklet containing "A glossary of computer terms" published by the BCS. Where other equivalent terms are also in common use in examinations they are drawn to the reader's attention. Notation is defined as it is introduced. As an extra study aid to the reader, when important terms are introduced or explained they are printed in bold. The reader is advised to learn such terms before leaving the chapter. A glossary checklist at the end of each chapter assists in this.

OTHER READING

13. The reader should find that this text provides the appropriate coverage of the reading material needed for those examinations for which the text is intended as a preparation. However, the reader might like to know that much of the more elementary material in this text is covered in more detail in *Computer Studies* by C.S. French. Greater detail of some aspects of data processing is provided in Oliver & Chapman's *Data Processing and Information Technology* (latest edition by C.S. French). The text has some material in common with *Computer Science*. These texts are published by DP Publications Ltd.

SUGGESTIONS AND CRITICISM

14. The author would welcome any suggestions or criticism from students or lecturers and would like to take this opportunity to thank all those who have written with their comments and suggestions in the past.

Carl French.

Note to the 4th Edition

1. This edition contains changes in content and layout which are aimed not just at covering the material on the latest syllabuses but at assisting the reader's study for the latest examinations.

2. The reader should note that syllabuses in Computer Science are increasingly written in terms which enable examination of contemporary topics not explicitly mentioned on the syllabus. The notes in the Part introductions address this matter by giving study hints which reflect trends in recent examinations.

3. As mentioned earlier, further study assistance has been added to this edition in terms of a more comprehensive and systematic use of bold type to emphasise important terminology best committed to memory. This is reinforced by the glossary checklist given at the very end of each chapter which is also intended to serve as a revision aid.

4. As for previous editions, the material has been extensively revised for this edition in order to give readers a full and up-to-date account of Computer Science and to reflect the content of the current examination syllabuses and trends in examination questions. New material has been included and obsolete material removed. Revisions are supported by numerous new illustrations.

5. The contents have been re-organised for this edition. Probably the most significant change is the introduction of a series of Parts targeted at contemporary computer applications and applications packages. This reflects a significant shift in emphasis in examinations over recent years. Additionally, the aim was both to present the subject from a modern viewpoint and to organise the subject matter in a way that would best help readers with their examinations and course work.

6. In addition to giving more emphasis to applications, in recent years the examination boards have, in general, continued to place less emphasis on numerical methods and the fine details of how the hardware works and have been placing more emphasis on the disciplines associated with developing and using computer systems. This trend is reflected in this edition of *Computer Science*. Topics given greater emphasis in this edition include: Graphical User Interfaces (GUIs), development methodologies, desktop computers, applications packages and databases.

7. The page format and typography has been improved so as to aid clarity and make the book less bulky.

8. Various minor changes have also been made to material where comments from readers had shown that clarifications were needed.

Carl French 1992

Contents

FOUNDATION TOPICS

1. The first four chapters contain introductory material, which will be developed in later chapters. Readers with prior knowledge are advised to read these chapters as a revision exercise.
2. Readers are also advised to read all of these chapters, irrespective of the examination course being studied, because of the general introductory nature of the material.

1: Introduction to Computers and Computer Science

INTRODUCTION

1.1   This chapter is primarily aimed at the reader who is new to Computer Science and who needs to know what the subject is about. The reader who has previously studied the subject is nevertheless advised to read the chapter to ensure that nothing to be referred to in later chapters has been missed.

As with most technical subjects, Computer Science has its own terminology. To ensure that the reader becomes familiar with the meaning of this "jargon", and feels confident in using it, great care is taken in this text to define terms as they are introduced. This chapter lays the foundations by introducing some basic terminology, which is then used to give an overview of what a computer is and the elements from which computers are made.

The reader is strongly urged to establish the good habit of learning the terminology as it is introduced, starting with this chapter. When important terms are introduced they are almost invariably printed in bold type. This can act as a prompt for the reader to learn them there and then. There is, of course, a lot more to studying Computer Science than just learning what the technical words mean, otherwise the subject would not be worthy of study at this level, but when it comes to passing examinations or being successful in other forms of assessment, the student who has not got the vocabulary cannot communicate and will not pass!

From the subject matter introduced in this chapter the reader may assume that Computer Science is concerned with answering questions about what computers are, how they work and how they are used. It is, but there is more to Computer Science than that. Computers are indeed some of the most interesting and complex items of technology in everyday use, but they are only around in such numbers because they are useful tools. Often, however, they are not as useful as they might be, or, worse still, they are more trouble than they are worth. When that happens it is usually largely the fault of those who designed and built the computer systems. Why?

A common reason is that those involved did not properly understand how to find out what was really required and then did not know how to build a computer system that met the requirement. Gaining the necessary understanding to be able to successfully carry out such tasks is a goal of Computer Science. It therefore means that **Computer Science is concerned with the application of scientific principles to the design, construction and maintenance of systems based upon the use of computers.**

Now we must turn our attention to the matter of mastering some basic ideas and terms.

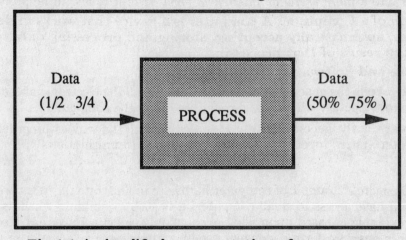

Data (1/2 3/4) → PROCESS → Data (50% 75%)

Fig 1.1 A simplified representation of a computer.

BASIC IDEAS AND TERMS

1.2   **Data.** "Data" is the name given to basic *facts*, eg, the number of items sold by a business, the name of a customer, a line of text, or the numerical values used in mathematical formulae. It has become standard practice to treat the word "data" as singular rather than plural.

1.3 **Computer.** A computer is a device that accepts data in one form and *processes* it to produce data in another form (see Fig 1.1). A more precise definition follows shortly. For now it is also worth noting that the data is normally held within the computer as it is being processed, and is often held much longer than that. Also, the nature of the processing may change according to the data entered. The forms in which data is accepted or produced by the computer vary enormously from simple words or numbers to signals sent from or received by other items of technology. So, when the computer *processes* data it actually performs a number of separate functions as follows.

a. Input. The computer accepts data from outside for processing within.

b. Storage. The computer holds data internally before, during and after processing.

c. Processing. The computer performs operations on the data it holds within.

d. Output. The computer produces data from within for external use.

This is summarised in Fig 1.2. A more detailed description of these functions is given later in this chapter.

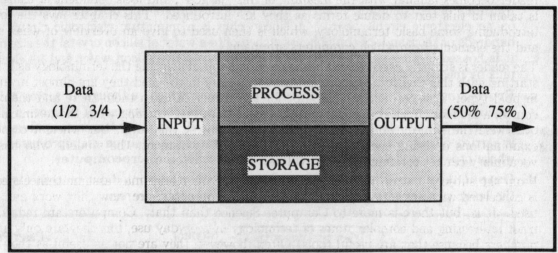

Fig 1.2 The basic functions of a computer.

1.4 **Program.** A program is a *set of instructions* that is written in the language of the computer. A program is used to make the computer perform a specific task, such as calculating interest to be paid to savings-account holders or producing a payroll. (Note the spelling **program** not **programme**.) The computer is only able to obey a program's instructions if the program has first been stored within the computer. This implies that the computer must be able to input and store programs in addition to data. So, the computer works under the *control* of stored programs.

1.5 **Information.** A distinction is sometimes made between *data* and *information*. When data is converted into a *more useful or intelligible form* then it is said to be processed into information.

1.6 **Definition of a Computer.** A computer is a device that works under the control of stored programs, automatically accepting, storing and processing data to produce information that is the result of that processing.

1.7 **Hardware and Software.**

a. Hardware is the general term used to describe *all* the electronic and mechanical elements of the computer, together with those devices used with the computer.

b. Software is the general term used to describe *all* the various programs that may be used on a computer system together with their associated documentation.

HARDWARE

1.8 Now for a concrete example of computer hardware to illustrate the ideas presented so far. Since most readers will have access to small computers it is such a computer which is used for the example. In fact, the example is based upon what is commonly called a **Personal Computer (PC)**, so called because it is designed for independent use by an individual at home or in the office.

1.9 Fig 1.3 illustrates the features of a typical PC. These features can be related to the functions of a computer listed earlier. A brief description now follows but *please : note that this is only an introduction with many points of detail deliberately being left till later.*

a. Input is performed primarily by typing data on the keyboard which is very similar to a typewriter keyboard. The mouse can also be used for input but the details will be given later.

b. **Storage** is performed by devices within the computer's cabinet so it is less easy to see what is going on. However, there are several external clues as to the features of this particular PC. For instance, there is a slot in the front of the cabinet into which a $3\frac{1}{2}$″**floppy disk** can be inserted. A floppy disk comprises a flexible circular disc coated in a magnetic material and held in a thin casing. When the floppy disk is inserted into the **disk drive** via the slot in the computer's cabinet it is rotated on a turntable. Then, in a way very similar to that in which the **heads** in an audio cassette recorder record or play back sound on the tape, **read-write heads** inside the disk drive **write** or **read** data.

Lights on the front of the computer cabinet show that it contains a disk drive for another kind of disk called a **hard disk** because it is rigid , unlike a floppy disk. This hard disk is not removable like the floppy disk but works on the same basic principles as the floppy disk. However, a typical hard disk is able to store much more data than a floppy disk of the same size because of technical differences which will be covered in later chapters.

Also out of view within the computer's cabinet is another form of storage called the **main memory** of the computer. Main memory takes the form of microelectronic **silicon chips** housed on an electronic circuit board. A silicon chip is a miniature electronic circuit equivalent to hundreds or thousands of components etched onto a wafer of silicon crystal the size of a fingernail. It is housed in a plastic case just big enough to hold the silicon wafer and its electrical contact pins by means of which it is plugged into the circuit board.

c. **Processing** is carried out my a **microprocessor** which, although it serves a very different function, is very similar in construction to main memory because it is another kind of silicon chip. It is also situated on an electronic circuit board. On many larger computers the processing is carried out by a number of separate chips, instead of a single microprocessor. A computer whose processing is done by a microprocessor is called a **microcomputer**.

d. **Output** takes two alternative forms. Data can either be printed out onto sheets of paper using the **laser printer** or it can be displayed on the **monitor's** screen.

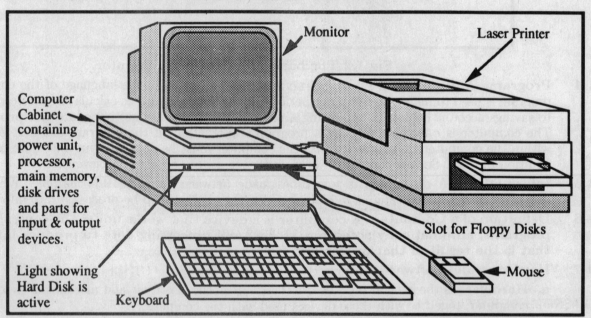

Fig 1.3 An example of a Personal Computer with Laser Printer.

COMPUTER TYPES

1.10   The PC just described is just one of many types of computer. There are several methods of classifying computers too. The main distinction between digital and analog devices is given next, followed by a classification by purpose and use. A further classification by age of technology is given later in the chapter.

BASIC TYPES

1.11   **Digital, Analog and Hybrid.**

a. **Digital** computers are so called because they process data that is represented in the form of discrete values (eg 0, 1, 2, 3 ...) by operating on it in steps. Discrete values occur at each step in the operation. Counting on one's fingers is probably the simplest *digital operation* we all know.

Digital watches have special, tiny, digital computers within them.

b. **Analog** computers are akin to measuring instruments such as thermometers and voltmeters with pointers on circular dials. They process data in the form of electrical voltages, which are variable like the variable positions of a pointer on a dial. The output from analog computers is often in the form of smooth graphs from which information can be read.

c. **Hybrid** computers, as their name suggests, are computers that have the combined feature of digital and analog computers.

Note. This book is mainly concerned with digital computers, which are by far the most widely used.

PURPOSE

1.12 Special purpose and general purpose.

a. **Special purpose computers**, as their name suggests, are designed for a particular job only; to solve problems of a restricted nature. Examples are computers designed for use in digital watches, in petrol pumps or in weapons guidance systems.

b. **General purpose computers** are designed to solve a wide variety of problems. Within the limitations imposed by their particular design capabilities, they can be adapted to perform particular tasks or solve problems by means of specially written programs. This book is mainly concerned with general purpose digital computers.

Note. This distinction is not as sharp as it first appears because a general purpose computer can temporarily become special purpose through adaptation.

The Apple Macintosh computer model IIci.
An advanced type of personal computer.
Picture courtesy of Apple Computer UK Ltd.

CLASSIFICATION BY USE

1.13 It is possible to provide a very long list under this heading. Here, just a few varied examples are given so as to give an impression of the variety.

a. A **Word Processor** is a *special purpose* computer used in the production of office documents, letters, contracts, etc.
   Note. A general purpose computer can run a word processing program and hence temporarily become special purpose.

b. A **Home Computer** is a low-cost microcomputer of limited capability designed for domestic use with programs that typically are used for such things as computer games or controlling family finances.

c. A **Personal Computer (PC)**, as mentioned earlier, is a microcomputer designed for independent use by an individual at work or in the home mainly for business purposes. Some PCs are portable. Many can be connected to minicomputers and mainframe computers so that the PC user can also gain access to the facilities offered by the larger machine (see Fig. 1.3).

    d. A Desktop Computer is any computer designed for use on a desk in an office environment. Therefore, home computers and PCs are types of Desktop computer.

    e. A Workstation is another kind of desktop computer. Although larger more powerful PCs are sometimes called workstations the term is normally used to imply the presence of advanced features not provided by all PCs. These include inbuilt capabilities for their interconnection and operation in conjunction with other computers, and for them to process pictorial data as well as that presented in the form of text.

    f. A Lap-top computer is a PC sufficiently small and light for its user comfortably to use it on his or her lap. A typical lap-top computer operates on mains electricity or by rechargeable batteries and is small enough to fit inside a brief case, still leaving room for other items. Lap-tops normally have in-built disk drives and flat screens. The latter are commonly Liquid Crystal Displays (LCDs).

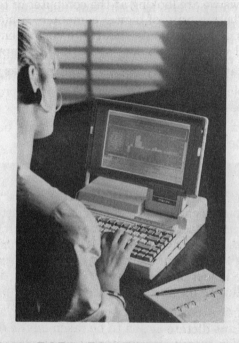

The Toshiba "T1600 PORTABLE DESKTOP 286" lap-top computer.
Photograph supplied by courtesy of Toshiba.

    g. An Embedded Computer is one that is within some other device or system but is not accessed directly. For example, there are embedded computers operating within petrol pumps, watches, cameras, video recorders and many types of domestic and industrial equipment.

SOFTWARE

1.14 In the preceding paragraphs the emphasis was on basic differences in hardware. We will now look at the general classification of the software applicable to all machines, before we go on to consider the elements of the computer.

1.15 Types of Software. The two main classes are as follows.

    a. Applications software. This is software that is designed to be put to specific practical use. This broad classification may be further sub-divided into:

        i. Specialist applications software, that is, programs, with associated documentation, designed specifically to carry out particular tasks, for example, solving sets of mathematical equations or controlling a company's stock of goods.

        ii. Applications packages, that is, suites of programs, with associated documentation, used for a particular type of problem. Many packages are designed in such a way that they can be used for a variety of similar problems. For example, payroll packages are sometimes produced in forms that enable them to be set up and used by different companies each having slightly different ways in which they need to produce their payroll. The most abundant selection of packages is available on personal computers, with the more popular packages selling in tens of thousands of copies or even hundreds of thousands of copies. For example, there are numerous word-processor packages that can enable PCs to be used as word processors (see 1.13a).

b. Systems software. These are programs, with associated documentation, that control the way the computer operates or provide facilities that extend the general capabilities of the system. Within the set of systems software for a given computer there is usually a program, or suite of programs, called the **operating system**. The operating system controls the performance of the computer by doing a variety of jobs to ensure the proper, orderly and efficient use of hardware by applications programs. Most applications programs can only work when used in conjunction with the operating system. Other systems software may extend the capabilities of the operating system further, for example, by providing programs that can monitor how efficiently the hardware is being utilised by the software.

BASIC ELEMENTS (FUNCTIONS) OF A COMPUTER

1.16 Now we resume the examination of the hardware functions of the computer introduced earlier in the chapter. In what follows we are looking at the computer in terms of a set of basic elements each with a specific function. The majority of digital computers conform to this view even though they may differ greatly in terms of the particular hardware components used to provide these functions. It is therefore a very useful way for us to deal with what a computer is in general terms.

1.17 The basic elements that make up a computer system are as follows:

a. Input.

b. Storage.

c. Control.

d. Processing.

e. Output.

1.18 A brief description of each element.

a. **Input.** Most computers cannot accept data in forms customary to human communication such as speech or hand-written documents. It is necessary, therefore, to present data to the computer in a way that provides easy conversion into its own electronic pulse-based forms. This is commonly achieved by typing the data into keyboard devices that convert it into **machine-sensible** forms. A keyboard device is just one of many kinds of **input device**. In some cases machine-readable documents or media are produced as part of the input process. Data finally enters **Storage**.

b. **Storage.** Data and instructions enter **main storage**, and are held until needed to be worked on. The **instructions** dictate action to be taken on the **data**. Results of action will be held until they are required for output. Main storage is supplemented by less costly **auxiliary storage**, also called **backing storage**, (eg, hard disks (1.9b) for mass storage purposes. Backing storage serves an important role in holding **"maintained data"**, ie data held by the computer so that it can provide information to the user when required to do so.

c. **Control.** Each computer has a **control unit** that fetches instructions from main storage, *interprets* them, and issues the necessary *signals* to the components making up the system. It directs all **hardware** operations necessary in obeying instructions.

d. **Processing.** Instructions are obeyed and the necessary arithmetic operations, etc, are carried out on the data. The part that does this is called the **Arithmetic-Logical Unit (ALU)**. In addition to arithmetic it also performs so-called "logical" operations. These operations take place at incredibly high speeds, eg, 10 million numbers may be totalled in one second.

e. **Output.** Results are taken from main storage and fed to an **output device**. This may be a printer, in which case the information is automatically converted to a *printed form* called **hard copy**, or alternatively data may be displayed on a monitor screen similar to that used in a television set.

1.19 The elements are shown in Fig. 1.4, which shows what is often referred to as "the Logical Structure" of the computer. Notice particularly the following points:

a. Data normally flows from input devices or backing storage into *main storage* and from main storage to output devices or backing storage.

b. The processor performs operations on data from main storage and returns the results of processing to main storage.

c. In some cases, which will be discussed in later chapters, data flows directly between the processor and input or output devices rather than as described in (a).

d. The Arithmetic-Logical Unit (ALU) and control unit *combine* to form the **processor**. (It needs to be stressed that when referring to "units" here we are only talking of distinct functions not

7

separate hardware components.) The processor is sometimes also called the **central processor (CP)** or **central processing unit (CPU).** However, the term CPU is also sometimes taken to mean not only the ALU and control unit but main storage too. To avoid possible confusion the term CPU is not used in this text.

e. There are two types of flow shown in Fig 1.4. Some lines carry data or instructions but other lines carry commands or signals.

f. Data held on backing storage may be input to main memory during processing, used and brought up to date using newly input data, and then returned to backing storage.

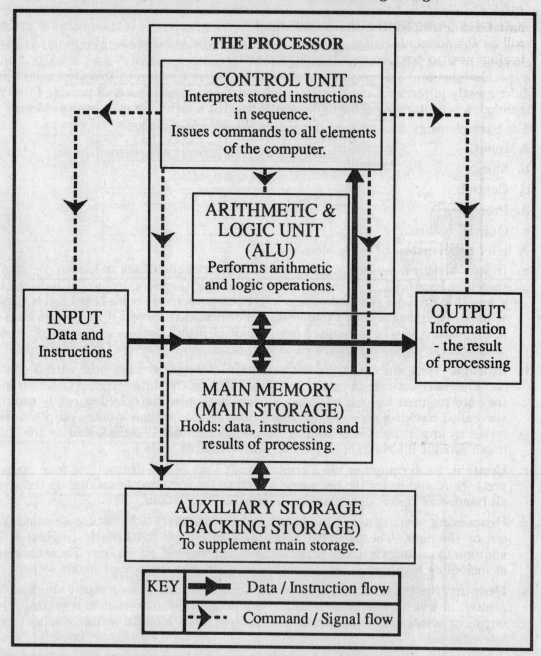

Fig 1.4 The elements of a Computer System showing its "Logical Structure"

COMPUTER GENERATIONS

1.20 The first *electronic* computers were produced in the 1940s. Since then a series of radical breakthroughs in electronics has occurred. With each major breakthrough the computers based upon the older form of electronics have been replaced by a new "**generation**" of computers based upon the newer form of electronics. These "generations" are classified as follows:

a. **First Generation.** Early computers using electronic valves (*circa* 1940s). Examples were EDSAC, EDVAC, LEO and UNIVAC1.

b. **Second Generation.** More reliable computers, using transistors, that replaced the first generation (*circa* 1950s). Examples were LEO mark III, ATLAS and the IBM 7000 series.

c. **Third Generation.** More powerful, reliable and compact computers using simple integrated circuits (ICs) (*circa* 1960s and early 1970s). Examples were the ICL 1900 series and the IBM 360 series.

d. **Fourth Generation.** The computers in use today and which contain more sophisticated microelectronic devices such as complex integrated circuits which are classified as "Large Scale Integration" (**LSI**) or "Very Large Scale Integration" (**VLSI**).

e. **Fifth Generation.** There are many predictions that by early in the 21st century computers will have been developed that will be able to converse with people in a human-like manner and that will be able to mimic human senses, manual skills and intelligence. The term "Fifth Generation" is often used to describe such computer systems.

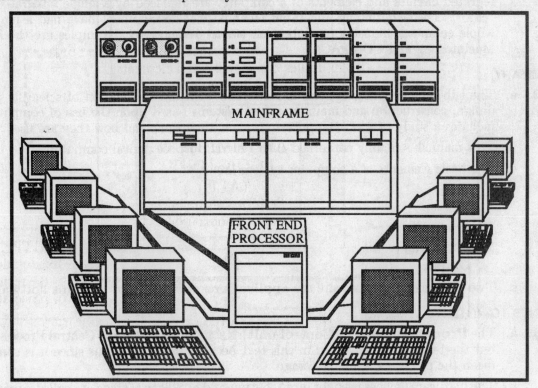

Fig 1.5 A Mainframe Computer

Fig 1.6 A Minicomputer Computer

FURTHER CLASSIFICATION

1.21 Mainframe, minicomputer and microcomputer.

The following classification is in order of decreasing power and size. However, there are no sharp dividing lines in that, for example, a model at the top of a manufacturer's range of minicomputers might well be more powerful than the model at the bottom of a range of mainframes.

a. **Mainframes.** Large general purpose computers with extensive processing, storage and input/output capabilities (see fig 1.5). The market for these computers is dominated by IBM.

b. **Minicomputers.** Physically smaller computers compared with mainframes (see fig 1.6). They are used for special purposes or smaller scale general purpose work. Examples are DEC's VAX RANGE.

c. **Microcomputers.** These represent a further step in miniaturisation in which the various integrated circuits and elements of a computer are replaced by a single integrated circuit called a "chip". Their continuing and rapid technological development have had a major effect on the whole computer industry over the past twenty years or so. Examples are the IBM PCs, Apple Macintoshes, and COMPACs.

SUMMARY

1.22 a. The subject Computer Science is concerned with the application of scientific principles to the design, construction and maintenance of systems based upon the use of computers. It therefore includes a study of what computers are, how they work and how they are used.

b. This manual is mainly concerned with general purpose digital computers.

c. The basic elements of a computer system are:

   i.   Input.
   ii. Storage.
   iii. Control.
   iv. Processing.
   v.   Output.

d. Two main classes of software are **applications software** and **systems software.**

POINTS TO NOTE

1.23 a. The **Processor (ALU + Control unit)** is sometimes called the Central Processing Unit (CPU), but the term CPU is avoided in this text because it is ambiguous since it is sometimes taken to mean the processor + main storage.

b. The hardware devices used for input, output and auxiliary storage are called **peripheral devices.**

c. Another name for a floppy disk is **diskette.**

d. A complete software product is not just programs but programs with their associated documentation.

e. The name "Computer Studies" is sometimes used instead of "Computer Science", but often the choice of name indicates a difference in emphasis. For example, compared with Computer Science, examinations in Computer Studies often place more emphasis on the use of computers by individuals, organisations and society in general, and less emphasis on the fundamentals of hardware and software. This book contains sufficient material to cover examination courses at this level with either title. Also, Computer Science is a different subject from Computer Engineering, although there is some overlap. The latter is a major specialist branch of Electronic Engineering. You do not have to understand any electronics to be a Computer Scientist. A Computer Engineer does need to know some Computer Science.

STUDENT SELF-TESTING QUESTIONS Note: Answers to all Student Self-Testing Questions set at the ends of chapters will be found in appendix 1.

1. Distinguish between the terms "data" and "information".
2. Identify the elements of a computer system and give a brief description of each.
3. Define what a computer is.
4. Identify the items labelled in Fig 1.7.

QUESTIONS WITHOUT ANSWERS

5. Find out whether the place where you are studying Computer Science has a mainframe, minicomputer or microcomputer and make a list of the hardware.

6. Computer Science is sometimes described as an "engineering discipline" rather than a "science" subject because of its concerns with building computer systems. You may like to discuss this idea with other students on your course because it may help you to form your own ideas as to what you want to get from studying the subject.

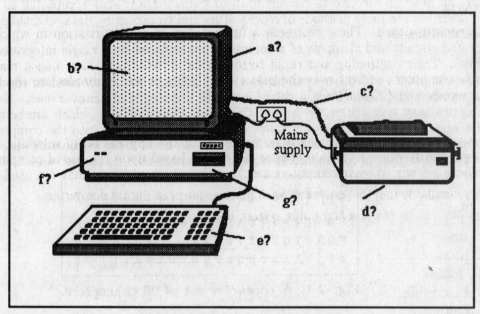

Fig 1.7 A Personal Computer

GLOSSARY CHECKLIST

2: Data Representation and Transmission

INTRODUCTION

2.1 Ideally we would like to communicate with computers in the spoken or written form of everyday language. In practice we have to convert data to forms more readily acceptable to a machine. This chapter describes the basic methods of representing and transmitting data, and takes commonly used methods as examples.

CHARACTERS

2.2 Sets of letters, digits and other symbols (see Fig. 2.1) are frequently used to represent data items such as names and prices. Such a set of symbols is called a **character set**. Keyboard devices, including ordinary typewriters, each have their own character sets, which are commonly engraved onto the keys. Keyboard devices are frequently used to input data into the computer. A character set, composed of 96 characters, is shown in Fig 2.1. In Fig 2.1 the keyboard's space bar and delete key are treated as part of the character set and are represented by "space" and "del".

```
s
p ! " # $ % & ' ( ) * + , - . / 0 1 2 3 4 5 6 7
a
c
e  8 9 : ; < = > ? @ A B C D E F G H I J K L M N O
   P Q R S T U V W X Y Z [ \ ] ^ _ ` a b c d e f g
   h i j k l m n o p q r s t u v w x y z { | } ~ d
                                                  e
                                                  l
```

Fig. 2.1. A character set of 96 characters.

CHARACTER TRANSMISSION

2.3 When a key on the keyboard of the computer input device is pressed the device produces an electrical signal that represents the key's character to the computer. The transmission passes through a cable from the device to the computer and the signal for each individual character is a series of electrical pulses called a **pulse train** (see Fig. 2.2).

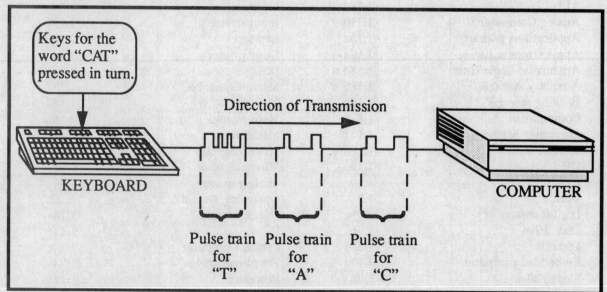

Fig. 2.2 A simplified view of data being transmitted from a keyboard device to a computer

CODE TRANSMISSION DETAILS

2.4 We will now look at pulse trains in more detail. As you read the next few paragraphs you may find it useful to refer to Fig. 2.3, which gives a detailed illustration of the pulse code for "T" shown in Fig 2.2.

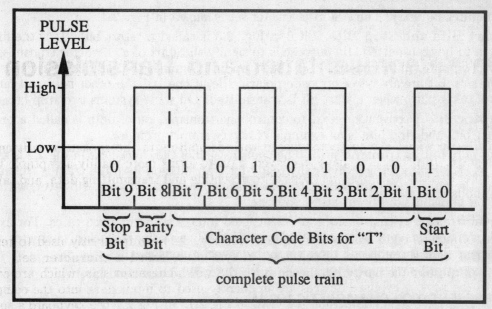

Fig. 2.3. Details of an asynchronous transmission of the ASCII character "T".

2.5 The complete pulse train in Fig. 2.3 comprises ten pulses in sequence that are each either at a high level or a low level. These two levels are represented by 1's and 0's respectively.

2.6 **BITs.** The system of representing pulse levels by the symbols "0" and "1" corresponds to a system of representing numbers called the **binary number system**. The binary number system also uses only the two symbols "0" and "1". Further details will be given in the next chapter. For the time being remember that **Binary digITS** are called **BITS** and note that the pulses in Fig. 2.3 are represented by the ten bits, which are labelled Bit 0 to Bit 9 inclusive.

2.7 **Character Codes.** The particular combination of 0's and 1's used for bits 1 to 7 inclusive in Fig. 2.3 has been chosen to represent the character "T". Thus we have a *"7-bit code"* representing the character "T".

Binary Code	Decimal Value	Char-acter	Binary Code	Decimal Value	Char-acter	Binary Code	Decimal Value	Char-acter	Binary Code	Decimal Value	Char-acter
0010 0000	32	space	0011 1000	56	8	0101 0000	80	P	0110 1000	104	h
0010 0001	33	!	0011 1001	57	9	0101 0001	81	Q	0110 1001	105	i
0010 0010	34	"	0011 1010	58	:	0101 0010	82	R	0110 1010	106	j
0010 0011	35	#	0011 1011	59	;	0101 0011	83	S	0110 1011	107	k
0010 0100	36	$	0011 1100	60	<	0101 0100	84	T	0110 1100	108	l
0010 0101	37	%	0011 1101	61	=	0101 0101	85	U	0110 1101	109	m
0010 0110	38	&	0011 1110	62	>	0101 0110	86	V	0110 1110	110	n
0010 0111	39	'	0011 1111	63	?	0101 0111	87	W	0110 1111	111	o
0010 1000	40	(	0100 0000	64	@	0101 1000	88	X	0111 0000	112	p
0010 1001	41	)	0100 0001	65	A	0101 1001	89	Y	0111 0001	113	q
0010 1010	42	*	0100 0010	66	B	0101 1010	90	Z	0111 0011	140	r
0010 1011	43	+	0100 0011	67	C	0101 1011	91	[	0111 0011	115	s
0010 1100	44	,	0100 0100	68	D	0101 1100	92	\	0111 0100	116	t
0010 1101	45	-	0100 0101	69	E	0101 1101	93	]	0111 0101	117	u
0010 1110	46	.	0100 0110	70	F	0101 1110	94	^	0111 0110	118	v
0010 1111	47	/	0100 0111	71	G	0101 1111	95	_	0111 0111	119	w
0011 0000	48	0	0100 1000	72	H	0110 0000	96	'	0111 1000	120	x
0011 0001	49	1	0100 1001	73	I	0110 0001	97	a	0111 1001	121	y
0011 0010	50	2	0100 1010	74	J	0110 0010	98	b	0111 1010	122	z
0011 0011	51	3	0100 1011	75	K	0110 0011	99	c	0111 1011	123	{
0011 0100	52	4	0100 1100	76	L	0110 0100	100	d	0111 1100	124		
0011 0101	53	5	0100 1101	77	M	0110 0101	101	e	0111 1101	125	}
0011 0110	54	6	0100 1110	78	N	0110 0110	102	f	0111 1110	126	~
0011 0111	55	7	0100 1111	79	O	0110 0111	103	g	0111 1111	127	del

Note. The binary codes corresponding to the decimal values 0 to 31 are used as "control characters", ie, they are used to control the transmitting device rather than to represent data. (Details later.)

Fig. 2.4. The ASCII character set

2.8 **ASCII.** The 7-bit code just described conforms to a standard called ASCII. ASCII stands for American Standard Code for Information Interchange. ASCII codes are widely used throughout the computer industry. The ASCII character set is shown in Fig. 2.4.

2.9   Start Bits and Stop Bits. Bit 0 in Fig. 2.3 is called a "start bit". It is the first bit in the pulse train to be transmitted. Its purpose is to signify the start of a character transmission to the receiver (the computer in this case). Bit 9, the "stop bit", signifies the end of the transmission. The start bit and stop bit are always of opposite polarity (ie, if one is 1 the other is 0) so that a change of pulse level takes place when a start bit is transmitted. On some systems two stop bits are used.

2.10   Protocols. A convention used to control the transmission of data is called a protocol. The use of start bits and stop bits is an example of a very simple protocol.

2.11   Asynchronous transmission. The transmission of the characters in Fig 2.2 is asynchronous. That is, as each character is individually ready for transmission its pulse train is *transmitted*. This means that the pulse trains are transmitted at *irregular intervals in time*. However, within each pulse train all bit transmissions occur at a fixed rate.

2.12   Synchronous transmissions occur at fixed intervals and at fixed rates. For example, a prepared set of characters may be transmitted synchronously as a single block of character, which will be more efficient than transmitting them singly by asynchronous means.

2.13   The purpose of the parity bit shown in Fig 2.3 will be discussed later.

DATA REPRESENTATION ON MAGNETIC MEDIA

2.14   Data in the form of character codes may also be represented on magnetic media. Invisible "spots" of magnetism are created in the magnetic surface of the medium. These spots, which can be magnetised in one of the two directions, correspond to binary 0 or 1 according to the direction of magnetisation. Fig. 2.5 shows an example of how data may be stored on magnetic tape, which is a common type of magnetic storage medium.

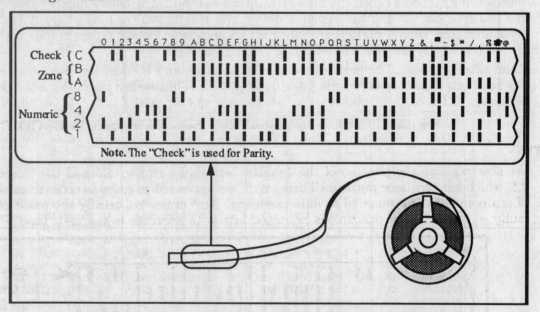

Fig. 2.5. How data is recorded on magnetic tape.

BINARY CODED DECIMAL (BCD)

2.15   BCD is a 4-bit code used for coding numeric values only, as follows:

DECIMAL DIGIT	0	1	2	3	4	5	6	7	8	9
BCD CODE	0000	0001	0010	0011	0100	0101	0110	0111	1000	1001

Example. The number 109 could be coded thus:

DECIMAL NUMBER	1	0	9
BCD CODE	0001	0000	1001

Note that each decimal digit is coded separately.

2.16   Standard BCD 6-bit code. This code is formed by extending the BCD 4-bit code by a further two bits in order to allow non-numeric characters to be coded. It is the code used on the magnetic tape shown in Fig. 2.5. The "check" bit is not part of the code. Note that zero is coded as 001010 on some machines rather than 000000 (see Fig 2.5).

ALPHA CHARACTER	BINARY CODE	ALPHA CHARACTER	BINARY CODE	ALPHA CHARACTER	BINARY CODE
A	11 0001	J	10 0001	–	–
B	11 0010	K	10 0010	S	01 0010
C	11 0011	L	10 0011	T	01 0011
D	11 0100	M	10 0100	U	01 0100
E	11 0101	N	10 0101	V	01 0101
F	11 0110	O	10 0110	W	01 0110
G	11 0111	P	10 0111	X	01 0111
H	11 1000	Q	10 1000	Y	01 1000
I	11 1001	R	10 1001	Z	01 1001

Fig. 2.6. Representation of alphabetic characters in BCD 6-bit code.

2.17 Extended Binary Coded Decimal Interchange Code (EBCDIC). EBCDIC code (usually pronounced "Eb-see-Dick") is sometimes called "8-bit ASCII" and is a newer code than 6-bit BCD. There are 256 characters in the EBCDIC character set but only 64 characters in the Standard BCD 6-bit code (see Fig. 2.7).

ALPHA CHARACTER	BINARY CODE	ALPHA CHARACTER	BINARY CODE	ALPHA CHARACTER	BINARY CODE
A	1100 0001	J	1101 0001	–	–
B	1100 0010	K	1101 0010	S	1110 0010
C	1100 0011	L	1101 0011	T	1110 0011
D	1100 0100	M	1101 0100	U	1110 0100
E	1100 0101	N	1101 0101	V	1110 0101
F	1100 0110	O	1101 0110	W	1110 0110
G	1100 0111	P	1101 0111	X	1110 0111
H	1100 1000	Q	1101 1000	Y	1110 1000
I	1100 1001	R	1101 1001	Z	1110 1001

Fig. 2.7. Representation of alphabetic characters in EBCDIC.

PARITY

2.18 We now examine the purpose of the **"parity bit"** shown in Fig. 2.3 and the **"check bit"** of Fig. 2.5, which has the same purpose. These extra bits are added to codes in order to allow the detection of errors in data transmission or data recording. Such errors are usually the result of using poor or faulty equipment. The principle is explained here with reference to magnetic tape (Fig. 2.5).

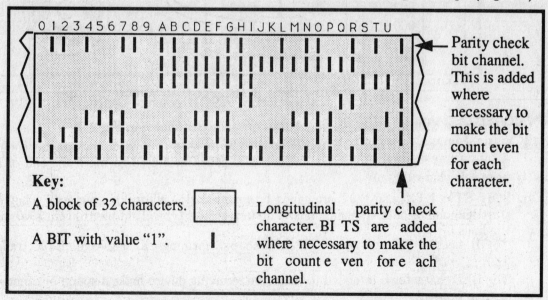

Fig. 2.8. Longitudinal parity checks.

2.19 Even parity. If you examine the magnetic tape codes of Fig. 2.5 you will discover that the parity bit has been added (vertical mark) to some codes on the tape so that the 7-bit code *including* parity always has an *even* number of bits. This is an even parity system. As each character code is read from the tape the number of bits, including the parity bit, is checked. Should an odd number of bits be discovered in an even parity system then an error must have occurred.

2.20   Odd parity. In an odd parity system the number of bits in the tape for each character code is made odd by the appropriate use of the parity bit.

2.21   Longitudinal parity checks. Parity bits may also be added to the end of blocks of characters so as to make the total number of holes along each channel even numbered. Longitudinal checks are most commonly used on magnetic media (see Fig. 2.8). Longitudinal checks can be used in synchronous data transmissions.

CONTROL CHARACTERS

2.22   **Protocols (2.10) for the transmission of characters make use of special **control characters. A control character is a particular control sign which can be sent between devices which are transmitting and receiving data. It is represented by a binary code in the same way as other characters but it does NOT have a printable character symbol. To illustrate the idea a selection of the ASCII character set's control symbols are used below to provide examples (see Fig 2.9) but *please note that there is no need to learn these codes.* Fig 2.4 illustrated the **printable characters** from the ASCII character sets.

Binary Code	Decimal Value	Character Name	Description
0000 0000	0	NUL	All zeroes
0000 0001	1	SOH	Start of heading
0000 0010	2	STX	Start of text
0000 0011	3	ETX	End of text
0000 0100	4	EOT	End of transmission
0000 0111	7	BEL	Bell or an attention signal
0000 1000	8	BS	Back space
0000 1001	9	HT	Horizontal tabulation
0000 1010	10	LF	Line feed
0000 1011	11	VT	Vertical tabulation
0000 1100	12	FF	Form feed
0000 1101	13	CR	Carriage return
0001 0001	17	DC1	Device control 1
0001 0010	18	DC2	Device control 2
0001 0011	19	DC3	Device control 3
0001 0100	20	DC4	Device control 4
0001 1011	27	ESC	Escape
0111 1111	127	DEL	Delete

Note. The full set of ASCII control characters is given in appendix 3.4.

Fig. 2.9. A selection of ASCII control characters.

**2.23   **Here are some additional details about the control codes shown in Fig 2.9.

   a.   NUL is effectively a blank character which can be used to provide a character code where one is required but none is applicable. NUL is also sometimes used to mark the end of a sequence of printable characters.

   b.   SOH, STX, ETX, and EOT are called "communication control characters". They appear at the start and end of data transmissions. The format of a typical simple transmission would be along the lines of:
   "SOH..header information...STX...characters forming a message...ETX..trailer information...EOT"

   c.   The BEL character is intended to make the receiving device make a sound or other signal to alert anyone present.

   d.   BS, HT, LF, VT, FF, and CR are called "format effector characters". They are intended to make the receiving device print out text messages with an appropriate layout. The following example illustrates a typical result of sending a character sequence:

i. Message sent.

```
NB BS BS _ _ The order is CR LF LF HT HT Mon HT 1 CR LF HT HT
Wed HT 5 CR LF HT HT Frid HT 7 CR The end."
```

ii. layout of the received message.

```
NB The order is

            Mon        1
            Wed        5
The end.    Frid       7
```

e. DC1, DC2, DC3 and DC4 control the operation of the sending and receiving devices. For example, DC3 is normally used to signal the sending device to suspend a transmission and DC1 is normally used to signal the sending device to resume a transmission.

f. The ESC character may be used to signal the need to exit from the current operation. Alternatively it is sometimes used to mark the beginning of a special sequence of characters intended to control a particular feature of the receiving device.

g. DEL indicates that the transmitted character immediately before DEL should be deleted.

2.24 Most control characters are not available as individual keys on computer keyboards. Common exceptions to this are keys for tab (HT), escape (ESC), delete (DEL or BS). Also, a RETURN or ENTER keys may correspond to a combination of CR and LF. Other control characters may be generated by means of a control key (often labelled CTRL) present on many keyboards. For example, if the normal keys produce ASCII characters, then the combination CTRL + "G" may produce a "bell" sound, CTRL + "S" will produce a DC3 and CTRL + "Q" will produce a DC1.

Fig 2.10 A digitised image.

INTERNAL AND EXTERNAL CHARACTER CODES

2.25 The binary codes used within input devices vary according to the types of devices and any input media they use. However, it is common practice to use just one particular binary code for all data within the processor and main storage so as to simplify and standardise the handling of data. This code is called the **internal code** and the choice of internal code differs from one manufacturer to another, eg. IBM uses EBCDIC for its mainframes, and most microcomputer manufacturers use ASCII. The codes used on the various peripherals are called **external codes**.

2.26 Code conversion from external to internal forms may take place

    a. within a peripheral device,

    b. within a device called an **interface** before data enters the processor or memory,

    c. within the processor itself.

NON-CHARACTER CODES

2.27 Not all data is represented by characters. Two non-character based forms of data deserving a particular mention are *images* (eg pictures or diagrams) and *sounds*. These non-character forms of data can nevertheless be represented by means of binary codes. Simple examples now follow to illustrate the principle. More details will be given in later chapters.

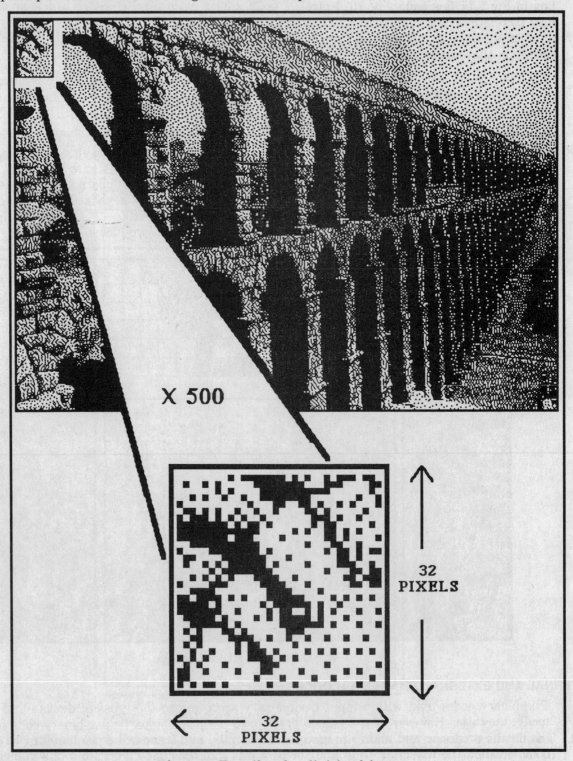

X 500

32 PIXELS

32 PIXELS

Fig 2.11 Details of a digitised image.

BIT-MAPPED IMAGES

2.28 An image such as photograph can be given a binary coded representation suitable for storage as "data" in a computer. A special input device called an **image scanner** can perform this task. The image is said to be **digitised**. An example of a digitised black and white image made from a photograph by an image scanner is shown in Fig 2.10.

2.29 On close inspection it can be seen that the digitised image is formed from a grid of tiny dots. The fineness of the grid's mesh determines how well the image's details are represented and therefore places a limit on the quality of the image. Fig 2.11 shows the details of the grid representation of a small area from the top left hand corner of Fig 2.10. The grid squares are called **pixels**. The detail box in Fig 2.11 is a square of 1024 pixels (ie 32 × 32). Each pixel is *either* black *or* white and may therefore be represented by a BIT. It is interesting to note that this tiny area requires the same number of bits to represent it as it would take to represent 128 8-bit characters! It is not surprising, therefore, that images can often take very large amounts of computer storage space.

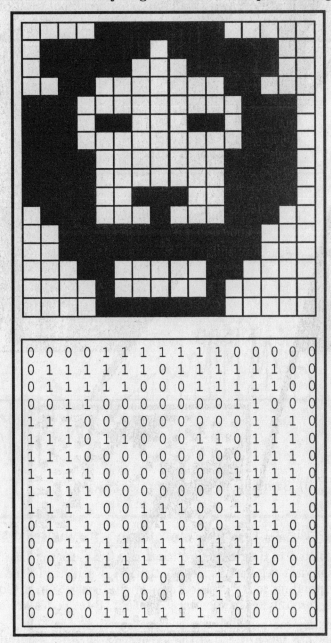

Fig 2.12 A simple image coded in binary.

2.30 The bits used to represent an image have to be organised into some well defined order corresponding to the positions they take in the grid. In other words there has to be a grid of bits which correspond to the grid of pixels. If an image is created or displayed from such a grid of BITs it is said to be **bit-mapped image**. There are other more sophisticated methods of representing images which do *not* use bit-mapping but they will be discussed in later chapters. A very simple bit-mapping is shown in Fig 2.12.

2.31 Close inspection of a typical monitor screen (Fig 1.3) reveals that the screen's display is a grid of pixels. The method of bit-mapping may be used to represent images for displays on such screens. Again, details will be discussed in later chapters.

2.32 The example just given was based upon a black and white image but colour images can be represented too. In the case of colour images each pixel may be able to take one colour from a "palette". A binary code can be assigned to each palette colour. The exact details will not be discussed here but it should be clear to the reader that the number of bits required will be considerably more than that required for a black and white image.

DIGITISED SOUND

2.33 Sounds can also be given a binary coded representation suitable for storage as "data" in a computer. In simple cases the input device is a combination of a microphone and a **"digitising sound sampler"**. It is the latter that produces a binary coded representation of the sound picked up by the microphone.

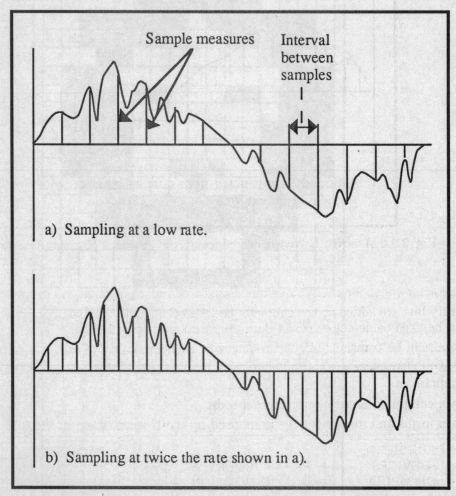

Fig 2.13 A sound waveform with digitised samples.

2.34 Sounds can be depicted in diagrammatic form as a **waveforms** (see Fig 2.13). The height of the waveform is measured at regularly spaced intervals. Each height measurement is represented as a binary code corresponding to its position on a digital scale. On a **Compact Disc (CD)** a 16-bit code is used for representing each such measurement. 8-bit codes are also commonly used.

2.35 The process of taking the regularly spaced measurements is called **sampling** and the frequency with which samples are taken is called the **sampling rate**. A sampling rate of 22,000 samples per second provides high quality sound representation but a sampling rate of half that frequency might be acceptable for many purposes. From these figures it can be deduced that to represent just *one second* of sound in 16-bit format at a sampling rate of 22,000 per second will take the equivalent storage space of 44,000 8-bit characters!

2.36 When sound is output the waveform is reconstructed from the coded samples (see Fig 2.14).

2.37 Further details will be provided in later chapters.

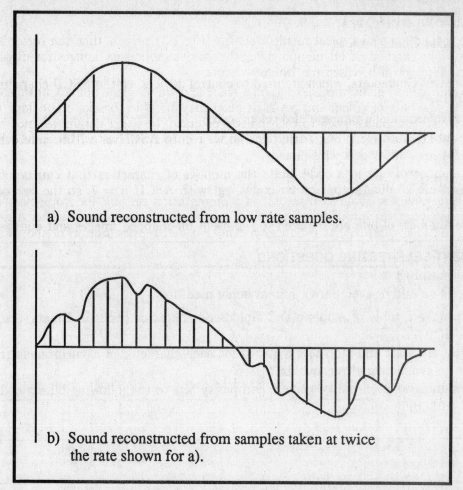

a) Sound reconstructed from low rate samples.

b) Sound reconstructed from samples taken at twice the rate shown for a).

Fig 2.14 A sound waveform reconstructed for a digitised representation.

SUMMARY

2.38 **a.** Character codes for the various input media can all be represented in binary form.

    b. Parity bits are added to the character codes so that parity checks performed at each code transfer can be used to detect errors in data preparation or transmission.

    c. Data may be transmitted synchronously or asynchronously in the form of pulse trains.

    d. Control characters are special characters used to control devices rather than represent character symbols.

    e. Each computer uses its own internal code.

    f. Data forms and movement is summarised by the block diagram in Fig 2.15.

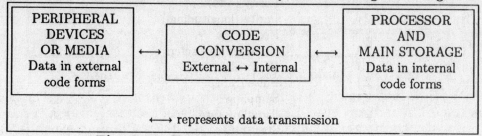

Fig. 2.15. Data movements in external and internal forms.

    g. Images and sounds are examples of "data" not based upon characters but they too can be digitised and thereby represented by binary codes

POINTS TO NOTE

2.39 Characters may be classified as

    a. Alpha-numeric, either

        i. Alphabetic, ie, A, B, C,.. Z,
        or

ii. Numeric, ie, 0, 1, 2,.. 9.

b. Special Characters, eg, . , - / +.
OR

c. Control Characters, which are used to control devices, eg the ASCII characters BEL, CR, LF and DEL.

By convention alpha-numeric also refers to **b**.

2.40 Codes are defined excluding parity bits, so we regard ASCII as a 7-bit code, which with parity gives an 8-bit.

2.41 The number of bits in a code limits the number of characters that can be coded. An n bit code can provide 2^n different character codes, eg, with ASCII $n = 7$, so the size of the character set is $2^7 = 128$.

2.42 Large numbers of bits are required to represent bit-mapped images and digitised sounds.

STUDENT SELF-TESTING QUESTIONS

1. Refer to Fig. 2.5
   a. Is an odd or even parity system being used?
   b. Make a table of numeric and alphabetic character codes in Binary (exclude the check digit).
2. Why are start and stop bits required for each character in asynchronous transmission but not in synchronous transmission?
3. Assuming an even parity system, add parity bits to the following binary codes:
   a. 1011100
   b. 0111101

QUESTIONS WITHOUT ANSWERS

4. What is meant by the term "character set"? Identify the character set on the computer keyboard you will be using on your course.
5. Look up the ASCII codes for the letter and spaces in the phrase "A Pulse Train" and draw a diagram like that in Fig. 2.2.
6. Explain two factors affecting the quality of a digitised sound.

GLOSSARY CHECKLIST

ASCII	2.8	Internal code	2.25
Asynchronous transmission	2.11	Parity bit	2.18
BCD	2.15	Parity (even)	2.19
Binary	2.6	Parity (odd)	2.20
BITS	2.6	Parity (longitudinal)	2.21
Bit-mapped image	2.30	Pixel	2.29
Character	2.1	Printable characters	2.22
Character codes	2.7	Protocols	2.10
Character set	2.1	Pulse train	2.3
Check bit	2.18	Sampling	2.35
Control characters	2.22	Sampling rate	2.35
Digitised image	2.28	Start bit	2.9
Digitised sound	2.33	Stop bit	2.9
EBCDIC	2.17	Synchronous transmission	2.12
External codes	2.25	Waveform	2.34
Image scanner	2.28		

3: Number Bases

INTRODUCTION

3.1 This chapter introduces numbers in base two, called binary numbers, which are used by digital computers when they store and process data. You will see that several other number bases also have uses in computing, and so the general idea of number bases, together with the methods we will need for converting from one base to another, are developed in this chapter.

3.2 **Decimal Numbers** are the numbers in everyday use, and are also known as **Denary** numbers, or numbers to **base 10,** because ten is the *basis* of the number system. To write a number in decimal we make use of the ten **digit** symbols 0, 1, 2, 3, 4, 5, 6, 7, 8 and 9 and also use the method of **place value** (ie, the position of a digit affects its meaning).

Example. The number "235" in decimals is made up thus:

PLACE VALUE	10^3 (100)	10^2 (100)	10^1 (10)	10^0 (1)		10^2 (100)	10^1 (10)	10^0 (1)
Digit "5" is in position 10^0				5	$= 5^0$	0	0	5
Digit "3" is in position 10^1			3		$= 3^1$	0	3	0
Digit "2" is in position 10^2		2			$= 2^2$	2	0	0
					TOTAL	2	3	5

BINARY NUMBERS

3.3 **Binary Numbers** are numbers to base 2. The binary number system uses just *two* symbols, 0 and 1, and place values increasing in powers of *two*.

Examples. (You should memorise these first 8 values for future use.)

BINARY NUMBER	$2^3 = 8$	$2^2 = 4$	$2^1 = 2$	$2^0 = 1$	DECIMAL EQUIVALENT
0 0 0 1	$= (0 \times 2^3)$ +	(0×2^2) +	(0×2^1) +	(1×2^0)	$= 1$
0 0 1 0	$= (0 \times 2^3)$ +	(0×2^2) +	(1×2^1) +	(0×2^0)	$= 2$
0 0 1 1	$= (0 \times 2^3)$ +	(0×2^2) +	(1×2^1) +	(1×2^0)	$= 3$
0 1 0 0	$= (0 \times 2^3)$ +	(1×2^2) +	(0×2^1) +	(0×2^0)	$= 4$
0 1 0 1	$= (0 \times 2^3)$ +	(1×2^2) +	(0×2^1) +	(1×2^0)	$= 5$
0 1 1 0	$= (0 \times 2^3)$ +	(1×2^2) +	(1×2^1) +	(0×2^0)	$= 6$
0 1 1 1	$= (0 \times 2^3)$ +	(1×2^2) +	(1×2^1) +	(1×2^0)	$= 7$
1 0 0 0	$= (1 \times 2^3)$ +	(0×2^2) +	(0×2^1) +	(0×2^0)	$= 8$

3.4 **Subscripts** are used to indicate the base of a number as in its written form. For example when we see 101_2 the subscript 2 tells us we are looking at a binary number, which from our table we identify as being equivalent to 5 in decimal. Without the subscript we should probably read 101 as meaning one hundred and one in decimal. So *at all times use subscripts* to indicate the base used if there is any risk of confusion without them. The subscript itself is always in decimal.

3.5 **Conversion from Binary to Decimal.**

Example Convert 1101101_2 to Decimal.

PLACE VALUES	2^6 (64)	2^5 (32)	2^4 (16)	2^3 (8)	2^2 (4)	2^1 (2)	2^0 (1)	DECIMAL VALUE
BINARY NUMBERS	1	1	0	1	1	0	1	
CONVERSION	$(1 \times 64) + (1 \times 32) + (0 \times 16) + (1 \times 8) + (1 \times 4) + (0 \times 2) + (1 \times 1)$							$= 109$

3.6 **Conversion from Decimal to Binary.** We use repeated *division* by 2.

Example. Convert 109 Decimal to Binary. *Arrows* are used here to emphasis the direction in which the Binary Number should be read.

23

USUAL LAYOUT OF WORKING		DETAILS
109	1	109 ÷ 2 = 54 Remainder 1
54	0	54 ÷ 2 = 27 Remainder 0
27	1	27 ÷ 2 = 13 Remainder 1
13	1	13 ÷ 2 = 6 Remainder 1
6	0	6 ÷ 2 = 3 Remainder 0
3	1	3 ÷ 2 = 1 Remainder 1
1	1	1 ÷ 2 = 0 Remainder 1 1 0 1 1 0 1

We have thus checked our previous result, $109_{10} = 1\ 101\ 101_2$

OCTAL NUMBERS

3.7 **Octal numbers** are numbers to **base 8.** There are eight symbols used in the octal system (0, 1, 2, 3, 4, 5, 6 and 7) and place values increase in powers of 8. Octal numbers are used as a shorthand for binary.

3.8 **Conversion between Octal and Decimal.**

Example. Convert 109_{10} to octal and convert back to decimal as a check.

a. Conversion to octal is done by repeated division by 8. In other respects the method is the same as conversion from decimal to binary.

WORKING			DETAILS
109	5	↑	109 ÷ 8 = 13 Remainder 5
13	5	↑	13 ÷ 8 = 1 Remainder 5
1	1	↑	13 ÷ 8 = 0 Remainder 1

Thus $109_{10} = 155_8$

b. Conversion *to* Decimal *from* Octal.

PLACE VALUES	8^2 (64)	8^1 (8)	8^0 (1)	DECIMAL VALUE
OCTAL NUMBER	1	5	5	
CONVERSION	$(1 \times 64)\ +$	$(5 \times 8)\ +$	(5×1)	= 109

Thus $155_8 = 109_{10}$

3.9 **Conversion between Octal and Binary.** A simple relationship exists between octal and binary, because eight is the cube of two. To do conversions it is merely necessary to remember binary equivalents for the eight octal symbols. Octal is often used as a "shorthand" for binary because of this easy conversion.

Conversion Table.

OCTAL NUMBERS	0	1	2	3	4	5	6	7
BINARY EQUIVALENTS	0 0 0	0 0 1	0 1 0	0 1 1	1 0 0	1 0 1	1 1 0	1 1 1

Example a. Convert 155_8 to Binary.

OCTAL NUMBER	1			5			5		
BINARY EQUIVALENTS FROM THE CONVERSION TABLE	0	0	1	1	0	1	1	0	1

Thus $155_8 = 001\ 101\ 101_2$

Example b. Convert 1110111000010_2 to octal.

In order to use the conversion table we group the binary digits into threes working from right to left, adding extra zeroes at the left end if necessary.

GROUPED BINARY DIGITS	0	0	1	1	1	0	1	1	1	0	0	0	0	1	0
OCTAL EQUIVALENTS FROM THE CONVERSION TABLE	1			6			7			0			2		

Thus $1\ 110\ 111\ 000\ 010_2 = 16\ 702_8$

Note. Conversions between Decimal and Binary are often quicker via Octal, ie, using Binary to Octal to Decimal, or Decimal to Octal to Binary.

HEXADECIMAL NUMBERS

3.10   Hexadecimal numbers, usually abbreviated to **"Hex"** are numbers to base **16**. The sixteen symbols using in the Hex system are 0, 1, 2, 3, 4, 5, 6, 7, 8, 9, A, B, C, D, E, and F and place values increase in powers of sixteen. We need to remember that A, B, C, D, E and F are equivalent to 10, 11, 12, 13, 14, and 15 DECIMAL. Hex numbers are used as a shorthand for binary.

3.11   **Conversions between Hexadecimal and Decimal** follow the same pattern used for binary and octal.

Example. Convert 109_{10} to Hex and back again.

a. Conversion *to* Hex *from* Decimal.

WORKING			DETAILS			
109	$13 = D_{16}$	↑	$109 \div 16$	=	6	Remainder 13
6	$6 = 6_{16}$	↑	$6 \div 16$	=	0	Remainder 6

Thus $109_{10} = 6D_{16}$

b. Conversion *to* Decimal *from* Hex.

PLACE VALUES	16^2 (256)	16^1 (16)	16^0 (1)	DECIMAL VALUE
HEX NUMBER	0	6	D	
CONVERSION	(0×256) +	(6×16) +	(13×1)	= 109

Thus $6D_{16} = 109_{10}$

3.12   **Conversion between Hex and other bases.** Conversion between hex, octal and binary is done in much the same way as the octal/binary conversions in paragraph 3.9. A conversion table is given below.

Conversion Table.

DECIMAL	0	1	2	3	4	5	6	7
HEX	0	1	2	3	4	5	6	7
BINARY	0000	0001	0010	0011	0100	0101	0110	0111
OCTAL	0	1	2	3	4	5	6	7

DECIMAL	8	9	10	11	12	13	14	15
HEX	8	9	A	B	C	D	E	F
BINARY	1000	1001	1010	1011	1100	1101	1110	1111
OCTAL	10	11	12	13	14	15	16	17

Example a. Convert $6D_{16}$ to Binary and Octal. A conversion between hex and octal is most easily made via binary.

Stage 1. (Hex to Binary)

HEX NUMBER	6				D			
BINARY EQUIVALENT FROM THE TABLE	0	1	1	0	1	1	0	1

Stage 2. (Binary to Octal)

BINARY	0	0	1	1	0	1	1	0	1
OCTAL		1			5			5	

Example b. Convert 1110111000010_2 to Hex.

We group binary digits into fours from the right, then use the conversion table.

GROUPED BINARY DIGITS	0 0 0 1	1 1 0 1	1 1 0 0	0 0 1 0
HEX EQUIVALENTS FROM THE CONVERSION TABLE	1	D	C	2

SUMMARY

3.13 a. A Numbering system is characterised by the base and symbols used. The table summarises those considered.

NUMBER SYSTEM	BASE	SYMBOL USED
Binary	2	0, 1.
Octal	8	0, 1, 2, 3, 4, 5, 6, 7.
Decimal or Denary	10	0, 1, 2, 3, 4, 5, 6, 7, 8, 9.
Hexadecimal or Hex	16	0, 1, 2, 3, 4, 5, 6, 7, 8, 9, A, B, C, D, E, F.

b. The base of a number is indicated by a subscript.

POINTS TO NOTE

3.14 a. Another name sometimes used instead of "base" is **"radix"**.

b. Octal and hex numbers can be used as "shorthands" for binary.

c. You will need to use the methods described in this chapter, so practise with the questions given here.

d. The simplest sequences to adopt when converting between bases are shown here:

i. Decimal $\rightleftharpoons$ Octal $\rightleftharpoons$ Binary.

ii. Hexadecimal $\rightleftharpoons$ Binary $\rightleftharpoons$ Octal.

STUDENT SELF-TESTING QUESTIONS

1. Convert these decimal numbers to (a) Octal (b) Binary (c) Hex.

    i.   22   ii.   26   iii.   31   iv.   44   v.   53

    vi.   58   vii.   93   viii. 751   ix.   1453

2. Convert these Octal numbers to (a) Decimal (b) Hexadecimal (c) Binary.

    i.   73   ii.   347   iii.   152   iv.   2354   v.   3733

3. Convert these Hexadecimal numbers to decimal.

    i.   6A   ii.   EF   iii.   2C8   iv.   347   v.   6DA

4. Express this binary number in Octal and Hex. 110111010101101011.

GLOSSARY CHECKLIST

Base	3.2	Hexadecimal number	3.10
Binary number	3.3	Octal number	3.7
Decimal number	3.2	Place value	3.2
Denary	3.2	Radix	3.14

4: An Overview of Hardware and Software

INTRODUCTION

4.1   This chapter concludes the series of chapters on "Foundation Topics". Its purpose is to extend the introductory material given in chapter 1 so as to provide an overview of hardware and software which will act as a suitable preparation for the more detailed and specialised chapters that follow. The chapter first deals with hardware and then with software.

4.2   **Hardware** is the name given to all the physical devices found in a computer system. Whether looking at a small computer on a desktop or at a large computer in the computer room, where the devices look like large inert metal cabinets, there is little visible evidence of the phenomenal speeds at which data is being processed within. It is the programs, that is the **"Software"**, that put life into the Hardware.

4.3   In this chapter common types of hardware are introduced by the use of suitable examples. Software is described in terms of how it is organised and used.

HARDWARE HEADINGS

4.4   The six main headings under which hardware is discussed in this chapter are:

    a. Semi-conductor processors and memories

    b. Data Storage

    c. Backing Storage

    d. Data entry

    e. Data transmission and networks

    f. Output

4.5   Although the basic uses of hardware are mentioned in this chapter, a full discussion of its uses is deliberately excluded, because a full knowledge of hardware capabilities and limitations must precede any evaluation of which hardware is best suited to a particular application.

SEMI-CONDUCTOR PROCESSORS AND MEMORIES

4.6   Although the computer carries out a number of different functions (Fig. 1.2), from a hardware viewpoint the basic electronic components of a modern computer are all very similar. Many of the main components are of a similar shape and size too. This similarity arises from common manufacturing processes.

4.7   Complex circuits such as those found in the ALU, control unit or main storage are manufactured on single minutely sliced wafers of silicon crystal. Such devices are called **"silicon chips"** or **"semi-conductor devices"** (see Fig. 4.1). Individual components can be as narrow as 0.0000015 inches.

4.8   **Microprocessors.** A microprocessor is an entire small computer processor (usually excluding main memory) manufactured on a single chip. Computers built around such devices are called **"microcomputers"**, or more correctly **"microcomputer-based systems"**.

4.9   The first production microprocessor was produced in 1972 by the Intel corporation. It was the model 4004 and its chip contained about 2,300 transistors. Transistors operate as electronic switches each having two binary states (ON or OFF). Over the intervening years the technology for constructing microprocessors has been improved so that the microcomputers of today are much more powerful than minicomputers were in 1972. An example of a typical microprocessor used in PCs is the Intel 386. It has a chip some half inch square set in a protective case with connectors on its sides. The chip itself contains 275,000 transistors! Many early models of PC used the Intel 8086 microprocessor which contained about 29,000 transistors. That was followed by the Intel 286 which had about 130,000 transistors. The trend continues with the Intel 486 having about 1,200,000 transistors and the Intel 586 having an even greater number of transistors. Another major chip manufacturer, Motorola, has brought out a series of processors which have also progressed in a manner comparable to the Intel chips. These are the M68000, M68030 and M68040 processor chips also used on some PCs notably the Apple Macintosh range of computers

4.10   Most microprocessors do not contain main storage, which is normally produced on separate silicon chips.

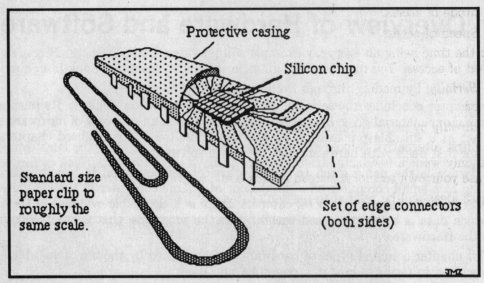

Fig. 4.1 A Computer Component Containing a Silicon Chip.

4.11   **Semi-conductor memory** is the name given to main storage manufactured on silicon chips. Semi-conductor memory rapidly replaced a former main storage medium, called *"core store"*, during the mid-seventies.

4.12   The most common types of semi-conductor memory are **"volatile"**, which means that all data is lost if the power supply is removed. The most common type of volatile memory is called **RAM** (Random Access Memory). Most computers normally contain a small proportion of **non-volatile** memory too. The most common type of non-volatile memory is called **ROM** (Read Only Memory).

4.13   **Main features.** The semi-conductor devices within the computer have the following features:

a.   Their operation is *wholly electronic*, and consequently they are very fast and reliable.

b.   Despite the complexity of these devices, modern manufacturing methods have enabled them to be produced at costs that represent only minor portions of the total costs of whole computer systems, eg, in a microcomputer costing £1000, the microprocessor may only constitute £10 of the total cost or even less.

c.   These devices are *highly miniaturised*. This feature may be exploited in order to provide computer hardware that can be accommodated comfortably in the office, home, petrol pumps, washing machines, cars, etc.

DATA STORAGE

4.14   Some specific aspects of data storage have just been discussed under the heading of semi-conductor processors and memories, but now we turn our attention to *general hardware aspects of data storage* applicable to both main storage and backing storage.

4.15   There are several different common types of hardware used for data storage. This variety stems from the fact that there are a number of physical characteristics that must be considered in deciding the appropriateness of a particular device in a given situation.

4.16   Data storage devices will be discussed under these headings:

a.   Storage capacity.

b.   Access facilities.

c.   Size.

d.   Robustness.

e.   Relative costs.

STORAGE CAPACITY

4.17   Storage capacities may be expressed and compared in terms of the number of **"characters"** stored (2.2). For example, *main storage* of a small computer may be expressed in terms of tens or hundreds of thousands of characters whereas *backing storage* of a larger computer may be expressed in terms of tens or hundreds of millions of characters.

ACCESS FACILITIES

4.18 Broadly speaking, the two main factors are:

    a. Mode of access.

    b. Speed of access.

4.19 For the time being an everyday example will provide a basic distinction between mode of access and speed of access. You may "access" data (ie. get facts) from this book in two modes:

    a. *Serially,* by reading through from the first page to the last,

    or

    b. *directly* by using the index to go straight to the data you need.

4.20 The first alternative is more efficient if you require most or all of the facts, but the latter is faster if you only want a few facts. If you require to have the *immediate recall* of facts, then you may need to use your own memory, instead of this book, as your "data storage medium".

4.21 These ideas will be related to particular items of hardware later.

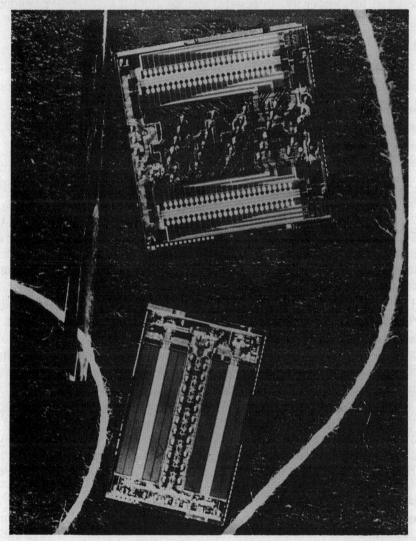

An IBM 64,000 Bit Dynamic Ram Chip, older model and new model (40% smaller) compared with a needle and thread.
Picture courtesy of IBM.

SIZE

4.22 Despite major strides in miniaturisation (the components within modern chips are more densely packed than the cells of the human brain, although they do not have the same intelligence as brains), some backing storage devices and media remain undesirably bulky. Most backing storage devices have some electro-mechanical parts, which contribute to their bulk. When data is to be stored for long periods with minimal access the most compact backing storage media are favoured because of the value of saving space.

4.23   Compared with normal paper-based data storage, as in the form of rows of filing cabinets, computer storage methods are all incredibly more compact.

ROBUSTNESS

4.24   Compared with paper-based storage, computer data storage may appear to be less robust. Such a view is based upon the fact that most computer storage media need handling with care and may only be used in carefully controlled environments. In practical terms this is seldom a serious problem for commercial applications, since the "office environment" is one which is suitable for most computer hardware. In industrial environments, such as on the factory floor, environmental problems are less easy to solve.

RELATIVE COSTS

4.25   There are sharp differences in costs between the various types of computer storage. Awareness of the various alternatives allows the most economical alternative to be selected in a given situation. Conversely, if the storage requirements have not been properly specified, an unduly expensive alternative may be selected unnecessarily. In general semiconductor storage is more expensive than storage on magnetic media.

BACKING STORAGE

4.26   The main backing storage media in use today are:

a. Magnetic Disk (hard or floppy).

b. Magnetic Tape (reel-to-reel or cartridge).

c. Optical Disk.

These media will be described in detail in later chapters.

4.27   **Magnetic Disks** are flat rotating circular plates coated with magnetic material. Some magnetic disks are rigid and called **hard disks**, others are *flexible* and are called **floppy disks or diskettes**. Hard disks are more expensive but are faster, more reliable and bigger.

4.28   Disks provide direct data access whereas Tapes provide serial data access. (4.19)

4.29   **Magnetic Tapes** are similar in principle to the tapes used domestically for audio or video recording. Tape, being a serial medium (4.19), is mainly used as a **"back-up"** or archiving medium. Tape is sometimes also used as an input medium because data on other media may be converted onto magnetic tape prior to input in order to give faster input.

4.30   **Magnetic media problems.** The common forms of backing storage media in use today are similar in principle to the medium of the domestic tape of cassette recorders. Consequently they are susceptible to stray magnetic fields and to dust.

4.31   There are some advantages associated with these features of magnetic media. For example, whereas confidential data on paper may prove difficult to dispose of, magnetic media are not directly readable by humans and may be wiped clear magnetically.

4.32   **Optical Disks** are currently less common than magnetic disks but are growing in popularity. Some are physically the same as **Compact Disks (CDs)** used in home audio systems. Other optical disks look similar to CDs but work on a slightly different principle. They have the advantage of being less susceptible to damage than magnetic media, but most, including the normal CD, have the disadvantage of recording permanently, unlike magnetic media which can be overwritten.

DATA ENTRY

4.33   There are problems associated with entering data into computers because humans communicate less quickly than computers and in a different way, ie, by speech, writing, etc. A computer's internal communication is based upon codes formed from high-frequency electronic pulses (2.3).

4.34   The basic problems are overcome by using devices that can encode our data into a form that is usable by the computer.

Modern methods fall into three broad categories:

a. Keyboard entry.

b. Document reading.

c. Data capture.

4.35   **Keyboard entry.** The keyboard was introduced in chapter one (1.9) where it was shown being used with a PC. Data typed on the keyboard is displayed on the monitor screen. In the case of a PC there is just one user so the keyboard and monitor are connected directly to the computer. This arrangement is not satisfactory for large computers with many users. Instead separate keyboard input devices are used.

4.36 One typical keyboard input device is the **VDU** (Visual Display Unit). See Fig. 4.2. The **VDU** is really two devices in one; one for input, one for output. Data is fed in via a keyboard, which is like a typewriter keyboard, and is both passed into the computer and displayed on the screen. The VDU can also receive and display messages from the computer.

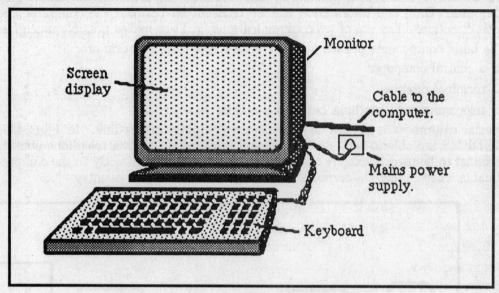

Fig 4.2 A VDU (Visual Display Unit).

4.37 The main way of using a VDU is to connect it directly to the computer. This is known as **on-line data entry**. Any device used for on-line data entry in this manner is called a **terminal**.

4.38 There are many different types of VDU (details later). Although VDUs look rather like PCs they do not have the same processing capabilities. For this reason they are sometimes called **dumb terminals**.

4.39 In the past it was also common to use VDUs in conjunction with some other special purpose data entry system in order to prepare data on a fast and reliable input medium, the most popular modern example of this, still in use, is the **key-to-floppy-disk** or **key-to-diskette** system. These are microcomputer-based systems that take in data from the VDU and store it on floppy disks. At some later stage the floppy disks are used for input to the main computer. However, such systems are in rapid decline because the same job can be carried out by a normal PC. This use of a PC is another example of a general purpose computer being able to carry out a special purpose task.

4.40 In a key-to-floppy-disk system, or its PC based equivalent, the data can be *checked and corrected* as it is being input and no non-reusable medium is being wasted.

4.41 **Terminal emulation.** Most personal computers, and many home computers, can mimic VDUs by means of special **"terminal emulation"** programs. Under the control of the terminal emulation program, the personal computer's keyboard acts as a VDU keyboard and its screen acts as a VDU screen. Of course, the personal computer must be fitted with a suitable connector and cabling to the main computer. This is yet another example of a general purpose computer acting as a special purpose computer by means of specialist software. VDUs can cost nearly as much as a small micro-computer so it has become quite common for some organisations to spend the extra money needed to buy PCs plus emulation software instead of buying VDUs.

4.42 **Document reading.** The idea behind document reading is to get a machine to read source documents (ie, the documents on which the data is originally recorded). This avoids the problems associated with transcription and verification of data when using keyboard devices. The data is recorded on the documents using special marks or characters, and is read by optical or magnetic reading techniques. Details will be given later.

4.43 **Data Capture.** This heading covers a wide variety of methods, all of which try to combine data creation with data entry, ie, the data is "captured" at source in a machine-sensible form. For example, prerecorded, or preprinted data on some suitable medium attached to goods may be read or collected as the goods are sold. This application is known as **PoS** (Point of Sale) data capture. Further details of this and other data capture methods will be given later.

DATA TRANSMISSION AND NETWORKS

4.44 Used in a general sense the term "data transmission" refers to the movement of data from one location to another. Data in a physical form such as documents can be moved by despatching through the post, by using a car or van, or by employing a courier service.

4.45 Nowadays, **"data transmission"** is usually understood to mean the movement of data by telecommunications systems. It is possible by this means to link a number of remote terminals to a central computer. Data and information can be transmitted between the computer and the terminals in both directions. The use of telecommunications facilities makes possible much faster transmission.

4.46 The basic components of such a simple data transmission system are:

a. a central computer.

b. terminal devices.

c. telecommunications links between **a** and **b**.

4.47 Special equipment is needed to provide the communications link. In Fig. 4.3 the devices called MODEMS are able to send data along and receive data from a telephone circuit. This enables the terminal to be used in exactly the same way as if connected directly to the computer by a short piece of cable when in fact the terminal could be in another city or country.

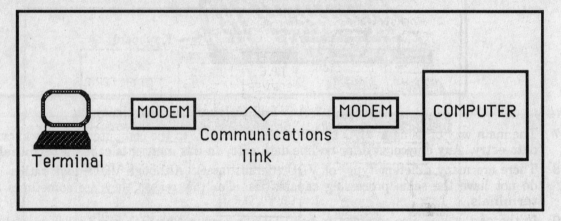

Fig 4.3 Point-to-point Data Communications

4.48 When they were first introduced the basic data transmission systems, like the one just described, were regarded as another part of the data entry system. It took no time at all to recognise and exploit the possibilities of *two-way* **point-to-point transmission**.

4.49 Many organisations set up their own *local private systems*. British Telecom (BT) set up *public services* in the UK with the trade name DATEL.

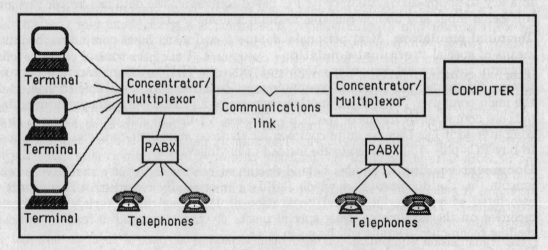

Fig 4.4 Data Communications Links

4.50 Fig 4.4 provides an example of a more advanced form of communications link but one still based upon the same basic idea shown in Fig 4.3. The devices called **concentrators** are able to use one communications link to the computer for a number of terminals that are close to one another, ie, the data to and from the set of terminals is *concentrated* into a single data stream. The method of using one single communications link to carry a number of separate signals is known as **multiplexing** and hence the device is called a **multiplexor**.

4.51 Another feature of Fig 4.4 is the use of the same communications link for telephone messages. The telephones are connected to the concentrator/multiplexor via a **PABX** (Private Automatic Branch Exchange). There are many different types of PABX but the significant point to note is the integration of two technologies; computer and telecommunications.

4.52 **Modern methods.** From its simple origins the whole concept of data transmission has been extended in two ways:

a. Many systems now have computers *at both ends* of the telecommunications link, and several computers may be inter linked in a similar manner to form a complete **computer network**. In some cases, the inter linking may be so sophisticated that the separate computers appear to act as one single system, a **"distributed computer system"**.

b. The networks are able to do more than pass data from point to point. **Messages** can be despatched from one point in the network and passed by the network to one or more destinations specified when the messages are sent. This is a form of **"electronic mail"**.

4.53 There are local, national and international networks in current use, and most major networks are interconnected.

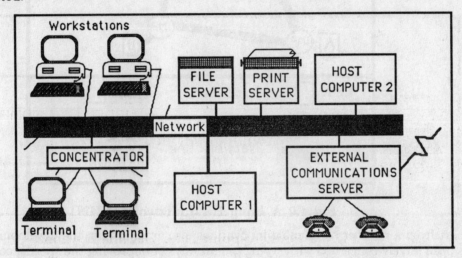

Fig 4.5 A Local Area Network (LAN)

4.54 In Fig 4.5 there is an example of a **Local Area Network (LAN)** as may be used on a single site within an organisation. The purpose of the LAN is to *connect* a variety of pieces of equipment by means of a shared link in order to allow their intercommunication. The terminals and workstations in Fig 4.5 are able to connect to either one of two "host" computers at will. The network also has a **file server** and a **print server**. The former is a special computer that provides a form of auxiliary storage, which can be used by any other computer on the network, and the latter is a special computer that can receive data from other computers on the network and print it. There is also an **external communications server** on the LAN that enables communication between equipment on the network and systems elsewhere by means similar to those described in 4.44 - 4.47.

4.55 LANs cannot be used over long distances. Instead **Long Haul Networks (LHNs)** are used. The feature of a typical LHN are show in outline in Fig 4.6. Computers at separate locations each have their own connection to the network. The point of connection is often called a **gateway**. When the network is used for electronic mail the gateway connection normally takes the form of some kind of **IMP (Interface Message Processor)**, which has the ability to receive, store and forward messages. A general purpose computer such as a minicomputer may perform this function if suitably programmed. The communications links between IMPs can take a variety of forms such as cable, optical fibre or satellite transmission.

4.56 Data transmission equipment has also been exploited as part of local or national **information retrieval systems.** For example, in the UK, BT offer a computer-based service connected to users by telephone links. Its trade name is "PRESTEL" and is one example of a **"Viewdata"** system. More details will be covered in later chapters.

OUTPUT

4.57 At the present time much information produced by computers is output in the form of printed paper documents, reports, etc. Many computer systems are used for "on-line" information retrieval and this means that considerable volumes of data are also merely displayed on screens instead of being produced in printed form.

4.58 In both these cases the information is expressed in terms of characters (2.2), but gradually more and more information is being provided in the form of images (ie, pictures or diagrams, possibly combined with text) (2.28). Such uses are already very common for such activities as producing original copies for reprinting in the form of reports, newsletters, textbooks and newspapers. Indeed, the author of this edition of this text has typeset the entire book using a home computer (A Macintosh).

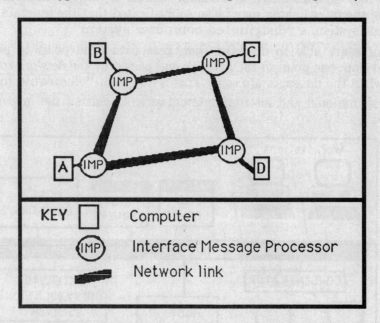

Fig 4.6 A Long Haul Network (LHN)

4.59 Quite apart from a number of valuable innovations over many years, the development of output devices has been largely concerned with trying to find ways of improving the speeds, costs and reliability of printers. Print quality and quietness have been additional aims for some printer applications.

4.60 The three main types of printer currently in use are:

    a. character printers.

    b. line printers.

    c. laser printers.

4.61 **Character printers** are low-speed printers that mimic the action of typewriters by printing *one character at a time*. The better character printers can produce output of sufficient quality to be used for business letters. Others may produce NLQ ("Near Letter Quality") output.

4.62 **Line printers.** The majority of high-speed printers *print whole lines at a time* (or appear to) and are consequently called *line printers*. Line printers usually have a considerable work load on mini or mainframe computers used for DP (Data Processing), ie, Business applications.

4.63 **Laser printers.** The first laser printers, which appeared on the market in the late 1970s, were very expensive ultra-high-speed devices intended to compete with the fasted line printers. The use of such printers is now well established. More recently, economical small-size lower-speed laser printers have become available and have been rapidly adopted for uses where high-quality output is important. The spelling "Lazers" is sometimes used.

4.64 This concludes the overview of hardware. The remainder of this chapter provides an overview of software.

SOFTWARE'S FLEXIBILITY

4.65 As stated previously, **software** is the term used to describe programs and associated documentation. Compared with hardware, the software used on a given computer is relatively easy to change and it is that capability which gives computers their flexibility of purpose.

4.66 The point is demonstrated well by the home computer used for playing games. Instead of buying a new machine each time a new game is wanted, as would be necessary if the game was solely hardware (ie, wholly built into electronic components), all that is needed is for a new program to be "loaded" into the machine each time a different game is needed. Better still, it is relatively easy to chop and change between games at will. This kind of flexibility is soon taken for granted, but it is in sharp contrast to most other items of everyday technology that have far less flexibility of purpose. It is this ability readily to change the computer's function which originally lead to the term **"software"** being used. Additional flexibility is also provided by software because not only is it relatively easy to change from one program to another but also individual programs can be changed, although such changes cannot necessarily be carried out by the computer user.

An Apple Macintosh SE with an Apple LaserWriter II laser printer
Courtesy of Apple Computers UK Ltd.

THE ORGANISATION OF SOFTWARE IN THE COMPUTER

4.67 The following diagram (Fig 4.7) gives a simplified illustration of how the various main items of software are organised and used in a general purpose computer. At the top of Fig 4.7 two types of computer user are shown above the software that they may directly access. Lower down, and not directly accessible, to the users, is the Operating System (1.15). The operating system is a special suite of programs that controls the way in which the software above it accesses and uses the computer's hardware. At the very bottom is the hardware that ultimately carries out the instructions it is given by the programs above it.

END USERS			
APPLICATIONS USERS		COMPUTER SPECIALISTS	
APPLICATIONS PACKAGES	SPECIALIST APPLICATIONS SOFTWARE	SYSTEM FACILITIES	COMMAND INTERPRETERS
OPERATING SYSTEM			
HARDWARE			

Fig 4.7 How Software is Organised and Used.

4.68 The next few paragraphs provide an interpretation of Fig 4.7.

4.69 The individuals who actually sit at computer terminals or at their own Personal Computers are called **"end-users"**. This distinguishes them from individuals who may be "users" but who do not get personally involved with "hands-on" activities.

4.70 The end-users of a general purpose computer may be broadly classified as either **applications users** or **computer specialists** according to the kinds of software they use.

    a. An applications user is an end-user who puts the computer to some specific practical purpose by using applications software (1.15). An applications user is not normally technically knowledgeable about the computer but may be trained to use a particular specialist applications program or applications package (1.15). In business organisations applications users most frequently use software to aid them in carrying out some clerical or administrative tasks. Some management tasks are aided by computers too. In industrial organisations applications users may use software that can monitor or control industrial processes for them, or may use software to perform complex computations.

    b. Some end-users are computer specialists whose work it is to set up, control or monitor the computer, or to produce new systems. In an organisation using large minicomputers or mainframes there may be many such staff. They may have specific roles and job titles such as "Computer Operator", "Systems Manager" or "Technical Support Officer". Alternatively they may be involved in developing new software. The most common example of such a person is a "programmer". As might be expected, these individuals use software that is often very different in nature from that used by end-users.

    Note. In the case of small computers, such as home computers and personal computers, there may only be one end-user who therefore may be both an applications user and, to some degree, a computer specialist.

4.71 Many specialist business applications make use of screens which are set out as **forms**. An example of a form used to enter the details of a new customer is shown in Fig 4.8.

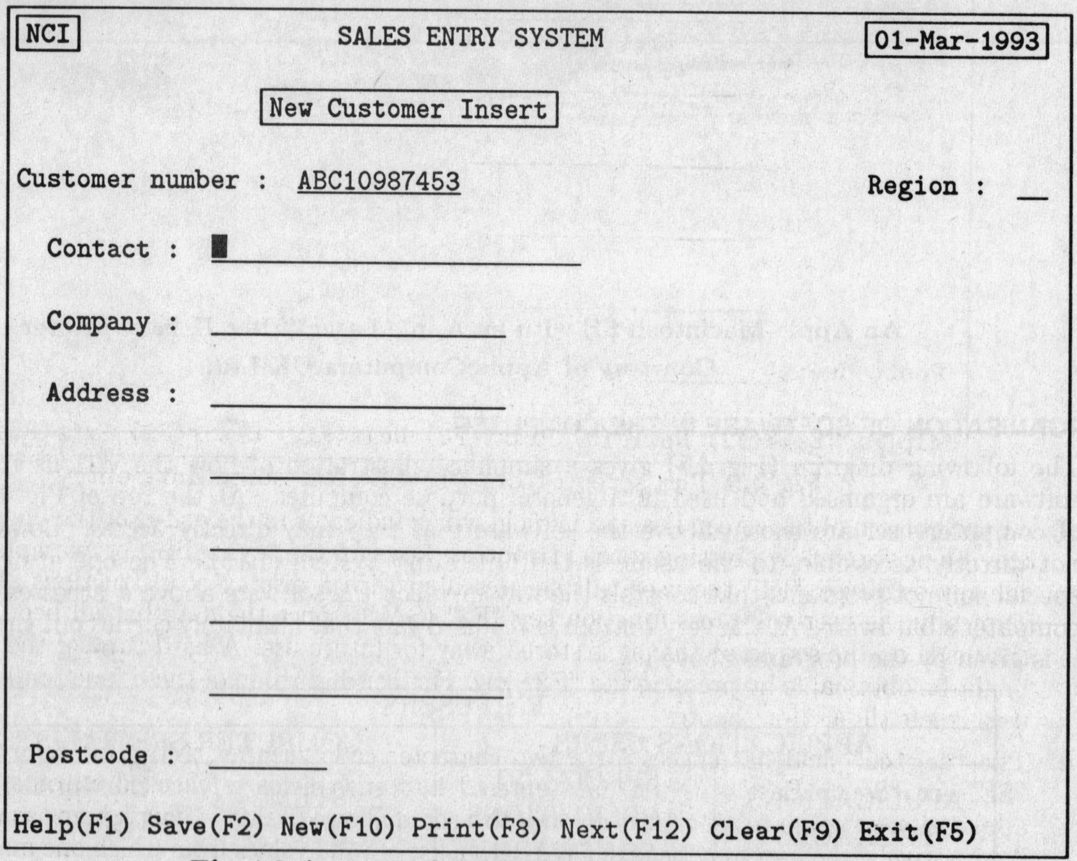

```
┌─────────────────────────────────────────────────────────────────┐
│ ┌─────┐                                              ┌───────────┐ │
│ │ NCI │          SALES ENTRY SYSTEM                  │01-Mar-1993│ │
│ └─────┘                                              └───────────┘ │
│                ┌──────────────────────┐                            │
│                │ New Customer Insert  │                            │
│                └──────────────────────┘                            │
│                                                                    │
│  Customer number :  ABC10987453                  Region : __       │
│                                                                    │
│     Contact :  █_____                          │
│                                                                    │
│     Company :  _____                           │
│                                                                    │
│     Address :  _____                           │
│                                                                    │
│                _____                           │
│                                                                    │
│                _____                           │
│                                                                    │
│                _____                           │
│                                                                    │
│                _____                           │
│                                                                    │
│     Postcode :  _____                                           │
│                                                                    │
│ Help(F1) Save(F2) New(F10) Print(F8) Next(F12) Clear(F9) Exit(F5)  │
└─────────────────────────────────────────────────────────────────┘
```

Fig 4.8 A screen based form used for data entry.

4.72 A number of general points about **forms**-based data entry can be made by reference to Fig 4.8 as follows.

    a. At various positions on the screen there are labelled places for entering data. For example, there are positions for five lines of an address. These are called **fields**. More precisely, the places used for individual data values are called **data fields** and the places occupied by the labels are called **trim fields**. The main heading "SALES ENTRY SYSTEM" is also a trim field. Some fields are contained within boxes while others are denoted by underlines.

b. In a **boxed field** at the top right hand corner of the screen the date is displayed. Normally data such as the current date is generated and displayed automatically by the computer and does not require entry by the end-user. Indeed, the user may be prevented form overwriting the value, in which case the field is said to be a **display-only** field. Other display-only fields are those giving the long name and short name of the screen currently being used. These are "New Customer Insert" and "NCI" respectively. The purpose of the short name will be discussed later.

c. A special symbol appears at the start of the field labelled "Contact :". This is called a **cursor** and is used to indicate the point at which data will appear if it is typed on the keyboard. When the user has completed typing the contents of a field then he or she may move on to the next field by typing an appropriate special key, typically an ENTER, RETURN or TAB key. For example, if the user types "Mrs A B Robinson" followed by the RETURN key the screen could appear as shown in Fig 4.9. Note how the cursor has moved to the start of the next data field.

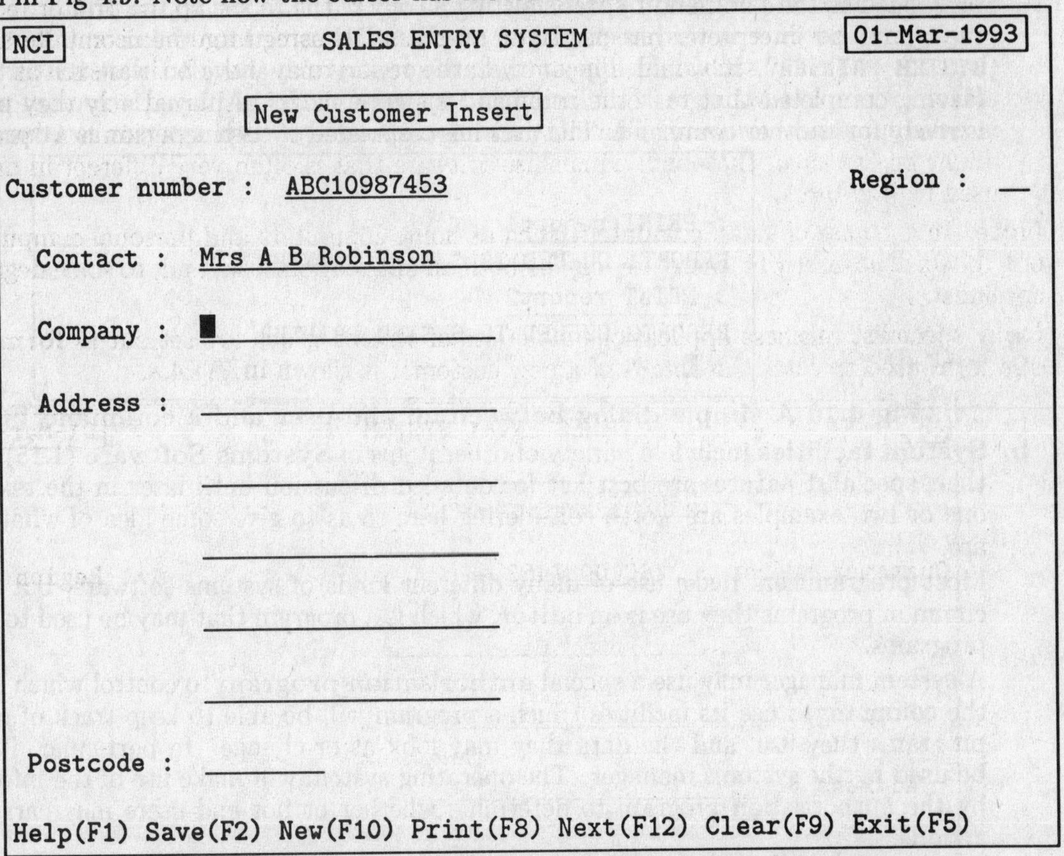

```
┌─────────────────────────────────────────────────────────────────────┐
│ ┌─────┐                                                   ┌───────────┐│
│ │ NCI │              SALES ENTRY SYSTEM                   │01-Mar-1993││
│ └─────┘                                                   └───────────┘│
│                    ┌──────────────────────┐                           │
│                    │  New Customer Insert  │                          │
│                    └──────────────────────┘                           │
│                                                                        │
│  Customer number :  ABC10987453                      Region :  __     │
│                                                                        │
│     Contact :  Mrs A B Robinson_____                                │
│                                                                        │
│     Company :  █_____                                  │
│                                                                        │
│     Address :  _____                                   │
│                                                                        │
│                _____                                   │
│                                                                        │
│                _____                                   │
│                                                                        │
│                _____                                   │
│                                                                        │
│                _____                                   │
│                                                                        │
│    Postcode :  _____                                                │
│                                                                        │
│ Help(F1) Save(F2) New(F10) Print(F8) Next(F12) Clear(F9) Exit(F5)      │
└─────────────────────────────────────────────────────────────────────┘
```

Fig 4.9 The screen from Fig 4.8 after some data entry.

d. At the bottom of the screen is a special field which indicates to the end-user the operations which may be performed by pressing special **function keys** on the keyboard. For example, by pressing the key engraved "F1" the user will be presented with a display of instructions of what to do. Typically the user will press function key "F2" (SAVE) once the data has all been entered onto the fields on the screen so that it is stored away for future use. A hard copy of the screen's data might be obtainable by pressing the "F8" key. Further discussion of these function keys and there uses is left till a later chapter.

e. The "Region" field has spaces for a two character code such as "NW" for "North West" and "SE" for "South East". Often data entered into such fields is checked automatically by the application program to see that it belongs to a set of allowed values. This is know as a **validation**. Alternatively, the user may be presented with a list of valid values from which one may be selected.

4.73 Further discussion of forms based data entry is left till later chapters.

4.74 In Fig 4.7 the applications users are shown using either specialist applications software or applications packages (1.15). The computer specialists are shown using two types of software, which will now be explained.

a. **Command Interpreters** are programs that provide a general-purpose means of instructing the computer to carry out operational tasks. For example, there will be commands that cause the computer to copy data from one magnetic disk to another. Other commands may cause particular information about the system or its users to be displayed on a screen or be printed out. Yet other commands may enable the computer to be set up so that applications packages can be used by particular end-users. More detailed examples will be provided later in this text.

The program is called a **command interpreter** because of the way in which it works. A user sitting at a terminal using the command interpreter will be able to type in simple standard instructions which the command interpreter will decipher and carry out straight away.

Fig 4.10 shows a screen at which a user has typed a command. In Fig 4.10 the letters shown in plain type are those which are generated by the command interpreter. Those underlined are the commands typed in by the user. The symbol ">" at the start of each line is called a **prompt**. Its purpose is to inform the user that the interpreter is ready to accept a command. The first command typed in PRINT report1 tells the command interpreter to print a copy of a report called "report1" on the computer's printer. The word PRINT is a special word that the command interpreter can understand. Such words are called **key words**. The command interpreter has responded to the command by transmitting a copy of the report to the printer. From the message the command interpreter has displayed on the VDU screen for the user ''REPORT1 QUEUED TO SYSTEM PRINTER", it would appear that the report may have to wait its turn to be printed. Having completed that task the command interpreter has displayed a prompt signifying that it is ready for another command. The user has responded by typing a similar command, and so on.

```
> PRINT report1
REPORT1 QUEUED TO SYSTEM PRINTER
> PRINT report2
REPORT2 QUEUED TO SYSTEM PRINTER
> █
```

Fig 4.10 A simple dialog between an end-user and a command interpreter.

b. **System facilities** include a variety of other items of **Systems Software** (1.15) that, because of their specialist nature, are best left for detailed discussion until later in the text. Nevertheless, one or two examples are worth considering here so as to give some idea of what these programs are.

Most programmers make use of many different kinds of systems software, but one of the most common programs they use is an **editor**, which is a program that may be used to create or amend programs.

A system manager may use a special **authorisation** program to control which users may *access* the computer to use its facilities. Such a program will be able to keep track of named users, the programs they use, and the data they may look at or change. In particular, it may itself only be used by the systems manager. The operating system will make use of the information created by the authorisation program to determine whether or not end-users may carry out particular actions.

In practice, the system software achieves part of this control by the use of **"user accounts"**, which are set up by the authorisation program. As with accounts in other situations, such as banking, a user must have an account before being able to use the facilities on offer. To use the software provided on the system the user must first **"log in"** to the system. Logging in is similar to using a command interpreter in that the system gives prompts to the user to which the user must type in appropriate responses. An example of logging in is shown in Fig 4.11

```
login:  Bloggs
Password Typed in but not displayed.
Welcome to the XYZ Ltd Company Computer


Please note the computer will close down at 18:30 today


The time now is 09:15

At this point the user will gain access to whatever software he or she
has been authorised to use.
```

Fig 4.11 An example of an end-user logging in to a computer.

In the example given in Fig 4.11 the end-user typed his or her user name, "Bloggs". The system software controlling the login was able to check that "Bloggs" was an authorised user so then went on to prompt for a password. Bloggs then typed the password at the keyboard, but, for security reasons, the letters were not displayed on the screen. Apparently the password was correctly typed because the system responded with a message and displayed the time.

Note. On many small computers, such as Personal Computers or Home Computers, such elaborate procedures may not be necessary. Some smaller computers operate as **turnkey systems**, which means that when they are switched on, perhaps by *turning a security key*, the computer automatically gives the user the use of just one particular applications program.

4.75 The **Operating System** has a special role to perform, in that most other programs are not able to work without it. In effect, the operating system provides facilities that enable the other programs to use the hardware in a safe and controlled way. The mechanisms by which this takes place are too complicated to discuss in detail at this stage but the ideas are simple. For example, a program that wishes to display some data on a user's screen makes a request to the operating system, giving it the data concerned. The operating system then displays the data. The end-user is totally unaware of all this. As far as he or she is concerned a single program is being used.

4.76 Having considered the way software is organised and used we now turn to what can be expected of professionally produced software. Amateur programmers often consider that their job is done once they have produced a program that seems to work. Indeed, if the program is for their own private and personal use that may be perfectly satisfactory. However, most of the software people use is produced as a product for sale and therefore must be more finished, as we will now see.

SOFTWARE AS A PRODUCT

4.77 When software is purchased for use on a particular computer the purchaser obtains a copy of the programs plus a number of items of documentation. Remember that the term software means *programs plus their associated documentation.* Software is normally purchased directly or indirectly from either a computer manufacturer or a "software house". A software house is a company that specialises in producing software and related services.

The purchaser of software usually pays for some or all of the following:

a. A licence. Sometimes the purchaser pays outright for all rights associated with using the software but usually that is not the case. Instead, the purchaser pays a licence fee, which gives the right to use the software on a particular computer or a specified number of computers on a particular site. Alternatively, a **site licence** may be paid for which entitles the purchaser to use the software on any computer at a particular place. Sometimes the licence specifies the number of users that may use the software at any one time, and, in the case of a single-user licence, may require that the user's name be registered. Using software in breach of licence agreements is a serious offence for which the user may be sued for damages or subjected to criminal prosecution. Companies are normally very careful to observe licence agreements, but many cases of **pirated software** (ie, illegally copied software) have been reported in recent years.

b. An installation guide. This guide may be part of a single documentation manual in simple cases or a completely separate manual in the case of larger suites of software. Normally, the guide starts by providing information about what hardware is needed to enable the programs to run satisfactorily. It then goes on to describe the procedures to be followed in order to set up the software so that it can be used satisfactorily and efficiently on a particular kind of computer. According to the complexities of the software involved this may involve some work being carried out by a computer specialist.

c. The installation of the software. A purchaser may not have the necessary expertise to set up the software, or may find it too time consuming or troublesome to carry out. In such cases the purchaser may be able to pay an additional fee to have the software installed.

d. Maintenance and updates. It is unfortunately not uncommon for programs to be supplied which may be faulty in some way. Sometimes these faults, called **bugs**, do not come to light until some time after the software has been delivered and put to use. A good supplier will make every effort to correct bugs as and when they are discovered and will provide a new corrected version of the program containing the necessary "bug fixes". The correction of bugs, ie, maintenance, is often combined with enhancements to the software, to make it better in some way. Enhancement normally involves increased **"functionality"** (ie, making it do more things) or improvements to performance (eg, making it work faster). Licensed purchasers may get some of these changes provided free of charge, perhaps during the first year of use. Subsequently the purchaser may be able to pay an annual fee for maintenance and updates.

e. A support contract. A purchaser experiencing problems with software, not necessarily caused by bugs, will want to be able to turn to the supplier for help. If a high level of assistance is required it may be available as an additional service subject to a separate contract. Some "mission critical" software in large corporations may be under 24-hour support contracts. The user can call for help on-site at anytime of the day or night. Obviously such support contracts are not the norm. However, it is very common for businesses to have support contracts that provide telephone assistance during the working day on what is often called a "hot line".

f. User guides. A user guide is usually a manual provided for an end-user to enable him or her to learn how to use the software. Such guides usually use suitable examples to take the user through the stages of carrying out various tasks with the software.

g. A reference manual. A reference manual is normally intended to be used by a user who already knows how to use the software but who needs to be reminded about a particular point or who wants to obtain more detailed information about a particular feature. Reference manuals normally have topics organised in alphabetical order.

h. A quick reference guide. These are single sheets or cards, small enough to fit into a pocket, which the user may keep handy for help with common tasks carried out with the software. For example, a quick reference guide for a Command Interpreter might list the commands alphabetically in key words order showing how they should be typed.

i. Training. In addition to providing user guides the software supplier may provide training courses on how to use the software. Sometimes some initial training is provided free as part of the initial purchase. Although training is often quite costly it may pay for itself if the software user becomes proficient much more quickly as a result.

j. Membership of a user group. A user group is a club for individuals or organisations who use a particular hardware or software product. The club is often run and partly sponsored by the supplier. Members of user groups may have meetings or receive newsletters which enable them to find out more about the product and how to use it.

4.78 It should be clear to the reader from what has just be stated that there is a lot more to producing a software product than merely producing the programs themselves. Even so, the programming is still a key task in the production of a software product. In later chapters a considerable amount of space is devoted to many of the basic methods, tools and languages used in programming. Always remember that, in addition to the production of a well-finished and reliable program with the right functionality, there are numerous other tasks to be done. These include considerable work by such people as those who produce all the documentation (manuals, guides, etc), the **"technical authors"**.

APPLICATIONS PACKAGES

4.79 Applications packages are suites of programs, with associated documentation, used for a particular type of problem or variety of similar problems. Software packages are sold as complete products and in this respect differ from most user applications programs, which are normally produced by an organisation for internal use to perform specific tasks.

4.80 Applications packages may be classified as either:

a. Application Specific

or

b. Generalised.

4.81 An application specific package is aimed at providing all the facilities required for a particular class of application problem such as payroll or stock control. A generalised applications package is one that provides a completely general set of facilities that are of use in dealing with similar types of task which arise in a wide variety of *different* applications problems. Well known packages of this type such as **spreadsheet** packages and **word processing** packages will be examined in detail in later chapters.

First, consider applications packages that are applications specific.

PACKAGES FOR SPECIFIC APPLICATIONS

4.82 Many users have the same type of problem to deal with by means of a computer, and thus manufacturers and specialist software writers have written standard programs to solve these problems and sell them to the many users who want them. Examples are stock control, sales invoicing, network analysis and payroll.

4.83 Applications packages are of major importance to small computer-system users who do not have the necessary resources or expertise to produce their own software.

4.84 **Advantages of packages.**

a. The main advantage is the saving of programming effort and expense on the part of the user. Development costs are effectively shared between the purchasers.

b. The user gets a well-tried and tested program, which he or she is able to use with confidence.

c. Relatively quick implementation results from the use of packages.

4.85 Disadvantages of packages.

a. The purchaser does not have direct control over the package in the same way as would be the case if the software was produced in-house.

b. The package will have been produced to meet general needs and may therefore not be ideal for a particular customer.

4.86 Practical considerations.

a. Many users' systems will differ in some detailed area, especially if there is a relationship between applications, as there is, for example, between labour cost analysis and payroll.

b. A solution would be for the users to modify their system to suit the package, but this has its problems.

c. Some users may decide arbitrarily to design a system to suit the package.

d. Some software houses build packages on the modular principle and thus are able to combine the various modules to suit a particular user's requirement.

e. The question of cost must not be ignored and will be reflected in the service provided by the supplier of the package.

f. A number of trade associations, etc, have sponsored the writing of packages for particular industries. The Motor Manufacturers Association has set up packages for its dealers.

g. Thorough research should be made into the reliability of the package and the particular software house offering it for sale. It is a good idea to ask current users of the package about their experience.

h. A program maintenance agreement should be sought where changes to the package are likely, eg, a payroll package could be affected by government legislation.

4.87 How the package is supplied. A package normally consists of:

a. A program (or suite of programs) actually written onto a suitable medium, eg, magnetic tape, or floppy disk.

b. Documentation, which specifies:

   i. How to set up the package.
   ii. How to use the package.
   iii. Necessary technical details.

4.88 Any software that the user buys is likely to be supplied in similar form to that just described. Suppliers tend to provide no more than the necessary technical detail in order to protect their trade secrets.

SUMMARY

4.89 a. The chapter has provided an overview of computer hardware under these main headings.

   i. Semi-conductor processors and memories.
   ii. Data storage.
   iii. Backing storage.
   iv. Data entry.
   v. Data transmission and networks.
   vi. Output.

b. General characteristics have been introduced, with examples, so that when the reader encounter details of particular hardware in later chapters, he or she will have some basic criteria by which to evaluate them.

c. End-users may be broadly classified as either applications users or computer specialists according to the types of software they use.

d. Many specialist business applications use forms on screens whereby data is entered into fields on the screen.

e. Command interpreters provide a general-purpose means of instructing the computer to carry out operational tasks.

f. Access to the computer is often controlled by software. One method requires the user to log in and give a password. Another method involves the use of turnkey systems.

g. The operating system controls the way in which all other software uses the hardware.

h. Software was considered as a product to highlight the various requirements of the software user.

i. Application packages are suites of programs, with associated documentation, used for a particular type of problem or variety of similar problems and normally sold as complete products.

j. Applications packages may be broadly classified as

   i. Application specific, eg, a stock-control package,
      or

   ii. Generalised, eg, a spreadsheet.

POINTS TO NOTE

4.90
a. Note the difference between **"on-line"**, ie, connected to the computer and under its control, and **"off-line"**, ie, away from the computer.

b. The hardware examples given in this chapter represent the most widely used types and have a commercial bias: Approximately 80% of all money spent on computer systems is spent on systems for commercial purposes. However, there are many important types of hardware used in industrial applications such as manufacturing. Examples of these will be given in later chapters. In terms of numbers of processors in use the majority of computer use is now industrial, with processors found in everything from watches to weigh-bridges.

c. With the hardware remaining unaltered the user can completely change the function of the computer merely by changing the software.

d. The term "applications package" has been used in this chapter as a very broad category for software. Even so, not all software products sold as "packages" would be called applications packages. For example, some database software is sold in very much the same way as applications packages but provides facilities "on top of" those provided by the standard systems software and can be used by applications software. Such packages are often referred to as **"layered software products"** because of their position between standard systems software, which they add to, and the applications software.

STUDENT SELF-TESTING QUESTIONS

1. Define the term "volatile" in the context of computer memory.
2. Name two common backing storage media.
3. Name three categories of data entry methods.
4. What is "data transmission"?
5. What do LAN, LHN and IMP stand for?
6. What is a command interpreter and who might use it?
7. What is a turnkey system?
8. List ten things that the purchaser of software might require as part of the purchase.

QUESTIONS WITHOUT ANSWERS

9. What kind of main storage and backing storage is used on the computer system that you use? Try to find out what capacity it has.
10. What is a terminal emulator and who might use it?
11. Think of some possible problems caused by software piracy and discuss them with your fellow students.
12. What is an applications package?

GLOSSARY CHECKLIST

APPLICATIONS I

1. This text contains a number of Parts aimed at covering various aspects of computer applications. The inclusion of this material in this new edition of the text reflects a significant trend in computer examinations in recent years, especially in A levels. Each Part deals with a different aspect of computer applications.
2. In this Part a single chapter deals with document processing which is one of the most common application of computers today.
3. Readers are strongly urged to gain first hand practical experience as well as reading the material.
4. Readers are also advised to read all chapters dealing with applications irrespective of the examination course being studied, because the general information provided.

5: Document Processing

INTRODUCTION

5.1 Computers are very widely used for the creation, manipulation and storage of documents but there is enormous variation in the methods used and in the levels of sophistication. This chapter surveys computer document processing from the most basic forms to the more complex and specialised.

5.2 When considering software used for a particular kind of application it is always important to judge it by its appropriateness for its purpose and by whether the benefits justify the costs. This applies to document processing software where the simpler and less costly software is aimed at purposes very different from those served by more sophisticated and expensive software.

DOCUMENT FILES

5.3 Each document is stored in the computer individually *by name* in what is called a **file**. Many document files take the form of a formatted sequence of characters. In their simplest form such files are called **text files** because they consist of printable characters (2.22) organised into lines of text. A small number of format effector characters (2.23d) signify tabs, page breaks and the divisions between lines. If the text file is output the control characters cause the output device (eg, printer or monitor) to give the document the required format. This is illustrated by Fig 5.1 which shows an example of a text file as stored and output. The format effector characters in the stored file are represented in Fig 5.1 by ⌷HT⌷ ⌷CR⌷ and ⌷LF⌷.

⌷HT⌷On 2nd November 1988⌷CR⌷⌷LF⌷ the Internet Worm program⌷CR⌷⌷LF⌷ invaded nationally⌷CR⌷⌷LF⌷ networked computer in⌷CR⌷⌷LF⌷ the USA causi ng havoc.⌷CR⌷⌷LF⌷ ⌷HT⌷The program's author⌷CR⌷⌷LF⌷ was subsequently tried⌷CR⌷⌷LF⌷ and convicted.⌷CR⌷⌷LF⌷

a. The text file is stored as an unbroken sequence of characters.

```
          On 2nd November 1988
the Internet Worm program
invaded nationally
networked computer in
the USA causing havoc.
          The program's author
was subsequently tried
and convicted.
```

b. The text file is output as a series of formatted lines.

Fig 5.1 An example of how a text file may be stored and output.

EDITORS

5.4 Text files can be created and modified with the aid of a special program called an **editor** (or more precisely a **text editor**). Many documents not requiring anything but a very basic page layout are prepared in this way. This applies to most computer programs.

5.5 The most basic types of editor provide means of editing text files on a line by line basis with each line being identified by a line number. These **"line editors"** are rather outdated and do not merit further discussion.

5.6 Modern text editors normally display the file's text on the screen in a form like that shown in Fig 5.1b. There are numerous text editors in use today and they are often associated with particular operating systems (4.75). For example, the editor "Vi" is commonly found on computers using an operating system called "Unix". However, the functions provided are broadly the same.

5.7   The common functions of text editors are illustrated by the following example based upon a text file with the name "mydoc.txt". The ".txt" at the end of the file name follows a common practice of indicating the type of file by means of a suffix following a ".". Here "txt" is a common abbreviation for "text".

5.8   If the computer user is using a command interpreter (4.74) then he or she may start editing the text file "mydoc.txt" by typing a command such as "edit mydoc.txt" at the prompt. Normally the editor will create a new text file if one does not exist. If one does already exist the editor "reads" the characters from the file and displays them on the screen. The editor may also display the cursor in the top left hand corner as shown in Fig 5.2.

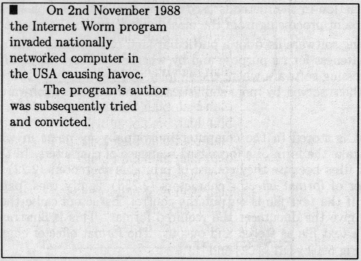

Fig 5.2 A screen display when using a simple text editor.

5.9   The cursor can be moved around the document by means of the four **cursor keys** normally engraved "←", "→", "↑" and "↓". So, for example, if the "↓" cursor key is depressed three times followed by four depressions of the "→" cursor key the cursor will end up as shown in Fig 5.3.

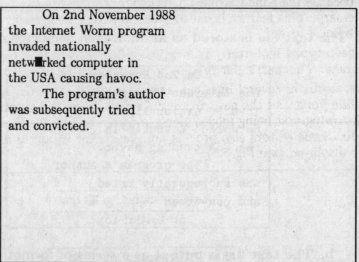

Fig 5.3 The display from Fig 5.2 with the cursor moved.

5.10   The text file will normally hold far more characters than can fit onto one screen display. A typical screen is 80 characters wide and may only display about 24 lines of text (slightly less than half of a printed page). The document size is not limited to this size. As more lines of text are typed, the earlier lines move off the top of the screen. Although they have disappeared from view they are still retained within the computers memory.

5.11   The screen thus acts like a **window** on the text, which can be moved up or down by means of the **cursor keys**. For example, if the cursor is at the bottom of the screen then a further depression of the "↓" cursor key will cause the next line of text to appear at the bottom of the screen, with all other lines being moved up one position causing the top line to no longer be displayed. The text file is like text on a scroll, only a small part of which can be seen at any one time through the window (see Fig. 5.4). The scroll is rolled up or down by moving the cursor, a process referred to as **scrolling**.

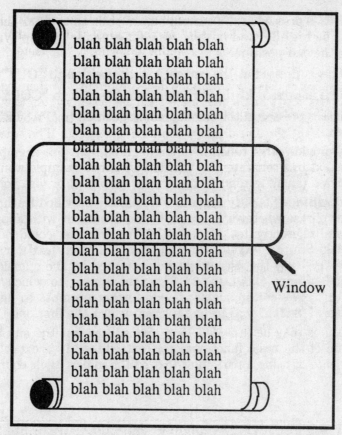

Fig 5.4. Scrolling text seen through a window.

5.12 As characters are typed across the screen there comes a point when a new line is required. A typist has to decide if the word about to be typed will fit on to that line. In some editors this is catered for automatically because the editor counts the number of spaces remaining and forces the word onto a new line if necessary. This feature is called **word wrap**. The carriage return key is thus used only to force a blank line.

5.13 If a word has been typed incorrectly it is quite easy to move the cursor to the offending word and correct the mistake. This particular process is also referred to as **editing**.

5.14 New characters, words or several lines can also be inserted into existing text. The cursor is moved to the appropriate point and the new characters typed. They will automatically be inserted into the text with the following text being moved along to accommodate the changes. The editor is said to be in **insert mode**. Some editors also provide an **overstrike mode** in which the typed text replaces that previously displayed (see Fig 5.5).

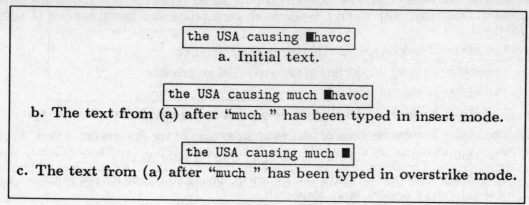

Fig 5.5. Modes of editing.

5.15 Most editors also incorporate "cut and paste" facilities whereby a section of text can be selected and moved to a different part of the document. A variation on this is to *copy* the selected section of text, without removing it from its original position. Such operations often require the use of special function keys. The selection is normally made by first "marking" a start position and then moving the cursor to the end position. A typical set of operations would be as follows.

    a. **Key F5.** This is pressed at the current cursor position to mark the start of a selection. Normally the text will be **highlighted** in some way, for example by displaying it underlined, as the cursor is moved to the end position.

    b. **Key F2.** This is pressed at the current cursor position to "CUT" the marked highlighted text.

    c. **Key F3.** This is pressed at the current cursor position to "COPY" the marked highlighted text.

    d. **Key F4.** This is pressed at the current cursor position to "PASTE" the text which was previously cut or copied.

5.16   The editor may provide other function on highlighted text. For example, it might be possible to save the highlighted text in a separate new text file. Another example would be changing the highlighted text from lowercase (small letters) to upper case (capitals) or visa versa.

5.17   A "**search and replace**" facility is another frequently provided feature. It allows the user to replace a single word or phrase wherever it occurs in the document with another word or phrase. A report containing several references to "Mr. Smith", for example, could be changed quite easily to refer to "Mr. Reginald Smith". Again, function keys are often used for such functions. For example, on pressing the "F5" key the user might be prompted by the question "FIND ?". On typing "Mr. Smith" a second prompt "REPLACE BY ?" might appear to which the user might respond "Mr. Reginald Smith". The editor might provide further prompts to determine whether or not every occurrence of "Mr. Smith" was to be replaced or just the first one.

5.18   Many more features may be provided by a text editors but the aim here has merely been to make the reader aware of the basic functions of a text editor. It is expected that readers will also gain practical experience of using a particular text editor as part their courses so further discussion is not merited here.

WORD PROCESSING

5.19   As was mention in chapter 1, a **word processor** (1.13) is a specialist computer used for the production of documents. However, these days most word processing is actually carried out using specialist **word processing** software on ordinary PCs. Indeed, the term **word processor** is increasingly used to describe a word processing program or complete word processing software package rather than a specialist computer. Examples of very popular word processing software packages are **WordPerfect** produced by the WordPerfect Corporation and **Word** produced by Microsoft.

5.20   A word processing program allows the user to create, edit, format, store and print text documents. A document is anything that can be typed: a memo, a letter, a report or a book.

5.21   At face value a word processing program is very similar to text editor because the two have many functions in common. In fact, some advanced text editors may reasonably be called word processing programs. However, a typical word processing program has far more capabilities than a normal text editor and operates on document files which have a far more complex format than normal text files. To qualify for the title **word processing program** the software must provide facilities not just to edit documents but to define their layout and to enable them to be printed.

5.22   In most offices word processors have virtually replaced typewriters as the means of producing documents. Compared with using a typewriter, word processing has a number of advantages which include:

    a. The ability to store typed documents in the computer.

    b. The ability to view the document on screen before printing.

    c. The ability to correct mistakes.

    d. The ability to insert or delete words, sentences or paragraphs.

    e. The ability to move sections of text to another part of the document.

    f. The ability to store documents on backing store for later recall.

    g. The ability to incorporate other text without having to retype it. For example, a standard form or letter can be re-used again and again.

    h. The ability to change the layout of the document.

    i. The ability to print the document many times.

5.23   Many professional writers (journalists, authors, novelists etc.) also use word processing packages.

5.24   Most word processing programs work in a similar way to text editors although they commonly display more useful information on the screen for the benefit of the user. For example, it is common for the word processor to display a **status line** at the bottom of the screen as is illustrated by Fig 5.6. Often, a printed plastic overlay for the keyboard, called a "template", is provided too. The template is used to label the function keys with their word processing operations.

```
        On 2nd November 1988
the Internet Worm program
invaded nationally
networked computer in
the USA causing havoc.
        The program's author
was subsequently tried
and convicted.▪






Page:  1   Line:  8   Document: mydoc.wpd
```

Fig 5.6 A word processor screen display.

5.25 Many packages claim to provide **"WYSIWYG"** or "what you see is what you get". This means that the representation of the document on screen is very close to how it will appear when printed. Assuming that a printer is connected to the computer, the document can be printed out at any time as often as is required.

```
A word processing program allows the
user to create, edit, format, store and print
text documents. A text document is
anything that can be typed: a memo, a
letter, a report or a book.

            a.  Left-justified

    A word processing program allows the
    user to create, edit, format, store and print
            text documents. A text document is
        anything that can be typed: a memo, a
                letter, a report or a book.

            b.  Right justified

A word processing program allows the user
to create, edit, format, store and print text
documents. A   text doc ument i s anyt hing
that c an be typed: a memo, a letter, a report
or a book.

            c. Fully justified
```

Fig 5.7. Examples of text justification.

5.26 The document is viewed on screen before printing and changes to the layout or format of the document can also be made. Controls over the format of the document include:

a. setting and changing the page size;

b. setting and changing page header and footer text;

c. setting and changing the width of the left-hand or right-hand margins for particular paragraphs;

    d. setting and changing the page numbering style and position;

    e. setting and changing the style and size of printed characters (eg, bold, italic, normal size or subscript size).

5.27 Another common formatting technique is **text justification** which means the alignment of text against a margin. **Left justification** means alignment against the left margin, **right justification** means alignment against the right margin and **full justification** means both left and right justification (see Fig. 5.7). For full justification, extra spaces are inserted by the program into lines of text to ensure a straight right hand edge to the document. Another example is the centering of text. Adjusting these formatting parameters is often achieved by means of special function keys on the computer keyboard.

5.28 When a document has been completed it can be saved for long term storage onto backing store as a file. The file normally has a format much more complex than that of a text file and is usually only directly usable by the word processing program which created it. The same document can be loaded back into the word processing program at a later time without it needing to be retyped. Further corrections or amendments can then be made.

5.29 This facility also allows other files to be merged into a new document. For example, a file containing a document of a current price list can be added to a letter to be sent out to a potential client. Only the letter needs to be typed. The technique of building up a document from standard paragraphs, such as clauses in a contract, is known as **boilerplating**.

5.30 Within a word processing software package there may be a number of ancillary programs which can be used in conjunction with word processed documents to enhance the standard facilities. One such facility is the process known as **mail-merge**. In this it is possible to produce a standard letter into which the name and address (and other details) of a number of clients in turn are merged and a series of individual letters printed. Each recipient of the letter receives an original print.

5.31 **Spell checkers.** Many word processing packages now include spell checking facilities. The spell check program comes with its own dictionary of from 20,000 to 100,000 words and is able to scan through the document and report wherever a word is found which does not exist in its dictionary. The user is then able to correct the word or leave it as it was originally spelt. Unless they have facilities for adding new words to the dictionary spell checkers have difficulty recognising peoples names and postcodes as correct "words".

5.32 Some spell checking programs can be left to search through a document and mark every doubtful word for later checking by the user (useful for very long documents) rather than provide interactive facilities. Others can check against their dictionary of words so quickly that they can provide immediate feedback to the user as each word is typed in.

5.33 Many spell checkers provide the user with a list of alternative words which are similar in spelling or sound to the doubtful word. Some also allow the user to create and maintain their own dictionary of words, which is very useful if the user constantly refers to specialised or "jargon" words in a particular subject area (eg, chemical compounds).

5.34 It should be pointed out that spell checking programs cannot guarantee that every spelling mistake will be detected in a document. The words "there" and "their", for example, are correctly spelt only if used in the correct context. The words "fore examples" are both correctly spelt in themselves, but are incorrect if "for example" was intended. Another common mistake in documents is double-typing of the the same word, as in this sentence. Programs aimed at detecting these types of mistakes are often referred to as **grammar checkers** or **style checkers**.

5.35 Style checkers also help to identify unnecessary words or wordy phrases which appear in the document. To help eliminate repetition, these programs can check to see if particular patterns of words appear again and again in the document, and they can also indicate if sentences seem too long.

5.36 Yet another useful facility is a **thesaurus**. This is a program which allows the user to choose an alternative word to a selected word. A thesaurus is basically a dictionary of synonyms (similar words) and antonyms (dissimilar words), and the user points to a particular word and is presented with a list of alternatives.

5.37 Many text documents also need to include tables and charts, and some word processing packages incorporate limited graphics capability to allow lines and borders to be drawn around such tables. There is often a need to bring data into a document which has been produced on another application package such as a spreadsheet, for example a table of numbers, and many word processing packages allow for this **"importing"** of data files from other packages including the importing of document produced by other word processors. An **export** facility is also often provided whereby the document is saved as a simple text file or in the file format used by another word processor.

5.38 More advanced word processors allow for many different fonts to be used in the printed document. The size of each printed character in these fonts can also be changed.

5.39 If the word processing software is sufficiently advanced in its control over page layout, printed fonts, diagrams and typography in general it may be said to perform **computerised typesetting**. The use of such computerised typesetting software on small computers such PCs and Workstation has given rise to the term **Desktop Publishing (DTP)**. However, there is more to DTP than merely using advanced word processing software and, indeed, some forms of DTP do not used word processors for text preparation.

Times Roman 9pt

Times Roman 10pt

Times Roman 12pt

Times Roman 14pt

Times Roman 18pt

Times Roman 24pt

Times Roman 36pt

Times Roman 9pt

Times Roman 10pt

Times Roman 12pt

Times Roman 14pt

Times Roman 18pt

Times Roman 24pt

Times Roman 36pt

Times Roman 9pt

Times Roman 10pt

Times Roman 12pt

Times Roman 14pt

Times Roman 18pt

Times Roman 24pt

Times Roman 36pt

Fig 5.8. The Times Roman Type Family.

DESKTOP PUBLISHING (DTP)

5.40 A **Desktop Publishing System** is a desktop computer with the necessary hardware and software to enable the user to carry out **computerised typesetting**. Typically, a DTP system will be able to handled document layouts involving not only printed text but diagrams and images too. For this reason the monitor screens used in DTP system are normally **bit-mapped** (2.30) with the grid of **pixels** (2.29) on the screen being used to represent both images and text characters. The binary codes corresponding to what is on the screen are stored in the computers memory from where they can be *mapped* onto the screen. Printed output also requires the use of devices which can print text and images. A **laser printer** is a common choice.

5.41 We will examine various key areas of DTP in turn starting with the details of type families and leading through to general aspects of page layouts.

5.42 Fig 5.8 shows an example of a popular **type family** called *Time Roman*. Although there is considerable variation within the examples there is clearly some basic similarity too. Within the type family shown in Fig 5.8 there are three **typefaces**. Each typeface is a different **style** of the same type family. At the top is a **plain** typeface. In the middle is a **bold** typeface. At the bottom is an **italic** typeface. Each typeface comes in a number of sizes. A typeface in a specified size is called a **font**. The size is commonly expressed in terms of **points** normally abbreviated to **pt** (details later). So, "**Times Roman bold 12pt** is a description of a font belonging to the **typeface Times Roman bold** which in turn belongs to the **type family** Times Roman.

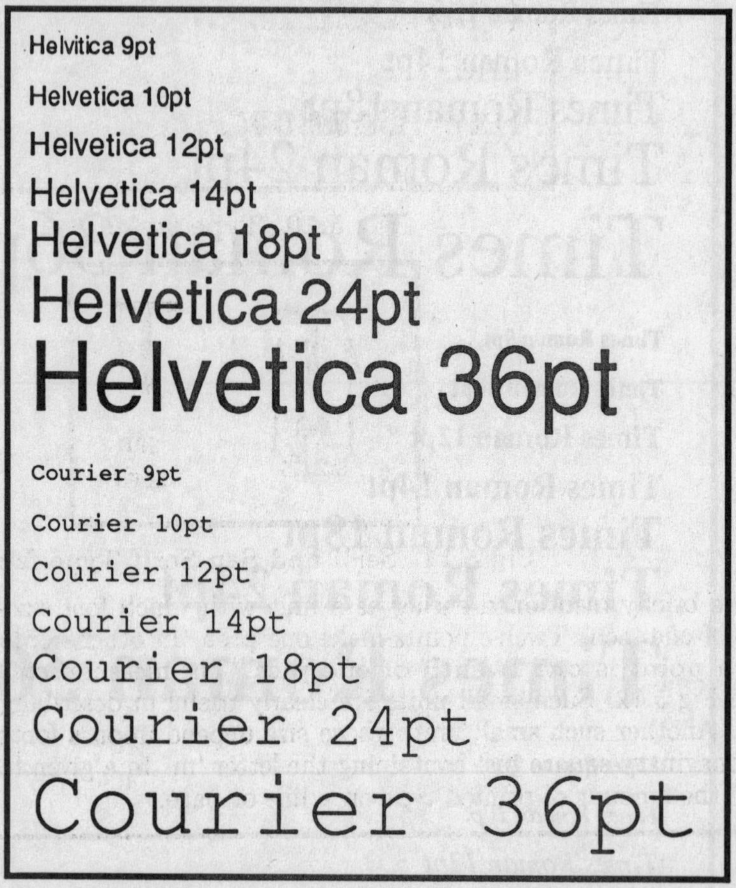

Helvitica 9pt

Helvetica 10pt

Helvetica 12pt

Helvetica 14pt

Helvetica 18pt

Helvetica 24pt

Helvetica 36pt

Courier 9pt

Courier 10pt

Courier 12pt

Courier 14pt

Courier 18pt

Courier 24pt

Courier 36pt

Fig 5.9. Helvetica Plain and Courier Plain Type Faces.

5.43 In Fig 5.9 two further popular typefaces are shown. They are both in the same style but belong to different type families. By way of contrast Fig 5.10 shows a series of different styles in the Times Roman type family.

5.44 Serifs are the ornate extra strokes which put decorations on individual characters in a font (see Fig 5.11). Characters in the Times Roman type family have serifs whereas the characters in Helvetica do not. Helvetica is therefore said to be a **sans serif** type family (*sans* meaning *without*). Plain typefaces with serifs tend to create a more serious impression but, more importantly, they are the most readable for large volumes of type. Research has shown that reading speed and accuracy is much higher when such fonts are used which is why most books and newspapers use type families with serifs. San serif typefaces are clearer and are most commonly used for headlines and titles. Also, san serif typefaces photocopy more clearly than typefaces with serifs and are therefore often used for documents such as news sheets or technical papers which may need to be photocopied for a small circulation.

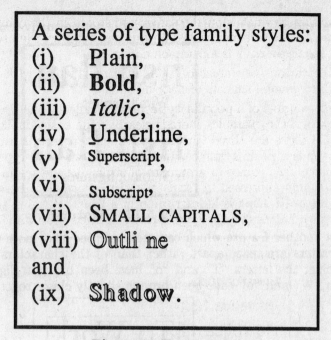

Fig 5.10. Type styles.

Fig 5.11. Serif and San Serif Type faces.

5.45 **Points** were briefly mentioned earlier as a unit with which font sizes are commonly expressed. A point is $\frac{1}{72}$ of one inch. Twelve points make one **pica**. In other words **a pica is one sixth of one inch and a point is one twelfth of one pica.** The measurement used to specify the point size is shown in Fig 5.12. Such small units are clearly useful in describing something so small as a text characters. Another such small unit, whose size depend upon a fonts size, is the **Em** which is the size of an imaginary square just containing the letter 'm' in a given font. It can be used to measure or estimate the amount of printed type on a line or page.

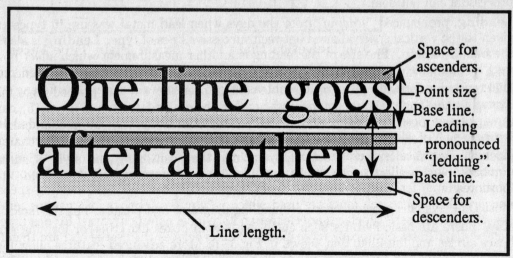

Fig 5.12. Layout spacing.

5.46 **Ligatures** are characters formed from the combination of two character symbols. Two examples are shown in Fig 5.13. Originally, the term referred to the strokes combining or binding the two letters together. Ligatures are not only elegant they are another feature which contribute to making a typeface more readable even though the reader is not normally consciously aware of their presence.

Fig 5.13. Ligatures.

5.47   **Kerning** is yet another feature which can make printed text more readable but it a feature of how particular characters are space apart rather than of the characters themselves. In Fig 5.14 notice how, with kerning, the letters "T" and "o" have been brought slightly closer together in the first word and again "W" and "o" have been brough slightly closer together in the second word.

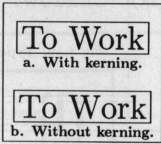

Fig 5.14. Kerning.

5.48   The particular adjustments made to spacing by kerning are quite separate from the normal spaces given between characters. Typewriters and many computer printers use fonts which take equal horizontal space for all characters. These fonts are said to be **monospaced** since there is only one spacing used. All fonts in the **Courier** type family (Fig 5.9) are monospaced. Monospaced fonts have the advantage of simplicity and make vertical tabulations easier, especially with columns of numbers, but they are far less easy to read in volume.

5.49   For volumes of text **proportionally spaced** typefaces are superior to monospaced typefaces (ie, *non* proportionally spaced). In a typeface with proportional spacing the horizontal space allowed for each character depends upon its shape . So, for example, "o" is allowed more space than "i". It is far more complicated to make text fully justified (5.27) when a proportionally spaced typeface is used. This is one of the many complexities which a DTP system must handle and with which many word processors can not deal.

5.50   **Leading**, pronounced *"ledding"* from the days when lead metal was use in typesetting, is the name given to the vertical space allowed between successive lines of type. **Leading** is also sometimes called the **baseline skip**. The size of the leading is another measurement which affect how readable a text may be and which may adjustable in a DTP system but fixed in a normal word processor.

5.51   DTP systems normally give considerable control over the way the printed page may be formatted. Normally the basic layout, comprising **header**, **body** and **footer** (Fig. 5.15) can be specified in terms of size position and format. Additionally, the body may be subdivided into a number of **frames** each of which contains a separate portion of the page such as a column of picture.

Controls over headers and footers may include the positioning and style of such things as, page numbers, page headers (eg, italic left justified on even page and right justified on odd), dates and footnotes.

5.52   Most DTP systems provide means of handling diagrams and pictures but the facilities vary considerably. There are basic features such enclosing text in boxes like this or forming simple figures from boxes circles and lines like that shown in Fig 5.16. More advanced features allow for the inclusion of whole diagrams and pictures as in the case of the DTP system used to produce this book.

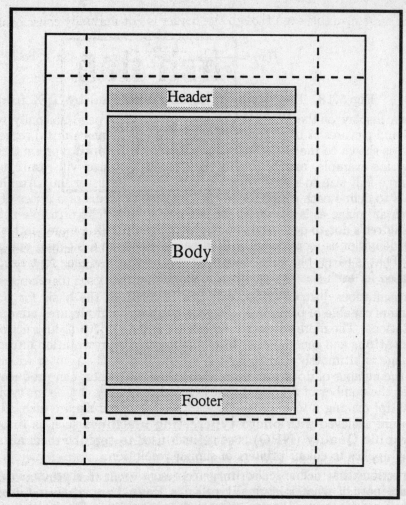

Fig 5.15. Page Layout.

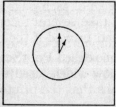

Fig 5.16 Simple graphics used in typesetting.

5.53   Before a document is output to the printer the user will normally wish to have an indication of what it will look like. In the case of a WYSIWYG system (5.25) this is simple, although the screen display never looks exactly like the printed output. If WYSIWYG is not use a **preview** option is normally available which creates and displays a close approximation to what the final document will look like. This becomes particularly important in typesetting systems which use special symbol codes to define the way the text is to be typeset. For example, a high quality typesetting system called TEX was produced by Donald Knuth with particular features for defining complex mathematical formulae. In the special version of TEX called LATEX formulae are defined using standard symbols in a normal text file. The text file is processed by a TEX program to produce a typeset version of the document which can be previewed on the screen or printed. An example of the text file version of a LATEX formula and its corresponding typeset form is shown in Fig 5.17 and Fig 5.18 respectively.

```
\[  f(x) =  \frac{1}{\sigma \sqrt{2\pi}}
e^{-\frac{(x -\mu)^{2}}{2\sigma^{2}}}
\mbox{\ \ \ for} -\infty < x < \infty \]
```

Fig 5.17. The text definition of a LATEX formula.

$$f(x) = \frac{1}{\sigma\sqrt{2\pi}}e^{-\frac{(x-\mu)^2}{2\sigma^2}} \quad \text{for} -\infty < x < \infty$$

Fig 5.18. The typeset formula produced by TEX from Fig 5.17.

5.54 The screen display of the WYSIWYG page or preview page normally represents font characters, diagrams and pictures as bit-mapped images. In Fig 5.19 an enlarged representation of a bit-mapped letter "A" is shown to the left. Clearly, a different bit-mapped representation is needed for each font size since, for example, merely scaling up a small font size will result in a jagged image. Scaling down a large font size to a small one typically result in distortion. An alternative approach to this problem is to define each character in the typeface in terms of a series of dots which can be joined up to form an image as is shown to the left in Fig 5.19. The principle is basically the same as that used in children's dot-to-dot puzzle books, although done in a more mathematically precise way. The character definition is more complex than one based upon a bit-map but has the advantage of being scalable. That is to say the same definition can be used for each font size. The best bit pattern can be generated for each size as and when required.

5.55 The representations just described can also be used as the basis for printed output. The more basic printers capable of printing characters, diagrams and pictures are only able to use bit-mapped representations. The more advanced models are able to interpret instructions defining **scaled image representations** and generate the "best" bit-mapped representation internally. However, the quality of the image is ultimately limited by the **resolution** of the printer which is normally expressed in terms of the number of **dots per inch (dpi)** that the printer can produce. The higher resolution, ie the higher the number of dpi, the better the image quality can be. A typical laser printer can print 300 – 400 dpi making a total of 90,000 – 160,000 dots per square inch. Higher resolutions of about 1,200 dpi are achieved with **photo typesetting machines** such as **linotronics**. The term **Near Photographic Quality (NPQ)** is sometimes used to describe them although the term NPQ more commonly applies to colour printers of similar resolution.

5.56 The instructions that define scaled image representations of characters to a printer, mentioned previously, are part of what is normally called a **Page Description Language (PDL)**. A PDL is essentially a set of standard instruction for drawing shapes. The shapes may be the scalable characters in a typeface, scalable geometric figures or fixed size bit patterns. Printers able to process DPLs contain small microcomputers dedicated to that task. The printer receives the PDL instructions and then generate the bit-mapped image of each page in its own memory before printing it out. In the case of a complex figure this can take several seconds, or even minutes in extreme cases. Complex images can also only be formed and printed if the printer's computer has enough memory.

5.57 By far the most common PDL is one called **PostScript** which was devised by the Adobe Corporation for Apple's Laser printer but is now widely used with many differnt makes of computer. The term **PostScript Printer** merely means that the printer is able to interpret PostScript instructions.

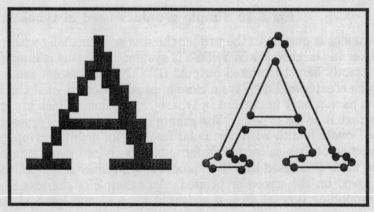

Fig 5.19. A bit-mapped character and its scaled character representation.

SUMMARY

5.58   **a.** Documents in the form of text files may be created and modified by text editors.

     b. Documents used in word processing typically have more complex forms than text files because of the more advanced document features and are specific to the word processor being used.

c. Typical word processing programs provides more facilities than typical text editors. In particular, they provides more controls over the layout and printing of documents with regard to such things as page size, text justification and page headers or footers.

d. A DTP system uses specialist software and hardware on a desktop computer to perform computerised typesetting. Some advanced word processing packages may be used for DTP but a variety of specialist programs are frequently used too.

e. When documents contain text and images bit-mapping techniques are commonly used and the quality produced depends upon the resolution available and the techniques employed to generate the images.

POINTS TO NOTE

5.59 **a.** The term **word processor** is often used as a *very broad classification* of any program which can be used to created and edit documents.

b. It is not normally possible to interchange documents in different formats between different document processing programs unless special import or export facilities are provided. Even simple text files come in a variety of formats. For example, in an ASCII text file the breaks between lines may be marked by $\boxed{\text{LF}}$ alone rather than by $\boxed{\text{CR}}\boxed{\text{LF}}$.

c. Many word processors are able to export versions of documents as simple text files but most of the document formatting information is lost in the process.

d. PostScript printers are able to print out simple text documents as well as the more complex ones required for DTP. When printing simple text documents a PostScript Laser printer may print 8–10 documents per minute but the same printer may take several minutes to print a single page if complicated typesetting features have been used.

STUDENT SELF-TESTING QUESTIONS

1. A file contains the text of a draft document. The order of the paragraphs needs to be changed, a new paragraph requires insertion and the word "cheap", which occurs several times in the document, is to be replaced by "inexpensive". Explain how this may be done.
2. What are the typical similarities and differences between a text editor and a word processing program?
3. Explain the terms **type family**, **typeface** and **font**.

QUESTIONS WITHOUT ANSWERS

4. What features of a PostScript printer make it suitable for use with a DTP system?

GLOSSARY CHECKLIST

Boilerplating	5.29	Grammar checker	5.34
Bold typeface	5.42	Importing	5.37
Computerised typesetting	5.39	Insert mode	5.14
Cursor key	5.9	Italic typeface	5.42
Cut and paste	5.15	Kerning	5.47
Desktop publishing	5.39	Leading	5.50
dpi	5.55	Left justification	5.27
DTP	5.39	Ligatures	5.46
Editing	5.4	Line editor	5.5
Em	5.45	Mail merge	5.30
Exporting	5.37	Monospaced	5.48
File	5.3	NPQ	5.55
Font	5.42	Overstrike mode	5.14
Frame	5.52	Page description language	5.56
Full justification	5.27	PDL	5.56

STORAGE

1. This Part of the text builds on the introductory material covered in the Foundation Topics to give a detailed account of storage. The emphasis in the following two chapters in on the features of the hardware used for storage rather than on methods of using the hardware. The latter is covered later in the text.
2. **Main Storage** is described in chapter 6. Main Storage holds data and programs currently in use.
3. **Backing Storage Devices** are described in chapter 7. They are used to provide mass storage of data and programs.
4. Again, the material in this Part is relevant to all examinations for which this text is a preparation.

6: Main Storage

INTRODUCTION

6.1 We were introduced to main storage in chapter 1, where it was seen to be an important element of a computer because it holds data and program instructions for use by the processor. The general features of main storage are described in this chapter. Another very appropriate name for main storage is **Main Memory**, because, like the human memory, it is able to retain or store information that may later be recalled or accessed.

6.2 **Features of Main Storage**

    a. Its operation is wholly electronic, and consequently very fast and reliable. In the most modern computers the electronic memory circuits are also highly miniaturised.

    b. Data is almost instantly accessible from main memory because of its electronic operation and close proximity to the processor. For example, an item of data may be retrieved from main storage in much less than one-millionth of one second. For this reason main storage has yet another name, **immediate access storage.**

    c. Data *must* be transferred to main storage before it can be processed by the processor. High access speeds then contribute to fast processing.

6.3 **Uses of Main Storage.** Ideally, main storage would be used to store all data requiring processing, in order to achieve maximum processing speeds. However, there are practical limitations on the size of main storage that processors can easily be made to operate with. Main storage is also relatively expensive, although its price has come down in recent years as the manufacturing methods have improved. So, the practical solution is to limit the size of main storage and supplement it with less expensive backing storage (1.18). Thus, limited capacity, coupled with the need to hold data in main storage for processing, results in main storage being *used* as a short-term memory.

It stores

    a. Instructions awaiting to be obeyed,

    b. Instructions currently being obeyed,

    c. Data awaiting processing,

    d. Data currently being processed,

    e. Data awaiting output.

6.4 An area of main storage being used for data currently being processed is called a **working storage area** and an area being used for data awaiting processing or output is called a **buffer area.**

THE OPERATIONAL FEATURES OF MAIN STORAGE

6.5 To understand the principles of how data is placed into main storage we will imagine it to be arranged like a set of boxes, and deal with the physical details of main storage later. The boxes are numbered from zero upwards so that each box can be identified and located. What is usually called a **"location in main storage"** corresponds to one of our boxes, and the **"location address"** corresponds to the number of the box (Fig 6.1).

Once data is stored in a location in main storage it remains there until it is replaced by other data. Data placed into the same location will destroy what was there previously (rather like the latest recording made on a tape recorder destroying the previous one). Accessing and fetching data from main storage is really a copying action which does not result in the data being deleted from main storage (just as playing a tape recorder does not erase the tape).

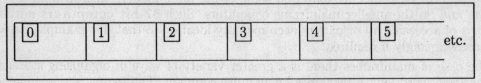

Fig 6.1. Locations in Main Storage.

6.6   Random Access. It is possible to fetch data from the locations in main storage in any order, and the time taken does not depend on the position of the locations. We summarise this by saying we have **random access** to data in main storage. This is also known as **direct access.**

6.7   Volatility. Depending on its physical characteristics, main storage may be either **volatile,** in which case data is lost once the power is turned off, or **non-volatile,** where no such data loss occurs.

6.8   Details of a single location. Each location in main storage consists of a set of tiny devices each of which can be in one of two states at any one time (eg, On or Off). The two states of each device are used to represent binary **0** (Off) and **1** (On), and hence the complete set of **two-state devices** in each location provides a method of coding data, rather like that used with input media such as magnetic tape. We may thus talk of a location in main storage as being so many bits long. For a given computer the number of bits in each location will be the same fixed number for all locations, eg, *each* location could contain 16 bits, and each location would be addressable.

BYTES AND WORDS

6.9   Each location in main storage is usually said to hold a unit of data called a **word.** Words can often be subdivided into smaller units called **bytes.** The real situation is much more complicated than this because of the many different approaches to computer design. The next few paragraphs discuss common design approaches.

6.10   Fixed Word-length Computers (Word Machines). In a fixed length computer **one word = one location in main storage,** ie, data is transferred into main storage one location at a time. The number of bits in each location (ie in each word) is known as the **word length** and depends on the make and model of computer. Typical word lengths are, 8, 16 and 32 bits. Several characters might be placed or "**packed** " into one word.

6.11   Microcomputers are normally fixed word-length machines and the smaller ones often have a word length of 8 bits. A single storage location of such a machine is large enough to hold one ASCII character, one BCD character, one EBCDIC character or two BCD numeric values. A microcomputer using this method of storage is called an **8-bit microcomputer** (see Fig. 6.2).

6.12   On larger microcomputers the most common size for a memory location is 16 bits and computers with memory locations of this size are called **16-bit computers.** Currently most PCs are 16-bit computers. A few minicomputers are 16-bit machines too. A single storage location on a 16-bit computer will be able to hold two characters (eg. ASCII or EBCDIC) but will normally "pack", characters two to a location for that reason (see Fig. 6.2). Such computers usually have facilities for accessing the right half and left half of each word separately in order to handle individual characters.

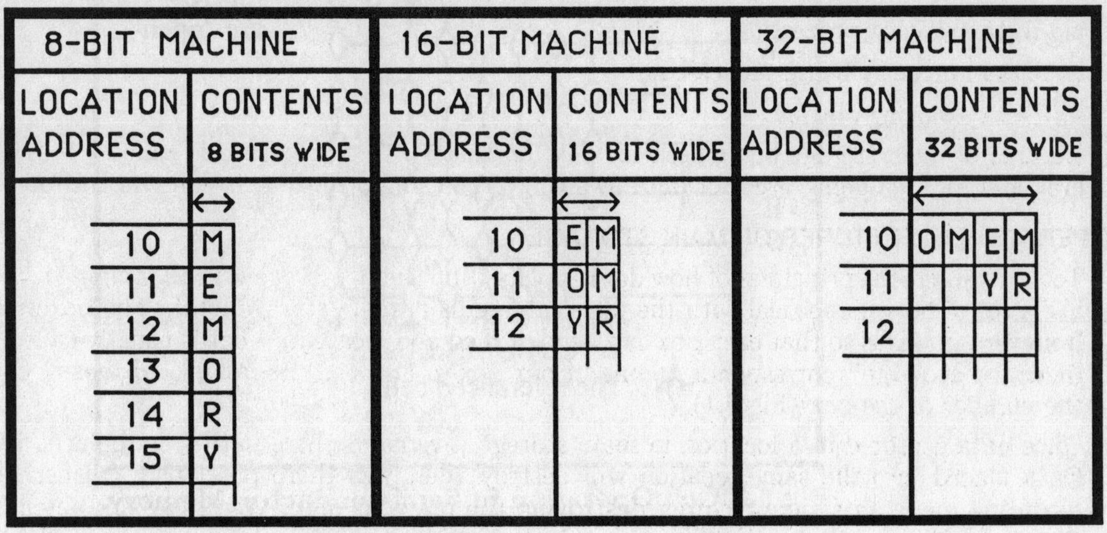

Fig 6.2. Alternative Storage Designs.

6.13   32-bit storage locations are found on some of the more modern microcomputers, on most minicomputers and on the smaller mainframe computers. Such **32-bit computers** normally have a variety of ways of accessing all or part of each memory location so that, for example, packed characters may be accessed singly if required.

6.14   In the case of mainframes there is a greater variety of ways of organising storage with alternatives to the fixed word-length machines being quite common. The reason is that in general, storage space tends to be wasted by using fixed-length units of storage for variable-length data, eg, having to use a 16-bit word to store one 8-bit character. As this problem occurs in most situations where data is to be transferred or stored, some designers have produced variable word-length computers.

6.15 Variable Word-length Computers. In these computers a word is one or more whole locations in length, and is set to the required length at each data transfer. Instructions may be of fixed or variable length but are more commonly of variable length in these machines. By setting the word length correctly at each transfer any whole instruction can be transferred in a single operation.

There are two types of variable word-length machine:

a. Byte machines in which each location is 8 bits long.

b. Character machines in which each location is 6 bits long.

6.16 Instruction storage. In both fixed-length and variable-length machines, locations may be used to store instructions instead of data, and **the stored codes are indistinguishable**. In principle there is nothing to prevent a stored instruction from being used as data or vice versa! In practice storage must be used carefully to avoid such errors.

6.17 Variation with machine size. The smaller computers tend to be fixed word-length machines. The larger microcomputers and small mini-computers tend to have word lengths of 16 bits and sometime 32 bits. Larger minicomputers and some mainframes have word lengths of 32 bits, and so on.

6.18 Parity check. We have been referring to storage as consisting of, eg, 8, 16 or 32 bit groups. In fact each one of these groups may have a parity bit added to it in the same way that transmitted codes do (see Fig. 2.3). The parity bit aids the detection of errors caused through bits being "lost" in the process of storing or transmitting the data.

Note. Small computers do not always incorporate parity-checking memory systems and this can bring their reliability into question in some situations.

PHYSICAL FEATURES OF MAIN STORAGE

6.19 To have a sound understanding of main storage we need to be aware of some features of its construction and technology. These features are illustrated here by reference to the most common type of main storage called **semi-conductor memory**.

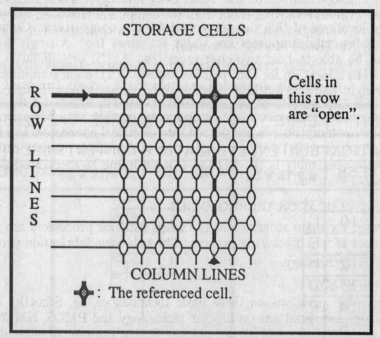

Fig 6.3 Cell Operation in Semi-conductor Memory.

6.20 Semi-conductor memory. The common type RAM (Random Access Memory) is described here.

    a. Each bit of semi-conductor memory is represented by a single cell, which may be regarded as a microscopic electronic circuit with two distinguishable stages used to represent "0" and "1". Cells arranged into rows and columns are built onto a single "chip" of silicon some 3mm × 3mm, in what is clearly a most advanced manufacturing process, since 2,048,000 cells may be formed on a single chip and many times more on the larger chips.

    b. Each cell can be *electrically charged* or *not electrically charged* representing "1" and "0" respectively. If a row line is made electrically active it causes all cells in that row to switch open so that they can be charged or discharged through a column line. A column line for one cell in the row may then be switched on, **either** to pass a charge into the cell (State "1") **or** to allow the cell to discharge (State "0") (Fig 6.3). Since charge can only flow from a charged cell, an observable discharge reveals the state of a cell and provides the means of reading from memory. A cell discharged by reading from it must be recharged to preserve its state.

    c. Charge slowly leaks from the cells and has to be topped up constantly. This is called "refreshing". Strictly speaking this is a feature of one type of RAM called **dynamic RAM.** Refreshing is not required in the other type of RAM, which is called **Static RAM.** In static RAM the "cells" stay "latched" in a '1' stage or '0' state by the provision of a constant power supply. This dependence on a constant power supply by both static and dynamic RAM means RAM memory is *volatile* (ie, data is lost if the power supply is removed).

6.21   **ROMS.** A non-volatile semi-conductor alternative to the RAM is the ROM (Read Only Memory) in which all cell states are set permanently during manufacture. A set of instructions stored in this way is said to be **"hard wired",** and is often called **firmware.** This technique is often used to extend the instruction set of the computer by storing special-purpose subroutines. These are called **microprograms.** ROM is also frequently used to store data or instructions which the computer needs all the time from the moment it is switched on.

6.22   **Other types of ROM.** Apart from the basic types of ROM just described, there are several variations, which are briefly described here:

    a. PROM (Programmable Read Only Memory). In contrast to normal ROM, in which the pattern of stored data is permanently incorporated into the chip using a "Mask" during the last stage of manufacture, the PROM can be programmed by the user. However, the data is held permanently once the PROM has been programmed.

    b. EPROM (Erasable Programmable Read Only Memory). This is like PROM in that it may be programmed by the user but has the advantage that it may be erased and reprogrammed. The EPROM must be removed from the computer in order to be erased. Special devices called "EPROM erasers" and "EPROM programmers" are used for these tasks.

    c. EAROM (Electrically Alterable Read Only Memory). These memories can be read, erased and rewritten without removing them from the computer. However, the erasing and rewriting process is very slow compared with reading, which limits their use. For this reason they are sometimes called **RMMs** (Read Mostly Memories).

    d. EEROM (Electrically Erasable Read Only Memory). Essentially the same as EAROM.

6.23   Memory chips are normally assembled onto electronic boards (**printed circuit boards (PCBs)**). They may either be assembled onto the **motherboard**, which is a main PCB also occupied by the processor and other main electronic components, or they may be assembled onto separate memory boards. These memory boards are slotted into electrical connectors inside the computer. Sometimes spare "slots" are provided during manufacture so that more memory can be added later. A common type of memory assembly is the **SIMM** (Single Inline Memory Module), which is widely used on small computer systems.

SEMI-CONDUCTOR FABRICATION TECHNOLOGIES

6.24   The chips used for main storage and the chips used for processors are normally made from one of two basic types of manufacturing process. The two basic fabrication processes are:

    a. BIPOLAR Technology.

    b. MOS Technology.

6.25   There are several variations on these basic technologies, eg, Schottky bipolar and I^2L (Integrated Injection Logic) are variations on bipolar technology and PMOS, NMOS, CMOS, SOS, VMOS and HMOS are all variations on MOS technology. Do not attempt to remember all these variations; they are mentioned here merely to show the wide variety of technologies that exist. Indeed, the details of this technology are largely outside the scope of computer science and are more the concern of electronic engineering or computer engineering. It is the consequence of using a particular technology which is the concern of Computer Science.

6.26   These types of fabrication technology have a direct bearing on the operational features of the semi-conductor devices. Factors affected include

    a. Cost.

    b. Power consumption.

    c. Speed of access.

    d. Reliability.

6.27 Very broadly speaking, MOS technology is more widely used on microcomputers and BIPOLAR technology is mostly used on minicomputers and mainframe computers, which should indicate some general differences between the two technologies.

BUSES

6.28 Data is normally transferred between main storage and the processor along a device called a bus which is effectively a means of sending multiple bits of data in parallel (Fig 6.4). For example, all the bits of a word may be transferred in parallel in a single operation.

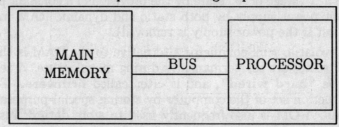

Fig 6.4. Main storage connected to the processor by a bus.

6.29 On close inspection the bus is constructed from a number of lines. It is the **data lines** which carry the data bits (Fig 6.5). For example, a 16-bit computer might have a bus connecting the processor to main memory with 16-data lines so that the contents of one whole 16-bit word could be transferred at a time between main memory and the processor. The *wider* the bus, that is to say the more bits it can transfer in parallel, the faster the rate of data transfer may be. The **bus width** typically matches the word size with, for example, an 8-bit bus being used with a computer having 8-bit memory. In general, therefore, the combination of word-size and bus width is one of the significant factor influencing the speed of a computer. There are many types of bus, as will be seen in later chapters.

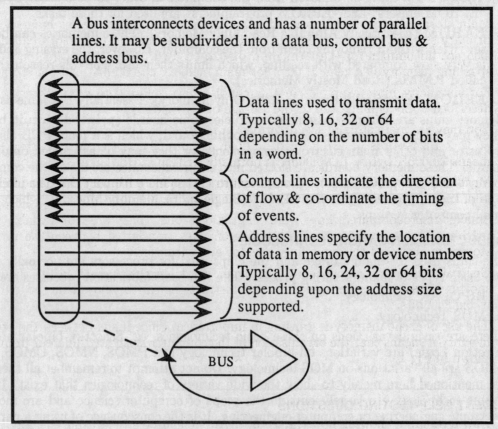

Fig 6.5. Details of a Bus.

CACHE MEMORY

6.30 In recent years it has become common practice to use memory chips with extra high access speeds to supplement those in main memory. The chips tend to be too expensive to use for the whole of main memory. These memory chips are used to provide a "cache", which is a temporary holding area for data which is currently subject to repeated access. The processor can access this data more quickly and there is therefore an overall speed improvement. The cache effectively sits between main storage and the processor acting as a holding area through which all data and instructions pass (Fig 6.6). Old data in the cache is overwritten by new because the cache has limited capacity. To make best use of the cache an appropriate strategy must be adopted to decide what data to overwrite. Common methods are the **LFU** (Least Frequently Used) and **LRU** (Least Recently Used) rules for determining which data items to overwrite.

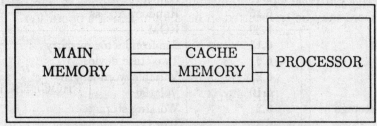

Fig 6.6. The use of cache memory.

SUMMARY

6.31 **a.** Main storage (also called main memory) is a fast, wholly electronic, random access memory which is used as a short-term memory for data awaiting processing or output, or which is being processed.

b. Data stored in main memory is identified and located by the memory location address.

c. Computers are described as "Character", "Byte" or "Word" machines according to the units of data transfer to and from main storage.

d. Modern main storage is made from semi-conductor memory chips.

POINTS TO NOTE

6.32 **a.** Main storage has several names, eg, main memory, immediate access memory, internal storage, primary storage, core storage (because of an obsolete form of technology called core store). It is also not uncommon for the term **memory** to be used to mean main memory although, strictly speaking memory is a general term for main memory *and* on-line backing storage.

b. For simplicity most examples in this chapter have referred to data storage, but the methods described apply equally well to the storage of instructions.

c. You may see main storage size described in terms of K. ($K = 2^{10} = 1024$.) Therefore 32K words $= 32 \times 1024$ words $= 32768$ words. 1000K is normally written M (for Mega). eg. 20M bytes means 20,000K bytes. 1,000,000K is normally written G (for Giga).

d. Most microcomputers are fixed word-length computers with word lengths of either 8 bits or 16 bits, hence the common terminology "8-bit micro" and "16-bit micro".

e. Smaller microcomputers have word lengths of 8 bits. They are **not** variable word-length byte machines, however, because the number of bytes transferred between the processor and main storage is always of the same fixed size for every transfer.

f. Generally speaking computers with longer word lengths operate faster than computers with shorter word lengths because data and instructions can be moved in and out of main storage in bigger units.

g. The use of cache memory is growing in importance. Since it sits between the processor and main memory it means that the organisation of the computer is slightly different from the arrangement shown in Fig 1.4.

STUDENT SELF-TESTING QUESTIONS

1. Draw a diagram showing how the word "RAM" could be stored using the ASCII code in:
   a. An 8-bit microcomputer's memory.

   b. A 16-bit microcomputer's memory.

GLOSSARY CHECKLIST

7: Backing Storage

INTRODUCTION

7.1 Ideally, all data for processing should be stored in main storage so that all internal operations can be carried out at maximum speed. As it is, main storage is relatively expensive and is therefore only used for storing the necessary instructions and the data currently being operated on. **Backing storage** is provided for the mass storage of programs and files, ie, those programs and files not currently being operated on but which will be transferred to the main storage when required.

7.2 Although data in the form of files held on backing storage is not immediately accessible, as it would be if held in main storage, it is nevertheless within the computer system. It can therefore serve an important purpose as part of a pool of maintained and accessible data.

7.3 There are many media for backing storage. The *main* devices and media, which will be described here, are:

a. Magnetic disk unit – magnetic disk.

b. Magnetic diskette unit – magnetic diskette (floppy disk).

c. Optical disk unit – optical disk.

d. Magnetic tape unit – magnetic tape.

e. Magnetic tape cartridges and cassettes.

f. Solid state storage devices.

g. Mass storage devices and media.

EXCHANGEABLE MAGNETIC DISK UNIT AND MAGNETIC DISK PACK

7.4 Features of an exchangeable disk unit

a. The **disk unit** is the device in which the disk pack is placed. The disk *pack* is placed into the *unit* and connects with the drive mechanism. Packs vary in size both in terms of the number of "platters" and in terms of the diameter of the platters. The photograph show a pack with eleven 10 inch platters which is more likely to be found on a minicomputer or mainframe. Disk packs with single platters are sometimes called disk **cartridges**. Disk cartridges tend to have platters of 5 inch diameter or less. Disk cartridges are mostly used on microcomputers but are also used on some minicomputers. In what follows assume that what is said of a disk pack also applies to a disk cartridge unless otherwise stated.

An exchangeable disk pack removed from its protective cover.

b. Once the pack (or cartridge) is loaded into the unit the read-write mechanism located inside the unit positions itself over the first track of each surface. The mechanism consists of a number of arms at the ends of which there is a read-write head for each surface. All arms are fixed together and all move together as one when accessing a surface on the disk page. See Fig. 7.1.

c. The disk when loaded is driven at a high number of revolutions (several thousand) per minute and access can only be made to its surfaces when the disk revolves.

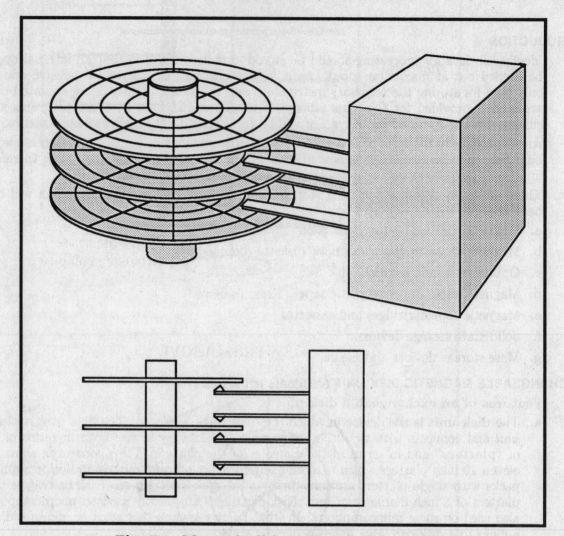

Fig. 7.1. Magnetic disk with read-write heads.

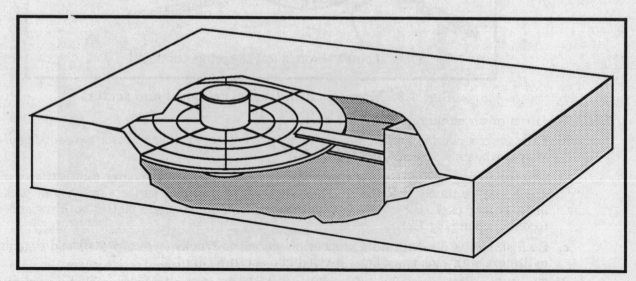

Fig. 7.2. A Single double-sided magnetic disk.

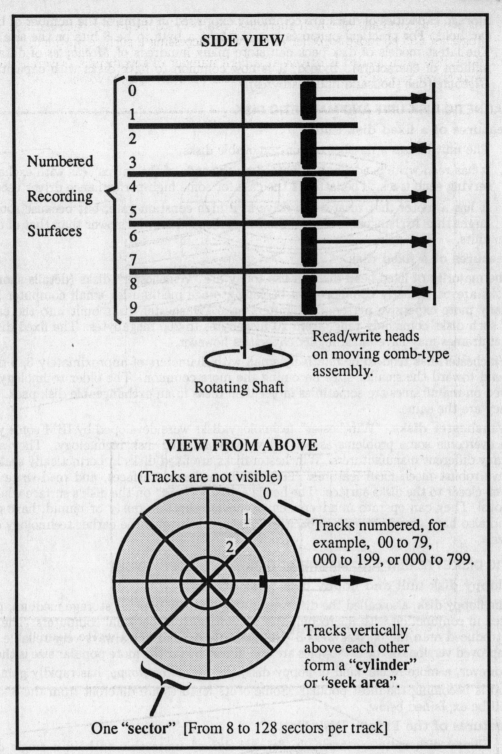

Fig. 7.3. Magnetic disk tracks, cylinders and sectors.

7.5 Features of an exchangeable disk pack

a. Disks are of a size and shape similar to a long-playing record although some have smaller diameters of approximately 5 inches or 3 inches.

b. The surfaces of each disk are of magnetisable material (except the outer-most surfaces of a pack which may be purely protective). Thus there are 10 recording surfaces in a 6-disk pack and 20 in an 11-disk pack. For a disk cartridge constructed from a single platter both surfaces may be recorded upon (Fig 7.2).

c. Each surface is divided into a number of *concentric* tracks (typically 200) and organised into **cylinders** with each track being divided into sectors (Fig 7.3).

d. The disks within a *pack* are inseparable, ie, the pack, of 6 or 11 disks, is *always* used as a single unit.

e. Storage capacities of disks are commonly expressed in terms of the number of bytes of data they can hold. For practical purposes one can take a byte to be 8 bits or the size of one character. The latest models of disk pack can store many hundreds of *Megabytes* of data (ie, hundreds of millions of characters). Indeed, it is now common to have disks with capacities in excess of *1 Gigabyte* (one thousand millions bytes).

FIXED MAGNETIC DISK UNIT AND MAGNETIC DISK

7.6 **Features of a fixed disk unit.**

a. The unit houses a number of non-removable disks.

b. It has read-write heads, either located on the ends of the "arms" (as with exchangeable disks) or serving each track. The latter is the case for some high-performance drives used on mainframes.

c. It has a motor that rotates the drive at a high constant rate, but because some fixed disks are larger than exchangeable disks the rotational speed may be slower than that of exchangeable disk units.

7.7 **Features of a fixed disk.**

7.8 The majority of fixed-head disks in use today are "Winchester" disks (details shortly). Winchester disks are particularly common as a backing storage medium for small computer systems. Indeed, many more expensive personal computers have Winchester disks built into the casing. Capacities of such disks commonly range from 20 megabytes to 200 megabytes. The fixed disks used on some mainframes may have much higher capacities however.

7.9 Winchester disk tend to be relatively small with diameters of approximately 3, 5 or 8 inches with a trend toward the smaller sizes becoming the more common. The older technology fixed-head disks used on mainframes are sometimes *larger* than disks in an exchangeable disk pack. In other respects they are the same.

7.10 **Winchester disks.** "Winchester" technology disks were developed by IBM some years ago in order to overcome some problems associated with established disk technology. They are now made by many different manufacturers. Winchester disks are fixed disks in hermetically sealed disk units and have robust mechanical features. They have toughened surfaces, and read-write heads that move even closer to the disks surface. The heads actually "land" on the disk's surface when the disk finally stops! They can operate in adverse environments that are dusty or humid, have greater reliability and also have greater storage capacities in comparison with the earlier technology disks of the same size.

MAGNETIC DISKETTE UNIT AND MAGNETIC DISKETTE (FLOPPY DISK)

7.11 **Floppy disk unit and floppy disk (diskette).**

The floppy disk, also called the diskette, is an extremely popular storage medium, particularly when used in conjunction with microcomputer systems such as personal computers. The first floppy disks introduced onto the market were 8", of low capacity and not always very reliable. Although a few improved versions of the 8" floppies are still in use, by far the more popular size is the $5\frac{1}{4}$" floppy disk. However, a more recent kind of floppy disk, the $3\frac{1}{2}$" *microfloppy*, has rapidly gaining in popularity and is becoming the most popular. Some of its features are different from the 8" and $5\frac{1}{4}$" disks as will be explained below.

7.12 **Features of the Floppy Disk Unit.**

a. Floppy disk units are normally "single-drive" units able to hold a single disk. Some free-standing floppy disk units are **dual-drive** units, ie, able to hold two separate floppy disks at a time. Single-drive units are often incorporated physically into the body of personal computers, sometimes in addition to hard disks such as Winchesters. They are then called **internal disk drives** as apposed to the free-standing **external disk drives**.

b. Each disk is inserted into a narrow slot in the front of the disk drive. The slot has a small flap over it, which must be clipped shut once the disk is inserted. Sometimes a push button or lever is used for shutting instead of a flap.

c. The action of closing the flap engages a turntable, which rotates the disk and also brings a "read-write head" into contact with the disk. The read-write head is moved to and fro across the disk in order either to record data on the disk surface (a "write"), or to "read" back data which has previously been recorded.

d. A typical floppy disk rotates at about 360 rpm compared with a hard disk which rotates about ten times faster.

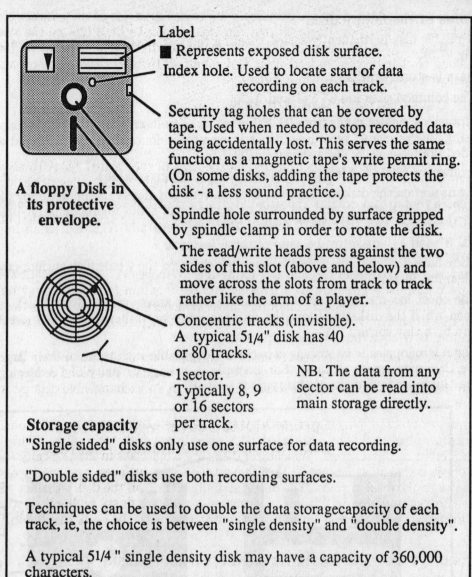

Label
■ Represents exposed disk surface.

Index hole. Used to locate start of data recording on each track.

A floppy Disk in its protective envelope.

Security tag holes that can be covered by tape. Used when needed to stop recorded data being accidentally lost. This serves the same function as a magnetic tape's write permit ring. (On some disks, adding the tape protects the disk - a less sound practice.)

Spindle hole surrounded by surface gripped by spindle clamp in order to rotate the disk.

The read/write heads press against the two sides of this slot (above and below) and move across the slots from track to track rather like the arm of a player.

Concentric tracks (invisible). A typical $5\frac{1}{4}$" disk has 40 or 80 tracks.

1 sector. Typically 8, 9 or 16 sectors per track.

NB. The data from any sector can be read into main storage directly.

Storage capacity

"Single sided" disks only use one surface for data recording.

"Double sided" disks use both recording surfaces.

Techniques can be used to double the data storagecapacity of each track, ie, the choice is between "single density" and "double density".

A typical $5\frac{1}{4}$ " single density disk may have a capacity of 360,000 characters.

Fig. 7.4. Floppy Disk (Diskette) Details.

Fig. 7.5. 8˝ floppy disk with part of its cover removed, with $5\frac{1}{4}$˝ floppy disk by its side.

7.13   Features of the floppy disk.

    a. A pliable disk permanently sealed within a rigid, smoothly lined, protective plastic envelope (see Fig. 7.5).

    b. Data is stored on tracks.

    c. The common sizes are 8″ $5\frac{1}{4}$″ and $3\frac{1}{2}$″.

    d. Storage capacities range from 60,000 bytes to $1\frac{1}{4}$ million bytes. The latter capacities are achieved using "high density" recording, which is even more dense than that achieved with normal double-sided double-density disks shown in Fig 7.5.

7.14   Microfloppy disks.(Also merely called $3\frac{1}{2}$″ floppy disks.)

One variation on the diskette that has become very popular is the microfloppy disk. These disks are normally $3\frac{1}{2}$″ in diameter and are used on a variety of small microcomputer-based systems, eg, the Apple Macintosh and IBM PS/2 series. They are generally regarded as an improvement over the normal 8″ and $5\frac{1}{4}$″ diskettes because of these features:

    a. They have a more rugged plastic cover, which keeps the whole disk surface covered and protected when not in use.

    b. The cover has a slot giving the disk drive heads access to the disk, which is automatically slid open while the diskette is inserted into the drive but otherwise is held closed against dust and dirt by a tiny spring.

    c. The microfloppies have storage capacities comparable with those of their larger counterparts and are thus more space efficient. For example, a storage capacity of 1.4 Megabytes is common on the "high density" disks of this type.

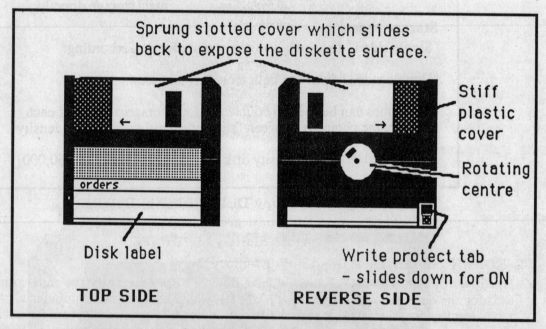

Fig 7.6 $3\frac{1}{2}$″ Microfloppy disk.

7.15   It is quite probable that the microfloppy diskette will supersede the $5\frac{1}{4}$″ just as the $5\frac{1}{4}$″ has superseded the 8″ floppy disk.

7.16   Although floppy disks are sometimes used as a primary medium for backing storage on small microcomputer systems they are mainly used for other purposes, such as:

    a. A medium on which to supply software for use on microcomputers.

    b. A medium on which to collect or input data, for subsequent transfer and input to another system, possibly at a remote site.

    c. As a **back-up** medium for small hard disks. For example, the contents of a 20 megabyte Winchester disk could be copied onto about 20 floppy disks so that if the Winchester disk becomes unusable for any reason its contents can still be recovered.

    Note. This is directly comparable to the way in which magnetic tape may be used to back-up hard disks on larger systems.

7.17   There are two variants on the floppy disk which have been introduced in recent years and have gained some degree of success. These are as follows.

    a. Bernoulli Boxes. A Bernoulli box is essentially a "souped-up" floppy drive in which a 8″ or $5\frac{1}{4}$″ disk housed in a cartridge is rotated at much higher speed than is normal for a floppy disk thus making the disk more stiff and stable and thus more like a hard disk. Capacities of 40 – 90 megabytes are possible at very competitive prices.

    b. Megafloppy drives. These are really effectively a very much more technologically advanced form of the conventional $3\frac{1}{2}$″ floppy disk drive. Capacities of 5 – 20 megabytes are possible and the speed of access is significantly faster than for a conventional floppy disk.

OPTICAL DISK UNIT AND OPTICAL DISK

7.18   There are three basic types of optical disk but all of them use lasers to write or read data. All three provide a means of storing very large volumes of data.

CD-ROM Disks optical data and audio storage.
Picture courtesy of PHILIPS

7.19   **CD-ROM (Compact Disk Read-only Memory).**

    a. Features of the CD-ROM unit. These devices work on exactly the same principle as that used for the domestic audio compact disk (CD), which has become so popular in recent years as a replacement for the vinyl LP record. Indeed, some units are manufacture for dual use both for playing audio CDs and accessing data CDs. This is not so surprising since CDs actually record sound in digital form, as was indicated in 2.34. The devices *are only able to read back prerecorded sound or data* by using a laser at lower intensity and detecting the pattern of light reflected from its beam by the surface of the disk as the CD rotates on a turntable (Fig 7.7).

    b. Features of the CD. The CDs are constructed in the same way as an audio CDs. A CD may hold about 55 megabytes of data. Access speeds tend to be slower than for magnetic disks.

    c. Jukebox options. Some CD units are incorporated into what is called a "jukebox". The name "jukebox" is borrowed from the audio device used in pubs and clubs. A jukebox is able to load one of a number of individual CDs into the disk unit under the control of suitable software. The facility greatly extends the volume of data which can be automatically accessed on-line.

    d. Uses. CDs are of use in providing reference works, catalogs, directories, encyclopedias, software, font descriptions, graphical images and sounds.

7.20   **WORM (Write Once Read many).**

    a. Features of the WORM unit. The device is similar in appearance to a fixed device magnetic disk unit, but data is written into the disk by burning a permanent pattern into the surface of the disk by means of a high-precision laser beam. A similar method may be used in the manufacture of a CD. The reading of data is conducted in the same way as that used for a CD. That is, data is read back by using the laser at lower intensity and detecting the pattern of light reflected from its beam by the surface of the disk as it rotates on a turntable. The WORM disks are exchangeable.

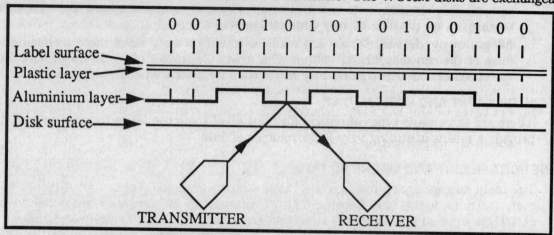

Fig. 7.7. Read data from a CD.

b. Features of the WORM disk. A typical disk looks like a CD and has a surface of 40,000 tracks each divided into 25 sectors and a total capacity of a staggering one Gigabyte (ie, 1,000 million bytes). (CDs have a lower capacity than this because of their mass produced nature.) The WORM disks are less prone to data loss than magnetic disks but are non-reusable at present. It is for this reason these optical disks are referred to as "WORM" storage. WORM stands for "Write Once Read Many times". As for CDs, access speeds tend to be slower than for magnetic disks.

c. Variants. 12" WORM drives are also available with capacities of 13.5 Gigabytes and better transfer rates. When fitted with a jukebox unit of 6 disks they can provide access to 27 Gigabytes, with cartridge exchange times of approx. 2.5 seconds.

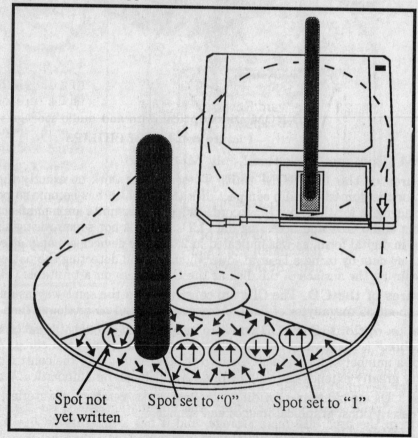

Fig. 7.8. Data recording on an EO disk.

d. **Uses.** Exchangeable WORM drives have become popular for systems where large amounts of data have to be archived and occasionally put on-line for reference purposes.

7.21 EO (Erasable Optical).

a. **Features of the EO unit.** The EO disk unit is similar to that used for WORM but works on a slightly different principle. Instead of burning a pattern onto the disk surface the laser heats spots on the disk surface which is made of a special alloy. Magnetic molecules in the alloy surface can be aligned by a magnetic field when warmed by the laser but cool again to leave a semi-permanent magnetic pattern comparable to that found on a magnetic disk. (Fig. 7.8.) The data can therefore be deleted and re-written when required. However, the speeds of writing and reading are much slower than those of a WORM drive.

b. **Features of the EO disk.** Again the disk is similar in appearance and size to a CD but enclosed in a casing which looks like that used for a $3\frac{1}{2}''$ floppy disk. The capacity of a typical EO disk is about 650 megabytes.

MAGNETIC TAPE UNIT AND MAGNETIC TAPE

7.22 The main magnetic tape medium is $\frac{1}{2}''$ tape which traditionally has come in reel-to-reel form. However, cartridge forms have become popular alternatives because they are easier to use. Magnetic cartridges come in a number of shapes and sizes and vary in the mechanism by which they operate. A lesser alternative to the magnetic tape cartridge is the magnetic tape cassettes which also comes in a variety of forms. In order to bring out the basic principles more clearly the following description deals with $\frac{1}{2}''$ "reel-to-reel" versions. Special features of tape cassettes and cartridges are covered later.

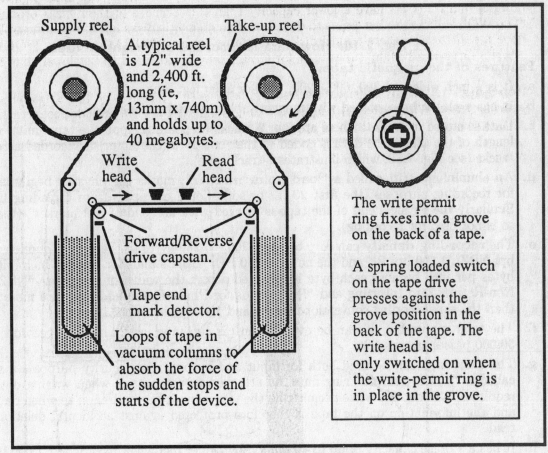

Fig. 7.9. Main features of a Magnetic Tape Unit.

7.23 Features of the tape unit

a. It holds the magnetic tape reel and also a second reel for "taking up" the tape (similar in concept to a tape recorder) (see Fig. 7.9).

b. It has a "read head" for "reading" the information stored on the tape, ie, for transferring data from the tape into main storage, and it has a separate "write head", for recording the information. Usually an individual tape is mounted onto the tape drive either to be read from or to be written to.

    c. The tape moves past the read head at up to 200 inches per second (ips). Typical speeds are 30, 45, 75 and 125 ips. When the tape is travelling at these speeds data can be read from them at rates between 100,000 and 200,000 bytes per second or even higher!

    d. The tape can be accelerated to maximum speed or decelerated from maximum speed to a halt in approximately 5-15 ms, while the tape travels about $\frac{1}{4}$ to $\frac{3}{8}$ of one inch.

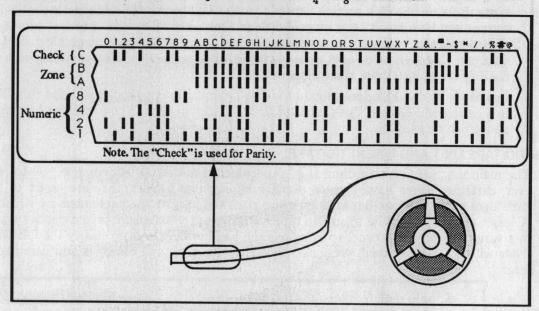

Fig. 7.10. How data is recorded on magnetic tape.

7.24 **Features of the magnetic tape.**

    a. It is $\frac{1}{2}$ inch wide and 300, 600, 1200, 2400 or 3600 feet long.

    b. It has a plastic base, coated with magnetisable material on *one* side.

    c. Data is stored in tracks. There are 7 or 9 tracks (depending upon the tape unit), which run the length of the tape. The data is coded so that one byte (character) is recorded across the 7 or 9 tracks (see Fig. 7.10, which illustrates 7-track tape).

    d. An aluminium strip, called a **"load point marker"**, marks the physical beginning of the tape for recording purposes (the first 20 ft. or so is not used, apart from threading into the unit). Similarly the physical end of the tape is marked with an "end of reel marker" (the *last* 20ft. or so is not used for recording).

    e. The **recording density** can *vary* between 200 – 6,250 bytes to the inch. Common forms are 800 bpi NRZI, 1,600 bpi PE and the newer 6,250 PE. "bpi" stands for bits per inch but is effectively bytes per inch because each byte is recorded across the width of the tape. "NRZI" stands for Non-Return Zero Inverting and "PE" stands for Phase Encoding. Both are more sophisticated than the simple coding conventions for 0's and 1's explained in 2.14.

    f. The tape is reusable, ie, can be overwritten (as can tape used with tape recorders) — 20,000 – 50,000 passes are possible.

    g. The same tape can be used both for input and output. For security purposes a special device called a **"write permit"** ring must be attached to a tape reel when writing onto the tape is required. Without the write permit ring the tape cannot be written on to when on the tape unit and the information on the tape is therefore protected against accidental deletion while being read.

    h. It has a storage capacity of up to 40 million bytes per reel when recorded at 1,600 bpi depending upon the size of the reel.

7.25 **Manner of recording.** Data is recorded (written) in blocks as the tape moves past the "write" head at a *constant* rate. After a block has been written, the tape slows down and stops. On being instructed to write again, the tape accelerates up to the speed required for writing and another block is written onto the tape. No writing takes place during the acceleration and deceleration time and this therefore leaves a gap between each block of data on the tape. This **Inter Block Gap (IBG)** measures some $\frac{3}{4}''$.

7.26 Unlike a tape recorder, the tape on a magnetic tape unit stops and starts between **blocks** of recorded data.

7.27 Reading takes place when the tape is moving at a high, *constant*, speed past the read head. Reading automatically ceases when the inter-block gap is sensed by the read head. The tape decelerates to a stop on termination of one "read" and accelerates up to its reading speed at the commencement of the next "read".

7.28 The speed with which the tape can be moved past the read or write head and the density of bytes combine to give the data transfer speed, ie, the number of bytes per second that are transferred between main storage and the tape. A *rate* of up to 1,250,000 bytes per second can be achieved on the latest models.

A magnetic tape (reverse side) with a write permit ring visible and removed from the back of the tape.

The pen tip is pointing to the "Load point marker" at the start of the tape.

7.29 The theoretical storage capacity (ie, length × maximum density) is not achievable in practice because of the inter-block gaps that are required, each taking up about $\frac{3}{4}$". Thus the practical capacity can be as little as 20 million bytes on a tape with a theoretical capacity of 40 million bytes. The size of blocks can have a significant effect on the practical capacity. The bigger the blocks, and therefore the fewer the gaps, the more data is stored.

MAGNETIC TAPE CARTRIDGES AND CASSETTES

7.30 **Cartridges and Cassettes** come in a number of different forms. They operate on the same principles as $\frac{1}{2}$" reel-to-reel tape. Indeed, many cartridges are designed mainly to overcome the bother of loading and unloading tapes. The cartridge just pops in a slot which is clearly simpler than threaded tape onto a reel. Apart from convenience, a tape cartridge also gives greater protection against dust and dirt and thereby makes the tape more trouble free. The more basic cartridges and cassettes are exactly the same as, or very similar to, the tapes and cartridges used for home audio. However, tape cartridges specially designed for computer use are of more advanced construction. Several computer manufacturers use their own particular designs. For example, DEC have a series of $\frac{1}{2}$" tape cartridges.

7.31 A variety of forms of tape cartridge have established themselves as **backup media** in recent years. The *primary purpose* of these tape cartridges is to provide an effective way to copy the contents of disks to guard against data loss. Data loss can occur for a number of reasons ranging from simple human error in deleting data by mistake to a mechanical failure such as a "disk crash" in which the read-write heads smash into the disk's surface. If data is backed up from a disk onto a tape cartridge on a regular basis, perhaps daily, then when a data loss occurs the backup copy can be read back again onto a replacement disk. Tape cartridges are also used as a means of distributing large volumes of software or data from one computer to another.

7.32 $\frac{1}{2}$" **cartridges.** A typical $\frac{1}{2}$" tape cartridge contains 600 feet of tape and holds from 60 Megabytes to 600 Megabytes depending on the recording density. Longer, high capacity models can record up to 2.5 Gigabytes. When a typical unit is operating at full speed data may be read or written at a rate of about 2.5 Megabytes per second. Large volume backups can be carried out using multi-hopper cartridge stacker units (Fig 7.11). The cartridges are automatically loaded and unloaded one at a time so that very large volumes of data can be backed-up unattended (ie, without the need for an operator).

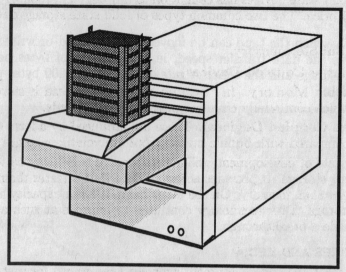

Fig. 7.11. A multi-hopper magnetic tape cartridge stacker unit.

7.33 $\frac{1}{4}''$ **cartridges.** A typical $\frac{1}{4}''$ tape cartridge (Fig 7.12) contains 1,000 feet of tape and holds from 250 Megabytes.

Fig. 7.12. A $\frac{1}{4}''$ magnetic tape cartridge.

7.34   **8mm cartridges.** 8mm tape cartridge have a more compact and modern design than the cartridges mentioned above. A single compact 8mm cartridge may store up to 10 Gigabytes in some cases.

7.35 $\frac{1}{8}''$ **cassette.** The more basic cassettes are generally slower than tape cartridges and store up to 340,000 bytes at 800 bytes to the inch on a 280-foot tape.

7.36   **Digital Audio Tape (DAT).** DAT tapes are produced in the form of 4mm cassettes (Non DAT 4mm cassettes are also in use). The DAT tape was first devised as a digital tape alternative to the CD for domestic music systems. DATs have so far had more success as a means of computer storage. DAT tapes units use rotating read-write heads similar to those used in domestic video recorders. The heads are placed at a slight angle to the tape and are made to spin in the opposite direction to the moving tape. The high relative speed of the heads and tape mean that reliable high density recording can be attained. This "helical scan" method is similar to that used in 8mm video camcorders and, as a result, the 4mm DAT tapes look like small scale versions of the 8mm camcorder cassettes. A standard DAT tape has a capacity of 1.3 Gigabytes.

SOLID STATE STORAGE DEVICES

7.37   Other forms of storage have been developed which are called **solid state** (ie, no moving parts). The (comparative) slowness of current disks and tapes is caused by the physical movement of the recording surface and (with disks) of the heads. There is no such physical movement in solid-state devices. These devices are another category of semi-conductor memory but give somewhat slower access speeds to the data than RAM and ROM and are therefore not suitable for main storage.

7.38 None of these solid state devices has caught on to any degree, probably because they are not competitive in terms of price. The two common types of solid state storage devices used for backing storage are:

a. **Magnetic bubble memory.**

b. **CCDs (Charge Coupled Devices).**

7.39 **Magnetic Bubble Memory.** In "bubble memories" data is stored as tiny magnetic domains (the bubbles) which continually circulate past read-write heads.

7.40 **CCDs (Charge Coupled Devices).** These are produced by a form of MOS technology. They are relatively fast compared with bubble memory but are volatile whereas bubble memory is not.

7.41 In the current state of development, solid-state storage is halfway between established memory systems and backing storage. It provides access to data that is faster than conventional backing storage devices but slower than memory. On the other hand, it has a capacity higher than memory but lower than backing storage. Disk technology continues to improve at such a pace that solid state devices have not yet made a breakthrough.

MASS STORAGE DEVICES AND MEDIA

7.42 Some large corporations and government agencies have a need for vast data storage capacities. This need can be met by mass storage devices. These devices are "automated libraries" of disk and tape cartridges, rather like the jukeboxes mentioned earlier. The total capacity of such a system tends to be expressed in terms of Gigabytes (thousands of millions of bytes). Further detail is not merited.

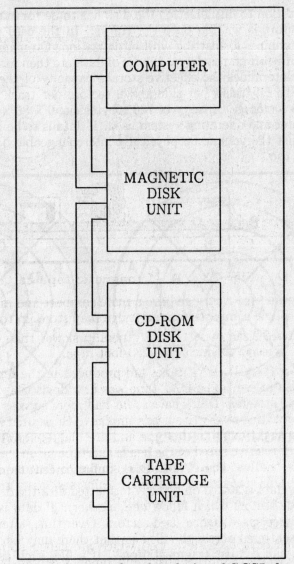

Fig 7.13. An example of a chain of SCSI devices.

SCSI INTERFACES

7.43 SCSI stands for "Small Computer Systems Interface" and is normally pronounced "scuzzy". SCSI is a *standard* for high speed communication between devices to which peripheral connections may be built. SCSI has become widely adopted in recent years. As its name suggests, the SCSI interface is aimed at small computer systems where there is often a need to connect several different types of external storage devices and other peripherals. A SCSI "host adaptor" circuit board in the computer is connected to a single plug-in socket on the computer's cabinet into which a chain of "**SCSI devices**" can be connected with each also fitted with an adaptor circuit board. Each device has two sockets to enable it to be chained to the next by a cable. At one end of the chain is the computer, and at the other end is a "**terminator**". (No cracks about "I'll be back"!) (Fig 7.13.)

7.44 Data is transferred at high speed between the devices which makes SCSI suitable for connecting disk devices to a computer. A transfer rate of 1 – 5 Megabytes per second is not uncommon and devices built to the new SCSI-2 standard can transfers data at about 10 Megabytes per second.

PHYSICAL STORAGE CONSIDERATION

7.45 "Volume" is a general term for any individual physical storage medium that can be written to or read from. Examples include: a fixed hard disk, a disk pack, a floppy disk, a CD-ROM, a disk cartridge or a tape cartridge.

7.46 **Initialization.** Before a disk volumes may be recorded upon it normally has to be **initialized** which involves writing zeroes to every data byte on every track. A special program is normally supplied for this purpose. Clearly, the re-initialization of a disk effectively eliminates all trace of any existing data.

7.47 **Formatting.** In addition to initialization the disk has to be **formatted** which means that a regular pattern of blank sectors is written onto the tracks. In the case of floppy disks the "formatting" program normally combines formatting with initialization. On magnetic tapes the **format** is defined when the tape is **mounted** on the drive. Blocks of data are then formatted as they are written to the tape. The **format** determines the effective storage capacity of the volume. For example, a double sided floppy disk with 80 tracks per side and 9 sectors per track with each sector containing 512 data bytes will have a storage capacity of 720 Kbytes (ie, 9 × 80 × 2 × 512 bytes.) Formats depend upon the manufacturer and operating system used. If data is to be transferred from one computer to another not only must the volume be physically interchangeable between drives the volume format must be compatible too.

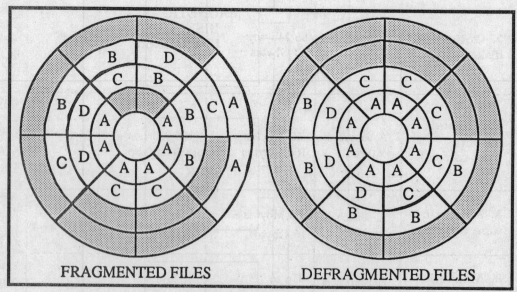

Fig. 7.14. Disk defragmentation.

7.48 **Fragmentation.** As data is stored on a newly formatted disk the data is written to unused **contiguous** sectors (ie, those sectors which follow one another). If data is erased then the deleted sectors may leave "holes" of free space among used sectors. Over time, after many inserts and deletes, these free sectors may be scattered across the disk so that there may be very little contiguous free space. This phenomenon is called "disk fragmentation". If a file, such as a document file say, is written to the disk the read-write heads will have to move about as they access the fragmented free space. This slows down the writing process and will also slow down any subsequent reads. Therefore, performance suffers. When this happens it may be possible to use a special disk defragmenter program to re-organise the data on the disk so as to eliminate the fragmentation. (Fig 7.14.)

SUMMARY

7.49   **a.** Auxiliary storage is used, as its name suggests, to supplement main storage.

     b. The descriptions have concentrated on the physical features rather than uses, which will be discussed later in the text.

     c. The main auxiliary storage media are in *magnetic* form.

     d. The main hardware devices and media for auxiliary storage are:-

         i. Magnetic disk unit – magnetic disk.

         ii. Magnetic diskette unit – magnetic diskette (floppy disk).

         iii. Optical disk unit – optical disk.

         iv. Magnetic tape unit – magnetic tape.

         v. Magnetic tape cartridges and cassettes.

         vi. Solid state storage devices.

         vii. Mass storage devices and media.

     e. The comparative performance of backing storage media and devices is shown in Fig. 7.15.

Devices and Media.	Typical Access Time.	Typical Storage Capacities.	Typical transfer Rates.	Types of Storage SAS † or DAS‡	Where used as primary medium.
1. Floppy disk (diskette)	260ms	180 K bytes to 1.25 M bytes	24,000 bps – 50,000 bps (bytes per second	DAS	Small micro-computer-based systems — otherwise as a back-up medium for hard disk.
2. Magnetic disk	20 – 60ms	60 Mbytes – 5 Gbytes	312,000 bps – 2,000,000 bps	DAS	Minicomputers and mainframes.
3. Optical disks	100ms	55 Mbytes – 10 Gbytes	200,000 bps	DAS	Minicomputers and mainframes — for archiving or on-line back-up.
4. Magnetic tape (reel-to-reel)	A search is required.	40 Mbytes – 160 Mbytes	160,000 bps – 1,250,000 bps	SAS	Minicomputers and mainframes — mostly as a back-up medium for disk.
5. Magnetic tape cartridge	A search is required.	50 Mbytes – 10 Gbytes	160,000 bps – 2.6Mbps	SAS	Microcomputer and minicomputers.
6. Magnetic tape cassette	A search is required.	Up to 145,000 bytes.	10 bps – 33,000 bps	SAS	Small micro-computer systems.

†SAS (Serial Access Storage) ‡DAS (Direct Access Storage)

Fig. 7.15. Comparative performance of backing storage media and devices.

POINTS TO NOTICE

7.50   **a.** Note the terms "on-line" and "off-line". "On-line" means being accessible to and under the control of the processor. Conversely, "off-line" means *not* accessible to or under the control of the processor. Thus, *fixed* magnetic disks are *permanently* "on-line"; a magnetic tape reel or an exchangeable magnetic disk pack is "on-line" when placed in its respective units, but "off-line" when stored away from the computer, terminals, *wherever* their physical location, are said to be "on-line" when directly linked to the processor.

b. On exchangeable disks, the read-write heads serving each *surface* will be positioned over the *same relative track* on *each surface* because the arms on which they are fixed move simultaneously.

c. The "jukebox" was introduced in this chapter as an option used with CDs but jukeboxes are available for a variety of disk devices.

d. The term *"cartridge"* is ambiguous unless prefixed by *"tape"* or *"disk"*.

e. The devices and media have been separated for ease of explanation. It should be noted, however, that in the case of the *fixed* disk the media are permanently fixed to the device, and therefore they cannot be separated.

f. Backing storage is also called **auxiliary storage.**

g. Input, output and storage devices are referred to collectively as peripheral devices.

h. Disk packs normally have several platters and are top-loading whereas disk cartridges are side-loading with just one or two platters.

i. Simplified versions of magnetic tape cartridge units used solely for back-up are sometimes known as **"streamers"**.

GLOSSARY CHECKLIST

INPUT AND OUTPUT

1. This Part of the text gives detailed coverage of computer input and output. It builds on the introductory material covered in the Foundation Topics but also introduces some new material.

2. One of the most common ways of using a computer for general purpose is for an end-user to have an on-line connection to the computer via a device such as a VDU terminal or workstation. The use of the computer is said to be **interactive**. The situation for the user of a home computer or personal computer is essentially the same, with the screen and keyboard performing a similar function to that provided by terminals or workstations. There are a variety of different devices that provide this kind of facility to input and output data. Chapter 8 looks at them in detail.

3. Terminals are not particularly suitable for outputting large volumes of data nor do they provide permanent copies. All data has to be entered via the keyboard and the forms in which data can be output have their limits too. Therefore, a number of other methods of data input and output are needed. Chapter 9 describes a number of special devices and media for output. They are used to receive data from the processor and to produce the data in a humanly sensible form (or in a machine-sensible form for later re-input).

4. Chapter 10 deals with the problems of how best to get data into the computer. It describes the methods and media that can be used to overcome these problems. The chapter also examines the choices that have to be made when deciding what is the best way to carry out input and output in particular situations.

5. Chapter 11 returns to the issue of interactive on-line computing, but instead of just considering devices, as in chapter 8, it examines the issues that concern making computers easy for users to interact with. This interaction between end-users and the computer is said to take place at the **"Human Computer Interface"** (HCI). The term "Human Computer Interface" is meant to cover *all* aspects of this interaction, not just the hardware. Of particular interest is what makes one HCI better than another one.

6. This Part is relevant to all examinations for which this text is a preparation. However, there is some difference in emphasis according to the examinations. A level examinations all require candidates to have a thorough understanding of the material in this Part. Readers taking other courses are advised to seek the advice of there lecturer about what to concentrate on since essential know-how varies on a course by course basis depending on course options, assignments and projects.

8: Workstations and Terminals

INTRODUCTION

8.1 This chapter deals with a range of devices used for interactive on-line computing. The chapter's title "Workstations and Terminals" reflects the range of devices covered. Some introductory material given in earlier chapters is revised and taken further.

8.2 The subject matter will be covered under the following headings:

a. Terminals

b. Personal computers as terminals

c. Workstations

d. Computer graphics

e. Windowing systems

All these devices are **"keyboard devices"**, which merely means that their primary means of entering data to the computer is via a keyboard. The keyboards resemble the QWERTY typewriter keyboard, but usually have several additional keys, which are used for other purposes depending upon the type of device.

TERMINALS

8.3 By far the most common form of **terminal** is the VDU which was introduced in 4.36. Terminals have a keyboard for input and a display screen or printer to show both what is typed in and what is output by the computer. Terminals which have a printer instead of a screen are called **terminal typewriters**. They are now rather outdated and rare, so the name "terminal" is now normally synonymous with **VDU** and is often used instead. There are many different types of VDU terminals in use today. Only the more common features and variants will be described.

8.4 **Features of the VDU Terminal.**

a. It is a dual-purpose device with a keyboard for data input and a cathode ray tube screen for output. The latter is similar to a TV screen. The screen is normally housed along with the device's electronic components in a cabinet similar to that used for a PC's monitor.

b. The keyboard resembles the QWERTY typewriter keyboard, but usually has several additional keys, which are used to control and edit the display.

c. Characters are displayed on the screen in a manner that resembles printed text. A typical full screen display is 24 rows by 80 columns (ie, 1920 characters).

d. The display can normally be generated in two different modes:

   i. **Scrolling mode** in which lines appear at the bottom and move up the screen rather like credits on a movie screen.

   ii. **Paging mode** in which one complete screen-full is replace by another, rather like a slide projector display.

e. Most VDUs have features that allow particular parts of the display to be highlighted or contrasted, eg,

   i. Inverse (Reverse) video, ie, black on white instead of white on black.

   ii. Blinking displays.

   iii. Two levels of brightness.

   iv. Colour - on the more expensive models.

f. **Cursor controls.** A cursor is a small character-size symbol displayed on the screen, which can be moved about the screen both vertically and horizontally by means of special keys on the keyboard. During data input, the display may resemble a blank form. In this case data may be entered by first moving the cursor to a space on the "form" and then typing in the data. Further keys may allow the data to be edited or corrected.

g. **Inbuilt microprocessors.** The numerous internal functions of almost all modern VDUs are controlled by inbuilt microprocessors. The more expensive models are often called **intelligent**

terminals. These more advanced devices are sometimes capable of limited amounts of processing, and with further enhancements they can often be turned into small microcomputer systems in their own right which may be called **"workstations"** in some cases. However, a typical "workstation" is a device with far more advanced facilities than a VDU and with different capabilities. Workstation will therefore be discussed separately later in this chapter.

An IBM 3277 model 2 Information Display Station and Light Pen.
Picture courtesy of IBM.

8.5   **How it works.** When a key is pressed on the keyboard the character's code (in ASCII, say) is generated and transmitted to the computer along the lead connecting the terminal to the computer. Normally the character code received by the computer is immediately "echoed" back out to the terminal by the computer. When a character code is received by the terminal it is interpreted by the control circuitry and the appropriate character symbol is displayed on the screen, or printed depending upon the type of terminal. In what follows the basic operation of a VDU is covered in more detail.

8.6   For the more basic VDU models the character codes are stored in a memory array inside the VDU with each location in memory corresponding to one of the 24 × 80 character position on the screen (Fig 8.1). The VDU is able to interpret control characters affecting the text format. Each character in the character set has its display symbol defined in terms of a grid of bits. These predetermined patterns are normally held in a special symbol table in ROM. Common grid sizes are 8 × 14 and 9 × 16. The character array is scanned by circuitry in the VDU and the character map generator refers to the ROM to produce the appropriate bit-map image for each character to be displayed on the screen. Often the device is able also to interpret sequences of control characters (often beginning with the ASCII control character "ESC") which may alter display characteristics such as reverse video or colour. This kind of VDU is only able to form images on the screen by constructing them from character symbols by means of the character map generator. It is therefore called a **character terminal.** The superior alternative is a **graphics terminal.**

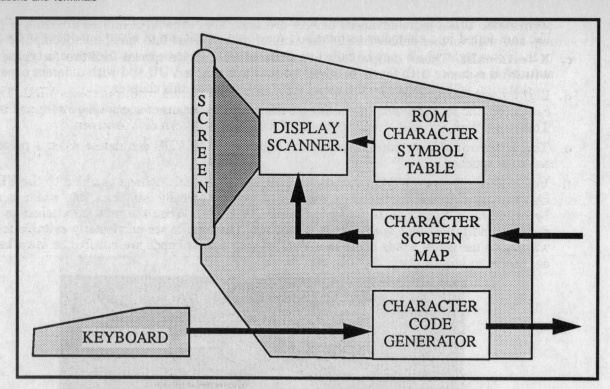

Fig 8.1 Simplified operation of a VDU

8.7 Variations on the VDU

a. **Graphics terminals.** Some VDUs have high quality displays that can be used for line drawings, draughtsmen's drawings, etc. These more advanced models are not limited to displaying characters but can handle screen sized images too. There are many kinds of graphics terminal but just one common example will be given here to explain the basic ideas.

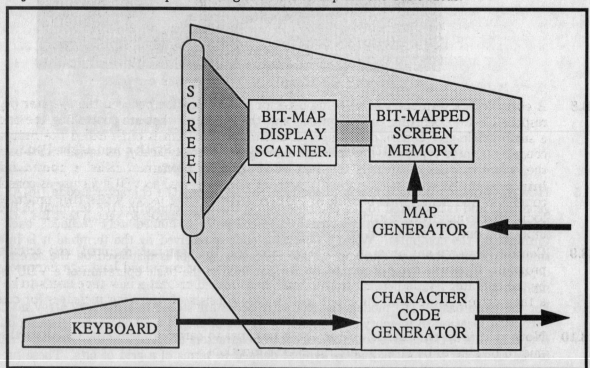

Fig 8.2 Simplified operation of a graphics terminal with bit-mapped display

b. In a **Raster Scan Display**, which is just one of many types of display technology, the character codes received from the computer are interpreted by the terminal's map generator which then loads the appropriate bit patterns into special memory ("video RAM") acting as a bit-map for the whole screen. This bit-mapped memory is organised into rows and columns of pixels which are a copy or "mapping" of a corresponding image representation to be displayed on the screen. The bit-mapped memory is scanned repeatedly with the corresponding image being displayed on the screen. (Fig 8.2.) The graphics terminal may also contain a ROM character symbol table like that found in a character terminal. It may hold definitions of a small number of fonts.

c. **X-terminals.** These are graphics terminals which provide special facilities for using the **X-windows** system. Details will be given later in this chapter.

d. **Light pens.** A light pen is a special pen used in conjunction with a graphics VDU. The VDU can detect the location of light shining on the screen by means of special hardware and software. This is a design aid that simplifies input of details of positions on the screen.

e. **Touch terminals.** An alternative to the light pen. The VDU can detect when a point on the screen is touched.

f. **Voice Data Entry (VDE).** Additional circuitry plus a microphone is added to the VDU. The unit can be switched to "learn" a number of words, typically less than 200, which it achieves by recording a "sound pattern" for each word typed in. When the unit is switched to input it displays and inputs any word that it recognises. These units are particularly suitable for people wishing to use a few words again in situations where their hands are not free to use a keyboard, eg, people in laboratories, invalids, etc.

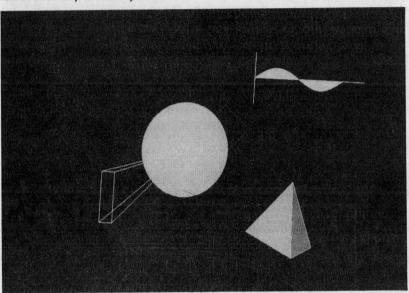

Fig 8.3 Simple VDU graphics output.

8.8 A **console** is a terminal that is being used for communication between the *operator* (ie, the person responsible for operating the computer) and the programs that are controlling the computer. For a small single-user computer the special controlling program is often called the **monitor** and the console operator types one-line monitor commands. More typically, on larger multi-user computers the operator types commands that are acted upon by a program called a **command language interpreter.** At one time terminal typewriter were preferred to VDUs for use as consoles on mini-computers and mainframes because of the permanent printed record which they produced. However, today this requirement is achieved by programming the computer to keep a text file "log" copy of all input and output carried out on the console.

8.9 Control messages are keyed in by the operator (eg, the next task required) and acted upon by the program. Messages can also be output by the monitor or command language interpreter for action by the operator (eg, indicating that a "run" has finished or that a new tape needs to be placed onto a tape drive). Note that the input in this case consists of *operating messages* for controlling the system.

8.10 **Note** that if an end-user is able to use a terminal to carry out operator functions the terminal is said to be able to be able to perform *console* functions.

PERSONAL COMPUTERS USED AS TERMINALS

8.11 There are many situations in which people who use terminals connected to minicomputers or main-frames also use Personal Computers (PCs). To save on the cost of hardware, and on desktop space, they may use their PC as a terminal instead of having a separate terminal. For this to be possible the PC must be fitted with the correct hardware and use **terminal emulation** software.

8.12 **PC features.** The PC's hardware must have suitable features that may require the fitting of some extras. There must be a suitable socket on the outside of the PC to which a terminal lead can be connected. Although this sounds a simple requirement there are a number of things that have to be set up correctly for such an arrangement to work. Usually, small computers such as PCs have a number of sockets fitted to them each of which has been designed to be connected to a particular type of peripheral device. These external points of connection are called **ports**. A "**communications port**" normally has the properties needed for connecting the PC to a terminal lead. It is helpful to be familiar with some of the issues involved.

a. **Interfaces.** A special piece of circuitry is fitted inside the computer and sits between the computer and the port. Its purpose is to provide a compatible connection between the two. Such a device is called an **interface**.

b. Interfaces are either **serial** or **parallel**. A serial interface sends or receives the bits comprising each character code one at a time, whereas a parallel interface sends the set of bits for each character all at once. As a consequence, more socket pins are used in parallel ports. A very common standard serial interface is the **RS232C**. A SCSI port is an example of a parallel port.

c. Most ports are **bidirectional**, ie, they can send and receive data. Some printer ports can only send data and can therefore not be used with a terminal connection.

d. The sending and receiving of signals at a port is usually governed by a set of rules known as **protocols**. For example, the **X-on X-off** protocol involves sending the ASCII code 19, which means "stop transmission" and the ASCII code 17, which means "start transmission". This facility may be available to the terminal user by typing the control key plus "S" for X-off (ASCII 19) and the control key plus "Q" for X-on (ASCII 17).

e. The speed with which data can be transmitted through the port can usually be varied. Such speeds are often expressed as **baud rates** (details later). Common settings are 330, 1200, 2400, 4800 and 9600. Divide these figures by 10 to get a *rough* approximation of the corresponding speeds in characters per second.

8.13   **Terminal emulation.** By themselves the hardware connections are useless without a suitable program running in the PC to make the PC behave like a VDU. Such a program is called a **terminal emulator**. Many different terminal emulators are on sale as standard "packages". A typical terminal emulator has the following features:

a. The emulator normally provides a set-up facility, which enables the user to choose the appropriate characteristics and settings needed. For example, the baud rate may be selected. Also, the emulator may present the user with a choice of standard VDU types. Very common options are VT100 and VT220, which are the model numbers of two popular VDUs manufactured by Digital and since copied by various other manufacturers.

b. The PC's keyboard is made to behave just like a VDU keyboard even to the extent of making special "function keys" behave in the same way if the emulation is a good one.

c. The screen behaves and looks just like the VDU screen. In a good emulation even special graphics symbols will display the same way.

d. In addition to making the PC behave like a VDU many terminal emulation packages also provide a **file-transfer** facility, ie, a means by which data and programs may be copied directly between a disk in the PC and the disks on the main computer to which the PC is connected as a terminal.

Note. Although this discussion has been about the use of PCs as terminals it is possible to use some home computers as terminals too and in much the same way as PCs.

WORKSTATIONS

8.14   A typical workstation looks similar to a PC because it is a desktop computer with screen and keyboard attached. However, it is different in a number of respects as will be seen from the following list of essential features.

a. It is larger and more powerful than a typical PC. For example, many popular workstations use 32-bit microprocessors whereas PCs are typically 16-bit microcomputers.

b. It is fully connected into a computer network as another computer on the network in its own right and not just running a terminal emulator.

c. It has high-resolution graphics on bit-mapped screens as a standard feature. So it incorporates the capabilities of the graphics terminal described earlier.

d. It has a **multitasking** operating system which means that it is able to run multiple applications at the same time. This is a feature not found in most PCs.

8.15 **Uses.** Workstations are normally used by professionals for particular kinds of work such as Finance (dealer rooms), Science and Research, and Computer Aided Design. They are also very popular for programming.

8.16 **Examples** of workstations are the Digital VAXSTATIONs and the SUN SPARCstations.

8.17 **PCs as workstations.** Most workstations are purpose built to provide the essential features listed above. It may be possible for a powerful PC to meet these requirements. The requirements may be met as follows.

    a. Higher powered processors such as the higher speed Intel 486 or Motorola M68040 will be desirable. Supplementary **co-processors** will also be preferable. **Maths co-processors** can take computational loads of the main processor and graphics co-processors can take load of the main processor in the construction and maintenance of images.

    b. The PC will normally be fitted with an extra circuit board able to control and operate a high speed network port.

    c. Suitable **Graphics cards** will be fitted to provide graphics capabilities of sufficiently high standard. Details later.

    d. A multi-tasking capability must be available through suitable software. The operating systems **PC-DOS** and **MS-DOS** found on the majority of IBM compatible PCs are *not* capable of multi-tasking. Only one application program can be run at a time. A form of multi-tasking is available through Microsoft Windows 3 which may be run under these operating systems. Alternatively, operating systems such as OS/2 and SCO Unix may be run on the same hardware and do provide full multi-tasking. On the Apple Macintosh "pseudo-multi-tasking" has been available for some time but full multi-tasking is only available under version 7 of Apple's MacOS operating system or under A/UX, Apple's version of Unix.

The Sun SPARCstation 1
Photograph courtesy of Sun Microsystem Ltd.

COMPUTER GRAPHICS

8.18 One feature of some terminals, many PCs and all workstations is Computer Graphics. A wide variety of pictures, diagrams, graphs, line drawings, animated cartoons, etc, can be produced on computer output devices and the general term for all such forms of output is computer graphics. The two basic methods of producing graphical images are:

    a. Block-based images.

    b. Pixel-based images.

8.19 Block-based images are simple and effective and can be performed on **character terminals**. The basic building blocks are graphics characters, which the device can display or print in addition to the ordinary alphabetic and numeric characters (see Fig. 8.4). The graphics characters available vary from device to device. One standard and very simple form of block-based image is that used on the British TV Ceefax and Oracle services.

8.20 Pixel-based images are of a higher quality than block-based images and are used on **workstations, graphics terminals and PCs fitted with "Graphics Video Adaptors"**. The image is built up from an appropriate combination of dots. To achieve this the whole screen is organised into rows and columns of individual "dot" positions called pixels. On a black and white screen each pixel can simply either be **on** (black) or **off** (white) (see Fig 8.4). On a colour screen each pixel may comprise a cluster of red, green and blue primary-coloured dots which can be on and off in different combinations.

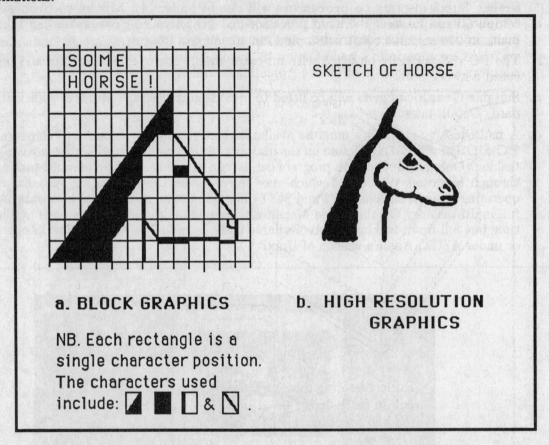

Fig 8.4. Computer Graphics.

8.21 The more pixels there are, the more detail can be represented, ie, the higher the resolution. A screen with more than 30,000 pixels will normally be classified as a **high-resolution graphics (HRG)** screen and will be capable of representing reasonably smooth curves and accurate drawings. Specialist graphics terminals are available, however, with more than 700,000 pixels.

8.22 A graphics terminal uses its own internal memory to hold the bit-mapped image. Similarly, a PC or workstation may have memory separately available dedicated to this purpose. The area of memory used to hold the data is sometimes called a **frame buffer**. Alternatively, in a PC or workstation main memory may be set aside for storing data corresponding to the pixels being displayed on the screen.

8.23 Normally the kind of display available on a PC or workstation depend upon the quality of the monitor used and the type of **"video adaptor"** which has been fitted. The video adaptor is a special circuit board fitted inside the PC or workstation with an external connection to the monitor. The bit-mapped memory on the board is called **"Video RAM"**. Software in the PC or workstation sends control instructions to the video adaptor informing it which pixels to turn on and off and in which colours. Without a powerful processor this can be a very slow process because of the amount of work that has to be done by the processor. One way of alleviating this is to fit a **graphics co-processor** which is a specialist processor which can take over the pixel-level operations and is driven by high level instruction to draw lines, circles, boxes etc. Graphics co-processing is common in workstations but there are many different ways in which it may be achieved depending upon how the extra processors are incorporated into the workstation's design.

8.24 **Examples** of video adaptors found on IBM PCs, and those PC operating to the same standard, known as "IBM compatibles" are as follows.

a. **Colour Graphics Adapter (CGA).** This was the original adaptor provided and is now obsolete. It supported 4 colours at a time, chosen from 16, and had a resolution of 640 × 200 pixels. Characters were generated in 8 × 8 pixel grids. It is mentioned here for completeness and to show how the technology has progressed.

b. **Enhanced Graphics Adapter (EGA).** This low grade adaptor supports 16 colours at a time, chosen from 64, and had a resolution of 640 × 350 pixels. Characters are generated in 8 × 14 pixel grids.

c. **Video Graphics Array (VGA).** This adaptor is in widespread use. It supports either 320 × 200 pixels in 256 colours or 640 × 480 pixels in 16 colours. Characters are generated in 9 × 16 pixel grids. As a comparison, a grid of 640 × 480 pixels in either 16 or 256 colours is common on video adaptors and monitors used on the Apple Macintosh II.

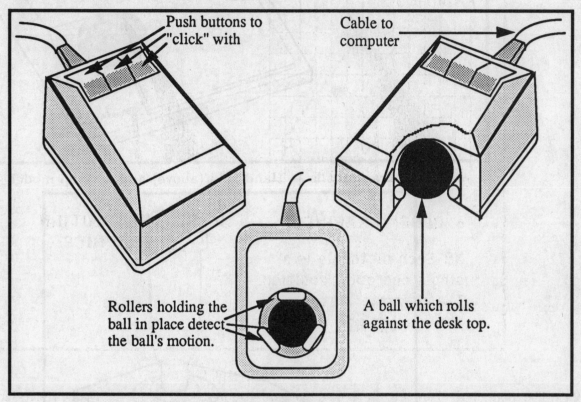

Fig 8.5. The operation of a mouse.

8.25 **Mice, trackerballs and joysticks.** These devices have a variety of uses complementary to the keyboard and are of particular value when used in conjunction with graphical displays. In simple cases they can be used to move the cursor about the screen.

a. **Mice.** As the mouse is moved about the desktop the cursor moves about the screen. A button on top of the mouse can be pressed when the desired position is reached. The motion of the mouse is sensed by a rolling ball, which is mounted in the underside of the mouse and in contact with the desktop.(Fig 8.5)

b. **Trackerballs.** A trackerball is really a variation on the mouse. The ball is on the top side of the trackerball, rather than on the underside as in a mouse. The ball is moved by passing the palm of the hand over it. Trackerballs are intended for use where desktop space is limited or not available, for example, when using a lap-top computer away from a desk.

c. **Joysticks.** A joystick is an alternative to a mouse. They have proved more popular for computer games than they have for serious applications. The joystick can be moved left, right, up or down to move the cursor and also has a button used like that on the mouse. The movements of the joystick are detected by cause electrical contacts to be made. (Fig 8.7)

d. Many graphics workstations provide software that allows pictures to be created by the use of devices such as mice. For example, by holding down the button on the mouse while moving the mouse across the desk top a line may be drawn across the screen. The graphics facilities can also be used to allow the user of the device to operate it in simpler and more visually interesting ways.

For example, alternative operations available to the user may be represented by simple graphical images called **icons**, which the user can select by means of a mouse. A pointer on the screen is moved by using the mouse so that the pointer is above the required icon. The mouse button is then clicked to select the operation represented by the icon (see Fig 8.8).

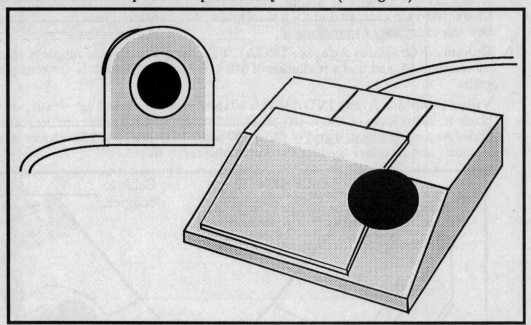

Fig 8.6. Trackerballs — Hand held (above) and desktop model.

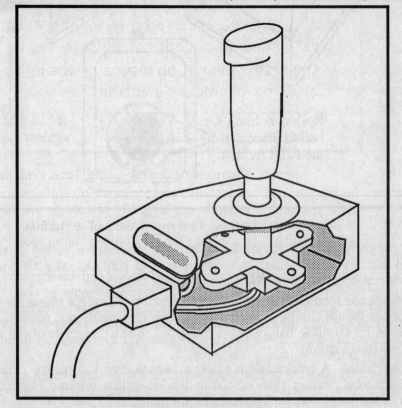

Fig 8.7. A Joystick.

WINDOWING SYSTEMS

8.26 A **window** is a rectangular area on a display screen in which text or graphical images may be displayed. Several windows may be displayed on a screen at the same time. Most workstations and some PCs use software that handles all screen displays by means of windows. These **windowing systems** normally have a number of common features:

a. **Windows** are displayed on the screen, normally using bit-mapped graphics, in a manner resembling rectangular pieces of paper placed on a desktop. Indeed, one large window, "beneath" all the others, is normally called the "desktop window" (Fig 8.9). A window designated as being "on-top" obscures the view of any part of any window beneath it. For example, in Fig 8.9 the desktop window has three file windows on it. The window with title "A" is on top. "B" is below it and "C" is underneath "B".

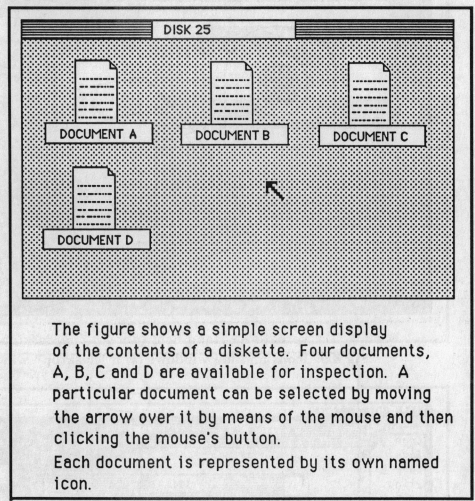

DISK 25

DOCUMENT A   DOCUMENT B   DOCUMENT C

DOCUMENT D

The figure shows a simple screen display of the contents of a diskette. Four documents, A, B, C and D are available for inspection. A particular document can be selected by moving the arrow over it by means of the mouse and then clicking the mouse's button.

Each document is represented by its own named icon.

Fig 8.8. Graphics Display using Icon and Mouse.

b. **Mice** may be used in conjunction with windows to provide additional means for the user to interact with the system. The mouse can be made to move a pointer on the screen to an item which is to be selected. For example by moving the pointer to a position above the window with title "B" (Fig 8.9) and then clicking the mouse's button the window "B" will be made to appear on top instead of "C".

c. **Icons** may be displayed in windows on the screen and used in conjunction with a mouse in the manner described earlier. A user may move the mouse so that the pointer is over an icon representing a document and then double click the mouse button to "open" the document. The document opens with the creation of a new window on the screen in which the document's contents may be seen. In Fig 8.9 the desktop window has four icons on it representing: a hard disk, a floppy disk, a CD-unit and a waste bin.

d. **Pull-down menus** are special-purpose windows associated with text headings displayed at the top of windows, especially the desktop's. In Fig 8.10 the pull-down menu under the screen heading "File" has been pulled down. *While the mouse key has been held down* the pointer has been moved to the "New" option which is highlighted. To select the highlighted operation the user merely releases the mouse button. Had the floppy disk icon previously been selected this might result in a window being displayed on the desktop showing documents on the disk (eg, see Fig 8.8). When looking at a document in an open window, there may be a heading at the screen top called "EDIT". If the mouse is moved above the word "EDIT" and then pressed a small window appears beneath it, *while the mouse key is held down*. Again, this **pull-down menu** will list a set of options available to the user (eg, FIND or CHANGE). If the user moves the mouse over an option and then lets go of the mouse button then the computer will carry out the selected action, in much the same way as it would if it was receiving typed commands.

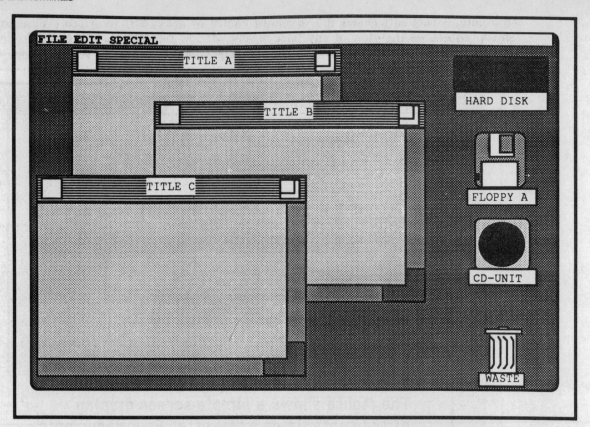

Fig 8.9. Icons and file windows on a "desktop" window.

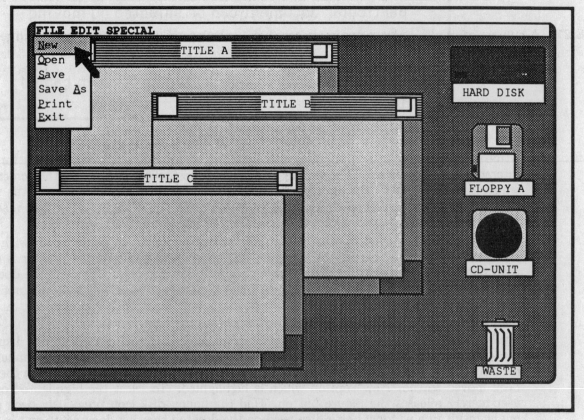

Fig 8.10. Pull-down menus.

e. **Pop-up windows.** In Fig 8.11 there is an example of a pop-up menu which has been displayed because the user has selected the "SAVE" option on a pull-down menu for a file which already exists. In this case the user is presented with three choices any one of which can be selected by clicking upon the appropriate box by means of the mouse controlled pointer. Once the selection has been made the pop-up window will disappear.

This combination of features is sometimes known as a WIMP interface (Windows Icons Mice and Pull-down menus).

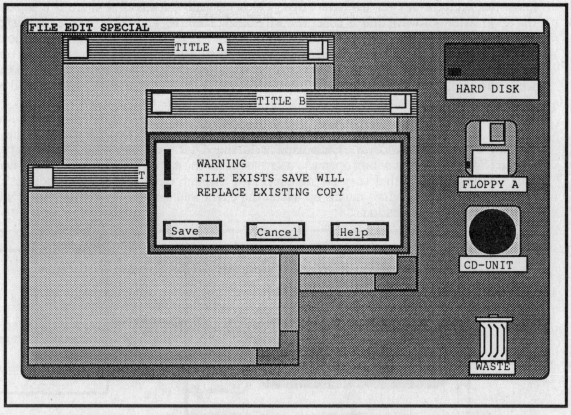

Fig 8.11. Pop-up windows.

8.27 A number of windowing systems are in common use today and the reader is strongly urged to get first-hand experience of using one. Two possible alternatives are the system used on the Apple Macintosh or the Microsoft Windows 3 package, which is available on some IBM PCs and compatibles.

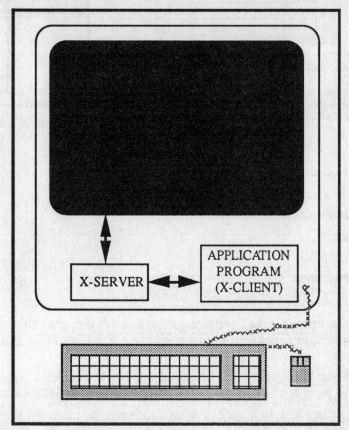

Fig 8.12. A workstation running an X-client and an X-server.

8.28   X-windows. Rather more advanced windowing capabilities are available on most workstations, many of which conform to a standard known as **X-windows**. The X-window system uses what is known as a **client-server architecture**, which basically means that there is a separation between the application software that is using the windowing facilities and the software that actually manages and controls the screen, keyboard and mouse in the intended fashion. The application is the **client** and the software managing the windowing environment is the **server**. The client and server programs may either both be executed in the workstation or, alternatively, the server may run in the workstation while the client runs on another computer in the network. Fig 8.12 shows a simplified representation of a workstation in which an **X-client** program and the **X-server** are both running. Fig 8.13 shows an X-terminal running the X-server software connected to two computers via a network with the computers acting as X-clients. The X-terminal is like a workstation except that the *only* program running on it is the X-server. Each window in the X-terminal can be used as a separate terminal screen. So, with four windows open the user has much the same facilities as he or she would have with four terminals except that they are all controlled through one keyboard and mouse. The X-window system provides a standard means by which the client and server may communicate with each other irrespective of their locations.

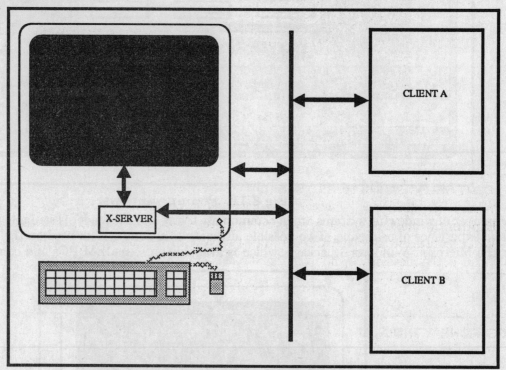

Fig 8.13. An X-terminal running an X-server.

SUMMARY

8.29   The following topics have been covered.

   a. Terminals

   b. Personal computers as terminals

   c. Workstations

   d. Computer graphics

   e. Windowing systems

POINTS TO NOTE

8.30   a. A **desktop** computer is, as the name suggests, any computer that can be used on a desk or table. The three common types of desktop computers are Home Computers, Personal Computers and Workstations.

   b. Some intelligent terminals, called X-terminals (or **X-stations**), are specifically designed to work as X-window servers without having full workstation capabilities in any other respect.

   c. When using graphical displays heavy demands can be made on the memory used to store images if the image is of high resolution or uses many colours. If the video RAM memory is of fixed size there is a trade off between the level of resolution and the number of colours which can be displayed.

The Macintosh portable
Courtesy of Apple Computers UK Ltd.

STUDENT SELF-TESTING QUESTIONS

1. What is the difference between "scrolling" and "paging" on a VDU?
2. Explain the meaning of the expression "high-resolution bit-mapped graphics display".
3. What features would you expect a workstation to have?
4. What is the meaning of the term "multi-tasking"?

QUESTIONS WITHOUT ANSWERS

5. Find out exactly what features are present on the VDU or PC display that you use.
6. What is an X-terminal?

GLOSSARY CHECKLIST

Baud rate	8.12e	Graphics terminal	8.7
Bidirectional port	8.12c	HRG	8.21
CGA	8.24a	IBM compatible	8.24
Character terminal	8.6	Icon	8.27c
Client	8.29	Intelligent terminal	8.4g
Client-server	8.24	Interface	8.12
Communications port	8.12	Joystick	8.25c
Console	8.8	Keyboard device	8.3
Co-processor	8.17a	Light pen	8.7d
Desktop window	8.27a	Maths co-processor	8.17
EGA	8.24a	Mice	8.25
File transfer	8.13d	Multi-tasking	8.14d
Frame buffer	8.22	Page mode	8.4d
Graphics card	8.17	Parallel interface	8.12b
Graphics co-processor	8.17a	Pop-up menu	8.27

9: Output Devices

INTRODUCTION

9.1 The following devices and media will be described:

    a. Printers — Single sheet or continuous stationery.

    b. Microform recorder — Microfilm or Microfiche.

    c. Graph Plotters — Single sheet or continuous stationery.

    d. Actuators.

    e. Others.

PRINTERS

9.2 A basic classification of printers is:

    a. **Character printers** which print one character at a time. The most common example is the **dot matrix printer**.

    b. **Line printers** which print whole lines at a time.

    c. **Page printers** (also called **image printers**) which print whole pages at a time. The most common example is the **laser printer**.

9.3 **Print Speeds** tend to be expressed in terms of **cps** (characters per second), **lpm** (lines per minute) or **ppm** (pages per minute). Printers may be classified as

    a. **Low speed** (10 cps to approx. 300 lpm) — usually character printers.

    b. **High speed** (Typically 300 lpm – 3000 lpm) — usually line printers or page printers.

9.4 Basic methods of producing print.

    a. **Impact or non-impact printing.** Impact printers *hit* inked ribbons against paper whereas non-impact printers use other methods of printer, eg, thermal or electrostatic. Most impact printers are noisy.

    b. **Shaped character or dot-matrix printing.** The difference is explained in Fig. 9.1. A dot matrix can also be used to produce a whole **picture** or **image** (9.2c) similar in principle, but superior in quality, to the minute pattern of dots in a newspaper picture.

LOW-SPEED PRINTERS

9.5 **Dot matrix impact character printers.** These are the most popular and widely used low-speed printers. They are often loosely referred to as **"dot matrix printers"**.

9.6 Features

    a. As with all character printers the device mimics the action of a typewriter by printing single characters at a time in lines across the stationery. The print is produced by a small **"print head"** that moves to and fro across the page stopping momentarily in each character position to strike a print ribbon against the stationery with an array of wires.

    b. According to the number of wires in the print head, the character matrix may be 7 × 5, 7 × 7, 9 × 7, 9 × 9 or even 24 × 24. The more dots the better the image.

    c. Line widths are typically 80, 120, 132, or 160 characters across.

    d. Speeds are typically from 30 cps to 200 cps.

    e. Multiple print copies may be produced by the use of carboned paper (eg. 4 – 6 copies using **NCR** (No Carbon Required) paper).

    f. Some higher quality versions have:

        i. Inbuilt alternative character sets.

        ii. Very good print quality. The term **NLQ** (Near Letter Quality) is sometimes used to describe them.

        iii. Features for producing graphs, pictures, and even colour by means of multiple-print ribbons.

g. Small versions of these printers are often used in conjunction with computerised tills in shops and service stations, especially for dealing with purchases by credit card.

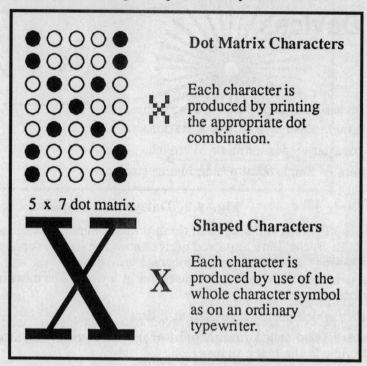

Fig. 9.1. Shaped and Dot Matrix Character.

9.7 **Daisywheel printers.** This is another popular type of low-speed printer that is favoured when high print quality is demanded.

9.8 **Features**

a. An impact shaped-character printer.

b. These printers are fitted with *exchangeable* print heads called **daisywheels** (see Fig. 9.2). To print each character the wheel is rotated and the appropriate spoke is struck against an inked ribbon.

c. Speeds are typically 45 cps.

d. They **are** similar to dot matrix printers in terms of page size and multiple-copy printing.

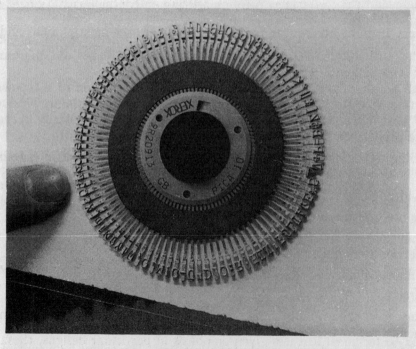

A daisywheel.

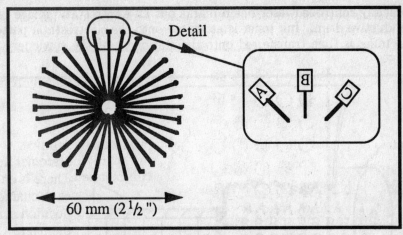

Fig. 9.2. Daisywheel Details.

9.9   Inkjet printers. The original models of these printers were character matrix printers and had only limited success. In recent years improved designs have resulted in very successful page printers which have been competing favourably with daisywheel printers.

9.10   Features.

    a. These are non-impact page printers.

    b. They operate by firing very tiny ink droplets onto the paper by using an "electrostatic field". By this means a medium quality bit-mapped image can be produced at a resolution of about 300dpi.

    c. They are very quiet but of low speed (4ppm).

    d. Some models print colour images, by means of multiple print heads each firing droplets of a different colour.

9.11   Other low-speed printers. There are many other low-speed printers too numerous to mention. One worth a mention is the **Thermal printer** which is a non-impact character matrix printer which prints onto special paper using a heated print head. It is very quiet and this gives it a big advantage for some applications.

HIGH-SPEED PRINTERS

9.12   There are two basic types of high-speed printer:

    a. Line Printers.

    b. Page Printers.

Line printer and the faster page printers operate on continuous stationery but most of the less fast page printers operate on single sheets of paper.

9.13   Line printers. These are impact shaped-character printers which, as their names suggest, print whole lines at a time. They are the printers traditionally used on Mainframes and minicomputers. There are three main types:

    a. Drum printers — Fig. 9.3.

    b. Chain printers — Fig. 9.4.

    c. Band printers — Fig. 9.4.

9.14   It will suffice to indicate how *b* and *c* work. A principle of operation typical of the faster models is that of a moving chain, with the links being engraved character-printing slugs, moving at a high constant speed past printing positions. The band printer has an embossed steel loop instead of a chain. Magnetically controlled hammers force *the paper* against the appropriate print slugs. Typically, there are 120 printing positions to a "line". Speeds of up to 50 lines per second *can* be achieved although, as yet, 20 (approx.) per second is a more typical speed. Using continuous stationery with interleaved carbons, up to 7 copies can be obtained (see Fig. 9.4).

The bands in a band printer may be exchanged quite readily to provide a variety of character sets.

9.15   Page printers. These printers print an "image" of a whole page at a time. The image may consist of conventional print, diagrams, pictures, or a combination of these, thus making pre-printed stationery unnecessary.

9.16   According to technical features given emphasis in particular designs, these printers are also known as **laser printers**, **optical printers** or **xerographic printers**.

9.17 An electronically controlled laser beam marks out an electrostatic image on the rotating surface of a photo conductive drum. Ink toner is attracted onto the electrostatic pattern on the surface of the drum. The toner is then transferred onto the stationery as the stationery comes into contact with the drum.

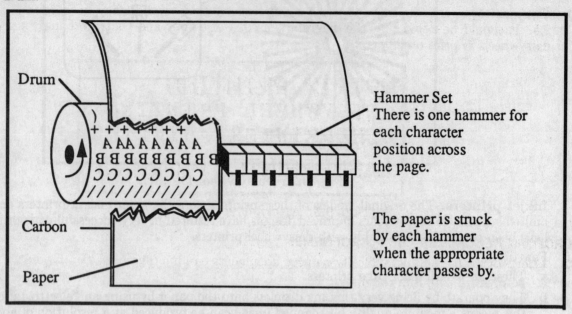

Fig. 9.3. A Drum Printer.

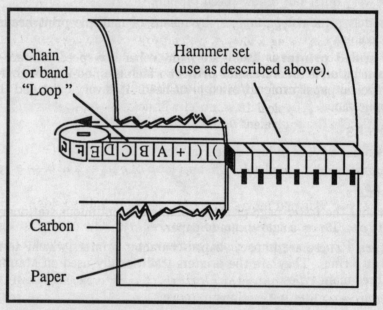

Fig. 9.4. A Chain or Band Printer.

9.18 A typical **high-speed laser printer** will print 146 pages per minute. When printed at a normal 6 lines per inch vertically, this represents a speed of 10,500 lpm, but with smaller spacing, speeds up to 30,000 lines per minute may be achieved on some models. These printers are very large and noisy.

9.19 A typical **Desktop laser printer** is suitable for use in an office environment and looks very similar to a photocopier. It has paper trays rather like those used in a photocopier too. Speeds are normally no more than ten pages per minute, but the quality of output is very high indeed (400 – 1200dpi), being much better than that produced by a daisywheel printer. Since it is a page printer the laser printer can print a combination of text and diagrams or pictures and is therefore very useful for producing reports, manuals and other small publications. These printers are therefore often used in conjunction with word processors and more advanced document creation systems, such as those provided on the Apple Macintosh, for what is often called **desktop publishing**.

9.20 Many desktop laser printers are fitted with **Postscript interpreters**. As was mentioned in chapter 5, postscript is a "**page description language**". Programs written in postscript are used to describe the way in which text and diagrams are to appear on a printed page. If a Postscript program is output from a computer to a laser printer the printer's postscript interpreter can follow the program's instruction to construct a page of printed output.

PRINT QUALITY

9.21 Comparing print quality. A *rough* comparison of print quality may be obtained from Figure 9.5. It should be noted that the diagram is a copy of a copy and that *some* matrix printers rival daisywheels in print quality.

```
MATRIX PRINTING
DAISYWHEEL PRINTING
LINEPRINTER PRINTING
LASERPRINTER PRINTING
```

Fig. 9.5. Alternative types of print.

MICROFORM RECORDERS AND MICROFORMS.

9.22 Microforms are photographically reduced documents on film. There are two types:

a. Microfilm – 16 mm roll film.

b. Microfiche – sheet film 105 mm x 148 mm.

Both types are produced in the same manner.

9.23 Output is written onto magnetic tape, which is then fed into a machine called a microform recorder, which reads the magnetic tape and copies the data onto microforms. The information can subsequently be inspected by using a viewer, which projects onto a screen. Full-size copies can be printed if required. This technique is useful when large volumes of information are used internally, since economies can be made in stationery costs and storage space. It is usually referred to as a **COM** (Computer Output on Microform/Microfilm/Microfiche).

9.24 Storage capacities. A typical 16 mm roll will hold the equivalent of 3,000 A4 pages. *One* typical microfiche will hold the equivalent of about 98 A4 pages.

GRAPH PLOTTERS

9.25 These devices provide a completely different form of output and have a variety of applications. Two basic types are:

a. Flatbed type. The pen moves up, down, across or side to side.

b. Drum type. The pen moves up, down and across. The paper provides the sideways movement.

Note. The up/down movements allow the pen to move from point to point with or without making a line.

9.26 Digital plotters and incremental plotters. The difference between these two types of plotter is in the way they are given instructions to move:

a. Digital plotters receive digital input that specifies the position to which the pen should move, ie, like a map reference.

b. Incremental plotters receive input that specifies changes in position, eg, move 2 mm left.

9.27 Colour. Many plotters have multiple pens of different colours that may be changed under machine control.

9.28 Some plotters use "electrostatic" printing rather than pen and ink.

Applications. Graph plotters are used for scientific and engineering purposes. One special application is CAD (Computer Aided Design) in which, for example, machine or architectural designs are created by computer and then output on graph plotters.

ACTUATORS

9.29 Computers are frequently used to control the operation of all manner of devices, appliances, mechanisms and processes. Any computer output device which is used to communicate some required action to a machine may be called an **Actuator**. For example a microcomputer operating a washing machine would use actuators to operate the motors and pumps. In a chemical plant controlled by computer **actuators** would operate valves, pumps, etc.

a. **A desktop, A3-size flatbed, 8-pen plotter from CalComp designed for plotting business and scientific graphs and charts on paper or on clear acetate for projection. Photograph with caption by courtesy of CalComp Ltd.**

b. **A high-speed desktop drum plotter from CalComp that uses A4-size continuous fan-folded paper or clear film. Photograph with caption by courtesy of CalComp Ltd.**

OTHER DEVICES

9.30 It is becoming increasingly common for small loudspeakers to be fitted in desktop computers. Although this facility is often used for computer games there are a number of serious uses. One general use is as a means of providing messages to the user, the simplest form of which is a warning "bleep" sound when something is wrong. However, loudspeakers really come into their own when used in conjunction with digitised sound (2.33). For example, by means of special software a desktop computer may be turned into a sound synthesizer unit which can be hooked up to a audio system.

9.31 Most other output devices are limited in use in specific applications. One notable exception is synthesized speech output.

9.32 **Speech output.** In principle, spoken output should be an extremely useful medium. Unfortunately the devices currently available produce unnatural sounds and are limited to a few specialist applications. The situation is likely to improve over the next few years.

SUMMARY

9.33 The *features* of the *main* hardware units and media for the output of data from the computer have been covered. They are:

a. Printers — Single sheet or continuous stationery.

b. Microform recorder — Microfilm or Microfiche.

c. Graph Plotters — Single sheet or continuous stationery.

d. Actuators.

e. Others.

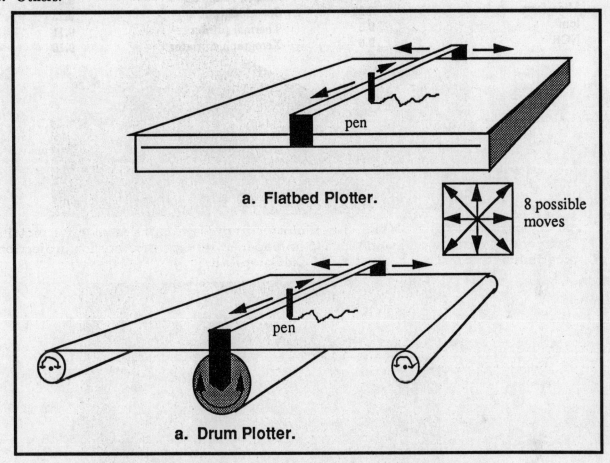

a. Flatbed Plotter.

8 possible moves

a. Drum Plotter.

Fig. 9.6. Flatbed plotter (above) and Drum plotter.

POINTS TO NOTE

9.34 a. Line printers can print in *Optical Character Recognition* form, ie, allowing later re-input without further transcription.

b. Some matrix printers can be used to produce bar-coded strips, eg, for use as stock labels.

GLOSSARY CHECKLIST

Actuator	9.29	Digital plotter	9.25
Band printer	9.13	Dot-matrix	9.7
CAD	9.28	Dot-matrix printer	9.5
Chain printer	9.13	Drum plotter	9.25
Character printer	9.2	Drum printer	9.13
COM	9.23	Flatbed plotter	9.25
cps	9.3	Graph plotter	9.25
Daisywheel	9.7	Image printer	9.2
Desktop laser printer	9.19	Impact printer	9.4

10: Data Capture and Data Entry

INTRODUCTION

10.1 These days the majority of computer end-users input data to the computer via keyboards on PCs, workstations or terminals. However, for many medium and large scale commercial and industrial applications involving large volumes of data the use of keyboards is not practical or economical. Instead, specialist methods, devices and media are used and these are the subject of this chapter. The chapter begins by examining the problems of data entry. It goes on to consider the stages involved and the alternatives available. It then examines the factors that influence the choice of methods, devices and media for data input. Finally, the chapter examines the overall controls that are needed over data as it is entered into the computer for processing.

10.2 The selection of the best method of data entry is often the biggest single problem faced by those designing commercial or industrial computer systems, because of the high costs involved and numerous practical consideration.

10.3 The best methods of data entry may still not give satisfactory facilities if the necessary controls over their use are not in place.

PROBLEMS OF DATA ENTRY

10.4 The data to be processed by the computer must be presented in a **machine-sensible** form (ie, the language of the particular input device). Therein lies the basic problem since much data *originates* in a form that is *far* from machine sensible. Thus a painful error-prone process of transcription must be undergone before the data is suitable for input to the computer.

10.5 The process of data collection involves getting the original data to the "processing centre", transcribing it, sometimes converting it from one medium to another, and finally getting it into the computer. This process involves a great many people, machines and much expense.

10.6 A number of advances have been made in recent years towards automating the data collection process so as to bypass or reduce the problems. This chapter considers a variety of methods, including many that are of primary importance in commercial computing. Specialist methods used for industrial computer applications will be covered in later chapters.

10.7 Data can originate in many forms, but the computer can only accept it in a machine-sensible form. The process involved in getting the data from its point of origin to the computer in a form suitable for processing is called **Data Collection**.

10.8 Before dealing with the individual stages of data collection it should be noted that data collection *starts* at the source of the raw data and *ends* when valid data is within the computer in a form ready for processing.

10.9 Many of the problems of data entry can be avoided if the data can be obtained in a computer-sensible form at the point of origin. This is known as **data capture**. This chapter will describe several methods of data capture. The capture of data does not necessarily mean its immediate input to the computer. The captured data may be stored in some intermediate form for later entry into the main computer in the required form. If data is input directly into the computer at its point of origin the data entry is said to be on-line. If, in addition, the method of direct input is a terminal or workstation the method of input is known as **Direct Data Entry (DDE)**. The term **Data Entry** used in the chapter title usually means not only the process of physical input by a device but also any methods directly associated with the input.

STAGES IN DATA COLLECTION

10.10 The process of data collection may involve any number of the following stages according to the methods used.

  a. Data creation, eg, on clerically prepared source documents.
  b. Transmission of data.
  c. Data preparation. ie, transcription and verification.
  d. Possible conversion from one medium (eg, diskette) to another (eg, magnetic tape).
  e. Input of data to the computer for validation.

f. Sorting.

g. Control — all stages must be controlled.

10.11 Not all data will go through every stage and the sequence could vary in some applications. Even today, a high proportion of input data starts life in the form of a manually scribed or typewritten document and has to go through all the stages. However, efforts have been made to reduce the number of stages. Progress has been made in preparing the source document itself in a machine-sensible form so that it may be used as input to the computer without the need for transcription. In practice, the method and medium adopted will depend on factors such as cost, type of application, etc. This will be discussed further in a later chapter.

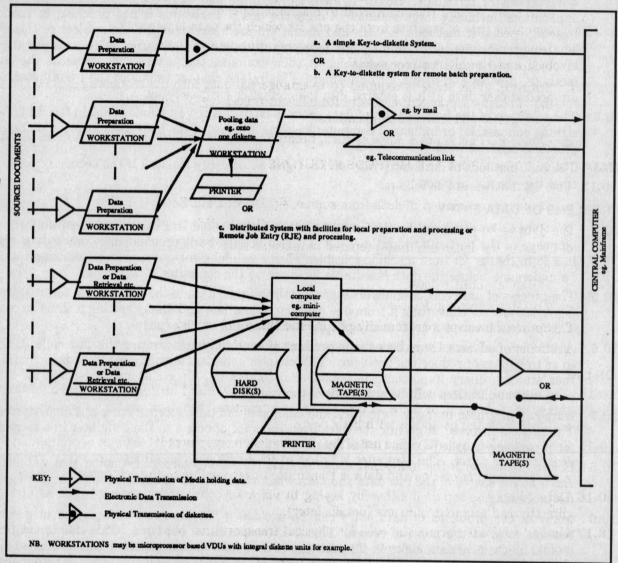

Fig 10.1 Some Typical Data Entry Systems.

STAGES EXPLAINED

10.12 a. Data creation. There are two basic alternatives, the first of which is the traditional method:

    i. Source documents. A great deal of data still originate in the form of clerically prepared source documents.

    ii. Data capture. Data is produced in a machine-sensible form at source and is read directly by a suitable device, eg, a bar code reader (details later).

   b. Data transmission. This can mean different things according to the method and medium of data collection adopted.

    i. If the computer is located at a central point, the documents will be physically "transmitted", ie, by the post office or a courier to the central point, (eg, posting batches of source documents).

ii. It is also possible for data to be transmitted by means of telephone lines to the central computer, in which case no source documents would be involved in the transmission process, (eg, transmitting data captured at source). A variant on this method is the use of FAXes.

c. **Data preparation.** This is the term given to the *transcription* of data from the source document to a machine-sensible medium. There are two parts; the original transcription itself and the verification process that follows.

Note. Data Capture eliminates the need for transcription.

d. **Media conversion.** Very often data is prepared in a particular medium and converted to another medium for faster input to the computer, eg, data might be prepared on diskette, or captured onto cassette, and then converted to magnetic tape for input. The conversion will be done on a computer that is separate from the one for which the data is intended.

e. **Input.** The data, now in magnetic form, is subjected to validity checks by a computer program before being used for processing.

f. **Sorting.** This stage is required to re-arrange the data into the sequence required for processing. (This is a practical necessity for efficient processing of sequentially organised data in many commercial and financial applications.)

g. **Control.** This is not a *stage* as such, because control is applied throughout the *whole* collection.

DATA-COLLECTION MEDIA AND METHODS IN OUTLINE

10.13 The alternatives are as follows.

a. On-line transmission of data from source, eg, Direct Data Entry (DDE).

b. Source document keyed directly into diskette (key-to-diskette) from some documents.

c. The source document itself prepared in machine-sensible form using Character Recognition techniques.

d. Data Capture Devices.

e. Portable encoding devices.

f. Source data captured from "Tags", Plastic Badges or strips.

g. Creation of data for input as a by-product of another operation.

ON-LINE SYSTEMS

10.14 The ultimate in data collection is to have the computer linked *directly* to the source of the data. If this is *not* feasible then the next best thing is to "capture" the data as near as possible to its source and feed it to the computer with little delay.

10.15 Such methods may involve the use of data transmission equipment if the point of origination is remote from the computer. The computer is linked to the terminal point (the source of data or nearby) by a telecommunication line and data is transmitted over the line to the computer system.

10.16 Data enters the terminal either by keying in via a keyboard or by a device such as one that can directly read source documents (details later).

10.17 On-line methods obviate the need for physical transportation of source documents to the processing point. There is also less delay in producing processed information, especially if the data link provides for two-way transmission of data (ie, from terminal to computer and computer to terminal).

10.18 Such systems can involve large capital outlay on the necessary equipment, which is usually justified in terms of speed of access to the computer's data and quicker feed-back of information.

10.19 On-line systems are the only practical choice for some applications. One example is the computer that controls a machine or factory process. It must receive input directly from source in order to be able to respond at a moment's notice.

10.20 If Direct Data Entry (DDE) is used then data is keyed in to a VDU or workstation by the operator. It is checked, displayed on the screen and then entered for processing.

10.21 A DDE station can also be used to interrogate the computer's stored data so that data can be checked for validity at the time of input. For example, if a customer's order is being entered, it is possible to check details of the customer's account and the availability of stocks.

10.22 Some specialised on-line systems are used by the general public. Probably the most common examples are the "hole in the wall" machines, more correctly called **on-line cash service tills**, which are provided by many banks and building societies for cash dispensing and other services outside normal office hours.

KEY-TO-DISKETTE

10.23 Key-to-diskette systems are a popular alternative to on-line systems in some organisations where data is generated at a number of different places.

Note. The key-to-diskette methods need not necessarily involve the use of special hardware. In many cases the same facility is provided by means of PCs running special programs. In what follows the features of specialist equipment are descibed.

10.24 The simplest key-to-diskette system is a stand-alone specialist "workstation" consisting of a high-quality VDU with inbuilt dual diskette units and microprocessor (Fig. 10.1a).

10.25 The workstation operates under the control of its own programs, which format the screen like a document, verify and validate input data, and transfer the data onto diskette. Programs for dealing with different source documents may be held on diskette and loaded by the workstation user when required.

10.26 The workstations are compact, robust, reliable, portable and operate autonomously. They therefore enable distributed data entry (close to the source of the data) together with a simple means of transferring data to a central computer.

10.27 Larger systems often include local printers to provide **hard copy** (ie, on paper) of the disk output (eg, for audit trail purposes, and electronic data transmission facilities) (Fig. 10.1b). The largest systems normally form part of a distributed data-processing system in which workstations are multi-purpose devices and facilities for data storage and transmission are varied and flexible, eg, a workstation may act as an interactive terminal to the main computer, or large volumes of data on diskette may be converted to magnetic tape for faster bulk input (Fig. 10.1c).

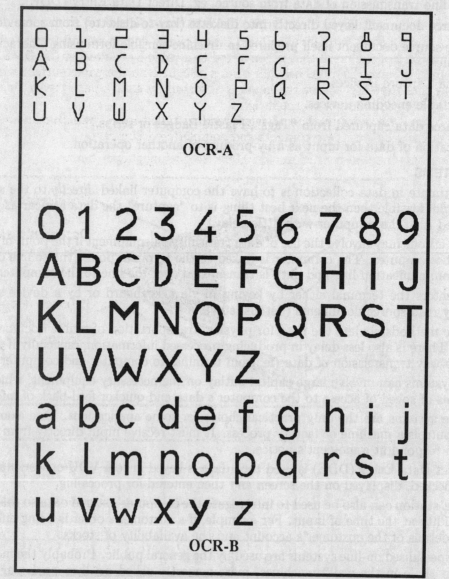

OCR-A

OCR-B

10.2 Specimen Characters from Two Common OCR Character Sets.

110

CHARACTER RECOGNITION

10.28 The methods described so far have been concerned with turning data *into* a machine-sensible form as a prerequisite to input. By using Optical Character Recognition (**OCR**) and Magnetic Ink Character Recognition (**MICR**) techniques, the source documents *themselves* are prepared in a machine-sensible form and thus *eliminate* the transcription stage. Notice, however, that such characters can *also* be recognised by the human eye (see Fig. 10.2 and 10.5).

We will first examine the devices used.

DOCUMENT READERS

10.29 Optical readers and documents. There are two basic methods of optical document reading:

a. **Optical Character Recognition (OCR).**

b. **Optical Mark Recognition (OMR).**

These two methods are often used in conjunction with one another, and have much in common. Their common and distinguishing features are covered in the next few paragraphs.

10.30 Features of an optical reader.

a. It has a document-feed hopper and several stackers, including a stacker for "rejected" documents (Fig 10.3).

b. Reading of documents prepared in optical characters or marks is accomplished as follows:

i. **Characters.** A scanning device recognises each character by the amount of reflected light (ie, OCR) (see fig. 10.2). The method of recognition, although essentially an electronic one, is similar in principle to matching photographic pictures with their negatives by holding the negative in front of the picture. The best match lets through the least light.

ii. **Marks.** A mark in a particular position on the document will trigger off a response. It is the *position* of the mark that is converted to a value by the reader (ie, OMR) (see fig. 10.4). The method involves directing thin beams of light onto the paper surface which are reflected into a light detector, unless the beam is absorbed by a dark pencil mark, ie, a mark is recognised by the reduction of reflected light.

Note. An older method of mark reading called **mark sensing** involved pencil marks conducting between two contacts and completing a circuit.

c. Documents may be read at up to 10,000 A4 documents per hour.

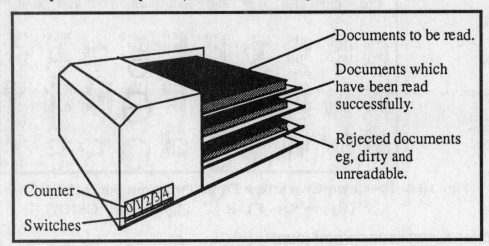

10.3 A Document reader.

Number to be coded										
3	0	1	2	3	4	5	6	7	8	9
5	0	1	2	3	4	5	6	7	8	9
1	0	1	2	3	4	5	6	7	8	9

10.4. A Marked Document Ready for OMR.

10.31 Features of a document.

    a. Documents are printed in a stylised form (by printers, etc, fitted with a special type-face) that can be recognised by a machine. The stylised print is also recognisable to the human eye. Printing must be on specified areas on the document.

    b. Some documents incorporate optical marks. Predetermined positions on the document are given values. A mark is made in a specific position using a pencil and is read by the reader.

    c. Good-quality printing and paper are vital.

    d. Documents require to be undamaged for accurate reading.

    e. Sizes of documents, and scanning area, may be limited.

10.32 Magnetic ink reader and documents. The method of reading these documents is known as Magnetic Ink Character Recognition (MICR).

10.33 Features of magnetic ink readers.

    a. Documents are passed through a strong magnetic field, causing the iron oxide in the ink encoded characters to become magnetised. Documents are then passed under a read head, where a current flows at a strength according to the size of the magnetised area (ie, characters are recognised by a magnetic pattern).

    b. Documents can be read at up to 2,400 per minute.

10.34 Features of documents

    a. The quality of printing needs to be very high.

    b. The characters are printed in a highly distinctive type style using ink containing particles of iron oxide, which gives the required magnetic property, (see Fig. 10.5). Examine a bank cheque for a further example.

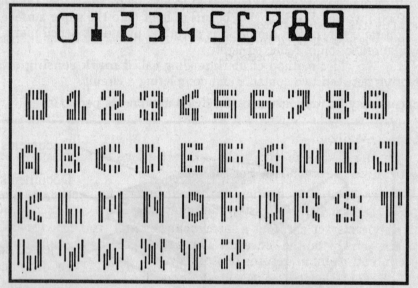

Fig. 10.5. Specimen Characters From Two Common MICR Character Sets.
(Upper Set: E13B   Lower Set: CMC7)

OPTICAL CHARACTER RECOGNITION (OCR)

10.35 a. Technique explained.

    i. Alphabetic and numeric characters are created in a particular type style, which can be "read" by special machines. The characters look so nearly like "normal" print that they can *also* be read by humans.

    ii. Characters are *created* by a variety of machines (eg, line printers, typewriters, cash registers, etc) fitted with the special type face.

    iii. The special optical character-reading machines *can* be linked to a computer, in which case the data is read from the document into the processor.

    b. Applications. OCR is used extensively in connection with billing, eg, gas and electricity bills and insurance premium renewals. In these applications the bills are prepared in OC by the computer, then sent out to the customers, who return them with payment cheques. The documents re-enter the computer system (via the OC reader) as evidence of payment. This is an example of the "turnaround" technique. Notice that no transcription is required.

c. **OCR/keyboard devices.** These permit a combination of OCR reading with manual keying. Printed data (eg, account numbers) is read by OCR; hand-written data (eg, amounts) is keyed by the operator. This method is used in credit card systems.

OPTICAL MARK READING (OMR)

10.36 a. **Technique explained.** Mark reading is discussed here because it is often used in conjunction with OCR, although it must be pointed out that it is a technique in *itself*. Positions on a document are given certain values. These positions when "marked" with a pencil are interpreted by a machine. Notice it is the "position" that the machine interprets and that has a predetermined value.

b. **Application.** Meter reader documents are a good example of the use of OMR in conjunction with OCR. The computer prints out the document for each customer (containing name, address, *last* reading, etc,) in OC. The meter reader records the current reading in the form of "marks" on the same document. The document re-enters the computer system (via a reader that reads OC *and* OM) and is processed (ie, results in a bill being sent to the customer). Note that this is another example of a "turnaround document".

MAGNETIC INK CHARACTER RECOGNITION (MICR)

10.37 a. **Techniques explained.** Numeric characters are created in a highly stylised type by special encoding machines using magnetic ink. Documents encoded thus are "read" by special machines.

b. **Application.** One major application is in banking (look at a cheque book), although some local authorities use it for payment of rates by instalments. Cheques are encoded at the bottom with account number, branch code and cheque number *before* being given to the customer (ie, pre-encoded). When the cheques are received *from* the customers the bottom line is completed by encoding the *amount* of the cheque (ie, post-encoded). Thus all the details necessary for processing are now encoded in MIC and the cheque enters the computer system via a magnetic ink character reader to be processed.

DATA CAPTURE DEVICES

10.38 These devices are mostly special-purpose devices intended for use in particular applications. Common, special and typical examples are described in the next few paragraphs.

10.39 **Direct Input Devices.**

a. Special sensing devices may be able to detect events as they happen and pass the appropriate data directly to the computer. For example:

   i. On an automated production line, products or components can be "counted" as they pass specific points. Errors can stop the production line.

   ii. At a supermarket checkout a **laser scanner** may read coded marks on food packets as the packets pass by on the conveyer. This data is used by the computerised till to generate a till receipt and maintain records of stock levels (details later).

   iii. In a computer-controlled chemical works, food factory or brewery industrial instruments connected to the computer can read temperatures and pressures in vats.

b. **Voice data entry (VDE) devices.** Data can be spoken into these devices. Currently they are limited to a few applications in which a small vocabulary is involved.

10.40 **Features**

The specific feature of these devices tends to depend upon the application for which they are used. However, the data captured by the device must ultimately be represented in some binary form in order to be processed by a *digital* computer. For some devices, the input may merely be a single bit representation that corresponds to some instrument, such as a pressure switch, being on or off.

10.41 **Data loggers/recorders.** These devices record and store data at source. The data is input to the computer at some later stage.

10.42 **Features**

a. The device usually contains its own microprocessor and data storage device/medium or radio transmitter.

b. *Magnetic tape cassettes* are often used for data storage. The cassettes are just like those used for domestic audio systems.

c. Data entry to the device is usually by means of a small keyboard, like a calculator keyboard, or by some special reading attachment.

10.43 A basic device, using only a keyboard for data entry, and able to transmit data, is effectively a portable terminal.

10.44 Popular attachments to both portable and static devices are the **light-pen** and **magnetic-pen**. These attachments resemble pens at the end of a length of electrical flex. More bulky hand held alternatives are sometimes called "wands". They can read specially coded data in the form of either optical marks/characters, or magnetic codes, which have previously been recorded on strips of suitable material. A common version is the **bar-code reader** (see Fig. 10.6).

Fig 10.6. A Bar-coded Strip Readable by a Light-pen, light-wand or laser scanner.

TAGS

10.45 The use of tags as a data collection technique is usually associated with clothing retailing applications, although they are also used to some extent in other applications.

a. The original tags were miniature punched cards. Today most tags in use have magnetic strips (details below) on them instead of holes.

b. Using a special code, data such as price of garment, type and size, and branch/department are recorded on the tag by a machine. Certain of the data is also *printed* on the tag.

c. Tags are affixed to the garment before sale and are *removed* at the point of sale. At the end of the day's trading each store will send its tags (representing the day's sales) in a container to the data processing centre. Alternatively, the tags may be processed at the point of sale (see later).

d. At the centre the tags are *converted* to more conventional diskette or magnetic tape for input to the computer system.

e. Note that data is "captured" at the source (point of sale) in a machine-sensible form and thus needs no transcription and can be processed straightaway by the machine (see Fig. 10.6).

BAR-CODED AND MAGNETIC STRIPS

10.46 Data can be recorded on small strips, which are read optically or magnetically. Optical reading is done by using printed "bar codes", ie, alternating lines and spaces that represent data in binary (see Fig. 10.6). Magnetic reading depends on a strip of magnetic tape on which data has been encoded. The data are read by a **light-pen, magnetic-pen** or wand which is passed over the strip. Portable devices are available that also include a keyboard. An example of their use is in stock recording; the light pen is used to read the stock code from a strip attached to the shelf, and the quantity is keyed manually. The data are recorded on a magnetic tape cassette. This technique is also used at check-out points in supermarkets. Goods have strips attached and stock code and price are read by the light pen. The data thus collected are used to prepare a receipt automatically, and are also recorded for stock control purposes (see the photograph later in this chapter).

BY-PRODUCT

10.47 All the systems described up to now have been designed specifically with data collection in mind but data can very often be collected as a by-product of some other operation. A good example is that found in some modern cash registers.

10.48 **Cash registers.** These are fitted with magnetic tape cassette units. A mass of statistical data is captured at source without any intermediate operation. The cassettes, etc, are forwarded to the data processing centre for input to a computer. Alternatively, the cash register may be connected on-line (see below).

POINT-OF-SALE TERMINALS

10.49 The Point-of-Sale Terminal (PoS) is essentially an electronic cash register that is linked to a computer, or that records data onto cassette or cartridge.

In its simplest form, it may simply transmit the details of a transaction to the computer for processing. The more complex terminals can communicate with the computer for such purposes as checking the credit position of a customer, obtaining prices from file and ascertaining availability of stock. If the customers bank or credit account is debited this is **EFTPOS** (Electronic Fund Transfer at Point of Sale).

The terminal usually includes a keyboard for manual entry of data. A bar-code reader may also be provided, typically to read stock codes.

10.7. A Stylised Example of an Application of Bar-coding.

10.50 The type of bar-coding shown in stylised form in Fig 10.7 is used on packets of consumable products such as foods. The numbers are coded in bar-coded strips and printed in OCR characters. The code is called a **UPC** (Universal Product Code) in the USA and an **EAN** (European Article Number) in Europe. The left-hand digit, "5" in Fig 10.6 represents the country of origin eg, "0" is the USA, "5" is the UK. The digits represent the manufacturer's code and the product number.

10.51 Such details would not be asked for in an examination but serve as a good illustration of a specialised coding system. In Fig 10.7 each digit is represented by a set of seven bit codes with a different code set being used depending upon the digit position and the country of origin. The example is based upon the UK EAN format.

FACTORS IN CHOICE

10.52 The choice of data collection method and medium may be influenced by the following factors:

10.53 Appropriateness.

    a. Magnetic Media such as magnetic tape and magnetic disk are primarily storage media, but are often used at an intermediate stage of data input. For example, data may be captured onto a diskette or magnetic cassette and then converted to magnetic tape on one computer prior to final input to the main computer needing the data. These magnetic media are reusable and can be input at much higher speeds than direct keying by DDE. Moreover, key-to-diskette systems provide an advanced method of data collection, with facilities for checking and control as the data are keyed, plus reducing the need for verification on the main computer. Tape and diskette are relatively cheap.

    b. Character recognition.

        i. MICR is largely confined to banking. It was developed in response to the need to cope with large volumes of documents (in particular cheques) beyond the scope of conventional methods. It is a very reliable but expensive method.

        ii. OCR is more versatile than MICR and less expensive. It is suited to those applications that use a turnaround system such as billing in gas and electricity where volumes are too high for conventional methods. It is limited to applications in which a "turnaround" document can be used — eg, a bill printed by the computer, part of which is returned with the payment.

iii. **OMR** is very simple and inexpensive. The forms can however be prepared only by people who have been trained in the method.

All character recognition techniques suffer from the possible disadvantage of requiring a standardised document acceptable to the document reader.

c. **Terminals** provide a very fast and convenient means of data collection and provide the main means of carrying out **Direct Data Entry**. They may also provide a fast means of output direct to the point of use. But costs are increased by the need to provide terminals at a number of different points and possibly by the additional use of data-transmission equipment.

d. **Special media** such as tags and bar-coded strips reduce costs, but are essentially tailored to particular types of application.

10.54 Cost This must be an overriding factor. The elements of cost are:

a. **Staff** (probably the biggest).

b. **Hardware** (capital and running costs).

c. **Media** Paper-based source documents are *not* reusable and magnetic media can only be reused a limited number of times.

d. **Changeover** There is normally a cost associated with changing over to a new method of data input.

10.55 Time. This can be quite fundamental in the choice of method and medium and is very much linked with cost because the quicker the response required the more it generally costs to get that response.

On-line systems will cut down this delay; so will methods, like OCR, that prepare source documents in a machine-sensible form.

10.56 Accuracy. This is linked with appropriateness and confidence, and is a big headache in data collection. Input must be "clean" otherwise it is rejected and delays occur. Errors at the preparation stage also are costly. Substitution of the machine for the human is the answer in general terms.

10.57 Volume. Some methods will not be able to cope with high volumes of source data within a reasonable time scale.

10.58 Confidence. It is very important that a system has a record of success. This is probably why many promising new methods take so long to be adopted.

10.59 Input medium. The choice of input medium is very much tied up with data collection. Often it will be an integral part of data collection, eg, on-line systems. Key-to-diskette methods have the advantage of collecting data on what is a fast input medium. These two examples are enough to demonstrate the way in which input medium is a prime consideration when looking at the collection of data.

THE OBJECTIVES OF CONTROL

10.60 The objectives of control are:

a. To ensure that all data is processed.

b. To preserve the integrity of maintained data.

c. To detect, correct and re-process all errors.

d. To prevent and detect fraud.

10.61 The different controls are dealt with under the following headings:

a. Manual controls — applied to documents prior to computer processing.

b. Data preparation controls.

c. Validation checks.

d. Batch controls.

e. Other controls.

DESIGN CONSIDERATIONS

10.62 Controls are a major consideration of the systems designer. They must be designed into the system and thoroughly tested. Failure to build in adequate control has caused many expensive system failures. Although the emphasis here is on data entry, many of the considerations also apply to other areas.

10.63 The need for controls must be clearly defined at the outset to enable the appropriate action to be taken to provide them. User staff and auditors should be fully consulted.

IMPORTANCE OF CONTROL

10.64 Control must be instituted as early as possible in the system. The quality of input data is of vital importance to the accuracy of output. Everything possible must be done to ensure that data are complete and accurate just before input to the computer.

TYPES OF ERROR

10.65 The systems designer must guard against the following types of error:

a. Missing source documents.

b. Source documents on which entries are omitted, illegible or dubious.

c. Transcription errors (eg, errors in copying data from one form to another).

d. Data preparation errors (eg, errors made when keying onto diskette).

e. Program faults.

f. Machine hardware faults.

Note. Machine hardware faults are less common in practice than is often supposed. Modern computers are self-checking to a very considerable extent (eg, parity) and usually signal any internal failure. The machine is very often blamed for what are really faults in systems design or programming.

10.66 **Verification.** The process of checking that data has been correctly transcribed is called **verification**. A common verification method is to compare a second transcription with a first. Password changes are often verified in this way.

MANUAL CONTROLS

10.67 Even in advanced systems, considerable checking of source documents is often necessary. Such checks may be:

a. **Scrutiny** to detect:

   i. missing entries.
   ii. illegible entries.
   iii. illogical or unlikely entries.

b. **Reference** of the document to stored data to verify entries.

c. **Re-calculating** to check calculations made on the document.

DATA COLLECTION CONTROLS

10.68 The collection of data for processing involves transcribing it into a form suitable for machine processing. There is a very real possibility of error at this stage, and control must be imposed to prevent or detect transcription errors. The type of control depends on the method of data collection used.

a. **On-line systems.** These depend on the data displayed (by a VDU) or being printed and checked by the operator before being released for processing.

b. **Character recognition.** With these techniques, accuracy depends on the character reader detecting any doubtful character or mark. Some readers provide facilities for display of the character and its immediate manual correction by the operator. Otherwise, the document is rejected by the machine.

VALIDATION CHECKS

10.69 A computer cannot notice errors in the data being processed in the way that a clerk or machine operator does. Validation checks are an attempt to build into the computer program powers of judgement so that incorrect items of data are detected and reported. These checks can be made at two stages:

a. **Input.** When data is first input to the computer, different checks can be applied to prevent errors going forward for processing. For this reason, the first computer run is often referred to as **validation** or **data vet**.

b. **Updating.** Further checking is possible when the data input are being processed. The consistency of the input data with existing stored data can be checked by the program. It is possible to perform checks of this type during the input run if the stored data is on-line at the time.

10.70 The following are the main types of validation check that may be used:

a. **Presence.** Data are checked to ensure that all necessary fields are present.

b. **Size.** Fields are checked to ensure that they contain the correct number of characters.

c. **Range.** Numbers or codes are checked to ensure that they are within the permissible range (eg, costs codes within the series allocated).

d. **Character check.** Fields are checked to ensure that they contain only characters of the correct type (eg, that there are not letters in a numeric field).

e. **Format.** Fields are checked to ensure that the format is correct (eg, that a part number contains the correct number of alphabetic and numeric characters in the correct sequence).

f. **Reasonableness.** Quantities are checked to ensure that they are not abnormally high or low (eg, that the amount of a certain type of goods ordered is "reasonable").

g. **Check Digits.** Use of a check digit enables a number to be self-checking. It is calculated using a mathematical formula and then becomes part of the number (see Appendix 3.3). When the number is input to the computer, the Validation Program performs the same calculation on the number as was performed when the check digit was generated in the first place. This will ensure that the number is correct, eg, no digits have been transposed.

10.71 The checks described above are usually applied during a first processing run unless all the processing is being carried out on-line. Further checks may be made when the data is processed. Discussion of such checks is left later chapters.

BATCH CONTROLS

10.72 Batch controls are fundamental to most computer-based accounting systems. The stages of batch control in a computer-based system are:

a. **Batching.** At an early stage in processing, documents are arranged in batches by being placed in a wallet or folder, or clipped together. The number of documents in a batch may be standard (eg, 50) or may represent a convenient group (eg, one day's orders from one sales office). A **batch cover note** is attached to the batch.

b. **Numbering.** Each batch is allocated a unique number, which is entered on the batch cover note.

c. **Batch registers.** Each department or section responsible for processing the batch records its receipt and despatch in a register. It is thus possible to check that all batches have been received and dealt with, and to trace any batch that gets lost or delayed.

d. **Batch totals.** Control totals are obtained for each batch, usually using a desktop adding or calculating machine. The control totals comprise:

   i. the total number of documents in the batch,

   ii. totals of the fields that it is required to control (eg, total value of invoices; total value of overtime payments; total quantities of orders).

   These totals are entered on the **batch cover note**.

e. **Data preparation.** When input is prepared, the batch totals are included (eg, if key-to-diskette is used, batch totals are typed in first and checked against the entered data).

f. **Reconciliation.** When the input data are read by the validation program, batch totals are reconciled. The input items are accumulated and the total agreed to the input batch control total. If the two totals do not agree, an error is reported. The report shows the two totals, the difference, and may provide a listing of all the items in the batch. The batch does not go forward for processing; it is re-input after the error has been found and corrected.

g. **Hash totals.** Batch totals are usually used to control the number of forms processed and the quantities they contain. It is also possible to apply the technique to numbers such as customer or payroll numbers. When batch totals are obtained the numbers are also added and entered on the batch cover note. The totals are input and reconciled in the way just described. Since the totals are meaningless and useful only for control, they are called "hash" or "nonsense" totals.

OTHER CONTROLS

10.73 It is essential to ensure that data is not only input correctly, but also maintained correctly and processed correctly right through the system. Further details of such controls will be given in later chapters.

COST OF CONTROL

10.74 The cost of control should be measured against the cost of *not* having it. It is possible to have too much control as well as too little. The inability of the computer to detect by itself faults in programs or data should always be kept in mind. Controls should be designed in relation to the consequences of an error going undetected, and after investigations into the types of error likely to occur. Controls should be inserted into the system at the point where they give maximum benefit. It is often necessary to adjust controls (particularly validity checks) in the light of practical experience.

SUMMARY

10.75 a. Data collection is the process of getting data into a form suitable for processing against master files.

    b. Data collection is accomplished in stages from source document through to actual processing against master files.

    c. Data collection is a costly, time-consuming and, in many cases, cumbersome process. Therefore methods of reducing cost and of reducing the time involved will be worthwhile.

    d. Remember the factors that influence choice of system:

        i. Appropriateness or suitability.

        ii. Cost.

        iii. Time.

        iv. Accuracy.

        v. Volume.

        vi. Confidence.

    e. Specialist methods such as tags and strips are in the minority but are important in their particular fields.

    f. Controls need to be designed into a system carefully.

    g. Controls have been considered under the following headings:

        i. Manual.

        ii. Data Preparation.

        iii. Validation checks.

        iv. Batch controls.

        v. Other controls.

    h. Control is costly. Consideration should be given to what *should* be controlled rather than what *can* be controlled.

POINTS TO NOTE

10.76 a. Many traditional methods require data preparation, eg, Key-to-disk, key-to-tape, etc.

    b. Many modern methods collect data in machine-sensible form thereby eliminating data preparation, eg, character recognition, source capture, etc.

    c. **Data collection.** The process of getting data to the computer in a machine-sensible form for processing.

    d. **Data capture.** Sometimes used as a substitute term for data collection, but more specifically refers to data "captured" in a machine-sensible form at its *source*.

    e. **Tags.** A major manufacturer of systems based on punched tags is Kimball and thus you may find tags referred to as **Kimball tags**.

    f. Note that data preparation is a part of the data collection process.

    g. Data is often captured or prepared in one machine-sensible medium and converted to another before input to computer.

    h. OCR and MICR "readers" can be of the type that are used off-line or on-line to the computer. The off-line readers may be linked to a magnetic tape unit so that the optical character/magnetic ink documents can be converted to tape for much faster input.

    i. Note the importance of detecting an error as quickly as possible so that it may be put right and the data re-enter into the system quickly.

    j. Long delays are caused by rejected input. It has to "go round again" and this can cause days of delay.

k. The unit of control for input is usually the batch.

l. Note the use of the check digit. Its use preserves the integrity of the number field and when used in conjunction with the record key it ensures a transaction is processed against the correct master record.

m. Note that good source-document design is important. It helps legible entries to be made and eases the task of the data-preparation operator.

n. This chapter deals only with system controls. Other types of control designed to ensure that the DP department functions efficiently and that its files are secure are dealt with later.

STUDENT SELF-TESTING QUESTIONS

1. At what stages in data collection is control applied?
2. Distinguish between "human-sensible" and "machine-sensible". Give an example of a form of computer input that is both machine sensible and human sensible.
3. What do you consider to be the advantages and disadvantages of the various methods/media of data collection?
4. Compare the relative advantages of a VDU and printer terminals for on-line computing.
5. Explain how the factors identified in this chapter could influence the choice of printer to be used on a system.
6. What is the difference between verification and validation in the context of data collection?
7. Name six types of error that can occur in data collection, and , for each type, give an example of one measure that can be used to prevent the error.
8. Details of payments to, and withdrawals from, a savings account are recorded on small paper slips. Each slip contains the following data:

   i. Date.

   ii. Account holder's name(s).

   iii. Account number.

   iv. Amount (in pounds).

   v. Account holder's signature.

   a. Suggest ways in which this data might be validated.

   b. Suggest a suitable layout for a simple batch-control slip (batch cover note).

   c. Suggest possible record formats if this data is to be stored in a transaction file.

QUESTIONS WITHOUT ANSWERS

9. There is an advantage to retailers in keeping track of how many of each stock item are sold. Assuming that a computerised system is to be used, suggest a variety of methods and media that could be used to collect the data required for this purpose. State under what circumstances you think each of your suggestions would be most appropriate.
10. It is required to test a program written to the following specification: valid input data is a date in the form DD/MM/YY where D, M and Y represent digits. The program validates the data, calculates the date a week later and outputs it in a full form; eg, if the input is 17/02/90 then the output should be: 24 February 1990, invalid input will be rejected with a message.

    Describe the validation checks that can be carried out and construct a set of test data that if presented to the program would establish that the program works according to the specification. Your test data should be chosen to show that invalid input is rejected and that the program can successfully calculate the date of a week later in all possible cases (including leap years).

    NB. You may like to design and implement this program too!

The IBM 3660 Supermarket System incorporates a high-speed optical scanner. As an item is pulled across the scanner's window a laser beam reads the European Article Number (or Universal Product Code in the US) bar code printed on the side of the package, and the system automatically decodes and registers the information on the symbol.

The item can be of any shape and size and the bar code can be passed over the window in any direction. Picture and details courtesy of IBM.

GLOSSARY CHECKLIST

Batch controls	10.72	Document reader	10.30
Batch cover note	10.72	EAN	10.50
Batch register	10.72	EFTPOS	10.49
Batch total	10.72	hash total	10.72
Check digit	10.70	Key-to-diskette	10.23
Data capture	10.12aii	Kimball tag	10.76e
Data collection	10.7	Laser scanner	10.39
Data entry	10.9	Light-pen	10.44
Data logger	10.41	Machine-sensible	10.4
Data preparation	10.12c	Magnetic pen	10.44
Data recorder	10.41	Mark sensing	10.30
Data transmission	10.12b	Media conversion	10.12d
Data vet	10.69	MICR	10.32
DDE	10.9	OCR	10.29
Direct data entry	10.9	OMR	10.30
Direct Input device	10.39	PoS	10.49

11: Human Computer Interfaces

INTRODUCTION

11.1 The interaction between end-users and the computer is said to take place at the "**Human Computer Interface**" (HCI). The term "Human Computer Interface" is meant to cover *all* aspects of this interaction, not just the hardware. Of particular interest is what makes one HCI better than another one.

This chapter provides an introduction to issues concerning the HCI. Some of ideas are taken further in the next chapter.

11.2 When computers were first developed the only people who could operate them were highly trained engineers and scientists. Today almost everyone operates a computer as part of daily life. Of course, individuals may not necessarily think about the fact that they are operating a computer as when, for example, they make adjustments to their digital watch or operate a cash-dispensing machine at "the hole in the wall". With so many people operating computers it is very important to make computers as easy to use as possible. Not only that, specialist users of computers, such as engineers in nuclear power stations, need to have an HCI available to them which will minimise the risk of them making mistakes when operating the computer systems under their control.

11.3 It is not surprising, therefore, that in recent years a great deal of research and development work has gone into gaining a better understanding of what constitutes a good HCI and how to create one. Despite all this effort much of what is and is not considered good practice is still a matter of opinion or experience rather than a matter of straightforward scientific result. What follows is therefore a set of important issues to consider rather than a set of hard and fast rules. Always remember that **the primary purpose of the HCI is to enable communication to and fro between the user and the computer.**

USER FRIENDLINESS

11.4 One of the most important features normally required in an HCI is that it be "**User Friendly**". As the name suggests, a user-friendly interface is one that the end-user finds helpful, easy to learn and easy to use. It is easy to recognise unfriendly interfaces but not so easy to design one that is certain to be user friendly.

11.5 What makes an HCI user friendly? There is no simple answer but the following points are important.

a. It should be relatively easy for the user to start using the system.

b. As far as possible, the system should be self-contained so that the user is not forced into accessing manuals or dealing with things that should be kept outside the system.

c. The amount of effort and information required of the user to get the system to complete required tasks should be kept to a minimum.

d. The user should be insulated from unexpected or spurious system actions. This includes protection against being the cause of a system failure and implies that the system should also be robust and reliable.

e. The system should be able to adjust to different levels of expertise between users, and as users grow in competence.

f. The user should be made to feel in control of what is going on.

g. The system should behave in a logical and consistent manner enabling the user, to reason about what is going on and apply what has been learned.

Of course these points are rather general in nature. We now turn to a number of specific practical issues.

TYPES OF INTERFACE

11.6 There are many different types of user interface available. They may be broadly classified as follows:

a. Command Driven Interfaces

b. Menu Driven Interfaces

c. Direct Manipulation Interfaces

d. User Interface Management Systems (UIMS)

e. Special Purpose Interfaces

Note. In some situations two different kinds of interfaces may be combined, eg, a menu interface with command options.

COMMAND DRIVEN INTERFACES

11.7 One of the long-established methods by which users can interact with the computer is by the use of commands. The use of commands has already been introduced with an example of a simple command interpreter 4.74). Commands enable the user quickly and simply to instruct the computer what to do. However, they require the user to already have a knowledge of what commands are available, what they do and the rules governing how they should be typed, so they are more suited to experienced users than to beginners. For these reasons commands tend to be most popular in situations where the end-user is a technical person, such as a computer operator or programmer, or where the end-user continually works with the same program and therefore can gain mastery of the commands.

11.8 To make commands more user friendly the following points need to be observed.

a. The command words used should be VERBS that clearly and unambiguously convey the intended action, eg, PRINT, COPY, DELETE.

b. Unique abbreviations should be provided for more experienced users, eg, PRI, COP, DEL. Even better is the provision of a means by which users may define their own abbreviations.

c. The format for more complex commands or variations on a single command should observe a simple and consistent set of rules. For example, the command **PRINT** might be used in the following ways:

i. `PRINT report1`
ie, print the document called report1 on the default printer.

ii. `PRINT report1 report2 report3`
ie, print the three documents called report1, report2 and report3 on the default printer.

iii. `PRINT -PprinterB report2`
ie, print the document called report2 on the printer called printerB.

If the end-user can guess from this example how to write the correct command to cause reports called report4 and report5 to be printed on the printer called printerC then the command language is working well. The command language is working better still if the end-user can also correctly guess how to type other commands, eg, the command that will cause report2 and report3 to be deleted.

Note

i. In the example given, separate items on a command line are ALWAYS separated by space, ie, the rule is simple.

ii. In the example given a "switch" or "command qualifier" -P is used to signify an alteration to the default meaning of the command. Without the use of -P the printer called printerA is used.

MENU-DRIVEN INTERFACES

11.9 Menus provide another popular form of user interface. There are many different alternative forms of menu. The simplest menus provide the user with a number of options and a simple means of selecting between them (see Fig 11.1).

11.10 The user is presented with a choice and therefore does not need to have remembered any commands. The interface is therefore suitable for beginners and infrequent users. All the user has to do is make a choice.

11.11 In the example given the user is expected to type "1", "2" or "3", which would appear in the box next to "OPTION". Where only a single keystroke is necessary, as in this case, the keystroke itself may cause the **activation** of the menu, ie, the system starts to act upon the information given. More generally, the pressing of an additional key is needed to activate the menu. Common choices of keys for menu activation are the keys called "RETURN", "ENTER" or "DO".

11.12 Suppose that the user has typed 1 and activated the menu. The activation causes the "MAIN MENU" to be replaced by the "PRINT MENU" (see Fig 11.2). One box on the screen already contains the name of the printer to be used (ie, the default printer). The contents of the box can be changed if required by moving the cursor to the box and then over typing the name of the new choice of printer. The cursor is normally moved by the use of arrow keys or by the use of the TAB key, which moves the cursor from one box to the next. Places on the screen where data items are entered or displayed, such as the boxes shown in Fig 11.2, are called fields.

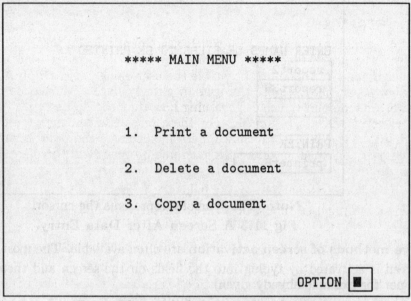

Note. The symbol ■ represents the cursor.

Fig 11.1 A Simple Menu.

11.13 Another box on the screen shown in Fig 11.2 contains a number of fields into which the names of reports may be typed. Fig 11.3 shows what the screen would look like once filled in, and before activation, if the user wanted reports called report2 and report3 to be printed on printerB.

11.14 Users like to be reassured of what is going on when they have activated a screen. In the example given, the activation of the PRINT MENU would cause the message `Printing...` to appear at the bottom of the screen.

11.15 **Help** is normally made available to the user of a menu-driven system by means of screens of information that can temporarily be called up and displayed on the screen during normal activities. It is best if the help information displayed is as specific as possible to the user's current activity. Help screens are normally activated by a special key. Some keyboards even have a key labelled "HELP". Similar facilities are often available in command-driven systems and are invoked by typing a command such as "HELP".

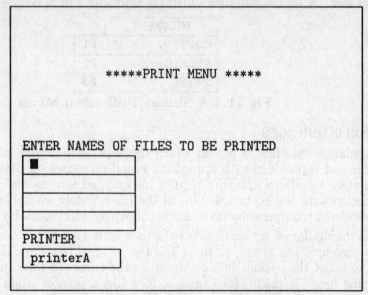

Note. The symbol ■ represents the cursor.

Fig 11.2 A Screen for Data Entry.

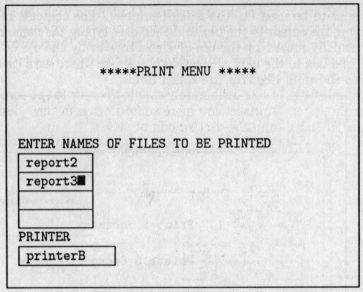

```
          *****PRINT MENU *****



  ENTER NAMES OF FILES TO BE PRINTED
  ┌─────────────────┐
  │ report2         │
  ├─────────────────┤
  │ report3■        │
  ├─────────────────┤
  │                 │
  ├─────────────────┤
  │                 │
  └─────────────────┘
  PRINTER
  ┌─────────────────┐
  │ printerB        │
  └─────────────────┘
```

Note. The symbol ■ represents the cursor.

Fig 11.3 A Screen After Data Entry.

11.16 Alternative methods of screen activation are often available. The most common ones are:

   a. The screen is activated by typing into the fields on the screen and then pressing an activation key (as per the example already given).

   b. The screen is activated by pressing a function key associated with a desired choice of activation. For example, instead of typing 1, 2 or 3 followed by an activation key the user might press one of the function keys labelled "F1", "F2" and "F3".

   c. The screen is activated by first moving the cursor until it is positioned at the desired choice and then pressing an activation key such as "DO".

11.17 In large menu systems it is common to find several levels of menu, starting with a top-level main menu from which level-two menus can be activated, which in turn can activate level-3 menus. A lower-level menu is said to be **nested** inside the menu that activates it. The user normally returns from a low-level menu to the one from which the activation was made by means of an "EXIT MENU" key. It is best not to nest menus very deeply because it can become difficult for the user to "navigate" around the system.

11.18 Pull-down menus are a special type of menu used in windowing and were briefly introduced in 8.26d. Some variations on the same idea are **pop-up menus** and **pop-down menus**. As the names suggest these menus are made to appear above or below an item on the screen in order to elicit a choice from the user. A simple pull-down menu is shown in Fig 11.4.

```
┌──────────────────────┐
│ DOCUMENT             │
├──────────────────────┤
│ COPY...         F1   │
├──────────────────────┤
│ DELETE...       F2   │
├──────────────────────┤
│ PRINT...        F3   │
└──────────────────────┘
```

Fig 11.4 A Simple Pull-down Menu

DIRECT MANIPULATION INTERFACES

11.19 A direct manipulation interface is one in which the user *at all times* is made visibly aware of the options available and is provided with immediate visual responses on the screen to any action taken. Direct manipulation interfaces normally require bit-mapped screens and input devices such as mice used in conjunction with the keyboard. One of the most widely available software products using a general-purpose direct manipulation interface is the Apple Macintosh Hypercard system.

11.20 A typical direct manipulation screen presents the user with a set of options that are often represented by icons. The user uses the mouse to move the cursor until it is over the icon and then clicks the mouse button to select the option. It is common for the cursor to take on different shapes according to how it is being used. It might, for example, look like a pointer when being used to select icons, look like a vertical bar if it is used to mark a place in a data field and look like a paint brush or spray can when being used for graphical design work. A very simple direct manipulation interface is shown in Fig 11.5. The cursor has the form of a pointing hand. The user can move the hand to point to a button to select one of three printers. The button with the solid centre signifies which has been selected. The pointing hand can also be used to select which action is required. For example, if a document is to be deleted, the hand may be pointed at the crossed-through document icon and the mouse button clicked to activate the delete. Alternatively, by clicking on the exit arrow the user can finish using the current screen.

11.21 The example given in Fig 11.5 is deliberately simple in order to get across the basic ideas. However, most direct manipulation interfaces are more sophisticated in their design whilst at the same time being simple and effective from the user's point of view.

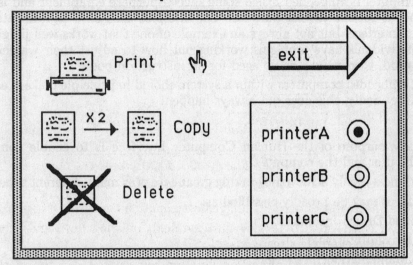

Fig 11.5 A simple Direct Manipulation Interface.

USER INTERFACE MANAGEMENT SYSTEMS (UIMS)

11.22 The aim of a user interface management system is the creation of a means by which a consistent interface with the same "look and feel" can be provided for any number of different applications within the same system. In a full implementation, *every* user interface will have the desired properties. Examples of UIMS are the system used on the Apple Macintosh computer, OSF/MOTIF from the Open Systems Foundation and the "Open Look" system developed by Sun for AT&T.

11.23 The UIMS achieves this goal as follows.

a. The UIMS provides a set of standard facilities for handling the user dialog. These facilities are available to the programmer as a set of tools. Some tools, called **widgets**, provide the basic standard components of the interface, such as a facility to display a box on the screen for data entry.

b. The UIMS provides some standard software, which manages the way in which each application program uses the interface.

c. A set of rules governs the way in which various features should appear or behave. For example, there may be a strict rule about how the mouse is to operate, such as:

   i. A single click selects an item.

   ii. A double click activates an item.

   iii. Dragging the mouse along with the button held down selects all items passed over by the cursor.

11.24 Most general-purpose UIMSs are based upon windowing systems. Such a system might be built using X-windows (8.29) and make use of some kind of WIMP (8.27). It is important to realise that, by themselves, windowing systems and interfaces like WIMPs do not necessarily provide a satisfactory interface because there is nothing to prevent such facilities from being used in an inconsistent and poorly organised way. It is the UIMS which provides and enforces the consistent interface.

11.25 Apart from the obvious benefits obtained from having a user-friendly interface the use of a UIMS also results in the saving of effort in programming and training. The savings in training are most noticeable when users come to learn their second application and discover they can already do lots of things because of its close similarity to the first application they learnt. The price sometimes paid for these benefits is the extra processing load placed upon the computer which may affect performance or require the purchase of more expensive hardware.

SPECIAL-PURPOSE HUMAN COMPUTER INTERFACES

11.26 There are two main types of special-purpose HCIs.

a. A general-purpose computer may be used, BUT some parts of the HCI is provided by special hardware and software. For example, the computer may be used to control some industrial process and so there may be video monitors in use which simulate the appearance of traditional, pre-computerised instrument dials. Another example is the cash-dispensing machine used by banks and building societies.

b. The computer is embedded inside some special-purpose equipment and is controlled by an interface that is specific to that purpose. The interface used on a digital watch is a good example of such an interface, but not always an example of one that works well judging by the way in which some individuals have problems working out how to adjust their watches. If the interface was really good, there might be no need for an instruction book.

11.27 The use of embedded computers within a system should in principle make it easier to provide a better user interface. Sadly, this does not always happen.

SUMMARY

11.28 The primary purpose of the Human Computer Interface is to enable communication to and fro between the user and the computer.

11.29 User friendliness is only achieved by taking great care over many different aspects of the user interface.

11.30 User interfaces may be broadly classified as:

a. Command Driven Interfaces

b. Menu Driven Interfaces

c. Direct Manipulation Interfaces

d. User Interface Management Systems (UIMS)

e. Special Purpose.

POINT TO NOTE

11.31 a. The term "user interface" or even "interface" is sometimes used instead of HCI when the context is clear, but take care not to use the term "interface" by itself where it might be mistaken for a hardware device (8.12).

b. There are many different types of menu but the methods of selecting items can be the same on the different menus. For example, a full screen menu, such as that shown in Fig 11.1, may allow selection by means of: typing the option's number or letter; pressing a function key or using a mouse.

STUDENT SELF-TESTING QUESTIONS

1. Name four types of human computer interfaces.
2. How might help be provided to the user of a command language?
3. What is a "field" and how might it be activated?

QUESTIONS WITHOUT ANSWERS

4. Critically examine the user interface of a computer application that you use and identify any features that could be improved.

GLOSSARY CHECKLIST

Command driven interface	11.7	Pop-down menu	11.18
Command qualifier	11.8cii	Pop-up menu	11.18
Direct manipulation interface	11.19	Pull-down menu	11.18
Field	11.12	Switch	11.8cii
Full screen menu	11.31	Screen activation	11.16
HCI	11.1	UMIS	11.22
Help facility	11.5	User friendly	11.4
Menu-driven interface	11.9	Widget	11.23
Nested menu	11.11		

APPLICATIONS II

1. This is the second Parts aimed at covering various aspects of computer applications. It contains a single chapter that deals with Graphical User Interface (GUIs) and Multimedia. The material relates to some of the material covered in the previous Part on "Input and Output".
2. GUIs are growing in importance and this is reflected in the kinds of questions which have appeared in examinations in recent years. All readers are therefore urged to become familiar with this subject matter. On the other hand Multimedia is, as yet, a less common examination topic but may well appear on an A level paper before too long. It also provides further modern applications examples.
3. Again, readers are advised to gain practical experience for themselves if possible.

12: GUIs and Multimedia

INTRODUCTION

12.1 A **Graphical User Interface** (GUI, commonly pronounced "guey" like "gluey") is an HCI based upon a graphical display. GUIs are most commonly found on workstations or PCs fitted with graphics adaptors able to support high resolution graphics. Some aspects of GUIs were introduced in earlier chapters, notably chapters 8 and 11. In this chapter the subject matter is taken further with the emphasis being upon the use of GUIs. Particular reference is made to their role in User Interface Management Systems (**UIMS** – see 11.2) especially those based on **WIMPs** (Windows Icons Mice and Pull-down Menus) (8.27). The software controlling a windows based HCI, such as that provided by a WIMP interface, is called a **Windows Manager** or **Windows Management System.**

12.2 Following on the success of computer GUIs there is growing interest in the use of computers in conjunction with other media such as video and digital sound. The computer performs a coordinating and controlling function. The name **"multimedia"** is used for such an arrangement but there are many forms of multimedia depending upon which combination is used. This chapter introduces multimedia systems and their uses.

12.3 The very nature of the subject matter of this chapter means that there are limits to what can be learned by the reader merely reading the contents. Therefore, the reader is urged to gain some first-hand practical experience of using GUIs. Suitable systems on which to gain GUI experience include: an Apple Macintosh, an IBM compatible PC running Microsoft Windows 3 or a Unix workstation running OSF/MOTIF or Open Look. In addition, the system needs to have a variety of graphically oriented applications packages installed.

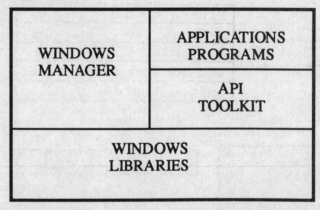

Fig 12.1 The organisation of GUI software.

THE ORGANISATION OF GUI SOFTWARE

12.4 Before examining the features of GUI software here is a brief description of how the various software items fit together.

12.5 Fig 12.1 is a simplified representation of how software is organised in a general purpose windows-based GUI system.

a. At the lowest level there are the **windows libraries**. These consist of sets of standard operation which can be used by the higher level software to interact with the GUI. For example, there may be a standard operation for drawing a line between any two specified points on the display screen, or there may be an operation to check the status of a mouse button. These standard low level operations are sometimes call **intrinsic functions**. Graphical objects created, manipulated, and removed by these standard operations are called **widgets**.

b. In most GUI systems the windows libraries are not used directly. Instead, a **toolkit** is provided which enables the GUI to be constructed from a set of standard widgets all conforming to a coherent and consistent style. This toolkit provides what is called an **Applications Program Interface (API)**. Programmers writing specialist applications programs or applications packages to be used in conjunction with the GUI do not themselves have to write instructions to manipulate the widgets or other components of the GUI interface, such a the keyboard or mouse. Instead, all they do is get their programs to use the toolkit. Their programs are said to **call toolkit functions**.

c. As indicated in Fig 12.1 each application program can call directly upon the toolkit to manipulate its own widgets. However, there is a need for some overall control of these activities so that, for example, one application does not interfere with the widgets in a window belonging to a separate application currently using the same display screen. This controlling and coordinating task is carried out by the **windows manager**.

OSF/Motif ...|... Open Look	Windows 3	Presentation Manager	Finder and Toolkit
X-WINDOWS	MS-DOS	OS/2	MacOS
Various Operating Systems			

Fig 12.2 Diverse GUI Software Configurations.

12.6   Fig 12.2 shows how the simplified arrangement of Fig 12.1 may be set up in practice. Each box on the top layer of Fig 12.2 represents a well established GUI comprising a windows manager with its associated API toolkit. The next layer down is the layer which provides the windows libraries. The GUIs on the right of Fig 12.2 are proprietary, each belonging to a particular manufacturer: (Windows 3 on MS-DOS — Microsoft; Presentation Manager on OS/2 — IBM; Finder with toolkit on MacOS — Apple Computers). The GUIs on the left side are used by a number of different manufacturers and utilize the X-windows system which was introduced in 8.28 with reference to its client-server architecture. The X-windows system provides a standard, system independent windowing system which is non-proprietary and therefore *open* to widespread use on a variety of systems. A system based upon such non-proprietary standard facilities is sometime called an **Open System**.

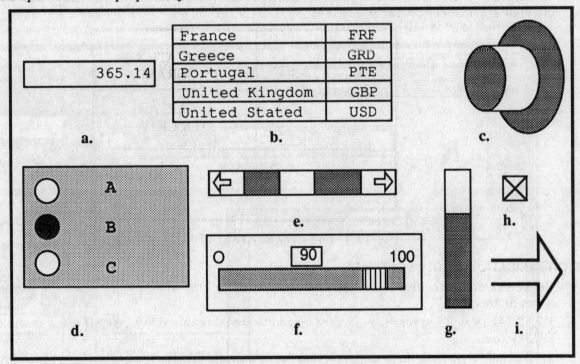

Fig 12.3 Some common Widgets.

GUI WIDGETS

12.7   As was indicated above, when a GUI interface is used the various displays tend to be constructed from a series of common components called **widgets**. Widgets are created, operated upon and removed, by the applications software through the API toolkit. The widgets used for document processing or graphics tend to be specialised and specific to the application. Such widgets are normally constructed from simpler standard ones. However, general purpose applications tend to be built from a small set of standard widgets. For example, commercial application may require screens which resemble the menus and forms shown in the previous chapter. Fig 12.3 shows a variety of widgets commonly used to construct GUI interfaces. A brief description of each widgets referenced in Fig 12.3 is given below.

a. A simple **box field** is one of the simplest widgets. It can be used to display text or numbers or it can be used for data entry. It may be possible to tab to such a field in addition to using the mouse to select it.

b. A **table field** is normally used for multiple items of text and numbers. The example shows names of countries and their associated international standard currency code. In some cases a table field acts as a window onto a larger number of rows of data. Some scrolling mechanism is then required.

c. A **button** is commonly used as a simple mechanism for turning options on or off by means of a simple click selection on a mouse button.

d. A **radio field** is normally used to allow the user to choose between a limited number of fixed options.

e. A **scroll bar** provides a means of scrolling up and down or left to right within a document. Slide bars may also be used with table fields.

f. A **slider bar** is similar in appearance to a scroll bar and is sometimes used in much the same way but it is more like a volume control. The reading in the box shows the current setting. Slider bars may also be used to select from one of a range of numbered pages in a document, whereas within each page the scrolling may be performed using a scroll bar.

g. A **bar field** is normally used as a means of graphically representing a reading. Perhaps the most common use of bar fields is one in which several are put together side by side to form a statistical bar chart.

h. A **toggle field** is normally used to turn options on or off and to show their current status. A blank toggle field box usually indicates that the option is not selected and a cross in the toggle field box indicates that the item is selected.

i. An **arrow field** is normally used as a means of navigation from one window display to the next or previous one in a series. The user uses the mouse to click on the arrow. The arrow is in effect a special type of button.

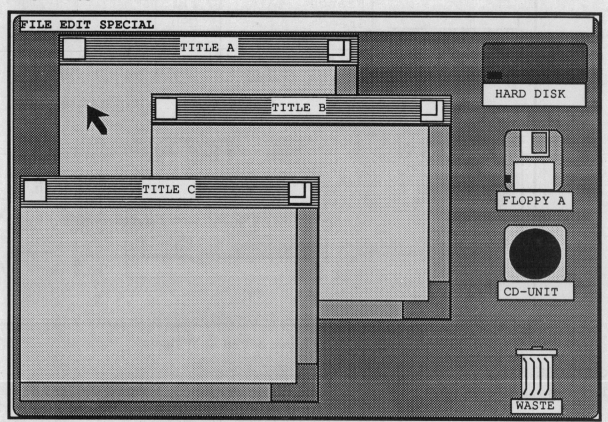

Fig 12.4 A Desktop with a WIMP interface.

THE DESKTOP METAPHOR

12.8   Fig 12.4 shows a simplified representation of a workstation screen. The appearance of the screen resembles a desktop upon which various items have been placed. For example, there are three documents named "Title A", "Title B" and "Title C" on the "desktop" with "Title C" on top, and "Title A" at the bottom. The **icons** on the right hand side resemble objects standing on the desktop, although it's a little odd having the waste bin on top of the desk! The visual similarity with an actual desktop implies to the user of the system a comparison, or analogy, between the visual objects on the graphical desktop and actual objects on a real desktop. This analogy is useful to the user. For example, the user understands the action of putting an unwanted document in a waste basket and may therefore expect to be able to apply the same idea to a document on the graphical desktop. When such a resemblance is used in the construction of a HCI it is called a **"metaphor"**.

12.9   On closer examination the **desktop metaphor** is not a single metaphor but several. For example, the "waste bin" provides a metaphor in its own right. To exploit the metaphor the user needs a little more information about how to make things work. This usually means learning how to use a keyboard and mouse. The use of a keyboard, including function keys, was covered in earlier chapters so in what follows the emphasis will be on the use of a mouse.

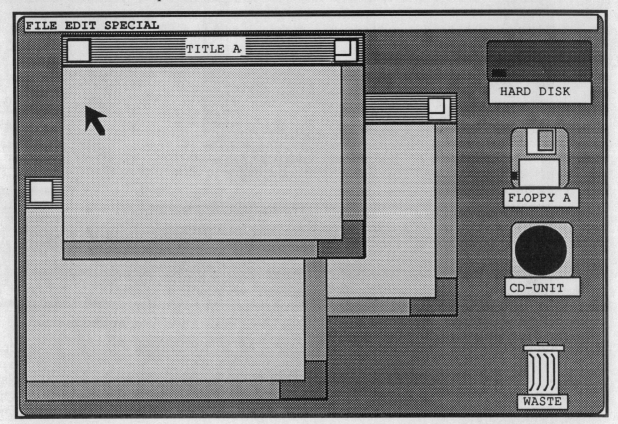

Fig 12.5 A selected window "TITLE A" brought to the top by a mouse click.

USING WIMPS

12.10 **Mice.** There are several common conventions for using mice with WIMP style GUI interfaces such as the desktop. The conventions are all very similar but vary with the number of buttons on the mouse and the graphical style of the windows and icons. It is easier to switch from one convention to another if the different types of operation are recognised. For the sake of simplicity in what follows the operations will be described in terms of the actions taken with a mouse having a single button.

Note that the WIMP interface is *not* part of the desktop metaphor. It is merely something commonly used in conjunction with a desktop display.

12.11 **Types of mouse operation.** Here is a brief description. More detailed examples follow shortly.

   a. **Select an item.** The mouse can be used to select an object or menu option. For example, the mouse may be moved so that the pointer on the desktop points at an object. By **clicking** on the mouse button the object can be selected. If an icon is selected its appearance normally changes in some way, for example to white on black instead of black on white. This operation normally involves a single click on the mouse button.

    b. Open an item. The mouse can be used to **open** a selected icon. For example, the mouse may be pointing at a selected icon for a document. To see the what is inside the document, ie to **"open"** it, the mouse button is given a rapid double click.

    c. Show an item's details. The mouse can be used to show details of an item such as an icon or menu. For example, the mouse may be pointing at a selected item such as a menu name. To see what is on the menu the mouse button is pressed and held down.

    d. Dragging an item. Items can be moved by means of the mouse. For example, by holding down the mouse button on a selected item, instead of merely clicking the button, and then moving the mouse, the item is moved along with the pointer.

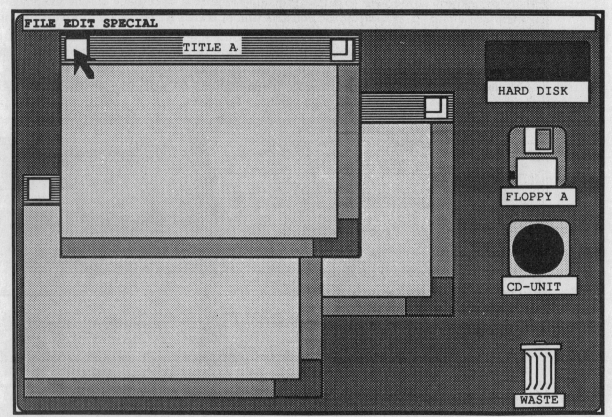

Fig 12.6 The window is closed by clicking the box at the arrow.

12.12 Launching an application. Icons on the desktop are often associated with a particular applications program. For example, documents only to be used with a particular word processing program will all have icons of the same design. When the first such icon is opened to reveal a window displaying the documents contents the Window Management System actually starts the execution of application software. This is know as **launching** the application. So, opening a word processing document by a double click of the mouse is comparable to executing a command such as **edit titlea** by means of a command line interpreter.

12.13 In Fig 12.4 the mouse has been used to move the pointer above the document "TITLE A". If the mouse button is clicked to select the document then the document is brought to the top as is shown in Fig 12.5. The documents on the desktop are **open** for use. If the little box in the top left hand corner of a document is selected (ie, clicked on) the document can be closed (see Fig 12.6). As each document is **closed** an icon representing it replaces it on the desktop. In Fig 12.7 the situation is shown as it would be after selecting the close box for all three documents shown in Fig 12.6). When a document is closed and replaced on the desktop by its icon it has been **"iconized"**.

12.14 To restore a document to the open state its icon can first be selected by a single click. It will become highlighted as "TITLE A" is in Fig 12.8. Then it can be opened by double clicking on the mouse button. Alternatively, having selected the item, the **open** option can be selected on the **pull-down** FILE menu as is shown in Fig 12.8. The mouse is first moved above the word "FILE" at which point the mouse button is held down thus causing the pull-down menu to appear. As the pointer is moved down the menu by means of the mouse, with the button held down all the time, each option is highlighted as the pointer moves over it. For example, in Fig 12.8 the option "Open" is highlighted. By releasing the mouse button when at this point the open operation is selected.

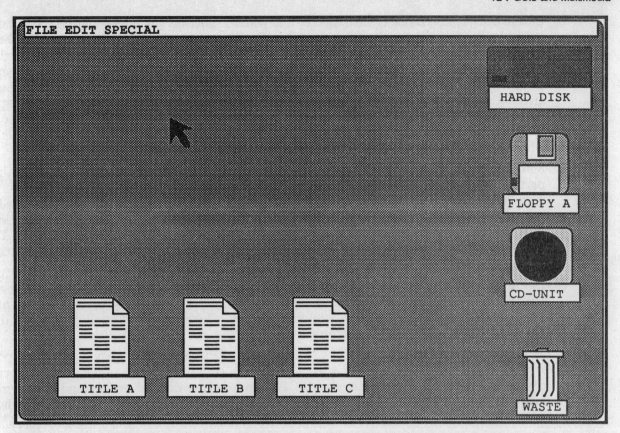

Fig 12.7 The documents have been closed and iconized.

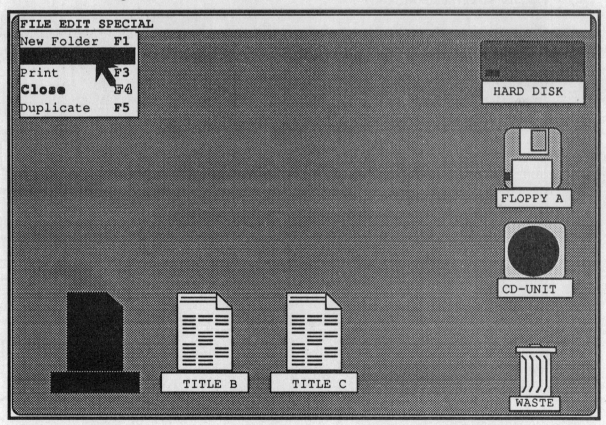

Fig 12.8 A pull-down menu being used to open the selected icon.

12.15 There are some further point to note about the pull-down menu in Fig 12.8.

    a. The menu names "FILE", "EDIT" and "SPECIAL" are displayed on what is called the **menu bar.** If a window has a menu bar it normally appears immediately below the **title bar** containing the window's name at the top of the window.

b. Beside each option name is the name of a keyboard function key which can be used *instead*. For example, "F2" is the function key for "Open". In general, there may be a combination of keys to use instead of a function key. Some WIMP systems allow for the use of alphabetic characters rather than function keys. Normally, the appropriate letters are underlined where they appear as options in the pull-down menu. For example, the "O" in "Open" might be underlined. Such alternatives to using the mouse are called **quick keys**. They are popular with more experienced users because they provide short cuts. This is an example of how an HCI can allow for different levels of expertise in the users. The novice may use the mouse and pull-down menu all the time whereas the expert may use the quick key short cuts.

c. Sometimes an option appearing on a menu may not be selected because it is not valid in the particular situation. For example, the "close" option is only available for an "open" document. This fact is normally indicated by some simple means on the menu, as in Fig 12.8 where the word "close" is shown in outline instead of normal print. Another popular way of representing this is to show the letters of the option word in grey instead of black. If the document "TITLE A" had not been selected, as shown in Fig 12.8, then only the menu option "New Folder" would have been available.

d. In Fig 12.8 the first option on the file menu is "New Folder". A folder is one aspect of the desktop metaphor. Just as on a real desktop there may be folders containing several documents, so on the GUI desktop there can be an icon representing a folder which if opened reveals a display of the icons of the documents it contains.

e. The menu headers such as "FILE" , "EDIT" and "SPECIAL" may vary depending upon which window is currently selected and what the window contains. For example, when a document is open and selected as in Fig 12.4. the "EDIT" options may depend on the kind of document. For example, if the document is a word processor document there may be lots of options whereas the option for the desktop might be limited to "CUT", "COPY", "PASTE" and "CLEAR".

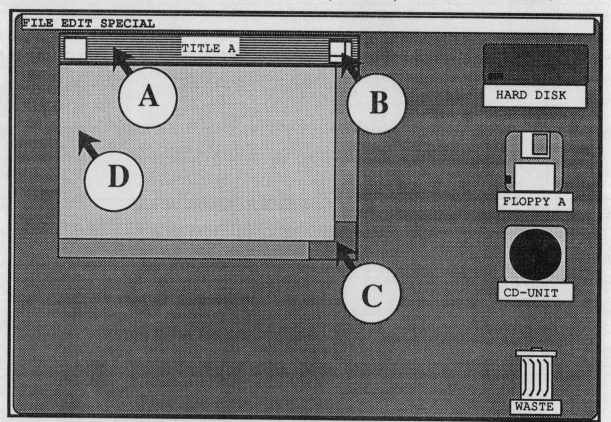

Fig 12.9 Feature of a basic window.

12.16 Within a given Windows Management System the windows all have a set of basic features and facilities. Typical examples are given below.

a. In Fig 12.9 there is a simple window called "TITLE A" whose name appears in the **title bar** (label "A"). If the window is iconized the icon has the same name as the window. If a document is stored in a file the document's window name is usually the same as the file name.

b. At the left end of the title bar there is normally a box which can be clicked on to close the window (Fig 12.9). If there is a menu bar below the title bar that sometimes has a box at its left end with a number of standard options on it similar to those shown under "FILE" in Fig 12.8

c. Label "B" in Fig 12.9 points to box at the right end of the title bar. Boxes in this position are often used to change the size of the window. In the simplest case a click on the box will alternately either expand or shrink the window.

d. Label "C" in Fig 12.9 points to another facility to **resize** a window. When this symbol is dragged the top right corner of the document stays where it is but the document becomes wider, narrower, longer or shorter depending upon the direction in which the symbol is dragged.

e. Label "D" in Fig 12.9 points to the window contents. These depend upon the type of window. For example, the window forming the desktop itself is merely a plain surface upon which icons or other windows are superimposed. A document window will normally contain text (Fig 12.10).

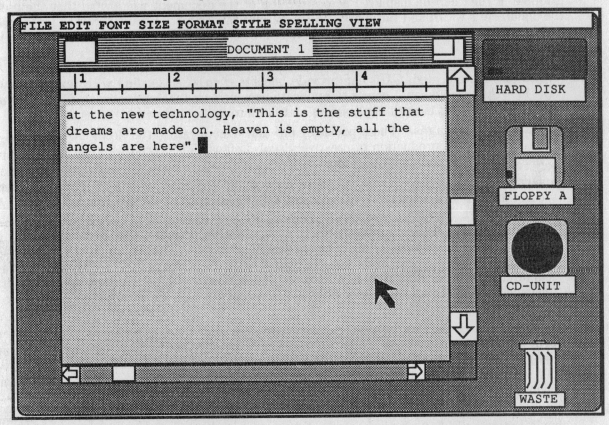

Fig 12.10 A word processor document open on the desktop.

DOCUMENT PROCESSING

12.17 Fig 12.10 shows a simplified representation of a desktop upon which a selected document is being edited by means of a word processor. Note that the menu bar has a series of headings associated with the functions of a word processor. Only one document is open, but in general there is no reason why several documents should not be open at the same time. The selected one will appear on top. If the user select a menu options or types something the actions will be applied to the selected window.

12.18 The cut and paste options on the EDIT menu can not only be used within a single document they can also be used to move text between one document and another. Also the user can be editing one document while referring to another. It is these kinds of WIMP features which help users and improve productivity.

12.19 Many aspects of document processing were described in chapter 5 so they need not be repeated here. However, there are a few windows related points which deserve a mention.

12.20 **Cursors and pointers.** In Fig 12.10 the cursor appears on the screen at the end of the text. This is displayed in addition to the pointer used in conjunction with the mouse. The cursor moves in the same way as it does in a normal situations. However, the cursor can also be moved to a different places in the document by means of the mouse. The pointer is merely moved to the new location and the mouse clicked once. The cursor appears at the new position. To move the pointer beyond the boundary of the visible window so as to scroll the document use is made of the **scroll bar** on the right side of the window. To scroll up the document the top arrow on the scroll bar is selected by means of the mouse. The document scrolls while the mouse button is held down or until the top of the document is reached. Similarly, scrolling down is achieved by performing the same action on the bottom arrow. Alternatively, the rectangular box in the middle of the scroll bar can be dragged up, or down. Its position down the scroll bar signifies the position of the window in the whole document.

12.21 Portions of text can be *selected* for such purposes as cutting, copying and spelling checking. This is done by using the mouse to drag the pointer across the area of text while holding the mouse button down. As the mouse pointer is dragged across the text the selected text becomes highlighted. When the button is released the selected text is left highlighted. Highlighted text normally appears as white on black instead of black on white. A further single click on the mouse, to reposition the cursor, de-selects the text.

12.22 Graphical features can be used to good effect to aid the appearance of the word processor. For example, a ruler can be displayed across the top of the document window so that the user can see the document's width and tab marks. Also, full use can be made of fonts so that the appearance of the document is a close approximation to WYSIWYG.

GRAPHICS PACKAGES

12.23 As has just be indicated, GUIs can provide benefits even when dealing with text. However, GUIs come into their own when it comes to applications which are inherently visual. **Graphics software packages** are aimed at such applications and fall into two broad categories as follows.

   a. **Painting Packages.** These packages are aimed at meeting the needs of artist and graphics designers in the production of creative visual designs. They produce good quality bit-mapped images in black and white or colour.

   b. **Drawing Packages.** These packages tend to have a more technical orientation with strict controls over scales and dimensions, although they often have "arty" features too. Although most modern drawing packages are able to produce output in bit-mapped form they tend to stored images in a more sophisticated ways as **scalable objects**. The principle used is the same as that used for **scalable characters** as described in 5.57. That is, an object is defined in terms of template of points and lines. For example, a rectangle is defined merely by the relative position of its four corners rather than as a fixed rectangular block of bits. This not only makes it possible to enlarge and reduce the size of objects individually it also make more economic use of storage space.

12.24 In practice the distinction between painting packages and drawing packages is far from clear cut. There are also some packages which are essentially hybrids of the two, such as Aldus Superpaint 3, which within the same package provides both bit-mapped paint facilities and object based draw facilities. Nevertheless, the distinction is a useful one when it comes to indicating the primary use at which the package is targeted.

12.25 **Painting packages** vary greatly but the more common features can be explained by reference to a simple example. Fig 12.12 shows a snapshot of a window taken from an Apple Macintosh running an application called "MacPaint" produced by Claris Ltd. MacPaint is a common and inexpensive package which was one of the' very first to be sold and become popular. Most paint packages in use today, even the much most sophisticated ones, show the influence of MacPaint. It therefore serves as a useful basic example.

12.26 The features of the example in Fig 12.11 are listed below.

   a. The main window below the title bar displays part of the complete picture. There are no scroll bars in this package, which is unusual. Instead, the picture is moved beneath the window by means of a "hand" whose symbol appears on the panel to the left of the picture window.

   b. The panel provides a series of tools which can be used by the user to "paint" a picture. Currently the **pencil** is selected. Its symbol is highlighted on the panel and it also appears on the picture window just above and to the right of an eye which it has been used to sketch. The mouse controls the pencil on the screen. A line is drawn if the mouse button is held down as the mouse is moved. Other tools on the panel include a brush, a spray can, a paint pot and an eraser. The pain brush was used to paint the eyes on the faces and the spray can was used to paint the hair.

   c. Some panel tools are used for drawing lines and shapes as indicated by their symbols. The panel shown bottom left determines line width. The mouse is used to select the required width which is then marked by a tick. One option is a thin dotted line. Lines and shapes are drawn by first selecting them on the main panel and then clicking the position of their start and end points. The remains of a rectangle is visible in the picture. Its top left and bottom corners have been removed by the eraser tool. When the rectangle was drawn the top left corner position was selected by a click on the mouse button. The pointer was then moved to the bottom right corner position which was selected by a second click. Once the rectangle was drawn a pattern was selected from the bottom palette. The selection is still visible in a rectangle at the left end of the palette. That pattern was used to fill the rectangle by clicking the paint pot within the rectangle.

d. The letter "A" on the panel signifies a tool for producing text on the picture, which is useful for putting labels on diagrams and other illustrations. When this tool is selected the required position for the start of text is selected on the picture by means of the mouse. The keyboard can then be used to type in the required words. Note that there are menu options available for controlling the text style etc.

e. There are two tools at the top of the panel, a lasso and a rectangle, for selecting parts of the picture in order to cut or copy. The lasso is used for irregular shapes.

f. The "GOODIES" menu provides a number of special facilities including a means of magnifying part of the picture so that fine details can be filled pixel by pixel by clicking them on or off with the pencil.

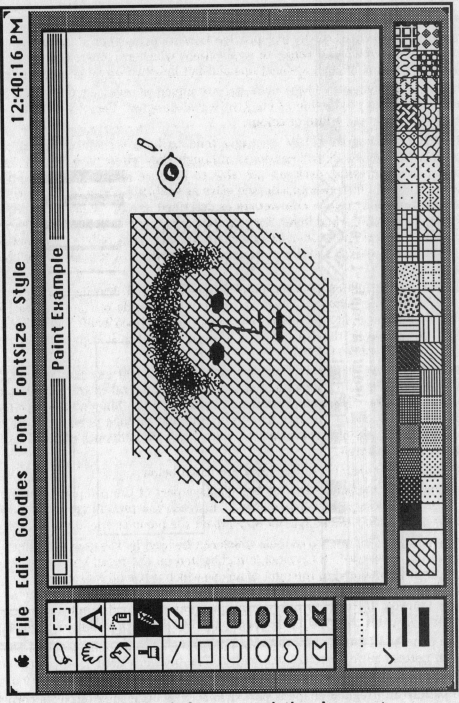

Fig 12.11 A window on a painting document.

139

12.27 Drawing packages also vary greatly but again the more common features can be explained by reference to an example. Fig 12.12 show a snapshot of a window taken from an Apple Macintosh running an application called "MacDraw Pro" produced by Claris Ltd. The package was used to produce many of the figures shown in this text. Since it is a drawing package alternative to MacPaint it provides an appropriate contrasting example.

12.28 The features of the example in Fig 12.12 are discussed below but the most obvious point to make is that in many ways it is similar to MacPaint. For example the same symbol "A" is used to represent the text tool on the left side panel. A new user already familiar with MacPaint will discover that he or she will be able to use many features of MacDraw immediately. This has obvious benefit. The two packages are said to have the same **look and feel**. Readers having the opportunity to try other painting and drawing packages will probably discover that some of the look and feel of these examples will be present in them, although probably to a lesser degree.

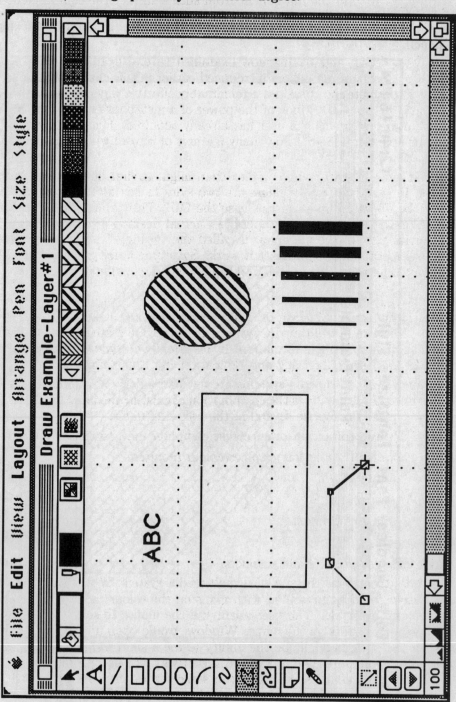

Fig 12.12 A window on a drawing document.

12.29 In the picture an irregular shape is part drawn. The little squares on its corners are only displayed because it is currently selected. The position of the corners are selected in turn by means of the mouse.

12.30 The different shapes shown in the picture are separate objects which can be individually moved about and manipulated. Object are selected my means of the mouse. Via options on the menus all manner of operations can be performed upon a selected object. For example, the object may be re-shaped, rotated, filled with a pattern, moved above or below another, enlarged, reduced, cut and pasted and so on.

12.31 A scaled grid is visible on the picture. This hints at the more technical orientation of the drawing package. In this kind of package it is possible to produce drawings to scale and to align objects accurately to a ruled grid or with one another.

12.32 Drawing packages can normally be used to produce very large drawing, covering many pages. The pages can be printed out separately, on a desktop laser printer say, and then pasted up onto one large sheet. However, to gain the full benefit from such a facility the computer needs to be connected to a high quality graph plotter.

FURTHER POINTS ON METAPHORS

12.33 Before leaving GUIs, and having now examined several examples, it is now possible to consider some further aspects of metaphors introduced earlier in this chapter with particular reference to the desktop. A good metaphor provides a remarkably effective way of enabling the user easily to perform complex tasks with a GUI. Much of the power of a metaphor comes from the way in which it is able to exploit know-how which the user has already acquired. For example, the user new to a desktop GUI may be able to reason out how many features of it work without having to be instructed because of prior knowledge.

12.34 Metaphors themselves are more complex than might at first be expected from something so easy to understand in practical terms. There are two sides to any metaphor. There is the primary subject literally to be operated upon, in this case the GUI. This primary subject is the **"tenor"**. There is also the figurative side to the metaphor, an actual desktop say, which provides the useful analogy. This figurative part of the metaphor is called the **"vehicle"**. It is the interaction between the two halves of the metaphor which makes it work. Sometime a metaphor still works even though it's odd in some way. The waste bin on the desktop is a good example of this.

MULTIMEDIA

12.35 **Multimedia** is the combination of audio, video, text and images into an interactive computer environment. The aim of multimedia systems is to provide a creative and effective way of producing, storing and communicating information. It has already become established in such applications areas as Sales and Marketing, Training and Education and Entertainment.

12.36 The components of multimedia systems are not particularly new or different in themselves. What is innovative about multimedia is the combination of existing media. The multimedia systems currently established typically comprise several of the following items.

   a. A small desktop computer, or specialist computer unit, to control the system.

   b. One or more high resolution graphics colour monitors.

   c. A stereo audio system.

   d. CD-ROM disk units.

   e. Video recording equipment.

   f. Video cameras.

   g. Colour graphics printers and scanners.

12.37 As an example, consider the use of a multimedia system by a travel agent. The user starting to use the system could be presented with maps on the colour monitor screen of various countries for which tours are available. The user might use the mouse to select a country and town by clicking on the appropriate spots on the maps. Windows would open up to show further details and options. Included in the options might be the ability to see a short video recording of the place in question together with a full stereo soundtrack. Alternatively, the user might look at tables of details about hotels charges and facilities, in much the same for as they are presented in a normal brochure. However, the system might be able to lead the user through a set of questions and answers so that the full cost of a holiday for them could be calculated. Extracts of material could be printed off on a colour printer as required.

12.38 Another example of multimedia is the **Graphical Information Service (GIS)** which is a term covering application based upon digitised maps and which ranges from town planning to computerised in-car navigation. One widely publisised example of this was the GIS systems used during the Gulf War to guide missiles and soldiers to targets.

12.39 Virtual Reality provides an unusual example which pushes the limits of what is currently possible in HCIs. The user of a virtual reality system normally wears a helmet, rather like a motor cycle helmet, except that the visor is replaced by small scale video monitor on which the wearer sees an animated representation of what is outside. More commonly what is seen is a fictitious view. This three dimensional environment changes in the same way as a real view would change as the user moves his or her head. Sensors in the helmet detect head movements and feed the information back to the controlling computer. The user often also wears a special glove containing sensors to detect hand movements. An object may be displayed on the user's video screen. The user's hand may be moved as if to hold the object. The movements are detected and the video display is modified to show an animated hand holding the animated object. While this is going on sounds are played in earphones in the users helmet. The net effect of all this is that the user feels as if he or she is in "another world". Nevertheless, there are serious limits to the quality of images used in the animations and to the speed with which such systems can respond.

12.40 These systems are often demonstrated by allowing a new user to play a virtual reality computer game. There are serious application, however, such as using a virtual reality harness to enable a user to control a vehicle or craft. For example, a "pilot" might sit in an office while wearing a harness while remotely controlling a diving craft, missile, or buggy.

INPUT DEVICES

12.41 Associated with GUIs and multimedia is the need to input images and sounds into the computer system. This obviously requires the used of specialist input devices but such devices have become quite common in recent years.

12.42 Sound is input by means of a microphone and **digitising sound sampler**, as was described in 2.33. The software controlling the sampler normally gives the user menu driven options for starting, pausing or stopping the recording and may also allow adjustment to the sampling rate and resolution.

12.43 Images are normally input to the computer by means of an **image scanner** (2.28). Most scanners are desktop models, similar in size to a desktop laser printer, but there are also hand held scanners about the same size as a large decorating paint brush. Some scanner are able to deal with coloured images but the majority are monochrome only. They all work on basically the same principles.

12.44 The flatbed or desktop scanner has a glass plate on which the sheet of paper containing the image is placed face down in much the same way as is done with many photocopiers. A well focused but wide beam of very bright light is shone across the width of the paper from a platform which moves along the whole length of the document, again in much the same way as many photocopiers. Light reflected from the document passes into a photoelectric light detector. The image is **digitised**, that is, the analog electrical signals from the detector are converted into a digital representation which is a bit-mapped image. The resolution of this bit-mapped image depends upon the scanner's design but resolution are normally between 300 dpi and 1,200 dpi.

12.45 An applications package is often supplied with the scanner. This package usually provides facilities for controlling the scanner and for setting such things as the resolution, brightness and contrast. Some packages provide similar facilities to those provided in a drawing package so that the scanned image can be edited or "touched up" like a photograph. Also, multiple scans of strips of a very large picture can sometimes be "stitched together to form a single image again. When the image is finally satisfactory to the user it is possible to save it in a file. There are many different formats in which such image files may be stored. Some represent the image in a simple bit-mapped form while others save a scalable image. The aim is to store the image in a file format which can be read by other software such as a painting package, a drawing package or a word processor. The latter are sometimes able to incorporate images into the text although they may not be able to alter the image very much if at all.

12.46 Some image file formats are in widespread use and provide a means of transferring images from one system to another. Of these one of the more popular ones is **TIFF** a variant of which is used by FAX machines.

12.47 Scanned images of text can also be processed by some OCR software packages to produce text files, or even word processor files.

SUMMARY

12.48 a. The GUI software is organised in layers including components such as windows libraries, API toolkits and windows managers.

b. Widgets are the basic graphical objects from which GUIs are constructed.

c. The desktop metaphor, in combination with WIMP provides a very successful and popular GUI.

d. Applications packages such as word processors benefit considerably from the use of GUIs but GUIs are specially suited to painting and drawing packages.

e. Multimedia applications are based upon a combination of audio, video, text and images used in an interactive computer environment and range from presentation system through GIS to virtual reality.

f. Input devices such as scanners and sound samplers are able to digitise sounds and images

POINTS TO NOTE

12.49 a. A GUI has particular advantage over the traditional **"character based interface** notably the following.

    i. **Graphical symbols** are more easily recognised and memorised than text.

    ii. **Direct manipulation**, for example by pointing and clicking on graphical objects with a mouse, reduces learning time for users and gives them a greater feeling of control over the HCI.

b. There is no substitute for first-hand experience of GUIs. The reader is urged to gain such experience and to be ready to describe the use of GUI based applications packages in examinations.

STUDENT SELF-TESTING QUESTIONS

1. Suggest ways in which a GUI might aid document processing.
2. What is a scalable graphical image and how does it differ from other types of image?
3. Explain the terms:
   a. Widget,
   b. API,
   c. Quick key.

QUESTIONS WITHOUT ANSWERS

4. Explain typical features and possible uses of a multimedia system.
5. Give an example of **direct manipulation** used in a GUI. What advantages does direct manipulation have over other methods?
6. What is the meaning of the term **metaphor** in the context of GUIs?

GLOSSARY CHECKLIST

COMPUTER SYSTEMS ORGANISATION I

1. The next two chapters look at how computer systems are organised. Chapter 13 examines the ways in which the various hardware and software components can be organised to form a complete computer system.

2. Chapter 14 deals with the ways in which individual computers can communicate with one another either as independent systems or as a single integrated system.

3. Although the material is of general importance there is considerable variation in the extent to which knowledge of this material is required by examining boards. The reader is probably best advised to check the particular syllabus which he or she is studying in order to identify the most important topics since the situation my well alter within the lifetime of this edition. Nevertheless, an initial read of all the material is recommended in order for the reader to obtain an appropriate overview.

13: Computer Systems Architecture

INTRODUCTION

13.1 The style of construction and organisation of the many parts of a computer system are its "architecture". Although the basic elements of the computer are essentially the same for almost all digital computers, there are variations in construction that reflect the differing ways in which computers are used. In this chapter we first consider the basic architectural features common to all systems. Then we consider variations in architecture that arise through differences in system use and size.

LEVELS WITHIN COMPUTER ARCHITECTURE

13.2 There are a number of levels at which we must study the construction and organisation of computer systems. The simplest distinction between levels is that between hardware and software (Fig 13.1). We may view hardware as the lowest and most basic level of the computer onto which a "layer" of software is added. The software sits above the hardware, using it and controlling it. The hardware supports the software by providing the operations the software requires.

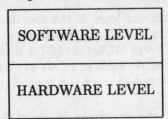

| SOFTWARE LEVEL |
| HARDWARE LEVEL |

Fig 13.1. Basic levels of computer architecture.

13.3 The idea is easily extended by viewing the whole computer system as a "multilayered machine" consisting of several layers of software on top of several layers of hardware (Fig 13.2). In this chapter we are primarily interested in the higher levels of hardware and the lower levels of software. A discussion of the higher levels of software is postponed until later chapters. However, in order to give an overall picture a brief description of all the layers is given below starting at the lowest layer.

7.		Applications Layer
6.	SOFTWARE LEVEL	Higher Order Software Layer
5.		Operating System Layer
4.		Machine Layer
3.	HARDWARE LEVEL	Microprogrammed Layer
2.		Digital Logic Layer
1.		Physical Device Layer

Fig 13.2. Multilayered Computer Architecture.

13.4 The **Physical device layer** which is in practice an **electrical and electronic component layer** is very important, but it is largely outside the subject of Computer Science and more in the province of computer technology. We do need to be aware that even the most sophisticated modern computer devices are built from simple electronic components such as transistors, capacitors and resistors (not normally as discrete components) and that these components rely on suitable power supplies and operating environments.

13.5 We need to know little more than that, however, except that **the transistor can act as an electronic switch** that is either ON (binary "1") or OFF (binary "0").

13.6 At some time in the future computers may be based upon some different technology such as optics or biochemistry. There is little chance of such a revolutionary change in the immediate future, however.

13.7 The **digital logic layer** is of considerable importance in Computer Science. All the most basic operations of the machine are provided at this level. The basic elements at this level can store, manipulate and transmit data in the form of simple binary representations.

13.8 These digital logic elements are called **gates**. A gate is normally constructed from a small number of transistors and other electronic components. However, many gates may be combined onto a single chip, as has already been outlined in 4.6 – 4.13.

13.9 Digital logic will be discussed more fully in chapter 25. For the time being it is sufficient for the reader to realise that standard digital logic devices are combined together to form computer processors, computer memories and major components of the units used for input and output.

13.10 The next two levels are more easily understood if considered together.

13.11 The **microprogrammed layer** interprets the **machine language** instructions from the **machine layer** and directly causes the digital logic elements to perform the required operations. It is, in effect, a very basic inner processor and is driven by its own primitive control program instructions held in its own private inner ROM. These program instructions are called **microcode** and the control program is called a **microprogram**. They are one example of **firmware** (ie, software in ROM).

13.12 There was no microprogrammed layer in the early generations of computers nor is there one in some of the small microprocessors of today. In machines without a microprogrammed layer the processor is constructed directly from a combination of digital logic components.

13.13 The use of a microprogrammed layer enables a manufacturer to produce a **family of processors** all of which process the same set of machine instructions at the **machine layer** but which differ in terms of construction and speed. In this way the manufacturer can offer a range of machines of differing power and price. Software can be moved from one machine to the next one in the range without alteration. As the technology is improved the manufacturer may replace an older model processor by a new one. So, the customer can **upgrade** the hardware without having to rewrite the software.

13.14 The details of this microprogrammed level of the architecture are not always disclosed by the manufacturers in order to protect trade secrets. For example, Motorola have not disclosed all details of the micro-programmed level of their MC68000 16-bit microprocessors. The details of the microprogrammed levels of larger computers, such as minis or mainframes, are sometimes published by the manufacturers. The microprogrammed layer is a special subject and further discussion is outside the scope of this book.

13.15 As has already been indicated, the **machine layer** is the lowest level at which a program can be written and indeed it is only **machine language** instructions which can be directly interpreted by the hardware.

13.16 The **operating system** layer controls the way in which all software uses the underlying hardware. It also hides the complexities of the hardware from other software by providing its own facilities which enable software to use the hardware more simply. It also prevents other software from bypassing these facilities so that the hardware can only be access directly by the operating system. It therefore provides an orderly environment in which machine language instructions can be executed safely and effectively.

13.17 The **Higher Order Software Layer** covers all programs in languages other than machine language which require translation into machine code before they can be executed. Such programs, when translated, rely upon the underlying operating system facilities as well as their own machine instructions.

13.18 The **applications layer** is the language of the computer as seen by the end-user.

13.19 The underlying computer as viewed from each layer is sometimes called a "**virtual machine**". For example, the operating system is a virtual machine to the software above it because, for practical purposes, it is the "machine" the software uses.

PHYSICAL ORGANISATION OF THE COMPUTER

13.20 We now turn to a more detailed examination of the physical organisation of the computer that were not covered earlier. However, what follows is *not* a description of the internal properties of the electronic components because they are not of particular concern in Computer Science. Instead attention is directed to how the complete microelectronic components are deployed.

13.21 Designing and building a new computer from scratch is an expensive process. Also, the unit costs of individual components are high unless the components are mass produced. These factors cause most computer manufacturers to construct their computers from varied combinations of standard components. For example, many *different microcomputers* contain the *same microprocessors*.

13.22 This principle of **modular construction** applies to different levels of design. At one level it might be a matter of "plugging in" one peripheral device instead of another. At a lower level it might be a matter of using one type of memory chip instead of another.

13.23 Standard components are much easier to interconnect if the means of interconnection is also standardised. One important method for doing this is using **"buses"** (6.28).

13.24 A **bus** is a collection of parallel electrical conductors called "lines" onto which a number of components may be connected. Connections are made at points along the length of the bus by means of connectors with multiple electrical contacts.

There are two basic types of bus:

a. **Internal buses,** used within the processor and an integral part of its construction.

b. **External buses,** used to connect separate hardware elements together, eg, connecting the processor to main memory.

13.25 Buses may be used to convey:

a. data signals,

b. data address signals,

c. control signals,

d. power.

13.26 Further details of the use of buses at the digital logic level follows shortly.

13.27 **The influence of size on construction** deserves some discussion before we move on to look at the architecture of complete systems. Three distinctly different forms of construction are, from smallest to largest:

a. Single-chip computers.

b. Single-board computers.

c. Multiple-board bus-based computers.

13.28 **Single-chip computers** are those found in such devices as watches, cameras, etc. The processors are specialised, they are programmed to do a specific task and, apart from the remarkable operations some of these devices do, they are not immediately recognisable as computers.

13.29 **Single-board computers.** These computers are usually much bigger than single-chip computers but are still relatively small. They are constructed on thin flat sheets of electrical insulator onto which the components can be fixed and interconnected. **Printed circuit boards (PCBs)** are often used for **volume** production.

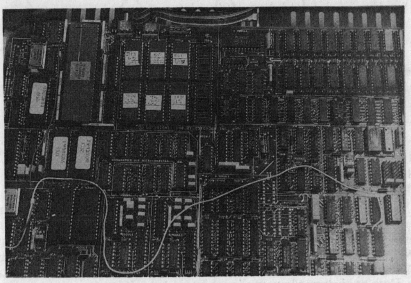

A computer on a single board. The larger chip (top left) is a 16-bit microprocessor. To its right is a block of 6 ROM chips. Further to the right is a block of 18 RAM chips. The remaining chips are for various input/output ports, etc.

13.30 The single-board computers fall into two broad categories:

a. Small general-purpose microcomputers such as the small home computers and many more basic PCs.

b. Small special-purpose computers, which are often used for applications involving the control of physical processes. Typical examples would be systems controlling a small-scale chemical distillation plant or controlling the operation of complex milling machines.

In both cases buses are used but as integral parts of the board's circuitry.

13.31 Multiple-board, bus-based computers are usually general-purpose computers. They are normally too large to fit onto a single board. Instead, each board has a particular function and all boards are interconnected by plugging them into individual slots on one ore more general-purpose buses. One board may contain the processor, another board may contain main storage, and so on. Many minicomputers and mainframes are based upon this type of construction. Sometimes there is a primary board, called a **motherboard**, for the processor and other main components into which other boards may be slotted.

13.32 Having considered some specific issues of size and use relating to the physical organisation of the computer it is now time to move on and examine the same issues in the broader context of system architecture at the digital logic level.

MAIN COMPONENTS OF DIGITAL LOGIC LAYER

13.33 As was indicated earlier, the standard digital logic devices are combined together to form computer processors, computer memories and major components of units used for input and output. Such devices have to be interconnected in organised way to form a complete system. In the vast majority of modern computers **buses** (6.28) provide the interconnections. Remember that a bus interconnects devices through a set of parallel **lines** and that the lines are classified as data lines (data bus), address lines (address bus) and control lines (control bus).

13.34 One of the simplest architectures is one based upon a single **general purpose bus**. (Fig 13.3). This arrangement tend to be used only on the microcomputer based systems. It is simple and effective but data transfers between the processor and memory can be held up by slower transfers involving input or output units.

13.35 Note that within the context of this discussion storage devices such as disk units and tape units are regarded as input and output devices. In what follows the common practice of using "I/O" as a shorthand for "Input or Output" is adopted.

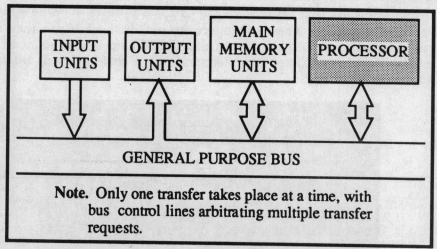

Fig 13.3 A system based on a general purpose bus.

13.36 Most architectures are based upon two buses and follow one of the two basic alternatives shown in Fig 13.4 and Fig 13.5. In both cases the bus used for data transfers between memory and the processor is separate from the bus used by input unit and output units. This reflects differences in speed. The data transfers between memory and the processor use a faster bus and are also not held up waiting for the slower devices used for input and output. Fig 13.4 shows a two bus arrangement commonly used on larger microcomputers and in many minicomputers. The processor has direct connections to both buses. Data only passes between memory and the (I/O) units via the processor. An alternative arrangement, more commonly found on larger minicomputers and mainframes, is that shown in Fig 13.5 in which the the processor only accesses data via the memory bus. In such arrangements the processor effectively delegates some of its detailed I/O controlling powers to subsidiary **peripheral processors**, also called **I/O channels**. Although details are not shown in Fig 13.5 the processor still has overall control over I/O. The exact arrangements and terminology varies from one manufacturer to another but in all cases the aims are the same:

a. to maximise the use of the processor by freeing it of the burden of controlling low level I/O operations;

b. to maximise the speed and efficiency of I/O data transfers to and from memory.

13.37 Another factor affecting the speeds of data transfers is the **bus width** (6.29). In simple arrangements such as that in Fig 13.3 the width of the data bus may only be 8-bits or 16-bit whereas in Fig 13.5 the data bus width may be 32-bits or 64-bits.

13.38 At this point we turn to a detailed examination of the role of the processor. The basic features of a processor will be described, including the functions and operations of its elements.

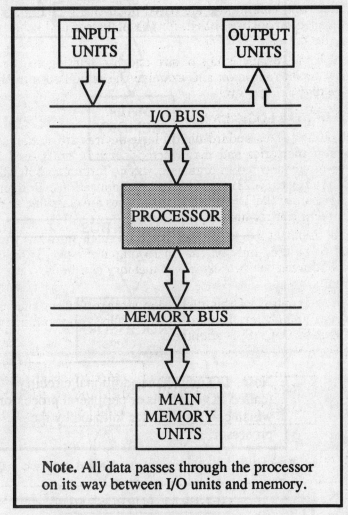

Fig 13.4 A system based on two buses.

THE PROCESSOR

13.39 In chapter 1 a figure of the elements of a computer system (Fig. 1.4) showed the processor as consisting of two primary elements. They are:

  a. The **Control Unit (CU)**.

  b. The **Arithmetic and Logic Unit (ALU)**.

13.40 Although Fig 1.4 provides a useful overview, the real situation is actually more complicated than that. The CU and ALU operate in conjunction with a number of additional processor components (details shortly). All components of the processor are wholly electronic.

13.41 The **functions of the processor** are:

  a. to control the use of main storage to store data *and* instructions,

  b. to control the sequence of operations,

  c. to give commands to all parts of the computer system,

  d. to carry out processing.

13.42 The processor controls the input of data and its transfer into main storage, processes data, and then sends the result to output units. At all stages data transmission is electronic.

13.43 As has already been indicated the processor is connected to other elements of the computer by means of buses. When looked at more closely the single buses shown in Figs 13.3 – 13.5 comprise multiple buses as shown in Fig 13.6.

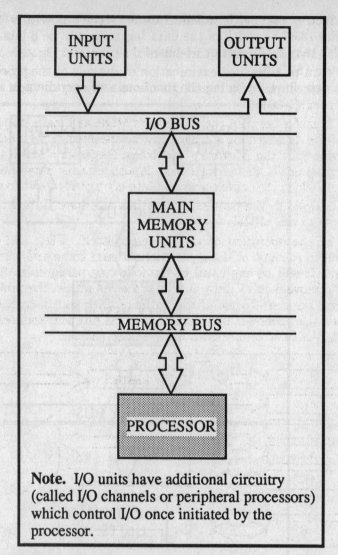

Note. I/O units have additional circuitry (called I/O channels or peripheral processors) which control I/O once initiated by the processor.

Fig 13.5 Another system based on two buses.

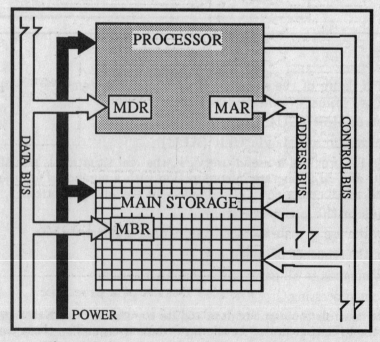

Fig 13.6 An example of Bus connections.

13.44 Registers. Fig 13.6 also illustrates the use of some registers. **Registers** are special-purpose temporary-storage locations within the processor or other devices. They are quite separate from the locations in main storage, although they can be similar in structure. The uses of registers shown in Fig 13.6 are as follows.

a. All data and instructions pass in and out of the processor through a register called the **Memory Data Register (MDR).**

b. All data and instructions pass in and out of main storage through a register called the **Memory Buffer Register (MBR).**

c. Prior to each transfer between the processor's MDR and main storage's MBR the exact source or destination of the data in main storage must be specified. This is done by loading the appropriate location address into the **Memory Address Register (MAR).** Main memory receives this address information via the address bus. It also receives control signals from the processor via the control bus which it is able to decode into commands for it to save or retrieve data.

d. I/O units connected to the processor via a bus also have **data buffer registers** which serve a similar purpose to the MBR.

13.45 Now for details of the operation of the processor itself. Fig. 13.7 gives an overall view of the processor and the movement of data, instructions and command signals within it and between it and main storage. It will be explained in the following paragraphs. The figure also shows the role of registers in the movement of data and instructions within the processor. The reader is advised first to try to gain an overall view of the paths of data and instructions through the registers. In the example given the processor has a single internal bus plus connections to external buses. *Some feature of Fig 13.7 will not be discussed until a later chapter.*

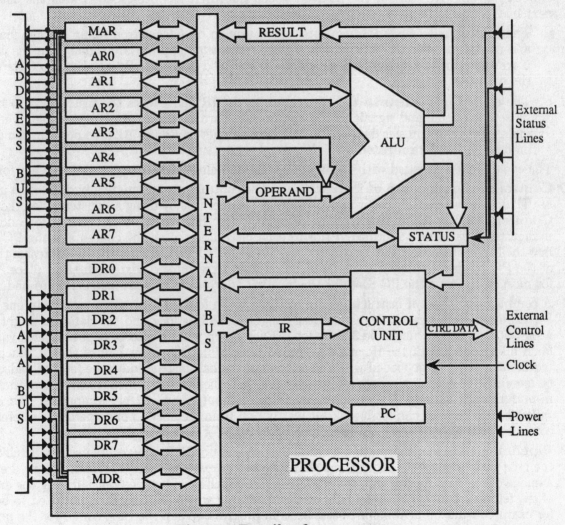

Fig 13.7 Details of a processor.

13.46 **Registers in the processor** are constructed so that their contents can be accessed and altered much faster than the contents of locations of main storage. They have many uses, for example:

a. An instruction that is about to be obeyed will first be taken from main storage via the MDR and placed in a register called the **Instruction Register (IR).** Once in the IR the instruction can be rapidly decoded and performed.

Note that the IR is also sometimes called the **Current Instruction Register (CIR)**.

b. Data to be processed (eg, numbers about to be added or subtracted) is taken from main memory via the MDR and placed in registers called **Data Registers (DRs)** within the ALU. The required arithmetic or logic operation (eg, add) is then rapidly performed. The ALU will provide the result in one data register, from which it can be taken and stored in main storage. The processor shown in Fig 13.7 has eight data registers labelled DR0 ... DR7.

Note that the DRs is also sometimes called **Accumulators**.

c. The processor shown in Fig 13.7 has eight address registers labelled AR0 ... AR7. The value in these registers are addresses which can be loaded into the MAR. Their role will be discussed fully in a later chapter.

d. The STATUS register shown in Fig 13.7 is used by the control unit as a means of detecting conditions which have occurred such as the ALU detecting the arithmetic error of division by zero.

13.47 Primary components of the processor will now be considered in detail.

CONTROL UNIT

13.48 Function. The control unit is the nerve centre of the computer. It coordinates and controls all *hardware* operations, ie, those of the peripheral units, main memory and the processor itself.

13.49 How it operates. It deals with each instruction in turn in a two-stage operation called the fetch-execute cycle. We start at the point at which the MAR has been loaded with the *address* of the next instruction to be performed.

a. The control unit causes the requisite instruction to be *fetched* from main storage via the MDR and placed into the IR. When main storage receives an appropriate signal from the control unit it transfers the instruction, whose address is specified in the MAR, into the processor's MDR via the data bus.

b. The control unit *interprets* the instruction in the IR and causes the instruction to be *executed* by sending command signals to the appropriate hardware devices. For example, it might cause main storage to transfer data to the MDR or it might cause the ALU to perform some operation on data in the data registers.

The cycle is then repeated with the next instruction being fetched as detailed in what follows.

13.50 Control of the sequence of instructions. The control unit automatically deals with instructions in the order in which they occur in main storage. It does this by using a register called the **Program Counter (PC)** or **Sequence Control Register (SCR)**, which holds the location address of the *next* instruction to be performed. Prior to each instruction fetch the contents of the PC are copied into the MAR. Each time the control unit fetches an instruction, it immediately increases the contents of the PC by one, so that it is ready to be referred to when the next fetch takes place. Therefore, for most of the time the PC contains the location address of the *next instruction* to be fetched.

13.51 A complication arises if instructions are too long to be fetched from main storage in one operation. For example, each location in main storage might be 16 bits long and the data bus might be 16-bits wide but instructions might be 32-bits long. Each **fetch** will have to be a *double fetch* with the first fetch filling one half of the IR and the second fetch filling the other half of the IR. Each fetch will require the MAR to be loaded with the address of the half-instruction to be fetched and the PC will be increased by one twice – once after each fetch. It is such factors which contribute to the differences in performance between 8-bit computers, 16-bit computers and 32-bit computers. For example, a *fully* 32-bit computer can fetch a 32-bit instruction from memory in one operation whereas an 8-bit computer will have to carry out four fetch operations for a 32-bit instruction.

13.52 Pipelining is the name given to a method of speeding up the fetch execute cycle by fetching not just the next instruction but the next few that follow it in main storage. The instructions are placing in a queue of registers feeding into the IR. These **pre-fetches** are carried out if during the execute part of the fetch-execute cycle a brief interval occurs during which memory does not need to be accessed, for example while an arithmetic operation is in progress. When the time comes for the normal fetch to take place it has already happened! The execute phase can commence immediately.

ARITHMETIC AND LOGIC UNIT (ALU)

13.53 Functions. The ALU has two main functions:

a. It carries out the arithmetic, eg, add, subtract, multiply and divide.

b. It performs certain "logical" operations, eg, testing whether two data items match.

13.54 How it operates.

a. Data items about to be processed are taken from main storage, as directed by the control unit, and pass via the MDR into the data registers (accumulators) in the ALU, where they are stored. This step is referred to as **"loading"** data into data register from main storage. It should be noted at this point that the location addresses of these data items will have been specified in instructions in the IR, from where they will have been transferred to the MAR prior to loading the data.

b. The ALU then performs the required operation(s) on the data (eg, adding) as directed by the control unit. The ALU leaves the result in a data register. While the ALU is carrying out an operation it may makes use of other registers of its own such as the "OPERAND" and "RESULT" registers shown in Fig 13.7. For example, it may build up a result in the RESULT register before sending the complete result to a designated data register.

c. Results are taken from data registers and placed in main storage, again under the direction of the control unit. This step is referred to as **"storing"** data.

13.55 The points made earlier about the effects of word length on the fetch-execute cycle also apply to the processing of the data. For example, if 32-bit long numbers have to be added in a 16-bit machine each number will require two load operations from memory and each arithmetic operation will be performed in two stages. There are some common alternative machine designs in which, for example, the internal bus and registers are 32-bits but the external buses are 16-bits. In such a situation the internal 32-bit operations will be performed singly but external loads and stores of 32-bit values will require double operations.

13.56 Decision making. Some logical operations of the ALU give the computer its decision-making ability. They do this by allowing the result of an operation to determine which instruction the control unit fetches next. For example, if two data items matched, then the IR (SCR) could be altered to some new value contained within an instruction in the IR. If the data items did not match it could be left unaltered. If pipelining is in use the previously pre-fetched queue of instructions will need to be discarded each time such a break in sequence of instructions occurs.

RISC AND CISC

13.57 Over the last twenty years or so there has been a steady trend towards computers having more extensive and complex sets of machine instructions so that some 16-bit microprocessors in use today have more complex instruction sets than mainframes used in the 1960s. Within the last few years an alternative approach to designing processors has become popular in which the processor has a simple instruction set based upon a small set of instructions. The name for such machines is **Reduced Instruction Set Computers (RISC).** For the purpose of distinction the traditional alternatives are called **Complex Instruction Set Computers (CISC).**

13.58 Under some circumstances RISC computers can have very high performance compared with CISC computers, but comparisons are difficult to make because it may take many RISC instructions to do what one CISC instruction could do in some situations, so the number of instructions carried out per second is not a sound basis for comparison. Also, machine language programs on RISC machines contain many more instructions than their CISC equivalents and can therefore take much more storage space. Common RISC machines are IBM's RS6000 range and those based on the MIPS chip or using the SUN SPARC architecture.

ARCHITECTURE OF SMALL COMPUTER SYSTEMS

13.59 The architecture of a typical configuration for a microcomputer-based system is shown in Fig. 13.8. Provided that sufficient slots are present in the bus, other units may be plugged in.

13.60 Memory organisation. In a small system like that shown in Fig 13.8 the main storage may be organised as shown in Fig. 13.9.

13.61 Firmware. Programs held in ROM are called **firmware.** They are stored permanently in the ROM and are ready for use when the computer is switched on.

13.62 When a microcomputer is switched on it is normally made to start executing the instructions held in ROM. This normally takes place automatically as part of switching on. Sometimes a "boot" button is be pressed instead. This is known as **"booting up** the system". The instructions in ROM sometimes perform a number of simple hardware checks such as finding out what RAM is fitted and working.

13.63 On most computers, not just microcomputers, the boot-up operation also causes a special "loader program" in firmware ROM to load a program into memory from predefined tracks on hard disk.

On some microcomputers the program may be loaded from floppy disk instead of hard disk. This first program loaded into memory is that part of the operating system which takes primary control over the hardware and which contains the facilities for higher level software to use it. This software has several alternative names including the **kernel**, the **executive** and the **supervisor**. On some microcomputers it is sometimes rather vaguely called the **system**.

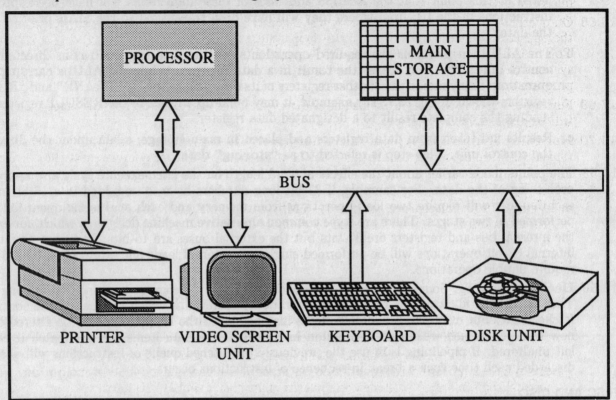

Fig 13.8. Simplified Typical Architecture of a Small Microcomputer-Based System.

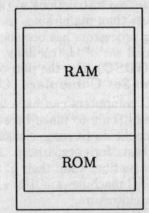

Fig. 13.9. Organisation of Main Storage in a Typical Microcomputer.

13.64 At some point the firmware program completes its loading operation and start the execution of the operating system kernel. Another file on disk sometime provides "configuration information" which determines how the operating system uses the hardware resources available to it. For example it might specify how much memory the operating system may reserve for its own purposes. This configuration information often specifies which higher level program is the first to be executed once the operating system has completed its start-up procedures.

13.65 Normally the first program to be executed is a **shell** program. A shell is a high level program which sits above the operating system kernel and provides the user with a means to operate the computer. A common form of shell is a command language interpreter such as that used on MS-DOS or PC-DOS whereby the user types commands. Some shells provide a GUI instead of a command language as is the case with the Apple Macintosh "Finder". The terms "shell" and "kernel" draw on an analogy with a nut in which the shell surrounds the inner kernel. The shell is normally regarded as part of the operating system.

13.66 On the older 8-bit microcomputers the kernel and shell were sometimes both stored in ROM and were often know as the **monitor.**

13.67 Some microcomputers may have much more firmware in ROM, even to the extent of being able to accept, "interpret" and execute programs written in a programming language such as BASIC. The microcomputer is then said to have "BASIC in ROM". GUI toolkit are sometimes held in ROM too.

13.68 On microcomputers designed for use by just one user at a time through a single keyboard and monitor the operating system operates a **single-user** system in which **multitasking** (8.14) is not available. This is the case with MS-DOS, PC-DOS, Apple MACOS prior to version 7 and CP/M. On these systems the user effectively takes turns at either using the shell or running a particular applications program such as an applications package.

13.69 Further details of operating systems and the interpretation and execution of languages such as BASIC will be given in later chapters.

13.70 **Hardware features of typical microcomputer-based systems.** In what follows the features of *typical* 16-bit microcomputer are given as the main example but for completeness the corresponding figures for the older 8-bit microcomputers which they have largely replaced are given in parentheses.

    a. A single 16-bit microprocessor plus 1 – 5 Mbytes of 16-bit RAM. (64 Kbytes of 8-bit RAM). There is move towards 32-bit machines led by many of the more advanced 16-bit processors having 32-bit internal buses.

    b. A single non-exchangeable winchester disk drive of 20 – 80 Mbytes capacity plus a $3\frac{1}{2}''$ or $5\frac{1}{4}''$ floppy disk drive. (Dual $5\frac{1}{4}''$ floppy disks on the majority of machines, and small Winchester disks on the larger models. Magnetic tape cassettes on the very small machines.)

    c. Low-speed printers, eg, dot matrix, or daisywheel character printers but with an increasing use of desktop laser printers and inkjet printers. (Dot matrix and some daisywheel character printers.)

    d. Usually a single monochrome or colour monitor with some, possibly good, graphics capabilities plus a keyboard with function keys, numeric keypad and possibly a mouse too. (A single monochrome monitor with very limited graphics plus a simple keyboard)

    e. Optional facilities for connecting the computer to a network. (Little networking capability if any.)

Note. In many machines several different items are built into the same cabinet, eg, the disk drives may be in the same cabinet as the computer itself.

THE ARCHITECTURE OF MINICOMPUTER AND MAINFRAME COMPUTER SYSTEMS

13.71 The smaller minicomputer systems can be indistinguishable from the larger microcomputer-based systems. However, a typical minicomputer has noticeably different features from a microcomputer and is essentially a scaled-down version of its "big brother" the mainframe computer.

13.72 **Hardware features of a typical minicomputer system.**

    a. Medium-size 32-bit processor and main storage sufficient to handle the data processing needs of a number of terminals or workstations (eg, 10 – 100 Megabytes of main storage).

    b. Multiple Hard disk units, both fixed and exchangeable, and magnetic tape storage (cartridge or reel-to-reel) in some cases. These devices typically have higher capacities and faster access speeds than those used on microcomputers.

    c. Line printer, eg, 300 lpm versions or desktop laser printers.

    d. Multiple terminals, eg, 20 VDUs or workstations.

    e. Standard means of interconnecting multiple machines via a network

13.73 It is also difficult to draw a line of demarcation between the larger minicomputers and small mainframe computers. The hardware in a mainframe may be similar to the hardware in a minicomputer, but there is usually much more of it, eg:

    a. Very large processors with massive amounts of main storage, eg, hundreds of Megabytes.

    b. Large number of magnetic disk and tape units with very large capacities. For example, the disks have capacities measured in hundreds of megabytes or even gigabytes.

    c. High-speed line printers, eg, 1,200 lpm.

    d. The ability to support large numbers of terminals, eg, 100 or more VDUs.

13.74 **Front End Processors (FEPs).** Many mainframe computers incorporate minicomputers, which are used to handle input and output from various terminals, thus relieving the main computer of some tasks associated with input and output. The minicomputer being used for this purpose is called a Front End Processor (FEP).

13.75 The front end processor may not only deal with terminals close to the main computer it may also deal with *remote* terminals situated at the end of data transmission lines.

OTHER ARCHITECTURAL FEATURES

13.76 **Cache memories.** These are high-speed RAMs, which work at speeds that match the processor. They are used to hold data that has recently been accessed from disk in anticipation of its use in the near future. Subsequent accesses, if they occur, will be fast because the disk will not require accessing again. The least accessed data in cache memory is replaced by newly accessed data. Alternatively, very high-speed cache memory may be used temporarily to store data read from main memory.

13.77 **Content Addressable Storage (CAS).** This storage works in a different way from normal storage. The principle will be explained by means of the following simplified example. Suppose that each word in memory can hold 4 characters and that location 200 contains "FRED". In normal storage the address, 200 would be used to load "FRED". In content addressable memory "FRED" would be passed along a data bus and the memory would pass 200 back, indicating the location of "FRED". Thus a paragraph of stored text could be retrieved by supplying a word contained in the paragraph. CAS is very useful for rapid data selection or retrieval but is expensive at present. A variant on CAS is **Content Addressable File storage (CAF)** in which CAS logic is part of a disk unit's circuitry and storage set-up. For example, the processor may request the input to main memory of all text file lines on the disk contain the word "FRED". The disk unit finds the appropriate lines and transfers them into memory. The processor is saved the job of searching for the data. CAFs are gradually gaining ground. A leader in this field is ICL.

MULTIPROCESSOR SYSTEMS

13.78 Here we are considering single computers with multiple processors as opposed to situations in which multiple computers are combined into a single system by means of networks and modern data transmission systems. Further details of the latter is left until chapter 14.

13.79 Traditionally, multiprocessor systems have been very large computers with two or more main processors and large main storage that has been wholly or partially shared. This arrangement not only serves to handle a large processing load but also provides back-up in the case of breakdown (ie, if one processor fails the system can continue to operate). Such systems are called **multiprocessing systems** (see Fig. 13.10).

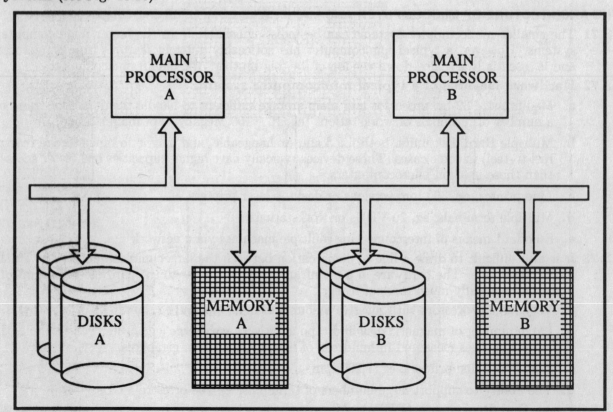

Fig 13.10 A Multiprocessing System with Duplicated Disk Storage and Memory.

13.80 In broad terms any computer containing more than one processor may be called a **multiprocessor computer**. However, the term is usually taken to imply processors that are sharing the same main memory. If the processors each have their own main storage but share disks and other peripherals the system is sometimes called **a clustered system**. The extra processors may be used as either of the following:

a. as additional main processors sharing the normal processing load,

b. as special-purpose processors catering for some particular function. For example, a **maths co-processor** may be used in conjunction with a single main processor to perform some standard complex computations.

13.81 Where there are a number of main processors, as in Fig 13.10, there are two basic methods of using the processors:

a. **Asymmetric multiprocessing (AMP)** In an asymmetric multiprocessing machine one processor is the master processor and all other processors are subordinate to it. The master processor has special privileges over the operating system. These allow it to work in what is called **kernel mode**, which basically means that it is able to carry out specially controlled operating-system operations on the hardware that ordinary applications programs are not allowed to do. The subordinate processors are therefore limited to processing applications programs and may have to wait for the master processor if the programs require the operating system to carry out some operation on their behalf. This can potentially cause a processing bottleneck at the master processor.

b. **Symmetric multiprocessing (SMP)** In a symmetric multiprocessing machine all processors have equal status, with each one able to carry out kernel mode operations. This removes the processing bottleneck, which occurs with asymmetric multiprocessing. This major advantage means that symmetric multiprocessing is a much more popular option even though it is technically much more difficult to achieve. Examples of machines that perform symmetric multiprocessing are the Digital VAX 6000 series computers running under the VMS version 5 operating system and all computers made by SEQUENT.

13.82 It must be pointed out that both kinds of multiprocessing are very sophisticated and are currently only available from a few manufacturers.

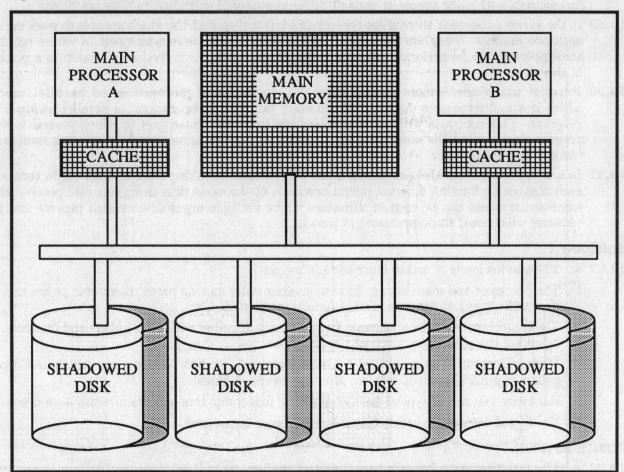

Fig 13.11. A Multiprocessing System local cache and shadowed disks.

13.83 Local cache. Some performance improvements may be gained in a multiprocessor machine by using a separate cache in close proximity to each of the processors. Thus, each processor has its own "local cache". Data can be read from main storage into the cache and then processed more quickly while it is in cache because of the higher access speeds. Any changes in the data must be written back to main memory before any other processor reads it. The accesses to main memory from the various processors can cause another bottleneck. Sophisticated methods of managing the cache, such as those used in SEQUENT computers, can help to alleviate these problems.

13.84 A further measure employed on such systems is to use **disk shadowing** whereby disks are used in pairs with the second disk storing exactly the same data as the first. If either disk fails for any reason the other one can continue operating so that no data is lost and the running of the system is not interrupted. This ability to continue despite a failure is called **resilience**. Fig 13.11 shows a multiprocessor system with local cache and shadowed disks.

13.85 Although the feature just described are quite sophisticated by general standards the components used can be quite ordinary. For example, one symmetric multiprocessing machine uses a standard Intel 486 microprocessor.

ALTERNATIVE ARCHITECTURES

13.86 All the examples in this chapter that have been considered so far have been concerned with single or multiple processors, all of which conformed to same basic design. However, in recent years there have been moves to create computers to radically new designs.

13.87 Many of these computers have been designed with the object of gaining greater computational speed. Two approaches that have had some measure of success are:

a. **Pipeline machines.**

b. **Array processors.**

13.88 In the **pipeline machine** architecture each stage in the fetch-execute cycle is handled by a *separate* machine hardware unit. This is similar in concept to the method of pipelining described earlier but is different in that the hardware is organised very differently to make maximum use of the method. The first unit fetches and instruction from memory. At any one time there may be four or five instructions within the processor each at different stages of execution in different units.

13.89 In the **array processor** there is one control unit but multiple ALUs, which are able to work in parallel with one another. They are particularly suited to applications in which sets of values require the same operation to be performed on each value, eg, converting every value in a table to a percentage of the total.

13.90 Parallel machines A more general alternative to the array processor is the **parallel machine**, which is a multiprocessor machine able to carry out various operations in parallel *within a single program*. This contrasts with some ordinary multiprocessor machines in which several individual programs may run at the same time, but in which at any one time a single program is unable to use more than one processor.

13.91 In a simple case of parallel processing a computer might be taking a set of numbers in turn and for each number performing different operations on it at the same time using separate processors. The same arrangement can be used in situations where multiple input devices each provide instrument readings which need to be processed in parallel.

SUMMARY

13.92 a. The various levels of architecture were introduced.

b. The processor and main storage have no mechanically moving parts. Electronic pulses moving at nearly the speed of light are used in data transmission.

c. The control unit and the arithmetic and logic units together with their buffers and interconnecting buses are the constituent parts of the processor.

d. Modern computer "architecture" is characterised by *modular components*, which are linked together in a building-block fashion, often by means of *buses*.

e. Hardware features of typical microcomputers, minicomputers and mainframes were described.

f. Newer and alternative architectural features were introduced.

POINTS TO NOTE

13.93 a. The fact that some larger microcomputers perform as well as some smaller minicomputers and some larger minicomputers perform as well as smaller mainframes is just one indication that some applications can be computerised in a number of different ways. It also shows the limited value of using rigid classification of computers.

b. A technical difference between a microcomputer and a minicomputer is that in a microcomputer the processor is contained on a single microprocessor chip, but in minicomputers the processor is larger and is often composed of a number of chips. This technical difference has minor practical significance to the user. Indeed, a larger multiboard microcomputer-based system will tend to be classified as a minicomputer, at least as far as the user is concerned.

c. A greater understanding of the processor will come after studying programming and the chapters on machine operation and language.

d. Most registers are also known by other names. Be prepared for this by noting these alternatives:

   i. The **Sequence Control Register (SCR)** is also known as **Program Counter (PC)**, **Instruction Counter (IC)**, **Instruction Address Register (IAR)**.

   ii. The **Current Instruction Register (CIR)** is also known as the **Instruction Register (IR)**.

   iii. The **Memory Data Register (MDR)** is also known as the **Memory Buffer Register (MBR)**, although the terms have been used with different meaning in this chapter.

   iv. Computer systems developed for special purposes in which the computer is largely hidden within the application, as is the case for many single-chip and single-board computers, are often referred to as **"embedded systems"**.

e. The idea of viewing the computer's architecture as a set of layers is quite common but the there are several alternative ways of classifying the layers. The reader should therefore merely take the classification used in this chapter as an example of a convenient one rather than as THE classification.

f. Although the **machine layer** is *always* regarded as part of a machines hardware, when it is implemented my means of microcode it is really firmware.

g. The description of the operation of the computer given in this chapter assumes that the memory used for data and program instructions is completely interchangeable. This is the norm, and machines based on this principle are often said to have a **von Neumann architecture**, after a computer pioneer who helped to establish such a design. However, some computers segregate the storage space into areas for data and areas for programs. This is sometimes referred to as the bf Harvard architecture. A series of Intel microprocessors, starting with the 8086, may be described as having a version of the Harvard architecture.

STUDENT SELF-TESTING QUESTIONS

1. Describe the functions of the processor.
2. Describe and distinguish between the following:

   i. Instruction Register.

   ii. Program Counter.

   iii. Memory Address Register.

   iv. Memory Data Register.

3. Define and distinguish between the terms:

   i. hardware

   ii. firmware

   iii. software

   iv. ROM

   v. RAM

   vi. EPROM.

4. Define the term "Front End Processor".

STUDENT SELF-TESTING QUESTIONS CONTINUED

5. A computer is required simultaneously to process the data input continually from a set of digital instruments. What architecture might be suitable for this?

6. The number 973 is to be stored in main storage using a 4-bit BCD code. Show how it might be stored in: A word with 16 bits.

7. a. What is the difference between the main store and the backing store of a computer? [3]

   b. Explain the terms speed of access, cost per bit, and capacity for backing stores, and give an account of the ways in which they are related. [3, 3, 3, 4]

   c. Explain why most backing stores are at present based on magnetic devices which need to be in motion. What advantages might be gained if they could be replaced by devices without moving parts, and why is this not done? [5, 4]

Oxford

QUESTIONS WITHOUT ANSWERS

8. Describe the notion of a "bus" in computer architecture and identify an advantage of using buses over alternatives.

9. Identify the computer you use on your course as either a mainframe, minicomputer or microcomputer and justify your choice of category.

GLOSSARY CHECKLIST

Accumulator	13.46	IC	13.39
ALU	13.53	Instruction address register	13.93
AMP	13.81	Instruction register	13.46
Architecture	13.1	Internal bus	13.24
Arithmetic and Logic Unit	13.53	I/O	13.35
Array processor	13.89	I/O channel	13.46
Asymmetric multiprocessing	13.81	IR	13.46
Booting up	13.62	Loader	13.46
CAF	13.77	Local cache	13.83
CAS	13.77	MAR	13.44
CIR	13.46	MBR	13.44
CISC	13.57	Memory address register	13.44
Clustered system	13.80	Memory buffer register	13.44
Control Unit	13.48	Memory data register	13.44
CU	13.48	MDR	13.44
Current instruction register	13.46	Microcode	13.11
Data buffer register	13.44	Microprogram	13.11
Data register	13.46	Modular construction	13.22
Disk shadowing	13.84	Monitor	13.66
DR	13.46	Motherboard	13.31
Embedded system	13.93	Multiboard system	13.31
External bus	13.24	Multilayered machine	13.3
Family of processors	13.13	Multiprocessor system	13.80
FEP	13.74	Multiprocessing system	13.79
Fetch-execute cycle	13.49	Parallel machine	13.90
Firmware	13.11	Peripheral processor	13.36
Front-end processor	13.74	PC	13.50
Gate	13.8	PCB	13.39
General purpose bus	13.34	Program counter	13.50
Harvard architecture	13.93	Pipeline architecture	13.88
IAR	13.93	Pipelining	13.52

14: Data Communications and Networks

INTRODUCTION

14.1 This chapter explains the traditional and modern methods of data transmission. It also looks at the broader subject of computer networks and distributed systems. Computer networks have been rapidly developed in recent years and support a growing number of important applications. Examples of these developments and applications will be covered within this chapter.

14.2 You are advised to re-read the following passages before you continue: 2.3 – 2.13 and 4.44 – 4.56.

BASIC IDEAS IN DATA TRANSMISSION

14.3 Consider the simple signals shown in Fig 14.1 and then note the points that follow.

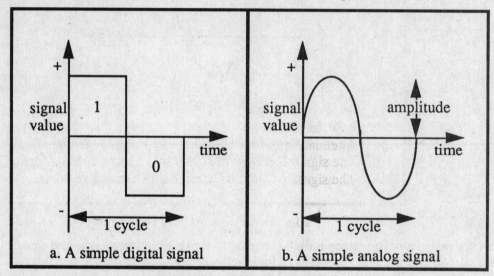

Fig 14.1. Simple Signals.

14.4 Data transmission speeds are related to signal **frequencies**. The frequency of a signal is the number of cycles per second and is often expressed in units called **hertz** (Hz for short). 1 Hz is 1 cycle per second.

14.5 Various physical factors limit the maximum and minimum frequencies that a given medium can carry. A transmission link is called a **channel**. The range of frequencies over which a transmission may take place over a channel is called the **bandwidth** of the channel. **Broadband** channels (ie, those with broad bandwidth) have the ability to carry more data. Broadband channels are also called **wideband** channels.

14.6 The data-carrying capacity of a channel is of prime interest to us and can be related to the channel frequency as follows. You may see from Fig. 14.1a that there are two pulses per cycle (a "0" and a "1"). The number of pulses per second is a unit called a **baud**. In simple situations like the one in Fig. 14.1a the baud rate is twice the frequency. We have already seen (Fig. 2.3) that data can be encoded and transmitted in terms of pulses with the binary values "0" and "1". However, not all the bits carry data, as is the case for the stop and start bits in Fig. 2.3. The rate of data flow, called the **data transfer rate**, is therefore less than the baud rate. Data transfer rates are often expressed in terms of the number of data bits transmitted per second. The actual units may be Kbits/s (thousands of bits per second) or Mbits/s (millions of bits per second).

14.7 This is an appropriate point to give some practical examples. **A coaxial cable** (see your TV aerial lead) may have a data transfer rate of 140 Mbits/s, enough to carry, at any one time, the information for two TV channels **or** nearly 300 music channels **or** about 2000 telephone channels. Optical fibres have even greater data transfer rates of 500 Mbits/s or more!

14.8 Transmitted signals become degraded during transmission because of:

   a. Noise ie, random unwanted signals picked up by the channel. The quality of the channel may be expressed in terms of its **signal-to-noise ratio**, which is measured in decibels, dB. The lower the value the better.

b. **Distortion** ie, changes to the shape of the signal caused by such things as absorption of the signal (**attenuation**) and delays by the medium, (see Fig. 14.2).

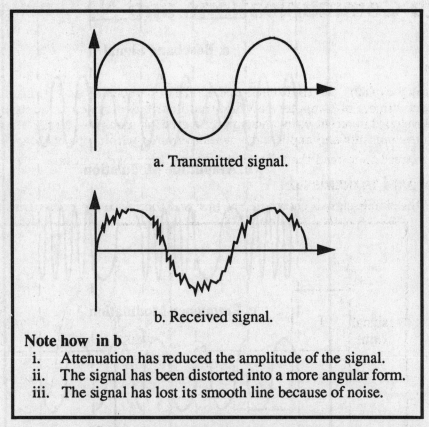

a. Transmitted signal.

b. Received signal.

Note how in b

i.   Attenuation has reduced the amplitude of the signal.

ii. The signal has been distorted into a more angular form.

iii. The signal has lost its smooth line because of noise.

Fig. 14.2. Signal Degradation.

14.9   It is relatively easy to restore a digital signal to its original amplitude and free it of noise by means of a unit called a **digital repeater**. However, **analog repeaters** are only able to restore amplitude and, worse still, they amplify noise. Therefore digital signals are preferable to analog signals.

14.10   **Baseband** transmission involves directly encoding the signal onto the channel medium, eg, using +5v for "1" and -5v for "0". Baseband transmission is satisfactory over relatively short distances, ie, less than 1km. For longer transmissions **"carrier waves"** must be used in order to overcome the degradation that occurs to baseband signals.

14.11   **Modulated carrier waves** are best explained with the aid of an example (Fig. 14.3). The basic form of the carrier wave is a simple signal that has the form of a smooth-rounded waveform. The characteristics of the carrier's waveform are regulated in accordance with changes in the signal to be carried (the baseband signal). This process is known as **modulation**. Various types of modulation may be used (see Fig. 14.3).

Note. If the carrier wave is thought of as a sound signal then amplitude modulation corresponds to defined changes in volume (amplitude), frequency modulation corresponds to defined changes in pitch (frequency) and phase modulation corresponds to defined displacements in a continuous tone.

14.12   **Multiplexing** is the term used in data transmission for using one data link to carry a number of separate data signals at the same time. There are two basic methods of multiplexing.

a. **Time Division Multiplexing (TDM),** in which the signals take frequent turns at using the carrier wave one after another.

b. **Frequency Division Multiplexing (FDM),** in which different ranges of the bandwidth are used for each signal.

When the signal is received it must be **demultiplexed** back into its constituent signals. Devices able to perform these functions are called **multiplexors** and **demultiplexors**. NB. Multiplexing may be used for both baseband and non-baseband signals.

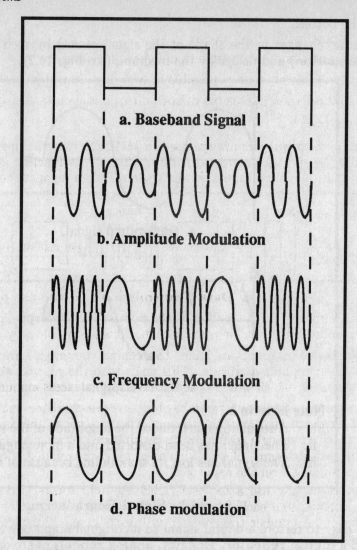

a. Baseband Signal

b. Amplitude Modulation

c. Frequency Modulation

d. Phase modulation

Fig. 14.3. Modulated Carrier Waves.

TRADITIONAL TELECOMMUNICATIONS METHODS

14.13 The next eight paragraphs outline the traditional methods used for data transmission.

BRITISH TELECOM (BT) AND MERCURY COMMUNICATIONS

14.14 In the UK, BT is a major carrier and once held a monopoly but now it has Mercury Communications as a competitor. If there is a requirement to set up a network within a single site (eg, a factory or office complex), private facilities may be used. In practice, most data in the UK is transmitted over the ordinary telegraph and telephone circuits, which are capable of carrying data as well as speech.

DATEL SERVICES

14.15 British Telecom offers a number of services under the name of DATEL. These are identified by numbers - DATEL 100, 200, 400, 600, 2400. The numbers indicate (roughly) the baud rate. The most common transmitting speed is 600 - 1,200 baud (bits per second). Much higher speeds can be achieved, up to 48,000 baud, by using "wide-band" circuits. Mercury Communications offer competing services.

PUBLIC AND PRIVATE LINES

14.16 Data can be transmitted over the ordinary *public* telephone circuits. The connection is made using a normal telephone handset and dialling the number of the computer from the terminal. The link is disconnected when the transmission has finished. Charges are based on the type of service and the amount of time used.

It is also possible to hire a *private* line. The public telephone network is used, but a line is reserved for the exclusive use of the hirer. A fixed charge is made regardless of the actual amount of traffic. The line can also be used for ordinary speech calls.

LINE SYSTEMS

14.17 Transmission is possible in three modes:

a. **Simplex.** Transmission is possible in only *one direction*.

b. **Half Duplex.** Transmission is possible in *both* directions, but not simultaneously.

c. **Duplex.** Transmission is possible in both directions simultaneously.

TRANSMISSION EQUIPMENT

14.18 a. Where public *telephone* circuits are used, a MODEM must be provided at each end of the line. " MODEM" is short for **modulator-demodulator**. Its function is to modulate the signals into frequencies suitable for transmission and to demodulate them at the receiving end (see Fig. 14.4).

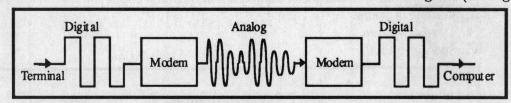

Fig. 14.4. Data Transmission and the use of Modems.

b. A cheaper alternative to the modem is the **acoustic coupler**, which makes it possible to use an ordinary telephone handset for transmission. This is suitable only for low-speed transmission.

c. When a number of terminals are linked to a central computer, a **multiplexor** has to be provided as part of the computer hardware. This deals with the routine work of handling incoming and outgoing messages, which would otherwise occupy an excess amount of processor time.

d. To reduce transmission costs, a **dataplex** or **concentrator** may be used. This connects a number of terminals that are close to each other but not to the central computer. The messages are transmitted in a single stream using multiplexing techniques. Trunk charges thus have to be paid for only one "stream" of data instead of for each terminal. Concentrators may also be used when the computer is on the same site.

Concentrators usually use a method called **asynchronous time-division multiplexing**, in which the signals from each terminal are transmitted at irregular intervals and must therefore be identified by a number transmitted with each item. This method is also called **statistical multiplexing.**

TERMINAL DEVICES

14.19 There is a very wide variety of terminal devices in use, ranging from a tele-typewriter to sophisticated devices that permit automatic sending and receiving of data. Any *peripheral device* can if required be used as a terminal, ie, a transmitting or receiving device at the end of a transmission line connected to a computer.

ON-LINE/OFF-LINE TRANSMISSION

14.20 If the remote terminal is linked directly to the computer, data is transmitted via the data link directly into the processor. Such a data-transmission system, as you might expect, is called an ON-LINE system.

The remote terminal can be linked to storage devices such as magnetic tape or disk units that are *not* themselves linked to the computer. Data is transmitted via the data link to the terminal device at the other computer's end. Such data is fed to the computer eventually. Such a data-transmission system is called an OFF-LINE system.

APPLICATIONS

14.21 a. The use of data transmission is increasing rapidly. Many systems are now designed with a communications network as their basis (details shortly). Other systems that operate on an "in-house" basis (ie, all data preparation and processing are carried out in one computer centre) are being re-designed to use data transmission.

b. The basic advantages are:

i. **Data collection** is much faster.

ii. **Information** in the files of the central computer is readily available at different locations.

iii. **Hardware** costs can be reduced by use of one large machine instead of a number of smaller ones at different sites.

    iv. Computing facilities can be made available to staff (eg, designers requiring complex calculations).

c. Some systems depend on immediate collection of data as soon as it originates. These are known as "on-line" and "real-time" systems and are dealt with later.

d. Off-line systems are simpler and less expensive, because the terminals are not connected to a computer. Such systems benefit from the speed with which data are transmitted, even though processing is not as fast.

e. Considerations in the choice of a system will be:

    i. Cost

    ii. Distance between computer and terminals

    iii. Volume of traffic

    iv. Type of system

    v. Speed required.

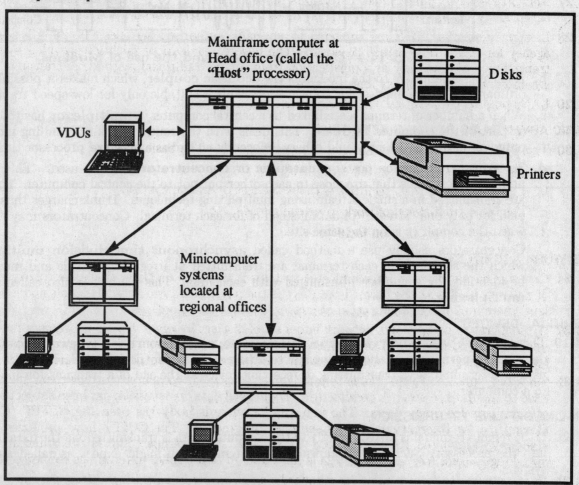

Fig. 14.5. A Distributed System.

NETWORKS AND DISTRIBUTED SYSTEMS DEFINED

14.22 An interconnected set of two or more computers may be called a **"computer network"**. However, if the computers in the network operate together as a single unit which to the user appears as a single computer, albeit physically dispersed, then the complete system is more accurately described as a **distributed system**. Therefore, although *any* interconnected set of computers is often conveniently referred to as a "computer network" the use of the term often implies an interconnected set of *independent* computers and not a distributed system. However, it may be useful to recognise distributed systems that are based upon particular types of network.

Note A computer that is *not* connected to other computers is a **"stand-alone system"**.

14.23 Distributed systems. Over recent years there has been a steady trend towards using computer systems that have several interconnected processors placed in separate locations. Each processor tends to have its own "local" peripherals (disks, printers, terminals) in addition to any peripherals attached to some central processor (see Fig. 14.5).

14.24 The advantages of distributing the processing include:

    a. Reduction in costs and delays in transmitting and processing data.

    b. Reduced load on the "host".

    c. Better local control and service.

14.25 Networks used to interconnect computers in a single room, rooms within a building, or buildings on one site are normally of a type called **Local Area Networks** (LANs). Sometimes multiple LANS are used on the same site. For example, there may be one LAN per floor in a multi storey building. Such LANs may all be connected onto one main network such as a **multidrop network** (Fig 14.6) called a **backbone**. Alternatively, they may be individually connected one to another across a cabled link known as a **bridge**.

14.26 Computers on a LAN may be regarded as a distributed system provided they operate in a sufficiently integrated way as to form a single processing system.

14.27 Networks used to interconnect computers on separate sites, or in separate cities or countries, are called **Long Haul Networks (LHNs)** or **Wide Area Networks (WANs)**.

14.28 In many countries LHNs are provided by specially authorised agencies. In the UK the principal agency for this is BT (British Telecom). The telecommunications facilities provided by BT for the transmission of data vary in sophistication from simple traditional methods of transmitting data to a computer using telephone lines to large LHNs.

14.29 LANs tend to be privately owned and to use baseband methods.

BASIC ADVANTAGES OF USING NETWORKS

14.30 There are many possible advantages in using networks. The basic ones are:

    a. The sharing of resources (eg, computers and staff) and information.

    b. The provision of local facilities without the loss of central control.

    c. The even distribution of work, processing loads, etc.

    d. Improved communication facilities.

NETWORK ARCHITECTURE

14.31 Communication between interconnected systems is a complex activity that takes place on a number of different levels. At the lowest level there is the physical transmission of signals and at the highest level there may be communication of messages in natural languages.

14.32 By deliberately organising a network into a set of distinct **levels** or **layers** it becomes much easier to understand and develop. The communications at each level have their own **protocols** (2.10). The layers plus their protocols constitute what is called the **architecture of the network.**

14.33 Since one purpose of networks is to interconnect dissimilar computer systems there is an important need to standardise network architecture. Traditional data transmission has been subject to a number of standards for many years. The influential standards body has been the CCITT (Consultative Committee for International Telephone and Telegraphy). The CCITT have produced a series of standards, numbered X1 to X29 and V1 to V57. For example, X25 is the standard for packet switching systems (see later) and V24 is the standard that applies to terminals connected to modems.

14.34 In an attempt to form a basis for standardising all layers in network architecture the International Standards Organisation (**ISO**) has devised a model of network architecture. This model is known as the Reference Model of Open Systems Interconnection (**OSI**).

14.35 The OSI model has seven layers. From lowest to highest they are as follows.

    a. **The physical-control layer** is the level of electrical connections, signal transmission and data in raw binary form.

    b. **The data-link layer** is the level at which data is transmitted in small units using suitable protocols to control and check correct transmission. The units of data are called "frames", ie, asynchronously transmitted characters or synchronously transmitted blocks of characters.

    c. **The network layer** is the level that provides the control between adjacent sending and receiving points in the network. The sending and receiving points that are able to *switch* transmissions are "**nodes**" in the network.

    d. **The transport layer** is the level that provides an **end-to-end** service between host computers. It deals with addressing, error controls and regulated data transfers.

e. **The session layer** is the level that handles the establishment of connections between hosts and the management of the dialog. Messages created at this level are addressed by the transport layer and split into packets at the network layer.

f. **The presentation layer** is the level that handles the standard forms for presenting data, eg, the layouts used for VDU displays.

g. **The application layer** is the level that the user has control over in determining what data is to be transmitted and how it is to be sent or received.

NETWORK STRUCTURES

14.36 A number of standard network structures are shown in Fig. 14.6.

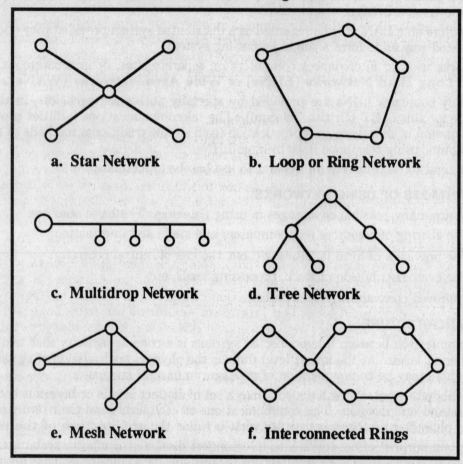

Fig. 14.6. Standard Network Structures.

14.37 The small circles in Fig. 14.5 represent **nodes** in the network which are connection points or switching points depending upon the kind of network. LHNs and LANs are organised rather differently from one another so they will be described separately.

14.38 In LHNs the nodes in Fig 14.5 are called **IMPs** (Interface Message Processors). This is a general name for what in particular networks may alternatively be called a **data switching exchange**, a **communications computer** or a **packet switching node**. In a LHN there are three basic ways of making a communications link across a network as follows.

a. **Circuit switching.** This is the normal method used on telephone networks. The **telephone exchanges** are **data switching exchange** nodes in the network. When the computer places a call the switching equipment at nodes in the telephone system seeks and establishes an unbroken path all the way from the sending computer to the receiving computer. This link is maintained until the transmissions are completed. The sender and receiver then disconnect thus freeing the circuit. The long set-up time, monopoly of bandwidth, and the need for sender and receiver to synchronise are disadvantages when using such a network for data communications.

b. **Message switching.** In these networks IMPs are special purpose **communications comput-ers**. Most computers or terminals would be connected to these IMPs. IMPs may communicate directly with one another if connected by cables or indirectly via other IMPs. An IMP may receive, **store and forward** messages received from one IMP and intended for another. There-fore, some disadvantages of circuit switching are overcome, notably the need to establish a path before transmission. For distances over approximately 400 km it is more economic to use satellite transmissions between IMPs rather than use cable. The IMPs are said to perform a **"message-switching"** function. **"Packets"** of information are transmitted at this level. A packet used in message switching is a variable length unit of data with two main components:

i. Header data, which specifies its destination address, (possibly its source address too).

ii. Data to be transmitted.

Unfortunately, long message packets can demand large amounts of storage space on IMPs which are *storing* and forwarding messages in their entirety and long messages can monopolise a particular link.

c. **Packet switching.** Packet switching also uses store and forward methods through IMPs called **packet switching node** but is aimed at overcoming the limitations of message switching by handling packets differently. In particular, packets have a fixed upper size limit which enables them to be held in an IMP's main storage instead of requiring disk space as often happens with message switching. The duration of each packet's transmission is also limited which ensures more balanced access to communication channels. The packet size limit means that a packet switching system handles messages as multiple packets. The first packet can be forwarded before the second one has arrived which improves throughput.

14.39 In the case of LANs the arrangements are different from those just described. For example, the circles in Fig. 14.6b might represent digital repeaters or access boxes on a ring. A device connected to an access box on a ring might be able to deposit data and addresses into empty packets circulating continuously on the ring. Another access box to which the message was addressed would be able to pick up the message, clear the packet and transmit an acknowledgement in a similar fashion. Some particular examples follow shortly.

NETWORKS CURRENTLY IN USE

14.40 There are numerous networks in use today. Many of them are proprietary. One of the earliest LHNs was **ARPANET** (a mesh network), the network of the Advanced Research Project Agency in the USA and part of the US Defense Department. ARPANET was set up partly for research purposes and many universities and private corporations have been allowed to use it, both in the USA and elsewhere. There are also networks in Britain and Europe that are connected together and to ARPANET.

14.41 One popular form of LAN is **Ethernet**, pioneered by XEROX but now used by a variety of manufacturers. Ethernet works on the same principle as a bus with network devices being connected to at various points. Each device has a unique address assigned to it. Standard Ethernet uses coaxial cable somewhat larger than that used for domestic TV aerials but there are several variants which use thin wires and high capacity versions which use optical fibre.

14.42 Another form of LAN is that based on the **Token Ring** in which special packets called **tokens** circulate around a ring networks. A PC or workstation connected to the ring sends a message by first setting a bit on a token to "capturing" it. It then send the message using the token and after transmission releases the token by resetting the token's bit to a free status.

APPLICATIONS AND RECENT DEVELOPMENTS

14.43 British Telecom have developed a digital telephone exchange system known as **System X**. Installation is due for completion in 1992. When it is completed analog MODEMS should be obsolete! The system will be compatible with the bottom three layers of the OSI model, which, incidentally, are compatible with X25.

14.44 A new version of the old **telex** service has been developed over the last few years. It will be able to send pictures as well as text and is called **teletex**. The intention is to link teletex devices into computer systems and to handle pictures as well as text. These developments will eventually lead to systems compatible with FAX (see below).

14.45 Facsimile devices (**FAX** for short) have been in use for some time to transmit pictures from one place to another using telephone links.

14.46 **Viewdata.** This is a service that has the international name **videotex** and the BT trade name "PRESTEL". Essentially it is a computer-based service that provides information, via telephone links, to a TV set connected to the user's telephone receiver point. It should not be confused with **teletext** (BBC's *CEEFAX* or ITV'S *Oracle*) which provides information by using "unused lines" on TV picture transmission. Private viewdata systems are used by a variety of different companies. One popular example is the use of viewdata systems by holiday tour operators. The tour operator has a central computer which provides holiday booking information. A travel agent can connect to the system via a viewdata terminal to check availability and make bookings for customers. Another rather different example is the use of a viewdata system by the International Stock Exchange London which provides share price information via a viewdata system.

NB. Note the *two* services **teletex** and **teletext**.

14.47 Many private organisations use their own automatic telephone exchanges as part of internal transmission. Such exchanges are known as **PABXs** (Private Automatic Branch Exchanges) as opposed to the older **PMBXs** (Private Manual Branch Exchanges). Some PABXs now have computers built into them and are able to be programmed to handle a variety of data transmission tasks. These PABXs are sometimes called **SPCs** (Stored Program-Controlled exchanges). Incoming and outgoing transmissions are also handled by the PABXs.

14.48 **Electronic mail.** As its name suggests electronic mail has features more familiar to the postal service than the telephone service. The main features are given here in outline:

   a. Each main user has a "mailbox" which is accessed via a computer terminal within the system by entering a password. Messages are drawn to the users' attention when they enter the system. When messages are sent they must consist of two parts, a "header" giving the "address" of the sender and the body of the text.

   b. The mailing system provides computerised ways of preparing, entering and editing text.

   c. The mailing system provides means of filing and retrieving messages.

14.49 The users of an electronic mail system may have the choice of sending messages within their own organisation, via a LAN, or possibly over a public LHN.

14.50 **Packet Switching Systems (PSS).**

In Britain BT operate a "packet switching system" PSS, which operates in and between major cities as an alternative to the telephone and telex services mentioned earlier. This is an LHN service. PSSs can be used to provide an electronic mail service.

SUMMARY

14.51 The basic ideas of data transmission were introduced, including the concepts of **signal frequency, channels, bandwidth, baud rates, data transfer rates, carrier waves, modulation** and **multiplexing**.

14.52 Traditional telecommunications methods were described, including the use of BT lines for data transmission.

14.53 Transmission equipment was described, including **modems, acoustic couplers, dataplexes** and **concentrators**.

14.54 Networks were defined and a distinction was made between **Local Area Networks (LANs)** and **Long Haul Networks (LHNs)**.

14.55 The advantages of networks were outlined.

14.56 Network architecture and the OSI reference model were introduced.

14.57 Network structures were described and current types of networks were discussed briefly.

14.58 Recent developments and applications were considered including:

   a. System X
   b. Teletex
   c. FAX
   d. Videotex
   e. PABXs
   f. Electronic mail
   g. Packet switching systems.

POINTS TO NOTE

14.59 a. Wide-band circuits make possible high-speed bulk data transmission.

   b. Some "terminals" are in fact microcomputers. They are called "intelligent terminals" because they have a small processor and can carry out "local" processing as well as transmitting data. Banks use them as part of their system for linking branches with their computer centre.

   c. It is also possible to use data transmission to link two large computers. One that is busy can then transfer work to the other. This is called "load shedding".

d. In some situations the same service to the user may be provided by systems of greatly differing design. For example, *one* moderately sized processor may support a number of user terminals, *or* alternatively a number of single-user computers might be connected into a network. The former is called **"shared logic"** the latter is called **"distributed logic"**.

e. The term **"distributed processing"** is now widely used in relation to micro- and minicomputers. It implies of course that a processing facility is made available at a number of sites instead of at a single computer centre. The term can imply:

   i. A number of micros and minis at different sites, not linked to each other.

   ii. A network of micros and minis linked to a central mainframe computer.

   iii. A network of micros and minis linked to each other without a central mainframe.

STUDENT SELF-TESTING QUESTIONS

1. Explain the meaning of these terms:
   a. Bandwidth
   b. LAN
   c. Baseband
   d. Multiplexing
   e. Carrier wave
   f. PSS
   g. OSI model
   h. Electronic mail.
2. Why are carrier waves needed for data transmission in LHNs?
3. What is the purpose of a MODEM and where would a MODEM be used?
4. Name one alternative to a MODEM if a portable terminal is to be used.
5. Explain the terms "distributed system" and "computer network".
6. Why was the OSI model created?
7. Explain the differences between and relative advantages of:
   i.   Circuit switching
   ii. Message switching
   iii. Packet switching

QUESTIONS WITHOUT ANSWERS

8. Explain why a transmitted signal using 4 signal levels, instead of two as shown in Fig. 14.1, can have a baud rate of 200 baud but a data-signalling rate of 400 baud.
9. Explain this statement: "The company uses a LAN in order to provide a distributed computer system on site".

GLOSSARY CHECKLIST

PROGRAMMING I

1. This Part of the text is intended to give an overview of what programming is and how to do it. It is also intended to act as a companion to any practical programming which occurs as part of the reader's course. If the reader's examination course requires no practical programming then the reader need not worry about mastering details of the techniques covered in this Part. Most readers will find that they have some choice over the amount of programming that they are required to do because projects and case studies encourage applications related work instead of just requiring programming tasks to be done. A level examinations and some BTEC courses have moved a long way in this direction in recent years. The reader may well like to read through this Part and see how he or she gets on with the ideas before deciding whether or not to concentrate further on these topics.

2. A set of instructions that describe the steps to be followed in order to carry out an activity is called an **algorithm** or **procedure.** If the algorithm is written in the computer's language then the set of instructions is called a **program.** The task of producing a computer program involves going through several stages, not all of which involve writing in the computer's own language. The complete task is called programming, but, as you will see, programming involves more than just *writing* programs.

3. Programs consist of sequences of instructions specifying controlled and ordered operations on data that are to be performed by a computer. This Part gradually builds up a complete picture of programs and programming by dealing with different aspects of the subject in turn.

4. Chapter 15 deals with **operations on data.** It considers various types of data, the ways in which we represent them and the ways we represent operations upon them. Since, ultimately, all operations upon data must be performed by the computer's hardware the representations of the data within the computer are considered too.

5. Chapter 16 deals with **program structures.** In other words it deals with the various component parts of programs and how they are organised. As with chapter 15 the material is also related to what goes on within the computer.

6. One important aspect of chapter 16 is a discussion of the basic features of a programming language. The chapter makes extensive use of a **pseudocode.** A pseudocode is a simple language with a few basic grammatical constructions which avoids the ambiguities and complexities of English but which can easily be converted into a programming language. *It is strongly recommended to the reader that, as an exercise, all examples given in pseudocode be converted into whatever programming language the reader is using for practical programming.*

7. Chapter 17 explains what **data structures** are. It gives examples of the more common and important data structures and explains the uses of data structures in programming.

8. Chapter 18 is concerned with **program design.** It examines the aims of programming and how the stages in programming must be followed systematically in order to achieve these aims. It makes use of methods and ideas introduced in chapter 15, 16 and 17.

9. Chapter 19, the last chapter in this part, discusses **program specification.** It examines a number of methods and notations which are used to specify what programs are required to do and how they are required to do them. Towards the end of the chapter **Formal Specifications** are introduced.

10. Some other aspects of programming are not included within this part because they fit more naturally into the subject matter of later chapters.

15: Operations on Data

INTRODUCTION

15.1 This chapter introduces some basic concepts that the reader needs to be familiar with before attempting to understand programming. It describes simple data types and their representation, and explains the operations that may be performed upon data of these simple types.

DATA TYPES

15.2 A **data type** consists of:

a. a set of data values

b. a set of operations that may be applied to the values.

15.3 Having defined data types we can classify individual data items. Some data items may be used singly whilst others may be combined together and arranged to form other data items. The former are classified as **simple data types** whereas the latter are classified as **data structures** or data **aggregates**. Data structures will be discussed in later chapters.

15.4 **Data type classification.** Several classifications are possible. The following classification is appropriate for study at this level. The simple data types are:

a. Numeric integer.

b. Numeric real.

c. Character.

d. Boolean (logical).

15.5 These data types will now be considered in two stages. First, the sets of values and methods representing them will be considered for each type in turn. Then the types will be considered in turn again in order to investigate the operations that may be performed upon them.

TYPE VALUES AND THEIR REPRESENTATION

15.6 Integers are the positive and negative whole numbers, and zero $(0, \pm1, \pm2, \pm3, \pm4, ...)$.

15.7 The positive integers $(0, +1, +2, +3, +4, ...)$ are called the **natural numbers,** or **cardinal values,** and are often written without the "+" sign. In practical work you will probably come across the terms **"unsigned integer"** (1, 2, 3, 4,...) and **"signed integer"** $(0, +1, +2, +3, ...)$. Of course, negative integers *must* be signed to distinguish them from positive integers.

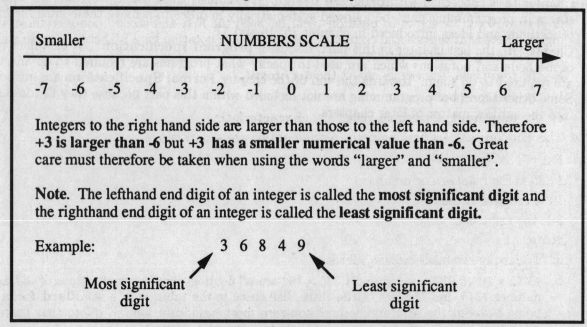

Fig 15.1. Representations of Integers.

174

15.8 The integers may be represented on a numerical scale (see Fig. 15.1).

15.9 **Real numbers.** These are **all** the numbers on the number scale shown in Fig. 15.1 (ie, including those between the integers). Real numbers include *all* the integers and *all* the fractions. These are all real numbers: $0, -0.5, 9, -1\frac{1}{7}, 39.864, \frac{7}{8}$. Positive real numbers may be represented in signed or unsigned forms.

15.10 The **numerical value** (or magnitude) of any real number, and hence any integer, is its value disregarding its sign. Thus $+3.2$ and -3.2 have the *same* numerical value. Another term for numerical value is **absolute value.**

15.11 **Fixed-point representation of real numbers.** The usual way of representing real numbers is to write the number with the decimal point **fixed** in its correct position between the two appropriate digits, eg, 13.75 or 3862.4. This is **fixed-point representation** and it proves very useful in data processing for example where sums of money are to be processed or printed. However, this representation becomes laborious and cumbersome when dealing with several very large or very small numbers, eg, 1375000000, 386240000, 0.000001375, 0.00000038624. The answer is to use floating-point representation.

15.12 **Floating-point representation of real numbers.** This concept is best introduced by some simple examples. See Fig. 15.2.

Fixed Point Representation	Floating Point Representation		Notation used in Computing
	Notation used in Science		
13.75	1.375×10^1	(Note $10^1 = 10$)	$.1375 \times 10^2$
137.5	1.375×10^2	(Note $10^2 = 100$)	$.1375 \times 10^3$
1375.	1.375×10^3	(Note $10^3 = 1000$)	$.1375 \times 10^4$
1375000000.	1.375×10^9		$.1375 \times 10^{10}$
1.375	1.375×10^0	(Note $10^0 = 1$ by definition)	$.1375 \times 10^1$
0.1375	1.375×10^{-1}	(Note $10^{-1} = \frac{1}{10}$ by definition)	$.1375 \times 10^0$
0.01375	1.375×10^{-2}	(Note $10^{-2} = \frac{1}{100}$)	$.1375 \times 10^{-1}$
0.001375	1.375×10^{-3}		$.1375 \times 10^{-2}$
3862.4	3.8624×10^3		$.38624 \times 10^4$
386240000.	3.8624×10^8		$.38624 \times 10^9$
.00000038624	3.8624×10^{-7}		$.38624 \times 10^6$

Fig. 15.2. Representations of Real Numbers.

15.13 In each of the floating-point representations just given in the table the decimal points have been moved or *floated* along the digits to position them between the first and second non-zero most significant digits. (Note that science and computer science differ in notation here.) There are three components to a floating-point representation:

a. the **mantissa**, sometimes called the **argument,**

b. the **radix** or **base,**

c. the **exponent**, sometimes called the **characteristic.**

15.14 The components of a floating-point representation are shown here:

For $\quad 1.375 \times 10^3$

1.375 is the mantissa or argument

10 is the base or radix

3 is the exponent.

Note.

a. The exponent takes integer values.

b. $13.75 \times 10^2, 0.01375 \times 10^5$ and 1.375×10^3 are *all* floating-point representations of the fixed point number 1375, but the last of the three, like those in the table, is in a **standard form** with the point between the first and second non-zero most significant figure. (Note that there are two "standard forms", one for science and one for computer science).

c. In some applications computer input and output of floating-point numbers is printed on one line as shown here:

Handwritten floating point representation	Computerised version
1.375^3	$+1.375E+3$
3.8624^{-7}	$+3.8624E-7$

The "E" separates the exponent from the mantissa and base 10 is assumed.

15.15 Characters. Characters have already been introduced (2.2). For practical purposes it is most useful to define the data type character by reference to some standard character set, eg, ASCII or EBCDIC. One consequence of such definitions is that each character has an associated ordinal value corresponding to its position in the character set (eg, ASCII "A" has ordinal value 65, see Fig. 2.4).

15.16 There are many situations when writing programs in which there is a need for simple data items consisting of characters, for example, when representing names like "Alex" or "James". Such sequences of characters treated as single data items are called **character strings** or merely **strings**. We cease to think of strings as simple data types the moment we cease to treat them as single invisible units and start to manipulate their individual character components. We then consider strings to be **data structures**.

15.17 Boolean (logical) data types. In one respect Booleans are the simplest data types of all because Boolean-type data items can only take one of two possible values at any one time. The two values are "True" and "False". The name "Boolean" comes from the name of a logician called George Boole, who did much pioneering work in the algebra of logic.

REPRESENTATION OF DATA TYPES WITHIN THE COMPUTER

15.18 The basic ideas of data representation within the computer were introduced in chapter 2 and were expanded upon in some later chapters. Here we relate these ideas to the data types under discussion in this chapter; some more detailed discussion will be provided in later chapters where appropriate.

15.19 Further classifications of numerical data types arise from the alternative ways in which numerical data types are coded for storage purposes. The basic types of representation are:

a. **BCD** representation, in which each decimal digit in the number is coded separately as in 2.19 (eg, 39 decimal is represented as 0011, 1001).

b. **Pure Binary** representation, in which the whole number is converted to binary, (eg, 39 decimal is represented as 10011).

15.20 Single and double precision.

This concept is best explained by a simple example. Suppose we wish to represent positive integers in pure binary in an 8-bit microcomputer. We might choose to use one memory location to store each number. The number 39 would be stored using 8 bits as 00100111. With this arrangement the largest positive integer we could store would be 11111111_2, which corresponds to 255 decimal. Clearly, this is rather small and so we might wish to use two 8-bit words instead. The largest positive integer we could store would then be 65536. The two alternatives here are between **single precision**, using 8 bits, and **double precision**, using 16 bits. A more practical example might involve using 16 bits for single precision and 32 bits for double precision.

15.21 Further details of numeric representation will be given in later chapters. We now turn to the representation of other data types.

15.22 Character representations within the computer have already been discussed in sufficient detail in chapter 2.

15.23 Boolean data items are easy to represent in binary. There is a simple choice between "1" for "True" and "0" for "False" or "0" for "True" and "1" for "False". In this book we will use the former when such a representation is required.

15.24 From the preceding paragraph it should be apparent that at machine level the binary representations of all these different data types are indistinguishable. That fact creates a potential source of error when data is processed and something to guard against when programming.

15.25 We now consider the other aspect of data types; the operations that may be applied to them.

OPERATIONS, OPERATORS AND OPERANDS

15.26 An **operation** is a defined action upon data. For example, the addition $3 + 5$ is an **arithmetic operation** on two integers. The **result** of the operation $3 + 5$ is 8. The **operator** used to signify this operation has the symbol '+'. The **operands** are the data items operated upon, in this example the operands are 3 and 5.

15.27 It is very important to recognise that particular operations can only be defined in terms of what happens to values of the data type to which they are applied.

15.28 Dyadic operations and unary operations. Operations that act upon *two* operands are called **dyadic operations** and operations that act upon single operands are called **unary operations.** The "+" and "−" signs are used both for dyadic operations and for unary operations.

15.29 Examples:

a. **Dyadic operations** $3 + 5$ and $5 − 3$.

b. **Unary operations** $+3$ and $−5$.

15.30 Dyadic operations are also called **"binary operations"** for fairly obvious reasons but ambiguities can arise from that choice of terms so beware! Unary operations are also called **"monadic operations".**

ARITHMETIC OPERATIONS

15.31 The arithmetic operations of addition, subtraction, multiplication and division are normally indicated by the use of the operators $+, −, \times,$ and $\div$. However, in computer programming languages other symbols are commonly used instead because of the limitations in character sets.

15.32 There are variations in symbols used between programming languages. Also, there are variations in symbols used that take account of differences between integers and reals.

15.33 Fig. 15.3 shows the more commonly used symbols.

OPERATIONS ON INTEGERS

15.34 All five operations in Fig 15.3 may be applied to integers, but in the case of division there are some special considerations. Dividing one integer by another does not necessarily give rise to an integer result. For example, 11/4 is 2.75, which is of type real. However, in some situations we might want to obtain the result of division in the forms of an integer quotient and integer remainder, for example, in asking the question how many lots of four items can be made from eleven items and how many will be left over. The remedy is to use **div** and **mod.**

15.35 Div and mod. These two operations apply to integers and produce integer results. **Div** produces an integer quotient and **mod** produces an integer remainder.

15.36 Examples

a. 11 **div** 4 has the result 2.

b. 11 **mod** 4 has the result 3.

+	+
−	−
×	*
÷	/ or div
3^2	$3 \uparrow 2$ or $3 * * 2$ or $3 \,\hat{}\, 2$

Fig. 15.3. Symbols for Arithmetic Operators.

OPERATIONS ON REALS

15.37 All five operations in Fig. 15.3 may be applied to reals, and division does not present the same problems encountered by integers. However, there is one more point to note regarding division which applies to integers and reals; the case of attempting to divide by zero. Division by zero leads **either** to an *infinite result* or, in the case of dividing zero by zero, to an *undefined result.* When writing programs that involve divisions the programmers should *always* consider these two special cases and allow for them.

OPERATIONS ON CHARACTERS

15.38 A few operations may be applied to individual characters and far more operations may be applied to character strings. It is more instructive to postpone the discussion of the operations for the time being and to give just one example here to illustrate the general idea.

15.39 Concatenation is an operation that adds one string onto the end of another string. The operator symbols commonly used for concatenation are either "+" or "&". Although the "+" sign is the same symbol as that used in arithmetic *it has a completely different meaning* when used as a string operator. When the same operator symbol is used for operations on different data types the operator is said to be **overloaded.** Determining the appropriate meaning of the operator in a given situation is known as **disambiguation**. To avoid any ambiguity or confusion "&" will be used to represent concatenation in this text. Some examples follow.

15.40 Examples.

    a. "ALEX" & "JAMES" has the result "ALEXJAMES"

    b. "ALEX" & " " & "JAMES" has the result "ALEX JAMES"

    c. "ALEX" & " AND " & "JAMES" has the result "ALEX AND JAMES"

LOGIC RELATIONAL OPERATORS

15.41 Before considering Boolean operators that apply to Boolean values to give Boolean results we will consider **relational operators** that give Boolean values when applied to data types such as integers, reals and characters.

15.42 The relational logic operators are set out in the following table.

OPERATOR	MEANING
=	equal to
≠ or <> or !=	not equal to
<	less than
>	greater than
≤ or <=	less than or equal to
≥ or >=	greater than or equal to

15.43 Examples.

    a. $3 = 4$ is **false**

    b. $3 \neq 4$ is **true**

    c. $3 < 4$ is **true**

    d. $3 > 4$ is **false**

    e. $3 \leq 4$ is **true**

    f. $3 \geq 4$ is **false**

15.44 The relational logic operators can only be applied to characters if the characters have a defined order. For example, the ASCII characters have a defined order (see Fig. 2.4). In fact, the order of the ASCII characters has been chosen very carefully so as to be consistent with the numerical order of the digits 0 to 9 and the alphabetic sequence A to Z. Note, however, that in ASCII "A" < "B" but "a" > "B"! (see Fig. 2.4).

15.45 Propositions. A proposition is a statement that can be either **true** or **false.** For example, the statement "You are reading this book" is true, but the statement "3=4" is false. NB. Questions and exclamations are **not** propositions. Propositions have Boolean values and Boolean operations may be applied to them.

OPERATIONS ON BOOLEANS

15.46 The three basic Boolean operations are:

    a. NOT.

    b. OR.

    c. AND.

15.47 The "NOT" operation. Application of the NOT operation to a Boolean value is called **negation**. Negating a true value gives a false result and negating a false value gives a true result. The two possible cases are set out in the following table.

p	NOT p	
true	false	When proposition "p" is true "NOT p" is false.
false	true	When proposition "p" is false "NOT p" is true.

15.48 Truth tables. Tables like the one just given are called truth tables. They define logic operations by tabulating all possible operation cases and results.

15.49 The "OR" operation. First consider this example of the OR operation.

(3 > 5) OR (8 < 4)	false
(3 > 5) OR (8 > 4)	true
(3 < 5) OR (8 < 4)	true
(3 < 5) OR (8 > 4)	true

15.50 The truth table for the OR operation is given here.

p	q	p OR q
false	false	false
false	true	true
true	false	true
true	true	true

15.51 Inclusive and Exclusive ORs

a. In everyday usage the word OR has two possible meanings:

    i. OR can mean one or the other or both. (The **inclusive** OR.)

    ii. OR can mean one or the other but **not** both. (The **exclusive** OR.)

b. **Examples.**

    i. **Inclusive OR.** To qualify for a competition you might have to subscribe to a magazine or you might belong to a club. (You might do both.)

    ii. **Exclusive OR.** You are rich or you are poor. (You can't be both.)

You can see from the truth table that this OR operation is in fact an inclusive OR operation.

15.52 The "AND" operation is defined by the following truth table.

p	q	p AND Q
false	false	false
false	true	false
true	false	false
true	true	true

Note that *both* p and q must be true for p AND q to be true.

REPRESENTING OPERATIONS BY DIAGRAMS

15.53 Diagrammatic representations of operations can often aid understanding.

15.54 Simple examples.

a. 3+5 can be represented by:

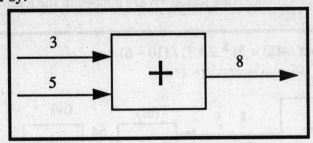

b. True OR False can be represented by:

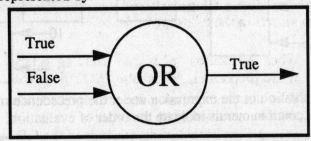

15.55 We will find a number of uses for these diagrams before we reach the end of this text. We will use them first in our discussion of *expressions*.

179

EXPRESSIONS

15.56 Expressions are formulae containing operations or combinations of operations. It is necessary to have rules that govern the order in which the operations are carried out. Such rules are called **rules of precedence**. Without rules of precedence many expressions would be ambiguous. For example, $3 + 4 * 5$ could mean *either* add 3 to 4 and multiply the result by 5 *or* multiply 4 by 5 and add the result to 3. The former evaluation gives the final result 35 whereas the latter evaluation gives the final result 23.

15.57 Here are examples that show how the potential ambiguities are overcome.

    a. The expression $3 + 4 * 5$ could mean

      either

      i. add 3 to 4 and then multiply that result (ie, 7) to 5 to give the final result (ie, 35).

      or

      ii. multiply 4 by 5 and then add that result (ie, 20) to 3 to give the final result (ie, 23).

    b. Case (a ii) is consistent with normal practice because, although it is natural to evaluate expressions by working from left to right, the rules of precedence require multiplication to be performed before addition.

    c. Parentheses may be used to override the order of operator precedence. So the expression $(3+4)*5$ would be evaluated as in a i because expressions within parentheses are evaluated first.

The following rules of precedence should be easier to follow if you relate them to the example just given.

15.58 Precedence rules for arithmetic expressions are:

    a. Operators of higher precedence are evaluated *before* operators of lower precedence.

    b. Operators of equal precedence are evaluated in the order they appear when scanning the expression from left to right.

    c. The inclusion of parentheses in the expression requires that the expression within parentheses be evaluated first by applying rules a, b and c.

The order of precedence is given in the following table.

ORDER OF PRECEDENCE	OPERATOR
4	− (unary)
3	↑
2	* mod div
1	+− (dyadic)

Fig. 15.4. Order of Precedence for Arithmetic Operators.

15.59 Example. The precedence rules just given are applied in the following expression and are illustrated by means of Fig. 15.5.

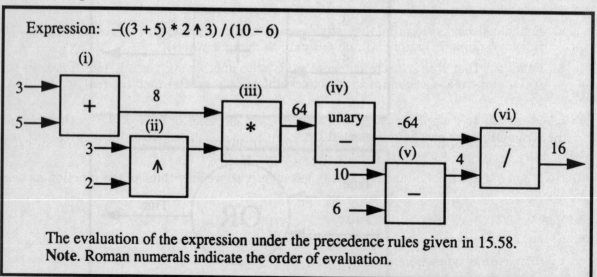

Expression: $-((3 + 5) * 2 \uparrow 3) / (10 - 6)$

The evaluation of the expression under the precedence rules given in 15.58.
Note. Roman numerals indicate the order of evaluation.

Fig. 15.5. Expression Evaluation.

15.60 For Boolean expressions the order of precedence is, from highest to lowest, NOT, AND, OR.

15.61 Mixed-mode expressions. It is possible for expressions to contain data of different types. Such expressions are called **mixed-mode** expressions. In most programming languages there are rules that restrict the use of mixed-mode expressions. For example, mixed-mode arithmetic, which involves mixing integers and reals, is governed by very strict rules in the programming language Pascal.

15.62 Mixed-mode expressions are always governed by carefully devised precedence rules. The precedence rules of 15.58 may be applied to mixed-mode expressions if used in conjunction with the orders of precedence specified in Fig. 15.6.

NB. Careful use of parentheses is needed for these expressions.

FUNCTIONS

15.63 Representing operations by means of operands and operator symbols proves to be unsatisfactory when devising new operations on a regular basis. In such cases the *functional notation,* borrowed from mathematics, is used.

At this point the reader familiar with mathematics should note that the things called "functions" in the subject computer science are defined differently from functions in mathematics, although they have many similar properties. Only computer science "functions" are discussed here.

ORDER OF PRECEDENCE	OPERATOR
8	− (unary)
7	↑
6	*/ div mod
5	+− (dyadic)
4	=≠<≤>≥
3	NOT
2	AND
1	OR

Fig. 15.6. Order of Precedence for General Expressions.

15.64 Functional notation. The operation "3 + 5" could be written in functional notation as "Add (3, 5)". Note the following points about this notation:

    a. Instead of using an operator symbol the action to be performed upon the data is identified by the function name, "Add" in this case.

    b. Function names help to convey the meaning of the function.

    c. What would be called operands in operation notation are called **arguments** (sometimes also called **parameters**) in functional notation.

    d. Function notation is easy to extend so as to allow for multiple arguments, eg, Add (3, 5, 2) could represent a function that performed 3 + 5 + 2.

15.65 Examples of functions.

    a. Functions that perform mathematical computations, such as Sine or absolute value. These functions use numeric arguments and evaluate to numeric results.

    b. Functions that *convert* from one numeric type to another such as an "Int" function, which has a real argument and evaluates to the largest integer not greater than the real, eg, Int(3.6) evaluates to 3.

    c. Functions that apply to characters to give their successor or predecessor in their character set.

    d. Functions that *convert* from characters to their integer ordinal value or vice versa. eg, a function with argument "A" that evaluates to 65 (see Fig. 2.4).

15.66 Note how the result of a function always has a type, so we may think of the function as being of that type.

SUMMARY

15.67 a. Data types were defined, including simple types and data structures.

    b. Simple data types were classified as:

        i. Numeric integer.

        ii. Numeric real.

        iii. Character.

      iv. Boolean (logical).

  c. Representations of data items of various types were discussed.

  d. Operations, operators and operands for various data types were introduced.

  e. Expressions and their precedence rules were introduced.

  f. Functions and functional notations were discussed.

POINTS TO NOTE

15.68 a. A data type is only fully defined if *both* its sets of values *and* its related operations are specified.

  b. Ensure that operator and operand used together are of consistent type when programming. That will guard against nonsensical operations being carried out at machine level, at which all data is in binary form. The rules of some languages enforce data type consistency.

STUDENT SELF-TESTING QUESTIONS

1. Show how the value 79_{10} may be represented in a 16-bit word as
   a. two BCD NUMERIC DIGITS
   b. two BCD 6-bit codes
   c. two ASCII characters, where an 8th bit is present in each code as an even parity bit.
   d. a pure binary natural number.
2. What two things must be specified in order to define a data type?
3. Distinguish between the terms "operation", "operator", "operand" and "function".
4. Suggest a probable fault with the way these expressions are written and a suitable correction.
   a. $15 <$ "26"
   b. $5 < 10$ **OR** 19
5. Evaluate these expressions:
   a. $((15 - 7)/2) * (-3 * 25)$
   b. $(3 < 9)$ **OR** $(7 < 2)$
   c. $((2 \uparrow 10 - 24) = 1000)$ **AND** $((2 \uparrow 3 = 16)$ **OR** $(24/2, 3 * 4))$
6. Suppose that a function called "ORD" takes an ASCII character as its argument and evaluates to the ordinal value of the character as defined in Fig. 2.4. For example ORD ("A") is 65. Also suppose that a function called "CHR" takes an integer argument and evaluates to the ASCII character as defined in Fig. 2.4. For example, CHR(65) = "A".
   Evaluate these expressions:
   a. ORD ("1") + ORD ("3")
   b. CHR(67) & CHR(65) & CHR(84)
   c. CHR(ORD("7") + 1)

QUESTIONS WITHOUT ANSWERS

7. What value does the binary code 01110101 represent in each of the following cases:
   a. A two-digit BCD numeric code.
   b. A pure binary integer.
   c. A single ASCII character.
   State any assumptions that you make.
8. Evaluate these expressions:
   a. $(17 \textbf{ div } 5) + (17 \textbf{ mod } 5 \geq (4 * (-2)))$
   b. **NOT** $((5 < 2)$ **OR** $(16 = 24))$
   c. $(2 \uparrow 7 = 128)$ **AND** $(2 \uparrow 9 - 512 = 0)$ **OR** $(12/4 \leq 5)$

GLOSSARY CHECKLIST

16: Program Structures

INTRODUCTION

16.1 This chapter introduces **program structures**, which are what we may call the forms in which program components are constructed, organised and interrelated.

16.2 In order to aid a clear understanding of the material covered in this chapter we start by providing the necessary background knowledge of programming languages and the forms in which programs are written.

16.3 When considering features of programs it pays to recognise how these features relate to the operational features of the computers for which the programs are written. Therefore the chapter is organised in a way that highlights these relationships.

16.4 Particular aspects covered in the chapter are:

    a. Language, its syntax and semantics.

    b. Data declarations.

    c. Basic operations on data.

    d. Control structures.

    e. Subprograms.

PROGRAMMING LANGUAGES

16.5 The subject of programming languages is covered fully in a number of later chapters. So, as was mentioned in the introduction, only background information needed for this chapter will be discussed here.

16.6 When learning a programming language we need to learn about two important aspects of the language:

    a. its **syntax** and

    b. its **semantics**.

16.7 The **syntax** of a language are the grammatical rules that govern the ways in which words, symbols, expressions and statements may be formed and combined.

16.8 The **semantics** of a language are the rules that govern its *meaning*. In the case of computer language, meaning is defined in terms of what happens when the program is executed.

16.9 **Natural languages and formal languages.** Languages used for everyday communication, such as English, French and Chinese, are called **Natural Languages**.

16.10 **Natural Languages** have complexities that make them unsuitable as computer-programming languages. Instructions written in such languages often suffer from ambiguities. For example, this simple English question has several interpretations: "Calculate 4 and 6 divided by 2".

It could mean add 4 to 6 and then divide that answer by 2, or divide 6 by 2 and then add that result to 4, or it could mean divide 4 by 2 to get one result and then divide 6 by 2 to get another result, and so on. Another example is "I want ham or eggs and chips".

16.11 **Formal Languages** differ from natural languages in that they have precise semantics. Properly defined programming languages are formal. Every instruction written in such languages has just one meaning.

16.12 In practical terms what all this boils down to is that when we learn a programming language, as we learn each new instruction, we must learn both its syntax (how to write it down correctly) and its semantics (what will happen when it is executed) so that we use it sensibly.

16.13 When we considered computer architecture in chapter 13, we saw that hardware could be viewed at different levels. The same is true of software. Some computer languages are at higher levels than others.

16.14 At machine level (13.15) the operations performed on data are very simple. Just to add together two numbers may take three of these simple operations. For each of these operations there will be one corresponding program instruction in what is called **machine language**. In the early days of computers all programs were written in machine language.

16.15 These days, programs are seldom written in machine language. Instead, programs are most frequently written in what are called **"high-level languages"**.

16.16 The program instructions in high-level languages are much closer to sentences in English or expressions in mathematics. This makes them easier to use than machine languages.

16.17 The price paid for using these easier and more powerful languages is that each high-level language program must first be translated into machine language because the computer can only operate using instructions in machine language. This translation is normally carried out by the computer.

16.18 Further details of programming languages at various levels, and of the translation processes involved, will be given in later chapters. In this chapter the examples will be given in forms akin to high-level languages. This should have the advantage of preventing the details of the hardware from obscuring programming concepts. This language form is a kind of **pseudocode** (See the Part introduction).

Note that program instructions written in high-level languages or pseudocode are normally called **statements.**

THE PROGRAM-LEVEL VIEW OF THE COMPUTER

16.19 When writing programs we need some concept of what the computer is doing when the program is used. This *program-level view of the computer* is much simpler than the "true" picture but is ideal for its purpose. This situation is comparable to a car driver's view of the car's controls. The driver merely thinks that when the accelerator is pressed harder the engine goes faster, without giving any thought to what actually happens under the car bonnet.

16.20 The main features of the computer are still visible in features of the language.

   a. Storage.

   b. Input and output.

   c. Operating on data.

   d. Control.

We will consider each of these in turn.

STORAGE

16.21 In all but the lowest level programming languages data items are identified by name rather than by their location addresses in main storage. The names that we associate with stored data values are called **identifiers** because an identifier is the name by which the data value may be identified.

16.22 **Constants and Variables.** An identifier is a **"constant"** if it is always associated with the same data value and it is a **"variable"** if its associated data value is allowed to change. Changing a variable's value implies changing what is stored.

16.23 **Literals.** When referring to letters or names in programs we must be careful to specify whether we mean them to be taken *literally* or be treated as identifiers. When names or letters are used literally we call them **literals,** and we enable them to be distinguished from identifiers by placing them within quotation marks. So the instruction PRINT "N" means print the letter N, and the instruction PRINT N means print the value associated with N. Note that PRINT 2+4 means print the values 6, but PRINT "2+2" means print the character "2" followed by the character "+" followed by the character "2".

DATA DECLARATIONS

16.24 The data types of constants and variables must be defined within a program so that the appropriate operations may be performed upon the data values and so that the appropriate amounts of storage space can be assigned. Such information should be given at the start of each program.

16.25 Some programming languages have special statements that might be used for this purpose. They are called **"declarative statements"** because they state properties of the data and are not executed. They differ in that respect from most of the statements to be discussed in the remainder of this chapter which are executed, and are called **"procedural statements"**.

16.26 A typical data declaration is given in Fig. 16.1. Most of the data items declared in Fig. 16.1 will be used in later examples. Two more have been added to make the example complete; the constant "pi", used in mathematics, and a Boolean value "rate-code-valid".

16.27 Some programming languages declare data types in very different ways. For example, in BASIC the use of a "$" sign at the end of an identifier declares the variable to be a string. The absence of the "$" declares the variable type to be numeric by default. In BASIC variables need not be declared in declarative statements. In the language "C" the data type name appears in front of the variable name. So, for example in C the integer variable "i" might be declared as "int i".

16.28 In the declaration of the real constant pi in Fig 16.1 a value has explicitly been **assigned** to the identifier "pi". All the other identifiers in the example have no values associated with them at the end of the declaration.

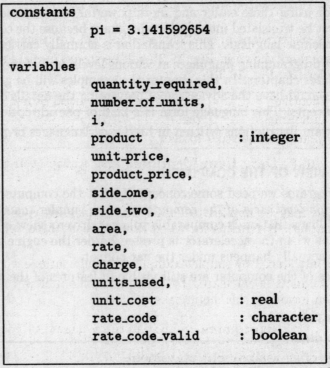

```
constants
        pi = 3.141592654

variables
        quantity_required,
        number_of_units,
        i,
        product                 : integer
        unit_price,
        product_price,
        side_one,
        side_two,
        area,
        rate,
        charge,
        units_used,
        unit_cost               : real
        rate_code               : character
        rate_code_valid         : boolean
```

Note. Variables of the same type are presented in a list separated by commas.

Fig. 16.1 An Example of a Data Declaration.

16.29 A variable name does not have an associated value until it has been assigned one. This may be done either by using an assignment statement (details follow in paragraph 39) or by using them as arguments in input functions (details follow in 15.33). This process of assigning values to variables before using them is called "initialisation".

16.30 Initialisation must be done in a systematic way. Otherwise, unexpected things may happen during the program's execution if non-initialised variables are used as operands. The programme may give an error message and stop, or possibly worse still, carry on and give the wrong results or cause something dangerous to happen.

INPUT AND OUTPUT

16.31 Programming languages have special functions for dealing with input and output. Common names for these functions are **input, read, get accept, output, write, print, put** and **display**.

16.32 It is not appropriate to consider all possible cases at this stage. Rather, we will take one typical example to illustrate the basic ideas.

a. PART OF THE PROGRAM (in pseudocode)	b. OUTPUT DURING PROGRAM EXECUTION (What appears on the monitor screen.)
output("Key in the unit price in pounds") input(unit_price) output("Key in the quantity required") input(quantity_required)	Key in the unit price in pounds 1.25 Key in the quantity required 20

Note.

i. The real number 1.25 and the integer 20 are keyed in by the user and are displayed on the monitor screen as they are keyed.

ii. Outputs of variables are also possible although not shown here.

Fig. 16.2. Programming Simple Input and Output.

16.33 Suppose the data is input at a keyboard input, that output appears on a monitor screen and that two numbers are to be input. Let us suppose that these two numbers represent the unit price and quantity purchased of some product from which it is intended to calculate the price for all the products. The instructions in the program dealing with the input might appear in a form similar to that shown in Fig. 16.2a. In Fig. 16.2b we see what would appear on the monitor screen when the program was executed.

16.34 Try to rewrite these instructions in the language that you are using as part of your course.

16.35 When input, the numbers shown in Fig. 16.2b will be stored in main storage and referred to by the appropriate identifier (see Fig. 16.3).

Identifier	Data Type	Associated Stored Data Value
unit_price	real	1.25
quantity_required	integer	20

Fig. 16.3. Data Item Identifiers and Associated Stored Values.

OPERATIONS ON DATA

16.36 The operations that may be applied to data items of various types were discussed in some detail in the previous chapter. It remains for us to examine how these operations are incorporated into programs.

16.37 The ideas are best introduced by simple example. We will continue with the example given in 16.33.

16.38 The price for all products is calculated by multiplying the unit price by the quantity required. A program instruction for doing this might take the form:

```
product_price := unit_price * quantity_required
```

This is an example of an **assignment statement**.

16.39 The **assignment statement** has three basic components:

a. An **assignment operator**, which is represented by some appropriate symbols (in the example ":=" is used).

b. A **result**, with an identifier ("products_price") to the left of the assignment operator;

c. an **expression**, to the right of the assignment operator.

16.40 Performing this instruction involves fetching the values associated with the operands in the expression from main storage, performing the required operations (multiplication in this case) and then storing the result in the location(s) in storage associated with the identifier "products_price". Thus, the outcome will be that the value of the result has been *assigned* to the identifier "products_price".

16.41 In some cases the same identifier may appear on *both* sides of an assignment statement. This often occurs when counting or accumulating totals.

16.42 **Examples.** Suppose we wished a program to count how many inputs had been made. To do this we could place this assignment statement at the start of a program to *initialise* the counter to zero:

```
number_of_inputs := 0
```

and place this assignment statement after each input instruction to count the inputs:

```
number_of_inputs := number_of_inputs + 1
```

NB. The result of evaluating the expression on the right-hand side of the assignment statement *replaces* the value associated with the identifier "number_of_inputs" *before* the expression is evaluated.

16.43 The exact form of the assignment statement varies from language to language. The examples just given take the form used in a number of languages including Pascal, Modula and ADA. Some readers may be using the language BASIC, which has an assignment statement in the form:

```
LET P = U * Q
```

In COBOL the assignment could take the form:

```
MULTIPLY U BY Q GIVING P
```

In C the assignment could take the form:

```
number_of_inputs := number_of_inputs + 1
```

or using a C shorthand for an **increment** ie, increasing a variable by 1, it could take the form:

```
number_of_inputs++
```

Note that decreasing a variable by 1 is called **decrementing**.

CONTROL

16.44 The order in which program instructions are performed by the computer must be carefully controlled, and programming languages contain features that allow the order of instruction execution to be controlled.

16.45 All programming problems, no matter how complex, may be reduced to combinations of controlled sequences, selections or repetitions of basic operations on data. This fact was established by two Italian computer scientists, C. Bohm and G. Jacopini in 1966. It is part of the important theory that is behind the concept of **"structured programming"**, a term first used by Professor E. Dijkstra in the mid-1960s and now widely used and misused!

CONTROL STRUCTURES

16.46 Program control structures are used to regulate the order in which program statements are executed. They fall into three categories:

a. **sequences**

b. **selections**

c. **repetitions** (sometimes called **iterations**.

We will consider these three categories in turn.

SEQUENCES

16.47 In the absence of selections or repetitions program statements are executed in the **sequence** in which they appear in the program:

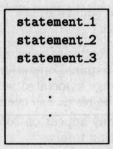

```
statement_1
statement_2
statement_3
        .
        .
        .
```

16.48 In the following paragraphs we will use the term **"statement sequence"** to mean a sequence of one or more statements.

SELECTIONS

16.49 **Selections** form part of the decision-making facilities within programming languages. They allow alternative actions to be taken according to the conditions that exist at particular stages in program executions.

16.50 Conditions are normally in the form of expressions that when evaluated give Boolean results (**true** or **false**).

16.51 **The if_then_else statement.** Versions of this simple selection statement appear in most high-level languages. A typical form of syntax for this statement is given here:

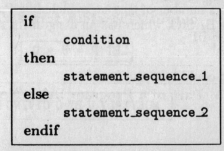

```
if
        condition
then
        statement_sequence_1
else
        statement_sequence_2
endif
```

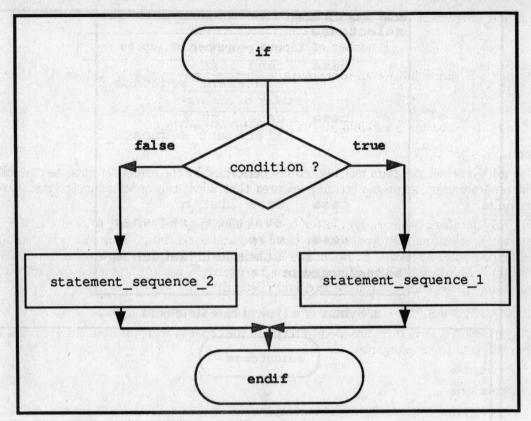

Fig. 16.4. The Semantics of the Selection if_then_else.

Note.

i. In this and further examples comments within programs will be enclosed between the symbols "(*" and "*)".

ii. In this example "side_1", "side_2" and "side_3" are all real numbers.

```
if
    (* The value of the sides are invalid *)
    (side_one <= 0)
    OR
    (side_two <= 0)
then
    output("The sides do not form a rectangle.")
else
    area := side_one * side_two
    output("The area is ", area)
    if
        side_one = side_two
    then
        output("The sides form a square.")
    else
        output("The sides form a rectangle.")
    endif
endif
```

Fig. 16.5. Part of a Program Using Nested if_then_elses.

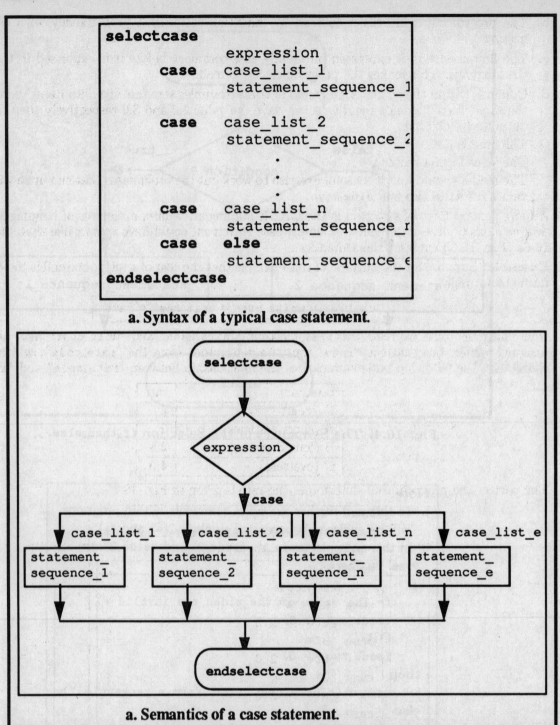

```
selectcase
            expression
    case    case_list_1
            statement_sequence_1

    case    case_list_2
            statement_sequence_2
                    .
                    .
                    .
    case    case_list_n
            statement_sequence_n
    case    else
            statement_sequence_e
endselectcase
```

a. Syntax of a typical case statement.

a. Semantics of a case statement.

Fig. 16.6. A Case Statement.

16.52 The semantics of this statement is as follows. When the statement is executed the condition's expression is evaluated. If the result of the evaluation is **true** then **statement_sequence_1** will be executed *otherwise* **statement_sequence_2** will be executed. After *either* **statement_sequence_1** or **statement_sequence_2** has been executed the statement following "endif" is executed (see Fig. 16.4).

16.53 **Example.** In this simple example we consider part of a program in which two real numbers representing the two sides of a rectangle are to be used to determine the area of the rectangle and to indicate whether or not the sides form a square (see Fig. 16.5).

16.54 Note the following points about this example.

    a. Within the first **if_then_else** statement there is another **if_then_else statement**. This is an example of **"nesting"**, ie, a structure containing other structures of the same type.

b. The program is made easier to read by indenting statements progressively with each level of nesting.

c. The first condition is expressed informally as a comment before it is expressed in the syntax of the language. This makes the program easier to read.

d. Commas within the output statements in these examples separate the data items to be output on the same line. If side_one and side_two have the value 2.0 and 3.0 respectively then the program output will look like:

The area is 6.0

The sides form a rectangle.

The reader should find it a useful exercise to work out the other cases that can arise with different values for side_one and side_two.

16.55 A more general form of selection is the **CASE** statement. Again, a number of languages have their own versions of case statements. A simple case statement could have syntax like that shown in Fig. 16.6a. Fig. 16.6b explains the semantics.

16.56 **Example.** Suppose for the purpose of this example that the cost of a telephone call is to be calculated from the formula

```
charge := units_used * unit_cost * rate
```

where all four items are reals. Also assume that "units_used" and "unit_cost" have already been assigned values, but that the "rate" must be determined from the "rate_code", which is a single character. The following table summarises the relationship between "rate_code" and "rate".

rate_code	rate
L (local)	2
A (short distance)	2
B (long distance)	2.5
C (overseas)	4.0

The part of the program that determines the rate is given in Fig. 16.7

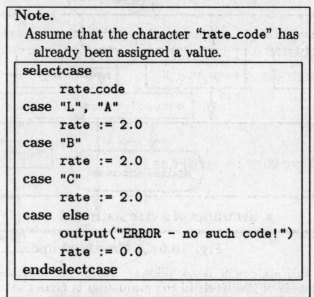

```
Note.
    Assume that the character "rate_code" has
    already been assigned a value.
selectcase
        rate_code
case "L", "A"
        rate := 2.0
case "B"
        rate := 2.0
case "C"
        rate := 2.0
case else
        output("ERROR - no such code!")
        rate := 0.0
endselectcase
```

Fig. 16.7. An Example of Using a Case Statement.

REPETITIONS

16.57 There are many programming problems in which the same sequence of statements needs to be performed again and again for a definite or indefinite number of times. The repeated performance of the same statements is often called **"looping"**.

16.58 Fig. 16.8 shows three common **"loop constructs"** for performing repetitions. The "while" and "repeat" loops are used for **indefinite repetitions**. That is, they do not define the number of repetitions that will occur when the loop is executed. They merely give conditions for looping to stop. The "for" loop is used for **definite repetition**. It defines the number of repetitions that will occur during execution.

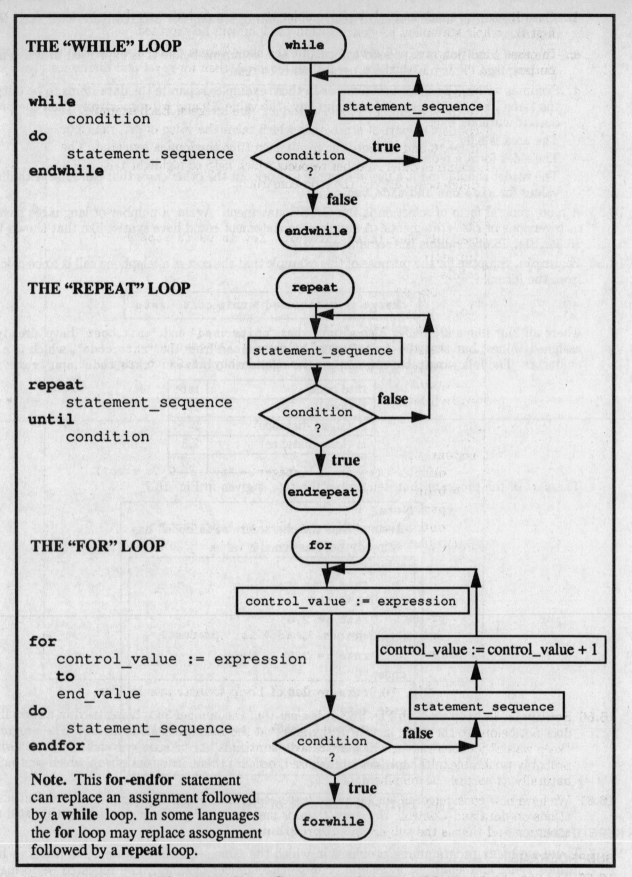

Fig. 16.8. Loop Constructs for Repetitions.

16.59 Examine Fig. 16.9, which gives examples of using the three loop constructs.

 a. In case A, if the number 99 is keyed in first then the statement sequence within the whole loop will not be executed at all.

b. Case B uses a repeat loop. It looks simpler than case A, but even if the number 99 is keyed in first the whole statement sequence within the loop will be executed.

c. In case C the program will always output the same values. The product will be calculated and output, first for i = 1, then for i = 2 then for i = 3, then for i = 4 and finally for i = 5.

Note.

In these example "i" and "product" are integers. Each example consists of part of a program which takes the value of "i", multiplies it by 16 and outputs the result each time the loop is repeated. The examples differ in other respects which help to highlight the differences between the loop constructs.

A.
```
output("Key in an integer.  Key in 99 to stop")
input(i)
while
    i <> 99
do
    product := i * 16
    output(i," times ", 15," is ",product)
    output("Key in an integer.  Key in 99 to stop")
    input(i)
endwhile
```

B.
```
repeat
    output("Key in an integer.  Key in 99 to stop")
    input(i)
    product := i * 16
    output(i," times ", 15," is ",product)
until i = 99
```

C.
```
for i := 1 to 5
    product := i * 16
    output(i," times ", 15," is ",product)
endfor
```

Fig. 16.9. Examples of Loop Constructs in Use.

16.60 Sentinels. In example A in Fig. 16.9 it is clear that the number 99 is being used in a special way. It does not belong to the data, instead it signifies that the data has come to an end. The program must "keep watch" for such values, which are called **"sentinels"** or **"rogue values"**. The term sentinel is probably preferable, although less widely used, because there are situations in which sentinels occur naturally as part of the genuine data.

16.61 We have now considered all the language features listed in 16.20: Storage, Input and Output, Operations on data and Control. However, there is one aspect of program structuring that still requires attention and that is the subject of **subprograms**.

SUBPROGRAMS

16.62 The term **"subprogram"** may be used to describe a component part of a program. Used loosely the term may merely refer to any set of statements forming part of a program used to perform a specific task. However, a properly constructed subprogram should be self-contained, perform well-defined operations on well-defined data and have an internal structure that is independent of the program in which it is contained. When a subprogram has all these properties it is sometimes called a program **module**.

16.63 The two basic types of subprograms are:

    a. functions

    and

    b. procedures.

Note that here the term "procedure" is being used with a far more precise meaning than that used previously (see the Part introduction). Unfortunately, there is some considerable variation in the use of terms such as "function", "procedure", "module" and "subprogram". Within this text every effort has been made to use the most widely adopted terms and to use them consistently. Where general and specific meanings exist the context should make it clear which sense is intended.

FUNCTIONS

16.64 Many high-level programming languages have inbuilt functions such as those mentioned in 15.65. A common example is the square root function "sqrt". The reader may remember that the square root of a number x is that number y with the property $y^2 = x$. thus the square root of 9 is 3 because $3^2 = 9$. We will assume, for the sake of mathematical simplicity, that the square root function in the following example is only to be used for positive arguments.

16.65 Fig. 16.10 shows a simple program using an inbuilt square root function.

```
program Find_root
    (*
    This program has the name "Find_root".
    It inputs a number and outputs the
    value of the square root of the number.
    *)
variables
    number,
    root     : real
Begin
    output("Key in the number whose square root you require.")
    input(number)
    if
        number < 0
    then
        output("No root is obtainable for negative numbers.")
    else
        root := sqrt(number)
        output("The square root of ",number " is ", root)
    endif
end
```

Fig. 16.10. A Simple Program Using an Inbuilt Function.

16.66 When a required function is not inbuilt it is sometimes possible for the programmer to define it for him or herself. Unfortunately, full facilities to do this are a less common feature of programming languages despite their usefulness.

16.67 Suppose we wish to have a function for calculating the area of a rectangle, as we did in Fig. 16.5. It may be argued that this operation is a little too simple to merit defining a special function but it serves as a useful example nevertheless.

16.68 The program that uses the function will contain a **function declaration**. This declaration *defines* the function. The function will also be used or "**called**" within the sequence of executable statements. Fig. 16.11 shows the relevant parts of the program.

16.69 The arguments used in the function declaration, ie, "`first_side`" and "`second_side`", are called "**formal arguments**". The arguments used in the **function call** are called "**actual arguments**".

PROCEDURES

16.70 Any defined way of carrying out some actions may be called a "**procedure**", but here we are using the term more precisely.

16.71 Programming procedures are defined operations on defined data and may be used as program components.

16.72 Procedure definitions are similar to function definitions, but procedure calls are statements whereas function calls appear in programs as expressions. These points should be clearer after the following example.

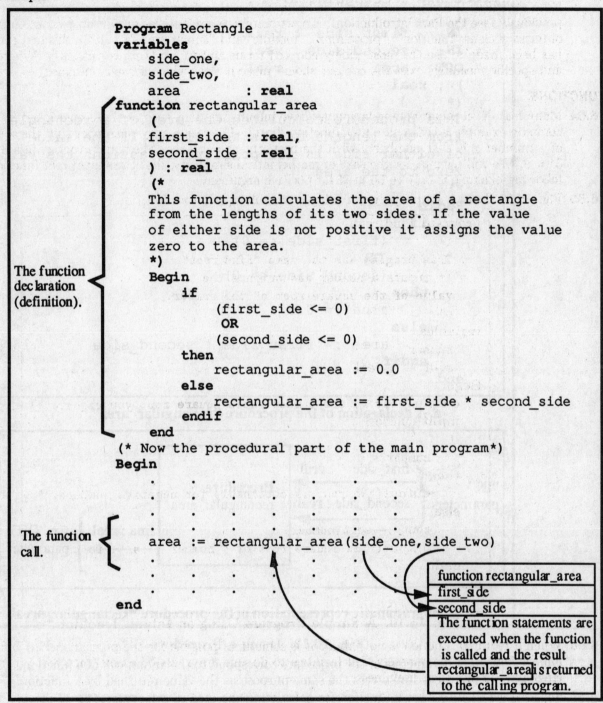

```
                    Program Rectangle
                    variables
                        side_one,
                        side_two,
                        area        : real
                    function rectangular_area
                        (
                        first_side  : real,
                        second_side : real
                        ) : real
                        (*
                        This function calculates the area of a rectangle
                        from the lengths of its two sides. If the value
                        of either side is not positive it assigns the value
                        zero to the area.
                        *)
                        Begin
                            if
                                (first_side <= 0)
                                 OR
                                (second_side <= 0)
                            then
                                rectangular_area := 0.0
                            else
                                rectangular_area := first_side * second_side
                            endif
                        end
                    (* Now the procedural part of the main program*)
                    Begin
                        .   .   .   .   .   .   .
                        .   .   .   .   .   .   .
                        .   .   .   .   .   .   .
                        .   .   .   .   .   .   .
                        area := rectangular_area(side_one,side_two)
                        .   .   .   .   .   .   .
                        .   .   .   .   .   .   .
                        .   .   .   .   .   .   .
                    end
```

The function declaration (definition).

The function call.

function rectangular_area
first_side
second_side
The function statements are executed when the function is called and the result rectangular_area is returned to the calling program.

Fig. 16.11. Declaring and Using Functions.

16.73 **A procedure call** is a program statement. This point will be easier to understand if we compare a procedure call with a function call. The function call in Fig 16.11 had the form:

```
area := rectangular_area (side_one, side_two)
```

Had an equivalent procedure been used instead the procedure call could have taken the form:

```
call rectangular_area (side_one, side_two, area)
```

16.74 **Parameters.** In the procedure example just given "side_one", "side_two" and "area" are the "actual parameters" of the procedure. The **formal parameters** are "first_side" and "second_side".

The reader will no doubt have noticed the similarity with the **"actual arguments"** and **"formal arguments"** of functions. However, there are some important differences. To see these, first consider Fig. 16.12.

```
procedure rectangular_area
    (
    IN      first_side  : real,
    IN      second_side : real,
    OUT     area        : real
    ) : real
    (*
    This procedure calculates the area of a rectangle
    from the lengths of its two sides. If the value
    of either side is not positive it assigns the valu
    zero to the area.
    *)
    Begin
        if
            (first_side <= 0)
            OR
            (second_side <= 0)
        then
            area := 0.0
        else
            area := first_side * second_side
        endif
    end
```

a. A declaration of the procedure "rectangular_area".

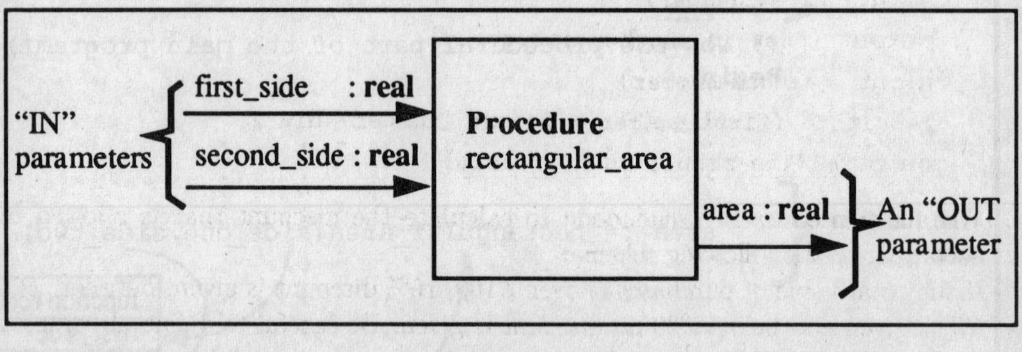

b. A diagrammatic representation of the procedure "rectangular_area".

Fig. 16.12. Using a Procedure.

16.75 Note that the **IN** parameters of the procedure correspond to the arguments of a function. The **OUT** parameter of the procedure serves the same purpose as the value returned by a function.

16.76 There is a third type of parameter not present in this example, the **IN-OUT** parameter, which is used when data is to be passed into a procedure, manipulated by it in some defined way and then passed out again.

16.77 There are a number of further features of functions and procedures still to be discussed but they fit more usefully into the remaining chapters in this Part.

SUMMARY

16.78 **a.** The idea of program structures was introduced.

b. The syntax, semantics and other basic properties of programming languages were introduced.

c. Data declarations were explained.

d. Identifiers, constants, variables and literals were defined.

e. Simple input and output functions were explained.

f. The assignment operation was discussed.

g. Control structures were introduced and explained including:

   i. **Statement sequences**

   ii. **Selections:** `if_then_else`, and `case`

   iii. **Repetitions:** `While-loops`, `Repeat-loops` and `For-loops`.

h. Subprograms were introduced, including the basic features and uses of:

   i. **functions**

   ii. **procedures.**

POINTS TO NOTE

16.79 a. This chapter has placed an emphasis on the "building blocks" from which programs are constructed. The *method* for designing complete programs from these building blocks *will be explained in the following chapters*. Also, later chapters go into more details of how the various program components work. For example, the mechanisms for dealing with parameters are explained.

STUDENT SELF-TESTING QUESTIONS

1. Explain the difference between syntax and semantics.

2. Distinguish between constants, variables and literals.

3. Using the definition of **input** and **output** given in 16.33 show what would be displayed on the monitor screen if the following statements were executed.

   NB. Assume

   i. the values input are 6 and 8.

   ii. all variables have been declared as integers.

```
output("Key in an integer.")
input (first_number)
output ("Key in another integer.")
input (second_number)
result := (first_number + second _number) div 2
output ("The result is ", result)
```

4. Write a procedure in pseudocode to calculate the discount that is allowed on purchases according to the following scheme:
   If the total value of purchases is over £100, 10% discount is given, between £20 and £100, 5% is given and below £20 no discount is given. Be careful to define all your variables.

5. Explain the differences in use between actual parameters and formal parameters.

QUESTIONS WITHOUT ANSWERS

6. Write a program that uses the procedure of question 4 and that deals with several purchase totals in turn terminated by a negative purchase total.

7. Use a case statement to write the following procedure. The IN parameter is a single character. If the character is an octal digit, then the corresponding binary value is output as a literal string. For example, if the parameter is "3" the string "011" will be output. Any other character should result in "not octal" being output.

GLOSSARY CHECKLIST

17: Data Structures

INTRODUCTION

17.1 This chapter explains what **data structures** are. It introduces the more important and common data structures and explains their uses in programming.

17.2 A **data structure** is an organised grouping of data items treated as a unit. They may be regarded as complex data types (15.3). Data structures are sometimes called **"data aggregates"**.

17.3 The principal data structures considered in this chapter are:

a. Arrays.

b. Strings.

c. Records.

d. Lists.

e. Trees.

17.4 The operations associated with these data structures will be explained and the most common programming methods related to these structures will be described with the aid of suitable examples.

17.5 There are so very many different types of data structure and so many related processing activities. Therefore, the discussion of some topics will be postponed until later chapters.

ARRAYS

17.6 In many situations, sets of data items such as the set of examination marks for a class, may be conveniently arranged into a sequence and referred to by a single identifier, eg:

$$MARK = (56\ 42\ 89\ 65\ 48)$$

Such an *arrangement* is a data structure called an **array**.

17.7 **Individual data items in the array** may be referred to separately by stating their position in the array. Thus MARK(1) refers to 56, MARK(2) refers to 42, MARK(3) refers to 89, and so on. The position numbers given in parentheses are called **subscripts**. Variables may be used as subscripts, eg, MARK(i), so when i = 2 we are referring to MARK(2), ie, 42, and when i = 4 we are referring to MARK(4), ie, 65.

SIMPLE ARRAY HANDLING

17.8 The basic methods used will be explained by means of examples. Suppose that individual exam marks are to be read into an array and, further, suppose that the largest mark, smallest mark, average mark, total mark and number of marks below the average are to be calculated and output.

17.9 The program to do this task will be easier to understand if taken in steps. First of all we can identify four main stages in the program:

a. Input all the data.

b. Calculate the largest mark, smallest mark, total mark and average mark.

c. Calculate the number of marks below the average.

d. Output the results.

17.10 These stages suggest four corresponding stages in the program. An outline program is shown in Fig. 17.1. Note that the first two stages of the program are in the form of procedures. The two accompanying procedure declarations have been omitted from Fig. 17.1 because they are to be discussed separately in the following paragraphs. The third stage is a function that is set as a question at the end of this chapter.

17.11 First we shall consider the input of the data into the array. Examine Fig. 17.2, which shows the details of the procedure declaration.

17.12 Note the following points about the procedure in Fig. 17.2:

a. The formal parameter "number_of_marks" and "marks" are both OUT parameter. In this example they have the same identifiers as the actual parameters used, but this makes no difference to their meaning.

```
Program    Marks
           (*
               This program inputs a set of not more than 100 marks into an array,
               determines the lowest mark, higher mark, total mark, average mark and
               number of marks below the average. It then outputs each of the values
               it has determined.
           *)
variables
               number_of_marks,
               number_below_average      : integer
               total_mark,
               smallest_mark,
               largest_mark,
               average_mark              : real
           (*
               The next declaration indicates that "mark" is an array able
               to hold up to 100 real numbers.
           *)
               mark      : array[1..100] of real
Begin
           (*
               Determine how may marks are to be input and input
               them into the array.
           *)
               call  input_marks(number_of_marks,mark)
               (* Calculate the required values. *)
               call  calculate_results
                                   (
                                   number_of_marks,
                                   mark,
                                   total_mark,
                                   smallest_mark,
                                   largest_mark,
                                   average_mark
                                   )
               number_below_average := below_average(number_of_marks, mark, average_mark)
               (* Output the results *)
               output("Number of marks entered ",number_of_marks)
               output ("Smallest mark: ",smallest_mark,"Largest mark: ",largest_mark)
               output ("Total mark: ",total_mark,"Average mark: ",average_mark)
               output("There were ",number_below_average,"marks below average.")
end
```

Fig. 17.1. Outline Program for an Array-Handling Problem.

b. The variable "subscript" is a **local variable**, ie, it is used within the procedure and is only defined there. In contrast, variables that are defined throughout the program are called **global** variables. In general terms it is bad practice to *use* variables globally. They should always be passed into procedures as parameters if they are to be used there. This matter will be discussed more fully in a later chapter.

c. If the user of the program repeatedly fails to key in a valid value for "number_of_marks" the procedure repeatedly outputs an error message and asks the user to try again. A more sophisticated procedure might be designed to abort the procedure after some specific number of errors.

d. In the for_loop in the last part of the procedure the subscript is increased by one each time the loop is repeated. So, for example, if `number_of_marks` = 3 the loop is equivalent to:

```
output("key in a mark")
input(mark(1))
output("key in a mark")
input(mark(2))
output("key in a mark")
input(mark(3))
```

17.13 Now for the second procedure, which is called "`calculate_results`" (Fig. 17.3). Note that this procedure relies upon the fact that there will be at least one mark value in the "mark" array. In this case it is a reasonable assumption because of the way "`input_marks`" is written. In general, however, it is a good idea to incorporate checks on IN parameters of procedures if their validity cannot be guaranteed.

```
procedure          input_marks
                           (
                           OUT number_of_marks :  integer
                                 mark                :  array[1..100]of real
                           )
            (*
                   This procedure gets the user to key in the number of marks
                   to be entered, which must be an integer between 1 and 100
                   inclusive.  Then it gets the user to key in the numbers which
                   it stores in the array.
            *)
variables
            subscript :  integer
Begin

            (* Get the user to key in the number of marks.  *)
            output("Key in the number of marks to be entered.")
            output("At least one mark and not more than 100 marks")
            output("may be entered.")
            input(number_of_marks)
            while
                   (* invalid number entered *)
                   (number_of_marks < 1)
                   OR
                   (number_of_marks > 100)
            do
                   output("ERROR - number must be between 1 and 100")
                   output("Please key in the correct value.")
                   input(number_of_marks)
            endwhile
            (* Get the user to key numbers into the array *)
            for subscript:  = 1 to number_of_marks
                output("key in a mark")
                input(mark(subscript))
            endfor
   end
```

Fig. 17.2. A Procedure for the Input of Numbers of an Array.

```
procedure   calculate_results
                                    (
                            IN   number_of_marks : integer
                                 mark             : array[1..100]of real
                            OUT  total_so_far,
                                 smallest_so_far,
                                 largest_so_far,
                                 average_mark   : real
                                    )
            (*
              This procedure finds the smallest mark, the largest mark, the
              total of all the marks and the average of all the marks.
            *)
variables
            subscript           : integer
Begin
            (* Initialise the total, smallest and largest values  *)
            total_so_far := 0
            smallest_so_far := mark(1)
            largest_so_far := mark(1)
            (*
              Take each mark in turn adding it to the total and checking it
              for any change to the smallest or largest value met so far.
            *)
            for    subscript := 1 to number_of_marks
                   total_so_far := total_so_far + mark(subscript)
                   if
                        mark(subscript) > largest_so_far
                   then
                        largest_so_far := mark(subscript)
                   else
                        if
                           mark(subscript) < smallest_so_far
                        then
                           smallest_so_far := mark(subscript)
                        endif
                   endif
            endfor
            average_mark := total_so_far/number_of_marks
            (*
              There must be at least one mark so division by zero cannot
              occur.
            *)
end
```

Fig. 17.3. A Procedure for Calculating Results.

OTHER FEATURES OF ARRAYS

17.14 Array elements. The individual data items in an array are often called its **elements**. Strictly speaking, however, a data item *occupies* an element, ie, elements, rather like pigeonholes, are regarded as locations into which data items may be placed and removed.

17.15 Main storage as an array. The reader may have observed a close similarity between arrays and the operational characteristics of main storage. Indeed we may regard main storage as an array in

202

which:

a. Locations correspond to elements, and

b. Location addresses correspond to subscripts.

One particular use of this fact is that skills learned in handling arrays are transferable to the handling of storage.

17.16 **Matrices** are arrays containing only numbers and no alphabetic data. (One **matrix**, many **matrices**.)

17.17 **Two-dimensional arrays** have elements arranged into rows and columns and are used for a variety of data tables. For example, the examination marks of a class for several subjects could be placed in a two dimensional array thus:

Pupil or Row Number	English Column 1	Maths Column 2
1	A(1,1) = 56	A(1,2) = 44
2	A(2,1) = 42	A(2,2) = 36
3	A(3,1) = 89	A(3,2) = 73
4	A(4,1) = 65	A(4,2) = 86
5	A(5,1) = 48	A(5,2) = 51

This table can be represented in an array called $A = \begin{bmatrix} 56 & 44 \\ 42 & 36 \\ 89 & 73 \\ 65 & 86 \\ 48 & 51 \end{bmatrix}$

Individual elements can be specified by two subscripts used like map references. **Rows** 1st, **Columns** 2nd. (To remember this order think of **Rhubarb and Custard**.) eg. A(3,1) = 88; A(4,2) =86. Again subscripts may be variables, as for a one-dimensional array, so for A(r,c), if r = 3 and c = 2 we are referring to A(3,2) = 73.

17.18 **Array handling.** In this example the data is entered row by row. The pseudo-code shown in Fig. 17.4 shows part of a procedure that reads data into the array. Assume that in the first part of the procedure valid values for the number of rows and columns in the array have been input.

```
Note.    "number_of_rows" and "number_of_columns" are
         integer numbers to which valid values have been assigned.
         "row_position" and "column_position" are local integers.
         "A" is an array of real numbers.

for      row_position := 1 to number_of_rows
             for column_position := 1 to number_of_columns
                 output("Key in value for row, ",row_position,
                         "column ",column_position)
                 input(A(row_position, column_position))
             endfor
endfor
```

Fig. 17.4. Part of a Procedure to Read Data into a 2D Array.

SORTING AN ARRAY

17.19 There are many situations in which the data items within elements of an array need to be rearranged into an ascending or descending sequence. The order of the sequence is often based upon the numerical or alphabetic order of the data. For example, the data in the "mark" array of 17.6 could be sorted (ie, re-arranged into order) from

$$MARK = (56\ 42\ 89\ 65\ 48)$$

into *ascending sequence* to become

$$MARK = (42\ 48\ 56\ 65\ 89).$$

```
procedure    sort_marks(IN        number_of_marks : integer
                        IN-OUT mark               : array [1..100] of real
              (*
                  This procedure takes in the array "marks", sorts it into
                  ascending numerical order using a straight insertion
                  sort and returns it.
              *)
variables
              current_value          : real
              current_value_position,
              pointer_position        : integer
Begin
              (* Start at element 1 *)
              current_value_position := 1
              while
                 (* some elements have not yet been reached *)
                 current_value_position < number_of_marks
              do
                 current_value_position := current_value_position + 1
                 (* get the current value *)
                 current_value := mark(current_value_position)
                 (*
                     put it in its correct position relative to the present
                     and lower elements
                 *)
                 (* set a pointer to the current value position *)
                 pointer_position := current_value_position
                 while
                        (* pointer not at insert position *)
                        (pointer_position > 1)
                        AND
                        (current_value < mark(pointer_position - 1))
                 do
                        (* copy adjacent value up to pointer position *)
                        mark(pointer_position) := mark(pointer_position - 1)
                        (* move pointer position down one *)
                        pointer_position := pointer_position - 1
                 endwhile
                 (* insert value *)
                 mark(pointer_position) := current_value
              endwhile
end
```

Note. The expression at the start of the inner while loop is assumed to evaluate to **false** when **pointer_position = 1**, ie, the left-most operand will be evaluated first so that **mark(0)** is not evaluated.

Fig. 17.5. A Straight Insertion Sort Procedure.

17.20 There are many methods of sorting data. The following example is based on a simple method called "**straight insertion sort**". This method is effective when sorting small arrays, but is rather slow when sorting larger arrays. A superior but more complicated method will be described later.

17.21 A procedure for the straight insertion sort is given in Fig. 17.5. Fig. 17.5 should be read in conjunction with the example in Fig. 17.6.

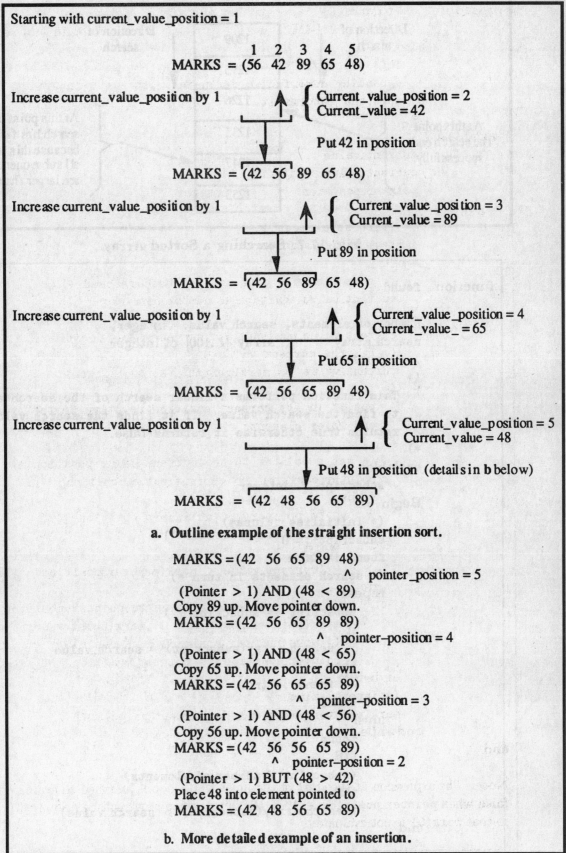

Starting with current_value_position = 1

$$\begin{array}{ccccc} 1 & 2 & 3 & 4 & 5 \end{array}$$
MARKS = (56 42 89 65 48)

Increase current_value_position by 1   Current_value_position = 2
Current_value = 42

Put 42 in position

MARKS = (42 56 89 65 48)

Increase current_value_position by 1   Current_value_position = 3
Current_value = 89

Put 89 in position

MARKS = (42 56 89 65 48)

Increase current_value_position by 1   Current_value_position = 4
Current_value_ = 65

Put 65 in position

MARKS = (42 56 65 89 48)

Increase current_value_position by 1   Current_value_position = 5
Current_value = 48

Put 48 in position (details in b below)

MARKS = (42 48 56 65 89)

a. Outline example of the straight insertion sort.

MARKS = (42 56 65 89 48)
         ^   pointer_position = 5
(Pointer > 1) AND (48 < 89)
Copy 89 up. Move pointer down.
MARKS = (42 56 65 89 89)
        ^   pointer-position = 4
(Pointer > 1) AND (48 < 65)
Copy 65 up. Move pointer down.
MARKS = (42 56 65 65 89)
      ^   pointer-position = 3
(Pointer > 1) AND (48 < 56)
Copy 56 up. Move pointer down.
MARKS = (42 56 56 65 89)
    ^   pointer-position = 2
(Pointer > 1) BUT (48 > 42)
Place 48 into element pointed to
MARKS = (42 48 56 65 89)

b. More detailed example of an insertion.

Fig. 17.6. Examples to Illustrate the Procedure of 17.5.

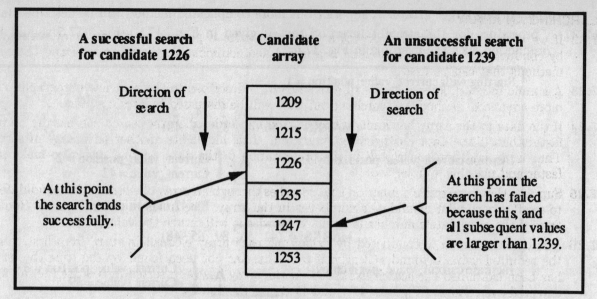

Fig. 17.7. Searching a Sorted Array.

```
function   found
           (
           number_of_elements, search_value:  integer,
           search_array      :   array [1..100] of integer
           ) :  boolean
           (*
              This function performs a linear search of the search array
              to find the search value.  If it finds the search value it
              returns true otherwise it returns false.
           *)
           variables
               subscript :  integer
           Begin
               (* Initialise values*)
               subscript := 0
               found := false
               (* search elements in turn *)
               repeat
                   subscript := subscript + 1
                   if
                       search_array(subscript) = search_value
                   then
                       found := true
                   endif
               until
                   found
                   OR
                   (subscript = number_of_elements)
                   OR
                   (search_array(subscript) > search_value)
           end
```

Fig 17.8. A Function for Performing a Linear Search of an Array.

SEARCHING AN ARRAY

17.22 If we wish to know whether or not a particular value is present within an array we may find out by conducting **a search.** Searching is a useful and common processing activity and there are many methods that can be used.

17.23 A simple method, known as the **linear search,** is described in the next few paragraphs. There are more advanced methods of searching but they will be discussed in later chapters.

17.24 If the data in the array has already been sorted into order then the search can usually be performed faster than if the data has been left unsorted. This highlights another advantage of sorting data. That is, in addition to helping in the presentation of the data, sorting may also make processing faster and possibly simpler too.

17.25 Suppose that we require a function that searches through an array of examination candidate numbers to see if a particular candidate's number is in the array. The function will return the Boolean value **true** if the candidate's number is found, otherwise it will return the value **false.**

17.26 The **linear search** is conducted by examining each array element in turn, from first to last, until the required value is found. Clearly, if the value has not been found by the time the last element has been examined the search has failed. If the array has been sorted into order the failure may be detected even sooner. Figures. 17.7 and 17.8 give the details.

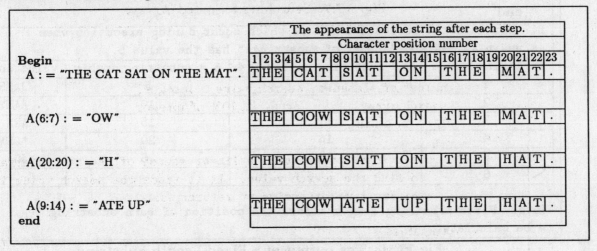

Fig. 17.9. Basic String-Handling Operations.

STRINGS

17.27 We now turn our attention to data structures that are used for text handling and related problems. As you may remember from 15.16, a sequence of characters handled as a single unit of data is called a **string.** For example,"ABC-, 3gh" and "THE CAT SAT ON THE MAT" are **literal strings.**

17.28 In other languages in which strings are used they are present in the form of one-dimensional arrays of characters. In the programming language BASIC all string identifiers have the "$" sign as a suffix. In paragraphs 17.29 to 17.35 assume that the variables A, B, C, V and F have been declared to be strings by a declaration such as

$$\text{A, B, C, V, F: string}$$

17.29 a. When strings are joined together they are said to be **concatenated** (15.39). So if A = "ALEX" and B="JAMES" the assignment

$$\text{C := A \& B}$$

concatenates A and B to form C where

$$\text{C = "ALEXJAMES"}$$

b. Part of a string is called a **substring,** eg, A = "ALEX" and B = "JAMES" are substrings of C = "ALEXJAMES".

17.30 In the following paragraphs we are primarily concerned with strings as *data structures* composed of substrings that can be operated upon individually, whereas in chapter 15 we merely considered strings as simple indivisible data items.

STRING HANDLING

17.31 String handling notation.

a. We number each character position in the string in sequence just like the elements in a one-dimensional array.

b. We refer to each substring by stating its *first* and *last* character position separated by a ":". The following pseudocode and table (Fig. 17.9) illustrate the method.

---

a.

```
(*
This is part of a procedure to output substrings of length 5 from a
string "F". The IN parameter "number_of_substrings" is of type integer,
as is the local variable "substring_number".
*)
Begin
    for substring_number = 1 to number_of_substrings
        output(F(5 * substring_number - 4 :  5 * substring_number))
    endfor
end
```

b. Here are the successive values which occur during execution when F is as in 17.33a and "number_of_substrings" has the value 5.

substring_number	5 * substring_number - 4	5 * substring_number	value output
1	1	5	JAMES
2	6	10	KATY
3	11	15	ANN
4	16	20	ALEX
5	21	25	JO
6			

Note. Fixed substring length allows the position of each substring to be calculate.

Fig 17.10. The output of a Fixed-Length Substring.

```
(*
    These few lines of pseudocode output the first substring of V.
    The local variable "position" is of type integer.
*)
Begin
    position :  =1
    while
        V(position :  position) <> "*"
    do
        output(V(position :  position))
        position := position + 1
    endwhile
end
```

Note i.   Further strings may be output in a similar fashion.

   ii.   An alternative storage strategy would be to have an integer at the start of each substring which indicated its length. eg.

   V = "05JAMES04KATY03ANN04ALEX02JO"

Fig. 17.11. Output from a Variable-Length String.

17.32 Fixed-length and variable-length strings. We return here to the concept of fixed-length and variable-length strings, which was introduced in 6.10 and 6.15.

   a. Fixed-length strings have a fixed number of character places available for data storage.

   b. Variable-length strings provide the data with just the number of spaces it needs.

The significance of these differences is illustrated by the following examples.

Note. These examples are important for two reasons:

   i. The manipulation of fixed-length and variable-length data is often needed in programming problems.

   ii. They illustrate the ways in which fixed-length and variable-length data is manipulated in main storage. The character positions in strings **F** and **V** in these examples may be compared with location addresses in main storage, where each location is able to store one character.

17.33 Example 1.

   a. This diagram shows five fixed-length strings concatenated into a single string called **F**. Each string is 5 characters long.

Details of F.

Character Position	1	2	3	4	5	6	7	8	9	10	11	12	13	14	15	16	17	18	19	20	21	22	23	24	25
Contents	J	A	M	E	S	K	A	T	Y		A	N	N			A	L	E	X		J	O			
Comment	1st String					2rd String					3rd String					4th String					5th String				

   b. This diagram shows five variable-length strings concatenated into a single string called **V**. The same data is used but the end of each string is indicated by a "*". Note the saving in storage space.

Details of V.

Character Position	1	2	3	4	5	6	7	8	9	10	11	12	13	14	15	16	17	18	19	20	21	22	23	24	25
Contents	J	A	M	E	S	*	K	A	T	Y	*	A	N	N	*	A	L	E	X	*	J	O	*		
Comment	1st String						2nd String					3rd String				4th String					5th String			Saved Storage	

17.34 Handling fixed-length strings. This example shows how the separate substrings in **F** can be printed in turn (see Fig. 17.10).

17.35 Handling variable-length strings is more difficult than handling fixed-length strings but does have the important advantage of saving space. This example shows how the first substring in **V** can be printed and the example in 17.36 will show how to handle all **V**. Here we assume we have no prior knowledge of the string's length and so we take out each character in turn until we meet the terminator "*".

17.36 A simple example of an **access table** is an array that holds details of the locations of data values. We will consider such a case now and leave more complicated examples for later discussion. An access table called **A** is shown in Fig 17.12. It provides a means of accessing the strings held in **V** of paragraph 17.33b.

Row number (corresponds to substring i)	Position of 1st character in string i	Position of last character in string i
1	$A(1,1) = 1$	$A(1,2) = 5$
2	$A(2,1) = 7$	$A(2,2) = 10$
3	$A(3,1) = 12$	$A(3,2) = 14$
4	$A(4,1) = 16$	$A(4,2) = 19$
5	$A(5,1) = 21$	$A(5,2) = 22$

Fig. 17.12. Details of Access Table A.

```
(*
    This is part of a procedure to output the substrings
    of V by using the access table "A".
    The local variable "i" is of type integer (see Fig.  17.12.)
    Other variables are as defined previously.
*)
begin
    for i := 1 to number_of_substrings
        output(V(A(i,1):A(i,2)))
    endfor
end

Note. For Fig. 17.12 number_of_substrings has value 5.
```

Fig 17.13. Part of a Procedure Using an Access Table.

RECORDS

17.37 Records will be easy to understand if we compare them with arrays. Records are like one-dimensional arrays in that they are comprised of a series of related data items. Records differ from arrays in that, whereas all the elements in an array have the same type, the successive data items in a record may differ in type. The following simple example should clarify these ideas.

17.38 **Example.** Suppose we wish to organise the following three items of data relating to an individual examination candidate into a single data structure:

```
candidate_number   :   integer
candidate_name     :   string
average_mark       :   real
```

17.39 Although the three data items belong together they cannot be stored in an array because they are of different types. The answer is to store them in a record. A suitable record declaration could take the form:

```
candidate. :=   record
                    candidate_number   :   integer
                    candidate_name     :   string
                    average_mark       :   real
                endrecord
```

17.40 In the example just given a record called "candidate" was declared. The three elements of the record each had their own identifiers, unlike array elements, which are merely referred to by subscripts. The elements of a record are called **fields**.

17.41 Reference to the individual fields of a record may be made as shown in the following example.

17.42 **Example.** Suppose we wish to create a record for candidate 1209, named "Smith", who gained an average mark of 55.2. The assignments of these values to the three fields of the record called candidate may be performed in two ways:

a. Using the **"dot"** notation. Consider these lines of pseudocode:

```
Begin
    candidate.candidate_number   :=1209
    candidate.candidate_name     :="Smith"
    candidate.average_mark       :=55.2
end
```

Each record field is identified by the record name followed by a "dot" followed by the field name. Clearly this notation is rather clumsy when referencing several fields from the same record. In such cases the following method is preferable.

b. The **"with"** notation. The following pseudocode is equivalent to that given in "a".

```
                    Begin
                        with       candidate
                        do
                                   candidate_number   := 1209
                                   candidate_name     := "Smith"
                                   average_mark       := 55.2
                        endwith
                    end
```

17.43 Not all high-level languages provide facilities for creating records. Pascal, C, COBOL, Modula and Ada do, but few versions of BASIC have such facilities.

ARRAYS OF RECORDS (TABLES)

17.44 Suppose we wish to store the following table of data for a set of examination students.

CANDIDATE NUMBER	CANDIDATE NAME	AVERAGE MARK
1209	Smith	55.2
1215	Brown	86.4
1226	Jones	49.2
1235	Robinson	66.0
1247	Finlay	59.8
1253	Johnson	71.3

17.45 This data could be stored in an array of records declared in the following manner:

```
        variables
            candidate:array [1..6]  of record
                                        number:  integer
                                        name:  string
                                        av_mark:real
                                    endrecord
```

17.46 Assuming that the data had already been assigned to records in the array, and that "i" had been declared as an integer, the data could be output using the following pseudocode:

```
        Begin
            for i:=1 to 6
                        with
                            candidate(i)
                        do
                            output(number, name, av_mark)
                        endwith
            endfor
        end
```

LISTS

17.47 Lists provide a flexible way of handling data items in order. Changes to the order can be achieved with minimal data movement and little loss of storage space.

17.48 Example. The sentence "Alex does not like cake" is written as a list.

$$\boxed{\text{ALEX}} \rightarrow \boxed{\text{DOES}} \rightarrow \boxed{\text{NOT}} \rightarrow \boxed{\text{LIKE}} \rightarrow \boxed{\text{CAKE}}$$

We regard each word in our sentence as a data-item or **datum**, which is *linked* to the next datum, by a **pointer**. Datum plus pointer make one **element** or **node** of the list. The last pointer in the list is a **terminator**. This list may be stored in an array of records as shown in Fig. 17.14. Each row of the array is one element in the list. Two other pointers are useful. A **start pointer** saying where the first datum is and a **free storage pointer** saying where the next datum can go.

	Row Number	Datum	Pointer to Next Datum	Comment
START POINTER	1 →			
	1	"ALEX"	2	Next datum is in row 2
	2	"DOES"	3	Next datum is in row 3
	3	"NOT"	4	Next datum is in row 4
	4	"LIKE"	5	Next datum is in row 5
	5	"CAKE"	-1	Last Datum: -1 is a terminator
FREE STORAGE POINTER	6 →	6		7	Empty
	7		8	Empty

Note. -1 is used as a terminator in this example.

Fig. 17.14. A List Stored in an Array of Records.

17.49 A data declaration of this list might take the form:

```
variables
    sentence:  array [1..7]  of record
                                  datum : string
                                  next : integer
                              endrecord
```

17.50 Assuming that the start pointer **"start"** and row value **"row"** have been declared as integers then the following pseudocode could be used to output the list elements in the correct order.

```
Begin
    (* Get first datum's row *)
    row := start
    while
        (* terminator not found *)
        row <> -1
    do
        (* output next datum *)
        output(sentence(row).datum)
        (* get next row *)
        row := sentence(row).next
    endwhile
end
```

17.51 Deletions. When elements are deleted from a list, the freed storage can be reused. In the example given here "NOT" has been deleted so the list now reads "ALEX DOES LIKE CAKE".

	Row Number	Datum	Pointer to Next Datum	Comment
START POINTER $\rightarrow$ 1	1	"ALEX"	2	
	2	"DOES"	4	Pointer to deleted item changed to deleted pointer
FREE STORAGE POINTER 3 $\rightarrow$	3		6	Deleted pointer replaced by free storage pointer
	4	"LIKE"	5	
	5	"CAKE"	-1	
	6		7	
	7		8	

The free storage point is replaced by the pointer to the deleted item.

17.52 Insertions. The free storage pointer is used for insertions. In this example the list is changed to "ALEX DOES LIKE CREAM CAKE" by inserting "CREAM".

	Row Number	Datum	Pointer to Next Datum	Comment
START POINTER 1 $\rightarrow$	1	"ALEX"	2	
	2	"DOES"	4	
	3	"CREAM"	5	Old pointer given to free storage
	4	"LIKE"	3	Old pointer given to new item. New pointer from free storage
	5	"CAKE"	-1	
FREE STORAGE POINTER 6 $\rightarrow$	6		7	
	7		8	

17.53 The pseudocode of 17.50 can be used to output the lists of 17.51 and 17.52. Extreme cases can be dealt with in these ways:

a. An empty list can be indicated by a terminator (eg, -1) in the start pointer.

b. A full list can be indicated by a terminator in the free storage pointer.

17.54 In the examples just given we have, strictly speaking, only been considering one method of **implementing** lists, namely linked lists in the form of arrays of records. A more general notation for lists is one in which the data elements are written in sequence thus:

$$< e_1, e_2, e_3, \ldots\ldots, e_n >$$

17.55 As with all data types what characterises a list is not only the set of values it takes but the operations that may be performed upon it. One would normally expect to be able to perform these operations upon a list:

a. Find the position and value of the first element.

213

b. Insert an element.

c. Delete an element.

d. Find the next element (sometimes the previous element too).

e. Find a specific element.

f. Output the list elements in order.

g. Create an empty list.

TREES

17.56 Trees are **hierarchical data structures** rather like the familiar family tree. They are constructed using a **rule of precedence** for the data items, eg, using alphabetic or numerical sequence. The **elements** of a tree are called **nodes** and each element consists of a datum and at least two pointers. In the example about to be given the examination marks used in 17.6 are entered into a tree so as to indicate their numerical order. Each element looks like this:

LEFT POINTER	DATUM	RIGHT POINTER

17.57 Example. These numbers are placed into a tree: 56, 42, 89, 65 and 48.

a. 56 is the *first* datum placed into the tree. Its node is therefore called the **parent** or **root node**.

b. We add 42 to the tree next using the precedence rule "lower numbers to the left, higher numbers to the right". The tree then looks like this:

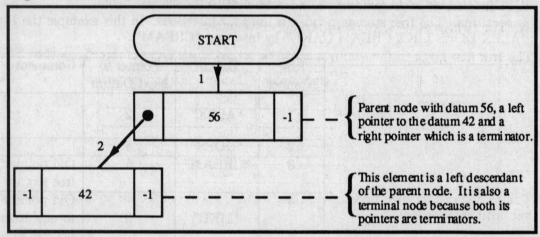

c. 89 is added next. It is larger than 56 so we add it to the right of the parent node thus:

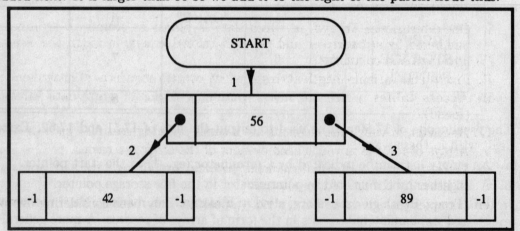

d. 65 is added next. It is larger than 56 so we go right at the parent node but left at 89 because it is smaller.

e. 48 is added next. We go left at 56 because it is smaller and right at 42 because it is larger. Our tree finally looks like this:

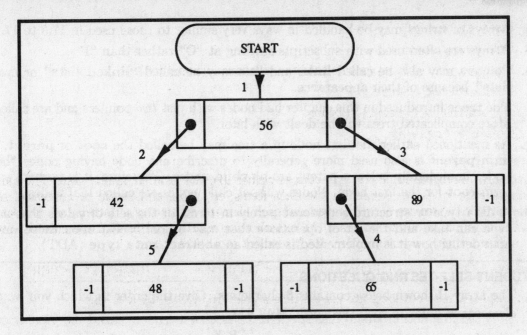

Note.

i. The leftmost node contains the smallest number.

ii. The rightmost node contains the highest number.

17.58 The tree just given in the example could be placed in an array of records as shown below.

Left Pointer	Datum	Right Pointer
2	56	3
-1	42	5
4	89	-1
-1	65	-1
-1	48	-1

17.59 The procedures for inserting and deleting items from trees together with other methods for trees are left until chapter 39.

SUMMARY

17.60 a. The data structures discussed were:

    i. **One-dimensional arrays**, in which data is placed in **elements** arranged into a sequence numbered by **subscripts**, and two-dimensional arrays, in which the elements are arranged into rows and columns.

    ii. Fixed- and variable-length **strings**, which contain sequences of characters.

    iii. **Access tables**, which are arrays containing details of where data values can be accessed (found).

    iv. **Records**, in which the elements are a series of **fields** that may each be of different types.

    v. Arrays of records in which each element of the array is a record.

    vi. **Lists**, in which individual elements (**nodes**) containing data and **pointers** are connected together by the use of the pointers.

    vii. **Trees**, in which data is organised in a hierarchical manner. Each **element** (**node**) has left and right pointers.

    b. **Sorting** and **searching** were introduced using simple examples.

POINTS TO NOTE

17.61 a. One-dimensional arrays may be called **vectors** and main storage may therefore be regarded as a vector.

    b. The terms "table" and "array" are synonymous most of the time, but for applications in main storage the term "table" is usually used. The term "table" is also commonly used to mean an array of records.

c. Arrays of strings may be handled in ways very similar to those used in 17.8 to 17.26.

d. Arrays are often used with subscripts starting at "O" rather than "1".

e. Pointers may also be called **links** and lists may be called **"linked lists"** or even **"threaded lists"** because of their appearance.

f. The **trees** introduced in this chapter had nodes with just *two* pointers and are called *binary* trees. More complicated trees will be dealt with later.

g. As mentioned earlier the first node in a tree may be called the **root** or **parent**. However, the term **parent** is also used more generally to describe *any* node having nodes "below" it. The nodes immediately below a parent are its **child** nodes. Therefore, it is perhaps safer to use the term **root** for the first node. Nodes without child nodes are called **leaf** nodes.

h. A data type or structure considered purely in terms of the sets of values that variables of the type can take and the set of operations that may be performed upon those variables *without* considering how it is implemented is called an **abstract data type** (ADT).

STUDENT SELF-TESTING QUESTIONS

1. The array B shown below contains 6 characters. Give the order in which you would select elements in order to spell the word "MATRIX".

T R X

I A M

2. Enter the letters of "MATRIX" into a tree one at a time in the order they are spelt. Use the rule "earlier in the alphabet to the left".

3. Write the function "below average" used in Fig. 17.1.

4. Write a procedure to reverse the order of elements in
   a. an array, eg, [3, 6, 2, 5] becomes [5, 2, 6, 3]

   b. a string, eg, "MATRIX" becomes "XIRTAM".

5. Describe a suitable data structure for details of stock items numbered in the range 1 to 100. Each stock item may be held at each of 20 locations. The numbers of items held at each location needs to be recorded.

QUESTIONS WITHOUT ANSWERS

6. The linked list shown in this chapter allows us to pass through the list in one direction only, ie, given only the location of an item we do not know its predecessor. Write a record declaration for a list so that from a single element we know both the location of its predecessor and its successor. How does this differ from a tree?

7. Write a function that determines the number of words in a string such as that shown in Fig. 17.9. State any assumptions that you make.

GLOSSARY CHECKLIST

Abstract Data Type	17.61	Leaf node	17.61
Access table	17.36	Linear search	17.23
ADT	17.61	Link	17.61
Array	17.6	List	17.42
Child node	17.61	Literal string	17.27
Data aggregate	17.2	Local variable	17.12
Data structure	17.1	Matrix	17.16
Datum	17.48	Node	17.48, 17.56
Dot notation (for records)	17.42	Parent node	17.61
Element	17.41	Pointer	17.48
Field	17.40	Records	17.37
Fixed length string	17.32	Root node	17.57
Global variable	17.12	Rule of precedence	17.56

18: Program Design

INTRODUCTION

18.1 Today there are many amateur programmers writing all kinds of programs. Just as the do-it-yourself enthusiast who builds a shed in the garden usually has only a rudimentary knowledge of building design, most amateur programmers have little knowledge of program design.

18.2 In this chapter we consider program design as it applies to the production of professional software. The chapter is only an introduction to program design because of the scope of the text. However, it must be stressed that although only a basic knowledge of program design is needed to write small programs of reasonable quality, a sound and detailed knowledge of program design is essential for the production of large-scale software. Would you let a do-it-yourself shed builder build a house for you?

THE IMPORTANCE OF GOOD PROGRAMMING METHODS

18.3 Today great reliance is placed upon computers for all kinds of applications, including banking, insurance, public and private administration, national defence and so on. Computers are only machines and will slavishly follow the program instructions given them.

18.4 The costs of programming have risen because the shortages of skilled personnel, as required for programming, have pushed up labour costs, whereas the costs of hardware have fallen because of technical innovation and increased automation. It is a false economy to reduce programming standards in order to achieve greater programmer output, because of potentially damaging effects of errors, high correction and maintenance costs and difficulties experienced in transferring substandard programs from one computer to another.

18.5 The need for good-quality programming is greater than ever, but there is also a need to reduce programming costs. Experience has shown that it pays to put greater effort into program **design** rather than into trying to get a badly designed program to work. The longer an error goes undetected the more costly it is to correct and so the early stages of program design are **very** important.

PROGRAM DESIGN AIMS

18.6 These are summarised as follows:·

   a. **Reliability**, ie, the program can be depended upon always to do what it is supposed to do.

   b. **Maintainability**, ie, the program will be easy to change or modify when the need arises.

   c. **Portability**, ie, the program will be transferable to a different computer with a minimum of modification.

   d. **Readability**, ie, the program will be easy for a programmer to read and understand. This can aid a, b and c.

   e. **Performance**, ie, the program causes the tasks to be done quickly and efficiently.

   f. **Storage saving**, ie, the program is not allowed to be unnecessarily long.

   Some of these aims are in conflict with others, eg, e and f.

PROGRAM SPECIFICATION AND CORRECTNESS

18.7 A programmer is usually given a specification of *what* the proposed program is required to do. The programmer must then design and implement the program so that it meets the specification. A program that meets its specification is said to be "correct".

18.8 There are some serious implications to this basic picture of design and implementation. First, the specification could be wrong in that it might not specify what was really required. This could lead to a program being "correct" but unsuitable! Secondly, even if the specification is right it may be very difficult to ensure that the program is correct. It is in this respect that good programming methods can be of great value.

18.9 The issues of how to provide good program specifications will be dealt with in later chapters. In this chapter we concentrate on program design and implementation with the emphasis on the design methods throughout.

18.10 What the general points made so far boil down to is this. We need to produce **correct** programs from specifications that truly express the requirements. The programs need to be reliable, maintainable, portable, readable and efficient. The programs must also be produced in reasonable time and without undue expense.

METHODS FOR PROGRAM DEVELOPMENT

18.11 There are a number of methods for designing and implementing programs. Broadly speaking, the methods are influenced both by the size of the programming problem and by the programming languages available for its solution.

18.12 We will start by considering the stages in programming that apply to program development for typical programs in most computer languages. Then we will look at how these stages may differ if more advanced methods are used.

STAGES IN PROGRAMMING

18.13 In the process of producing the necessary instructions making up a program, the following stages can be recognised:

 a. Understanding the problem.

 b. Planning the method of solution.

 c. Developing the methods using suitable aids, eg, pseudocode.

 d. Typing the instructions into the computer using a programming language.

 e. Testing the program. (The various components of the program are tested as well as the whole program.)

 f. Documenting all the work involved in producing the program. This documentation will be developed stage by stage.

18.14 If during testing the program an error is discovered, then *it is important to go back to earlier stages* in order to correct the error. If the error comes from misunderstanding the problem, it will probably be better to start again from the beginning. An outline of what happens at each programming stage now follows.

18.15 **Understanding the problem.** The programmer needs to know exactly what the program is required to do and normally works from a **program specification.** This program specification is normally part of a **"System Specification"**, which defines the whole system, of which the program may be only a small part. For example, the program might just be one of a suite of programs for use in a particular application.

18.16 Broadly speaking, the **program specification** will define the inputs, processing and outputs required. A good specification will normally specify *what* processing is needed by giving the exact relationship between outputs and the inputs from which they are derived rather than prescribing *how* the program should be written.

18.17 **Planning the method of solution.** Depending upon the extent of the task, the program preparation may be shared amongst many programmers. Such co-operation requires an overall plan. Large programs may require each programmer to write a separate part of the program. These separate parts are often called modules or segments. The modules may be prepared and tested separately, then linked together to be tested as a whole, a process known as **integration.**

18.18 **Developing the method by using suitable aids such as pseudocode.** Modern approaches to programming recognise the fact that complicated problems can be solved most easily if they are broken down into simpler, more manageable tasks in a step-by-step fashion. At each step the problem is broken down further and consideration of details is put off as long as possible. This general approach is known as **top down programming by stepwise refinement.** (More details later.)

18.19 **Typing the instructions in a programming language.** This may be regarded as the last step in stepwise refinement. The instructions written in pseudocode are written in a programming language. There are different types of programming languages and details will be given in later chapters. If programs have to be written in a very strict format, and are to be typed by someone other than the programmer, then they are first written on special forms called "coding sheets". The use of coding sheets is unusual today because most programmers type their own programs using VDUs or workstations.

18.20 **Testing the program.** Once written a program has to be subjected to various tests to check that it has been written out and transcribed correctly and does what it is supposed to do, ie, that it is correct. These tests invariably reveal errors, which have to be corrected. This can be quite a lengthy, and expensive, process. Careful and thorough design in the early stages of programming will help to minimise these errors. The later an error is discovered the more expensive and troublesome it will be to eliminate it.

18.21 It is good practice to test each component of a program as it is produced as well as testing the completed program. There are several stages of testing:

a. **Unit testing**, which involves testing the separate components as they are produced.

b. **Integration testing**, which involves testing the separate components as they are put together.

c. **System testing**, which involves testing the whole program once it is in the final form in which it is to be used.

d. **User acceptance testing**, which involves the user of the program (possibly the customer) testing the program to see that it is what was required.

18.22 **Documentation.** It is very important that the work of the programmer in producing a finished program is fully documented. This documentation will include a statement of the problem (system specification), pseudocode, coding sheets, test data and results. *Producing these documents should be done as part of each stage in programming and not as an afterthought.* If this is done the documentation will aid the maintenance of the program during its lifetime. Some programs have very long lives. For example, some programs written during the 1960s are still in use to day, although they may have been subjected to *regular maintenance*, eg, modification or bringing up to date.

COMPUTER STAFF

18.23 It is easier to see programming in context if at this stage we give some consideration to the work of the staff involved. An outline of the work is given in the following paragraphs. Greater detail will be given in a later chapter.

18.24 **Systems analyst.** The main jobs of the analyst are:

a. To examine the feasibility of potential computer applications.

b. Analysis of existing systems with a view to their computerisation.

c. Design of computer-based systems, their implementation and review.

18.25 It is very likely that systems analysts would work in project teams with a senior analyst in charge.

18.26 **Programmers.** Following the design process the job of programming begins. The programmer:

a. Encodes the procedures detailed by the analyst in a language suitable for the specified computer.

b. Will liaise very closely with the analyst and the user to ensure logical correctness of programs.

18.27 Programmers also frequently work in project teams.

CONCEPTS THAT LIE BEHIND PROGRAM DESIGN

18.28 There are a number of concepts of relevance to the general problems of program design that the reader should be aware of. Three particular concepts are:

a. Computability.

b. Complexity.

c. Correctness.

The last was introduced in 18.7.

18.29 **Computability.** Throughout this text we are concerned with what tasks computers can do and how they do them. Here we stop briefly to face the fact that there are many problems that computers cannot solve, not just for practical reasons but because the task can be proven to be theoretically impossible. A task may be said to be **computable** if it can in principle be performed by a machine.

18.30 Strange though it may at first seem, most tasks are not computable. It is relatively easy, for example, to discover non-computable mathematical functions. There are also some celebrated unsolvable problems in the theory of computability. One rather interesting problem in this category is "**the halting problem**". Put simply, there is no algorithm that can take an arbitrary program and its input and decide whether the program's execution will stop if the program is given that input. Such algorithm would have great practical value but cannot exist. Further discussion is beyond the scope of this book.

18.31 **Complexity** is measured in terms of the quantity of resources used. The main resources considered are time and storage.

18.32 The general idea is easier to understand by considering a simple example. Suppose that we wish to perform a processing operation on a set of "n" numbers. For a simple task, such as finding the total, the complexity in terms of storage requirements will not be affected by n because we need only store the cumulative total. The complexity, in terms of time taken, will be in direct proportion to n. For some other task, sorting say, not only will all the n values require storing but the time taken for methods such as the straight insertion sort is proportional to n^2.

18.33 Clearly, for many tasks there may be alternative algorithms and for practical reasons a knowledge of their complexity will help us make the best choice. Also we may be interested in average cases and worst cases.

18.34 **Correctness.** As was mentioned in 18.7, a program is correct if it meets its specification. Ideally, when we complete the implementation of any program we want to be able to say for certain the program is correct. Unfortunately this is seldom possible. To **prove** that a program is correct it is necessary to show for certain that for all permissible input to the program the program will produce the required results. Such proofs require methods comparable to those for proving theorems in mathematics and can become very complicated even for simple programs.

18.35 In practice, rather than attempt a proof, we **test** the program using a set of carefully selected "test data".

18.36 Testing may be conducted by executing the program on the computer or by simulating its execution by a manual pencil and paper exercise called a **"dry run"**. There are two basic types of testing:

    a. **Functional testing** (also called **black box testing**). This form of testing is based upon typical, extreme and invalid data values that are representative of those covered by the specification.

    b. **Logical testing** (also called **white box testing**). This form of testing is based upon examining the internal structure of the program and selecting data which gives rise to the alternative cases of control flow, eg, both paths through an if..then..else.

18.37 Functional testing is often used at the final stage of programming as a basis for accepting or rejecting the program. Functional testing is not adequate by itself and logical testing by the programmer during program development tends to be far more beneficial.

18.38 **Debugging.** A program fault that causes a program to fail during testing, or after it has been commissioned, is called a **bug**. The process of finding and getting rid of bugs is called **debugging**.

18.39 The presence of bugs in a program is often symptomatic of poor workmanship on the part of the persons who produced the specification or who wrote the program. When a bug is discovered it is important that the reasons for its occurrence are investigated fully and that the program's design and implementation are reworked where necessary. Quick and easy alterations to the program to remove bugs, often called **"fixes"** or **"patches"**, invariably produces "new bugs for old".

PROGRAMMING METHOD

18.40 Armed with the additional background knowledge provided by the preceding paragraphs we now return to the ideas introduced in 18.18.

18.41 Many of the terms used to describe programming methods have been so badly overused that they have become almost meaningless slogans. Even so, these "popular" terms deserve some explanation and the next few paragraphs will provide it where appropriate.

18.42 **"Top down"** and **"bottom up"** methods. It is clear that many problems that occur in programming, and system design, are too large to be solved all at once. The answer is to try to solve such problems in stages. But where should one begin? If the problem is different from anything met before, it may be necessary to set about solving a part of the problem that is understood, and then, as other parts of the problem become clearer, solving them until the whole problem is solved. Such an approach in which the whole situation is built up by joining together the completed parts is called a "bottom up" approach.

18.43 There is one severe danger inherent in the bottom up approach; the various parts may not fit together properly, and, in some cases, considerable effort may be necessary to overcome this problem. "Top down" methods attempt to avoid such problems by starting with the general concept of what is required, breaking the whole into component parts, and then tackling the component parts in the same manner. The interrelationships between components are decided upon before the components are created so that the final integration of the parts into the whole should be more straightforward. A number of methods in use today may be described as top down.

18.44 **Decomposition** is the term used to describe the process of breaking down a program into component parts. (When applied to rotten programs it seems even more appropriate!) Since there is almost invariably a choice over what the components should be, both for top down methods and for bottom up methods, it is possible to examine the completed program and classify it as a good decomposition or a bad one.

```
Program factor_checker
        (* See paragraph 18.48 for details.  *)
variables
        possible_factor,
        number_for checking :  integer
Begin
    (* get a value for the possible factor *)
    (* get numbers for checking and check the possible factor on each *)
end
        a. Stage 1
```

```
Program factor_checker
        (* See paragraph 18.48 for details *)
variables
        possible_factor,
        number_for_checking :  integer
Begin
    (* get a value for the possible factor *)
    output("Key in the number to be checked as a factor")
    input(possible_factor)
    (* get numbers for checking and check the possible factor on each *)
    output("Key in a number to be checked (Key in 0 to stop)")
    input(number_for_checking)
    while(* number keyed in is not zero *)
    do
        (* check the number and get the next number *)
    endwhile
end
        b. Stage 2
```

```
Program factor_checker
        (* See paragraph 18.48 for details *)
Begin
    (* get a value for the possible factor *)
    output("Key in the number to be checked as a factor")
    input(possible_factor)
    (* get numbers for checking and check the possible factor on each *)
    output("Key in a number to be checked (Key in 0 to stop)")
    input(number_for_checking)
    while(* number keyed in is not zero *)
            number_for_checking<> 0
    do
            if
                (* possible factor divides exactly into number entered *)
                number_for_checking mod possible_factor = 0
            then
                output(possible_factor,"is a factor of", number_for_checking)
            else
                output(possible_factor,"is not a factor of", number_for_checking)
            endif
            output("Key in number to be checked (Key in 0 to stop)")
            input(number_for_checking)
    endwhile
end
        c. Stage 3
```

Fig. 18.1. Stages in a Top Down Development of a Simple Program.

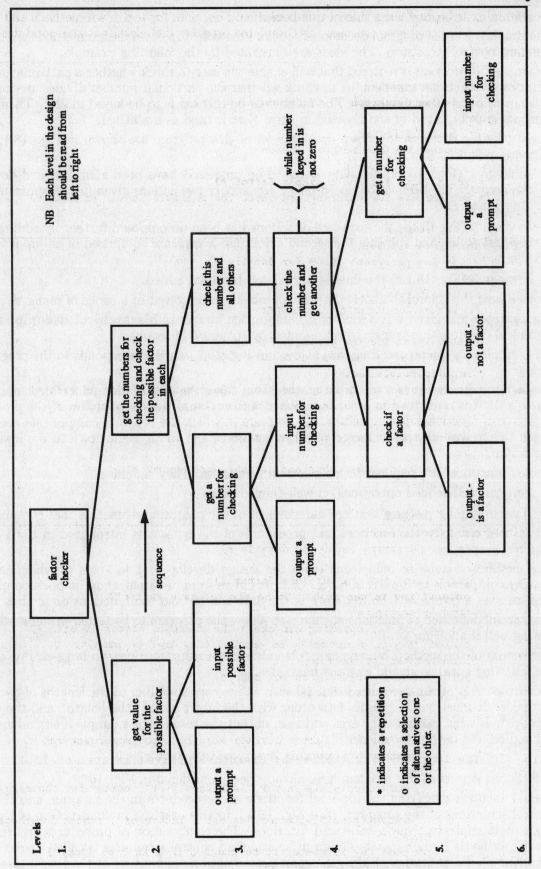

Fig. 18.2. A Structure Diagram.

18.45 Most standard methods of decomposition are **control oriented**, that is to say, they concentrate on working out the flow of control within the program. Methods based upon flowcharts and pseudocode are almost invariably control oriented. The alternative to control oriented programming is **object oriented** programming, in which attention is directed towards identifying objects such as data structures and the operations performed upon them. A detailed discussion of object oriented programming is beyond the scope of this book.

18.46 The simplest form of program decompositions produced by top down design methods are based upon standard control structures. The ideas are illustrated by the following example.

18.47 **Example.** A program is required that will enable the user to check whether a particular number is a factor of several other numbers (ie, to check whether the particular number divides an exact number of times into the other numbers). The number to be checked is to be keyed in first. Then a series of numbers is to be keyed in and checked in turn. Zero is used as a sentinel.

18.48 These possible stages in top down development of this program are shown in Fig. 18.1. Note the following points:

   a. In stage 1 (Fig. 18.1a) the data items to be processed have been identified and declared and the program has been decomposed into a *sequence* of two actions given in the comments between **Begin** and **end.**

   b. In stage 2 (Fig 18.1b) the sequence of actions has been decomposed further by adding details to the first action and splitting the second acton into a *sequence* comprised of an input followed by a loop.

   c. In stage 3 (Fig. 18.1.c) the final level of detail has been added.

   Notice how this approach allows the whole problem to be solved in a series of manageable steps.

18.49 The example just given was a kind of decomposition known as **hierarchical decomposition.** Hierarchical decompositions may be represented by structure diagrams.

18.50 An example of a **structure diagram** is given in Fig. 18.2, which corresponds to the program in Fig 18.1.

18.51 **Stepwise refinement** is a top down method that takes the idea of hierarchical decomposition and extends it. It is often used in order to arrive at a **functional decomposition** of the program. The objective of functional decomposition is a program in which the program components are functions, which themselves may be composed of other functions, and so on, right down to the lowest level of the design.

18.52 These "functions" are required to have certain properties. They should:

   a. Perform well-defined operations on well-defined data.

   b. Have internal structures that are independent of the program or function that contains them.

   When used correctly, the functions and procedures of the types first introduced in 16.63 have these required properties.

18.53 The method of stepwise refinement takes the design development in steps in which each step is broadly comparable to the *levels* in Fig. 18.2. It differs from hierarchical decomposition in that each step involves a complete definition both of the data and of *what* the functions do at that level.

18.54 The careful definition of functions at each step allows the program to be tested in steps, which makes testing better and simpler.

18.55 The merits of the method become more obvious when writing medium- to large-size programs, but the following example should give the basic idea.

18.56 **Example.** A program is required that takes in values corresponding to the lengths of two sides of a rectangle. It must put the values into order with the larger called "the length" and the other "the breadth". It must calculate the area and then output the result. For example if the values input are 3.0 and 5.0 the output should be:

   `The length 5.0 multiplied by breadth 3.0 gives an area of 15.0.`

   NB. Some aspects of this problem have already been considered in Fig. 16.11.

18.57 **Step 1** involves specifying the top-level functions and procedures in the program and the top-level control structures of the program. (See Fig. 18.3.) In this case the main structure of the program is a simple sequence of procedures and functions. The combination of procedures and functions at the higher levels of the program design using standard control structures is called **"program-level structure".** In contrast with this, the combination of basic operations at the lowest level of design using standard control structures is called **"code-level structure".**

18.58 Even at this first step the program can be transcribed into a programming language and tested for correct syntax. Some languages, such as Pascal, can act as their own pseudocode, thus making testing even easier.

18.59 Testing at lower levels is achieved by using "dummy" procedures and functions, sometimes called **"stubs".**

```
Program      Rectangle
             (* See paragraph 18.56 for details of the specification *)
variables
             side_one,
             side_two,
             area : real
procedure    get_two_valid_sides(OUT first_side,
                                        second_side : real )
             (*
             This procedure obtains positive values for the two sides
             from the user of the program.
             *)
             Begin
                 (* Code is written at the next step in refinement *)
             end
procedure    put_sides_into_order(IN_OUT first_side,
                                          second_side :  real)
             (*
             This procedure checks the value of the two sides and swaps
             them around if necessary to ensure that the larger value is
             first.  Equal values are not altered.
             *)
             Begin
                 (* Code is written at the next step in refinement*)
             end
function     rectangle_area(first_side :  real , second_side :  real ) :  real
             (* see Fig 16.11 *)
             Begin
                 (* Code is written at the next step in refinement *)
             end
procedure    output_results(IN first_side,
                               second_side,
                               area : real
             (*
             This procedure outputs the results.
             *)
             Begin
                 (* Code is written at the next step in refinement *)
             end
Begin
             call get_two_valid_sides(side_one,side_two)
             call put_sides_into_order(side_one,side_two)
             area := rectangle_area(side_one,side_two)
             call output_results(side_one,side_two,area)
end
```

Fig. 18.3. First Step in the Refinement of a Program.

18.60 Step 2 involves writing and testing the code for each of the functions and procedures defined in step 1. This may require the definition of functions at a lower level, in which case a further step in refinement will be necessary.

18.61 At this second step we may first write the "output_results" procedure. The procedure can be tested by creating dummy procedures. For example, the values 5.0 and 3.0 may be *assigned* to first_side and second_side respectively in the procedure "put_side_in_order" and the value 15.0 may be *assigned* to "rectangular_area".

18.62 Having established that the output results procedure is correct we might then write and test the "get_two_valid_sides" procedure.

18.63 As each procedure or function is written new local variables, procedures and functions may be created. For example, within the procedure "put_sides_into_order" we might have the following:

```
variables
              swap_value :   real
Begin
      if
              second_side > first_side
      then
              (* swap the values around*)
              swap_value := first_side
              first_side := second_side
              second_side := swap_value
      endif
end
```

Note. "Swap_value" is a variable local to this procedure.

18.64 Functions and procedures must be used with care when attempting to produce a good functional decomposition. We now turn to some basic principles concerning their use.

USING SUBPROGRAMS

18.65 Most programming languages have restrictions upon the ways functions, procedures, their arguments and their parameters may be used. Some restrictions may prevent the programmer from doing what is ideal and may also permit the programmer to indulge in bad practices. Either way, a greater burden of responsibility is placed upon the programmer.

18.66 Here is an outline guide to the main points to bear in mind:

a. Constants should always be declared in the main heading of the program rather than be hidden within the subprograms. Inclusion in subprograms may lead to inconsistencies between different values for the same constant.

b. Variables should only be passed between a calling program and the called subprogram by means of parameters or arguments. Neglect of this principle makes it harder to keep the program components independent of one another, which in turn complicates understanding the program, testing it or modifying it.

c. Use IN, OUT and IN-OUT parameters in the appropriate way. In particular do not allow a procedure to change an IN parameter, or a function to change its arguments. Neglect of this principle leads to confusion and errors. For example, we would not want a function that found the square root of "x" to change the value of x. A function or procedure that does change its argument or data external to it is said to have "side effects".

18.67 **Recursive Functions** are functions that are defined with reference to themselves. When recursive functions are executed they call themselves. These ideas are best understood by means of an example.

18.68 **Example.** Suppose we wish to have a function that generates powers of 2 and that the "↑" operator is not available, eg, given the argument 3 we want to obtain 2^3. In this particular case we could implement a solution without the need for recursion by calculating $y = 2^n$ in the following way:

NB. Assume that n is a non-negative integer and that "y" and "i" are declared as integers.

```
Begin
      y := 1
      i := 0
      while
            i < n
      do
            y := y * 2
            i := i+1
      endwhile
end
```

However, this is rather removed from the definition of what the function does.

18.69 A recursive definition of the function could take this form:

Note. Assume that the function is not used if n is negative.

```
function  two_to_power(n: integer) : integer
          (* finds the value of two to the power n *)
          Begin
               if
                    n = 0
               then
                    two_to_power := 1
               else
                    two_to_power := 2 * two_to_power(n - 1)
               endif
          end
```

18.70 Recursive functions, and the use of recursive definitions in general, are of considerable importance in Computer Science, but further discussion is inappropriate in a text at this level.

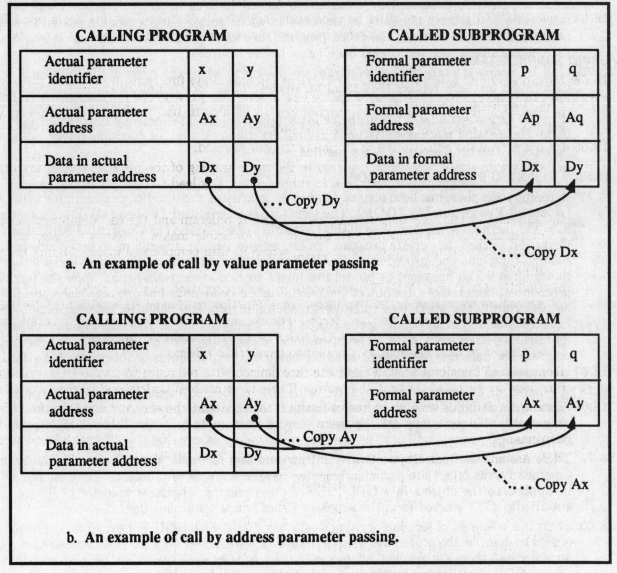

a. **An example of call by value parameter passing**

b. **An example of call by address parameter passing.**

Fig 18.4. Parameter Passing Mechanisms.

PARAMETER-PASSING MECHANISMS

18.71 There are a number of methods by which parameters may be passed from the calling program to the subprogram and back again. The principal methods are:

    a. **call by value**

    b. **call by address** (also known as "call by reference" and "call by location")

    c. **call by result**

    d. **call by value-result**

    e. **call by name.**

18.72 **Call by value** is an appropriate way to handle "IN" parameters or function arguments. When the subprogram is called the actual values of the parameter are placed in the memory locations associated with the formal parameters of the called subprogram (see Fig. 18.4a).

18.73 **Call by address** is an appropriate way to handle "IN-OUT" parameters. When the procedure is called the memory location of the actual parameter is passed to the called procedure so that it can access and alter the actual parameter. In call by address both the calling program and the called procedure access the same data, whereas in the case of call by value the calling program has no access to the formal parameter data (see Fig. 18.4b).

18.74 **Call by result** is an appropriate way to handle "OUT" parameters. When the procedure is called the formal parameter is not initialised. At the end of procedure execution the value is copied back in a similar manner to that used to pass values in call by value.

18.75 **Call by value-result** is an alternative way of providing IN-OUT parameter passing. The actual value is passed in as for call by value and is passed back as in call by result. There is a slightly more complicated form of call by value-result in which actual parameters are passed in and out by call by address but in which the called program uses local values, which are copied from the formal parameters after entry and copied back again before return.

18.76 **Call by name** is a rare method of parameter passing in which the *effect* of the call is as if the actual parameters textually replace the formal parameter. Thus, for example, if the actual parameter were "z" and an expression such as "x + y", and the corresponding formal parameters were "a" and "b", then the expression a := 2 * b in the called subprogram would effectively be z := 2 * (x + y). The parameter-passing mechanism is implemented by a special type of function rather oddly called a "**thunk**"! Further discussion is not merited.

OBJECT ORIENTED PROGRAMMING (OOP)

18.77 In recent years there has been a steady rise in popularity of a method of programming called **Object Oriented Programming (OOP)**. The term **Object Oriented Design (OOD)** is sometimes used too. The methods so far described in this chapter may be described as **Control Oriented** or **Process Oriented** in that they create program level structures based primarily upon processing components such as functions and procedures. In OOP the design concentrates upon **objects** which are the *things* upon which functions or procedures might be performed rather than upon the functions and procedures. For example, the object "rectangle" might be identified as one on which operations might be performed. The operations to be performed on a rectangle might include "**create**", "**remove**", "**get_length**", "**get_breadth**" **get_area**". This suggests that at the heart of any object is data representing its current state. The operations *belong* to the object whereas in a process oriented program the data may be thought of as *belonging* to the procedures or functions. Individual objects are created and combined into a complete programs.

18.78 A number of advantages are associated with object oriented methods including a rise in productivity and reliability because of the re-usability of code and the self-contained nature of program components. Objects may also be more easy to identify in real-life problems than procedures or functions.

18.79 There are a variety of Object Oriented Programming methods *not just one*. Some methods are general whereas others are particularly suited to specific types of problems. For example, OOP may be applied to the objects in a GUI. Popular programming languages used for OOP are C^{++} and **smalltalk**. C^{++} evolved form the language C but is a separate language.

18.80 There is a whole set of terminology specifically associated with OOP. For example, the term **method** is used to describe the procedures used in conjunction with objects. It is reasonable to have a different term because there are genuine differences in the way they work but it can be confusing for someone new to OOP. Another important concept is the idea of **inheritance** whereby a hierarchy of objects may be created with more complex objects being constructed from simpler ones but with **methods** of the simpler objects being available to ("inherited by") the more complex ones.

SUMMARY

18.81 a. Good program design is essential for the economic production of correct programs.

    b. Programming aims include:

        i.   Reliability.

        ii. Maintainability.

        iii. Portability.

        iv. Readability.

        v. Performance.

        vi. Storage saving.

    c. Programming takes place in stages.

    d. Computability, complexity and correctness are concepts that lie behind program design.

    e. Modern program design methods were introduced.

    f. Functional decomposition and stepwise refinement were discussed.

    g. The use of subprograms was discussed further, including parameter passing mechanisms.

    h. Recursion was introduced and explained.

    i. The work of computer staff was introduced.

POINTS TO NOTE

18.82 a. Good programs only come from good program design and good program design only comes from giving sufficient thought and effort in the early stages of programming.

    b. The programmer cannot solve a programming problem satisfactorily if the problem has not been properly stated.

    c. Subprograms are also sometimes called "subroutines".

    d. One subprogram may be called upon several times, in different places, within the same program.

    e. Functional decomposition as described in this chapter is a form of **modular decomposition**. "Modular decomposition" is a term that also applies to object-oriented programming (18.45) and so its use has been avoided here.

    f. Further aspects of parameter passing and memory allocation for subprograms will be covered in later chapters.

    g. Inbuilt functions are sometimes called **intrinsic functions.**

    h. A function call is sometimes called a **"function reference"**.

    i. Formal parameters and arguments are sometimes called **"dummy arguments"**.

    j. **"Structured programming"** is a term used to describe programming methods that employ program-level structuring and code-level structuring (18.57).

    k. If two functions both call each other they are said to be **mutually recursive.**

STUDENT SELF-TESTING QUESTIONS

1. State seven aims of program design and give possible reasons for these aims.
2. What is meant when we say that a program is "correct".

STUDENT SELF-TESTING QUESTIONS CONTINUED

3. The following program is required to obtain a set of real number values from the user in a "user-friendly" way and to output the total. The numbers are to be terminated by 999.

   a. Is the program correct? If not why not?

   b. What is wrong with the program design?

   c. Rewrite the program properly.

```
program a
variables
t, r:  real
Begin
repeat
input(r)
t := t + r
until r=999
output(t)
end
```

4. List the main sections of program documentation and explain the purpose of each section.

5. Distinguish between the roles of systems analysts and programmers.

6. Suppose that you may use an output function called "out", which is the same as "output" except that it does not cause a new line to be executed. For example, the statements:

```
out("a")
out("b")
```

give rise to the output "ab" on a single line.

NB. Assume **output** by itself cause a new line to be generated.

Produce a design, in pseudocode, for a program that for a given pair of positive integers outputs a suitably sized rectangle of asterisks. Suppose 5, 4 is input the output will be:

```
* * * * *
* * * * *
* * * * *
* * * * *
```

QUESTIONS WITHOUT ANSWERS

7. Distinguish between "program-level structure" and "code-level structure".

8. Explain the difference between "IN", "OUT" and "IN-OUT" parameters. "IN-OUT" parameters could be used instead of "IN" or "OUT" parameters but why shouldn't they be used in this way?

9. Assuming you may use the **"out"** function of question 6, produce a design in pseudocode for a program that takes in a single positive integer and outputs a triangle of corresponding size, eg, if 3 is input the output will be:

```
*
* *
* * *
```

GLOSSARY CHECKLIST

19: Program Specification

INTRODUCTION

19.1 This chapter examines methods and notations used to specify what programs are required to do and how they are required to do them.

19.2 A **program specification** is usually part of a **system specification**, which defines the whole system. In order to avoid needless repetition, the more general aspects of program specification are included in the chapters on system development (chapters 44 – 47) and are merely introduced in this chapter.

GENERAL REQUIREMENTS

19.3 Much of the detail within a program specification is specific to the particular problem to be solved. However, some general design aims (18.6) may be expressed explicitly as part of the program specification irrespective of the particular problem. The following requirements of a program design fall into this general category:

a. Program design style and its presentation.

b. Program reliability.

c. Program efficiency.

d. Program development time.

e. Program development costs.

f. Program documentation.

PROGRAM DESIGN STYLE AND ITS PRESENTATION

19.4 An insistence upon **structured programming** can directly contribute to the overall quality of programs and the achievement of many design aims. (18.6). Structured programs are not only more comprehensible they are also much easier to test and essential if program proving (18.34) is to be attempted.

19.5 Program presentation is another important issue. Aids to presentation include:

a. The use of long meaningful identifiers for programs, subprograms, variables and constants.

b. The indenting of code to highlight its structure.

c. The use of appropriate program structures.

d. Restricting the size of subprograms to manageable lengths, eg, insisting that no subprogram occupies more than one page.

e. Incorporating comments within the program that explain what is being done and how it is done.

19.6 The use of more advanced methods based upon **Object Oriented Programming OOP** may provide even further benefits. In these methods each data structure is contained solely within one program **module**. The idea is to keep all information about the data structure within the one module so that changes to its design and implementation can be localised. Access to the data is provided by a set of functions controlled by the module but visible outside it. For example, a module might be used for an array and provide functions to input data to the array and output values from the array sorted into sequence. Such methods are called **"data encapsulation"** or **"information hiding"** and use the idea of an **abstract data type**.

PROGRAM RELIABILITY

19.7 It is common for program specification to be accompanied by carefully laid down methods for testing the program. Appropriate methods were discussed in the previous chapter. A program that passes its test may be "certified" and put into use. If the program continues to work for some appreciable time without failure, it may be regarded as reasonably reliable. It is useful to quantify reliability in some way. One measure of reliability, borrowed from engineering, is **mean time between failures**. This is the average time that elapses between program failures being detected. A failure could be anything from the output of a wrong result to a non-recoverable and unexpected termination of execution called a **"crash"**.

PROGRAM EFFICIENCY

19.8 The efficiency of a program may be expressed in terms of its use of resources such as time and storage space. There are some obvious links between efficiency and complexity (18.31). For example, a less complex method of sorting an array will be more efficient than a more complex method. There is often a trade-off between time and storage saving.

19.9 Efficiency is better achieved by adopting a sound design method rather than by using programming "tricks" that result in compact but unreadable programs, which will undoubtedly fail to achieve any other requirements of the program's specification. It is better to design a program to work first and make it efficient later.

19.10 A well-written program containing a simple subprogram to sort an array, say, can easily be made to perform faster by merely rewriting that subprogram. The same idea applies on a larger scale. A good design may turn out to be efficient enough by itself. If it is not, it will be much easier to make efficient than a poorly designed program.

19.11 The use of subprograms may slow down execution speeds slightly because of the time taken for parameter passing, but this can be turned to advantage in dealing with the efficient use of restricted storage space. This happens when **segmentation** is possible.

19.12 A **segmented program** is one that, when executed, allows some parts of the program (segments) to take turns in occupying the same area of main storage. Segments will occupy main storage when they are executed and be held on disk, say, the rest of the time.

19.13 Overlays. Copying programs or subprograms into the same area of main storage during execution is known as performing an overlay.

PROGRAM DEVELOPMENT TIME

19.14 There is usually some limit set on the amount of time to be used in designing and implementing a program. Such limits may cause the quality of the program to suffer, but the quality should not be allowed to suffer unnecessarily. The urgent desire to get a program up and running can tempt the programmer to economise on the design and hurry on to the implementation. This "rushing to write the code" usually makes matters worse. The best strategy is to produce a good design from which a quick and simplified implementation can be produced if necessary.

19.15 Milestones. Some program specifications state dates by which specific parts of the programming task must be completed. These are called "milestones". To the programmer they may seem more like millstones!

PROGRAM DEVELOPMENT COSTS

19.16 Programs must usually be produced within specific budgets. The consequences of such limits are very similar to those for time.

PROGRAM DOCUMENTATION

19.17 Here, we build on the basic ideas of program documentation introduced in 18.22. Program documentation varies according to its intended use. Three main areas of use are:

a. For the programmer's own present or future use, as an aid to all stages in programming.

b. For the present or future use of other programmers, including the programmer's supervisor, eg, for maintenance, modification, debugging, etc.

c. For the users of the program, who may themselves vary in expertise.

19.18 The following items may be expected as part of the complete process of documentation:

a. A statement of the problem (system and program specification).

b. Documents specifying the format of inputs and outputs, including checks on the validity of data.

c. Details of the data structures used, plus details of how data in files is to be organised, accessed and kept secure (details later).

d. Details of the algorithms and procedures used to solve the problem. These must be in a suitable form, eg, pseudocode.

e. A carefully devised set of test data with evidence to show that the test data has been used to good effect.

f. Evidence to show that the program not only works but also that it has simple, effective, unambiguous and error-free methods of input and output for the program's users (ie, a good "user interface").

g. Detailed instructions to the user (or installer), eg,

    i. Limitations of the program.

    ii. Requirements in order to run the program (eg, hardware needed).

    iii. Details of how to run the program.

    iv. Instructions, with examples, on how to use the program. These may take the form of a **user manual** with additional instructions output by the program when it runs.

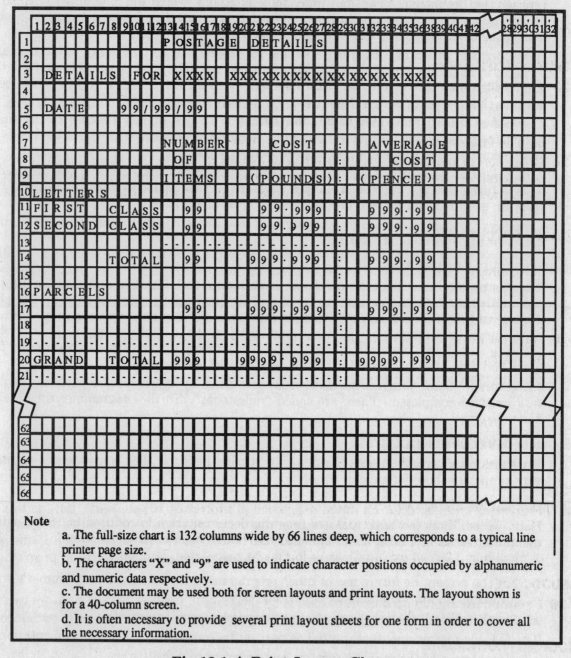

Note

a. The full-size chart is 132 columns wide by 66 lines deep, which corresponds to a typical line printer page size.

b. The characters "X" and "9" are used to indicate character positions occupied by alphanumeric and numeric data respectively.

c. The document may be used both for screen layouts and print layouts. The layout shown is for a 40-column screen.

d. It is often necessary to provide several print layout sheets for one form in order to cover all the necessary information.

Fig 19.1 A Print Layout Chart.

DETAILED SPECIFICATION

19.19 The discussion of documentation concluded the general aspects of program specification and also introduced some specific aspects, which need more detailed attention. The three areas of specification important to each particular application are the specification of:

    a. Inputs.

    b. Outputs.

    c. Processing.

INPUT SPECIFICATION

19.20 The two main considerations here are the definitions of:

a. The data items to be input, their data types, what values it is valid for them to take and what actions are to be taken if an attempt is made by a user to enter invalid data.

b. The formats in which input data values are to be entered. For example, the layout of screens may need specifying along with a description of how a dialogue with the user should take place.

19.21 **Screen layouts** for data input (or output) may be specified on special forms called **screen layout charts**, which consist of boxes set out in a grid in rows and columns that correspond to character positions on the screen. They are similar to print layout charts, which will be described shortly.

19.22 Many modern systems provide special programs that enable screen layout to be designed directly on the screen. This avoids the need for pencil and paper specifications.

OUTPUT SPECIFICATION

19.23 The main considerations are the definitions of:

a. What data is to be output, how it is to be derived from the input data, when it is to be produced and the form in which it is to be produced.

b. The formats in which the data is to be output.

19.24 **Print layout charts** are used to give precise definitions of how the output data is to be printed. One output report may take several print layout charts to define. One chart might provide a specimen layout, another might give a precise definition of the formats of the individual data items (see Fig. 19.1).

PROCESS SPECIFICATION

19.25 The specification of how the processing is to take place needs to give a precise definition of *what* processing is needed by giving the relationship between the input data and the output data. At times some details of *how* the processing is to be done are also given, but if the definition is too prescriptive of how the processing is to take place the definition has taken over a significant part of the task of programming and may exclude alternatives that merit consideration.

19.26 Some standard ways of specifying processing will now be considered. They are:

a. English.

b. Pseudocode.

c. Flowcharts.

d. Program structure block diagrams.

e. Warnier diagrams.

f. Decision tables and trees.

ENGLISH

19.27 English is often used for an initial expression of processing requirements, but, as was discussed in 16.10 - 16.18, English is a natural language that lacks the precision of meaning and simplicity needed when programming a computer. The chief use of English in producing specifications is as a means of providing informal explanations to formal languages and notations.

PSEUDOCODE

19.28 **Pseudocode** should need no introduction by this stage in the text. Its basic advantages have already been explained (16.18) and the reader can judge for him or herself how useful pseudocode is.

PROGRAM FLOWCHARTS

19.29 Flowcharts are traditional means of showing, in diagrammatic form, the sequence of steps in performing a programming task (see Appendix 3.2).

19.30 Program flowcharts are generally produced in two stages representing different levels of details:

a. Outline program flowcharts.

b. Detailed program flowcharts.

19.31 **Outline program flowcharts.** Outline program flowcharts represent the first stage of turning the systems flowchart into the necessary detail to enable the programmer to write the programs. As implied by the title they present the actual computer operations in outline only (see Fig. 19.2a).

19.32 **Detailed program flowcharts.** These charts are prepared from the outline charts and will contain the *detailed* computer steps necessary to perform the particular task. It is from these charts that the programmer will prepare his or her program coding sheets. Such is the amount of detail involved that these charts are often prepared by individual programmers each taking a segment of the outline charts (see Fig. 19.2b).

THE LIMITATIONS OF FLOWCHARTS

19.33 Flowcharts were originally introduced as aids to a systematic process of analysing problems and developing suitable computer-based solutions. In recent years flowcharts have been heavily criticised as being cumbersome and inefficient tools for the job. Newer alternatives have been introduced and widely adopted.

19.34 Particular limitations of flowcharts are:

a. Different levels of detail can easily become confused, eg, details of a particular implementation can be inadvertently introduced too early in the design.

b. There are no obvious mechanisms for progressing from one level of design to the next, eg, from system flowchart to outline program flowchart.

c. The essentials of *what* is done can too easily be lost in the technical details of *how* it is done.

d. Program flowcharts, although easy to follow, are not such a natural way of expressing procedures as writing in English, nor are they easily translated into programming languages.

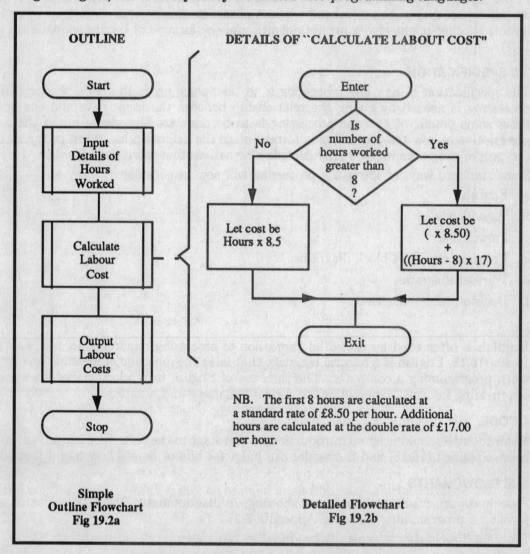

Fig. 19.2. Examples of flowcharts.

PROGRAM STRUCTURE BLOCK DIAGRAMS (See also structure diagrams Fig. 18.2)

19.35 There are many varieties of program structure block diagrams. They are all based upon the original idea proposed by **Nassi and Shneiderman** in 1973. Their "Nassi Shneiderman Structured Flowcharts" **NSSF** were intended as a replacement for traditional flowcharts that aided the writing of structured code. NSSFs and variations upon them have had some measure of success but are often criticised as only being suitable for low-level specifications. Typical examples are shown in Fig. 19.3.

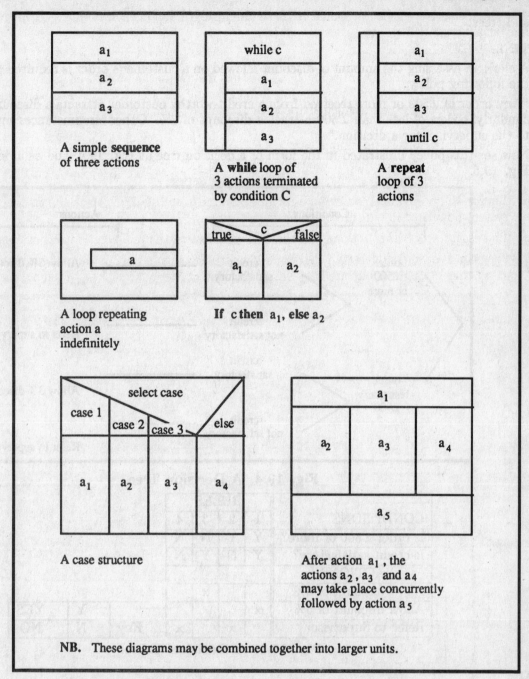

Fig. 19.3. Program Structure Block Diagram Examples.

WARNIER DIAGRAMS

19.36 Warnier diagrams are a simple way of writing out processing requirements in a structured form. They are mostly used for drafting out simple procedures before attempting to express the procedures in more precise forms such as pseudocode. They are no longer used to any extent so further discussion is not merited.

DECISION TABLES AND TREES

19.37 In considering a particular problem it is sometimes difficult to see all the possible factors involved and how they interact. **Decision tables** are used to analyse a problem. The conditions applying in the particular problem are set out, and the actions to be taken, as a result of any combination of the conditions arising, are shown. **Decision trees** are a graphical representation of decision tables. Their purpose is to aid the construction of decision tables.

19.38 Decision tables and trees are means of expressing process logic. They may therefore be used in conjunction with, or in place of, flowcharts or pseudocode.

19.39 We begin with a very simple example of a commercial situation involving conditions and actions. The example is then used in the succeeding paragraphs to illustrate the concepts of decision tables and trees.

EXAMPLE 1

19.40 A clerk, in assessing the amount of discount allowed on a customer's order is required to comply with the following policy:

"Any order of £500 or more received from a credit-worthy customer attracts a discount of 5% , and, similarly, orders of less than £500 attract a discount of 3%. Other circumstances must be referred to the supervisor for a decision."

Now see this policy illustrated in the form of a decision tree at Fig. 19.4, and as a decision table at Fig. 19.5.

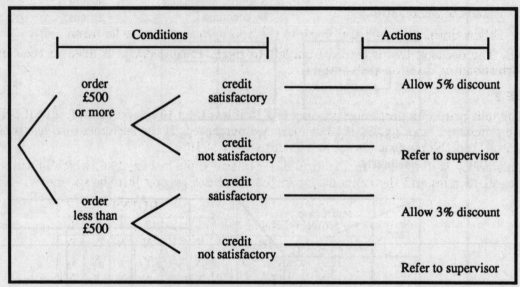

Fig. 19.4. A Decision Tree.

CONDITIONS	RULES			
	1	2	3	4
Is order £500 or more?	Y	Y	N	N
Is credit satisfactory?	Y	N	Y	N
ACTIONS				
Allow discount of 3%			x	
Allow discount of 5%	x			
Refer to Supervisor		x		x

Key	Y	YES
	N	NO

Fig. 19.5. A Decision Table.

FORMAT

19.41 Decision tables have a standardised format and are composed of four sections (separated by double lines):

    a. **Condition stub.** This section contains a list of all possible conditions that could apply in a particular problem, eg, "order of £500 or more", "satisfactory credit".

    b. **Condition entry.** This section contains the different *combinations* of the conditions, each combination being given a number termed a "Rule".

    c. **Action stub.** This section contains a list of the possible actions that could apply for any given combination of conditions, eg, give discount of "3%", "5%", "refer to supervisor".

    d. **Action entry.** This section shows the action to be take for each combination of conditions.

    NB. The decision tree contains the same information but in a less formal way.

METHOD OF PREPARATION

19.42 In constructing a decision table from a narrative given to you in an examination, go about it in an orderly way. The following steps are given for you to follow in constructing a decision table.

    a. List the conditions in the *condition* stub.

    b. Work out the possible number of combinations of conditions, ie, 2^n where n = the number of conditions. This will give you the number of rules and ensures that the table is complete.

In the worked example, there are 2 conditions, thus $2^2 (2 \times 2) - 4$ possible combinations (rules).

c. Rule up sufficient columns in the condition entry section for the number of combinations, ie, 4.

d. When entering "Y" or "N" the combinations must be *unique* (ie, no two columns must be alike). The "halve" rule is applied to each row of condition rules as follows:

    i. **Row 1.** Ys are inserted for half the number to rules (2 in our case) then Ns are inserted for the other half.

    ii. **Row 2.** Alternate the Ys and Ns, the groups being half the size of those in Row 1. (The group size in our example is 2, therefore the second row size will be 1, ie, Y, N, Y, N.)

In an example where there are more than two rows, the halve rule is continued for the other row.

e. Enter the action stub.

f. Follow down each rule and mark in the appropriate action to be taken.

NB. The decision tree is drawn from left to right. Each question is filled in the same order as the corresponding decision stub entry.

EXAMPLE 2

19.43 The unit price of a particular product is £15 if less than 10 are purchased, £14 if between 10 and 49 are purchased, and £13.80 if 50 or more are purchased. If the customer also has preferred customer status then the purchase is subject to a discount of 10%.

This policy is illustrated in the form of a decision table in Fig. 19.6, which is arrived at by setting out all 16 rules and then eliminating impossible cases leaving just the six shown.

CONDITIONS	RULES					
	1	2	3	4	5	6
order < 10	Y	Y	N	N	N	N
10 ≤ order < 50	N	N	Y	Y	N	N
50 ≤ order	N	N	N	N	Y	Y
Preferred Customer	Y	N	N	Y	N	N
ACTIONS						
charge £15 per item		x				
charge £13.5 per item	x					
charge £14 per item				x		
charge £12.6 per item			x			
charge £13.80 per item						x
charge £12.42 per item					x	

Fig. 19.6

19.44 The form of decision table dealt with is called **limited entry decision tables** because the *conditions* and *actions* are *limited* to the condition/action *stub* respectively. **Extended entry decision tables** are ones showing a *part* only of the condition/action in the *stub* with the balance in the *entry*, eg, in the action *stub* in Fig. 19.5 the first two actions could be combined as "allow discount" and in the action *entry* "3%" and "5%" shown in place of the crosses.

19.45 Limited entry format and extended entry format can both be used in a single table for individual conditions or actions. Where a table contains *both* types of format it is called a **mixed entry decision table**.

a. When one type of format is used in preference to another depends on particular circumstances. In general terms, extended entry and mixed entry tables use few conditions and actions and are thus more compact, but are not so easily checked for completeness as are limited entry tables.

b. It is possible to present processing requirements to the computer in the form of decision tables instead of programs, provided a special item of software called a "decision table processor" is available. Although some decision table processors have been available for a number of years, they have not been widely adopted.

FORMAL SPECIFICATION

19.46 A **formal specification** is one which each statement has *a single meaning*. Specifications written in pseudocode are said to be **precise** because although they are not strictly formal they do leave far less room for ambiguity than specifications written in a "natural language" such as English.

19.47 In this chapter various aspects of program specification have been examined together with some standard ways of specifying *what* processing is needed. The methods given have *not* been formal, although most have been precise. This lack of complete precision can result in a program written from such a specification not doing exactly what was required.

Such mistakes can be very costly, irritating, time consuming and, on occasions, downright dangerous.

19.48 A program itself *is* formal, but specifies not only **what** is required but **how** it is to be carried out. What is needed is a formal notation able to express **what** a program is required to do without specifying **how** it is to be done.

19.49 Several advantages can be gained from using a formal notation for program specifications:

a. Potential ambiguities can be identified and eliminated from the specification at an early stage in development.

b. It simplifies the overall task by separating concerns about what is required from matters of how to achieve it.

c. It avoids placing unnecessary and undesirable restrictions upon how the implementation is done.

d. It is at a sufficiently high level that it may serve as a specification for more than one implementation. For example, the specification may first be used for a simple, quick, low-cost but inefficient implementation that may later be replaced by a higher-quality alternative.

e. It is possible to carry out mathematical proofs using the notation showing that the implementation matches the specification. This is an aid to ensuring reliability. The methods used are outside the scope of this book.

19.50 The following examples show how some simple procedures may be specified. The intention is not to make the reader proficient at writing specifications; that would require several chapters. It should, however, provide the reader with an insight into what may be involved in working from a formal specification.

In each case the formal specification is preceded by an informal description.

19.51 Example 1.

a. **Informal.** A simple procedure called "min" takes as input the two integers "a" and "b" and produces as a result "r", which is also an integer and which has a value equal to the minimum value of "a" and "b".

b. **Formal.**

```
min:            Int Int → Int

pre-min(a,b):   true

post-min(a,b,r): (*
                r is no greater than a or b
                and is equal to one of them
                *)
                r ≤ a AND r ≤ b
                AND
                (r = a OR r = b)
```

Note.

i. The line **min: Int Int → Int** gives the **signature** of the procedure. In other words, it defines the data types of the input values (more correctly called **input parameters**) and the result. The result's type is to the right of the arrow.

ii. The line **pre-min(a,b): true** is a **pre-condition**. It states what must be true of the input parameters taken by the procedure for the procedure to give a result. The value "true" indicates that there are no restrictions on the parameters and therefore there is a result for all integer values of "a" and "b".

iii. The lines starting with **post-min** form the **post-condition**. The post-condition states what is true when the procedure gives a result.

c. Implementation – outlined in pseudocode.

```
if
    a < b
then
    r := a
else
    r := b
endif
```

19.52 Example 2.

a. **Informal.** A procedure called "grade" takes as input an examination mark "m" expressed as a percentage in the range 0...100. It gives as output a grade "g", which is "F" for a mark below 40%, "P" for a mark of 40% or more but less than 60% and "C" if the mark is 60% or more.

b. **Formal.**

```
grade:              Int → Character

pre-grade(m):       m ≥ 0 AND m ≤ 100

post-grade(m,g):    ( g = "F" AND m < 40 )
                    OR
                    ( g = "P" AND m ≥ 40 AND m < 60 )
                    OR
                    ( g = "C" AND m ≥ 60 )
```

c. **Note.** The significantly different feature in this example is the pre-condition, which indicates that the procedure only has **defined results** for values of "m" between 0 and 100 inclusive. The procedure should therefore not be used with values outside the specified range. If the procedure is used with values outside the defined range, there is no knowing what the function may do because nothing has been specified.

d. **Implementation**

```
if
    ((m < 0) OR ( m > 100))
then
    fail("Grade -- marks outside the range 0...1")
else
    if
        m < 40
    then
        g := "F"
    else
        if
            m < 60
        then
            g := "P"
        else
            g := "C"
        endif
    endif
endif
```

19.53 Note.
In the implementation it has been decided that the procedure will fail to give a result if the parameters taken do not satisfy the pre-condition. This is about the best that can be done under the circumstances. The **fail** statement will stop the execution of the program and leave a display on the user's terminal so that the source of the failure can be identified. Of course such failures should be avoided by only using procedures in a defined way. It is a poor-quality program that allows user actions to lead to such failures.

SUMMARY

19.54 a. General requirements present in all program specifications were discussed.

b. Detailed specifications of inputs, outputs and processing were described.

POINTS TO NOTE

19.55 a. Many of the problems of specifying, designing and implementing individual programs are present on a larger scale when specifying designing and implementing whole systems.

b. The "dash" rule can sometimes be used to simplify the problem when constructing decision tables. For example, if these two columns result in the same action.

Y Y
N Y

they may be replaced by the single column.

Y
-

where the data "-" means yes or no.

STUDENT SELF-TESTING QUESTIONS

1. Briefly describe eight items to be included in program documentation.
2. A programmer's salary scale has three points. Applications for posts are placed on the scale according to the following criteria: people over 25 years of age with either a degree in computing or three years' programming experience are placed on scale point two; where applicants over 25 have both of these qualifications they are placed on point three; applications under 25 with either a degree in computing or three years' programming are placed on point one, while those with both are placed on point two. All other applicants are rejected. Construct a decision table for the placing of candidates on the salary scale. Show that your table covers all possibilities and reduce the table to eliminate redundancy.
3. Work from the answer to question 3 to produce a program design in pseudocode that takes in the required data and generates suitable results.

   Before you write your pseudocode design suitable layouts for the inputs and outputs.

QUESTIONS WITHOUT ANSWERS

4. A publisher produces short books on topics in computing. These are published in two page sizes, A4 and A5; they are also available in paperback or hardback. The selling price will depend on these two factors and the expected sale. The A4-size books cost £2 more than the corresponding A5 book. The hardback copy costs £3 more than a paperback copy. The selling price for paperback A5 copies is £15 per copy if the expected sale is greater than 5,000 and £18 otherwise.

   Construct a decision table for this pricing scheme. Show that the table is complete and eliminate any redundancy if possible.
5. Design a program in pseudocode that can determine the selling price of a book from suitable input using the answer from question 5 as the basis of your design.
6. The stamp charge on a letter or postcard is based upon the class (1 or 2) and the weight in grams. Obtain up-to-date information from your post office and then design a decision table and program based upon the values you have obtained. The user of the program should be asked to key in the class and number of grams and the program should output the stamp required.

QUESTIONS WITHOUT ANSWERS CONTINUED

7. A common programming problem in computer payroll systems is **coin analysis**. Given a sum of money to be paid, the appropriate notes and coins required for payment must be determined. For example, given the sum £57.93, payment could be made as follows.

2 × £20 notes	40.00
1 × £10 note	10.00
1 × £5 note	5.00
2 × £1 coin	2.00
1 × 50p coin	.50
2 × 20p coin	.40
1 × 2p coin	.02
1 × 1p coin	.01
	£57.93

Design a program that is able to perform coin analysis on an input sum.

8. a. Define the term, and explain the importance of, subroutines. Explain two ways of passing information to and from a subroutine. **6**

   b. A list is held in store that contains the mark that each student gained in a particular examination. A subroutine must be produced to find the maximum mark gained, the minimum mark gained, and the mark that was gained by most students. **6**

   i. Using a flowchart, or some other suitable method, describe an algorithm for this subroutine. **6**

   ii. Describe how this subroutine may be used by another programmer. **4**

   iii. Explain how you would test this subroutine after it had been coded into a suitable high-level language. **4=20**

JMB

GLOSSARY CHECKLIST

FILES AND FILE PROCESSING

1. This is an important Part of the text for all examinations at which the text is aimed. However, the more detailed aspects of files organisation and access together with specific programming methods are not required for all examination courses so the reader would be wise to check syllabus details.
2. Files are named collections of stored data. Files tend to be too large to be held in main storage and are therefore held on backing storage devices such as magnetic disks and magnetic tapes. When data in a file is required for processing the file is read into main storage in manageable amounts.
3. Named programs are also often held on backing storage ready for use and may be regarded as "files" too. In this Part of the text we are primarily concerned with file stored for data processing which we may call **"data files"** to distinguish them from files containing programs. The term "data file" is interpreted broadly in this context to include text files.
4. Chapter 20 sets out the concepts of magnetic files. Chapter 21 describes the methods of organising a file on *disk* and magnetic *tape* and how access is made to the records in such a file.
5. In the interests of clarity only two storage devices are used as a basis for discussing computer files. These are:

   a. Disk (Magnetic hard or floppy, plus optical) – Direct Access Storage (DAS).

   b. Magnetic tape – Serial Access Storage (SAS).
6. The *general* principles discussed with regard to *disk* or magnetic *tape* can be applied to other media according to whether the media are SAS media or DAS media.
7. Chapters 22 and 23 describes methods of file processing. The emphasis in chapter 22 is on sequential files and can therefore be applied both to DAS and to SAS. In chapter 23 the emphasis is on non-sequential file processing and therefore is only applicable to DAS.
8. The chapters 22 and 23 not only describe basic methods they also deal with important aspects of controlling file processing. Additionally, they contrast the ideas of batch processing with transaction processing.

20: Computer File Concepts

INTRODUCTION

20.1 The purpose of this chapter is to look at the general concepts that lie behind the subject of computer files before going on to discuss the different methods of organising them. At all times the term "file" will refer to computer data files.

20.2 **Purpose.** A file holds data that is required for providing information. Some files are processed at regular intervals to provide this information (eg, payroll file) and others will hold data that is required at regular intervals (eg, a file containing prices of items).

20.3 There are two common ways of viewing files:

a. **Logical files.** A "logical file" is a file viewed in terms of *what* data items its records contain and *what* processing operations may be performed upon the file. The user of the file will normally adopt such a view.

b. **Physical files.** A "physical file" is a file viewed in terms of *how* the data is stored on a storage device such as a magnetic disk and *how* the processing operations are made possible.

20.4 A logical file can usually give rise to a number of alternative physical file implementations. These alternatives are considered in later chapters.

ELEMENTS OF A COMPUTER FILE

20.5 A file consists of a number of **records**. Records were defined in 17.37. Here we consider records in a slightly different way because we are concerned with the way they are commonly stored. Each record is made up of a number of **fields** and each field consists of a number of **characters**.

CLOCK NUMBER	EMPLOYEE'S NAME	DATE OF BIRTH	SEX	GRADE	HOURLY RATE
1201	P J JOHNS	06 12 45	F	4	850

Field   Field of characters "P", "J", "J", etc.

Notes: 1. Clock number is the Key field, (20.10.)
2. Grade is coded.
3. Hourly rate is expressed in pence.

Fig. 20.1. Payroll Record (part only).

a. **Character.** A character is the smallest element in a file and can be alphabetic, numeric or special, (2.2).

b. **Field.** An item of data within a *record* is called a field - it is made up of a number of *characters*, eg, a name, a date, or an amount.

c. **Record.** A record is made up of a number of related fields, eg, a customer record, or an employee payroll record (see Fig. 20.1).

ALTERNATIVE TERMINOLOGY

20.6 The terminology of 20.5 (ie, record, field and character) is firmly established as a means of describing the characteristics of files in general situations. However, the use of this terminology can lead to excessive attention being directed towards physical details, such as how many characters there should be in a field. Such issues can divert attention from matters of high priority, such as what fields should be recorded in order to meet the information needs of the user. To overcome this difficulty, two alternative sets of terms have been developed, one set for physical files, and the other set for logical files. They are:

a. For physical files.

  i. Physical record.

      ii. Field.

      iii. Character (a physical feature).

   b. **For logical files.**

      i. Logical record - an "entity".

      ii. Data item - "attributes" of the "entity".

20.7 Entities are things (eg, objects, people, events, etc.) about which there is a need to record data, eg, an item of stock, an employee, a financial transaction, etc. The individual properties of the entity, about which data is recorded, are its **"attributes"**, eg, the attributes of an invoice (entity) will include the "name"; "address"; "customer order number"; "quantity"; "price"; "description".

     A logical record is created for each entity occurrence and the logical record contains one **data item** for each **occurrence** of the entity's attributes, eg, the "customer's name" would be a data item and there would be **one** only in the logical record. Whereas the attributed "quantity" would have as many data items as there are entries on the invoice.

20.8 The relationship between the various terms used is summarised in the following table:

Things about which there is a need to record data	Entities	–	each entity has a number of *attributes*
How the data is recorded	Logical records (1 per entity occurrence)	–	each logical record contains a number of *data items*
Physical details of how the data is recorded	Physical record (1 or more per logical records	–	each physical record contains a number of *fields*

TYPES OF FILES

20.9 a. **Master file.** These are files of a fairly permanent nature, eg, customer ledger, payroll, inventory, etc. A feature to note is the regular *updating* of these files to show a current position. For example customer's orders will be processed, increasing the "balance owing" figure on a customer ledger record. It is seen therefore that master records will contain both data of a static nature, eg, a customer name and address, and data that, by its nature will change *each time* a transaction occurs, eg, the "balance" figure already mentioned.

   b. **Movement file.** Also called **transaction file.** This is made up of the various transactions created from the source documents. In a sales ledger application the file will contain all the orders received at a particular time. This file will be used to update the *master file.* As soon as it has been used for this purpose it is no longer required. It will therefore have a very short life, because it will be replaced by a file containing the *next* batch of orders.

   c. **Reference file.** A file with a reasonable amount of permanency. Examples of data used for reference purposes are price lists, tables of rates of pay, names and addresses.

ACCESS TO FILES

20.10 **Key fields.** When files of data are created one needs a means of access to particular records within those files. In *general* terms this is usually done by giving each record a "key" field by which the record will be recognised or identified. Such a key is normally a *unique identifier* of a record and is then called the **primary** key. Sometimes the primary key is made from the combination of two fields in which case it may be called a **composite key** or **compound key.** Any other field used for the purpose of identifying records, or sets of records, is called a **secondary key.** Examples of primary key fields are:

   a. Customer number in a customer ledger record.

   b. Stock code number in a stock record.

   c. Employee clock number in a payroll record.

20.11 Not only does the key field assist in accessing records but also the records themselves can, if required, be *sorted* into the sequence indicated by the key.

STORAGE DEVICES

20.12 Mention is made here of the two storage devices that will be considered in connection with the storage of files (ie, physical files).

a. **Magnetic or optical disk.** These are direct access media and are the primary means of storing files on-line.

b. **Magnetic tape.** This medium has significant limitations because it is a serial access medium.

20.13 These characteristics will loom large in our considerations about files in the chapters that follow. Note then that they are inherent in the *physical* make-up of the devices and will clearly influence the *type* of files stored on each one, and how the files can be *organised* and *accessed*.

PROCESSING ACTIVITIES

20.14 We will need to have access to particular records in the files in order to process them. The major processing activities are given below:

a. **Updating.** When data on a master record is changed to reflect a current position, eg, updating a customer ledger record with new orders. Note that the old data on the record is replaced by the new data.

b. **Referencing.** When access is made to a particular record to ascertain what is contained therein, eg, reference is made to a "prices" file during an invoicing run. Note that it does *not* involve any alterations to the record itself.

c. **File maintenance.** New records must be added to a file and records need to be deleted. Prices change, and the file must be altered. Customers' addresses also change and new addresses have to be inserted to bring the file up to date. These particular activities come under the heading of "maintaining" the file. File maintenance can be carried out as a separate run, but the insertions and deletions of records are sometimes *combined* with updating.

d. **File enquiry or interrogation.** This is similar in concept to referencing. It involves the need to ascertain a piece of information from, say, a master record. For example, a customer may query a Statement sent to him. A "file enquiry" will get the data in dispute from the record so that the query may be settled.

FIXED-LENGTH AND VARIABLE-LENGTH RECORDS

20.15 The question whether to use records of a fixed or variable length is one that usually does not have to be considered in manual systems.

a. **Fixed.** Every record in the file will be of the same fixed number of fields and characters and will never vary in size.

b. **Variable.** This means that not *all* records in the file will be of the same size. This could be for two reasons:

  i. Some records could have more *fields* than others. In an invoicing application, for example (assuming a 6-character field to represent "total amount for each invoice"), we would add a new field to a customer record for each invoice. So a customer's record would vary in *size* according to the *number* of invoices he had been sent.

  ii. Fields *themselves* could vary in size. A simple example is "the name and address" field because it varies widely in size.

20.16 It should be noted, however, that in the examples at 20.15b a fixed-length record *could* be used. In 20.15b.i the record could be designed in the first instance to accommodate a fixed number of *possible* invoices. This means the records with less than the fixed number of invoices would contain blank fields. Similarly in 20.15b.ii the field could be made large enough to accommodate the *largest* name and address. Again records with names and addresses of a smaller number of characters would contain blanks.

20.17 Fixed-length records make it easy for the programmer because he or she is dealing with a known quantity of characters each time. On the other hand they result in less efficient utilisation of storage. Variable-length records mean difficulties for the programmer but better utilisation.

HIT RATE

20.18 This is the term used to describe the rate of processing of master files in terms of active records. For example, if 1,000 transactions are processed each day against a master file of 10,000 records, then the hit rate is said to be 10%. Hit rate is a measure of the **"activity"** of the file.

OTHER FILE CHARACTERISTICS

20.19 Apart from **activity**, which is measured by hit rate, there are other characteristics of the file that need to be considered. These are:

a. **Volatility.** This is the frequency with which records are added to the file or deleted from it. If the frequency is high, the file is said to be **volatile**. A file that is not altered is "static". If the frequency is low, the file is said to be **"semi-static"**.

b. **Size.** This is the amount of data stored in the file. It may be expressed in terms of the number of characters or number of records.

c. **Growth.** Files often grow steadily in size as new records are added. Growth must be allowed for when planning how to store a file.

DATA HIERARCHY

20.20 The data structure of a file forms part of a **data hierarchy**, as shown below.

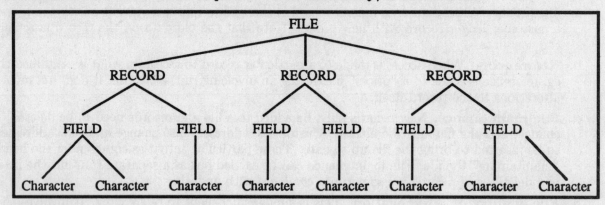

OTHER FILE TYPES

20.21 **Document Files** were introduced in chapter 5 with particular reference to the simplest form of document file the **text file** (5.3). Other common forms of document files are those used in conjunction with word processors or desktop publishing systems. More generally, "document files" may hold the files used by painting or drawing packages.

20.22 In a typical document file the records each have a single field of variable length and correspond to units of text such as lines or paragraphs. The records may not necessarily have key fields although a text line number is sometimes used as a key. A high-level language program may be stored as a text file.

20.23 Other types of files may also be referred to in the following ways:

a. **Program file.** A file in which the "data" held in the file is some item of software such as a simple program or collection of program parts.

b. **Data file.** The types of file described so far, as opposed to **program file**.

c. **Input and output files. Either** files formed from source documents but not sufficiently organised for use as transaction files (eg, not sorted) **or** files holding processed data awaiting output.

d. **Work file.** A file created during an intermediate stage in processing.

e. **Scratch file.** A file no longer needed which may be overwritten.

SUMMARY

20.24 a. A file is a collection of *related* records.

b. A file is made up of **records,** which are made up of **fields,** which are made up of **characters.**

c. It is often advantageous to distinguish between physical files and logical files.

d. Fields within logical records are normally called "data items" (or just "items")

e. A record is recognised or identified by the record KEY.

f. Files can be broadly classified as master files, movement (or transaction) files and reference files.

g. The physical nature of the storage device will have a direct bearing on the way files are organised on it, and also the method of access.

h. The physical nature of the storage device will have a direct bearing on the way files are organised on it, and also on the method of access.

i. Four processing activities are: updating, referencing, file maintenance and file enquiry or interrogation.

j. Referencing is usually carried out during updating and is incidental to it.

k. Files can consist of records of fixed length or variable length. The decision on which is adopted is a question of programming ease v storage utilisation.

POINTS TO NOTE

20.25 a. Magnetic tape is a serial-access medium, disk is a direct-access medium. Nevertheless disk can act as a serial-access medium if required.

b. Direct access should be distinguished from **immediate access**, which refers to access to main store.

c. Direct access is also called **random access** because it means access in no set order.

d. In terms of levels of storage direct access is below immediate access and above serial access.

e. A file may be described in terms of its **"structure"** and in terms of its **organisation**. Its *structure* is determined by which data items are included in records and how the data items are grouped within records. Its *organisation* is determined by how the records are arranged within the file.

f. Files are not normally held in **primary storage** (ie, main storage). They are normally held on an on-line backing storage (**secondary storage**) or on off-line backing storage.

STUDENT SELF-TESTING QUESTIONS

1. An organisation runs a simple savings scheme for its members. Members pay in sums of money to their own accounts and gain interest on the money saved. Data about the accounts is stored in a master file.
What would you suggest would be the entities used in this system? Also suggest what attributes these entities might have.
2. Define the term "key field". Discuss the suitability of the following data items as key fields.
   a. A person's surname in a personnel file.
   b. A national insurance number in a payroll file.
   c. A candidate number in an examinations file.
3. Define the terms "hit rate" and "volatility" with regard to computer files. Where else have you come across the term "volatility" in computer science?

QUESTIONS WITHOUT ANSWERS

4. Suppose the exam results for all students in your college or school were maintained in a master file. Comment on the probable characteristics of the file in terms of its
   a. Volatility,
   b. Activity,
   c. Size,
   d. Growth.

GLOSSARY CHECKLIST

Activity	20.18	Field	20.5
Attributes	20.7	File enquiry	20.14
Character	20.5	File maintainance	20.14
Composite key	20.10	Fixed-length record	20.15
Compound key	20.10	Hit rate	20.18
Data file	20.23	Input files	20.23
Data hierarchy	20.20	Items	20.24
Data item	20.7,20.24	Key fields	20.10
Document files	20.21	Logical files	20.3
Entities	20.7	Master files	20.9

GLOSSARY CHECKLIST CONTINUED

21: File Organisation and Access

INTRODUCTION

21.1 This chapter describes the ways in which files may be organised and accessed on disks and magnetic tapes. Before tackling this chapter the reader should be thoroughly conversant with the relevant hardware described in 7.4 – 7.36. Those paragraphs describe the physical attributes of magnetic tapes (in the form of reels or cartridges) and disks (fixed exchangeable). They also describe the "reading" and "writing" devices called the tape units and disk drives.

21.2 Today most file processing is carried out using files stored on hard magnetic disks. Optical disks only have a minority use at present although they are being used increasingly for applications requiring large volumes of archived or reference data. Floppy disks are only used as the main file processing medium on very small microcomputers. The principles covered by this chapter concerning the use of disks are applicable to all disk types. Any relevant differences will be highlighted when appropriate.

21.3 There is still a significant amount of file processing carried out using files stored on magnetic tape but it is almost all done on mainframes in large commercial, industrial or financial institutions. Magnetic tape continues to be an important backup medium especially in its cartridge forms.

21.4 Magnetic tape is in most respects a much simpler medium than disk. Indeed, the simplest methods of organising and accessing files on disk are very similar to the standard ones use for magnetic tape. Therefore, throughout this chapter the descriptions relating to tape are give before the corresponding descriptions for disk.

21.5 **File organisation** is the arrangement of records within a particular file. We start from the point where the individual physical record layout has been already designed, ie, the file "structure" has already been decided. How do we organise our many hundreds, or even thousands, of such records (eg, customer records) on magnetic tape or disk? When we wish to access one or more of the records how do we do it? This chapter explains how these things are done.

WRITING ON TAPE

21.6 Records are "written" in the first place from main storage onto the tape by the processor. Each record is written onto tape in response to a "write instruction". This process will be repeated until all the required records are written onto the tape, ie, until the file is complete. Fig. 21.1 illustrates what the tape will look like in diagrammatic form.

Cust. 1	Inter Record Gap	Cust. 2	Inter Record Gap	Cust. 3	Inter Record Gap	Cust. 4		etc...

Fig. 21.1. Diagram Illustrating Records on Magnetic Tape.

Notice the inter-record gap (IRG), which is caused by the tape slowing down at the conclusion of one "write" and accelerating at the beginning of the next.

READING FROM TAPE

21.7 Having created (ie, written) a file of records onto tape, we will later need to *process* the file. To do this, we take the reel of tape and mount it onto a tape unit. Records are now "read" *from* the tape into the main storage. Notice that when "reading", the tape automatically stops when the IRG is reached. It "knows" when to stop *either* because the length of the record is known in advance *or* because control data recorded on the end of the record marks the end of the record.

WRITING ON DISK

21.8 In order to process files stored on disk the disk pack must first be loaded into a disk unit. Records are "written" onto a disk as the disk pack revolves at a constant speed within its disk unit. Each record is written in response to a "write" instruction. Data goes from main storage through a read-write head onto a track on the disk surface. Records are recorded one after the other on each track.

Note. All references to "records" in this chapter should be taken to mean "physical records" unless otherwise stated.

READING FROM DISK

21.9 In order to process files stored on disk the disk pack must first be loaded into a disk unit. Records are read from the disk as it revolves at a constant speed. Each record is read in response to a "read" instruction. Data goes from the disk to the main storage through the read-write head already mentioned. Both reading and writing of data are accomplished at a fixed number (thousands) of bytes per second.

21.10 We will take for our discussion on file organisation a "6-disk" pack, meaning it has ten usable surfaces (the outer two are not used for recording purposes). But before describing how files are organised let us look first at the basic underlying concepts.

CYLINDER CONCEPT

21.11 Consult Fig. 7.3 where the disk pack is illustrated, and note the following:

  i. There are *ten* recording surfaces. Each surface has 200 tracks.

  ii. There is a read-write head for *each* surface on the disk pack.

  iii. *All* the read-write arms are fixed to *one* mechanism and are like a comb.

  iv. When the "access" mechanism moves all ten read-write heads move *in unison* across the disk surfaces.

  v. Whenever the access mechanism comes to rest *each* read-write head will be positioned on the equivalent track on *each* of the ten surfaces.

  vi. For *one* movement of the access mechanism access is possible to *ten* tracks of data.

21.12 In the case of a floppy disk the situation is essentially the same but simpler (Fig. 7.5). There is just *one* recording surface on a "single-sided" floppy disk and *two* recording surfaces on a "double-sided" floppy disk. The other significant differences are in term of capacity and speed.

21.13 Use is made of the physical features already described when organising the storage of records on disk. Records are written onto the disk starting with track 1 on surface 1, then track 1 on surface 2, then track 1 on surface 3 and so on to track 1 on surface 10. One can see that conceptually the ten tracks of data can be regarded as forming a CYLINDER.

21.14 Data is written onto successive cylinders, involving *one* movement only of the access mechanism for each cylinder. When access is made to the stored records it will be advantageous, in terms of keeping access mechanism movement to a minimum, to deal with a cylinder of records at a time.

21.15 Conceptually the disk can be regarded as consisting of 200 CYLINDERS. Cylinder 1 comprises track 1 on each of 10 surfaces; cylinder 2 comprises track 2 on each of the 10 surfaces and so on to cylinder 200, which comprises track 200 on each of the 10 surfaces. This CYLINDER CONCEPT is fundamental to an understanding of how records are organised on disks. An alternative term for cylinder is SEEK AREA, ie, the amount of data that is available to the read-write heads as a result of one movement or SEEK of the access mechanism.

HARD-SECTORED DISKS AND SOFT-SECTORED DISKS

21.16 The tracks on a disk are subdivided into **sectors** (see Fig. 21.2). There are two alternative design strategies for the division of tracks into sectors. One is called **soft sectoring,** the other is called **hard sectoring.**

In either case *whole* sectors of data are transferred between the disk and main storage.

Note. A disk said to have "no sectors" is effectively a soft-sectored disk.

21.17 A **soft-sectored** disk has sectors that may be varied in length, up to some maximum value that is never more than the size of a complete track. Sector size and position is *soft*ware controlled, hence the term "soft sectored".

21.18 A **hard-sectored** disk has sectors of fixed length. There may be anything from 8 - 128 sectors per track. Sector size and position is pre-determined by hardware, hence the term "hard sectored".

21.19 You may compare a sector with a physical record or block on magnetic tape (Fig. 21.1). In fact, it is common to use "sector" and "blocks" as synonyms. However, in the case of hard-sectored disks, blocks may be grouped together into larger units called "buckets" or "logical blocks". It is therefore prudent to call a sector a "physical block" so as to avoid any possible ambiguity.

BASIC ADDRESS CONCEPTS

21.20 As the disk is a direct-access device a record can be accessed independently of other records. To enable the disk to locate a record, the record must have some form of ADDRESS. The whole area of each disk can be subdivided to enable this to be accomplished.

  a. **Cylinder.** The major subdivision as we have seen is the cylinder.

  b. **Track.** Each cylinder is composed of a number of tracks (10 in our quoted example).

  c. **Block.** The smallest addressable part of a disk is a block (ie. a sector). This forms the **unit** of transfer between the disk and main storage.

  d. **Bucket.** When the block size is fixed (ie, when the disk is hard sectored) a number of blocks (ie, sectors) are grouped to form a larger unit of transfer. This unit is called a bucket or **logical block.**

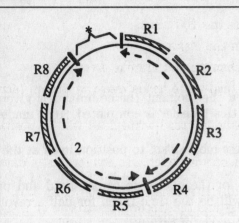

The start of each track is marked physically by a notch or hole. The start of each sector is marked by special data recorded there.

a. Soft-sectored Disk.

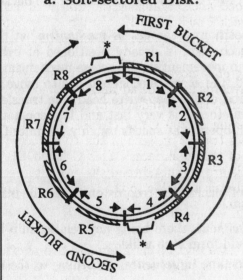

The start of each track and sector is marked physically by a notch or hole. There may also be recorded marks as on the soft-sectored disk.

Key
SECTORS (ie, BLOCKS)
    ARE NUMBERED 1, 2, 3 ....

LOGICAL RECORDS:
    ARE NUMBERED R1, R2, R3, ...

∗ INDICATES WASTED STORAGE SPACE.

b. A Hard-sectored Disk.

Note

Reading a bucket is treated as a single read operation, although in reality it is a sequence of hard-sector reads.

Fig. 21.2. Blocking Records on Magnetic Disks.

21.21 The block or the bucket is therefore the unit of input/output on disk. As on magnetic tape, records will be combined together to form one of these units. The optimum size for a block or bucket is determined by:

  a. the need to optimise fillage of a track — eg, if a size were chosen for a variable-length block that did not divide exactly into the track size, space would be wasted, (see Fig. 21.2).

  b. the need to minimise the number of transfers between main storage and disk storage. The larger the block or bucket size, the more records will be brought into main storage at each transfer, (eg, in Fig. 21.2b, four records are transferred at a time).

c. the need to economise in the use of main storage. A large block or bucket may occupy so much main storage that insufficient space is left for other data and programs.

21.22 In basic hardware terms, the address of a record is given thus:

a. cylinder number

b. track number

c. block number (which will be the first block in the bucket if this concept applies).

Note. On a single-sided floppy disk the address would be simply

a. "track" number
b. block number } (ie, one of a number of concentric tracks)

Thus the address 1900403 indicates

a. cylinder 190

b. track 4

c. block 3.

ACCESS TIME

21.23 Access time *on disk* is the time interval between the moment the command is given to transfer data from disk to main storage and the moment this transfer is completed. It is made up of three components:

a. **Seek time.** This is the time it takes the access mechanism to position itself at the appropriate cylinder.

b. **Rotational delay.** This is the time taken for the bucket to come round and position itself under the read-write head. On average this will be the time taken for half a revolution of the disk pack. This average is called the **"latency"** of the disk.

c. **Data transfer time.** This is the total time taken to *read* the contents of the bucket into main storage.

21.24 Access time will vary mainly according to the position of the *access mechanism* at the time the command is given. For example if the access mechanism is already positioned at cylinder 1 and the record required happens to be in cylinder 1 no movement of the access mechanism is required. If, however, the record required is in cylinder 200, the access mechanism has to move right across the surface of the disk. Once the bucket has arrived at the read-write head, the transfer of data to storage begins. *Speed of transfer* of data to main storage is very fast and is a constant rate of so many thousand bytes per second. A hard disk will operate at speeds roughly 10 times faster than a floppy disk.

FILE ORGANISATION ON TAPE

21.25 Organisation of a file on tape is simply a matter of placing the records one after the other onto the tape. There are two possible arrangements of files:

a. **Serial.** When records are written onto tape *without* there being any relationship between the record keys. *Unsorted* transaction records would form such a file.

b. **Sequential.** When records are written onto tape in *sequence* according to the record keys. Examples of sequential files are:

i. **Master** files.

ii. **Sorted** transaction files.

TAPE FILE ACCESS

21.26 a. **Serial files.** The only way to access a serial file on tape is SERIALLY. This simply means to say that each record is read from the tape into main storage one after the other in the order they occur on the tape.

b. **Sequential** files. The method of access used is still SERIAL but of course the file is now in sequence, and for this reason the term SEQUENTIAL is often used in describing serial access of a sequential tape file. It is important to note that to process (eg, update) a sequential master tape file, the transaction file must *also* be in the sequence of the master file. Access is achieved by first reading the transaction file and then reading the master file until the matching record (using the record keys) is found. Note therefore that if the record required is the twentieth record on the file, in order to get it into storage to process it the computer will first have to read in *all* nineteen preceding records.

Note. These limited methods of organisation and access have lead to tape becoming very much less common than disk as an on-line medium for the storage of master files. Tape continues as a major storage medium for purposes such as off-line data storage and back-up.

FILE ORGANISATION ON DISK

21.27 There are four basic methods of organising files on disk:

a. **Serial.** As for tape. Records are placed onto the disk one after the other with no regard for sequence.

b. **Sequential.** Again as for tape; records are written onto the disk but in a defined sequence according to the record keys.

c. **Indexed sequential.** Records are stored in sequence as for 21.27b but with one important difference - an *index* is provided to enable individual records to be located. Strictly speaking the records may not always be stored in sequence but the index will always enable the sequence to be determined.

d. **Random.** Records are actually placed onto the disk "at random", that is to say there is no *obvious* relationship between the records as with 21.27b and 21.27c

A mathematical formula is derived which, when applied to each record key, generates an answer, a bucket address (as illustrated in 21.22). The record is then placed onto the disk at this address, (eg, one possible formula might be: given key = 36713. Divide by 193 giving 190 remainder 43. (Address is taken as cylinder 190, track 4, block 3.)

ACCESS

21.28 a. **Serial files.** As for tape the only way to access a serially organised file is SERIALLY.

b. **Sequential files.** As for tape also, in fact the comments under 21.26b apply equally to sequentially organised files on disk.

c. **Indexed sequential files.** There are three methods of access:

i. **Sequential.** This is almost the same as in (b) above; the complete file is read in sequential order using the index. The method is used when the hit rate is high. The method makes minimal use of the index, minimises head movement and processes *all* records in each block in a single read. Therefore, the index is used once per block rather than once per record. Any transaction file must be pre-sorted into the same key sequence as the master file.

ii. **Selective sequential.** Again the transaction file must be pre-sorted into the same sequence as the master file. The transaction file is processed against the master file and *only* those master records for which there is a transaction are selected. Notice that the access mechanism is going forward in an ordered progression (never backtracking) because both files are in the same sequence. This minimises head movement and saves processing time. This method is suitable when the hit rate is low, as only those records for which there is a transaction are accessed.

iii. **Random.** Transactions are processed in a sequence that is not that of the master file. The transactions may be in another sequence, or may be unsequenced. In contrast to the selective sequential method, the access mechanism will move *not* in an ordered progression but back and forth along the file. Here the index is used when transactions are processed immediately - ie, there is not time to assemble files and sort them into sequence. It is also used when updating two files simultaneously. For example, a transaction file of orders might be used to update a stock file *and* a customer file during the same run. If the order was sorted to customer sequence, the customer file would be updated on a *selective sequential* basis and the stock file on a random basis. (Examples will be given in later chapters.)
Note. In c.i and c.ii the ordered progression of the heads relies upon an orderly organisation of the data and no other program performing reads from the disk at the same time, which would cause head movement to other parts of the disk. In multi-user systems these things cannot always be relied upon.

d. **Random files.** Generally speaking the method of access to random files is RANDOM. The transaction record keys will be put through the *same* mathematical formula as were the keys of the master records, thus creating the appropriate bucket address. The transactions in random order are then processed against the master file, the bucket address providing the address of the record required.

METHODS OF ADDRESSING

21.29 For direct access one must be able to "address" (locate) each record whenever one wants to process it. The main methods of obtaining the appropriate address are as follows:

a. **Index.** The record keys are listed with the appropriate disk address. The incoming transaction record key is used to locate the disk address of the master record in the index. This address is then used to locate the appropriate master record. We referred to this method in 21.28c.

b. **Address generation.** This is another method that was mentioned earlier, in 21.28d. The record keys are applied to a mathematical formula that has been designed to generate a disk hardware address. The formula is very difficult to design and the reader need not worry about it. The master records are placed on the disk at the addresses generated. Access is afterwards obtained by generating the disk address for each transaction.

c. **Record key = disk address.** It would be convenient if we could use the actual disk hardware address as our record key. Our transaction record keys would then also be the appropriate disk addresses and thus no preliminary action such as searching an index or address generation would be required in order to access the appropriate master records. This is not a very practical method, however, and has very limited application.

Note. Files organised as in 21.29b and 21.29c are said to be "**self-indexing**".

UPDATING MAGNETIC TAPE FILES

21.30 a. Because of the design of the tape unit it is not possible to write records back to the same position on the tape from which they have been read. The method of updating a tape file therefore is to form a *new* master file on a *new* reel of tape each time the updating process is carried out.

b. Updating a master file held on tape entails the following:

   i. Transaction file and master file must be in the same sequence.

   ii. A transaction record is read into main storage.

   iii. A master record is read into main storage and written straight out again on a new reel if it does not match the transaction. Successive records from the master file are read (and written) until the record matching the transaction is located.

   iv. The master record is then updated in storage and written out in sequence on the new reel.

The four steps are repeated until all the master records for which there is a transaction record have been updated. The result is the creation of a *new* reel of tape containing the records that did not change plus the records that have been updated. The new reel will be used on the next updating run (see Fig. 21.3).

MAGNETIC TAPE FILE MAINTENANCE

21.31 File maintenance is the term used to describe the following:

a. Removing or adding records to the magnetic file.

b. Amending static data contained in a record, eg, customer name and address, prices of stock items following a general price change.

The term generally applies to master files.

21.32 Removing a record entails leaving it off the carried-forward tape reel, while adding records entails writing the new record onto the C/F tape reel in its correct sequence. Variable-length records present no problems because there are no constraints on the size of records that can be written onto tape.

FILE LABELS

21.33 In addition to its own particular "logical" records (ie, the customer or payroll records) each *tape file* will generally have two records, which serve organisational requirements. They are written onto the tape in magnetic form as are the logical records. These two records are usually referred to as LABELS. One comes at the beginning of the file and the other at the end.

a. **Header label.** This is the first and its main function is to identify the file. It will contain the following data:

   i. A specified field to identify the particular record as a label.

   ii. File name - eg, PAYROLL; LEDGER; STOCK.

   iii. Date written.

   iv. Purge date - being the date from which the information on the particular tape reel is no longer required and from which the reel can be reused.

This label will be checked by the program before the file is processed to ensure that the correct tape reel has been mounted.

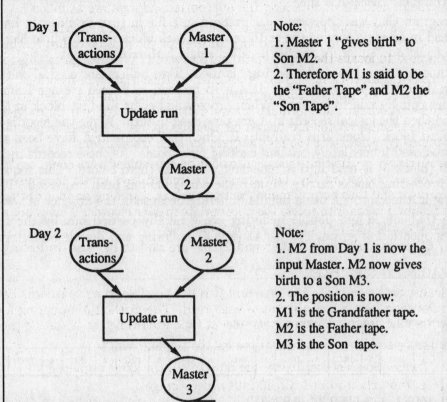

Day 1

Note:
1. Master 1 "gives birth" to Son M2.
2. Therefore M1 is said to be the "Father Tape" and M2 the "Son Tape".

Day 2

Note:
1. M2 from Day 1 is now the input Master. M2 now gives birth to a Son M3.
2. The position is now:
M1 is the Grandfather tape.
M2 is the Father tape.
M3 is the Son tape.

This can be carried on ad infinitum, but there will be a definite policy with regard to how *many* generations are kept; Grandfather – Father – Son should be adequate. If an accident should befall M3 on Day 3's Update run then no matter, we can re-create it by doing Day 2's run again. The keeping of the Master and appropriate transaction files ensures security of the system's files. Notice as new "generations" are born the oldest tapes are reused. The old information they contain is overwritten.

Fig. 21.3. File Security on Tape - the Father-Son Concept.

b. **Trailer label.** This will come at the end of the file and will contain the following data:

i. A specific field to identify the particular record as a label.

ii. A count of the number of records on file. This will be checked against the total accumulated by the program during processing.

iii. Reel number if the file takes up more than one reel of tape.

CONTROL TOTALS

21.34 Mention is made here of one further type of record found on tape files - one which will contain control totals, eg, financial totals. Such a record will precede the trailer label.

BLOCKING RECORDS

21.35 The gaps created between each record on tape represent wasted space, but more importantly they represent unproductive *time* spent by the tape unit in slowing down and accelerating in between each write and read operation. In order to reduce the number of IRGs and thus speed up the *total* time to process a tape file the technique of blocking records is adopted. Thus a single "read" or "write" instruction will cause a number of records to be read or written. See Fig. 21.4.

BUFFERS AND BUFFERING

21.36 The area of main storage used to hold the individual blocks, when they are read in or written out, is called a **buffer**.

21.37 In the example shown in Fig. 21.4 tape 2, where the blocking factor is 6, the buffer will be at least as long as 6 logical records because records are transferred between the tape unit and main memory one complete block at a time.

21.38 A program that was processing each record in a file in turn would only have to wait for records to be read in after processing the sixth record in each block when a whole block would be read in. The use of just one buffer for the file is called single **buffering.**

21.39 In some systems **double buffering** is used. Two buffers are used. For the sake of argument call them A and B and assume that data is to be read into main storage from the file. (The principle applies equally well to output.) When processing begins the first block in the file is read into buffer A and then the logical records in A are processed in turn. While the records in A are being processed the next block (block 2) is read into B. Once the records in A have been processed those in B can be processed immediately, *without waiting for a read.* As these records in B are processed the next block (block 3) is read into A replacing what was there before. This sequence of alternately filing and processing blocks carries on until the whole file has been processed. There can be considerable saving in time through using double buffering because of the absence of waits for block reads.

21.40 Note that single and double buffering are generally carried out by the operating system not by the application program. Further aspects of buffering and double buffering will be covered in later chapters.

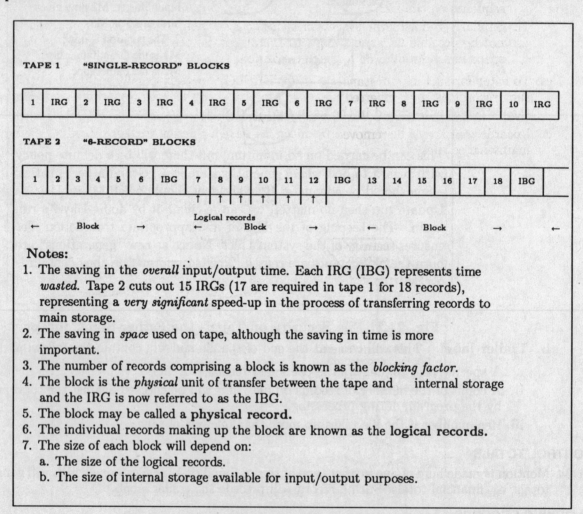

Fig. 21.4. Blocking Records on Magnetic Tape.

UPDATING DISK FILES

21.41 As individual records on disks are addressable, it is possible to *write back* an updated record to the same place from which it was read. The effect is therefore to *overwrite* the original master record with the new or updated master record. This method of updating is called "Updating in place" or "**overlay**". Note the sequence of steps involved:

a. The transaction record is read into main storage.

b. The appropriate master record is located on disk and is read into main storage.

c. The master record is updated in main storage.

d. The master record (now in updated form) is written from main storage to its original location, overwriting the record in its *pre*-dated form.

21.42 a. The method described can only be used when the *address* of the record is *known,* ie, when a file is organised as indexed sequentially or randomly.

b. Files organised on a serial or sequential basis are processed in the same way as magnetic tape files, ie, a physically different carry-forward master file will be created each time the file is processed. Such a new file could be written onto a different disk pack or perhaps onto a different area of the same disk pack.

21.43 The Grandfather-Son method of file security cannot be applied to "update in place". A common alternative is shown in Fig. 21.5.

FILE MAINTENANCE – DISK FILES

21.44 a. If disk files are organised and processed in the same manner as magnetic tapes then the remarks made in the previous chapter apply.

b. Disk files that are updated using the "overlay" method present certain problems:

i. When new records are to be inserted it may not be possible to put them, there and then, in sequence on the file.

ii. Similarly, if during the process of *updating* a variable record it were to be made longer, it may not be possible to write it back to the disk in its original place, unless, of course, sufficient space had been allowed for such expansion.

c. To cater for such circumstances , an OVERFLOW area is usually included in the disk file and such records as those referred to above are placed in this area temporarily and an indication of their whereabouts placed in the main part of the file (usually called the HOME area).

d. Records that are to be removed from the file have a deletion marker placed on them during a file maintenance run.

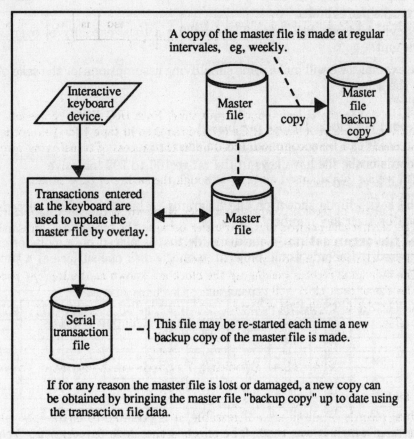

Fig. 21.5 An Example of File Security for Disk Files Updated by Overlay.

FILE REORGANISATION

21.45 As a result of the foregoing the number of records in the overflow area will increase. As a consequence the time taken to locate such a record will involve first seeking the home track and then the overflow track.

Periodically it will be necessary to reorganise the file. This will entail rewriting the file onto a new disk pack:

  i. Putting the records that are in the overflow area in the home area in the proper sequence.

  ii. Leaving off the records that have a deletion marker on them.

  iii. Rewriting any index that is associated with the file.

LABELS/CONTROL TOTALS

21.46 Header and trailer labels and control totals - akin to those on magnetic tape - are used on disk files too.

21.47 In index sequential files there is some extra data included in the header label. The extra data is called the **primary index**, which is used to locate records on the disk. When the file is "opened" the primary index is read into main storage and it is held there throughout the time the file is being processed. Each cylinder also contains its own **secondary index**, which supplements the primary index.

ILLUSTRATIONS OF FILE ORGANISATION

21.48 a. To put the problem in context we can consider these figures, which could be found in practice.

  i. 80 bytes per record

  ii. 4 records per block

  iii. 4 blocks per bucket

  iv. 8 buckets per track

  v. 10 tracks per cylinder

  vi. 200 cylinders per disk unit. Thus making a total capacity of over 20 million bytes on one disk unit.

b. In these examples we will make some simplifying assumptions for the sake of clarity. The principles remain the same.

Assume:

  i. 1 record per block, 1 block per bucket

  ii. 10 records can be accommodated on each track

  iii. Records in the file have keys in the range 100 to 299 inclusive

  iv. Not all keys are used.

Only the keys will be shown on the diagrams rather than whole records since the records are organised by their key numbers.

21.49 Sequential file organisation. Consider a file that is placed on a cylinder corresponding to all the tracks numbered 1. Records would be written on the disk one surface at a time in sequence as shown in this diagram.

Position on Track	Track 1 Surface 0	Track 1 Surface 1	Track 1 Surface 2	Track 1 Surface 3	Track 1 Surface 4	Track 1 Surface 5	Track 1 Surface 6	Track 1 Surface 7	Track 1 Surface 8	Track 1 Surface 9
			LOCATIONS OF RECORDS 101 to 299							
1	101	132	158	219	265					
2	104	137	167	224	270					
3	105	138	171	228	275					
4	107	140	177	231	277					
5	111	145	179	237	282					
6	113	146	183	241	287					
7	119	149	188	245	293					
8	123	151	197	252	294					
9	128	154	200	256	299					
10	130	156	206	263						

Note. Working from surface to surface on the same cylinder does not require movement of the read-write heads.

21.50 Index Sequential Organisation. (The example shown here is explained by the notes that follow.)

Position on Track	Track 1 Surface 0 (Secondary Index for Cylinder 1) see b.				Track 1 Surface 1	Track 1 Surface 2	Track 1 Surface 3	Track 1 Surface 4	Track 1 Surface 5	Track 1 Surface 6	Track 1 Surface 7	Overflow Tracks Track 1 Surface 8	Track 1 Surface 9
1	1	119	119	*	101	123	145	167	200	241	275		
2	2	140	140	*	104	128	146	171	206	245	277		
3	3	158	158	*	105	130	149	177	219	252	282		
4	4	197	197	*	107	132	151	179	224	256	287		
5	5	237	237	*	111	137	154	183	228	263	293		
6	6	270	270	*	113	138	156	188	231	265	294		
7	7	299	299	*	119	140	158	197	237	270	299		
8													
9													
10													

The Index sequential file is created from a file that is already in sequential order. The indexes are generated and included as the index sequential file is organised and stored. The indexes are subsequently updated as the file is updated.

a. The **primary index** is created in main storage as the file is organised, and stored on the disk when organisation and storage of the file is completed. It is loaded into main storage again at the start of any subsequent access. The primary index on surface "0" track "0" say would have a record such as this one:

Cylinder number	Highest key number on cylinder	Cylinder number "1" is comprised of all
1	299	tracks numbered "1".

b. A **secondary index** is also created in main storage while each cylinder is organised and stored. There is one secondary index per cylinder. During the organisation of each cylinder provision is made for **local overflow**, ie, the provision of spare storage on the *same* cylinder, for tracks that subsequently may become full and therefore unable to accommodate further records. (**Global overflow**, ie, overflow of the whole file, may be catered for in a similar way.) The secondary index for cylinder "1" would have records such as this one:

Surface number	Highest key number on the track	Highest key number in overflow from the track	Pointer to first overflow key
1	112	119	Track 1 T1S9B2, ie, Surface 9 Block 2

If there is no overflow the second and third field will contain the same number and the overflow pointer will be a terminator eg "*;".

c. Space has been left on each surface during the initial organisation so that a few additions can be made before overflow occurs. Finding the key numbered 188 on a subsequent access works as follows. Reference to the primary index directs us to cylinder 1. The secondary index on cylinder 1 directs us to surface 4.

d. The following diagram shows the same cylinder after a number of records have been added.

Position on Track	Track 1 Surface 0 (Secondary Index for Cylinder 1) see b.				Track 1 Surface 1	Track 1 Surface 2	Track 1 Surface 3	Track 1 Surface 4	Track 1 Surface 5	Track 1 Surface 6	Track 1 Surface 7	Overflow Tracks Track 1 Surface 8	Track 1 Surface 9
1	1	112	119	T1 S9 B2	101	123	145	167	200	241	275	119 *	118 T1 S8 B1
2	2	140	140	*	103	128	146	168	206	245	277	197 *	113 T1 S9 B1
3	3	158	158	*	104	130	149	170	219	252	282	188 T1 S8 B2	
4	4	185	197	T1 S8 B3	105	132	151	171	224	253	287		
5	5	237	237	*	106	137	154	177	228	254	293		
6	6	270	270	*	107	138	155	178	231	256	294		
7	7	299	299	*	108	140	156	179	237	263	299		
8					109		158	183		265			
9					111			184		270			
10					112			185					

Again use the index and pointers to find the key number 188.

21.51 Random file organisation. In this method the keys are used to allocate record positions on the disc. For example, a record whose key was 149 could be allocated the position surface 1 track 49. We say that the **disk address** of the record has been *generated* from the key and so the technique is called **address generation**. The generated disk address usually gives just enough detail to specify the block in which the record is to be placed or found; so that when a record is to be accessed the whole block is input, and the record is searched for within the block. We thus have **organisation by address generation** and **access by address generation**. Sometimes an index of generated addresses is produced as the file is created. This index in then stored with the file. It is then possible to access the file by means of this **random index**. We then have **organisation by address generation** and **access by random index**.

21.52 Hashed keys. When disk addresses are generated directly from keys, as in the example just given, there tends to be an uneven distribution of records over available tracks. This can be avoided by applying some algorithm to the key first. In this case we say the key is **hashed**. Examples:

a. Squaring, eg, for key number 188

188^2 =	3	5	3	4	4
DISC ADDRESS	Track Number	Surface Number	Bucket Number	Block Number

b. Division method, eg, for key number 188.

188 ÷ 7 = 26 Remainder 6. So we could use track 26 surface 6 say.

Hashing reduces the chances of overflow occurring, but when overflow does occur records are normally placed on the next available surface in the same cylinder so as to minimise head movement.

OTHER ORGANISATION AND ACCESS METHODS

21.53 The methods of file organisation and access described so far are closely related to the physical features of the disk. It is now common practice for much of this detail to be "hidden" from programmers or users of the system. Instead the operating system handles the physical levels of organisation and access, and provides standard *logical file* organisation and access methods.

21.54 Some examples of logical file organisation.

a. **Sequential files.** A programmer need merely regard the file as a sequence of records, and need have no concern for their physical location. A program instruction to read the next record will result in the appropriate record being transferred into memory, ie, the programmer's "view" may just be like this.

R1	R2	R3	R4	R5	R6	etc

R1.... R6 are logical records.

b. **Direct files.** These are files that provide fast and efficient direct access, ie, they are normally *random files* with *one* of a number of appropriate addressing methods. A common type of direct file is the **Relative file**. The logical organisation of a relative file is like this:

R1	R2	R3	R4	R5	R6		etc.
1	2	3	4	5	6		etc.

R1.... R6 are *logical records* with *logical* keys 1....6.

A relative file may be accessed sequentially or randomly.

c. **Index sequential files.** Logical versions of index sequential files are simpler than their physical counterparts, in that logical keys are used instead of disk addresses, and details of overflow are hidden from the programmer. The accessing methods are the same as those given in 21c.

FILE CALCULATIONS

21.55 Two basic types of calculation are often needed when using magnetic tape files:

a. The space occupied by the file.

b. The time taken to read or write the file.

A simple example now follows.

21.56 Example. (Note. Metric (S.I.) units are still seldom used in practice so they are not used here.)

a. Assume that a magnetic tape on which a file is to be stored has these characteristics.

    i.   1,600 bpi recording density
    ii. length 2,400 feet
    iii. IBG$\frac{1}{2}$"
    iv. Speed 75 ips (inches per second)
    v.   Stop/start time 10 ms

See 7.24 — 7.26

b. Assume a file of 10,000 records, each 200 bytes long, is to be stored on magnetic tape with four records to a block.

c. Find:

 i. The space occupied by the file.

 ii. The time taken to read the file if it is single buffered.

d. Solution.

 i. Space occupied. One block of 4 records is 800 bytes long. Therefore it occupies $\frac{800}{1,600}$ inches ie $\frac{1}{2}$"

 Therefore a block plus its BG will occupy 1".

 10,000 records occupy 2,500 blocks.

 Therefore the file occupies 2,500 inches or approximately 208 feet.

 ii. Time taken.

$$\text{Total time} = \left[\text{start time} + \left[\begin{array}{c} \text{time to read} \\ \text{one block} \end{array} \right] + \text{stop time} \right] \times \left[\begin{array}{c} \text{number} \\ \text{of blocks} \end{array} \right]$$

 If the speed of the tape is 75 ips and the recording density is 1,600 bpi then data will be transferred at a rate of $75 \times 1,600$ bytes per second.

 Therefore the time to read one block will be, in ms

$$\frac{800}{75 \times 1,600} \times 1,000 \text{ ms} = 6\frac{2}{3} \text{ ms}$$

 So the total time taken $= [10 + 6\frac{2}{3} + 10] \times 2,500$ ms

 $= 66,666$ ms

 ie approximately 1 minute.

21.57 Basic calculations of storage requirements and times are often needed for magnetic disk files, just as they are for files on magnetic tape.

21.58 From 21.23 we may deduce that

 average access time = seek time + latency + data transfer time.

21.59 For a random file where N records were read the total read time would simply be N × average access time. Note that a whole sector would have to be read in just to get each individual record.

21.60 For a sequential file, where the disk was not being used for any other accesses at the same time there would be a seek for each cylinder and then all sectors in the cylinder would be read. This suggests a formula such as:

$$\begin{array}{c} \text{Total read} \\ \text{time} \end{array} \left[\text{seek time} + \left[\begin{array}{c} \text{latency} + \text{data} \\ \text{transfer time} \end{array} \right] \times \left[\begin{array}{c} \text{number of} \\ \text{sectors per} \\ \text{cylinder} \end{array} \right] \right] \times \left[\begin{array}{c} \text{number of} \\ \text{cylinders} \\ \text{per file} \end{array} \right]$$

OTHER DIRECT-ACCESS MEDIA

21.61 The ability to access records independently of others within a file, ie, at random or *directly*, has resulted in the term *direct-access* devices being given to those devices able to offer this facility. The **magnetic drum** is another direct-access device having one read-write head per track which reduces the elements of access time to rotational delay and transfer time (no seek time being involved as with disks). As electro-mechanical movement is a major part of access time, the elimination of seek time makes access to drums faster than to disks. However, drums are expensive to manufacture and have a much lower capacity than disks. Drums are therefore seldom used these days and do not merit further discussion.

SUMMARY

21.62 a. An inter-block gap is created after each block is *written* on tape.

 b. When the tape is being read the IBG terminates the "read" operation (ie, the transfer of the data in that particular block).

 c. Tape is a serial medium and can only be accessed serially.

 d. Updating is achieved by creating a physically different file each time.

 e. File maintenance involves adding and deleting records and the amendment of static data contained in records.

f. Labels are provided for control/organisational purposes.

g. A diagram showing the components of a tape file is shown in Fig. 21.6.

Fig. 21.6. Diagram Illustrating Components of a Tape File.

h. Conceptually the disk is regarded as being composed of so many concentric CYLINDERS.

i. Disk is an addressable medium and therefore specific records can be accessed leaving the rest of the file undisturbed.

j. Organisation on disk is by cylinder, track and bucket (or block).

k. Access time on disk consists of three components seek time, rotational delay and data transfer time.

l. The overlay or "in-place" method of updating *can be* used on disk.

m. Methods of file organisation on disk are:

    i. Serial.

    ii. Sequential (with or without an index).

    iii. Random.

n. Methods of access to disk files are:

    i. Serial (for serial and sequential files).

    ii. Selective sequential (for indexed sequential files).

    iii. Sequential (for sequential and indexed sequential files).

    iv. Random (for random and indexed sequential files).

o. File maintenance on disk raises problems:

    i. When inserting new records.

    ii. When updating variable-length records.

p. Special overflow areas are designated on disk to take new records and overlength records temporarily.

q. A periodic file re-organisation run is required with disk files to place records residing temporarily in overflow areas into their correct sequence in the file and to leave off "deleted" records. Any index also has to be reconstructed during this run.

r. A summary of normally accepted methods of file organisation on disk and associated methods of access is given in Fig. 21.7.

FILE ORGANISATION METHOD		METHOD OF ACCESS	
1. Serial 2. Sequential }	(Sequential)	Serial Serial (Sequential) }	(Sequential)
		a. Sequential	
3. Indexed sequential		b. Selective sequential	
4. Random (direct or relative)		c. Random (Direct)	
		Random (Direct)	

Fig. 21.7. A summary of file organisation and access methods.

Note. Terms in parentheses are alternative terms normally used at a logical level.

POINTS TO NOTE

21.63 a. Note the amount of data transfer *time* saved by blocking records together on tape (Fig. 21.4).

b. When we talk of "transferring" or "reading" from tape, we really mean *copying* it from tape because the data is still *there* on the tape. This concept holds good *whatever* the medium on computers.

c. Data can also be written onto tape "off-line", ie, by a transferring from another medium to tape, eg, from diskette by means of a separate computer from that which will finally do the processing. Transaction files are generally associated with these methods of "preparing" tape.

d. The size of blocks is limited by the amount of main storage available for the input/output area.

e. Tape labels are *magnetic* labels for use by the computer program.

f. The expression "reading the master/transaction file" really means in effect "reading *one* block into main storage". A separate "read" instruction is required for each block on each tape to be "read" into main storage.

g. The use of the term "generation" in connection with master files (Fig. 21.3).

h. Magnetic tape is *not* normally used as a storage medium for master files undergoing processing, unless the files are only updated infrequently and are not required for on-line access between updates.

i. Magnetic tape is the most popular storage medium for off-line "back-up" of all kinds of files.

j. Some tape units may be operated in a mode in which data is transferred between the tape and main storage in a continuous stream for "back-up" or "recovery" purposes. This is known as **streaming.**

k. A file is "open" for input once its header label has been read and checked, and it is "open" for output once its header label has been written successfully.

l. The expression "the disk" has been used in this chapter. It is probably more correct to use the slightly more verbose expression "the disk pack".

m. "Seek area" or "cylinder" constitutes the amount of data available at any one time to the read-write heads for only one movement of the access mechanism. Note, however that data can only be read or written for *one* read-write head at one time.

n. Although it is a direct-access device, the disk is very often used without making use of the particular characteristic of direct access for reasons that will be stated later.

o. Updating in place (overlay) is generally adopted in conjunction with *fixed*-length records.

p. The methods of file organisation and access were dealt with separately in the text for clarity. They are, however, very much related.

q. If you are asked a question about "file organisation" the chances are you will be required to talk about the whole subject including, of course, access.

r. Although dealt with separately in the interests of clarity, file maintenance and file reorganisation are closely related and should both be included in an examination answer on either subject.

s. It is desirable to have a disk overflow area on the *same* cylinder as the home area. If the overflow area is on a different cylinder then the access mechanism has to move *twice* for one access; once to the home area and then to the overflow area. The second movement is not required if the home area and the overflow area are on the same cylinder.

t. Note the implication of an overflow area during the sequential access of an indexed sequential file on disk. Access is made to every record in their *logical* sequence, which may *not* be the same as the *physical* sequence because some of the records will be residing temporarily in an overflow area.

u. Index sequential access mode files (**ISAM** for short) are based upon a tree-like structures. One more advanced form of such a structure is called a **btree.** In a btree structured file the nodes of the index are split as the file grows so that the index maintains a balanced structure.

v. Details of file processing methods will be covered in later chapters.

STUDENT SELF-TESTING QUESTIONS

1. Why are gaps required between physical records on a magnetic tape file? What improvements are made by blocking records together?

2. Why is the updated master file stored on a new reel during a file update run?

STUDENT SELF-TESTING QUESTIONS CONTINUED

3. Firstly assume the tape characteristics given in 21.56 and secondly assume that a file has 15,000 records each of 250 bytes in length.

   a. Find the space occupied by the file.

   b. Find the time taken to read the file if it is single buffered.

   Compare the answers for blocks of 1 record only with those for 5 records per block.

   Explain the effect double buffering could have on the read time.

4. What factors would govern choice of storage media?

5. Outline the methods by which files may be organised and accessed on:

   a. magnetic tape,

   b. magnetic disk.

   For files on each medium, state the contents of file labels and explain how they are used.

   (AEB)

6. Describe a method of file organisation on a direct-access storage device, which involves a hash algorithm (address generation algorithm).

   A file on a direct-access device occupies 100 blocks, each block containing 1,000 bytes. The records are of variable length, terminated by *; the last record terminator in each block being followed by /. The key of each record is contained in the first 6 bytes, and the file is organised with a specified hash algorithm.

   a. Draw a flowchart to show how, given a key, you would obtain the required record, assuming that the record is not in an overflow block.

   b. Explain what is meant by overflow, and describe briefly how you obtain a record from an overflow block.

   (AEB)

7. Describe briefly each of the following methods of file organisation, listing the particular merits of each.

   a. Sequential

   b. Direct

   c. Index sequential.

   (BCS Pt 1)

8. Describe the way sectors are addressed on a disk pack.

9. Discuss the problems of file security on disk files.

10. Design an access method for a situation where records are stored in a relative file with physical record numbers 1...N but with logical records numbered 2,501 to 3,500. Design two methods:

    a. using address generation,

    b. using an index.

    State any assumption that you make.

QUESTIONS WITHOUT ANSWERS

11. A disk drive and its exchangeable disk pack have the following characteristics:

    i. The disk is hard sectored with 8 sectors per track each of 512 bytes and 200 tracks on each surface. There are six usable surfaces per pack.

    ii. The disk has a seek time of 20 ms when seeking an adjacent track but an average seek time of 40 ms.

    iii. The disk rotates once every 24 ms and has a data transfer rate of 256,000 bytes per second.

    A file to be stored on the disk consists of 19,200 records each 128 bytes in length.
    a. How many records can be stored in each sector?
    b. What percentage of available disk space will the file occupy?
    c. If the file is stored with sequential organisation, how long will it take to read the whole file sequentially?
    d. If the file is stored with random organisation, how long will it take to read the whole file in key sequence?

    State any assumptions made and comment on your results.

12. a. Information is stored in the form of records on a sequential file sorted on a particular key and held on a magnetic tape. Explain how records can be inserted into and deleted from such a file. (7)

    b. What is meant by an indexed file and how can it be accessed?

    An insurance company has records for each of its 700,000 clients, each record contains 300 bytes including a 20-character sort key. If the disk block size is 2,400 bytes, how could an index for the file be organised?

    Write down the operations that would have to be performed to find a record with a given key. (13)

    Welsh Joint Education Committee

13. What is the Father-Son concept with regard to the updating of magnetic tape files?

14. What data would you expect to find in header and trailer labels and comment on each item. Give an example of a header label and trailer label for a particular application.

15. Distinguish between the way sectors are located on a hard-sectored disk and the way they are located on a soft-sectored disk.

    Find out the kind of sectoring used on the types of disks you use.

16. Find out the operating characteristics of the types of disk you use, eg, seek time, latency. Calculate the time taken to read one record from the disk.

QUESTIONS WITHOUT ANSWERS

17. The characteristics of a particular disk drive are as follows:

   i.   the disk has a single recording surface consisting of 200 tracks;

   ii. the disk rotates at 3,000 revolutions per minute (ie, 20 ms per revolution);

   iii. moving the head from one track to another takes approximately 25 ms plus 10 ms per track moved;

   iv. after moving the head it takes on average half a revolution to find the marker that indicates the start of data on the track.

A file occupies tracks 151 to 200 of a disk and is to be moved to occupy tracks 1 to 50 of the same disk. A program exists that copies a file by reading a complete track, and then writing a complete track, continuing until all tracks of the file have been copied. Assuming that a complete track is transferred in a single operation and that the processor time involved in initiating read and write operations is negligible compared to the transfer times, calculate approximately the time taken to move the file.

If a second disk drive is available that may be accessed concurrently with the first one, by what method and by approximately how much may this time be reduced?

Explain all your timing calculations.

Cambridge

18. a. Explain the following terms:

   i.   file creation,

   ii. file reorganisation,

   iii. master file.

6

   b. A magnetic disk cartridge has 10 usable disk surfaces. Each surface has 200 tracks, with 10 blocks per track. The time for the disk is as follows:

Time for one revolution	25 msecs
One track seek	10 msecs
Average time for a random seek	40 msecs

   i.   For this disk calculate the file size for 20,000 records packed at 10 records/blocks.

   ii. The above file is to be updated with 200 records. Calculate the time for this update for both a sequential and a random update, stating any assumptions you make. Comment on your answers.

14 = 20

(JMB)

GLOSSARY CHECKLIST

GLOSSARY CHECKLIST CONTINUED

22: File Processing I

INTRODUCTION

22.1 The main purpose of this and the next chapter is to apply the basic ideas concerning storage media and processing requirements to file processing. This is a large subject area which is why the material has been split into two chapters. In order to place the subject matter in context this chapter considers factors affecting the choice of methods for file organisation and access. Methods associated with sequential file processing are discussed in detail in this chapter too.

22.2 Sequential file processing is an important feature of the simpler and long-established methods of batch processing. Such methods were established when magnetic tape was the main file-processing medium. Today, the same methods continue to be used but with magnetic disk as the usual choice of storage medium.

22.3 Most examples given in this chapter relate to business and commercial applications but a simple example of processing a text file is given first. The processing of text files is important in its own right but the example also serves as a simple introduction to sequential file processing operations.

22.4 The chapter contains three examples of file processing relate to business and commercial applications. The first is used to explain how a sequential master file is updated. The second example is more general and typifies sequential file processing. The example is followed by a discussion of the advantages and limitations of magnetic tape as a file storage medium. The third example illustrates file controls, ie, measures to ensure that data files are processed correctly.

PROCESSING TEXT FILES

22.5 Text files were introduced in 5.5. They may be regarded as a special type of sequential file. It is often possible to write or and read text file one character at a time. The "records" are the individual characters, and they have no key – just a physical order in the file. If this is the primary way of processing the text file it may be called a **stream file**. Normally, however, characters in text files are structures into variable length records as follows.

    a. Each line (or possibly a paragraph) in the text file is a variable length record containing one variable length field of characters.

    b. There may be no key as such for identifying individual records, although some text files may contain line numbers.

    c. Lines of text are written to the text file one after the other and may then be read back in the same order.

    d. It is normally possible to write or and read text file one character at a time too if required.

22.6 As an example suppose that a program is required which reads in a text file and outputs a copy of the same file to which line numbers have been added (Fig. 22.1).

22.7 The pseudocode of a program which does this processing is shown in Fig 22.2. Here are some notes describing the program.

    a. Files have to be "opened" by programs before the data in them can be processed. An "open" statement in a program is, in effect, a request to the operating system to give the program access to the data. The "open" statement normally specifies, the name by which the file is known to the operating system (eg, `"olddoc.txt"`), the file name to be used within the program (eg, `"old_text_file"`) and the mode of processing (eg, `text input`).

    b. In the program the input file is read in one line at a time within the while loop. Note that the while loop is terminated when the file's end is detected by a call to the function **end_of_file**. An empty line results in an empty string being input.

    c. The integer variable **line_number** is incremented each time through the loop. When the output line is constructed this line number is converted into a string variable by means of the function **text** so that the old line number can be concatenated onto it to form a new line.

    d. When all the lines have been processed the files are "closed". Again the close statements are, in effect, a request to the operating system. In fact all access to files is via the operating system so the calls to **end_of_file**, **readline** and **writeline** are all handled by the operating system for the program.

```
On 2nd November 1988
the Internet Worm program
invaded nationally
networked computer in
the USA causing havoc.

The program's author
was subsequently tried
and convicted.
```

a. The input text file without line numbers.

```
1 On 2nd November 1988
2 the Internet Worm program
3 invaded nationally
4 networked computer in
5 the USA causing havoc.
6
7 The program's author
8 was subsequently tried
9 and convicted.
```

b. The output text file with line numbers added.

Fig 22.1. Text files.

22.8   That concludes an introduction to the processing of text files.

CHOICE OF FILE ORGANISATION AND ACCESS METHODS

22.9   **Factors affecting choice:**

    a. **Size.**

      i.   Disks and tapes are both capable of storing very large files but very large files are stored more economically on magnetic tape. Small files can use disk space well if blocks are suitably sized and can be easily accessed, but may be troublesome to access if strung along magnetic tape because of the serial nature of tape.

      ii. The percentage of additions or deletions in file maintenance if low may allow satisfactory organisation of indexed or random files, but if high will make sequential organisation more attractive.

      iii. If a file is likely to increase in size then the design of an indexed or random file must allow for it.

    b. **Reference and enquiry.** If quick reference is essential then indexed or random files will be needed. If the file is only used for quick one-off reference then a random organisation may be best.

    c. **Hit rate.** This relates to b, in that low hit rates are suited by indexed or random files, and high hit rates are suited by sequential files. Putting together batches of enquiries to form a transaction file can raise hit rates.

    d. **Security and backup.** The "Father-Son" concept is an aid to security when using sequential files. Indexed and random files are overwritten *during processing* so they may need to be dumped onto tape or another disk *between processing,* as well as keeping a copy of all transactions between dumps.

271

```
Program    put_line_numbers_on_file
variables
           line_number :  integer
           input_line  :  string
           output_line :  string
Begin
           (* open files *)
           open old_text_file, "olddoc.txt" for text input
           open new_text_file, "newdoc.txt" for text output
           line_number := 0
           while
           (* There are lines to be read in the input file *)
               NOT(end_of_file(old_doc_file))
           do
               (* read in a line *)
               call readline(old_text_file, input_line)
               (* increment the line number *)
               line_number := line_number + 1
               (* construct the new output line *)
               output_line := text(line_number) & " " & input_line
               (* write the new line to the output file *)
               call writeline(new_text_file, output_line)
           endwhile
           (* close all files *)
           close old_text_file
           close old_text_file
end
```

Fig 22.2. Processing text files.

FILE-HANDLING TECHNIQUES

22.10 The techniques discussed in this chapter apply to the following file-handling activities.

a. **File creation.** The creation of transaction files **after** the validation stage will be considered.

b. **File updating (amendment).**

c. **File maintenance.**

The techniques described in this chapter apply mainly to sequential and index sequential file handling. During random file handling each record is handled separately, and so techniques used with sequential transaction files may either apply to single records or be irrelevant.

22.11 Prior to any sequential file update or maintenance it is necessary to get the transaction file into a suitable form. This usually involves:

a. **File conversion,** ie, converting from the input medium (eg, diskette) to storage medium (eg, magnetic tape say).

b. **Sorting** ie, the transaction file must be sorted into the sequence of the master file before processing can take place. The key fields of the transaction file may be sorted into either **numerical sequence** or **alphabetical sequence** according to the method used on the master file.

22.12 File conversion was discussed in chapter 10 and needs no further mention. Sorting was discussed in chapter 17. Details of file sorting methods will be covered in chapter 40.

22.13 Final sequencing.

A final check may be made to ensure that all records on the transaction file do lie in sequence.

22.14 Collating.

Collating can also involve merging and matching, eg, a transaction file is merged with a master file and unpaired records are removed, thus leaving only those records needed for updating.

VALIDATION CHECKS

22.15 When records on transaction files are matched with master files, further checks may be made. These are:

    a. **New records.** If a complete new record is input for insertion into the master file, a check is made to see that a record with the same key number is not already present.

    b. **Deleted records.** If input indicates that a record is to be deleted from the file, an error is reported if the record is not present on the file.

    c. **Consistency.** Before the master file record is amended, a check may be made to ensure that the new data is consistent with data already stored in the record (eg, before updating a payroll record with overtime payments, the record would be checked to ensure that the employee was not a salaried member of staff not entitled to overtime).

APPLICATION EXAMPLE

22.16 In order to illustrate file-processing activities we will now consider a simple stock control system. This example will be used both in this chapter and again in the next one.

22.17 Details about individual stock items may be stored as logical records in a stock master file, ie, a stock item is an "entity" (20.7). One "attribute" (20.7) of the stock item entity will be the number of items in stock.

22.18 Events taking place in the organisation will change the actual stock. The master file must be made to reflect these changes so that the required information about stock can be produced from it.

22.19 Events such as the introduction of new stock items, or the discontinuation of existing items, correspond to the *insertion or deletion* of entities in the master file.

22.20 Events such as the delivery of items as they are sold correspond to " *debiting*" or " *crediting*" the attribute value of the number of items in stock.

22.21 Events such as price increases of stock items correspond to changing the attribute value of the stock item price.

22.22 From the cases just considered the following basic file-processing activities can be identified:

    a. Insertions and deletions $\Big\}$ File maintenance (22.10c)
    b. Changes

    c. Debits and credits $\Big\}$ File update (22.10b)

    ' In fact these activities are typical of most file-processing applications. The reader should be able to see the parallels in other applications, eg, we may open or close an account, change a client's address or credit or debit the client's account.

22.23 Although file updating and file maintenance are different file-processing activities they are sometimes combined together for convenience. The term **"master file update"** is often used loosely to mean both update and maintenance and in the remainder of this Part the same meaning will apply.

22.24 **Transactions.** Relevant details of events need to be recorded and input to provide the data needed to update the master file. Since data is recorded about the events, the events are entities too. In traditional file terminology these entities are called transactions.

PROCESSING STRATEGIES

22.25 There are two basic strategies for processing transactions against the master file:

    a. **Transaction processing** - ie, processing each transaction as it occurs.

    b. **Batch processing** - ie, collecting transactions together over some interval of time and then processing the whole batch.

22.26 One method of processing is no better than the other. It is a matter of "horses for courses". Details of the different methods of file processing will be discussed in the chapter following this one. The relative advantages and disadvantages of the different methods will be included in the discussion.

22.27 Transaction processing will be considered in the next chapter. Batch processing is most commonly achieved by sequential file processing, so batch processing will now be explained before we continue with an example of sequential file processing.

22.28 The majority of commercial computer applications are involved in batch processing. Transactions are accumulated into batches of suitable sizes, then each batch is sorted and processed. The concept is not new, in fact it is also adopted in most manual systems of data processing. By its very nature a batch-processing system will involve a degree of "delay". Generally, the result of processing a particular *item* of data will not be known until the results of the *batch* are known.

EXAMPLE 1 — UPDATING A SEQUENTIAL MASTER FILE

22.29 This example illustrates the basic principles involved in the update of a sequential master file, by dealing with the update of a simple stock master file.

22.30 Each item of stock is an entity about which data is recorded in one logical record. Each logical record is identified by its own unique key (its stock number). At any one time only some of the set of available keys will be *allocated* to stock items, eg, if an account number is a key some account numbers are not allocated.

22.31 It will aid a clearer understanding of the master file update if we think of the master file as the *complete* sequence of available keys, although only some keys will be allocated to stock items at any one time. The *status* of a key, ie, allocated or not allocated, is signified by the fact that only allocated keys have records physically present within the master file.

22.32 **Processing operations.** There are different types of transactions, and each transaction corresponds to a particular operation on a master file record. The status of the key will determine whether or not the operation is a valid one in a particular situation. The possible combinations of valid and invalid operations are shown in the following table:-

		TRANSACTION TYPE				
		INSERT NEW RECORD	DELETE EXISTING RECORD	CHANGE EXISTING RECORD	CREDIT EXISTING RECORD	DEBIT EXISTING RECORD
Key Status Prior To Processing The Transaction	Allocated	×	√	√	√	√
	Not Allocated	√	×	×	×	×

Key: √: a valid operation.
      × : an invalid operation.
      eg, "Insert new record" is **not** a valid transaction if the key is already allocated, ie, present.
      Similarly, "Delete existing record" is **not** valid if the key is not allocated.

Fig. 22.3.

22.33 **Batched transactions.** Batches of transactions of different types are accumulated together into a transaction file. The means by which these transactions are entered into the system have been covered in earlier chapters.

22.34 In the case of a sequential master file update, the transaction file is sorted into the same key sequence as the master file prior to processing. This enables the processing to be carried out in an orderly and efficient manner.

22.35 Within one transaction file there are likely to be multiple transaction records with particular key values, eg, several debits from the same stock item. The sequence in which these transactions are processed should correspond to the chronological sequence of events that created them, eg, new stock must be introduced before it is removed, and similarly a key must be allocated before stock is debited from its record.

22.36 The way in which the transaction file and master file are related by key sequence is shown in Fig. 22.4.

22.37 **The update.** An overview of the update is provided by Fig. 22.5. Fig. 22.6 gives a further level of detail by showing how only one key is processed at a time, so that only a limited number of records need be present in main storage at any one time.

22.38 The procedure is given in outline in the structure diagram (Fig. 22.7) and in greater detail, in pseudocode, in Fig. 22.9. The procedure shown in these two diagrams may be easier to understand if read in conjunction with Fig. 22.8.

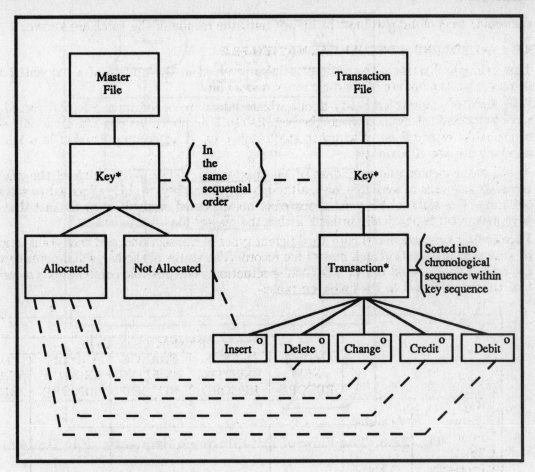

NB. - - - - indicates valid operations.

Note. Some master keys may not have any corresponding transactions.

Fig. 22.4. Structure Diagrams for the Two Files used in the Update.

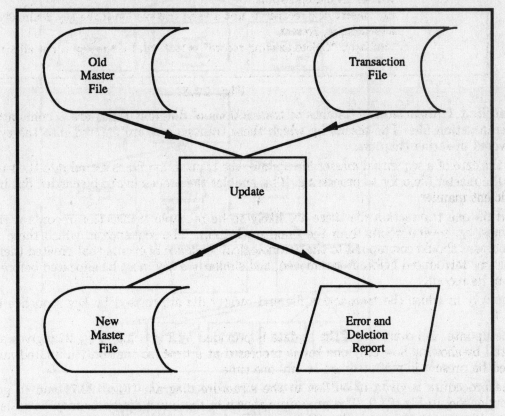

Fig. 22.5. Sequential Master File Update - System Flowchart

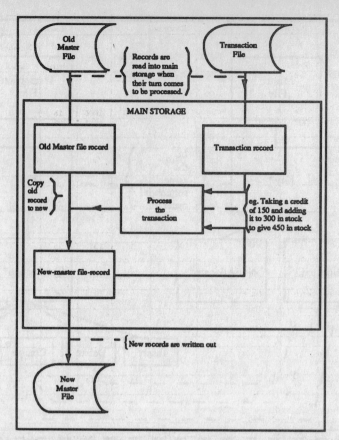

Fig. 22.6. The Flow of Data during a Sequential File Update.

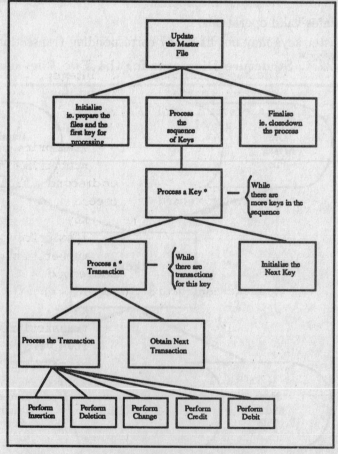

**Fig. 22.7. A Structure Diagram giving an Overview
of the Master File Processing.**

Key	Old Master File Records			Transaction File Records			New Master File Records			Comment
	Key	Item Price	Number in Stock	Key	Type	Value	Key	Item Price	Number in Stock	
1000	1000	15	300	1000	Credit	150				The number in stock takes the successive values 300, 450, 650, 350, as credits and debits are made
				1000	Credit	200				
				1000	Debit	300	1000	15	350	
1001	1001	25	450				1001	25	450	No transaction, so master record is unchanged
1002										Key not allocated
1003	1003	20	0	1003	Delete					Master record is deleted by not writing to new master
1004										Key not allocated
1005				1005	Insert	30				A new master record is created with an item price of 30 and zero stock. Stock is then credited with 250 items
				1005	Credit	250	1005	30	250	
1006										Key not allocated
1007	1007	15	300	1007	Change	20	1007	20	300	Assume for simplicity that change applies to price only
1008	1008	30	350	1008	Insert	35	1008	30	350	An invalid transaction - cannot insert existing record
1009	1009	25	400				1009	25	400	No transaction, so master record is unchanged
1010				1010	Debit	200				An invalid transaction - cannot debit nonexistent stock
1011										Key not allocated
1012				1012	Delete					An invalid transaction - can only delete existing record
1013	1013	30	200				1013	30	200	No transaction, so master record is unchanged
...............etc...............										And so on ....

Fig. 22.8. Detailed example showing how the file data is processed.

```
Program     Master_file_update
constants

            sentinel = 99999
variables

            the_key_to_process        : integer
            key_is_allocated          : boolean
            old_master_record :       record
                                          Key                 : integer
                                          item_price          : real
                                          number_in_stock     : integer
                                      endrecord
            new_master_record :       record
                                          key                 : integer
                                          item_price          : real
                                          number_in_stock     : integer
                                      endrecord
            transaction_record :      record
                                          key                 : integer
                                          transaction_type    : string
                                          item_value          : real
                                          stock_value         : integer
                                      endrecord
```

Fig. 22.9a.

277

```
Begin
       (*open files*)
       open old_master_file, "oldmaster.dat" for sequential input
       open new_master_file,"newmaster.dat" for sequential output
       open transaction_file for sequential input
           (*initialise records and keys*)
       call read(old_master_file, old_master_record)
       call read(transaction_file,transaction_record)
       the_key_to_process:  = min(old_master_record.key,
                                  transaction record.key)
       call initialise_the_key_to_process (the_key_to_process,
                                  old_master_record,
                                  new_master_record,
                                  key_is_allocated)
   (* process all keys *)
   while
       (* there is a key to process *)
       the_key_to_process <> sentinel
   do
       while (* there is a transaction for this key *)
         the_key_to_process = transaction_record.key
       do
         call process_the_transaction (new_master_record,
                                  transaction_record,
                                  key_is_allocated)
         call read (transaction_file, transaction_record)
       endwhile
       if
         key_is_allocated
       then
         call write (new_master_file, new_master record)
       endif
       the_key_to_process:  = min (old_master_record.key,
                                  transaction_record.key)
       call initialise_the_key_to process (the_key_to_process,
                                  old_master_record
                                  new_master_record
                                  key_is_allocated)
   endwhile
   (* close files *)
   close old_master_file
   close new_master_file
   close transaction_file
end
```

Fig. 22.9b.

```
procedure read(  IN    file_name    :  string
                 OUT   record_name  :  record)
(*
If there are more records in the named file yet to be read
this procedure reads the next record from the file into the
named record.  Otherwise, the procedure assigns the value
of the sentinel to the named record's key.
NB. In this case the sentinel is a value higher
than any key value
)


procedure write(  IN    file_name    :  string
                  OUT   record_name  :  record)
(*
This procedure writes the value of the named
record out to the named file
)


function min(first_key, second_key, :  integer): integer
(*This function returns the smaller value of its two arguments.*)
Begin
        if
                first_key < second_key
        then
                min := first_key
        else
                min := second_key
        endif
end

procedure      initialise_the_key_to_process(
    IN         the_key_to_process                    :  integer
    IN-OUT     old_master_record,
               new_master_record                     :  record
               key_is_allocated                      :  boolean)
  (*
Provided there are still records to be processed
this procedure sets key_is_allocated to the
appropriate state and sets up a new master record
if one is required.
 *)
Begin
    if
        (* there are still records to process *)
      the_key_to_process <> sentinel
    then
        if
            the_key_to_process = old_master_record.key
        then
            key_is_allocated := true
            new_master_record := old_master_record
            call read(old_master_file, old_master_record)
        else
            key_is_allocated := false
        endif
    endif
end
```

Fig. 22.9c.

```
procedure    process_the_transactions
            (IN-OUT                          new_master_record
            IN                               transaction_record
            IN-OUT                           key_is_allocated )
(* This procedure processes the five types of transaction.
ERROR messages should ideally show more information such as the key *)
Begin
            selectcase transaction type
                case insert
                    if
                                            NOT Key_is_allocated
                    then
                                            (* copy details from transaction
                                            to new_master_record *)
                                            key_is_allocated: = true
                    else
                                            output ("ERROR - record already exists")
                    endif
                case delete
                    if
                                            key_is_allocated
                    then
                                            key_is_allocated:= false
                                            (*output to deletion report*)
                    else
                                            output ("ERROR - record does not exist")
                    endif
                case change
                    if
                                            key_is_allocated
                    then
                                            (* make_changes to new_master_record*)
                    else
                                            Output ("ERROR - record does not exist")
                    endif
                case credit
                    if
                                            key_is_allocated
                    then
                                            (* add transaction value to new master value *)
                    else
                                            output ("ERROR - record does not exist")
                    endif
                case debit
                    if
                                            key_is_allocated
                    then
                                            (* subtract transaction value
                                            from new master value *)
                    else
                                            output ("ERROR - record does not exist")
                    endif
                case else
                                            (*the transaction is of an invalid type
                                            and should be reported*)
            endselectcase
end
```

Fig. 22.9c.

EXAMPLE 2 — MULTIPLE FILE UPDATES

22.39 This example, which deals with order processing, shows batch processing involving the update of two master files. The method typifies batch processing using magnetic tape. The reasons why magnetic disk is normally used in preference to magnetic tape will be given later.

22.40 The following systems flowcharts should be studied in conjunction with the notes that follow them.

FILE UPDATES USING MAGNETIC TAPE

This chart illustrates the computer runs necessary to update the stock and customer files and to produce invoices. Orders are entered at a terminal and the stock file (held in stock-number sequence) and customer file (held in customer-number sequence) are stored on magnetic tape.

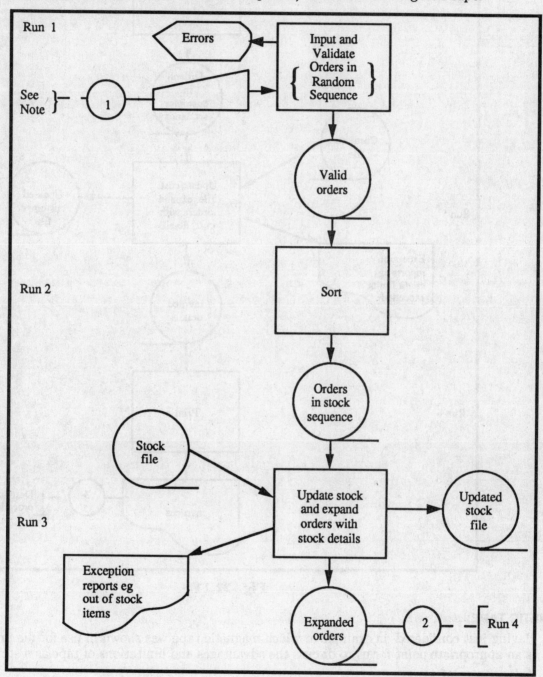

Note:

Connector symbol 1 shows the link between this part of the systems flowchart and another part of the chart, which contains the clerical procedures involved in preparing the documents for input.

Fig. 22.10.

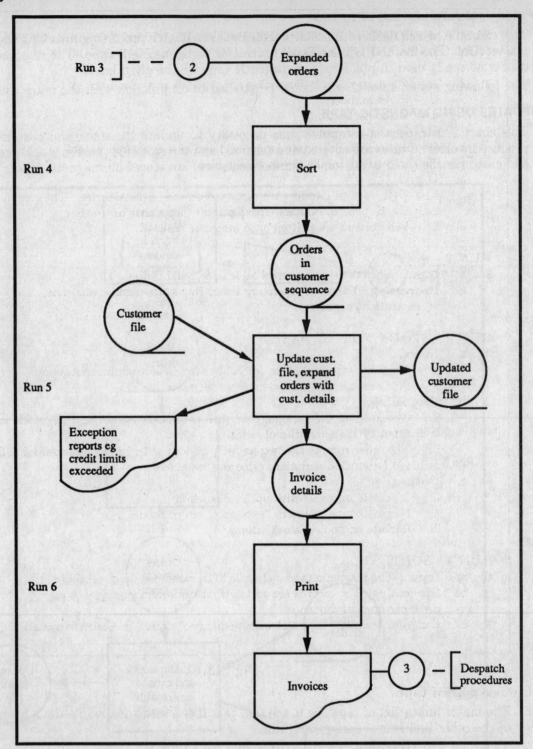

Fig. 22.11.

MAGNETIC TAPE

22.41 Having just considered an example in which magnetic tape was shown in use for file processing, this is an appropriate point for us to discuss the advantages and limitations of tape as a storage medium.

22.42 Advantage of tape.

    a. It is relatively cheap, (eg, approx. £10 per reel vs approx. £250 per disk pack).

    b. It has high capacity, enabling it to store the largest files.

    c. The data transfer speed is fairly high.

    d. It requires no complicated systems software for its operation.

    e. Industrial standards govern the way data is normally recorded on tape. This ensures compatibility between different computers and therefore allows bulk off-line data transfers between systems.

SYSTEM FLOWCHART SUPPORTING NARRATIVE TO FIGS. 22.10 and 22.11
RUN 1 DATA INPUT AND VALIDATION (KEY-TO-TAPE).

1. a. **Input** Details of each transaction are typed in at a terminal:
      i.   Stock number.
      ii. Customer number.
      iii. Quantity ordered.
  b. **Processing.** Each transaction is validated as it is entered, ie, the data is "vetted" by the key-to-tape system.
  c. **Output**
      i.   Data of invalid orders are displayed on the terminal screen. The errors may also be printed on a low-speed printer (not shown in the diagram).
      ii. Valid orders are written onto *magnetic tape.*

RUN 2 - SORT.
2. a. **Input.** The magnetic tape reel at 1c.ii, ie, valid orders.
  b. **Processing.** The valid orders are sorted into stock-number sequence, ie, *sequentially* organised.

RUN 3 - STOCK FILE UPDATE.
3. a. **Input.**
      i.   Magnetic tape reel at 2c, ie, valid orders in stock-number sequence.
      ii. Stock master file in stock-number sequence.
  b. **Processing.**
      i.   The order records are matched with the master records and the stock master file is updated by the quantities of items.
      ii. The order records are "expanded", ie, each order record has additional fields included for stock description, price and value.
  c. **Output.**
      i.   Magnetic tape reel with updated stock file.
      ii. Magnetic tape reel with "expanded" order details.
      iii. Reports on "out-of-stock" items.

RUN 4 - SORT.
4. a. **Input.** The magnetic tape reel at 3c.ii, ie, expanded order details:
  b. **Processing.** The records are sorted from stock-number sequence into customer-number sequence.
  c. **Output.** Magnetic tape reel with "expanded" orders in *customer-number* sequence.

Fig. 22.12

22.43 Limitations of tape.

a. The major limitation of tape lies in the fact that it is a serial non-addressable medium and many of the other limitations spring from this.

b. As tape is a serial medium all transaction files must be in the sequence of the appropriate master file. This involves a great deal of unproductive time spent in sorting and re-sorting input data.

c. Updating a master tape file involves reading and writing the complete file however small the transaction file may be. Notice that when the batches are very small (ie, the hit rate (20.18) is low) this will involve a high proportion of *redundant processing* (ie, the reading and writing of the inactive records).

d. Because tape is a non-addressable medium a particular record cannot be accessed directly. Information required from a particular record is *not available* until the whole batch has been processed.

e. Several runs are required to produce output and this may result in some files not reflecting a *true up-to-date position* at a given moment (Fig. 22.13 Note 5).

```
┌─────────────────────────────────────────────────────────────────┐
```

RUN 5 - CUSTOMER FILE UPDATE.

5. a. **Input**
      i.   The magnetic tape reel at 4c.
      ii. Customer master file in customer-number sequence.
    b. **Processing.**
      i.   The order records are matched with the customer master records and the invoice amount calculated. The customer master records are updated by the value of the invoices.
      ii. Name and address details are extracted from master records.
    c. **Output.**
      i.   Magnetic tape reel with updated customer file.
      ii. Magnetic tape reel with invoice details.
      iii. Reports on credit limits being exceeded (etc).

RUN 6 - PRINT OUTPUT.

6. a. **Input.** The magnetic tape reel at 5c.ii, ie, invoice details.
    b. **Processing.** The invoices are printed.
    c. **Output.** Printed invoices on the line printer.

Notes:

1. The use of tape as the storage medium requires that each transaction file and appropriate master *must* be in the same sequence in order to carry out processing.

2. Consequently there is need for much sorting and re-sorting of the transaction file.

3. Two updating runs were required (ie, updating the stock file and the customer file) and a sort was necessary before each.

4. Not all the information required could be obtained in one RUN and thus 6 separate runs were necessary to produce the final output.

5. a. If an order is found to be unacceptable on Run 5 (for reasons of "credit" for instance) then the stock file shows a false position. The order will have been recorded during Run 3, thus reducing the balance of the particular produce. Notice that all subsequent orders for that product on Run 4 will be processed in the light of the stock having been depleted by the amount involved; a situation which in fact does not exist, as Run 5 shows.

   b. The stock file is "put right" on the next run by means of a "receipt" transaction (ie, an adjustment voucher).

Fig. 22.13

22.44 These limitations have caused the steady decline of tape as an on-line storage medium, although tape is still of major importance for off-line storage, eg, back-up and data entry. Magnetic tape is still used in some applications where there is a high hit-rate, where "delay" as such is of no consequence, and where a direct-access facility is not required. Examples of such applications are payroll, which requires processing only once a week, and files of historical data, which are only required periodically.

FILE CONTROLS

22.45 It is essential to ensure that data are not only input correctly, but also maintained correctly and processed correctly right through the system. It is also necessary to ensure that data in master files are not corrupted by machine or program failures.

22.46 The necessary safeguards are provided by *file control totals*. At the end of each file there is a special block (sometimes blocks) that holds the total value of the items stored in the file. For example, the net total of the balances and a count of the number of records. When the file is processed, totals are accumulated from each record. At the end of the run, these totals are compared with those in the file control block. Any difference between the two totals indicates some error in processing or some corruption of data in the file.

22.47 File-control totals are derived from batch totals, and the following paragraphs explain how this is done.

   a. **Transaction files.** When batch totals have been reconciled, data are written onto a magnetic file for further processing. By adding all the correct batch totals for the run, a control for the transaction file is obtained. This total is used to ensure that the transaction file is correctly processed during subsequent runs, and that all transactions are processed when the master file is updated.

b. **Master file.** When the master file is updated from the transaction file, the processing of the transaction file is controlled as described above. The control totals in the master file are then adjusted by the amount of the transactions that have been inserted into it. Subsequent runs of the master file are reconciled to the control total.

c. **Clerical control.** It is possible to maintain an independent control on computer processing. Records are kept of the batch totals and are added to provide a run total, ie, the total value of transactions passed to the DP department for processing. When the computer outputs are received the control totals printed by the machine can be reconciled to the original batch figures. Adjustments have to be made, of course, for individual items rejected by the computer because they fail validity checks.

SYSTEM FLOWCHART

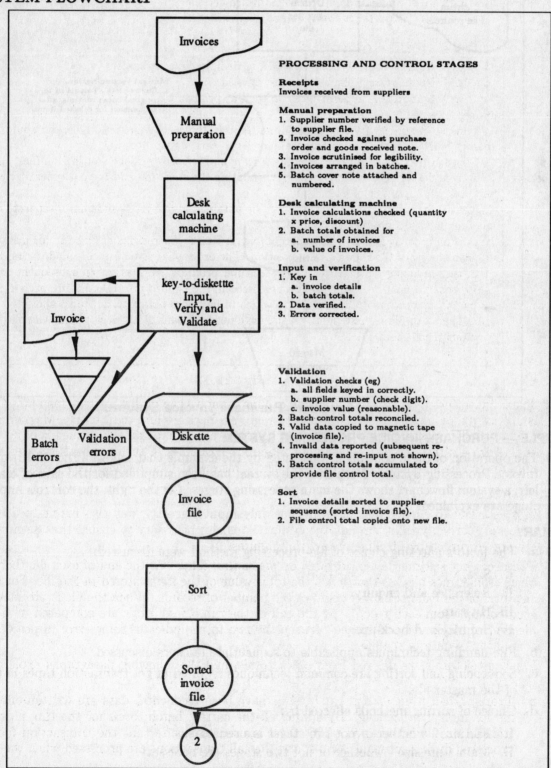

PROCESSING AND CONTROL STAGES

Receipts
Invoices received from suppliers

Manual preparation
1. Supplier number verified by reference to supplier file.
2. Invoice checked against purchase order and goods received note.
3. Invoice scrutinised for legibility.
4. Invoices arranged in batches.
5. Batch cover note attached and numbered.

Desk calculating machine
1. Invoice calculations checked (quantity x price, discount)
2. Batch totals obtained for
   a. number of invoices
   b. value of invoices.

Input and verification
1. Key in
   a. invoice details
   b. batch totals.
2. Data verified.
3. Errors corrected.

Validation
1. Validation checks (eg)
   a. all fields keyed in correctly.
   b. supplier number (check digit).
   c. invoice value (reasonable).
2. Batch control totals reconciled.
3. Valid data copied to magnetic tape (invoice file).
4. Invalid data reported (subsequent re-processing and re-input not shown).
5. Batch control totals accumulated to provide file control total.

Sort
1. Invoice details sorted to supplier sequence (sorted invoice file).
2. File control total copied onto new file.

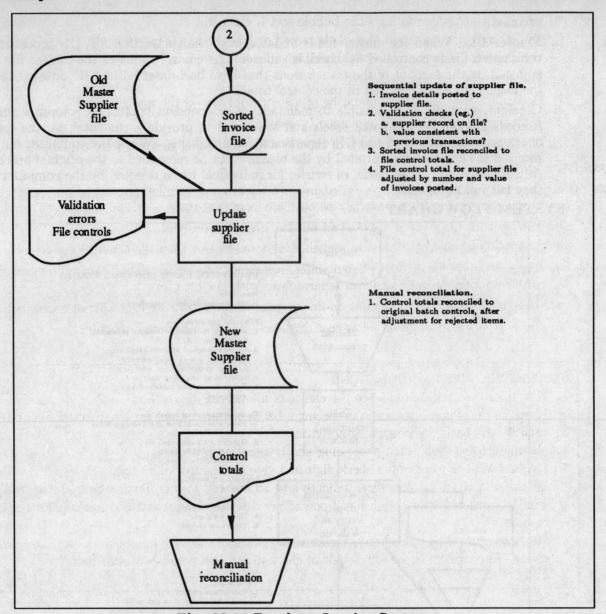

On the right of the figure:

Sequential update of supplier file.
1. Invoice details posted to supplier file.
2. Validation checks (eg.)
   a. supplier record on file?
   b. value consistent with previous transactions?
3. Sorted invoice file reconciled to file control totals.
4. File control total for supplier file adjusted by number and value of invoices posted.

Manual reconciliation.
1. Control totals reconciled to original batch controls, after adjustment for rejected items.

Labels in flowchart: Old Master Supplier file; Sorted invoice file; Validation errors File controls; Update supplier file; New Master Supplier file; Control totals; Manual reconciliation.

Fig. 22.15 Purchase Invoice System.

EXAMPLE — PURCHASE INVOICE PROCESSING SYSTEM

22.48 The operation of these controls is illustrated by the example that follows (Fig. 22.15) of a Purchase Invoice Processing System. Note that the system has been simplified for the sake of clarity. On the left, a system flowchart shows the main processing stages. On the right, the controls imposed at each stage are explained.

SUMMARY

22.49 a. The factors affecting choice of file-processing method were discussed:

    i. Size.

    ii. Reference and enquiry.

    iii. Hit rate

    iv. Security and back-up.

b. File-handling techniques applicable to sequential files were discussed.

c. Sequencing and sorting are common techniques required to get transaction tapes in the sequence of the master file.

d. Choice of sorting methods affected by:

    i. File size - whether or not two stages are necessary.

    ii. Main store size - whether or not two stages are necessary.

iii. Degree of pre-ordering - the bubble sort is quicker.

iv. Record size - whether the whole record or just the key is moved.

v. For final sequencing a serial check is sufficient.

e. Batch processing was explained.

f. A detailed example of the updating of a sequential master file was given.

g. Multiple file updates were explained by example.

h. The advantages and limitations of tape as a file-processing medium were explained.

POINTS TO NOTE

22.50 a. Internal sorting is sometimes called **in-core sorting**, a term left over from the days when main storage was made from cores, a now obsolete form of storage.

b. We say that the records are **sorted** but the file is **sequenced.**

c. The merge using the Fibonacci sequence is more efficient than the classical merge sort.

d. The example of file updating and maintenance shows a common method of combining maintenance with updating, thereby saving a separate run with low hit rate.

e. Tape is no longer an important on-line storage medium because it is a serial access medium.

f. Tape is very important as a low-cost, high-volume, off-line storage medium.

STUDENT SELF-TESTING QUESTIONS

1. How does the hit rate influence the choice of file-processing method?
2. Describe the stages involved in preparing a batch of transactions for a sequential file update.
3. Identify the basic file-processing activities.
4. Distinguish between batch processing and transaction processing.
5. Explain what is meant by a check digit and give an example of its use.

   By use of a chart or otherwise, indicate how an ordered master file can be updated using a similarly ordered transaction file if one allows deletions, insertions and amendments of the records.

   How can you protect this process against hardware or software failure?　　(15 marks)

   (Note. Appendix 3.3 give full details of check digits, less detail is needed here.)

   (London)

QUESTIONS WITHOUT ANSWERS

6. A supermarket uses a computer to keep a daily check on its stock levels. Information regarding the sale and delivery of goods is recorded, resulting in a transaction file containing records that consist of the following three fields:

   Item number: Quantity; Marker.

   For goods sold the marker is S, for goods received it is R. At the end of each day this file is used to update the master file, the records of which consist of the following fields:

   Item number; Description; Quantity in stock; Re-order level.

   Both of the above files are sorted into ascending item-number sequence.

   Construct a flowchart or an appropriate pseudocode description for a program to update the master file with the stock movements from the transaction file and to produce a report of all those items where the updated quantity in stock is less than the re-order level on one printer and an error report on another.

   You may assume that each file is terminated by a dummy record containing a "high-value" item number.　　(20 marks)

   (AEB)

GLOSSARY CHECKLIST

23: File Processing II

INTRODUCTION

23.1 The previous chapter introduced file processing by the use of examples that explained the basic methods of sequential file processing used with disk or magnetic tape. In this chapter we will see how the advantages of disk over magnetic tape make it possible to use disk for a wide variety of file-processing activities, including more sophisticated forms of batch processing. Several examples are used to illustrate the points that are made.

MAGNETIC DISK

23.2 Disk is a direct-access storage medium and therefore overcomes the major limitation of tape. This gives it a very real advantage over tape in this respect. Disk does require the use of systems software, although this is not a serious problem with the current range of computers. It has a higher data transfer speed than most models of tape and effectively has a greater storage capacity. The cost of disk is much higher than that of tape but it is a cost users seem willing to pay for the benefits of its use.

23.3 Not all the limitations of tape are overcome by the use of disk. However, the facility of direct access helps to solve some of the problems and help to alleviate others. We will now reconsider the limitations of tape in the same order as previously outlined (22.43) and see how the use of disk helps overcome them.

    a. The question of access has been covered already and disk does overcome this limitation completely.

    b. Despite the fact that disk provides a direct-access facility it is often expedient to sort a transaction file into the sequence of the master file. For example an Indexed Sequential File processed Selective Sequentially makes use of direct-access while not involving the access mechanism in back-tracking, provided no other use is made of the disk by the other users while the file is being processed. If the same file were processed in a random manner (ie, using an unsorted transaction file) a great deal more time would be spent by the access mechanism in moving to and fro across the face of the disk. The first method involves sorting time and seek time, the second involves no sorting but considerably more seek time. Individual circumstances will indicate the method to be used.

    c. If a very large file with a low hit rate is stored on disk then the direct-access capability makes it possible to access *only* those records requiring updating, thus eliminating the redundant processing that occurs with tape.

    d. Requests for information can be answered quickly. **File Enquiry** (as it is called) is accomplished by linking a terminal or workstation to the processor. A request for information can be answered by displaying the contents of a particular record on the screen. This could be done while the enquirer (a customer) is waiting at the other end of a telephone. Notice that by using a multi-programmed computer (ie, one that runs more than one program at a time), file enquiries can be answered during the running of another program, eg, an updating program. (An example will be given later.)

    e. In the example in Fig. 23.1 the use of disk storage solves the problem of a file not reflecting a true situation. The stock file is stored on disk and access is made to it at the same time as the customer file. Thus the two runs are combined and all the data required is available at *the same time*. The underlying principle is important because it represents a significant advance on tape processing.

    Notice that the "delay" problem is *still* present, because it is inherent in the batch-processing system itself.

23.4 Most small systems use either floppy disks or small hard disks and can exploit the direct-access capabilities of disks. However, few small systems can provide simultaneous file access by multiple programs as just described in d. although it is becoming more common on newer 16-bit or 32-bit microcomputers such as the Archimedes and those running the operating systems Unix or OS/2.

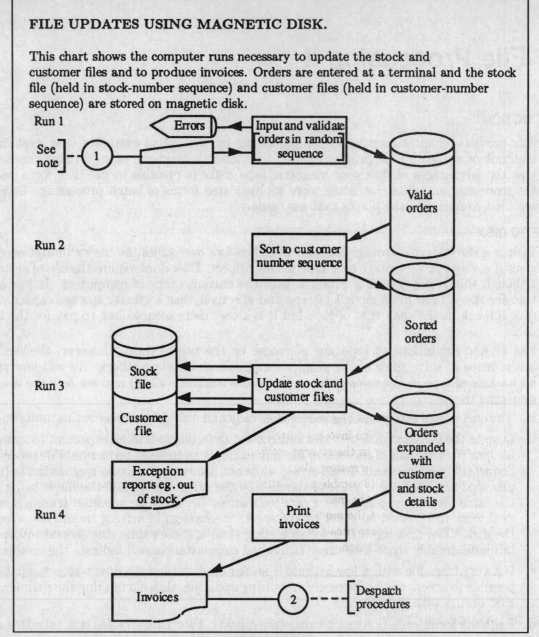

FILE UPDATES USING MAGNETIC DISK.

This chart shows the computer runs necessary to update the stock and customer files and to produce invoices. Orders are entered at a terminal and the stock file (held in stock-number sequence) and customer files (held in customer-number sequence) are stored on magnetic disk.

Fig. 23.1

PROCESSING APPLICATIONS USING DISK STORAGE

23.5 a. **File enquiry.** This has been mentioned already. The information required must be stored on a DAS medium. Random access would be necessary in this particular application in order to be able to deal with any enquiry as it arose.

b. **Random access.** Building societies and insurance companies have extremely large files with a very low hit rate. Random access is used in view of the small size of batches, thus saving the vast amount of redundant processing of inactive records which would be required with tape. Such files stored on tape can take some six hours to process completely, which will give you an idea of the problem.

c. **Simultaneous processing** of files. A customer file and stock file can be processed together provided the stock file is on a DAS medium.

23.6 So far we have considered the concept of batch processing purely in terms of computer processing and have seen how the use of disk storage can overcome many of the limitations of tape. We now want to extend our considerations to include the link with data collection so that we can see a more complete picture.

SYSTEMS FLOWCHART DISK PROCESSING - SUPPORTING NARRATIVE.

RUN 1 - DATA VALIDATION.
- a.　**Input.** See Fig. 22.12 para 1a.
- b.　**Processing.** See Fig. 22.12 para 1b.
- c.　**Output.** Onto disk instead of tape, otherwise the same as shown in Fig. 22.12.

RUN 2 - SORT.
- a.　**Input.** The magnetic disk used for output in Run 1.
- b.　**Processing.** Sorting of valid orders into customer-number sequence.
- c.　**Output.** Onto disk.

RUN 3 - UPDATE OF STOCK AND CUSTOMER FILES.
- a.　**Input.** The magnetic disk used for output in Run 2.
- b.　**Processing.** Access to the customer file is by the selective sequential method and to the stock file by the random method. Invoice values are calculated.
- c.　**Output.**
  - i.　Magnetic disk with details of invoices.
  - ii.　Exception reports.

NB. For file security details see Fig. 21.5

RUN 4 - PRINT OUTPUT.
- a.　**INput.** Invoice details.
- b.　**Processing.** Invoices are printed.
- c.　**Output.** Printed invoices on the lineprinter.

Notes: 1. Using disk as the storage medium it is not *essential* to sort each transaction file into the sequence of the master file.

2. Consequently, Run 3 combines updating of customer file (where transactions *are* in the sequence of the master file) with updating the stock files (where the transactions are *not* in the sequence of the master file).

3. Because of this, fewer runs are required than with magnetic tape, and the files always show a *true* position.

Fig. 23.2

LINK WITH DATA COLLECTION

23.7 For many years the delay spoken of earlier in terms of batch processing was *aggravated* by the time it took for data to pass through all the stages of data collection prior to processing. Newer methods of data-collection have helped to reduce data collection times. The change to key-to-disk eliminated media conversion. The use of OCR/MICR eliminated the transcription process.

23.8 Although these methods of data collection add delay to the time cycle of the system, nevertheless this time lag is perfectly acceptable to many users, which is why this form of DP is still widely used.

ON-LINE PROCESSING

23.9 The methods just discussed tend to involve some physical transportation of data or *manual intervention* in the data-collection process. The data source itself can be linked directly to the computer, in which case there is no manual intervention and the whole process is automatic. This **"on-line data entry"** may take place by means of data transmission equipment or as part of a distributed system. By one means or another data arrives at the main computer where the processing is to take place.

23.10 On receipt at the main computer, the data (which may be coming from hundreds of remote terminals, is at once stored on disk and after a suitable interval sorted and then processed (involving data validation, updating and production of output). Notice that in essence all we have done is to dramatically speed up the process of data collection. The batch-processing concept *still* applies.

MULTI-USER SIMULTANEOUS FILE PROCESSING.

This chart shows the simultaneous processing of two files and file enquiry in a multi-user, multi-programming system.

1. It is a multi-programming system because more than one program is running. In this example one program is the update program (as in Fig. 23.1 run 3), another is the file enquiry program.

2. The stock file and customer file are each being processed by both programs so simultaneous file processing is taking place.

NB. Careful controls on file access are necessary in order to deal with situations where two different programs try to access the same record at the same time. One method, called **record locking**, enables the first program accessing the record to prevent access by the other programs until the first program has completed processing the record.

3. This requires direct access storage and a file organisation method that supports random access.

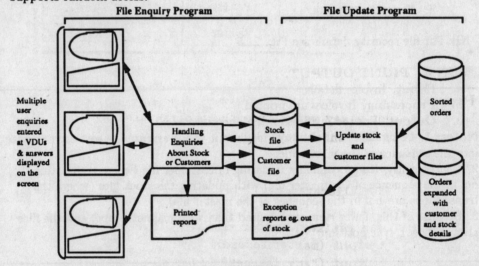

Fig. 23.3

23.11 The advantage of "on-line" processing is that data is less out of date on arrival in the computer. As a result, files reflect a much more up-to-date, more *real*, picture of a particular set of circumstances. Furthermore, the results of processing are available more quickly as they can be fed back to the same terminal if need be. Additionally the remote terminal can also be used for enquiries that arise at the source.

23.12 The major clearing banks have an on-line system of processing coupled with file enquiry.

23.13 It should be realised that on-line systems of batch processing are much more costly than the conventional method involving transporting the data by post. However the advantages lie in the time saved and the availability of more up-to-date information.

TRANSACTION PROCESSING

23.14 We have just seen how the time lag in batch-processing systems can be reduced by the use of various data collection techniques and more especially by the use of the techniques of on-line processing (coupled with the use of DAS). Most businesses *do not* require their files of data to be right "up to date" at all times and gear their activities to a time cycle that is acceptable.

23.15 There are situations, however, that require any data that arise to be immediately processed and the relevant file updated because any action taken must be based on the true current circumstances. Such a processing system is said to be working in **real time**. Real-time processing is the processing of data so quickly that the results are available to influence the activity currently taking place. Decisions are continually being made on the very latest information available because files are kept permanently up to date.

23.16 You could say that a single transaction becomes the batch, which is processed *on demand*. Thus the process of input, validation, updating and output must be gone through just as with batch processing, but for *each* transaction as and when it occurs. This real-time processing of individual transactions is known as **"Transaction Processing"**.

23.17 Transaction processing is just one kind of real-time processing. Other kinds of real-time processing are those concerned with the control of physical systems such as chemical plants or power stations.

23.18 Further details of transaction processing and its applications will be given in later chapters.

A SIMPLE PRACTICAL EXAMPLE

23.19 The following examples shows random access to a disk file to display and view **or** display, view and update records singly. Old records are overwritten by updated records. Each record is identified by its key, which is keyed in at a terminal.

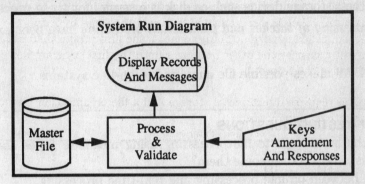

Fig 23.4.

```
Repeat
        (* get a key value from the program user *)
        output ("which key?")
        input (key)
        if
                key_allocated(key)
        then
                call get(key, master_record)
                Output (master_record)
                Output ("Any changes?  (yes or no")
                input (reply)
                if
                        reply = "yes"
                then
                        repeat
                                (* input record amendments *)
                                (* validate amendments *)
                                (* displaying errors messages where necessary *)
                        until record_valid
                        call put(key, master_record)
                endif
        else
                Output ("there is no record with this key")
        endif
        Output ("Any more records?  (yes or no)")
        input (response)
until response <> "yes"
```

23.20 The following pseudocode outlines how the main processing is performed. Assume that:

a. The file has been opened for random input and output.

293

   b. "Key" is an integer, reply and response are strings, record-valid is Boolean and master record is a record containing a key.

   c. The function **key-allocated** returns **true** when its argument has a record with that value in the file.

   d. The procedure **get** has **key** as an **IN** parameter and **master_record** as an **OUT** parameter. It reads and returns the master record with the specified key from the file.

   e. The procedure **put** has **key** and **master record** as IN parameters. It writes the master record to the appropriate position on the disk.

SUMMARY

23.21 a. The various non-sequential file-processing methods have been illustrated by example.

   b. A direct-access storage device such as disk is essential for these processing methods.

   c. *On-line processing of batches and transaction processing* have been explained.

POINTS TO NOTE

23.22 a. Note how DAS makes possible file enquiry and on-line systems.

STUDENT SELF-TESTING QUESTIONS

1. What are the limitations to file processing using magnetic tapes and how can the use of magnetic disks help to overcome them?

2. Distinguish between on-line processing and real-time processing.

QUESTIONS WITHOUT ANSWERS

3. This question is concerned with a file of student records with the following fields:

Student number	4 numeric characters
surname	20 characters
forenames	20 characters
address	40 characters
date of birth (YYMMDD)	6 characters
course code	4 numeric characters
subject details – a group of three items where each consists of –	
subject studied	3 characters
total mark to date	integer
number of items marked	integer

Each student may be studying up to three subjects, the subjects studied are coded so that each subject has a standard abbreviation, eg, STA - statistics, MAT - maths, ACC - accounts, etc. In the questions that follow invent your own abbreviations if you find it necessary.

a. Write a program that reads the student records for those students studying a particular subject, typed in by the user, into a table. Then for that group compute the average mark achieved so far in that subject and output a list of those students whose own average is below the group average.

b. Write a program to update the student file with transactions of the form:

student number	4 numeric characters
subject code	3 characters
mark for one piece of work	integer

Assume both files are sequential files sorted into ascending order of student number. Your algorithm should cater for a number of transactions for the same student - including several marks for the same subject and marks for a number of subjects; also check for errors such as student numbers not matching and students having marks for subjects they do not apparently study.

c. Design an algorithm to validate a file of transactions for the maintenance of the student file detailed above. The format for the transactions will be the same as the master file, except for the addition of an extra field of one character which denotes the record type - A for amendment, I for insertion, D for deletion.

Transactions indicating a deletion will consist of the record type and the student number, the rest of the record will be spaces. Transactions indicating an insertion will have all fields present, but the total marks and the number of pieces of work must be zero. Transactions for amendments will have the record type, the student number and any fields to be changed, other fields will be left blank.

The output will be a file of valid transactions and an error report containing the invalid transactions and an indication of the errors in each record. You must choose a suitable method for this.

QUESTIONS WITHOUT ANSWERS CONTINUED

4. Write an algorithm to produce invoices given data in the following files: an orders file and a customer-reference file; both are sequenced on customer number. There may be several order records for each customer but each order record gives rise to a separate invoice. The customer reference records consist of the following fields.

> customer number
> name
> address

The orders records consist of the following fields:

> customer number
> stock number of item ordered
> date of order (YYMMDD)
> number of items ordered.

The invoices consist of:

> customer number
> name
> address
> date of order
> stock number of items ordered
> number of items ordered
> price per item
> total price of items ordered
> VAT at 15% of total price
> total cost (total price + VAT)

You may choose the layout of the invoices.

The prices of the items are found from a table that is read into an array at the beginning of the program. There are 100 stock items. Each entry in the table consists of the stock number and its price per item, these are stored in sequential order of stock number. Hence, given the stock number you need to search the table to find the price.

GLOSSARY CHECKLIST

APPLICATIONS III

1. The single chapter in this Part deals with the subject of Spreadsheets. Spreadsheet Packages are a very popular type of applications software. Even where they are not mention explicitly on examination syllabuses a knowledge of them is normally implied by some general requirement. This is because of the great utility and importance of spreadsheets. All readers are therefore advised not only to study this chapter but to gain first hand practical experience.

24: Spreadsheets

INTRODUCTION

24.1 Spreadsheets are popular examples of a **generalised software package**. They are general-purpose tools which can be used for tasks which arise in a variety of different applications involving calculations on rows and columns of numbers.

24.2 Included in the many tasks to which spreadsheets may be applied are: analysing statistics; creating business plans; creating business budgets; estimating business cost, calculating profits or losses; sales forecasting and financial analysis.

24.3 One of the earliest spreadsheet packages was the software package called "Visicalc" produced by Visicorp Inc. for use on microcomputers. Newer, more advanced versions have since been produced by Visicorp and its competitors. Two very popular spreadsheet packages in widespread use today are LOTUS 1-2-3 and Microsoft's EXCEL. Indeed spreadsheet packages are some of the most widely sold items of software.

24.4 This chapter starts with some general features and then goes on to look in more detail at a windows based spreadsheet.

	:A	:B	:C	:D	
1:		CUSTOMER	F. Bloggs	ESTIMATE	
2:					
3:	MATERIALS	UNIT-COST	QUANTITY	TOTAL COST	
4:					
5:	White Gloss (Small)	2.00	0.00	0.00	← B5 × C5
6:	White Gloss (large)	3.50	2.00	7.00	← B6 × C6
7:	Coloured Gloss (Small)	2.50	3.00	7.50	← B7 × C7
8:	Coloured Gloss (Large)	4.00	1.00	4.00	← B8 × C8
9:	White Emulsion (Small)	2.50	0.00	0.00	← B9 × C9
10:	White Emulsion (Large)	4.50	1.00	4.50	← B10 × C10
11:	Coloured Emulsion (Small)	3.00	0.00	0.00	← B11 × C11
12:	Coloured Emulsion (Large)	5.50	3.00	16.50	← B12 × C12
13:	Cleaning Materials	3.00	1.00	3.00	← B13 × C13
14:					
15:				42.50	← sum of
16:					D5 to D13
17:					
18:	LABOUR	HOURS	RATE	TOTAL COST	
19:	Jim Brusher	35.00	10.00	350.00	← B19 × C19
20:					
21:			GRAND		
22:			TOTAL	392.50	← D15 + D19
23:					

Note.

a. If the values in columns B and C are changed then all other values can be recalculated automatically by using a recalculate command.

b. Since recalculation is so easy it is possible to handle "what if" questions such as "What if material costs rise by 5% ?".

Fig. 24.1. A simple spreadsheet layout showing how the values are calculated.

GENERAL FEATURES

24.5 Simple examples are shown in Fig. 24.1 – Fig. 24.3. They show some estimates relating to a painting and decorating job. You will notice that the spreadsheet (Fig. 24.1) comprises a grid of numbered rows and lettered columns. Each grid position is called a **cell** and can contain either text or numerical values. It is possible to define formulae by which values in some cells can be calculated from values in other cells. When using the spreadsheet package on the computer the user sees only part of the spreadsheet. The section of the screen displaying part of the spreadsheet is called a window (Fig. 24.2). In addition to the window the user also sees a display of details about the status of one cell currently being edited. The method of presenting this information varies from on package to another. A cell is selected for editing by moving the cursor about the screen until it is at that cell's position. This may be done by cursor keys or by means of a mouse. In Fig. 24.1 cell D6 is selected (ie, column D, row 6), whereas in Fig. 24.2 cell D10 is selected.

	:A	:B	:C	:D
1:		CUSTOMER	F. Bloggs	ESTIMATE
2:				
3:	MATERIALS	UNIT-COST	QUANTITY	TOTAL COST
4:				
5:	White Gloss (Small)	2.00	0.00	0.00
6:	White Gloss (large)	3.50	2.00	7.00
7:	Coloured Gloss (Small)	2.50	3.00	7.50
8:	Coloured Gloss (Large)	4.00	1.00	4.00
9:	White Emulsion (Small)	2.50	0.00	0.00
10:	White Emulsion (Large)	4.50	1.00	4.50

PRESENT CELL POSITION: D10

CELL TYPE : NUMERIC
CELL CONTENTS : + B10 *+ C10
CELL VALUE : 4.50

ENTER COMMAND OR VALUE : _____

Note.
a. Cell positions are specified like map grid references (column letter, row number), eg, D10.
b. A cell can contain numerical values or text, eg, A contains the text "MATERIALS", and cell D10 contains the value 4.50.
c. Numerical values may be entered directly OR calculated from other values, eg, values in columns B and C have been entered directly but values in column D are calculated by multiplying unit-cost by quantity. Formulae for calculating values are typed in in the same way as values.
d. Commands to save or print the display can be typed in too.

Fig. 24.2. A spreadsheet display showing a window of columns A–D and rows 1–10.

24.6 Numerical values can either be entered directly, by moving the cursor to the cell position, OR they may be calculated from other values. For example, values in columns B and C have been entered directly, but values in column D are calculated by multiplying unit-costs by quantity. Formulae are typed in the same way as values. The formula for cell D6 is B6 × C6. A SUM formula has been typed into cell D15 to obtain the totals of cells in the column from D5 to D13.

24.7 Having done the basic calculation the user can then carry out enquiries of the "what if?" variety such as "what if I mark up the material costs by 10%?" Various kinds of data manipulation are possible:

a. Inserting, deleting or copying rows and columns.
b. Changing the spreadsheet layout or the precision of calculations.
c. Printing the spreadsheet or saving a copy on disk for future use.
d. Performing comprehensive computation using mathematical functions and formulae.

24.8 With these functions the spreadsheet can be used for a wide variety of problems: job costing or production estimation; balance sheets and statements; simple forecasting; asset depreciation.

24.9 The more advanced packages, such as LOTUS 1-2-3 and Microsoft's EXCEL, also provide facilities to display data in graphical forms such as bar charts or pie charts.

24.10 The reader is advised to gain first-hand experience of using a spreadsheet if possible. For those readers with limited access to a spreadsheet package the following more detailed description is provided. The examples illustrate the basic features of a version of Microsoft Excel on an Apple Macintosh and can be compared with the simplified examples given earlier. These examples also illustrate the use of a package in a WIMP environment.

MATERIALS	CUSTOMER UNIT-COST	F. Bloggs QUANTITY	ESTIMATE TOTAL COST
White Gloss (Small)	2.00	0.00	0.00
White Gloss (large)	3.50	2.00	7.00
Coloured Gloss (Small)	2.50	3.00	7.50
Coloured Gloss (Large)	4.00	1.00	4.00
White Emulsion (Small)	2.50	0.00	0.00
White Emulsion (Large)	4.50	1.00	4.50
Coloured Emulsion (Small)	3.00	0.00	0.00
Coloured Emulsion (Large)	5.50	3.00	16.50
Cleaning Materials	3.00	1.00	3.00
			42.50
LABOUR	HOURS	RATE	TOTAL COST
Jim Brusher	35.00	10.00	350.00
		GRAND TOTAL	392.50

Fig. 24.3. How the spreadsheet may appear when printed.

FURTHER EXAMPLES

24.11 These examples start by illustrating some of the tasks carried out in setting up the spreadsheet shown in Figs 24.1 – 24.3.

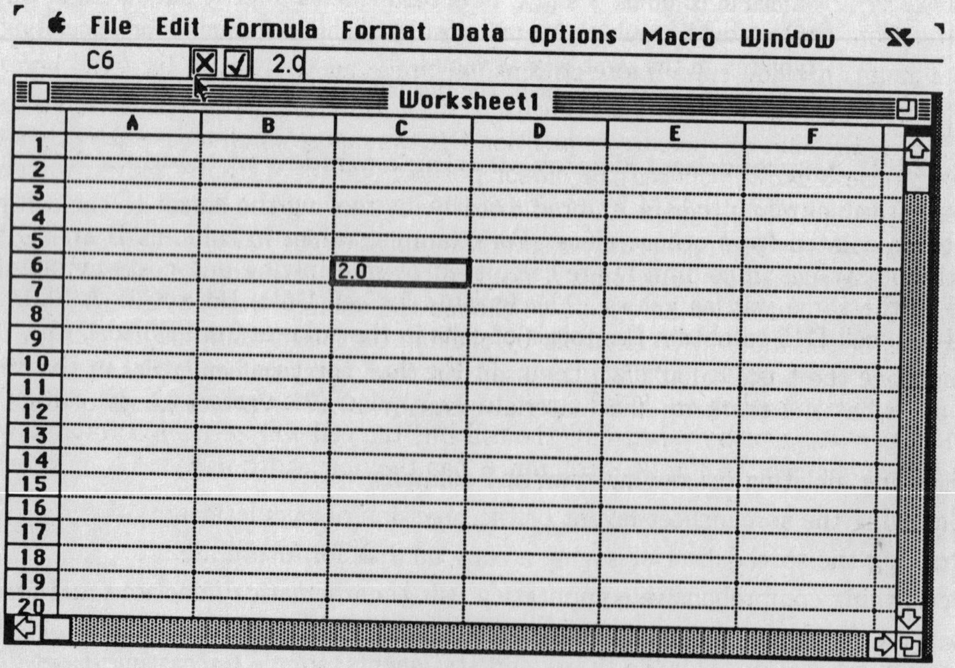

Fig 24.4.

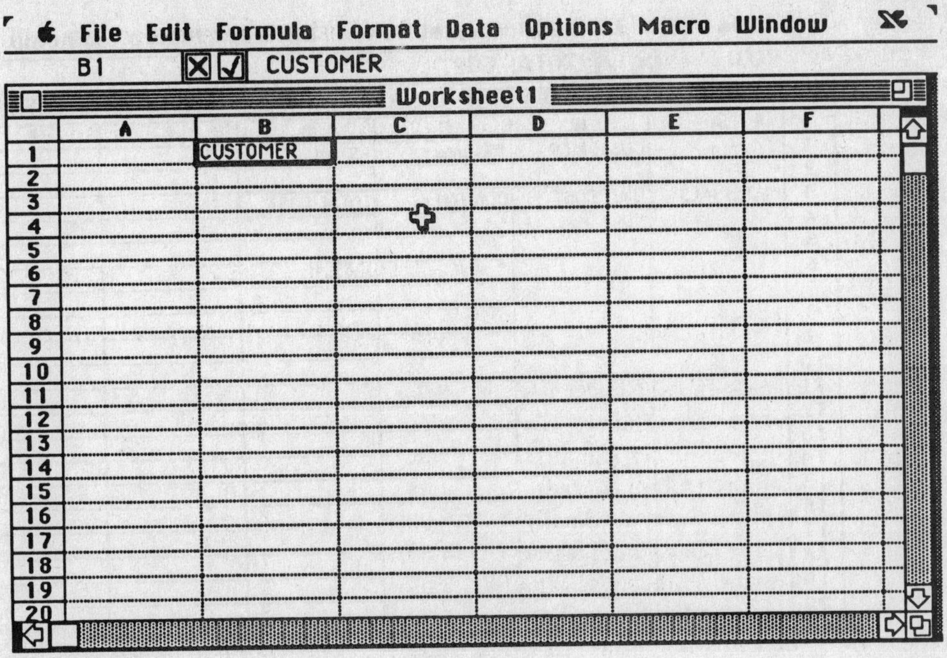

Fig 24.5.

24.12 Fig 24.4 merely shows a blank spreadsheet with cell C6 selected. Note how the number being typed in ("2.0") is also displayed in a field below the menu bar. This field is comparable to the one called "ENTER COMMAND OR VALUE" in Fig 24.2. The cell address , C6, is also displayed top left below the menu bar. Cells can be selected by means of the cursor keys or mouse. The latter may also be used to operate the scold bars to move to other areas of the spreadsheet.

24.13 The title bar contains the name of the current spreadsheet being worked on – "Worksheet1". The file menu provides the means to:

a. create a new spreadsheet,

b. open an existing spreadsheet from file,

c. print the current spreadsheet,

d. save the current spreadsheet as a file,

e. delete spreadsheets,

f. close the current spreadsheet,

g. quit from the package.

Other menus provide many more options, to numerous to mention in detail here.

24.14 In Fig 24.5 cell B2 has been filled with a title. The cell B2 is still selected and the box around "CUSTOMER" shows the cursors position but the mouse's pointer is currently sitting above cell C4. If the mouse button is clicked the cursor position will be instantly moved to cell C4. Alternatively the user may move to cell C4 by means of the arrowed cursor keys.

24.15 Fig 24.6 shows the spreadsheet after several more title cells have been added. From Fig 24.1 it can be seen that the row labels in column A need to be wider than the default width of 10 characters. The "Format" menu provides an option to change the column width. The user first selects the column by means of the mouse, for example by clicking on the column header cell "A". Then the column option is selected on the format menu. In Fig 24.7 the user has typed in the new column width of 24 and is ready to click on "OK" for it to be applied. Incidentally, if the column width is left at 10 then longer text can be typed into the cell but the cell will act as a scrollable window into the full contents of the cell. In Fig 24.8 column A has the new width of 24.

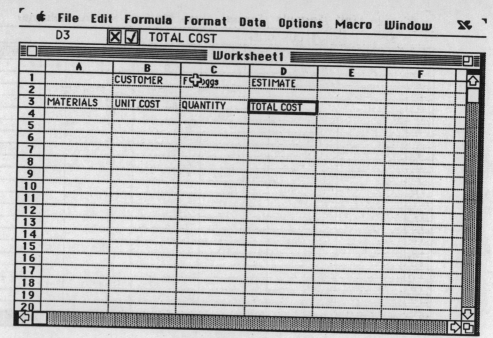

Fig 24.6.

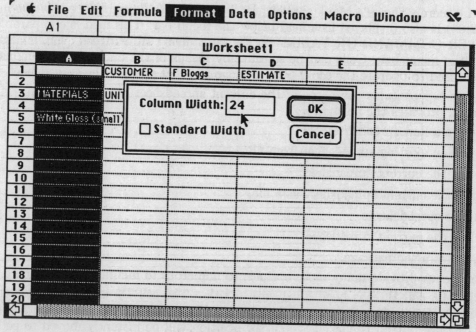

Fig 24.7.

24.16 Fig 24.8 also contains two columns of numbers. These have been typed in directly by the user cell by cell. The remaining values are to be calculated, rather than input, which requires the use of formulae.

24.17 Fig 24.9 shows the cursor on cell D5 with first formula being input. The spreadsheet program recognises a formula because it begins with a "=" sign. It recognises formulae by initial "+" and "-" signs too. The formula in cell D5 indicates that the contents of D5 should be calculated by multiplying the contents of cell B5 by the contents of cell C5. The formula for cell D6 will be like the formula for D5 except that the row number will be different. To save the laborious task of typing in the formula again a facility is provided for copying formulae from one cell to another and making the necessary adjustments on the way. So to get the formula into cell D6 the user may use the "Edit" menu to copy the formula in D5 and then paste automatically adjusted version of it into cells D6, D7, D 8, D9, D10, D11, D12 and D13. As the formulae are entered in each cell the cell values are automatically calculated. The calculated values are shown in Fig 24.10

**   File   Edit   Formula   Format   Data   Options   Macro   Window**

C4

	A	B	C	D	E
2					
3	MATERIALS	UNIT COST	QUANTITY	TOTAL COST	
4					
5	White Gloss (Small)	2	0		
6	White Gloss (Large)	3.5	2		
7	Coloured Gloss (Small)	2.5	3		
8	Coloured Gloss (Large)	4	1		
9	White Emulsion (Large)	2.5	0		
10	White Emulsion (Large)	4.5	1		
11	Coloured Emulsion (Small)	3	0		
12	Coloured Emulsion (Large)	5.5	3		
13	Cleaning Materials	3	1		
14					
15					
16					
17					
18					
19					
20					
21					

Fig 24.8.

**   File   Edit   Formula   Format   Data   Options   Macro   Window**

D5   ☒ ☑   =b5 * c5

	A	B	C	D	E
2					
3	MATERIALS	UNIT COST	QUANTITY	TOTAL COST	
4					
5	White Gloss (Small)	2	0	=b5 * c5	
6	White Gloss (Large)	3.5	2		
7	Coloured Gloss (Small)	2.5			
8	Coloured Gloss (Large)	4	1		
9	White Emulsion (Large)	2.5	0		
10	White Emulsion (Large)	4.5	1		
11	Coloured Emulsion (Small)	3	0		
12	Coloured Emulsion (Large)	5.5	3		
13	Cleaning Materials	3	1		
14					
15					
16					
17					
18					
19					
20					
21					

Fig 24.9.

24.18 Fig 24.10 also shows a formula being entered into cell D15. The formula uses the "SUM" function in which a range of cells in a row or column can be specified and added up. The expression "SUM(D5:D13)" means add all cell in column D from row 5 to row 13 inclusive. This is clearly much more convenient than writing a formula such as "= D6 + D7 + D8 + D9 + D10 + D11 + D12 + D13". Many other functions are available too for a number of different purposes in these areas:

a. General Mathematics.

b. Statistics.

c. Trigonometry.

d. Logic.

e. Text manipulation.

f. Logic.

g. Finance.

h. Dates.

These are in addition to basic operations such as "+", "−", "*", "/", ">", "<", "<=", ">=", "<>", and "&". The last one performs string concatenation.

File Edit Formula Format Data Options Macro Window

D15 [X] [✓] =sum(d5:d13)

Worksheet1

	A	B	C	D	E
2					
3	MATERIALS	UNIT COST	QUANTITY	TOTAL COST	
4					
5	White Gloss (Small)	2	0	0	
6	White Gloss (Large)	3.5	2	7	
7	Coloured Gloss (Small)	2.5	3	7.5	
8	Coloured Gloss (Large)	4	1	4	
9	White Emulsion (Large)	2.5	0	0	
10	White Emulsion (Large)	4.5	1	4.5	
11	Coloured Emulsion (Small)	3	0	0	
12	Coloured Emulsion (Large)	5.5	3	16.5	
13	Cleaning Materials	3	1	3	
14					
15				=sum(d5:d13)	
16					
17					
18					
19					
20					
21					

Fig 24.10.

File Edit Formula Format Data Options Macro Window

D15 | =SUM(D5:D13)

Worksheet1

	A	B	C	D	E
1		CUSTOMER	F Bloggs	ESTIMATE	
2					
3	MATERIALS	UNIT COST	QUANTITY	TOTAL COST	
4					
5	White Gloss (Small)	2.00	0	0.00	
6	White Gloss (Large)	3.50	2	7.00	
7	Coloured Gloss (Small)	2.50	3	7.50	
8	Coloured Gloss (Large)	4.00	1	4.00	
9	White Emulsion (Large)	2.50	0	0.00	
10	White Emulsion (Large)	4.50	1	4.50	
11	Coloured Emulsion (Small)	3.00	0	0.00	
12	Coloured Emulsion (Large)	5.50	3	16.50	
13	Cleaning Materials	3.00	1	3.00	
14					
15	ALL MATERIALS			42.50	
16					
17					
18					
19					
20					

Fig 24.11.

24.19 In Fig 24.11 the contents of cell D15 have been calculated but, with the cursor over this cell, the formula is shown on the second line of the screen so that the user can see how the value was obtained.

24.20 Also, in Fig 24.11 the untidy format of the number in Fig 24.10 has been changed so that all numbers in columns B and D are displayed to two decimal places. The format column has been used to change each format. This is another option on the "Format" menu. The action of setting the format is shown in Fig 24.12.

24.21 Further more complex arithmetic can be performed by spreadsheet packages by means of the use of macros. A spreadsheet is similar in principle to a procedure in a programming language. It provides a means of putting together a named set of spreadsheet formulae for execution as a group.

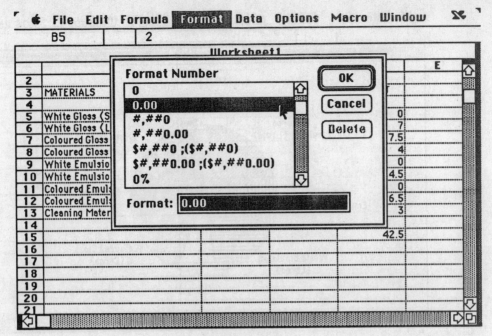

Fig 24.12.

24.22 Finally we come to two examples of the graphical capabilities of spreadsheets. Within the spreadsheet package it is possible to produce graphs and charts directly from the data on spreadsheets. Fig 24.13 shows an example of a bar chart produced from columns A and B of worksheet1 and Fig 24.14 shows a pie chart produced from the same data.

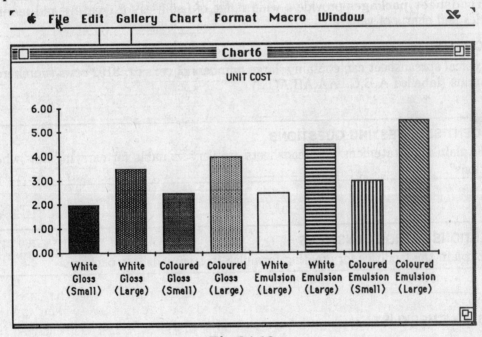

Fig 24.13.

24.23 There are still more features present in many modern spreadsheet packages, including means of connecting spreadsheets to databases and linking data across multiple spreadsheets and with text in word processors. However, the methods are somewhat specialised and product specific.

24.24 That concludes the more detailed examination of spreadsheets.

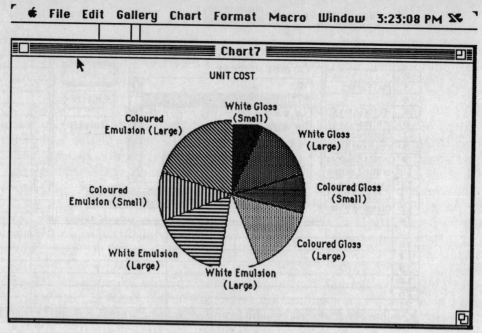

Fig 24.14.

SUMMARY

24.25 A **spreadsheet** comprises a grid of numbered rows and lettered columns intersecting in cells. A cell can contain either text or numerical values.

24.26 **Spreadsheet packages** provide a wide range of facilities for creating and manipulating formatted tables and charts of values.

POINTS TO NOTE

24.27 A typical spreadsheet can contain a large numbers of cells eg, 8192 rows (numbered 1,2,3...) and 256 columns (labelled A,B,C...AA,AB,AC...).

STUDENT SELF-TESTING QUESTIONS

1. Explain this statement. "Spreadsheets are very valuable for carrying out 'what if' calculations".

QUESTIONS WITHOUT ANSWERS

2. Explain the facilities for creating formulae in a spreadsheet package.

GLOSSARY CHECKLIST

Cell	24.5	Spreadsheet	24.25
Cell address	24.12	Spreadsheet packages	24.26
Generalised software package	24.1	What if	24.7
Macros	24.21		

LOGIC AND FORMAL NOTATIONS

1. Chapter 25 is an introduction to Boolean algebra, which is the algebra of logic. The chapter includes a discussion of the features of logic operations and truth tables along with methods of representing and simplifying logic expressions. At the time of publication of this text (1992) the only A level examination syllabus still to have a significant amount of this subject matter within it was the JMB's. Readers studying for other examinations would be wise to check the exact requirements. Some of the basic material is nevertheless of general importance so the reader may still benefit from reading the chapter once in order to gain an overview of the subject matter.

2. Chapter 26 shows how Boolean algebra applies to the operation of computer devices. In particular it deals with the logic operations of the ALU and the encoding and decoding circuits. The points made about syllabuses for chapter 25 apply to chapter 26 too except that some aspects of the computer's operation are more generally required.

3. Chapter 27 introduces Formal Notations and their use in specification and Language definition. There is considerable variation in examination syllabuses in this area but nearly all seem to contain some coverage. Most readers are likely to benefit from reading the whole chapter. When it comes to detailed methods it would be wise to check current syllabus requirements.

25: Boolean Algebra

INTRODUCTION

25.1   Boolean **algebra**, named after its pioneer George Boole, is the algebra of logic. The binary nature of logical propositions (true or false) means this subject has applications in computing. Indeed, we have already seen Boolean algebra, as applied to programming, in chapter 15. In this chapter we revise the basic ideas and take them a stage further.

PROPOSITIONS AND PREDICATES

25.2   **Propositions.** A proposition is a statement that can either be **true** or **false**. Propositions can be represented by letters.

    Examples.

    a. "p" stands for the proposition "You are reading this book" (TRUE)

    b. "q" stands for the proposition $3_{10} + 4_{10} = 10_{10}$ (FALSE)

    Questions and exclamations are **not** propositions.

    Examples.

    a. "Who are you?" (NOT A PROPOSITION)

    b. "Oh what a hot day!" (NOT A PROPOSITION)

25.3   **Negation.** The **negation** of a proposition "p" is the proposition that is false when p is true, and true when p is false. The negation of "p" may be written as $\bar{p}$, –p or ~ p. (and pronounced NOT p)

    Example.

        "p" is the proposition "You are reading this book"

        "$\bar{p}$" is the proposition "You are *not* reading this book"

25.4   **Truth tables.** The table shown below is a **truth table**. It shows the possible values of p and $\bar{p}$. It also serves as a concise definition of $\bar{p}$ in terms of p.

p	$\bar{p}$
T	F
F	T

    T stands for True. F stands for False.
    When p is true $\bar{p}$ is false
    When p is false $\bar{p}$ is true

Frequently the digits "0" and "1" are used instead of "T" and "F". *We will use "1" for True and "0" for False.* The truth table then appears as:

p	$\bar{p}$
1	0
0	1

    This binary representation should give you
    a clue as to how computers handle logic.

25.5   **Predicates** are like propositions in that they can either be **true** or **false**, but differ from propositions in that they contain variables, which, until specified, prevent the true or false value from being determined.

    Examples.

    a. x > 5 is a predicate. We need to know the value of x before we can determine whether or not it is true or false. Once a value is assigned to x (8 say) the predicate becomes the proposition 8 > 5, which is true.

    b. "It is red" is a predicate. We need to know what "it" is before we can determine whether or not the predicate is true or false.

25.6   Conditions in selections and repetitions in programming languages are examples of predicates.

25.7   Since the substitution of values into the variables in a predicate turns the predicate into a proposition, predicates are sometimes loosely called propositions. Try to avoid this practice if you wish to pursue this subject further.

LOGIC OPERATIONS (BOOLEAN OPERATIONS)

25.8 **Operations**, **Operands**, and **Operators** were defined in 15.26. Propositions and predicates may be combined together using logic operators. The propositions and predicates then become **operands** in **logic operations**.

25.9 **Logic operations** Propositions may be combined together. The propositions then become **operands** in **logic operations**.

Examples.

a. "p" stands for "You are reading this book". "q" stands for "You are drinking coffee". p AND q is a **logic operation** with "p" and "q" operands and AND as operator. p AND q stands for "You are reading this book *and* you are drinking coffee".

b. P(x) is a predicate that stands for

$$x > 5$$

Q(y) is a predicate that stands for

$$y = 9$$

P(x) AND Q(y) is a **logic operation** with P(x) and Q(y) as operands and AND as operator. P(x) AND Q(y) stands for "x > 5 *and* y = 9".

25.10 **Logic operations** may be defined by truth tables. **Negation** is a logic operation and it was defined by truth table in paragraph 25.4.

25.11 **The AND operation** is defined in the truth table given below. The symbols ∩ ∧ and are commonly used for AND. So $p \wedge q$ is pronounced "p AND q"

p	q	$p \wedge q$
0	0	0
0	1	0
1	0	0
1	1	1

Note:
a. All possible combinations of p and q are given. Only one combination gives $p \wedge q$ true.
b. The AND operation may also be called the **logical product**, **intersection** or **conjunction**.

25.12 **The OR operation** is defined in the following truth table. The symbols ∪, ∨ and + are commonly used for OR. The OR operation may also be called the logical sum, **inclusive OR, disjunction** or **union**.

p	q	$p \vee q$
0	0	0
0	1	1
1	0	1
1	1	1

25.13 **Inclusive and Exclusive ORs.**

a. In everyday usage the word OR has two possible meanings:
   i. OR can mean one or the other or both (the **inclusive OR**).
   ii. OR can mean one or the other but **not** both (the **exclusive OR**).

b. **Examples.**
   i. **Inclusive OR.** To qualify for a competition you might have to subscribe to a magazine OR belong to a club (you might do both).
   ii. **Exclusive OR.** You are rich OR you are poor (you can't be both).

You can see from the truth table that the OR operation, as defined here, is in fact an inclusive OR operation.

exclusive OR symbol ≢ is defined in the following truth table.

p	q	$p \not\equiv q$
0	0	0
0	1	1
1	0	1
1	1	0

Compare this with the inclusive OR.
NB p ≢ q is a shorter way of writing
$$\overline{p}.q + p.\overline{q}$$

25.14 The equivalence operation (match), symbol ≡ is defined in the truth table. Note that p = q is true when p and q are the same, ie, match. An alternative symbol for ≡ is ⟺.

p	q	$p \equiv q$
0	0	1
0	1	0
1	0	0
1	1	1

Compare this with non-equivalence where
p ≢ q *is* true if p and q do *not* match.
NB $p \equiv q$ is a shorter way of writing
$\bar{p}.\bar{q} + p.q$

25.15 Equivalence. Two operations are equivalent if they have the same truth table, and the equivalence operation is used to test equivalence. For convenience we use the = sign for cases where the equivalence operation is true, eg, $p = q$ means $p \equiv q$ is true.

25.16 Examples.

a. To show $\overline{p \vee q} = \bar{p} \wedge \bar{q}$ using truth tables.
   Truth Table.

p	q	$\bar{p}$	$\bar{q}$	$\bar{p} \wedge \bar{q}$	$p \vee q$	$\overline{p \vee q}$
0	0	1	1	1	0	1
0	1	1	0	0	1	0
1	0	0	1	0	1	0
1	1	0	0	0	1	0

Method.

i. $\bar{p}$ and $\bar{q}$ are filled in using the negation table.

ii. $\bar{p} \wedge \bar{q}$ is filled in using the AND table with $\bar{p}$ and $\bar{q}$.

iii. $p \vee q$ is filled in using the OR table.

iv. $\overline{p \vee q}$ is filled in using negation of $p \vee q$.

The truth table values for $\overline{p \vee q}$ and $\bar{p} \wedge \bar{q}$ match, so $\overline{p \vee q} = \bar{p} \wedge \bar{q}$, ie, $\overline{p \vee q} \equiv \bar{p} \wedge \bar{q}$ is "1" for *all* values of the expressions.

b. This example uses the alternative notation with . for AND and + for OR so that the reader becomes familiar with both sets of symbols.
   To show $A + \bar{A}.B = A + B$

A	B	$A + B$	$\bar{A}$	$\bar{A}.B$	$A + \bar{A}.B$
0	0	0	1	0	0
0	1	1	1	1	1
1	0	1	0	0	1
1	1	1	0	0	1

The columns are filled in left to right using the appropriate operations to build up the expressions.

c. To show $A + 1 = 1$ and $A.1 = A$

A	1	$A + 1$	$A.1$
1	1	1	1
0	1	1	0

VENN DIAGRAMS

25.17 Diagrams in which AREAS represent OPERATIONS or PROPOSITIONS are called **Venn diagrams.**

25.18 Examples. The area within the rectangle represents all the possible propositions and the shaded area represents the proposition under consideration. **NB. A letter within a circle refers to the WHOLE circle in all these examples.**

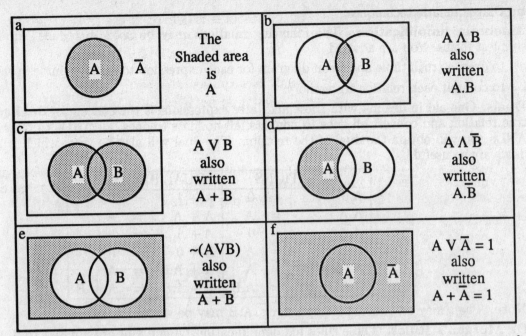

25.19 Using Venn diagrams. If two operations have the same Venn diagram they are equivalent. We use this fact to show equivalence.

Examples. Repeating the problems in paragraph 15.

a (i)

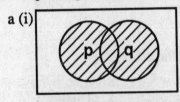

"p" refers to the **whole** of the lefthand circle and "q" refers to the **whole** of the righthand circle 1n a(i) and a(ii).
The shaded area represents pvq, so the unshaded area represents $\overline{pvq}$.

(ii)

'//, represents $\overline{p}$. \\\\` represents $\overline{q}$ so the double shaded area represents $\overline{p} \wedge \overline{q}$ and is the same as the unshaded area in a(i).
So $\overline{pvq} = \overline{p} \wedge \overline{q}$

b (i)

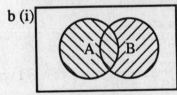

"A" refers to the **whole** of the lefthand circle and "B" refers to the **whole** of the righthand circle in b(i) and b(ii).
    \\\\ represents A. /// represents $\overline{A}$.B
So the total shaded area represents A + $\overline{A}$.B

(ii)

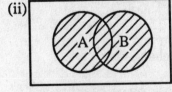

/// represents A + B and is the same as the total shaded area in b(i).
So A + $\overline{A}$B = A + B

c (i)

/// represents 1.\\\\` represents A but'//. also represents A+1 so A+1 = 1
The double shaded area is A.1 and is the same as \\\\. So A.1 = A

SIMPLIFICATION OF EXPRESSIONS

25.20 Broadly speaking simplification involves producing equivalent expressions that contain fewer operators.

Methods. The two methods covered by this book are:

a. Algebraic simplification using standard relations.

b. Diagrammatic techniques.

25.21 Algebraic simplification. The following relations may be used to reduce expressions to their simplest forms. You are advised

a. to draw a truth table and Venn diagram for each expression to satisfy yourself that they are true.

b. to commit each relation to memory.

25.22 Duals. One aid in dealing with these and later expressions is the concept of **duality**. If you take a true relation and convert all ones to noughts, all noughts to ones, all ANDs to ORs and all ORs to ANDs you will obtain the dual of the relation. The dual will also be true, which is the reason why duals are so useful.

RELATIONS		DUAL RELATION	
$A.0$	$= 0$	$A + 1$	$= 1$
$A.A$	$= A$	$A + A$	$= A$
$A.\overline{A}$	$= 0$	$A + \overline{A}$	$= 1$
$A.1$	$= A$	$A + 0$	$= A$
$A.(A + B)$	$= A$	$A + A.B$	$= A$
$A.(\overline{A} + B)$	$= A.B$	$A + \overline{A}.B$	$= A + B$

Note. The . may be omitted if implied, eg, A.B may be written AB.

25.23 De Morgan's Rules. These rules aid simplification. Again you are advised to draw truth tables and Venn diagrams for several expressions to get familiar with the results.

a. To apply De Morgan's Rules to simple expression (with a view to simplification) do the following.

i. change ANDs to ORs and ORs to ANDs.

ii. negate all variables.

iii. negate the expression so formed.

Examples. Apply the rule to either side to obtain the other.

$$\left. \begin{array}{rcl} \overline{A+B} & = & \overline{A}.\overline{B} \\ \overline{A.B} & = & \overline{A}+\overline{B} \end{array} \right\} \text{Duals}$$

$$\left. \begin{array}{rcl} \overline{A+B+C} & = & \overline{A}.\overline{B}.\overline{C} \\ \overline{A.B.C.D} & = & \overline{A}+\overline{B}+\overline{C}+\overline{D} \end{array} \right\} \text{Duals}$$

We use these expressions to simplify more complicated ones.

Note. The rules only apply to sum and product expressions.

b. For more elaborate expressions the rule is applied in stages.

Example

Consider $\overline{(p+q).\overline{r}}$

1st Stage $\overline{(p+q).\overline{r}} = \overline{p}.\overline{q}.r$ [Apply De M' to $\overline{(p+q)}$]

2nd Stage $\overline{p}.\overline{q}.r = \overline{p+q+\overline{r}}$ [Apply De M' to whole expression]

25.24 Other Rules.

a. Commutative Law (ordering of variables can be changed).

Examples.

   i.   A. B = B. A

   ii.   A + B = B + A

Examples.

   i.   A. (B. C) = (A. B). C = A. B. C

   ii.   A + (B + C) = (A + B) + C = A + B + C

   iii.   (A + B) + (C + D) = A + B + C + D

b. Distributive Law (similar rule to multiplying brackets in algebra).

Examples.

   i.   A. (B + C) = A. B + A. C

   ii.   (A + B) (A + C) = A. A + A.B + A.C + B.C = A + BC

25.25 Examples of Simplification.

a. To simplify $A + B(A + B) + A(\overline{A} + B)$

Solution

$$A + B(A + B) + A(\overline{A} + B)$$
$$= A + B + A(\overline{A} + B) \text{ (See paragraph 23)}$$
$$= A + B + A.B \text{ (See paragraph 23)}$$
$$= A + AB + B \text{ (Commutative law)}$$
$$= A + B \text{ (See paragraph 23)}$$

b. To simplify $\overline{A} + \overline{(B.C)} + \overline{C}.B$

Solution

$$\overline{\overline{A} + \overline{(B.C)} + \overline{C}.B}$$
$$= \overline{\overline{A}}.\overline{(\overline{B.C})}.\overline{\overline{C}.B} \qquad \text{(De M' applied as for } \overline{x + y + z} =$$
$$\overline{x}.\overline{y}.\overline{z})$$
$$= A.B.C.\overline{(\overline{C}.B)} \qquad \text{(since eg } \overline{\overline{A}} = A)$$
$$= A.B.C.(\overline{\overline{C}} + \overline{B}) \qquad \text{(De M' applied to } \overline{(\overline{C}.B)})$$
$$= A.B.C.(C + \overline{B})$$
$$= A.B.C.C + A.B.C.\overline{B} \qquad \text{(Distributive Law)}$$
$$= ABC \qquad (C.C = C \text{ and } B.\overline{B} = 0 \text{ and see}$$
$$\text{paragraph 23)}$$

c. To simplify $A + \overline{(\overline{B}.C)} + \overline{(\overline{B}.\overline{D})} = \overline{A}D$

Solution

$$A + \overline{(\overline{B}.C)} + \overline{(\overline{B}.\overline{D})} + \overline{A}D$$
$$= A + \overline{A}D + \overline{(\overline{B}.\overline{C} + \overline{B}.\overline{D})} \qquad \text{(Commutative Law)}$$
$$= A + D + \overline{(\overline{B}.\overline{C} + \overline{B}.\overline{D})} \qquad \text{(See paragraph 23)}$$
$$= A + D + \overline{(\overline{B}.\overline{C})}.\overline{(\overline{B}.\overline{D})} \qquad \text{(De Morgan)}$$
$$= A + D + (B + C).(B + D) \qquad \text{(De Morgan)}$$
$$= A + D + B + CD \qquad \text{(Distributive law see paragraph 25cii)}$$
$$= A + B + D + C.D \qquad \text{(Commutative Law)}$$
$$= A + B + D \qquad \text{(See paragraph 23)}$$

KARNAUGH MAPS (A stylized form of Venn diagrams)

25.26 There are different forms according to the number of variables in the expression to be simplified. We will consider expressions with up to 4 variables. Appropriate diagrams are shown below.

a. Two-variable case. The variables A,B and their negations can be combined in 4 ways and by cross reference of row and column labels (as with a map) each can be described.

	A	$\overline{A}$
B	represents A.B	represents $\overline{A}$.B
$\overline{B}$	represents A.$\overline{B}$	represents $\overline{A}.\overline{B}$

To represent an expression a "1" is placed in each square for which a term is present, eg, A = A.B + A.$\overline{B}$ is represented below.

	A	$\overline{A}$
B	1	
$\overline{B}$	1	

b. Three-variable case.

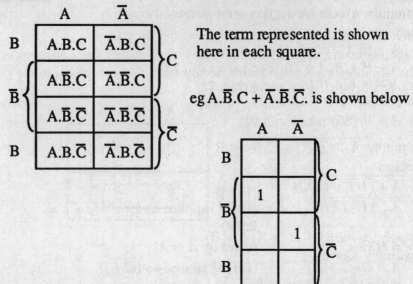

The term represented is shown here in each square.

eg $A.\overline{B}.C + \overline{A}.\overline{B}.\overline{C}$. is shown below

c. Four-variable case. The diagram is shown below and terms are written in.

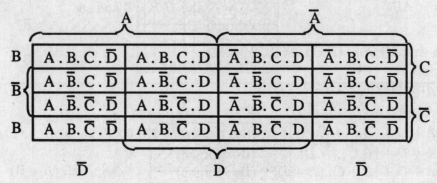

The expression $A.B + C.D$ is shown below.

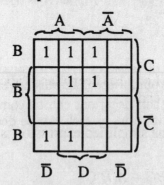

Simplifications using Karnaugh maps.

25.27 This is a very useful diagrammatic technique particularly when simplifying expressions that have several terms connected by ORs.

The procedure is as follows:

a. Do preliminary sketches to identify terms if you find it helpful.

b. On a new sketch fill in 1's for any term that is present in the expression. Use your preliminary sketches as a guide.

c. Draw loops around groups of 1, 2, 4 or 8 1's that correspond to simple expressions. The simplified expression will be a combination of these simpler expressions.

A little skill is needed to group the 1's correctly, but it soon comes with practice.

25.28 Examples.

a. To simplify $A\overline{B} + \overline{A}.B + AB$

Solution.

A preliminary sketch serves no useful purpose here.

i. Each term in the expression is represented by a 1.

ii. A loop is drawn around the 1's representing $\overline{A}$ and the 1's representing B.

iii. The two loops include all terms, so the simplified expression is $\overline{A}+\overline{B}$, ie, $A.\overline{B}+\overline{A}.B+\overline{A}.\overline{B} = \overline{A}+\overline{B}$

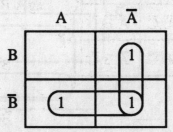

b. To simplify $A + B(A + B) + A(\overline{A} + B)$

Preliminary sketch 1

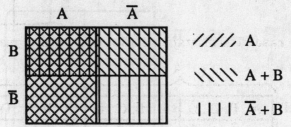

Preliminary sketch 2

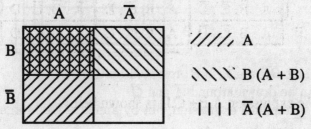

1's diagram with loops

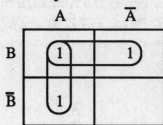

A Loop has been placed about A and B

The simplified expression is A + B

c. To simplify $ABC + A\overline{B}\,\overline{C} + \overline{A}B\overline{C} + \overline{A}BC + AB\overline{C} + \overline{A}\,\overline{B}\,\overline{C}$

i. Each term in the expression is represented by a 1.

ii. A loop is drawn around the terms representing $\overline{C}$.

iii. Another "broken loop" can be placed around the terms representing B.

The simplified expression is $B + \overline{C}$.

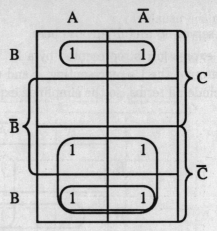

d. To simplify $\overline{A}C + B\overline{C} + \overline{B+C}$

Preliminary manipulation may help, ie, $\overline{A}C + B\overline{C} + \overline{B+C} = \overline{A}C + B\overline{C} + \overline{B}.\overline{C}$ (De M')

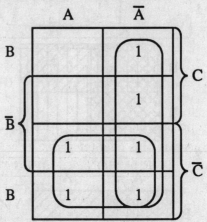

   i. $\overline{A}C$, $B\overline{C}$ and $\overline{B}\overline{C}$ are each represented by two 1's.

   ii. A loop can be drawn around $\overline{A}$ and $\overline{C}$.

  iii. $\overline{A} + \overline{C}$ is a simplified expression, but by applying De Morgan's rule we get a further simplification to $\overline{A.C}$.

(See if you can spot the result $\overline{A.C}$. just by inspecting the Karnaugh map).

e. To simplify $\overline{A}BCD + \overline{A}B C\overline{D} + AB\,\overline{C}D + \overline{A}\,\overline{B}\,\overline{C}D + \overline{A}\,\overline{B}\,\overline{C}\,\overline{D} + AB\overline{C}D + \overline{A}B\overline{C}D$

   i. Each term is represented by a 1.

   ii. A loop can be drawn around $\overline{A}.\overline{B}$ and $\overline{C}D$.

The simplified expression is $\overline{A}\,\overline{B} + \overline{C}D$

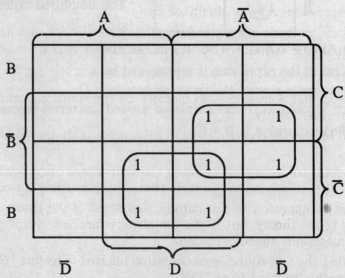

f. To simplify $ABD + \overline{B}CD + \overline{C}D + A\overline{B}C\overline{D} + \overline{A}BCD$

316

i. 1's are entered in the usual way

ii. Loops can be drawn for D and $A\overline{B}C$.

The simplified expression is $D + A\overline{B}C$.

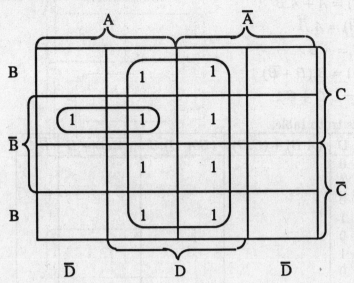

SUMMARY

25.29 a. The terms operation, operand and operator were defined.

   b. The operations introduced in this chapter were:

OPERATION	OPERATOR SYMBOL
NOT	- or ~
AND	. or $\wedge$ or $\cap$
OR	+ or $\vee$ or $\cup$
EQUIVALENCE	$\equiv$ or $\Longleftrightarrow$
NON-EQUIVALENCE	$\neq$ or $\oplus$

p	q	$\overline{p}$	p.q	$p+q$	$p \equiv q$	$p \neq q$
0	0	1	0	0	1	0
0	1	1	0	1	0	1
1	0	0	0	1	0	1
1	1	0	1	1	1	0

   c. Venn diagrams help in illustrating operations and simplifying expressions.

   d. Boolean expressions may be simplified by:

   i. Algebraic methods using standard relations and rules such as De Morgan's rule.

   ii. Diagrammatic techniques, eg, Karnaugh maps.

POINTS TO NOTE

25.30 a. It is essential that you commit to memory all the notation terminology and operations because they are used frequently.

   b. You should be completely competent in at least one of the methods of simplification and preferably both.

   c. It is important to distinguish between the equivalence operation that is performed on operands and the = sign, which is used to state that the equivalence of two expressions is true.

   d. An alternative approach to this subject makes use of the theory of SETS. There is no need for you to study set theory, but if you are already familiar with it you should be able to draw on some common skills already acquired.

   e. You may find the non-equivalence operation referred to as just "NEQ" or "XOR" and the equivalence operation referred to as "EQ".

317

STUDENT SELF-TESTING QUESTIONS

1. Use truth tables to find which of the following relations are true.

    i. $A(A + B) = A + A.B$

    ii. $A.(\overline{A} + \overline{B}) = A.\overline{B}$

    iii. $A = \overline{A}.B = A.B$

    iv. $B.(A + 1) = B.(B + \overline{B})$

    v. $A.0 + C = C.\overline{C} + C.1$

2. Complete this truth table.

A	B	C	D	$(A.B) + (C.D)$	$(B + D).C$	$(\overline{A}.\overline{D}) + B$	$\overline{B}.\overline{C}$
0	0	0	0				
0	0	0	1				
0	0	1	0				
0	0	1	1				
0	1	0	0				
0	1	0	1				
0	1	1	0				
0	1	1	1				
1	0	0	0				
1	0	0	1				
1	0	1	0				
1	0	1	1				
1	1	0	0				
1	1	0	1				
1	1	1	0				
1	1	1	1				

3. Simplify these expressions. (25.21).

    i. $A.\overline{B} + \overline{A}.B$

    ii. $A.B + \overline{AB} + \overline{A}.\overline{B}$

    iii. $\overline{A}.(B + C).\overline{D}$

    iv. $(x + \overline{x}.y) + v(\overline{v} + w)$

    v. $\overline{x.(x + y) + \overline{(y + yz)}}$

    vi. $\overline{(\overline{u} + 0).(\overline{v} + 0).(\overline{v}.0).(\overline{w} + \overline{w}).(\overline{x}.\overline{x})}$

4. Simplify these expressions using Karnaugh maps.

    i. $A\overline{B} + \overline{A}.B$

    ii. $A.B + \overline{A}.B + \overline{A}.B$

    iii. $(X + \overline{X}.Y) + V(\overline{V} + W)$

    iv. $\overline{A}\,\overline{B}CD + \overline{A}\,\overline{B}\,\overline{C}\,\overline{D} + AB\overline{C}\,\overline{D} + \overline{A}\,\overline{B}C\overline{D} + AB\overline{C}D + \overline{A}\,\overline{B}\,\overline{C}$

5. Simplify these expressions.

    i. $(\overline{A}BC + \overline{A}\,\overline{B}C) + (A\overline{B}\,\overline{C} + AB\overline{C}) + (\overline{A}\,\overline{B}\,\overline{C} + \overline{A}B\overline{C})$

    ii. $ABC\overline{D} + (\overline{A}B\overline{C}\,\overline{D} + AB\overline{C}\,\overline{D}) + (\overline{A + \overline{B} + \overline{C} + D})$

    iii. $\overline{X(X + Y) + \overline{(Y + YZ)}}$

6. Simplify the dual of $(A + B + C).(A + B + \overline{C}).(A + \overline{B} + C).(\overline{A} + B + \overline{C})$. The dual of the simplified dual is the simplest form of the original expression. Try checking it.

QUESTIONS WITHOUT ANSWERS

7. A logical operation called "implies" with symbol "$\Longrightarrow$" has the following truth table.

p	q	$p \Longrightarrow q$
0	0	1
0	1	1
1	0	0
1	1	1

Find an alternative expression for this operation given that you may only use the symbols for AND, OR and NOT.

8. Simplify these expressions:

a. $A.\overline{B} + \overline{B}.\overline{C} + A.\overline{C} + \overline{A}.B.\overline{C} + \overline{A}.B.\overline{C}.$

b. $A.B.\overline{C}.\overline{D}. + \overline{B}.\overline{C}.D. + A.C.\overline{D} + \overline{A}.B.\overline{C}.D + \overline{A}.C.\overline{D} + A.\overline{B}.C + A.\overline{B}.\overline{D}$

GLOSSARY CHECKLIST

Algebraic simplification	25.21	Karnaugh maps	25.26
Commutative law	25.11	Logical product	25.11
Conjunction	25.11	Logic operations	25.8
De Morgan's rules	25.23	Match	25.14
Disjunction	25.12	Negation	25.3
Distributive law	25.24	Predicates	25.5
Duals	25.22	Propositions	25.2
Equivalence	25.15	The AND operation	25.11
Equivalence operation	25.14	The OR operation	25.12
Exclusive	25.15	Truth tables	25.4
Inclusive OR	25.12,25.13	Union	25.12
Intersection	25.11	Venn diagrams	25.17

26: Machine Logic

INTRODUCTION

26.1 In chapters 2 and 6 we saw how data and instructions are coded and stored in binary form. This chapter shows how the computer handles binary data and instructions at what may be called the **digital logic level** of the machine (13.7).

26.2 Data and instructions are transmitted between the various parts of the processor or between the processor and peripherals by means of **pulse trains** (2.3). Various tasks are performed by passing pulse trains through "electronic switches" called **gates**. Each gate is an electronic circuit that may have provision for receiving or sending several pulses at once. Each gate may be regarded as a "black box" that controls the flow of pulses in a particular way.

26.3 Each gate normally performs some simple function (operation), eg, AND, OR, NOT, and for this reason gates are often called **logic elements**. It is the logic operations of gates which will concern us in this chapter, and we will not consider how they perform electronically, nor will we consider how they are made. The following background information should suffice.

BACKGROUND INFORMATION

26.4 Most of the background information needed for this chapter was given earlier. The key points are summarised here with references to earlier details.

   a. In modern computers a large number of components are made from small pieces of semi-conductor material called **silicon chips** (4.7). A single chip will contain several components (eg, all the components for one gate) and because of this electronic property may be referred to as an **integrated circuit (IC)**. IC memory, also called **semi-conductor memory**, was introduced in 4.11.

   b. Chips may be classified according to size as follows:

      i. Small Scale Integration (SSI) - containing at most 10 gates.

      ii. Medium Scale Integration (MSI) - containing between 10 and 100 gates.

      iii. Large Scale Integration (LSI) - containing between 100 and 100 000 gates.

      iv. Very Large Scale Integration (VLSI) - containing more than 100 000 gates.

   NB. This classification is not too strictly adhered to. For example, a circuit with 12 simple gates might be classified as SSI.

   c. To gain an idea of what these sizes mean we may note that typical microprocessor-units (MPUs), and memory chips used with them, are examples of LSIs. Many of the devices described in this chapter, adders, decoders, multiplexers, etc, may be made using MSI, or from a combination of SSI components.

   d. LSI design and manufacture is most economic if large numbers of chips are to be used. Therefore, special-purpose devices that could be manufactured using LSI may be constructed from common MSI components instead if the numbers required do not make LSI manufacture economic. General-purpose LSIs may also be used in such cases. One type, the **PLA (Programmed Logic Array)**, may be specially tailored to a particular purpose in a one-off operation broadly comparable to the programming of a PROM.

   e. To function properly, all chips require an adequate power supply. The operation of many chips requires precise timing and when this is the case electronic clocks are used to provide pulses to the chip. The operations that a chip performs on the inputs it receives may either depend upon the level of the input signal (0 or 1) or upon transitions in level (0 to 1 or 1 to 0). Where appropriate, these ideas will be discussed later.

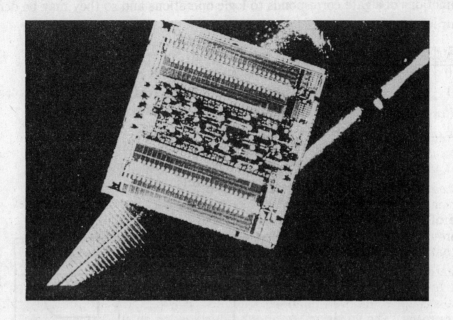

IBM 64K bit chip on a pen nib. Picture courtesy of IBM.

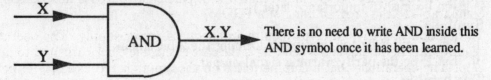

IBM 288K bit chip. Picture courtesy of IBM.

LOGIC DIAGRAMS

26.5 In logic diagrams *gates* are represented by *symbols* and *inputs* and *outputs* are represented by *arrowed lines* labelled by letters.

Example. In this diagram an AND gate (AND element) has two input signals, X and Y, and gives one output signal corresponding to X.Y.

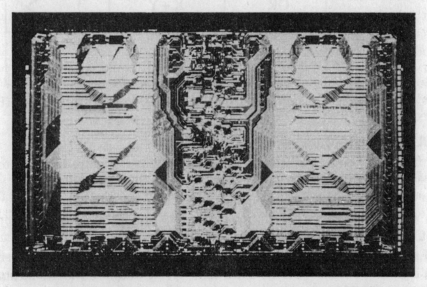

There is no need to write AND inside this AND symbol once it has been learned.

Simplified symbols may be used in which the name of the gate is written inside a circle as shown here.

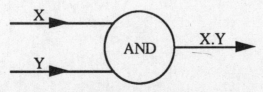

26.6   The functions of a gate corresponds to logic operations and so they may be defined by a truth table.
Example.

X	Y	X . Y
0	0	0
0	1	0
1	0	0
1	1	1

"1" means a "high" signal. "0" means a "low" signal. The AND gate will only output a "high" signal if it receives both X and Y "high" signals at the same time. **NB.** The convention "1" for "high", "0 for low is called **positive logic. Negative logic** may also be used, ie, "0" for high "1" for low. All examples in this text use positive logic.

26.7   **Table of logic symbols.**

OPERATOR	OPERATIONS	SYMBOL
AND	X . Y	
OR	X + Y	
NOT	X	

All other operations can be performed by a combination of these gates. Other useful gates will be introduced later.

SOLVING PROBLEMS IN LOGIC DESIGN

26.8   In designing a logic circuit we aim to reduce the number of gates used, thereby reducing cost. The method is outlined here and then illustrated with a simple problem.

Steps in the solution.

a.   Start with a well-defined description of the problem, eg, identify exact inputs and outputs.

b.   Select symbols to represent the input and output variables.

c.   Form a truth table in terms of these symbols referring to the problem definition throughout.

d.   Form logic expressions from the truth table giving output variables in terms of input variables.

e.   Try to simplify the output expressions using Karnaugh maps or algebra.

f.   Produce a logic diagram for the simplified outputs. Build up the diagram using ANDs, ORs, or NOTs and work "backwards" from output to input. The latter is not essential but the method helps later on.

26.9   **Example.**

a.   **Definition of problem.** Design a "parity detector" that produces a warning signal if it receives a 2-bit signal that does not have even parity (2.20). (This problem is not typical in all ways but is given because of importance later.)

b.   **Symbols.**

    i.   Let A and B be the two *inputs* forming the 2-bit signal.

    ii.   Let P be the parity warning signal *output*.

c.   **Truth table.**

A	B	P
0	0	0
0	1	1
1	0	1
1	1	0

d. Form Expression.

$p = \overline{A}.B + A.\overline{B}$ (Note also that $P = A \neq B$)

This requires *5 gates*: 2 NOTs, 2 ANDs and 1 OR.

e. Simplification.

i. Karnaugh map.

	A	$\overline{A}$
B	0	1
$\overline{B}$	1	0

ii. From the Karnaugh map we see that

$$P = \overline{A.B + \overline{A}.\overline{B}}$$
$$= \overline{A.B}.\overline{\overline{A}.\overline{B}} \quad \text{(de Morgan)}$$
$$= \overline{A.B}.(\overline{\overline{A}} + \overline{\overline{B}}) \quad \text{(de Morgan)}$$
$$= \overline{A.B}.(A + B)$$

This expression uses only *4 gates*:

1 NOT, 2 ANDs and 1 OR.

In our example the Karnaugh map does not lead to simplification in the usual way! A more typical simplification of $Q = \overline{A}.\overline{B} + \overline{A}.B + AB$ say is shown here.

i. Karnaugh map

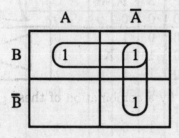

A	B	Q
0	0	1
0	1	1
1	0	0
1	1	1

ii. or by Algebra

$$Q = \overline{A}.\overline{B} + \overline{A}.B + A.B = \overline{A}.\overline{B} + \overline{A}.B + \overline{A}.B + A.B$$
$$= \overline{A}(\overline{B} + B) + B(\overline{A} + A)$$
$$= \overline{A} + B$$

f. Logic diagram for $P = \overline{A.B}.(A + B)$ The diagram is drawn from the expression working *right* to *left*.

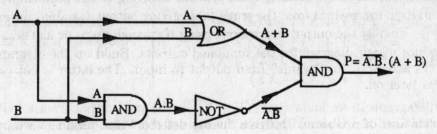

GATES FOR ARITHMETICAL PURPOSES

26.10 Addition of 2 bits. The four possible additions are represented in this truth table. The two inputs are X and Y and the outputs are S for SUM and C for CARRY.

X	Y	SUM "S"	CARRY "C"
0	0	0	0
0	1	1	0
1	0	1	0
1	1	0	1

From our table we see that

$$C = X . Y$$
and $$S = \overline{X}.Y + X.\overline{Y} = X \neq Y$$

S can be represented by $S = \overline{X.Y}(X+Y)$, as was demonstrated in paragraph 9. This is illustrated here by truth table.

X	Y	$C = X . Y$	$\overline{X.Y}$	$X+Y$	$S = \overline{XY} . (X+Y)$
0	0	0	1	0	0
0	1	0	1	1	1
1	0	0	1	1	1
1	1	1	0	1	0

26.11 A half adder. Gates can be combined to produce a device that gives both **sum** and **carry** outputs. The device is called **a half adder** and is shown here.

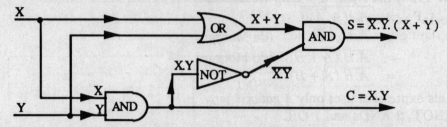

26.12 The adder (full adder) can deal with a carry from a previous 2-bit sum and has 3 inputs.

INPUTS			OUTPUTS	
P	X	Y	S	C
0	0	0	0	0
0	0	1	1	0
0	1	0	1	0
0	1	1	0	1
1	0	0	1	0
1	0	1	0	1
1	1	0	0	1
1	1	1	1	1

In this truth table, which defines the operation of the adder, the inputs are X, Y and carry from previous sum P. The outputs are S for Sum and C for Carry.

$$S = \overline{P}\,\overline{X}Y + \overline{P}X\overline{Y} + P\overline{X}\,\overline{Y} + PXY$$
$$C = \overline{P}XY + P\overline{X}Y + PX\overline{Y} + PXY$$

From these expressions we may get

$$S = \overline{P}(\overline{X}Y + X\overline{Y}) + P(\overline{X}\,\overline{Y} + XY)$$
$$= \overline{P}(\overline{X}Y + X\overline{Y}) + P(\overline{\overline{X}Y + X\overline{Y}})$$
$$\text{and } C = XY(\overline{P} + P) + P(\overline{X}Y + X\overline{Y})$$
$$= XY + P(\overline{X}Y + X\overline{Y})$$

See 25.12 and 25.13
Also please note $X \equiv Y$
$= \overline{X \equiv Y}$
$= \overline{X \not\equiv Y}$

From paragraph 10 we know that $\overline{X}Y + X\overline{Y}$ is the sum output from a half adder. A close look at the terms for S and C should provide the basis of the adder design shown here.

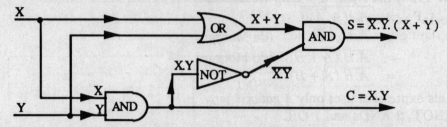

26.13 Parallel and serial addition. There are two basic methods of adding numbers that are several digits long.

a. Parallel addition, in which the columns are added side by side at the same time.

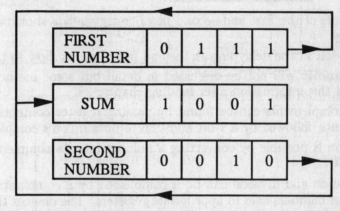

b. Serial addition , in which columns are added one at a time, the carry being held over and used in the next column addition.

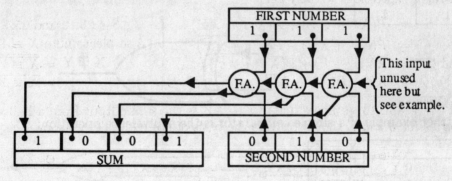

NB. A bit for the sum enters from the **left** as each column is added, working right to left. As this happens the successive values of the sum in this example are: 0000, 1000, 0100, 0010, 1001.

26.14 Relative merits. Parallel addition is faster than serial addition but requires more gates (hardware). The advantage of greater speed usually outweighs cost, making parallel addition more popular.

26.15 Registers. Data input to an adder must be held in an appropriate register.

a. In **parallel registers** all bits from the register are applied to the parallel adder simultaneously.

b. In **serial registers** all bits from the register are applied to the serial adder one at a time. The remaining bits in the registers are shifted along towards the end each time until output.

26.16 Example of a parallel adder.
The addition $111_2 + 010_2 = 1001_2$ is shown.

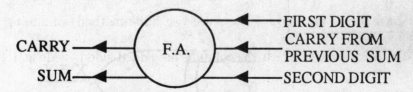

Details of full adders (F.A.)

CARRY ◀— F.A. —◀ FIRST DIGIT
                    CARRY FROM
                    PREVIOUS SUM
SUM —◀—   SECOND DIGIT

Note. In this example provision is made for a 4-digit sum of 3-digit number. Alternatively the *last carry* can be used to signal overflow. (An example will be given in 29.14-29.16.)

26.17 Example of a serial adder. It consists of:

a. **One full adder**, which receives pairs of X, Y bits from two serial registers starting with the least significant bits.

b. **A delay store**, which consists of a binary store, which holds the carry bit until it is needed for the next addition. The store is set to zero prior to the first addition.

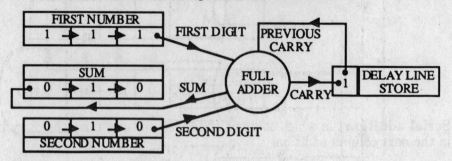

The *initial state* of the first and second number registers is shown along with the *final state* of the sum and delay.

Note. A one left in the delay line at the end indicates overflow in this example.

Other arithmetic will not be discussed in detail but some methods are outlined here. You may like to re-read this information after reading chapter 28.

a. Number complements can be found by passing register contents through a NOT gate for one's complements, followed by a 1-bit addition to obtain two's complements.

b. Subtraction is possible by converting a number into its complement prior to passing it through an ADDER.

c. Multiplication and division can be accomplished by a combination of shifts, additions and subtractions of numbers held in appropriate registers. The devices that perform the shift operations are called **shifters** and are normally constructed to perform parallel shifts from one register to another.

d. BCD arithmetic uses a combination of serial and parallel methods.

COMPARATORS

26.18 The exclusive OR (XOR), which we have already seen used in parity checking and arithmetic, is an example of a simple **comparator**. Its truth table and logic symbol are given here:

X	Y	X $\neq$ Y
0	0	0
0	1	1
1	0	1
1	1	0

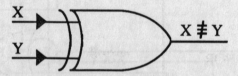

26.19 A further example of a simple comparator is the equivalence operation:

X	Y	X $\equiv$ Y
0	0	1
0	1	0
1	0	0
1	1	1

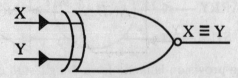

26.20 In general **comparators** are used to compare two registers, A and B say, to test for the conditions A = B, A $\neq$ B, A < B and A > B. Here is a simple example of testing A = B for two 3-bit registers.

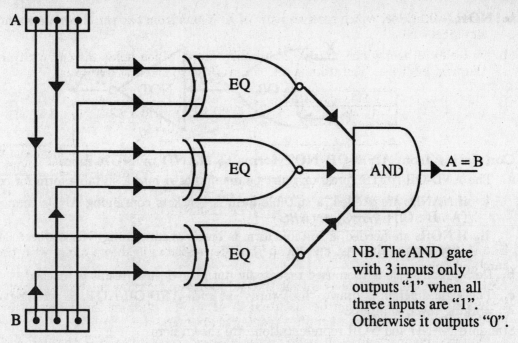

A comparator.

NB. The AND gate
with 3 inputs only
outputs "1" when all
three inputs are "1".
Otherwise it outputs "0".

NAND and NOR METHODS

26.21 Although AND, OR and NOT gate combinations are always sufficient for the construction of any logic operation, alternative methods using NAND and NOR gates are more economical and therefore more widely used. The NAND and NOR operations will be described in this section. *All* logic operations can be performed with combinations of just NANDs or just NORs, but a combination of NORs, with NANDs is usually preferable to one provided just by NANDs.

26.22

OPERATOR	OPERATION	SYMBOL	TRUTH TABLE		
			X	Y	$\overline{X.Y}$
NAND	$\overline{X.Y}$		0	0	1
			0	1	1
			1	0	1
			1	1	0
			X	Y	$\overline{X+Y}$
NOR	$\overline{X+Y}$		0	0	1
			0	1	0
			1	0	0
			1	1	0

26.23 The AND-OR-NOT representation of NAND and NOR is shown here.

  a. NAND.

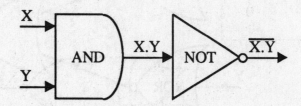

b. NOR.

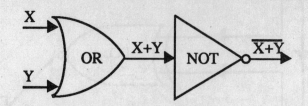

26.24 Converting from AND-OR-NOT forms to NAND or NOR forms.

a. The AND-OR-NOT expression must be manipulated into a suitable form for conversion:-

  i. if NANDs are needed, a suitable form is brackets containing ANDs connected by ORs, eg, $(A . B . C) + (\overline{A}BC) + (A\overline{BC})$

  ii. If NORs are needed, a suitable form is brackets containing ORs connected by ANDs, eg, $(A + B + C) . (\overline{A} + B + C) . (A + \overline{B} + \overline{C})$

b. De Morgan's rule is then used repeatedly until the desired result is reached.

c. The logic diagram is drawn "backwards" as with AND-OR-NOT, ie, starting with outputs and working towards inputs.

26.25 Standard NAND and NOR representations are shown here.

a. NOT

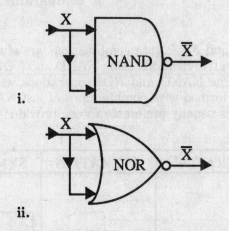

  i.

  ii.

b. AND

  i. Using NAND

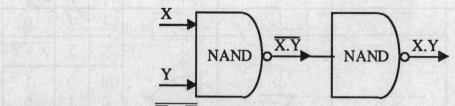

  ii. Using NOR. $X . Y = \overline{\overline{X} + \overline{Y}}$. (De Morgan).

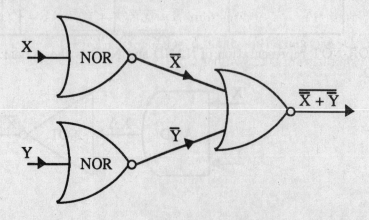

c. OR

i. Using NOR.

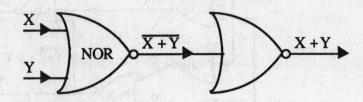

ii. Using NAND $X + Y = \overline{\overline{X}.\overline{Y}}$. (De Morgan).

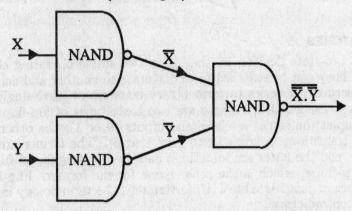

26.26 Example. Finding NAND and NOR forms for the sum of the half adder

$$S = \overline{X.Y}(X + Y)$$

a. NAND Form.

i. Manipulation into a suitable form. $S = \overline{XY}(X + Y) = \overline{XY}.X + \overline{XY}.Y$

ii. Apply De Morgans Rule $S = \overline{(\overline{XY}.X).(\overline{XY}.Y)}$

iii. The logic diagram is shown here. An extra NAND has been added to produce a CARRY. (Note that **a NAND with a single input acts like a NOT.**)

NAND HALF ADDER

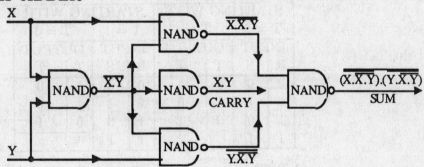

b. NOR Form.

i. Manipulation into a suitable form $S = \overline{XY}(X + Y) = (\overline{X} + \overline{Y}).(X + Y)$ (De Morgan)

ii. Apply De Morgan's Rule again $S = \overline{\overline{(\overline{X} + \overline{Y})} + \overline{(X + Y)}}$

iii. The logic diagram is shown here.

NOR HALF ADDER

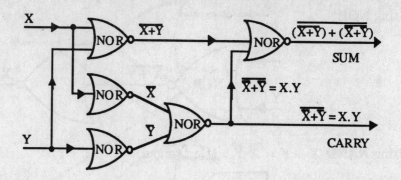

FLIP-FLOPS AND LATCHES

26.27 Flip-flops are two-state devices, ie, they have two stable operating states corresponding to binary "0" and "1". They can be switched from one state to another and can be used in multiples to form registers, "cascaded" in series to form binary counters or used singly as status registers (eg, 1 = Device ON, 0 = Device OFF). There are two basic types of flip-flop. One type has output states that depend upon the signal levels of the inputs (0 or 1), the other type has output states that depend upon transitions in levels (0 to 1 or 1 to 0). The former are often called **latches**, rather than flip-flops, and the latter are sometimes called **edge-triggered flip-flops** as opposed to **level-triggered flip-flops**, which is the other name for the former. Flip-flops are also called **bistable multivibrators** or just **bistables**. Unfortunately, the terminology in use is far from universal and is sometimes contradictory!

26.28 A common type of flip-flop is the Set=Reset flip-flop, which has two inputs, one to make the output "1" (the set) the other to make the output "0" (the reset).

26.29 The Set/Reset flip-flop. (This can be used as a 1-bit memory.)

Truth Table.

Note.

i. The combination S = 1 and R = 1 is not possible.

ii. The double *output* $T/\overline{T}$ is held and used as part of the next *input*.

STARTING WITH T = 0 $\overline{T} = 1$				STARTING WITH T = 1 $\overline{T} = 0$			
INPUT		OUTPUT		INPUT		OUTPUT	
R	S	T	$\overline{T}$	R	S	T	$\overline{T}$
0	0	0	1	0	0	1	0
0	1	1	0	0	1	1	0
1	0	0	1	1	0	0	1
1	1			1	1		

S(SET) ➤ ⟶ $\overline{T}$

FLIP FLOP (BISTABLE)

R(RESET) ➤ ⟶ T

Practical NOR implementation.

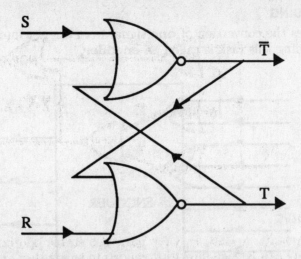

If the flip-flop is edge triggered then a *momentary* pulse will set this 1-bit store to a detectable state held *indefinitely*.

ALU and CONTROL

26.30 So far we have seen how gates can be combined to perform particular tasks such as addition. The ALU is composed a large number of such gate combinations, but is usually designed as a whole so as to work most efficiently. The selection of the appropriate operation (set of gates) can be handled by passing signals from the CONTROL UNIT through gates.

Example. This example is illustrative rather than practical and also uses one's complement. The inclusion of the half adder in the adder below allows the circuit to **either** add or subtract according to the CONTROL UNIT signal "S".

If S = 1 subtract Y from X. If S = 0 add Y to X.

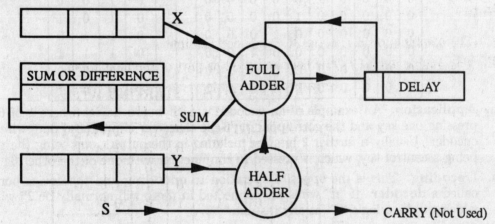

26.31 A typical diagrammatic representation for a complete ALU is shown here:

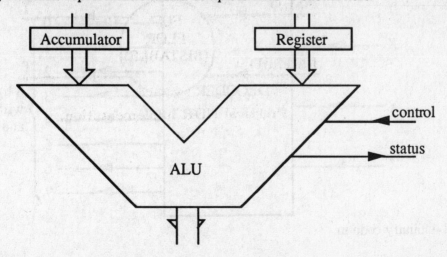

ENCODING AND DECODING

26.32 Encoding involves the conversion of **one** signal from one set into a **group** of signals of another set. A device performing this task is called an **encoder.**

    a. Example.

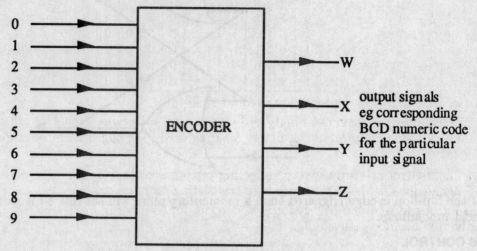

10 inputs, **only one of which is a "high signal"** at any time.

INPUT												OUTPUT			
0	1	2	3	4	5	6	7	8	9			W	X	Y	Z
1	0	0	0	0	0	0	0	0	0			0	0	0	0
0	1	0	0	0	0	0	0	0	0			0	0	0	1
0	0	1	0	0	0	0	0	0	0			0	0	1	0
0	0	0	1	0	0	0	0	0	0			0	0	1	1
0	0	0	0	1	0	0	0	0	0			0	1	0	0
0	0	0	0	0	1	0	0	0	0			0	1	0	1
0	0	0	0	0	0	1	0	0	0			0	1	1	0
0	0	0	0	0	0	0	1	0	0			0	1	1	1
0	0	0	0	0	0	0	0	1	0			1	0	0	0
0	0	0	0	0	0	0	0	0	1			1	0	0	1

1 = high signal
0 = low signal

    b. Application. An example of an encoder is a keyboard device where 1 of 64 lines is raised by pressing one key and the corresponding 6-bit character is produced on 6 wires coming out of the encoder. Usually a further 2 bits are included in the output, one being the parity bit, the other being a control key, which is pressed in conjunction with one of the other 64 keys.

26.33 a. Decoding. This is the opposite operation to **encoding** and the device performing the task is called a **decoder.** If "n" wires are connected in there will normally be 2^n wires out, only one of which will be a logic "1" at any instant.

    b. Example.

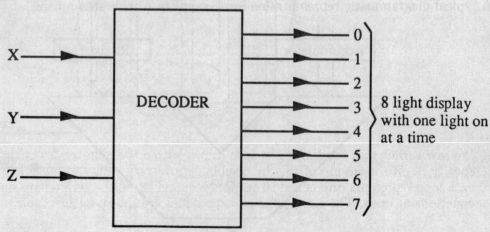

3-bit binary code in.

INPUT				OUTPUT							
X	Y	Z		0	1	2	3	4	5	6	7
0	0	0		1	0	0	0	0	0	0	0
0	0	1		0	1	0	0	0	0	0	0
0	1	0		0	0	1	0	0	0	0	0
0	1	1		0	0	0	1	0	0	0	0
1	0	0		0	0	0	0	1	0	0	0
1	0	1		0	0	0	0	0	1	0	0
1	1	0		0	0	0	0	0	0	1	0
1	1	1		0	0	0	0	0	0	0	1

26.34 Uses. Encoders and decoders are used for such things as:

a. Translations of **internal** binary codes to or from **external** signals for peripheral input or output actions such as printing characters, reading cards, moving pens in plotters or monitoring device status.

b. The control of hardware, eg, selecting output channels from device codes, translating control signals for disk-head movements or translating function codes.

26.35 An example of decoder design. A decoder for converting a 4-bit 8421-weighted BCD code into individual decimal equivalents.

BCD DIGIT	CODE BITS				LOGIC EXPRESSION
	A	B	C	D	
0	0	0	0	0	$\overline{A}\,\overline{B}\,\overline{C}\,\overline{D}$
1	0	0	0	1	$\overline{A}\,\overline{B}\,\overline{C}D$
2	0	0	1	0	$\overline{A}\,\overline{B}C\overline{D}$
3	0	0	1	1	$\overline{A}\,\overline{B}CD$
4	0	1	0	0	$\overline{A}B\overline{C}\,\overline{D}$
5	0	1	0	1	$\overline{A}B\overline{C}D$
6	0	1	1	0	$\overline{A}BC\overline{D}$
7	0	1	1	1	$\overline{A}BCD$
8	1	0	0	0	$A\overline{B}\,\overline{C}\,\overline{D}$
9	1	0	0	1	$A\overline{B}\,\overline{C}D$
10-15	Arbitrary because unused				

Karnaugh map. (Arbitrary unused terms called "don't care terms" are marked with a U).

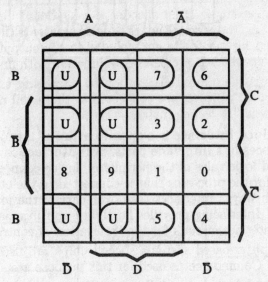

a. We saw earlier that the larger the loop drawn within the map the fewer variables are needed to specify it. We make use of this by combining arbitrary values to make larger loops. Note that each loop represents **one** of the 10 outputs required, so on the map we are simplifying 10 Boolean equations at once. The corresponding expressions are shown in this Table.

DECIMAL DIGIT	LOGIC EXPRESSION	ALTERNATIVE EXPRESSION
0	$\overline{A}.\overline{B}.\overline{C}.\overline{D}$	$\overline{A+B+C+D}$
1	$\overline{A}.\overline{B}.\overline{C}.D$	$A+B+C+\overline{D}$
2	$\overline{B}.\overline{C}.\overline{D}$	$\overline{B+\overline{C}D}$
3	$\overline{B}.C.D$	$\overline{B+\overline{C}D}$
4	$B.\overline{C}.\overline{D}$	$\overline{B+C+D}$
5	$B.\overline{C}.D$	$\overline{B+C+\overline{D}}$
6	$B.C.\overline{D}$	$\overline{B+\overline{C}+D}$
7	$B.C.D$	$\overline{B+\overline{C}+\overline{D}}$
8	$A.\overline{D}$	$\overline{A+D}$
9	$A.D$	$\overline{A+\overline{D}}$

b. An implementation using NOR gates.

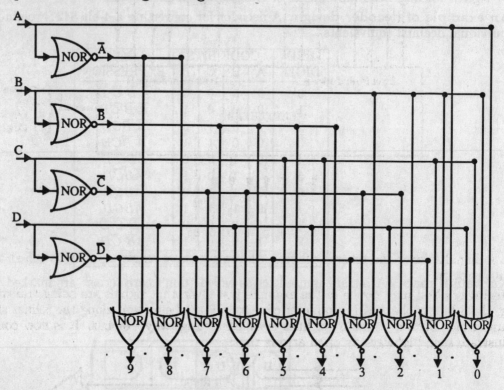

INTERFACING

26.36 Interface. A **standard interface** is a **specification** of the logic signals, electrical connections and logic rules of the processor's **interface** parts. An **interface** is a piece of hardware that converts the electrical signals and logic rules of the peripheral device connected to one side of it into those of the standard interface, for the processor that is connected to the other side of the interface. Conversions may take place both ways. Interfaces take over part of the job of controlling the devices to which they are connected. Interfacing provides flexibility and increases efficiency. Encoders and decoders form part of most interface circuits for the translation of control and data signals at the **interface.**

26.37 On most microcomputer-based systems special chips are used to provide input and output with suitable interfacing. Common chips used for this purpose are:

a. UARTs (Universal Asynchronous Receiver Transmitters), which handle two-way communication between the computer and a *serial device.*

b. On the computer side of the UART, data, such as individual characters, will be transmitted in parallel. On the serial device side data will be transmitted **serially** as a sequence of pulses in a pulse train.

c. USARTs (Universal Synchronous Asynchronous Receiver Transmitters), which differ from UARTs in that they can handle block transmissions of data synchronously between the device and the computer.

d. PIOs (Parallel Input/Output), which handle I/O between the computer and devices that can send or receive data in parallel.

e. Special controllers for CRTs (Cathode Ray Tube Screens), disk drives, etc.

NB. Devices such as printers are often described as "serial" or "parallel" according to the method of interfacing, eg, by UART or PIO.

MULTIPLEXERS (MULTIPLEXORS) (MUX for short)

26.38 Multiplexers are selection mechanisms. They have long had importance in handling multiple numbers of input and output devices. They have even more importance today in the way they handle the selection of data and instruction flow within modern computers. You may compare them with the points and signal box at a railway junction. Here is a simple example:

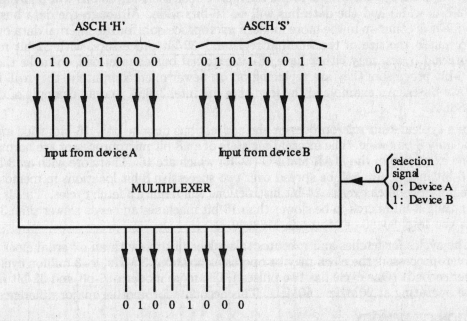

In a demultiplexer the reverse process takes place, ie, a single input is switched to an appropriate output path.

26.39 Highways. You may notice in the example just given that signals are being transmitted in parallel, eg, the 8 bits of the ASCII character code for 'H' are being sent along the 8 lines side by side at the same time. Such a "bundle" of lines is called a **"highway"** or bus. It is now common practice to illustrate such highways by open arrows thus:

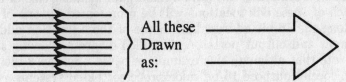

NB. The highway may contain any number of lines, not necessarily 8.

COMBINATIONAL AND SEQUENTIAL LOGIC

26.40 **A combinational logic** gate has outputs that are completely defined by the combination of inputs. A **sequential logic** gate differs from combinational logic in that the outputs depend not only on the combination of inputs but on the sequence in which they occur. AND, OR and NOT gates provide examples of combinational logic and a flip-flop provides an example of sequential logic. The idea of sequential logic will be familiar to you although the terminology may not be. For example, a TV set may have a single ON/OFF button and the set may be in one of two *states*, "ON" or "OFF". The "output" resulting from the single "input" of pressing the ON/OFF button will depend on the state the set is in when the button is pressed. Thus the "output" (set on or set off) resulting from the "input" (press button) depends on where we are in the on/off *sequence*. This is one example of sequential logic.

26.41 Another example of sequential logic may be supplied by the same TV set if it has a push-button for each channel. Pressing the button for a given channel may cause a change to that channel, or produce no change if the same button is pressed a second or third time in succession. The "output" from pressing a combination of ON/OFF button and channel-selector button will depend on the prior state of the set.

APPLICATIONS OF DIGITAL LOGIC

26.42 The remainder of this chapter is devoted to examples that illustrate the use of digital logic within the computer.

A SIMPLIFIED VIEW OF A MICROCOMPUTER-BASED SYSTEM

26.43 Examine Fig. 26.1, which shows a simplified view of a microcomputer-based system. The processor shown in Fig. 26.1 may be constructed along the lines of that shown in Fig. 13.7. The reader is advised to revise the details of Fig 13.7 before proceeding.

    a. In a typical system with a 16-bit microprocessor the address bus will be 24 bits wide (or possibly 32 bits wide) and the data bus will be 16-bits wide. Although the data bus is normally 16 bits wide it is common in the more modern microprocessors for the internal data bus to be 32-bits wide to match the size of the internal registers. 32-bit processors, with 32-bit registers AND 32-bit internal buses, may either have 16-bit external bus connections, to make them compatible with 16-bit processors they are replacing or, on newer microcomputers, they will have 32-bit external data buses. An example of the former is the Intel 386SX and an example of the latter is the Intel 386DX.

    b. In a typical 8-bit microprocessor the address bus may be only 16-bits wide and the data bus may be only 8 bits wide. The internal registers of an 8-bit microprocessor are normally 8 bits wide with the exception of the MAR and PC (SCR) which are 16. Therefore with an 8-bit microprocessor a 16-bit instruction will be spread over two successive 8-bit locations in memory and will therefore require two fetch cycles. 24-bit instructions will require 3 fetch cycles. This is an important factor causing 8-bit micros to be slower than 16-bit machines and even slower than 32-bit machines such as the Intel 80486 or Motorola M68040.

    c. The cycles for fetches and executes take place in time with an external clock. On the older 8-bit microprocessors the clock may be operating at about 3 MHz, ie, 3 million cycles (6 million pulses) per second. (One cycle has two pulses.) The more modern 16-bit and 32-bit microprocessors may be operating at 20MHz – 50MHz. This accounts for another major difference in speed.

ORGANISATION OF MEMORY

26.44 A typical 16-bit microcomputer has a theoretical maximum memory size which is so large that it not a practical constraint. In theory such a processor can directly address 4 gigabytes (4 thousand million bytes). In practice there are restriction placed on memory addressing but these are more commonly the result of using an operating system having inbuilt design limits as is the case with MS-DOS (PC-DOS) still widely used on many PCs.

26.45 A typical 8-bit microcomputer will have a maximum memory size of 64k words (ie, 65,536 memory locations). Each of these 64k locations will be represented by one of the 64k codes, which can be transmitted along the 16-bit address bus. Some of these location addresses may be "borrowed" as addresses to input and output ports. A simplified diagram showing such an arrangement is shown in Fig. 26.2. Note that although this example is based upon an 8-bit microprocessor the method is widely used on special purpose 16-bit microprocessor based systems.

26.46 The use of "borrowed" location addresses for input and output is known as **"memory mapped I/O"**. Such memory mapping is widely used on both microcomputers and minicomputers. It simplifies the provision of input and output, but the price paid for this simplicity is the loss of some memory space.

26.47 A typical allocation of 8-bit microcomputer memory addresses for various uses is illustrated in Fig. 26.3.

MICROCODED MACHINES

26.48 The idea of microprogrammed machines was introduced in 13.11. Here, we consider the idea in more detail with the aid of a simplified example (Fig. 26.4). Within the control unit of a microprogrammed computer is what appears to be another processor. There now follows a simplified version of how this machine works which is intended to convey the principle but which, because it is simplified, is not technically accurate in all respects.

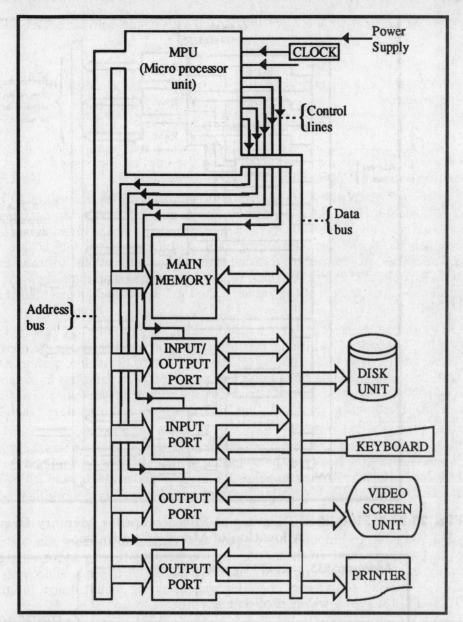

Fig. 26.1. A simplified view of a Microcomputer-based System.

26.49 The microprogrammed machine works as follows:

a. Start at the point when, at the conventional level of the machine, the next instruction to be executed has just been loaded into the IR (CIR) (Fig. 13.7). The part of this instruction that specifies the operation to be performed, called the **function code** or **opcode**, is decoded to obtain the start address of the appropriate sequence of microcoded instructions held in the control store. This address passes to the multiplexer.

b. The multiplexer passes the appropriate address to the MSCR, which is driven by clock pulses.

c. The next microcoded instruction, held at the address specified in the MSCR, is loaded into the **MMDR,** from where it is transferred to the MCIR.

d. The microcoded instruction may be quite long compared with conventional machine instructions because bit positions within the instruction may each correspond to individual control lines to particular hardware units. A "1" may indicate a control signal is to be transmitted and a "0" that it is not. Thus, each microcoded instruction holds a particular combination of control signals. When the MCIR receives a pulse from the clock these signals are transmitted.

e. Also within the MCIR will be an address for the next microcoded instruction. This address is used when the sequence of control is to be altered because of conditions signalled to the multiplexer by the ALU. For example, the ALU may signal that it has tested for, and found, a zero result.

f. Normally, the microcoded instructions will be executed in sequence by the contents of the MSCR being incremented by 1 and being reloaded into the MSCR via the multiplexer.

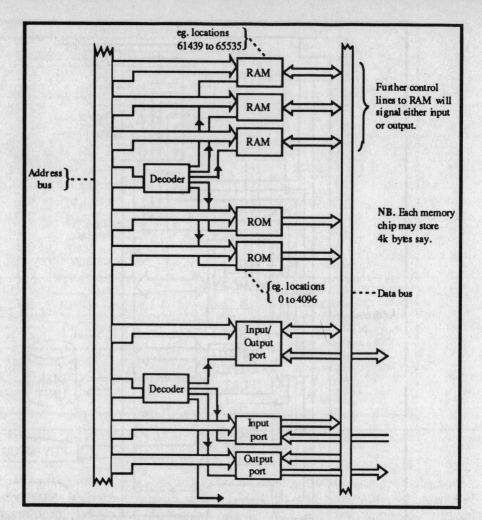

eg. locations
61439 to 65535

Further control
lines to RAM will
signal either input
or output.

Address
bus

NB. Each memory
chip may store
4k bytes say.

eg. locations
0 to 4096

Data bus

Fig. 26.2. A Simplified Diagram of Microcomputer Memory Organisation and Allocation of Memory Addresses.

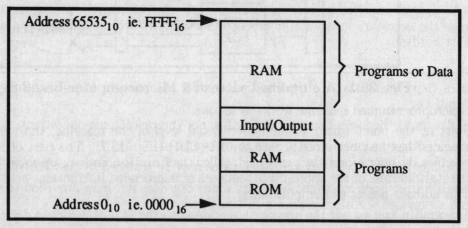

Address 65535_{10} ie. $FFFF_{16}$

RAM — Programs or Data

Input/Output

RAM — Programs

ROM

Address 0_{10} ie. 0000_{16}

Fig. 26.3. Microcomputer Memory with Memory-mapped I/O.

26.50 Not all computers are microcoded, although the exceptions tend to be among the smaller microprocessors. In most microcoded machines the control store is in ROM and cannot be altered after manufacture. In a few cases the control store contains RAM, which means that the instruction set of the machine may be altered. However, microcoding is normally not available to the user, only to the manufacturer.

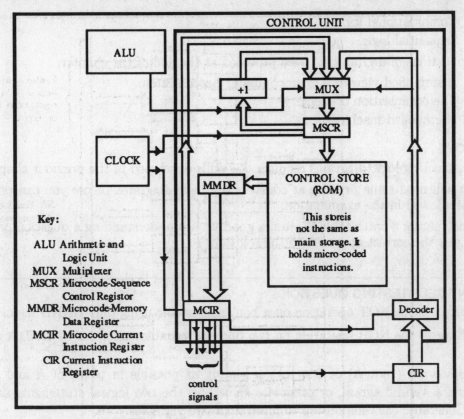

Fig. 26.4. A Simplified View of the Microprogrammed Level of the Computer.

26.51 One of the main advantages of using microcoded machines is that a whole range of different processors may be created by a manufacturer, all with the same basic conventional machine instruction set but differing in processing power and cost. This is the **virtual machine** principle mentioned in 13.91. This is the case for the IBM 370, 4300 and 3300 series of computers and for the digital (DEC) VAX minicomputer series. In the smaller machines in such a range one conventional machine instruction may give rise to many microcoded instructions and may be relatively slow. On larger machines in the range the necessary number of microcoded instructions will be reduced by the provision of more specialist hardware.

SUMMARY

26.52 a. Gates (logic elements) are devices that control the passage of pulses, thus facilitating logical operations.

    b. We discussed the logical operation of gates, not their electronic operations.

    c. In logic diagrams gates are represented by symbols.

    d. A combination of AND, OR and NOT gates may be replaced by just NAND or just NOR gates.

    e. A **half adder** adds together two binary digits but does not have provision to deal with the carry from a previous addition as does a **full adder.**

    f. Two basic types of addition are:

        i. Parallel addition (usually faster)

        ii. Serial addition.

    Data must be held in parallel and serial registers respectively.

    g. Gates can be used for:

        i. Arithmetical and logical purposes.

        ii. For control purposes such as selecting operations or devices, eg, by multiplexing.

        iii. Encoding and Decoding.

    h. Interfacing is used for the electronic and logical communication between the CPU and its peripherals and interfaces themselves have some control tasks.

    i. The two basic types of logic are:

i. Combinational logic.

ii. Sequential logic.

j. Applications of digital logic were provided at the end of the chapter:

i. A simplified view of a microcomputer-based system.

ii. The organisation of memory.

iii. Microcoded machines.

POINTS TO NOTE

26.53 a. Constructing logic diagrams requires the skills developed in the previous chapter.

b. You will need some practice at constructing logic diagrams before you can produce them in the time allowed in the examination.

c. Constructing a truth table is often a good way of understanding a question or problem and may suggest the correct approach to the solution.

STUDENT SELF-TESTING QUESTIONS

1. a. Express the NOT operation on a boolean variable using only NAND logic.

   b. Express the NOR operation on two boolean variables using only NAND logic.

   (AEB)

2. a. State not ((not A) or (not b)) as simply as possible in terms of A and B. By drawing a Venn diagram, or otherwise show how the two logical statements are connected. Generalise the relationship to more than two variables.

   b. The decimal digits 0 to 9 can be represented by a set of binary digits a, b, c, d of values 8, 4, 2 and 1 respectively. Devise a logical function of a, b, c and d that is true if they represent a decimal digit and false otherwise. Explain your derivation.   (Oxford)

3. Relate the differing scales of integration of electronic components to the differing generations of computer.

4. Distinguish between serial and parallel adders and draw a logic diagram for each. Why are parallel adders preferred to serial adders in most cases?

5. Explain the difference between an edge-triggered flip-flop and a level-triggered flip-flop.

6. Define:

   a. UART

   b. USART

   c. PIO

7. Distinguish between combinational logic and sequential logic and identify the category to which the following gates belong.

   a. adder

   b. comparator

   c. flip-flop

   d. decoder.

STUDENT SELF-TESTING QUESTIONS CONTINUED

8. Here is a simplified multiplexer:

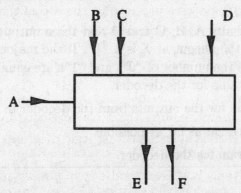

When the signal at A is "0" the output at F is the same as the input signal at D and the output at E is "0" regardless of the signals at B and C. When the signal at A is "1" the output at E is the same as the input signal at B and the output at F is the same as the input signal at C regardless of the signal at D.

a. Summarise these details in a truth table.

b. Construct expressions for the outputs E and F in terms of A, B, C and D.

c. Simplify your expressions.

d. Create a logic circuit for the multiplexer.

e. Justify your choice of gates in d.

9. Two 2-bit registers, X and Y, are both used to hold 2-digit positive integers where 00_2, 01_2, 10_2 and 11_2 represent 0,1, 2 and 3 respectively.

A comparator has four inputs, two from register X and 2 from register Y, and outputs a "1" when the contents of X are greater than Y, otherwise it outputs "0".

a. Represent this comparator diagrammatically.

b. Construct a truth table for the comparator.

c. Produce a simplified expression for the output of the comparator.

d. Derive a logic diagram for the comparator.

10. a. What practical advantage is there in employing NAND or NOR components in electronic circuits? (2 marks)

b. By using a truth (logic) table, or otherwise, show that the Boolean expressions below are all different:

$$\overline{A + B + C}$$
$$\overline{A + B} + C$$
$$B + \overline{C} + A$$
$$\overline{A} + B + \overline{C}$$

(5 marks)

c. Using the result in (b), express $(\overline{A.\overline{B}.\overline{C}}) + (A.B.C)$ in NOR logic. (3 marks)

d. A four-input decoder produces a zero output when any of the patterns 0000, 0001, 0010, 0100 or 1000 is input; for all other input combinations, the output is "1". Derive a Boolean expression for the decoder and convert the expression to NOR logic in a simplified form. (10 marks)

(AEB)

QUESTIONS WITHOUT ANSWERS

11. Design a demultiplexer for the multiplexer in question 8. It should have inputs A, E and F and outputs B, C and D.

12. A decoder has four inputs A, B, C and D and three outputs X, Y and Z. If the majority of the inputs are "1"s the output at X is a "1". If the majority of inputs are "0"s then the output at Y is a "1". If the number of "0"s and "1"s are equal then the output at Z is a "1".
    a. Construct a truth table for the decoder.
    b. Derive an expression for the outputs from the decoder in terms of the inputs.
    c. Simplify your expression as far as possible.
    d. Derive a logic diagram for the decoder.

GLOSSARY CHECKLIST

27: Formal Notations

INTRODUCTION

27.1 This chapter provides a brief introduction to the subject of Formal Notations. A formal notation is a succinct and unambiguous means of expressing things. It therefore has certain advantages over everyday language when there is a need to be as precise as possible. Formal notations consist of systems of symbolic expressions strictly governed by sets of well-defined rules. A common example of a formal notation in Computer Science is a programming language.

27.2 Statements written in formal notations are easy to manipulate and reason about, as is evident from their successful use in subjects such as mathematics and chemistry (chemical formulae). Misunderstandings over technical descriptions can be costly and annoying. The use of formal notations reduces the chances of such misunderstandings.

27.3 These benefits have resulted in formal notations being used increasingly in many areas of Computer Science, but especially for specifications. Formal specifications of programs were introduced in 19.46 – 19.53. Other examples are provided in this chapter to illustrate the technical possibilities. In particular, this chapter examines program language definitions and how programs written to such definitions are translated.

LEVELS OF FORMALITY

27.4 Before starting upon the detailed subject matter of the chapter it is useful to distinguish between the different levels of formality with which things may be stated in Computer Science.

27.5 Statements expressed in English are **informal** because, in general, they do not necessarily have *a single meaning*. Incidentally, languages used for everyday speech such as English and French are called **natural languages**. A language or notation in which each statement has *a single meaning* is said to be **formal**. A programming language is therefore formal. Statements expressed in intermediate notations between natural languages and formal languages may be called **precise** if they are not strictly formal but leave little room for ambiguity. Pseudocode may be called a precise notation.

27.6 In order to illustrate the possible uses of formal notations, this chapter covers areas in which they are already being used successfully. There are many other areas of potential application of formal notations, but at present they are still fairly new to the academic curriculum in polytechnics and universities and barely established in the computer industry apart from use in certain specialist fields.

METALANGUAGES

27.7 Anyone learning or using a programming language needs to understand:

a. its syntax – The structures of its statements and the grammatical rules governing them.

b. its semantics – The meaning of statements written in the language.

Of course, the individual will also need to have an understanding of programming methods too.

27.8 A language specially designed to describe languages is called a **metalanguage**. In general, metalanguages may be used to describe just the syntax or just the semantics or both.

27.9 A **syntactic definition of a language**:

a. names and describes language components;

b. shows how syntactically valid sentences in the language may be formed.

27.10 In Computer Science it is well-established practice to use metalanguages to describe the syntax of programming languages. The metalanguages used are formal and therefore are concise and unambiguous.

27.11 There are many syntactic metalanguages in common use. The following examples are based on the British Standard syntactic metalanguage BS6154. Other notations are illustrated later.

Note. This is *not* a full description of the metalanguage. It is merely intended to illustrate how such a notation may be used.

27.12 Syntax rules. Syntax rules all have the same basic form. A name appears on the left-hand side of an "=" sign, and to the right of the "=" sign is a definition of the thing named on the left. The rule ends with a ";" . Once a name has been defined it may be used on the right-hand side of subsequent rules.

Comments may be added to the rules in order to aid readability. They must be enclosed between an "(*" and an "*)".

27.13 Example 1. A rule to define a binary digit.

$$\text{binary digit} = "0" \mid "1" ;$$

Note that the vertical bar symbol means "OR" and should be pronounced as "OR".

27.14 Example 2. A rule to define an unsigned binary number.

$$\text{unsigned binary number} = \text{binary digit} , \{ \text{binary digit} \} ;$$

The comma means concatenate. The curly braces { and } contain items that may be repeated zero or more times. So, this definition says that an unsigned binary number consists of a series of one or more binary digits.

It is usually possible to find alternative definitions. The following **recursive definition** is equivalent to the one given. It is called a recursive recursive definition because the term being defined also appears within the definition.

```
unsigned binary number  =  binary digit
                           |
                           binary digit , unsigned binary number ;
```

27.15 Example 3. Rules to define a signed integer.

```
        digit  =  "0" | "1" | "2" | "3" | "4" |
                  "5" | "6" | "7" | "8" | "9" ;
unsigned integer  =  digit , { digit } ;
        integer  =  ["+" "-"] , unsigned integer ;
```

The square brackets "[" and "]" contain optional items.

27.16 Example 4. A rule to define upper-case letters.

```
binary digit  =  "A" | "B" | "C" | "D" | "E" |
                 "F" | "G" | "H" | "I" | "J" |
                 "K" | "L" | "M" | "N" | "O" |
                 "P" | "Q" | "R" | "S" | "T" |
                 "U" | "V" | "W" | "X" | "Y" | "Z" ;
```

27.17 Example 5. A rule to define an if-then-else statement.

The rule assumes that the following have already been defined:

spaces

newline

condition

statement sequences

```
if statement  =  "if" , [newline | spaces] ,
                 "condition", [newline | spaces]
                 statement sequence , [newline | spaces]
                 [ "else" , [newline | spaces ]
                 statement sequence, [newline | spaces]
                 "endif"
```

27.18 The reader is advised to gain further practise with a syntax definition for the programming language he or she is using for practical work.

LANGUAGE DEFINITION AND DESCRIPTION

27.19 Uses of language definition. Language definitions are of use in:-

a. Producing all legal sentences or expressions in a language.

b. Checking the legality of a sentence or expression. In computer applications this leads to the production of unambiguous code.

(b. is of more interest to us.)

27.20 Syntax, Lexicons and Semantics.

a. The **syntax** of a sentence is the structure of the sentence and the grammatical rules governing the structure.

b. A **lexicon** is a dictionary of valid words in a language, ie, a list of valid words.

c. **Semantics** is concerned with the meaning of words and sentences.

The following paragraphs are concerned **mainly** with a., **partly** with b., but **not** with c.

27.21 Language definition. A language may be defined by

a. a **generative** scheme, ie, a procedure for generating all legal sentences in the language, or

b. **recognition**, in which a procedure is defined for deciding the legality of any sentence.

The **generative** method is more common in the context of definition of programming languages, but **recognition** is closer to the implicit language definition provided by most **compilers** and **interpreters** which are programs which translate programming languages

27.22 Most schemes of language definition run into trouble when applied to natural languages like English, because of the inherent ambiguities, and metaphors and imprecise meanings, but these schematic methods work well on computer languages.

BNF GENERATIVE CLASSIFICATION

27.23 The BNF (Backus Naur Form) is syntactic metalanguage commonly used as a notation for presenting language generation.

27.24 Notation, Terminology and Method.

a. → means "is defined by" (sometimes::= or := is used instead of →); | means "or"; < > are used to enclose **syntactic variables**, as shown in these examples:

b. **Example 1.** A language rule defining operands used in the language.
< operand > → A | B | C | D means the syntactic variable (an operand) is defined by the terminal symbols A or B or C or D, ie, in the given language an operand is one of the characters A, B, C or D.

c. **Example 2.** A language rule defining operators used in the language.
< operator > → + | − | / | *. In examples 1 and 2 A, B, C, D, +, −, /, and * are all examples of **syntactic elements** and **terminal symbols**.

27.25 Producing legal sentences or legal expressions.

a. **Example.** Defining a legal expression. The following rules could be given.

   i. < expression >→< operand >< operator >< operand >
   ii. < operand >→ A | B | C | D
   iii. < operator >→ +| − |/|*

Such rules or definitions are called **productions**.

b. To **generate** or **produce** a legal expression **recursion** may be used, ie, the **left-hand sides** of **productions** are substituted into the right-hand sides again and again. Intermediate expressions containing both syntactic elements and syntactic variables are called **sentential forms**. (eg, i. < expression >→ A < operator >< operand > is a sentential form).

Once all syntactic variables have been replaced by syntactic elements we have produced a sentential form, which is a **legal expression** or **legal sentence** in the language, as shown in C.

c. Apply rules a.i., a.ii. and a.iii. to get a **legal expression**.

a.i	< expression >	→	< operand >	< operator >	< operand > } sentential
Use a.ii			A	< operator >	< operand > } forms
Use a.iii			A	+	< operand > }
Use a.ii			A	+	B } legal expression

27.26 Example of forming a legal sentence.

a. Given the following production

   i. < sentence >→< subject phrase >< verb >< object phrase >
   ii. < subject phrase >→< article >< adjective >< noun >
   iii. < object phrase >→< article >< adjective >< noun >

       iv. < verb >→ ate | has | saw

       v. < article >→ a | the

       vi. < adjective >→ bad | big | nice | small

       vii. < noun >→ boy | bird | chocolate

Note: The **lexicon** is defined by iv., v., vi. and vii., and each word in the lexicon is a **terminal symbol.**

b. Constructing a legal sentence.

	< sentence >
Using production i.	< subject phrase >< verb >< object phrase >
Using production ii	< article >< adjective >< noun > < verb >
	< object phrase >
Using production iii	< article >< adjective >< noun >< verb >< article >
	< adjective >< noun >
Using production iv.	< article >< adjective >< noun > ate < article >
	< adjective >< noun > etc

Until we arrive at legal sentences such as:

"the bad chocolate ate the small bird"

"the nice boy saw the big chocolate".

Note. The semantics may be incorrect, but syntactically these examples are legal.

27.27 Defining a statement in high-level languages.

Example. A simplified version of the PRINT statement in BASIC could be defined as follows:

< PRINT statement>	→ PRINT | PRINT < expression >
< expression >	→< variable > | < variable >,| < variable >;
< variable >	→< letter > | < letter >< digit >
< letter >	A | B | C | D | E | F | G | H | I | J | K | L | M | N | O | P | Q | R | S | T | U | V | W | X | Y | Z
< digit >	→ 0 | 1 | 2 | 3 | 4 | 5 | 6 | 7 | 8 | 9

So statements such as the following would be legal.

   i. PRINT

  ii. PRINT A

 iii. PRINT A,

  iv. PRINT B;

   v. PRINT C9

  vi. PRINT Z2.

27.28 Syntax diagrams are sometimes used as an alternative to BNF.

Examples.

a. < operand >→ A | B | C | D could be written in syntax diagram form as *operand*

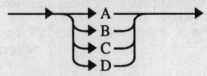

b. < assignment >→< variable >:=< expression >

assignment

$$\longrightarrow \text{variable} \longrightarrow := \longrightarrow \text{expression} \longrightarrow$$

PARSING (used in syntax analysis stage of compilation)

27.29 Parsing is the breaking down of sentences into their components. We will parse in order to check the legality of sentences. More precisely, parsing is defined as the process of defining the productions which when applied by recursion results in giving legal sentences or expressions.

27.30 Example of parsing.

    a. Given these language-definition productions.

        (1) < expression >→< operand >< operator >< operand >

        (2) < operand >→ W | X | Y | Z

        (3) < operator >→ +| − | * |/

    b. Parsing the expression W − X

    Using (2) < operand > −X

    Using (3) < operand >< operator > X

    Using (2) < operand >< operator >< operand >

    Using (1) < expression >

    The parse is described by the sequence of production, ie, (2, 3, 2, 1).

    c. The parsing of an expression can be represented by a TREE called a **syntax tree** or a **parse tree.** The syntax tree for the parse in b. is shown here.

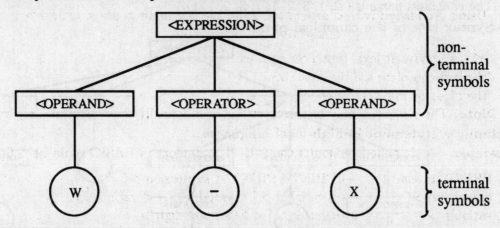

27.31 The canonical parse is a procedure that ensures well-defined parsing, as follows:

    a. **i.** Find a production that when applied, would have produced the **leftmost** syntactic elements and replace these elements by the syntactic variable from which they came.

        ii. The process is repeated on syntactic elements and variables (always working from the left) until a single expression is arrived at.

    b. The left-hand syntactic variable produced at each stage of the parse is called the **handle.**

27.32 A sentence (or expression) is **unambiguous** if only *one* canonical parse exists for that sentence. **Computer languages** must be defined so that *all* sentences in the language are unambiguous, in which case the language is said to be **unambiguous.** When a *canonical* parsing procedure is not adhered to, a sentence can only be unambiguous if just **one** parse exists for the sentence regardless of parsing procedure. The following example shows how a language definition can be unsatisfactory with non-canonical parsing producing ambiguous expressions.

27.33 Example.

Ambiguous language definition.

(1) < expression >→< operand > | < expression >< operator >< expression >

(2) < operand >→ W | X | Y | Z

(3) < operator >→ +| − | * |/

a. Canonical parse of W − X * Z

Using (2) < operand > − X * Z
Using (1) < expression > − X* Z
Using (3) < expression >< operator > X * Z
Using (2) < expression >< operator >< operand > * Z
Using (1) < expression >< operator >< expression > * Z
Using (1) <   expression   > * Z
Using (3) <   expression   >< operator > Z
Using (2) <   expression >< operator >
           < operand >
Using (1) < expression >< operator >
           < expression >
Using (1) <   expression   >

The canonical parse is (2, 1, 3, 2, 1, 1, 3, 2, 1, 1).

b. Syntax tree of the canonical parse.

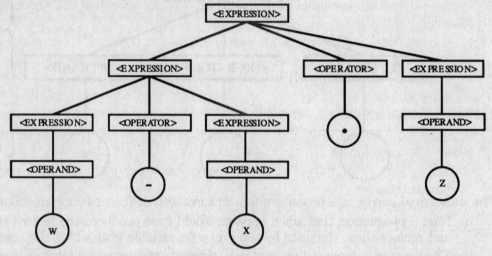

c. Note. A further deficiency of this language definition is apparent from this parse, namely that the order of operations is contrary to normal practice. We would normally expect to perform the * before the −. A good language definition for arithmetic expressions will provide the necessary precedence rules.

d. Alternate non-canonical parse of W − X * Z

2 < operand > − X * Z
3 < operand >< operator > X * Z
2 < operand >< operator >< operand > * Z
3 < operand >< operator >< operand >< operator > Z
2 < operand >< operator >< operand >< operator >< operand >
1 < expression >< operator >< operand >< operator > < operand >
1 < expression >< operator >< expression >< operator ><operand >
1 < expression >< operator >< expression >< operator >
   < expression >
1 < expression >< operator ><   expression   >
1 <   expression   >

The parse is (2, 3, 2, 3, 2, 1, 1, 1, 1, 1).

e. **Syntax tree of this parse.**

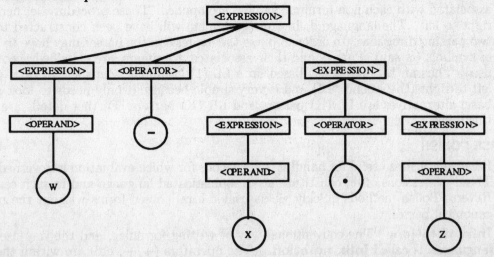

27.34 A language definition for simple arithmetic expressions providing the normal precedence rules for arithmetic operations.

(1)   < expression >→< term > | < expression > + < term > | < expression >
     − < term > |

(2)   < term >→< variable > | < term > * < variable > | < term > /
     < variable > |

(3)   < variable >→ W | X | Y | Z

a. A canonical parse of W − X * Z is performed here. Notice the need to **backtrack** when the parse fails to complete.

    i. Using (3) < variable > − X * Z) **NB.** No rule for < variable > followed by operator to try another rule.

    ii. Using (2) < term > − X * Z)

    iii. Using (1) < expression > − X * Z

    iv. Using (3) < expression > − < variable > * Z

    v. Using (2) < expression > − < term > * Z

    vi. Using (1) < expression > * Z

    vii. Using (3) < expression > * < variable >

    viii. Using (2) < expression > * < term

The parse fails here so we **backtrack** to step v.

vi Using (3) < expression > − < term > * < variable >

vii Using (2) < expression > − < term >

viii Using (1) < expression >

The canonical parse is (3, 2, 1, 3, 2, 3, 2, 1).

Note. Backtracking can also be used to search for ambiguous expressions.

27.35 From these parsing examples we may draw some useful conclusions.

a. Computer-language definitions should be unambiguous and cater for precedence rules where appropriate.

b. A satisfactory computer-language definition will allow the parsing procedure to:

    i. detect illegal expression (when the parse fails despite all backtracks),

    ii. find the legal parse. It is the correctly parsed form that is converted into code within a translator such as a compiler.

27.36 Awareness of what features of language definitions lead to efficient parsing methods has led to the development of standard forms of language definition together with parsing methods that work well with them.

27.37 In outline, the methods work like this. Expressions are scanned left to right. Parsing procedures associated with each non-terminal symbol are applied. These procedures either parse left to right or right to left. The language definition (grammar) will have been constructed to favour one of these two parsing directions. In order to parse the expression the parser may have to look ahead a number of symbols (K say). Parsers and their associated grammars, are classified according to the methods used. Thus an LL (1) parser, based on a LL (1) grammar, scans left to right (the first "L") parses left to right (the second "L") and is very simple because it only needs to look ahead 1 symbol. The basic alternatives are LL (K) parsers and LR (K) parsers. Further details are beyond the scope of this book.

REVERSE POLISH

27.38 Reverse Polish is useful for handling expressions for which evaluation is governed by precedence rules. These expressions often constitute an unsophisticated language and in such cases the application of Reverse Polish methods quickly yields usable legal parsed forms without the need for backtracking canonical parses.

27.39 Infix notation. The conventional way of writing formulae, and the way used in many high-level languages, is called **infix notation.** The operators (+, −, etc) are within the expression between the appropriate operands. For example:

$$(A + B) * (C - D)$$

(* means "multiply")

27.40 The problem of infix notation is that the order in which the expression is written down is not the same as the order in which the operands are required, or the operations are performed. This is even more apparent if we consider the order in which a computer might do the calculation, eg,

1 Fetch A
2 Fetch B
3 Add A and B (then store intermediate result (A + B))
4 Fetch C
5 Fetch D
6 Subtract D from C
7 Multiply by intermediate result (A + B)

The order in which the terms of the expression were used is indicated here:

```
1   3   2       7       4   6   5
(   A + B )  *  (   C   -   D   )
```

27.41 Reverse Polish notation. (First devised by a Polish logician, J. Lukasiewicz). In **Reverse Polish** notation each operator is written after the appropriate operands, eg, the infix expression (A + B) * (C − D) would be written as AB + CD − * which as you can see is the useful order shown in the previous paragraph. Reverse Polish notation is sometimes called **postfix notation.**

AIDS TO TRANSLATION

27.42 The unary minus. The + and − signs of normal arithmetic are used in two ways.

a. For binary operations, ie, those requiring **two** operands such as 3 + 5 or 7 − 4

b. For unary operations, ie, to designate sign value where only one operand is present such as + 4 or − 9.

In case b the − is called the **unary minus** sign and in conversion to Reverse Polish we may ignore the unary + but must treat the unary minus differently to the normal "binary" minus.

27.43 Restricting the use of the unary minus. The use of the unary minus is often restricted in a high-level language and may only be used after an : = or a (sign.

A further general restriction is that operands must always be explicit,

eg, A * B may **not** be written as AB

27.44 Operators. The following notation will be adopted to comply with the more usual notation of BASIC and FORTRAN. Note the use of "=" rather than ":=" for assignment in these examples.

Assigning values	=	eg, LET X = 3 (ie, X : = 3)
Parentheses	(or)	
Add	+	
Subtract	−	
Unary minus	~	(for identification only)
Multiply	*	
Divide	/	
Exponentiate	↑	eg, 3^2 written $3 \uparrow 2$ (note * * is also used in FORTRAN)

27.45 Precedence rules. In order to carry out the translation it is advantageous to give the operators a rule of precedence (ie, a rule to decide what to do when all else is equal). The following convention is adopted throughout this book, there are variations used elsewhere.

OPERATOR	PRECEDENCE
=	0
(	1
+ −)	2
* /	3
↑	4
~	5

TRANSLATION TO REVERSE POLISH FROM INFIX

27.46 Preliminary comments. The method will be described with the aid of pseudocode, but the following points should be noted first:

a. The infix expression will be regarded as a (one-dimensional) string called the infix string and will be scanned left to right one symbol at a time.

b. The Reverse Polish expression will be regarded as a (one-dimensional) string called Reverse Polish expression filled left to right.

c. Use will be made of LIFO stack of the type described in the chapter on data structures. The top entry in the stack will be called top-of-stack.

d. The symbol in the infix string currently being examined will be called current symbol.

e. The method used here is called Dijkstra's method.

f. Operands may be

    i. **Constants** eg, 5, 19, etc, or

    ii. **Literals** eg, A, B, C, etc.

g. You are advised to use the pseudocode to work through the table that follows it.

27.47 Pseudocode for converting well-formed infix strings to Reverse Polish. (Some error checks are included but none could be added to good effect.) This pseudocode merely gives an outline of the method. In many places comments are given instead of the actual code.

```
variables
    current_symbol,
    top_of_stack                    character
    infix_string
    reverse_polish_expression   string
    end_of_infix_string,
    error_found,
    stack_empty,
    process_needed                  boolean

Begin
  error_found:  = false
    while  (* more characters in infix_string *)
        AND NOT  error_found
    do
        if
            end_of_infix_string
        then
            (* empty stack into reverse_polish_expression
            but omit "(" or ")".  *)
        else
            (* assign next infix_string symbol to the *)
            (* current_symbol *)
            if
              (* current_symbol is an operand *)
            then
                if
                  (* the previous current_symbol was an operand *)
                then
                    error_found:  = true
                else
                    (* add current_symbol to the *)
                    (* reverse_polish_expression *)
                    endif
            else  (* current_symbol is an operator a "(" or a ")" *)
                if
                    stack_empty
                then
                    (* add current_symbol to stack *)
                else
                    if
                        current_symbol = "("
                    then
                        (* add current_symbol to stack *)
                    else
                        (* adjust stack NB. Details shown separately *)
                    endif
                endif
            endif
        endif
    endwhile
end
```

```
(* Details of "adjust stack")
process_needed : = true
repeat
    if
        (precedence of current_symbol)
        >
        (precedence of top_of_stack)
    then
        if
            current_symbol = ")"
            AND
            top_of_stack = "("
        then
            (* remove "(" from the stack *)
        else
            (* add current_symbol to the stack *)
        endif
        process_needed := false
    else
        if
            top_of_stack = "("
            OR
            top_of_stack = ")"
        then
            error_found := true
        else
            (* transfer top_of_stack *)
            (* to reverse_polish_expression *)
            if
                stack_empty
            then
                (* add current_symbol to stack *)
                process_needed := false
            endif
        endif
    endif
until (NOT process_needed) OR error_found
```

27.48 Examples using the Pseudocode.

Example 1. Convert (A + B) * (C − D) to Reverse Polish. Use the pseudocode and refer to the table given below. The table is filled by working through the pseudocode, so tick entries in pencil as you do them.

Current_symbol	Precedence (if an operator)	Stack top_of_stack to the right	Precedence of top_of_stack	Reverse_Polish_expression
(	1	(	1	
A				A
+	2	(+	2	
B				AB
)	2	(	1	AB+
*	3	*	3	
(		*(	1	
C				AB+C
−	2	*(−	2	
D				AB+CD
)	2	*(	1	AB+CD−
End of infix_string stack Empty				AB+CD−*

(A + B) * (C - D) is AB + CD - * in Reverse Polish.

27.49 Example 2. Convert $X = (-W + A * (5 * Y - Z \uparrow 3))/2$ into Reverse Polish (postfix) notation.

Note. We identify that the unary minus occurs after the "(" and rewrite the expression

$$X = (\sim W + A * (5 * Y - Z \uparrow 3))/2$$

27.50 This table illustrates the conversion of

$X = (\sim W + A * (5 * Y - Z \uparrow 3))/2$ to Reverse Polish notation.

So

$$X = (\sim W + A * (5 * Y - Z \uparrow 3))/2$$

is

$$XW \sim A5Y * Z3 \uparrow - * +2/ =$$

in reverse polish notation.

Note.

i. The operands are in the same order as the operands in the infix string.

ii. The operators are now in "operational" order.

Symbol currently scanned	Precedence (if an operator)	Stack (Top value to the right)	Precedence of top value	Reverse Polish Expression
X				X
$=$	0	$=$	0	
$($	1	$=($	1	
$\sim$	3	$=(\sim$	3	
W				XW
$+$	2	$=($	1	$XW \sim$
		$=(+$	2	
A				$XW \sim A$
$*$	3	$=(+*$	3	
$($	1	$=(+*($	1	
5				$XW \sim A5$
$*$	3	$=(+*(*$	3	
Y				$XW \sim A5Y$
$-$	2	$=(+*($	1	$XW \sim A5Y*$
		$=(+*(-$	2	
Z				$XW \sim A5Y*Z$
$\uparrow$	4	$=(+*(-\uparrow$	4	
3				$XW \sim A5y*Z3$
$)$	2	$=(+*(-$	2	$XW \sim A5y*Z3\uparrow$
		$=(+*($	1	$XW \sim A5Y*Z3\uparrow-$
		$=(+*$	3	
$)$	2	$=(+$	2	$XW \sim A5Y*Z3\uparrow-*$
		$=($	1	$XW \sim A5Y*Z3\uparrow-*+$
		$=$	0	
$/$	3	$=/$		
2				$XW \sim A5y*Z3\uparrow-*+2$
empty stack				$XW \sim A5Y*Z3\uparrow-*+2/=$

27.51 Well-formed Formulae (WFF) in Reverse Polish. Before generating code form, or evaluating expressions in Reverse Polish, the Reverse Polish expression should be checked for legality. (A legal expression is said to be **well-formed.**) The procedure for this check is simple to perform but must be carefully prepared.

Steps.

a. "Rank" value is assigned as shown and is used solely for this check.

Reverse Polish String Member	Rank Value
Variable or Constant	1
Unary operator, eg $\sim$	0
Other (binary) operators	-1

b. The Reverse Polish symbol string is constructed, rank values assigned and then rank value subtotals are evaluated as shown here.

For the expression $AB + CD - *$ (The letters h to m are annotations)

Symbol String	Rank Value		Rank Value Subtotal		Comment
$*$	-1	h	-1	h	subtotal ≤ 0
$-$	-1	i	-2	h+i	subtotal ≤ 0
D	1	j	-1	h+i+j	subtotal ≤ 0
C	1	k	0	h+i+j+k	subtotal ≤ 0
$+$	-1	l	-1	h+i+j+k+l	subtotal ≤ 0
B	1	m	0	h+i+j+k+l+m	subtotal ≤ 0
A	1	n	1 = (Total of all rank values)		total $=1$

c. The Reverse Polish string is well formed IF and ONLY IF

   i. Each subtotal is < 0

   ii. The total of all rank values $= 1$

27.52 Code generation and Reverse Polish string evaluation. The details of code generation are beyond the scope of this book, but if you can see how to write a set of machine instructions for the following example of string evaluation you will have grasped the basic principles.

27.53 Evaluating a Reverse Polish string. To illustrate the method we will assume that successive symbols in the string are stored in a table as shown below. The expression can be thought of as being in successive memory locations if you wish. (Numerical values are also shown to aid understanding.) For Reverse Polish expression $AB + CD - *$

LOCATION	CONTENT
1	A = 10
2	B = 14
3	+
4	C = 18
5	D = 15
6	−
7	*

Assume we can use a stack to store location values. The procedure is as follows.

a. Work through the table one location at a time.

b. If the contents are an operand, place its address on top of the stack.

c. If the contents are an operator then

   i. Remove addresses of the required number of operands from the stack. (Usually two, one in the case of unary minus.)

   ii. Perform the operation and replace the operator by the result.

   iii. Place the address of the result on top of the stack.

On completing the first scan the expression will be calculated. The table below shows successive contents of locations and stack when following the above procedure. The stack could be used to hold the operands rather than their addresses.

	LOCATIONS						STACK (Top to the right)
1	2	3	4	5	6	7	
A = 10	B = 14	+	C = 18	D = 15	−	*	1,
							1,2
		(A+B) = 24					3
							3,4
							3,4,5
					(C−D) = 3		3,6
						(A+B) * (C−D) = 72	7

Note. The final entry in the stack gives the location of the result.

TREE REPRESENTATION

27.54 A procedure for constructing the tree representation of a Reverse Polish string is as follows:

Start at the **right-hand** end of the expression and work right to left thus:

a. Take the symbols in turn. For each symbol form a new right node, place the symbol in the node and traverse to that node. When the node that has just been created contains an operand start step b. Nodes containing operands are terminal nodes.

b. Traverse backwards up the tree until a left node is required. Fill this with the next symbol in the Reverse Polish string.

c. i. If the symbol filled in in b. is an operand continue with b.

ii. If the symbol filled in in b. is an operator return to step a.

The tree representation of $AB + CD - *$ is shown here.

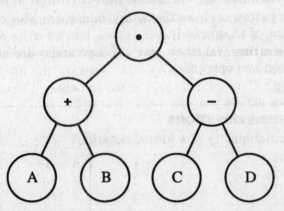

SUMMARY

27.55 a. The meaning of **formal notation**, **precise notation** and **informal notation** were introduced.

b. The meanings of **syntax** and **semantics** were explained

c. The uses of formal notations were illustrated by simple examples drawn from metalanguages and formal specifications.

d. Two further topics were discussed:

i. Language definition.

ii. Reverse Polish notation.

e. Languages may be defined by **generative schemes** or **recognition schemes**. BNF is a useful generative classification or metalanguage.

f. Computer languages require unambiguous definition.

g. Parsing is the process of defining the **production** which, when applied by recursion, results in the given legal sentence or expression.

h. Reverse Polish (postfix) notation places operands and operators in a more usable order than that found in infix notation.

POINTS TO NOTE

27.56 a. Methods also exist for formally defining the semantics of a programming language. They are more complex and mathematical than the formal definition of syntax and are outside the scope of this book.

b. Some care needs to be exercised in the choice of terminology used in this subject area with regard to the term "formal". For example, the term "formal method" may be used to mean two completely different things:

i. A method involving the use of formal notations.

ii. A set of well-defined rules to be obeyed when carrying out a set of tasks, such as following rules for writing programs.

c. Reverse Polish can equally well be applied to Boolean operations. A possible precedence rule is:

Operator	Precedence
=	0
(	1
+)	2
. −	3

d. Although Reverse Polish notation provides a more useful order of presentation of expressions, further improvement can be made to the methods described, which lead to more efficient ways of using machine instructions to perform operations.

e. You should be aware of this alternative terminology.

   i. **Syntactic elements** are also called **terminal symbols**.

   ii. **Syntactic variables** are also called **non-terminal symbols** or **metacomponents**.

   iii. **Unary operators** such as the unary minus are also called **monadic prefix operators** (fixed in front of an operand).

   iv. **Binary operators**, (ie, they have two operands) are also called **dyadic infix operators** (fixed between two operands).

STUDENT SELF-TESTING QUESTIONS

1. What is the essential quality of a formal notation?
2. Explain the terms:
   a. syntax
   b. semantics
   c. pre-condition
   d. post-condition
3. The following part of a language defines an arithmetic expression in Backus Naur Form (BNF):

   <expression> :: = <term> | <expression> + <term> | <expression> − <term>
   <term>:: =<variable> | <term> * <variable> | <term< / <variable>
   <variable>::= a|b|c|d

   Show that a + b * c is a syntactically correct expression in this language.　　*(4 marks)*
   　　　　　　　　　　　　　　　　　　　　　　　　　　　　　　　　　　　(AEB)

4. Write a set of productions that will generate from < date > all possible dates conforming to this description:
   A "data" consists of a day letter (eg, M for Monday) followed by a month letter (eg, F for February) followed by one of 32 day numbers for the month. Exceptions to the code are two-letter codes introduced when the day or month letter is not unique, eg, TH = Thursday, TU = Tuesday. The three components of the date are separated by a space, for which you may use the symbol ▽. Outline amendments necessary to exclude non-dates like M▽F▽31.

5. Parse this expression using the language definition given in 27.33.

   　　　　　　W / X + Z * Y (backtracking will be needed).

6. i. Convert the expression W / X + Z * Y into Reverse Polish. Then check that your answer is well formed.

   ii. Convert these expressions to Reverse Polish. Draw a tree for each expression.
   a. $A = (- X + C \uparrow E) * Y$
   b. $Y = (X + B) / (W - Z)$

7. Convert the following infix expression to postfix (Reverse Polish) and show how the postfix expression may be evaluated using a stack. $(3*4 + 5) - (1 + 6/3)$　　　*(5 marks)*
   　　　　　　　　　　　　　　　　　　　　　　　　　　　　　　　　　　　(AEB)

QUESTIONS WITHOUT ANSWERS

3. A first attempt to define a portion of the syntax of a programming language dealing with expressions involving only variables is made as follows:

    < expression >   →< variable > | < expression >< op >< expression >

    < op >   → + | * | ↑

    < variable >   → A | B | C | D

Show that this is unsatisfactory by drawing two different syntax trees for the expression
A   *   B + C   ↑   D
Subsequently, this inherent ambiguity is removed by replacing the definitions above by:

    < expression >→< term > | < expression > + < term >

    < term >   →< factor > | < term > * < factor >

    < factor >   →< primary > | < factor >↑< primary >

    < primary >→< variable >

    < variable >→ A | B | C | D

    i. Using a tree derived from the revised syntax rules, express

    A * B + C ↑ D

    in Reverse Polish (postfix) notation.

    ii. What change would you make to the definition of < primary > to allow for bracketed expressions in the language?

(London)

4. Arithmetic expressions are often represented in a computer either in Reverse Polish form, in which each operator is preceded by its operands, or by means of a binary tree structure. For example (A + B) * C has Reverse Polish form AB + C * and may be represented by the tree

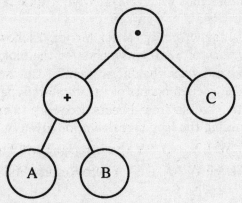

Why are these representations important?
Convert each of the following expressions to Reverse Polish form and draw an equivalent binary tree.

    a. (X + Y) * (X - Z)

    b. 2 * (3 * X + 1) ↑ 3

    c. (A + B − 3) * (F − G)/H) − K * (F − G)

    Describe in outline the steps involved in generating the Reverse Polish form of an expression from its binary tree representation.

(London Specimen Paper)

    d. Obtain a copy of the syntax definition of the language you currently use and experiment with trying to write the syntax definition for any extra feature you would like to see in the language.

GLOSSARY CHECKLIST

COMPUTER ARITHMETIC

1. In the next three chapters we deal with computer arithmetic in more depth and make use of the ideas on number bases introduced in chapter 3. There has been a decline in the extent to which this subject matter has been given emphasis in syllabuses and examination in recent years so in this edition of the text the material has streamlined accordingly.
2. Chapter 28 deals with arithmetical procedures. Chapter 29 introduces and develops fixed-point and floating-point arithmetic. Lastly, chapter 30 explores the problems of errors and accuracy associated with all computer calculations.

28: Arithmetical Procedures

INTRODUCTION

28.1 This chapter deals with the methods of addition, subtraction, multiplication and division that apply to computer arithmetic. It also introduces methods involving binary fractions, sign bits and number complements.

BINARY ADDITION

28.2 Binary addition is performed in a similar way to decimal addition. We apply these rules:

a.		b.		c.		d.	
	0		0		1		1
+	0	+	1	+	0	+	1
	0		1		1		10

28.3 **Example.** $00110_2 + 01101_2$ (Equivalent to $6_{10} + 13_{10} = 19_{10}$)

First Number	0	0	1	1	0	6_{10}
Second Number	0	1	1	0	1	13_{10}
Sum	1	0	0	1	1	19_{10}
Carried	1	1				—
Addition rules	a then b	b then d	d	c	b	—

28.4 **Further Examples** set out in the usual way. (The carry is shown where it occurs.)

a	b	c
1 0 1 1 0 0	1 1 0	1 0 1
+ 1 0 0 1 0	+ 1 0 1	+ 0 1 1
1 1 1 1 1 0	1 0 1 1	1 0 0 0
	1	1 1 1

These are respectively equivalent to the decimal sums $44 + 18$, $6 + 5$ and $5 + 3$.

28.5 To add more than two numbers we can apply the same method by adding the first two numbers, and then adding the next number to the subtotal. We repeat additions to the subtotal until all numbers are added. The subtotal is called a **partial sum**.

OCTAL ADDITION

28.6 Two methods may be readily employed:

   a. **i.** Convert to binary

       ii. Add

       iii. Convert back to octal.

   b. Use the Octal addition table shown here:-

OCTAL ADDITION TABLE								
+	0	1	2	3	4	5	6	7
0	0	1	2	3	4	5	6	7
1	1	2	3	4	5	6	7	10
2	2	3	4	5	6	7	10	11
3	3	4	5	6	7	10	11	12
4	4	5	6	7	10	11	12	13
5	5	6	7	10	11	12	13	14
6	6	7	10	11	12	13	14	15
7	7	10	11	12	13	14	15	16

The square $\boxed{11}$ in the table illustrates the addition $5_8 + 4_8 = 11_8$

Once familiar, both methods should be achieved without the need to refer to tables.

28.7 Examples of the addition $327_8 + 245_8 = 574_8$

Method (a)

OCTAL NUMBERS			CONVERSION (See 3.9)	BINARY REPRESENTATION		
3	2	7	→	011	010	111
+2	4	5	→	010	100	101
5	7	4	←	101	111	100

Method (b)

OCTAL NUMBERS	COMMENTS (Working Right to Left)
3 2 7	$7_8 + 5_3 = 14_8$ (From table) ie, 4 carry 1
+ 2 4 5	$2_8 + 4_8 = 6_8$ (From table) $6 + 1 = 7_8$ (ie, Add carry)
5 7 4	$3_8 + 2_8 = 5_8$ (From table)

Further example $654_8 + 176_8 = 1052_8$

	6	5	4
+	1	7	6
1	0	5	2

	110	101	100
+	001	111	110
001	000	101	010

1052_8 is obtained either way.

HEXADECIMAL ADDITION

28.8 Conversion to binary or the use of an addition table are acceptable methods. It is left to the reader to construct a table if he so wishes. An example using conversion to binary is given here.

Example of $CA3_{16} + 5FB_{16} = 129E_{16}$

HEX NUMBER			CONVERSION	BINARY REPRESENTATION			
	C	A	3	→		1100	1010	0011
+	5	F	B	→	+	0101	1111	1011
1	2	9	E	←	0001	0010	1001	1110

BCD ADDITION

The procedure here is longer but straightforward. We will take it in two stages.

28.9 Single-digit addition.

There are two cases to consider:

a. Example

DECIMAL NUMBERS	BCD NUMBERS
2	0010
+ 3	+0011
5	0101

Binary addition of the two BCD codes gives the correct BCD result 0101 directly. No further work is needed.

363

b. Example (This corresponds to a "decimal carry".)

DECIMAL NUMBERS	BCD NUMBERS	COMMENTS
8	1 0 0 0	Binary addition results in 1101_2, which is not a BCD code (2.15). To correct for this 0110_2 is added.
+ 5	+ 0 1 0 1	
13	1 1 0 1	
—	+ 0 1 1 0	Correction added to result
13	0 0 0 1 0 0 1 1	BCD codes for 1_{10} and 3_{10} (ie, BCD 13)

28.10 Multi-digit addition. To do this the methods of single-digit addition are applied as follows starting with the right-hand column.

a. Add the two BCD digits.

b. Add any carry digits to this sum.

c. Add 0110 if the sum is not acceptable BCD code.

d. Move to the next column and return to step a.

28.11 Example. The sum $159 + 473 = 632$ in BCD.

WORKING			COMMENT
0 0 0 1	0 1 0 1	1 0 0 1	First BCD number
0 1 0 0	0 1 1 1	0 0 1 1	Second BCD number
0 1 0 1	1 1 0 0	1 1 0 0	Two-digit sums
0 0 0 1 ←	0 0 0 1 ←	↓	Decimal carry
0 1 1 0 ↑	1 1 0 1 ↑	1 1 0 0	Sum
↓ CARRY	↑ CARRY		
↓ ↑	0 1 1 0 ↑	0 1 1 0	Correction
↓ ↑	0 0 1 1 ↑	0 0 1 0	Sum + carry
↓ 1	1	↓	
SUM	SUM	SUM	
↓	↓	↓	
0 1 1 0	0 0 1 1	0 0 1 0	Final BCD sum

28.12 You can see from these examples that BCD addition is no longer than pure binary addition. The time taken to convert to pure binary and to convert the pure binary result to BCD is avoided, however. In general for number representation and arithmetic pure binary is preferred because the representation is compact and provides computational ease and speed. BCD arithmetic, and other forms of "string arithmetic" performed on numeric codes, can be found in some commercial applications, eg, in many versions of COBOL and in BUSINESS BASIC. The conversions between character codes and BCD codes are relatively simple, as can be seen from inspecting the character codes. Also, some computers have hardware able to perform BCD arithmetic directly.

REPRESENTATIONS OF NEGATIVE NUMBERS

28.13 The familiar method of placing a "–" sign before a number to show that it is negative is not the only way to represent a negative number. We will now look at an alternative method and see how it provides certain advantages when using computers. A car milometer can be used to illustrate this alternative method. If the milometer is run backwards we see that, for example, 9997 represents –3 miles not +9997 miles. This is one example of the **numbers complement** method of representing negative numbers. It provides an **implicit sign**, but to avoid ambiguities we must sacrifice the representation of large numbers like +9997. We will now see how to convert to this method of representation.

FOUR-DIGIT MILOMETER READING	DISTANCE GONE
0 0 0 3	3 Miles
0 0 0 2	2 Miles
0 0 0 1	1 Mile
0 0 0 0	Start
9 9 9 9	— 1 Mile
9 9 9 8	— 2 Miles
9 9 9 7	— 3 Miles

28.14 Complements. There are two types of number complement. They are:

a. The radix-minus-one complement (also called the diminished radix complement).

    i. In the decimal system it is called the **nines complement.**

    ii. In the binary system it is called the **ones complement.**

b. The radix complement(also called the *true* or noughts complement).

    i. In the decimal system it is called the **tens complement.**

    ii. In the binary system it is called the **twos complement.**

28.15 Rules for finding complements of numbers.

    a. To obtain the radix-minus-one complement of a number, subtract each digit of the number from one less than the radix (base), eg, for decimal (base 10) subtract each digit from 9.

    b. To obtain the radix complement, add one to the radix-minus-one complement.

28.16 Examples for 30962 decimal and 10110 binary.

DECIMAL EXAMPLE	COMMENTS		BINARY EXAMPLE
	One less than the radix		
9 9 9 9 9 9	ie, 9	ie, 1	1 1 1 1 1 1
0 3 0 9 6 2	Subtract		0 1 0 1 1 0
	number to be complemented		
9 6 9 0 3 7	Result		1 0 1 0 0 1
	Nines complement	Ones complement	
1	Add 1		1
9 6 9 0 3 8	Tens Complement	Twos Complement	1 0 1 0 1 0

Also see note (i) below.

Note: For binary numbers the rules simplify to:

    i. change ones to zeroes and zeroes to ones to obtain the ones complement.

    ii. add one to this result for the twos complement.

28.17 Reverse process. The reverse of complementation can be accomplished by using **exactly the same rules** as those used to obtain the complement, hence the complement of a number has the number as its complement, one reason for the choice of the term "complement".

28.18 Using Complements.

    a. Complements are mainly used for:

        i. Representing negative numbers

        ii. subtraction.

    b. Reasons for their use are:

        i. Convenience: Complementation is easy with two state devices.

        ii. Efficiency: Only one procedure, **addition,** is needed because to subtract a number one can add its complement.

        iii. No provision is needed for separate *explicit* sign representation. The sign is *implicit*.

28.19 Examples of use. Assume for simplicity that we are using a representation with just two decimal digits. We can use the numbers 00 to 99. However, if we use tens complement representation for negative numbers we must "borrow" some positive number forms. An arbitrary but convenient choice would be to use 00 – 49 to represent positive numbers and 50 – 99 to represent negative numbers, eg:

DECIMAL NUMBER	TENS COMPLEMENT REPRESENTATION
27	27
16	16
– 16	84
– 27	73
49	49 (Most positive number)
– 1	99
– 50	50 (Most negative number)

To *subtract* a number *add* its complement.

CALCULATION OF 27 + 16		COMMENT	CALCULATION OF 27 – 16		COMMENT
2	7	Normal methods apply	2	7	To subtract 16 its complement, 84, is added. The last carry is lost in the absence of a third column
1	6		8	4	
4	3		1	1	

CALCULATION OF 16 – 27		COMMENT	CALCULATION OF 27 + 27		COMMENT
1	6	The complement of 27 (ie, 73) is added. The result 89 is the tens complement representing –11.	2	7	The result is too large to be represented since 54 is the representation for –46!
7	3		2	7	
8	9		5	4	

Binary examples are given in 28.20 and 28.21.

BINARY REPRESENTATIONS OF NEGATIVE NUMBERS

28.20 The different methods of representation can be compared by using the simple 3-bit examples given here. In each example the most significant (ie, leftmost) bit indicates the number's sign (0 for "+" and 1 for "−"), and is called the **sign bit**.

a. Explicit sign method ie, sign bit plus positive representation				b. Ones Complement Method (The sign is implicit)				c. Twos Complement Method (The sign is implicit)			
Decimal Integer	Sign	Binary Representation		Decimal Integer	Sign	Binary Representation		Decimal Integer	Sign	Binary Representation	
+3	0	1	1	+3	0	1	1	+3	0	1	1
+2	0	1	0	+2	0	1	0	+2	0	1	0
+1	0	0	1	+1	0	0	1	+1	0	0	1
0	0	0	0	0	0	0	0	0	0	0	0
(Redundant) −0	1	0	0	(Redundant) −0	1	1	1	−1	1	1	1
−1	1	0	1	−1	1	1	0	−2	1	1	0
−2	1	1	0	−2	1	0	1	−3	1	0	1
−3	1	1	1	−3	1	0	0	−4	1	0	0
Range: +3 to −3				Range: +3 to −3				Range: +3 to −4			

28.21 The use of twos complement representation is preferred for these reasons:

a. There is no redundant representation of zero. (The twos complement of 0000 is 0000.)

b. The range of representation is extended by one bit as a consequence of a.

Representation using a greater number of bits can be constructed in the same manner. Here we show the 12-bit representation of 107_{10} and -107_{10} in twos complement with the leftmost bit as sign bit.

Decimal Integer	Sign	Twos Complement Binary Representation									
+ 107	0	0	0	0	0	1	1	0	1	0	1 1
– 107	1	1	1	1	1	0	0	1	0	1	0 1

c. Twos complement arithmetic is more straightforward than ones complement arithmetic, eg, when adding two negative numbers:

USING TWOS COMPLEMENTS   USING ONES COMPLEMENTS

$$111_2 \qquad -1 \Big\} \text{ ADD} \qquad\qquad 110_2 \qquad -1 \Big\} \text{ ADD}$$
$$\underline{111_2} \qquad \underline{-1} \qquad\qquad\qquad \underline{110_2} \qquad \underline{-1}$$
$$\underline{1110_2} \qquad \underline{-2} \qquad\qquad\qquad \underline{1100_2} \qquad \underline{-3} \quad \text{Wrong Answer !}$$

$\hookrightarrow$ ignore $\hookrightarrow 1$ Add Cary (An 'End Around Carry')

$$\underline{101_2} \qquad -2 \quad \text{Correct Answer}$$

See 26.16 for the implementation of end around carry.

OTHER METHODS

28.22 Complements in BCD. The method for finding the nines and tens complement is shown in this example. Note that the codes 1010 and 1111 are used to represent the signs "+" and "−" respectively.

LAYOUT (To Complement 275_{10})				COMMENTS
+	2	7	5	Decimal number
1 0 1 0	0 0 1 0	0 1 1 1	0 1 0 1	BCD Representation with sign
0 1 0 1	1 1 0 1	1 0 0 0	1 0 1 0	Produce ones complement of each BCD digit
1 0 1 0	1 0 1 0	1 0 1 0	1 0 1 0	Add 1010 to each BCD digit
1 1 1 1	1 0 1 1 1	1 0 0 1 0	1 0 1 0 0	Result of adding 1010
1 1 1 1	0 1 1 1	0 0 1 0	0 1 0 0	To obtain the nines complement: Bring down the first 4 bits of each sum
0 0 0 0	0 0 0 0	0 0 0 0	0 0 0 1	Add one to obtain the tens complement
1 1 1 1	0 1 1 1	0 0 1 0	0 1 0 1	Tens complement
−	7	2	5	Decimal form of tens complement

28.23 Excess −3 (XS3) code. This is an alternative code to 8421-weighted BCD code and has the advantage of having a simpler procedure for complementation. Each decimal digit has a code *3 higher* than its 8421 BCD equivalent, as can be seen in this table:

DECIMAL DIGIT	EXCESS-3 CODE	DECIMAL DIGIT	EXCESS-3 CODE
0	0 0 1 1	5	1 0 0 0
1	0 1 0 0	6	1 0 0 1
2	0 1 0 1	7	1 0 1 0
3	0 1 1 0	8	1 0 1 1
4	0 1 1 1	9	1 1 0 0

Note: Other advantages include:

i. No code is null (all zeroes)

ii. Some arithmetic is simpler and quicker.

iii. Each digit is self-complementing.

28.24 Example. Finding the nines and tens complements of 275 in XS3,0000 is used for "+" and 1111 for "−" if required.

LAYOUT (To complement 275_{10})				COMMENTS (A zero in the right-hand column must be corrected (See 11))
+	2	7	5	Decimal number
0000	0101	1010	1000	XS3 representation
1111	1010	0101	0111	The ones complement gives the nines complement
0000	0000	0000	0001	Add one to get the tens complement
1111	1010	0101	1000	XS3 form of tens complement
−	7	2	5	Tens complement in decimal

BINARY FRACTIONS

28.25 Examples of binary fractions are given in this table.

BINARY FRACTION	$2^{-1} = \frac{1}{2}$ $2^{-2} = \frac{1}{4}$ $2^{-3} = \frac{1}{8}$ $2^{-4} = \frac{1}{16}$	DECIMAL EQUIVALENT
.1000	$= (1 \times \frac{1}{2}) + (0 \times \frac{1}{4}) + (0 \times \frac{1}{8}) + (0 \times \frac{1}{16})$	$= \frac{1}{2} = 0.5$
.0100	$= (0 \times \frac{1}{2}) + (1 \times \frac{1}{4}) + (0 \times \frac{1}{8}) + (0 \times \frac{1}{16})$	$= \frac{1}{4} = 0.25$
.0010	$= (0 \times \frac{1}{2}) + (0 \times \frac{1}{4}) + (1 \times \frac{1}{8}) + (0 \times \frac{1}{16})$	$= \frac{1}{8} = 0.125$
.0001	$= (0 \times \frac{1}{2}) \times (0 \times \frac{1}{4}) \times (0 \times \frac{1}{8}) \times (1 \times \frac{1}{16})$	$= \frac{1}{16} = 0.0625$

28.26 Conversion from binary to decimal.

Example 1. Convert 11.101_2 to a decimal value.

PLACE VALUE	2^1 (2)	2^0 (1)	.	2^{-1} ($\frac{1}{2}$)	2^{-2} ($\frac{1}{4}$)	2^{-3} ($\frac{1}{8}$)	DECIMAL VALUE
BINARY NUMBER	1	1	.	1	0	1	
CONVERSION	\multicolumn{6}{l}{$(1 \times 2) + (1 \times 1) + (1 \times \frac{1}{2}) + (0 \times \frac{1}{4}) + (1 \times \frac{1}{8})$}	$3\frac{5}{8} = 3.625$

28.27 Decimal to Binary Conversion. (The whole number part is converted as in 3.6.)

Example 1. Convert 0.625_{10} to binary.

WORKING	COMMENT
.625 × 2	Multiply by 2 and write result beneath.
1.25	Remove digit before the point to form
.25 × 2	the binary fraction.
0.5	Repeat process until a zero fraction
.5 × 2	value occurs, or the required accuracy
1.0	is reached.
.0 × 2	
.1 0 1	

28.28 Example 2. Convert $\frac{1}{3}$ to binary using 5 bits for your representation and twos complement form. Note: We convert $+\frac{1}{3}$ and then find its complement.

WORKING		FURTHER WORKING TO 5 BITS	
	$\frac{1}{3} \times 2$	0.0101	$\frac{1}{3}$ to 5 bits including sign
0 +	$\frac{2}{3} \times 2$	1.1010	Ones complement
1 +	$\frac{1}{3} \times 2$	1.1011	Twos complement
.0 1	$\frac{1}{3} \times 2$ [Repeats]		

Note: When fractions are stored in words or registers the position of the point is not shown but recorded separately, eg, 1.1011 could be stored as:

$$\boxed{1}\,\boxed{1}\,\boxed{0}\,\boxed{1}\,\boxed{1}$$

SHIFTS.

28.29 If the bits in the word or register are moved leftwards or rightwards, then a **shift** is said to have taken place. A shift one place left corresponds to multiplication by 2 and a shift one place right corresponds to division by 2, provided certain conditions are satisfied.

These conditions are:

a. The sign of the number must be preserved.

b. Arithmetic meaning must be preserved.

Shifts that satisfy these conditions are called **arithmetic shifts**.

28.30 Examples. (Further examples will be given in Chapter 31.)

AFTER ONE SHIFT LEFT				STARTING WITH			AFTER ONE SHIFT RIGHT			
Bit lost in shift 0 ←	Sign bit	Value + 4	Bit inserted ← 0	Sign bit	Value + 2		Bit inserted 0 →	Sign bit	Value + 1	Bit lost →0
0 ←	0	1 0 0	← 0	0	0 1 0		0 →	0	0 0 1	→0
Bit lost 1 ←	Sign bit	Value −4	Bit inserted ← 0	Sign bit	Value −2		Bit inserted 1 →	Sign bit	Value −1	Bit lost → 0
1 ←	1	1 0 0	← 0	1	1 1 0		1 →	1	1 1 1	→ 0

MULTIPLICATION AND DIVISION

28.31 In general.

a. Binary multiplication is achieved by a combination of shifts and additions.

b. Binary division is achieved by a combination of shifts and subtractions.

The details of these procedures are difficult to grasp, so the reader may wish to leave this for a later reading, and the less mathematical reader may prefer to leave this section completely.

28.32 Binary multiplication (A computer-based procedure).

The two numbers being multiplied together are called **multiplicand** and **multiplier**. The result obtained at each stage of the calculation is called the **partial product sum**. Its final value is that of the product of the two numbers.

Steps. (These should be read in conjunction with the example.)

a. Negative multiplicands or multipliers should be converted to positive representations and the result complemented back to a negative representation at the end if necessary.

b. Set the partial sum to zero.

c. Start with the leftmost bit of the multiplier and take multiplier bits in turn until all have been considered. Perform these steps for each multiplier bit:-

    i. Shift the partial product sum left by one bit position.

    ii. If the multiplier bit is a *one*, add the multiplicand to the partial product sum.

28.33 Example. To perform $-13_{10} \times 6_{10} = -78_{10}$ in binary.

$(13_{10} = 1101_2, 6_2 = 0110_2)$.

Partial Product Sum Successive Values (Last Value is the Product) (First set to zero)								Multiplier Bits Labelled A, B, C, D to Aid Explanation A B C D	Comments The partial product sum is the combined length of multiplier and multiplicand
0	0	0	0	0	0	0	0	0 1 1 0	
0	0	0	0	0	0	0	0		Left shift (Step c.i.) Multiplier bit (A) is zero (c.iii.)
0	0	0	0	0	0	0	0		Left shift (Step c.i.)
0	0	0	0	1	1	0	1		Multiplier bit (B) is *one* so add multiplicand (c.ii.)
0	0	0	0	1	1	0	1		Result of sum.
0	0	0	1	1	0	1	0		Left shift (Step c.i.)
0	0	0	0	1	1	0	1		Multiplier bit (C) is *one* so add multiplicand (c.ii.)
0	0	1	0	0	1	1	1		Result of sum.
0	1	0	0	1	1	1	0		Left shift (Step c.i.). Multiplier bit (C) is *zero* (c.ii.)
0	1	0	0	1	1	1	0		This product, 78_{10} must be complemented (Step a.)
1	0	1	1	0	0	1	0		Twos complement representing -78_{10}

28.34 Binary Division. (A computer-based procedure called the **restoring method**.) In the decimal division $-19 \div 6 = -3$ remainder 1, -19 is the **dividend**, 6 is the **divisor** and 3 is the **quotient**.

Steps. (These should be read in conjunction with the example.)

a. The division should be performed on positive values and the sign corrected at the end.

b. Shift the divisor left until the most significant bits align with the divisor (beneath the left-hand end of the dividend). Record the number of shifts made.

c. Subtract the divisor from the dividend (by adding the twos complement).

d. Shift the quotient one place left.

e. i. If the result of Step c. is negative, *restore* the dividend to its previous value by adding back the divisor.

 ii. If the result of Step c. is positive, add one to the quotient.

f. Shift the remainder one place left.

g. With the remainder as the new dividend return to Step c.

h. Repeat these steps as many times as the divisor was shifted in Step b.

28.35 Example. To evaluate $-19 \div 6.$ ($19_{10} = 10011_2$, $+6_{10} = 0110_2$, $-6_{10} = 1010_2$)

Sign Bit	WORKING ON DIVIDENDS & REMAINDERS					COMMENTS — Three lines of preliminary work followed by main steps.		Q					
0	1	0	0	1	1	Dividend							
0	1	1	0	0	0	Step b. The divisor "6" has been shifted 2 places left.							
1	0	1	0	0	0	Twos complement of the divisor		QUOTIENT					
0	1	0	0	1	1	Dividend	Start with zero quotient	0	0	0	0	0	0
1	0	1	0	0	0	Subtract divisor (Step c.)	No change	0	0	0	0	0	0
1	1	1	0	1	1	Result of subtraction	(Step d.) Shift left	0	0	0	0	0	0
0	1	1	0	0	0	Restore dividend (Step e.i.)	No change	0	0	0	0	0	0
0	1	0	0	1	1	Remainder, ie, restored dividend	No change	0	0	0	0	0	0
1	0	0	1	1	0	Shift left (Step f.)	No change	0	0	0	0	0	0
1	0	1	0	0	0	Subtract divisor (Step c.)	No change	0	0	0	0	0	0
0	0	1	1	1	0	Result of subtraction	(Step d.) Shift left	0	0	0	0	0	0
0	1	1	1	0	0	Shift remainder left (Step f.)	(Step e.ii.) one added	0	0	0	0	0	1
1	0	1	0	0	0	Subtract divisor (Step c.)	No change	0	0	0	0	0	1
0	0	0	1	0	0	Result of subtraction	(Step d.) Shift left	0	0	0	0	1	0
0	0	0	1	0	0	Remainder = 1. The 2 shifts (Step b.) tell us the point is 2 places in from the right	(Step e.ii.) One added	0	0	0	0	1	1
0	0	0	1	0	0		Twos complement	1	1	1	1	0	1

At this stage we have the result -19 divided by 6 is -3 remainder 1. The procedure can be continued to obtain the quotient to greater accuracy.

GRAY'S (OR CYCLIC) CODE

28.36 This is also BDC code, but **not** 8421 weighted. The weighting is twice the binary power less one. Zeroes may be ignored, but in calculating values one works from the **leftmost** 1 to the **rightmost**, alternately adding and subtracting weighted values. The table below should make this clearer.

Note.

i. This bizarre code has the feature that the addition of one to any number results in only one bit being altered.

ii. The feature mentioned in i. makes it suitable for use in mechanical, optical or electronic counting mechanisms, because the load or signal changes evenly and aids accurate readings (see iii).

iii. Gray's Code is sometimes used for disc and drum drives for the purpose of reading rotational positions.

iv. the code is *not* useful for arithmetic purposes.

Decimal	Weightings n	Gray's Code 8 4 2 1	Comment
	2n - 1	15 7 3 1	
0		0 0 0 0	
1		0 0 0 1	
2		0 0 1 1	3 less 1
3		0 0 1 0	3
4		0 1 1 0	7 less 3
5		0 1 1 1	7 less 3 plus 1
6		0 1 0 1	7 less 1
7		0 1 0 0	7
8		1 1 0 0	15 less 7
9		1 1 0 1	15 less 7 plus 1

SUMMARY

28.37 a. Complements are used for representing negative numbers and for subtraction because they are convenient and efficient.

b. Two types of complement are used.

c. Binary multiplication uses shift and add. Binary division uses shift and subtract.

d. The range of numbers stored in a given word or register depends on the word size, position of the point, and choice of complementation method.

POINTS TO NOTE

28.38 a. A computer that uses BCD arithmetic or some other form of string arithmetic is called a "decimal computer".

b. BCD arithmetic is favoured for some commercial purposes because of the saving in conversion time, but pure binary arithmetic is usually preferable.

c. The methods illustrated in this chapter are computer-based methods as required in examinations. Quicker, manual methods are inappropriate.

d. When BCD is referred to we should strictly speaking call it 8421-weighted BCD code because there are alternative BCD codes. XS3 is one example of an alternative BCD code. Another example is Gray's Code.

e. Re-read the note to 26.17 for further understanding of machine methods.

STUDENT SELF-TESTING QUESTIONS

1. Find
   a. $1101_2 + 1001_2$

   b. $110110_2 + 100111_2$

   c. $10101_2 + 11011_2$

   d. $11110_2 + 10101_2$
2. Do these octal additions.
   a. $27 + 53$

   b. $46 + 675$
3. Do these Hex additions.
   a. $D5F + 4AC$

   b. $BCA + E23$

STUDENT SELF-TESTING QUESTIONS CONTINUED

4. Do these decimal sums using BCD. Check your answer.

    a. $7 + 4$

    b. $294 + 328$

5. Give these 8-digit binary ones and twos complement representation of

    a. -21_{10}

    b. -39_{10}

6. Use 4-bit representation and twos complement to do this decimal subtraction in binary: $7 - 4 = 3$

7. Convert these binary numbers to decimal.

    i.   0.11

    ii. 0.1101

    iii. 0.0111

    iv. 10.101

    v.   101.011

8. Convert from decimal to binary.

    i.   0.3125

    ii. 0.9375

    iii. 6.1875

    iv. 0.53125

    v.   0.2

9. a. Given that you can convert octal fractions to binary by writing down the binary equivalent of each octal digit, convert these octal fractions to binary (eg, $0.3_8 = 0.011_2$)

        i.   0.36

        ii. 0.65

        iii. 0.742

    b. Using a similar rule for hexadecimal fractions (eg, $0.3_{16} = 0.0011_2$) convert these hex fractions to binary.

        i.   0.2B

        ii. 0.3CF

        iii. 0.5B9

    c. Evaluate 11×3 and $11 \div 3$ decimal using binary multiplication and division.

QUESTIONS WITHOUT ANSWERS

11. Convert 1101 1101 1011. 1110 0011$_2$ to decimal, octal and hex.

12. Convert $C4F.B_{16}$ and $EB4.5_{16}$ to binary. Subtract the larger value from the smaller one using twos complements and then express your answer in base 10.

GLOSSARY CHECKLIST

29: Fixed-point and Floating-point Arithmetic

INTRODUCTION

29.1 This chapter introduces the two basic methods of number representation used in computers. A method of representation is judged in terms of the range, scale and accuracy that it provides, so these features are also explained. The basic ideas of number representation were introduced in chapter 15 as part of the description of numerical data types. In that chapter emphasis was placed on considering number types from the point of view of a programmer using a high-level language. Here, the emphasis is upon the details of the binary representation of stored numbers and any reference to programming is in the context of low-level languages, where details of storage are more visible to the programmer than they are in high-level languages.

FIXED-POINT NUMBER REPRESENTATION

29.2 For fixed-point number representation the programmer requires:

    a. A computer-storage location or register of sufficient size to store all the digits of the number.

    b. The ability to keep track of where the point lies himself. Convention dictates a **fixed** position for the point at the right-hand side of the units column.

29.3 Example. ♦ indicates the position of the point.

    a. Decimal example for a 5-digit representation.

        i. If the programmer assumes the point position to be:

$$\boxed{}\boxed{}\boxed{}\;♦\;\boxed{}\boxed{}$$

        then $\boxed{0}\boxed{1}\boxed{3}\boxed{7}\boxed{5}$ represents 13.75

        and $\boxed{3}\boxed{8}\boxed{6}\boxed{2}\boxed{4}$ represents 386.24

        ii. If the programmer assumes the point position to be:

$$\boxed{}\boxed{}\;♦\;\boxed{}\boxed{}\boxed{}$$

        then $\boxed{1}\boxed{3}\boxed{7}\boxed{5}\boxed{0}$ represents 13.75

        and $\boxed{3}\boxed{8}\boxed{6}\boxed{2}\boxed{4}$ represents 38.624

    b. Binary example for an 8-digit representation.

        i. If the programmer assumes the point position to be:

$$\boxed{}\boxed{}\boxed{}\boxed{}\boxed{}\boxed{}\;♦\;\boxed{}\boxed{}$$

        then $\boxed{0}\boxed{0}\boxed{1}\boxed{1}\boxed{0}\boxed{1}\boxed{1}\boxed{1}$ represents 13.75

        and $\boxed{0}\boxed{0}\boxed{0}\boxed{1}\boxed{0}\boxed{0}\boxed{1}\boxed{0}$ represents 4.5

        ii. If the programmer assumes the point position to be:

$$\boxed{}\boxed{}\boxed{}\boxed{}\;♦\;\boxed{}\boxed{}\boxed{}\boxed{}$$

        then $\boxed{0}\boxed{1}\boxed{1}\boxed{0}\boxed{1}\boxed{1}\boxed{1}\boxed{0}$ represents 13.75

        and $\boxed{0}\boxed{0}\boxed{0}\boxed{1}\boxed{0}\boxed{0}\boxed{1}\boxed{0}$ represents 2.25

29.4 Usage.

    a. Only by knowing the assumed position of the point is it possible to determine the value of a stored number, eg, compare the storage of the numbers 4.5 and 2.25 in 29.3b.

    b. When using fixed-point representation it is the *responsibility of the programmer* to keep track of the point position. This task is simplified by

    i. maintaining the same assumed point position throughout all calculations
    or,

    ii. restricting the type of number representation. This leads to three basic classifications of fixed-point representation:

        A. Mid-point representation in which there are digits both before and after the point.

        B. Integer representations in which there are no digits after the decimal point.

        C. Fraction representations in which there are no digits before the decimal point.

29.5 The decimal examples given in paragraph 3, and those given later, could be represented in BCD. However, the same principles apply to BCD representations and so the details have been omitted in the interests of clarity.

FLOATING-POINT NUMBER REPRESENTATIONS

29.6 For floating-point number representations the programmer requires:

    a. A computer-storage location or register of sufficient size to store all the significant digits of the number. (This part is called the **mantissa**.)

    b. Additional storage space to store the position of the point. This additional space may be within the same or a separate location. (This part is called the **exponent**).

29.7 Examples.

    a. Decimal examples with a 5-digit mantissa and a 3-digit exponent.

MANTISSA ie, 5 digits of the number					EXPONENT ie, position of point from the left				Number represented. **Note** The position of the point "floats" between the digits
1	3	7	5	0	0	0	2		$.13750 \times 10^2 = 1.375$
1	3	7	5	0	0	0	1		$.13750 \times 10^1 = 1.375$
3	8	6	2	4	0	0	3		$.38624 \times 10^3 = 386.24$
3	8	6	2	4	0	0	0		$.38624 \times 10^0 = .38624$

    b. Binary examples using a total of 12 bits and twos complement for negative values.

MANTISSA Sign bit				Fraction				EXPONENT				Number represented
0	1	1	0	1	1	1	0	0	1	0	0	$.110111_2 \times 2^4 = 1101.11_2 = 13.75_{10}$
0	1	0	0	1	0	0	0	0	0	1	1	$.1001_2 \times 2^3 = 100.1_2 = 4.5_{10}$
0	1	0	0	1	0	0	0	0	0	1	0	$.1001_2 \times 2^2 = 10.01_2 = 2.25_{10}$
0	1	0	0	0	0	0	0	1	1	1	1	$.1_2 \times 2^{-1} = 0.01_2 = 0.25_{10}$
1	0	0	1	0	0	1	0	0	1	0	0	$-.110111_2 \times 2^4 = -1101.11_2$ $= -13.75_{10}$

    c. These examples suggest the **general form**, which is $n = f.r^e$
    where

        i. "n" is the number,

        ii. "f" is the **mantissa**, which is a *fraction* sometimes called the **argument**,

        iii. "r" is the **radix** or base, and

        iv. "e" is the **exponent**, which is an *integer* sometimes called the **characteristic**.

29.8 Take care over the following unfortunate features of this terminology.

    a. In **fixed-point** computer representations of numbers the points position *between* two bits *need not remain* in a *fixed position* in a storage location since the programmer may move it.

    b. In **floating-point** computer representations of numbers the point *remains fixed* at the left-hand end of the mantissa.

COMPARING FIXED POINT AND FLOATING POINT

29.9 Speed. Computers can perform fixed-point arithmetic faster than floating-point arithmetic because extra work is involved in calculations with floating-point numbers. Hardware may be used to do floating-point arithmetic, but this is usually an option costing extra. Floating point saves the programmer work but is still not as fast as fixed-point arithmetic.

29.10 Range, Scale and Accuracy.

   a. Fixed-point representation limits the range and scale of the numbers being represented.

   b. Floating-point representation gives greater flexibility in range and scale, usually at the cost of accuracy.

29.11 Examples. We take a simple case to clarify ideas. Suppose just 3 decimal digits may be used to represent positive numbers. We can now see how they may be utilised.

   a. Fixed-point case. *Three-figure accuracy* is possible. The point position determines range and scale.

   i. With the point to the extreme left fractional representations $\blacklozenge$ 000 through $\blacklozenge$ 999 are possible. The **range** (difference between largest and smallest) is 0.999. The **scale** is such that the right-most digit represents units of .001.

   ii. With the point to the extreme right, integers from $\blacklozenge$ 000 through $\blacklozenge$ 999 are possible. The **range** is 999 and the **scale** unit is 1.

   b. Floating-point case. No more than *two-figure accuracy* is possible. We will consider that case, ie, assume a 2-digit mantissa and single-digit exponent.

   i. **Range.** The smallest number possible is $\blacklozenge$ 00 $\times 10^0 = 0$ and the largest number is $\blacklozenge$ 99 $\times 10^9 = 990\,000\,000$. Hence the range is 990 000 000.

   ii. **Scale.** When the exponent is 0 the mantissa is in units of 0.01 and when the exponent is 9 the mantissa is in units of 10 000 000.

   iii. **Accuracy.** Reducing the accuracy to single-digit values could allow a 2-digit exponent with even greater range and scale change.

   Note: Floating-point scale is adjusted automatically for each number represented.

FIXED-POINT ARITHMETIC

29.12 The procedures introduced in chapter 28 apply directly to fixed-point arithmetic. It remains for us to examine the range and accuracy of binary representations in detail.

29.13 Examples of binary representations. An 8-bit register holds numbers in twos complement form with the leftmost bit as sign bit. Maximum and minimum positive and negative numbers are represented. Seven-bit accuracy is available.

   a. Example of integer representation.

REPRESENTATION								VALUE (in decimal)	COMMENT
Sign bit									
0	1	1	1	1	1	1	1	$= 2^7 - 1 = 127$	Maximum positive
0	0	0	0	0	0	0	1	$= 2^0 = 1$	Minimum positive
1	1	1	1	1	1	1	1	$= -2^0 = -1$	Least negative
1	0	0	0	0	0	0	1	$= -2^7 = -128$	Most negative

   b. The example is repeated here with a fractional representation.

REPRESENTATION								VALUE (in decimal)	COMMENT
Sign bit	← Point Position								
0	1	1	1	1	1	1	1	$= 1 - \frac{1}{2^7}$	Maximum positive
0	0	0	0	0	0	0	1	$= \frac{1}{2^7}$	Minimum positive
1	1	1	1	1	1	1	1	$= -\frac{1}{2^7}$	Least negative
1	0	0	0	0	0	0	0	$= -1$	Most negative
1	0	0	0	0	0	0	1	$= -1\left(1 - \frac{1}{2^7}\right)$	Most negative fraction

If arithmetic produces results beyond the range of representation they must be handled in some way. We now see how this problem is overcome.

29.14 Overflow and Underflow.

  a. Overflow occurs when the result of an arithmetic operation is too large to be stored in the location allocated to it.

  b. Underflow occurs when the result is too small to be stored in the location allocated to it.
  All overflow and underflow should be detected and corrected if possible.

29.15 Examples given a 5-bit word with 4-bit accuracy and leftmost bit as sign bit. All numbers are integers.

a. Sign Bit	BINARY SUM (ADDITION)				DECIMAL VALUES
0	1	1	0	0	12
0	0	1	1	0	6
1	0	0	1	0	18

	b. Sign Bit	BINARY SUM (ADDITION)				DECIMAL VALUES
	1	0	1	0	0	−12
	1	1	0	1	0	− 6
1	0	1	1	1	0	−18

a and b are examples of overflow. The results are too large, which is easily detected since the sign bit of the sum is different to the sign bits of the two numbers being added together.

  c. If 6 were divided by 12 in this representation the result $.1_2$ would be too small to represent, ie, underflow would occur.

29.16 Detecting overflow. (Detected values will be lost unless they are stored elsewhere immediately they occur.)

  a. Using an extra bit, which is added to the left of the sign bit. Procedure:

    i. The extra bit is set to the same value as the sign bit before addition or subtraction.

    ii. The modified numbers are added or subtracted.

    iii. If the extra bit and sign bit differ after the operation then overflow has occurred.

  b. An alternative method not requiring an extra bit can be used but it is more complicated:

    i. With ADD, if signs differ, and with SUBTRACT, if signs are the same, overflow cannot occur.

    ii. In other cases the sign can be predicted, ie:
    For A + B if sign (A) = sign (B) then result should be sign (A)
    For A − B if sign (A) ≠ sign (B) then result should be sign (A)

    A wrong sign will indicate overflow.

Examples of (a) and (b) above.

a. Extra bit	Sign bit	BINARY SUM (ADDITION)				DECIMAL VALUES
0	0	1	1	0	0	12
0	0	0	0	1	1	3
0	0	1	1	1	1	15
0 = 0		Bits the same: no overflow				

b. Extra bit	Sign bit	BINARY SUM (ADDITION)				DECIMAL VALUES
0	0	1	1	0	0	12
0	0	0	1	1	0	6
0	1	0	0	1	0	18
0 ≠ 1		Bits differ: overflow				

29.17 Double precision. One way to reduce overflow is to increase the storage length allocated to each number representation. If one location in memory is not long enough then two adjacent locations can be used. A number stored in this way is called a **double-precision number** or **double-length number.** Double precision is used:

  a. When the use of a single location will not give sufficient accuracy or range, as is often the case with small computers with word lengths less than 24 bits.

  b. For multiplication where products will be double the length of the multiplicands.

29.18 Double-precision arithmetic is arithmetic using double-precision numbers. It is slower, but machines with longer words tend to be more expensive so this method is often employed. The details go beyond the scope of this book, but the ideas involved are indicated by this example in which for simplicity we assume each location is 4 bits long.

DOUBLE PRECISION NUMBERS								COMMENT
First Location				Second Location				Example of
Sign bit	More significant bits			Carries "C"	Less significant bits			$25_{10} + 15_{10}$ ie $11001_2 + 1111_2$
0	0	1	1	0	0	0	1	$25_{10} = 11001_2$
0	0	0	1	0	1	1	1	$15_{10} = 1111_2$
0	0	0	1	1	0	0	0	Pseudocode Step 1
0	0	0	1	1	0	0	0	Pseudocode Step 3
0	0	1	0	0	0	0	0	and Step 4
0	0	1	1	0	0	0	0	Pseudocode Step 5
0	1	0	1	0	0	0	0	Result $101000_2 = 40_{10}$

```
Begin
        Add less significant halves          (* Step 1)
        if
                carry = 1                     (* Step 2*)
        then
                Add 1 to the more significant half
                   of the number             (* Step 3 *)
                carry := 0                    (* Step 4 *)
        endif
        Add more significant halves          (Step 5 *)
end
```

FLOATING-POINT ARITHMETIC

29.19 Standard form. You will see that 0.125×10^2 and 0.0125×10^3 are alternative floating-point representations of the same number. It proves useful in practice to use only those representations which have mantissa values within some specified range. Such representations are said to be in **Standard form**.

29.20 Example. In decimal we can specify the mantissa "m" by

$$+0.1 \leq m < +1 \text{ and } -1 < m \leq -0.1$$

So for example 0.125×10^2 *is* in standard form but 0.0125×10^3 *is not*. The representation of zero is a special case which will be dealt with later.

29.21 Standard form for binary floating-point numbers.

The range for the mantissa "f" is $\frac{1}{2} \leq f < 1$ and $-1 \leq f \leq -\frac{1}{2}$. This choice of mantissa range enables the detection and correction of **temporary overflow** of the mantissa during floating-point arithmetic. A 7-bit floating-point number is used to illustrate the important points in the following examples. Note carefully that the exponents are powers of 2.

29.22 Examples with this representation:

MANTISSA (fraction)				EXPONENT (Integer)		
sign bit	●			sign bit		

STANDARD FORM MANTISSA							
Positive Mantissa $\frac{1}{2} \le f < 1$				Mantissa Values	Negative Mantissa $-1 \le f < -\frac{1}{2}$			Mantissa Values

Positive Mantissa				Mantissa Values	Negative Mantissa				Mantissa Values
0	1	0	0	$\frac{1}{2}$	1	0	0	0	-1
0	1	0	1	$\frac{5}{8}$	1	0	0	1	$-\frac{7}{8}$
0	1	1	0	$\frac{3}{4}$	1	0	1	0	$-\frac{3}{4}$
0	1	1	1	$\frac{7}{8}$	1	0	1	1	$-\frac{5}{8}$

Assume an exponent value of zero, in which case the mantissa value is the value represented.

Note: The sign bit and adjacent bit differ in *all* cases. *Any* representation in which the sign bit and adjacent bit are *equal* will be *detected* as an illegal (overflow) representation, (ie, representation is out of range).

29.23 Normalisation (Standardisation).

The mantissa 0.001 for $\frac{1}{8}$ is not in standard form. To convert its representation into standard form, ie, to **normalize** it, we can apply this general procedure for **normalisation**:

a. Shift the mantissa n bits left or right as necessary.

b. If shifted left, subtract n from the exponent.

c. If shifted right, add n to the exponent.

Examples.

a. Subtracting $\frac{1}{2}$ from $\frac{5}{8}$ could give rise to this unconventional representation of $\frac{1}{8}$, which must be corrected.

MANTISSA				EXPONENT			COMMENT
0	0	0	1	0	0	0	$\frac{1}{8}$ **not** in standard form.
0	1	0	0	1	1	0	Mantissa shifted two places left so 2 subtracted from exponent, ie, $\frac{1}{2} \times 2^{-2}$

b. Adding $\frac{5}{8}$ to $\frac{7}{8}$ could give rise to this unconventional representation of $1\frac{1}{2}$, which must be corrected.

MANTISSA				EXPONENT			COMMENT
1	1	0	0	0	0	0	$1\frac{1}{2}$ **not** in standard form (could be confused with $-\frac{1}{2}$)
0	1	1	0	0	0	1	Mantissa shifted 1 place right so 1 added to exponent, ie, $\frac{3}{4} \times 2^1$

29.24 During addition or subtraction temporary overflow often occurs, but normalisation is easy, as can be seen from these further examples.

	REPRESENTATIONS			COMMENTS
	MANTISSA	EXPONENT	DECIMAL WORKING	
a.	1 0 0 0	0 0 0	-1×2^0	Signs differ so a left shift
	0 1 0 0	0 0 0	$+\frac{1}{2} \times 2^0$ ADD	will be required.
	1 1 0 0	0 0 0	$-\frac{1}{2} \times 2^0$	Correct result but not in standard form.
	1 0 0 0	1 1 1	-1×2^{-1}	Mantissa shifted left 1 bit NORMALISED RESULT
b.	0 1 1 1	0 0 0	$+\frac{7}{8} \times 2^0$	Signs differ so a left shift
	1 0 1 1	0 0 0	$-\frac{5}{8} \times 2^0$ ADD	will be required.
	0 0 1 0	0 0 0	$+\frac{1}{4} \times 2^0$	Correct result but not in standard form.
	0 1 0 0	1 1 1	$\frac{1}{2} \times 2^{-1}$	Mantissa shifted left 1 bit
c.	0 1 0 0	0 0 0	$+\frac{1}{2} \times 2^0$	Signs same so a right shift
	0 1 1 0	0 0 0	$+\frac{3}{4} \times 2^0$ ADD	will be required.
	1 0 1 0	0 0 0	$+\frac{5}{4} \times 2^0$	Correct result but not in standard form.
	0 1 0 1	0 0 1	$+\frac{5}{8} \times 2^1$	Mantissa shifted right 1 bit Least significant bit is lost.
d.	1 0 0 0	0 0 0	-1×2^0	Signs same so a right shift
	1 0 1 0	0 0 0	$-\frac{3}{4} \times 2^0$ ADD	will be required.
	0 0 1 0	0 0 0	$-\frac{7}{4} \times 2^0$	Correct result but not in standard form
	1 0 0 1	0 0 1	$-\frac{7}{8} \times 2^1$	Mantissa shifted right. Sign bit replaced. Least significant bit is lost.
e.	0 1 0 0	0 0 0	$+\frac{1}{2} \times 2^0$	Sign same so a right shift.
	0 1 0 1	0 0 0	$+\frac{5}{8} \times 2^0$ ADD	will be required.
	1 0 0 1	0 0 0	$+1\frac{1}{8}$ (Taken for $-\frac{7}{8}$ if left!)	Correct result but sign indicates overflow.
	0 1 0 0	0 0 1	$+\frac{1}{2} \times 2^1$	Mantissa shifted right 1 bit. Least significant bit is lost so value becomes 1 not $1\frac{1}{8}$.

29.25 Range of standard-form floating-point representations.

a. In floating-point representations:

i. The most positive number occurs with the largest positive mantissa and largest positive exponent.

ii. The least positive number occurs with the smallest positive mantissa and largest negative exponent. **This number is often used as the standard form representation of zero since a zero mantissa is out of range.** Alternatively, zero must be handled as a special case.

iii. The least negative number occurs with the least negative mantissa and largest negative exponent.

iv. The most negative number occurs with the most negative mantissa and most positive exponent.

Note.

i. **Floating-point overflow** occurs if the *exponent* overflows.

ii. Some machines automatically set underflow values to zero.

b. Examples. Zero representations shown here are not typical. Typical values would be $\pm 10^{-30}$ or smaller.

MANTISSA				EXPONENT			COMMENT
0	1	1	1	0	1	1	Most positive number
$+(1 - \frac{1}{2^3})$				+3			$(1 - \frac{1}{2^3}) \times 2^3 = \frac{7}{8} \times 8 = +7$
0	1	0	0	1	0	0	Least positive number (Represents zero)
$+\frac{1}{2}$				−4			$(\frac{1}{2}) \times 2^{-4} = +\frac{1}{32} = +0.03125$
1	0	1	1	1	0	0	Least negative number (Alternative representation of zero).
$-(\frac{1}{2} - \frac{1}{2^3})$				−4			$-(\frac{1}{2} - \frac{1}{2^3}) \times 2^{-4} = -\frac{1}{2^5} + \frac{1}{2^7} = -0.0234375$
1	0	0	0	0	1	1	Most negative number
−1				+3			$-1 \times 2^3 = -8$

29.26 General method for addition and subtraction.

a. Line up points by making the exponents equal. (Right-hand shifts should be used so as to lose least significant digits instead of most significant digits.)

b. Add or subtract mantissas.

c. Normalise result.

29.27 Examples. The method is demonstrated in decimal for simplicity.

a.	$(0.28 \times 10^3) + (0.12 \times 10^2)$					
	0	2	8	0	× 10^3	
	0	0	1	2	× 10^3	Shifted right to align points
	0	2	9	2		Mantissa added, result in standard form
b.	$(0.2 \times 10^3) - (0.24 \times 10^3)$					
	0	2	8	0	× 10^3	
	0	2	4	0	× 10^3	Points already aligned
	0	0	4	0	× 10^3	Result needs normalisation
	0	4	0	0	× 10^2	Result in standard form

29.28 Multiplication and division of floating-point numbers.

a. Multiplication rule:

i. Multiply the mantissas

ii. add the exponents

iii. normalise.

b. Division rule:

i. divide the mantissas

ii. subtract the exponents

iii. normalise.

ie

If the numbers are $n_1 = f_1 . r^{e_1}$ and $n_2 = f_2 . r^{e_2}$

Then

$$n_1 \times n_2 = (f_1 \times f_2) \times r^{e_1 + e_2}$$
$$n_1 / n_2 = (f_1 / f_2) \times r^{e_1 - e_2}$$

29.29 Examples.

a.	$(0.12 \times 10^2) + (0.253 \times 10^3)$						
	0 • 1	2	0	×	10^2		Assume 3 digit accuracy in mantissa fraction.
	0 • 2	5	3	×	10^3		
	0 • 0	3	0	×	10^{2+3}		Mantissa multiplied. Result is .03036; partial underflow. Exponents added
	0 • 3	0	0	×	10^4		Result in standard form
b.	$(0.156 \times 10^3) \div (0.12 \times 10^2)$						
	0 • 1	5	6	×	10^3		
	0 • 1	2	0	×	10^2		
	1 • 3	0	0	×	10^{3-2}		Mantissa divided. Exponents subtracted
	0 • 1	3	0	×	10^2		Result in standard form

29.30 Guard bits. If in example 29a we had provided a temporary extra digit for the result, then our result in its final standard form would have been 0.303×10^4, and a more accurate value. An even more serious problem is the temporary underflow of an exponent, which can be handled by placing an extra bit at the right-hand end of the accumulator. This extra bit is called a **guard bit** and preserves floating-point accuracy.

29.31 Exponents of floating-point numbers are often represented by **excess 64 code**. This exponent is a 7-bit code in the range -64 to $+63$ and each value is coded as a positive value in binary by adding 64, eg, 5 is coded as $(64 + 5) = 69$ and -12 is coded as $(64 - 12) = 52$.

SUMMARY

29.32 a. The two basic methods of binary number representation used in computers are fixed-point representation and floating-point representation.

b. The two methods may be contrasted in terms of range, scale, accuracy, and convenience, speed and cost in doing arithmetic.

c. Floating-point numbers are stored in **normal** or **standard** form with limits to the range of representation of the mantissa to allow overflow checks.

d. Double precision may be used to provide greater accuracy.

e. The use of extra bits at the end of the accumulators can aid overflow checking and guard bits can protect accuracy during temporary overflow.

POINTS TO NOTE

29.33 a. The physical features of the computer, notably word length, have a direct bearing on the magnitude of numbers representable in single precision.

b. It is the responsibility of the programmer to see that his program keeps track of the point when using fixed-point arithmetic.

c. Fixed-point arithmetic is preferred for most commercial computing because of its speed, and commercial computers usually have an adequate word length to deal with all numbers in single precision. Commercial computers using the language COBOL often store numerical values in fixed-point BCD form. This saves the time needed to convert the numbers into fixed-point pure binary, but arithmetic in BCD is slower. On balance, the saving in conversion time pays off because of the small amount of arithmetic performed compared with the number of data items that would be converted.

d. Floating-point arithmetic is often required for scientific computing in order to handle the variety of number ranges and scales. To cater for the accuracy sometimes required double-precision floating-point facilities are often available on scientific machines.

e. Extending precision as in double-precision fixed-point arithmetic is just one example of **extended precision**, eg, a microcomputer with 8-bit words may use 7 words to represent a floating-point number.

f. To estimate the number of bits required to store a decimal number as a fixed-point binary number you may assume that it requires *roughly* $3\frac{1}{3}$ bits per decimal digit.

STUDENT SELF-TESTING QUESTIONS

1. A 12-bit register is to be used to hold fixed-point numbers. State the largest and smallest positive and negative numbers that can be represented in arrangements a and b below. Use twos complement representation.

   a.

   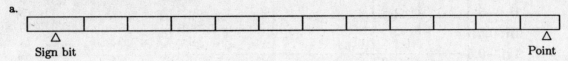

   Sign bit   Point

   b.

   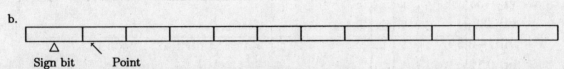

   Sign bit   Point

2. Place these decimal numbers into this standard form: $n = f \times r^e$ where n is the number, f is a mantissa (fixed point part), $r = 10_{10}$ is the radix and e is the exponent.
   Take $0.1 \leq f < 1$ or $-1 < f \leq -0.1$
   eg $25 = 0.25 \times 10^2$

   i. 36

   ii. 159

   iii. -276

   iv. -56724

   v. 376.992

   vi. 36.5×10^2

   vii. -0.0498×10^3

   viii. 9.824×10^{-3}

   ix. -15.62×10^{-5}

   x. -0.026×10^{-6}

3. Give the relative advantages and disadvantages of fixed- and floating-point representation of numbers in computers.

4. a. How are signed binary integers represented in digital computers and what are the advantages and disadvantages of each representation?

   b. Express each of the following numbers, given in the scale named, in each of the other three named.

      i. Binary $+0.101$

      ii. Decimal -97

      iii. Octal $+237$

      iv. Hexadecimal $+E8$

   (B.C.S.Part 1)

5. a. What is the numerically largest negative integer that can be represented by 8 bits, using twos complement fixed-point storage? Give your answers in binary and denary.

   b. The floating-point representations of numbers are usually normalised. Why?

   (London)

STUDENT SELF-TESTING QUESTIONS CONTINUED

6. a. Show how each of these decimal numbers would be represented in a binary register using the floating-point representation indicated below.

    i. 5

    ii. −5

    iii. 0.5

    iv. −0.5

    v. 35

    vi. −35

    vii. 3.5_{10}

    viii. −3.5

    ix. 0.125

    x. −0.125

Mantissa (fraction twos complement)   Exponent (signed integer twos complement)

Sign bit   Point   Sign bit   Point

range of mantissa "m" $-1 \leq m < -\frac{1}{2}$ $\frac{1}{2} \leq m < 1$

b. State in decimal for this representation

    i. the most positive number

    ii. the least positive number

    iii. the most negative number

    iv. the least negative number

QUESTIONS WITHOUT ANSWERS

7. A 16-bit word is to be used to store floating-point numbers with 6 bits allocated to the exponent and 10 bits allocated to the fraction.

  a. Suggest how the format of the word could be organised.

  b. What is the largest positive number that can be represented?

  c. How many decimal digits accuracy can be guaranteed?

8. Consider the contents of the following 16-bit word:

1	0	0	1	0	1	1	1	0	0	1	0	0	1	0	1

What value is being represented if:

  a. The word holds an integer in fixed-point BCD 8421-weighted code?

  b. The word holds a mid-point binary number with 4 bits after the point?

  c. The word holds a binary integer?

State any assumptions that you make.

GLOSSARY CHECKLIST

30: Errors and Accuracy

INTRODUCTION

30.1 This chapter deals with types of errors, sources of errors, ways of dealing with errors in computer arithmetic and methods of preserving accuracy or avoiding errors.

30.2 **Errors (numerical errors).** An **error** occurs when the value used to represent some quantity is not the true value of that quantity, eg, errors occur if we use approximate values such as 2.5 instead of 2.53627. **Note that:**

a. A value may be *intentionally* used despite the fact that it may incur an error. The reasons for this may be those of:

   i. simplicity,

   ii. convenience,

   iii. cost,

   iv. necessity.

b. An error may be caused by a **mistake,** which is said to occur if the value used is other than the one intended, eg, writing 5.2 when meaning to write 2.5.

30.3 **Other errors.** The term "error" may also be used to describe situations that occur when a program **either** is not executed in the manner intended **or** produces results that are not correct. Causes for such errors include:

a. Faulty data.

b. Faulty software.

c. Faulty hardware.

(The last is by far the least common.)

30.4 **Absolute and relative errors.** (These definitions are general; computer-orientated examples come later.)

These are the two main types of error. They have both theoretical and practical importance.

Definitions:

a. **Absolute error.** This is the difference between the true value of quantity and the number used to represent it.

ie, Absolute error = Value used − True value.

eg, True value = 2.5, Value used = 3

Absolute error = 3.0 − 2.5 = 0.5

b. **Relative error** = $\dfrac{\text{Absolute error}}{\text{True Value}}$

for example, using the figures just given

Relative error = $\dfrac{0.5}{2.5}$ = 0.2

We may express the result algebraically as $E = \dfrac{U - T}{T}$

where E is the relative error, U is the used value and T is the true value. This formula can be rearranged into a useful form, which is

$$U = T\,[1 + E]$$

Note:

i. Alternative definitions of the absolute error ignore its sign, ie, they define it in terms of **numerical values** or **absolute values.**

ii. Since the true value may not always be known, the relative error may be approximated by using:

$$\text{Relative error} = \frac{\text{Absolute error estimate}}{\text{Used value}}$$

For small absolute errors this gives a reasonably accurate value.

SOURCES OF ERROR

30.5 These may include:

a. Data errors.
b. Transcription errors.
c. Conversion errors.
d. Rounding errors.
e. Computational errors.
f. Truncation errors.
g. Algorithmic errors.

We will now define and discuss these various sources of error.

30.6 Data errors. The data input to the computer may be subject to error because of limitations on the method of data collection. These limitations may include:

a. the accuracy to which it was possible to make measurements,
b. the skill of the observer, or
c. the resources available to obtain the data.

30.7 Transcription errors. These are errors (mistakes) in copying from one form to another.

a. Examples

i. Transposition, eg, typing 369 for 396.
ii. "Mixed doubles", eg, typing 3226 for 3326.

b. These errors may be reduced or avoided by using

i. Direct encoding (eg, OCR/OMR)
ii. Validation checks.

30.8 Conversion. When converting data from its input form, BCD say, to its stored form, pure binary say, some errors may be unavoidably incurred because of practical limits to accuracy. On output similar errors may occur. Further discussion will follow later.

30.9 Rounding errors frequently occur when doing manual decimal arithmetic. They may occur with even greater frequency in computer arithmetic.

a. Examples.

i. Writing 2.53627 as 2.54
ii. Writing $\frac{1}{3}$ as 0.3333.

b. A rounding error occurs when **not all the significant digits** (figures) are given, eg, when writing 2.54 we omit the *less significant digits* 6, 2 and 7.

30.10 Types of rounding.

a. **Rounding down,** sometimes called truncating, involves leaving off some of the less significant digits, thus producing a *lower* or *smaller* number, eg, writing 2.53 for 2.53627.

b. **Rounding up** involves leaving off some of the less significant digits, but the remaining least significant digit is increased by 1, thus making a *larger* number, eg, writing 2.54 for 2.53627.

c. **Rounding off** involves rounding up or down according to which of these makes the least change in the stated value, eg, 2.536 would be rounded up to 2.54 but 2.533 would be rounded down to 2.53. What to do in the case of 2.535 can be decided by an arbitrary rule such as "if the next significant digit is odd round up, if even round down." So using this rule 2.535 would round to 2.54 because "3" is odd.

30.11 Significant digits (figures) and decimal places. These are the two methods of describing rounded-off results. They are defined as follows.

a. **Decimal places.** A number is given to n decimal places (or nD) if there are n digits to the right of the decimal point.

Examples. 2.53627 is 2.54 to 2 decimal places

ie 2.53627 = 2.54   (2D)
    2.53627 = 2.536 (3D)
    4.203 = 4.20   (2D)
    0.00351 = 0.0035 (4D)

b. Significant figures. A number is given to n significant figures (or nS) if there are n digits used to express the number but excluding

i. all leading zeros and

ii. trailing zeros to the *left* of the decimal point.

Examples.	2.53627	=	2.54	(3S)
	57640	=	58000	(2S)
	0.00351	=	0.0035	(2S)
	4.203	=	4.20	(3S)

30.12 Computational errors occur as a result of performing arithmetic operations and are usually caused by overflow or rounding of intermediate results.

30.13 Truncation errors. We first need to define some terms. When numbers are placed in some specified order they form a **sequence**, eg, 1, 3, 5, 7, 9... or $\frac{1}{2}$, $\frac{1}{4}$, $\frac{1}{8}$, $\frac{1}{16}$ ... When a sequence is added it is called a **series** eg, $1 + 3 + 5 + 7 + 9 + ...$ or $\frac{1}{2} + \frac{1}{4} + \frac{1}{8} + \frac{1}{16} + ...$ Some series have many practical uses. For example the quantity π, used extensively in mathematics, can be evaluated to *any* required accuracy by using the formula:

$$\pi = 4 \times (1 - \frac{1}{3} + \frac{1}{5} - \frac{1}{7} + \frac{1}{9} - \frac{1}{11} + \frac{1}{13}......)$$

The series is an **infinite** series since it goes on as far as we care to take it. In practice we might only use the first few terms to get an approximate value. We **truncate** a series if, when we calculate its sum, we leave off all terms past a given one, eg,

$$1 - \frac{1}{3} + \frac{1}{5} - \frac{1}{7}$$

is a truncated series. A **truncation** error is an error resulting from the truncation of a series.

Note. *Rounding down* is also sometimes called **truncation**.

30.14 Algorithmic errors. An **algorithm** is a set of procedural steps used in the solution of a given problem and can be represented by pseudocode. Errors incurred by the execution of an algorithm are called **algorithmic errors**. A computer program is one type of algorithm. If two programs are available to perform a specified task, the one that produces the result with the greatest accuracy will have the smaller algorithmic error. Since each step in an algorithm may involve a **computational error**, the algorithm that achieves the result in fewer steps *may* have a smaller algorithmic error.

ERRORS IN COMPUTER ARITHMETIC

30.15 In manual arithmetic calculations we may wish to estimate the accuracy of the result given the accuracy of the data used in the calculation. The same problem exists with computer calculations, but we have to focus our attention on the errors introduced when the computer stores and handles data.

30.16 Rounding errors in stored data. Since all computers have a **finite word length** there is always a limit to the accuracy of the stored data, and many values will be **rounded** each time they are stored. The following factors are relevant.

a. For **fixed-point integer representation** there is good control over accuracy within the allowed range since there is no fractional part to be rounded.

b. In **other fixed-point representations**, where part or all of the number is fractional, rounding will occur often, but the precision provided may still allow reasonable control over accuracy during addition and subtraction.

c. In **floating-point representations** almost all number storage and calculations can lead to rounding errors.

d. Rounding should be **unbiased** if possible, ie, numbers should be rounded **off** rather than **up** or **down** when stored.

30.17 Unbiased rounding in binary.

Example. Consider a very simple case where only the first two binary fraction places are available, as shown here. Consider values between $\frac{1}{4}$ and $\frac{1}{2}$. Unbiased rounding is indicated by this diagram. (N is the number to be rounded.)

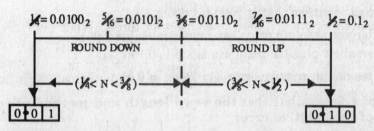

PLACE VALUES			NUMBER REPRESENTATION
1	½	¼	
0	0	0	0
0	0	1	¼
0	1	0	½
0	1	1	¾
1	0	0	1

$\frac{1}{4} = 0.0100_2$ $\frac{5}{16} = 0.0101_2$ $\frac{3}{8} = 0.0110_2$ $\frac{7}{16} = 0.0111_2$ $\frac{1}{2} = 0.1_2$

ROUND DOWN   **ROUND UP**

$\leftarrow (\frac{1}{4} < N < \frac{3}{8}) \rightarrow$ $\leftarrow (\frac{3}{8} < N < \frac{1}{2}) \rightarrow$

0	0	1

0	1	0

Note. The numbers with the *third* binary place "0" are rounded down whilst those with the same place "1" are rounded up. This suggests a general rule, which is: To round off a binary fraction to n places:

If the $(n+1)^{th}$ bit is zero, round down.
If the $(n+1)^{th}$ bit is one, round up.

30.18 Conversion errors. In converting fractions from decimal to binary for storage, rounding errors are often introduced.

Example. $\frac{4}{5}$ is easily represented as the decimal fraction 0.8. However, if we convert 0.8 to binary we discover that it can only be represented as a recurring fraction, ie, 0.1100110011001100 .... Suppose we are able to store only 6 bits of this fraction, ie, 0.110011. If we convert this stored value back to decimal we will get the value 0.796875 **not** 0.8! *Conversion errors like this are very common.*

30.19 Computational errors.

a. In general every arithmetic operation performed by a computer may produce a rounding error. The cause of this error will be one of:

   i. The limited number of bits available to store the result, ie, finite word length.

   ii. Overflow or underflow (also a consequence of ai).

   iii. Rounding in order to normalise a result.

b. The size of the error will depend on these two main factors:

   i. The size of the word length.

   ii. The method of rounding, up down, or off.

Control over these errors depends on factors listed in paragraph 16.

30.20 Relative errors in floating-point representation depend on the word length and method of rounding, as will now be demonstrated. For simplicity we will consider a decimal example. The results apply equally well to binary representations.

Suppose we have a representation that provides **3-digit accuracy** in the mantissa and adequate representation of the exponent and sign. So the 4-digit number 2594 will be *rounded* when stored as $+.259 \times 10^{+4}$. The relative error in this case is clearly

$$= \frac{-0.0004 \times 10^4}{0.2594 \times 10^4} \simeq -0.0015$$

You should notice that since the exponents cancel we need only consider mantissas. This we will do in the general case that follows.

30.21 Maximum relative error (denoted by $\in$). For a given representation we expect to obtain the largest relative error when we have the smallest possible mantissa with the largest absolute error (because we divide the latter by the former to obtain a value for $\in$).

Examples. (We continue with the previous example but disregard the sign of the error.)

a. For a *3-digit mantissa* that is *rounded off*

   i. The largest absolute error has numerical value 0.0005.

   ii. The smallest possible mantissa (see 20.19) is 0.100.

   iii. The maximum relative error $\in = \dfrac{0.0005}{0.100} = 0.005$.

b. For a *4-digit mantissa* that is *rounded off*

   i. The largest absolute error has numerical value 0.00005.

   ii. The smallest possible mantissa again is 0.100.

   iii. The maximum relative error $\in = \dfrac{0.00005}{0.100} = 0.0005$.

c. For a *3-digit mantissa* that is *rounded down*

   i. The largest absolute error has numerical value 0.001.

   ii. The smallest possible mantissa again is 0.100.

   iii. The maximum relative error $\in = \dfrac{0.001}{0.100} = 0.01$.

These examples demonstrate that **the word length and method of rounding affect the maximum size of the relative error**

30.22 Errors in stored results. All results stored in mantissas of the same length will be subject to the *same* maximum relative error $\in$. This will be the case for *any* floating-point arithmetic operation; add, subtract, multiply or divide.

30.23 The floating-point error formula. This formula is used to find the maximum error in the result of a floating-point arithmetic operation. This topic is somewhat more specialised than is required by most readers and so details are given in appendix 3.

FURTHER ERRORS IN COMPUTER ARITHMETIC

30.24 Order of operations. It is better to add "floating-point" numbers in order of magnitude if possible.

Example. To calculate $0.273000 + 0.001480 + 0.000862$.

The true value is 0.275342. We will do this sum two numbers at a time and round intermediate results just as a computer would do it. We have a choice of working (scanning) from right to left or from left to right. Assume the computer truncates intermediate results when it stores them with mantissas only 3 digits long.

a. WORKING LEFT TO RIGHT IN DESCENDING ORDER OF MAGNITUDE	COMMENTS	b. WORKING RIGHT TO LEFT IN ASCENDING ORDER OF MAGNITUDE
0.273000 0.001480	ADD	0.000862 0.001480
0.274480	Results	0.002342
0.274000 0.000862	Truncated to 3 figs Add next Number	0.002340 0.273000
0.274862 0.274000	Results Rounded to 3 figs	0.275340 0.275000

The third figure is wrong in a. but correct in b. As a general rule therefore do additions in order of magnitude of the numbers from smaller to larger.

30.25 Algorithmic errors. The errors produced when using an algorithm will frequently depend on

a. the order of the operations performed.

b. The number of operations performed.

If the errors from one stage of the algorithm are carried over to successive stages then the size of the error may "grow". These **accumulated errors**, as they are called, may ultimately make the result obtained very unreliable.

30.26 Example. To keep the example simple we will consider an artificial situation, but with modifications it becomes a common practical problem. Suppose the solution of a problem requires the same calculation to be performed on successive values of X from $\frac{1}{3}$ to 6 in steps of $\frac{1}{3}$, ie, X takes values $\frac{1}{3}$, $\frac{2}{3}$, 1, etc. Assume the problem is performed in decimal using *3-digit accuracy* at each stage. Two possible algorithms are shown here:

ALGORITHM A			ALGORITHM B
variables	SUCCESSIVE X VALUES	SUCCESSIVE X VALUES	variables
x : real			n : integer
	0.333	0.333	x : real
Begin	0.666	0.667	
x : = 0	0.999	1.00	Begin
repeat	1.33	1.33	n : = 0
x : = x + 333	1.66	1.67	repeat
(*Perform	1.99	2.00	n : = n + 1
Calculation*)	2.32	2.33	x : = n / 3
until x > 6	2.65	2.67	(*Perform
end	etc.	etc.	Calculation*)
			until n > 18
			end

Both sets of X values suffer from rounding, but algorithm A accumulates errors so that successive values become too low. Many simple decimal fractions become recurring fractions when converted to binary (see paragraph 18). An algorithm requiring steps of 0.1_{10} would need to deal with this problem for example.

METHODS THAT REDUCE ERRORS AND MAINTAIN ACCURACY

30.27 Nesting. This reduces the number of operations, thereby reducing error accumulation.

Example. To evaluate $3x^3 + 2x^2 + 5x + 1$ for a given x value use $((3x + 2)x + 5)x + 1$, starting with the innermost bracket and working outwards.

30.28 Batch adding. This is an extension of the method in paragraph 28. A set of numbers to be added is grouped into several batches containing numbers of similar magnitude. Each batch total is found, then the batch totals are added.

30.29 Finding a "small" root of a quadratic equation. When solving $ax^2 + bx + c = 0$ using the well-known formula

$$x = \frac{-b \pm \sqrt{b^2 - 4ac}}{2a}$$

difficulties arise if one root is close to zero. Suppose the roots are α and β then $(x - \alpha)(x - \beta) = 0$ ie, $x^2 - (\alpha + \beta)x + \alpha\beta = 0$

By comparison with $ax^2 + bx + c = 0$ we see that $\alpha\beta = c/a$ or $\beta = c/\alpha a$. So given one root we can find the other.

Example. To solve $100x^2 + 2502x + 50 = 0$

a = 100, b = 2502, c = 50

Working to 3-figure accuracy

$$x = \frac{-b \pm \sqrt{b^2 - 4ac}}{2a}$$

gives $x = -25$ or 0

but taking $\alpha = -25$

$\beta = \dfrac{c}{\alpha A} = \dfrac{50}{-25 \times 100} = -0.02$, the correct value for the other root.

ILL CONDITIONING

30.30 A problem is **ill conditioned** if small errors in the data used for its solution lead to large errors in the answer. **Equations are ill conditioned** if small changes in coefficients lead to large changes in the solution.

30.31 Example.

To solve $50x^2 - 215x + C = 0$ where C = 231 (3S).

Using C = 231 in the formula $x = \dfrac{-b \pm \sqrt{b^2 - 4ac}}{2a}$

we get $x = 2.1$ or $x = 2.2$. But $C = 231 \pm 0.5$ and if we use $C = 231.5$ in the formula we get no real solution!

SUMMARY

30.32 a. The two types of numerical error are the absolute error and relative error.

    b. Sources of numerical errors are:

        i. Data errors.

        ii. Transcription errors.

        iii. Conversion errors.

        iv. Rounding errors.

        v. Computational errors.

        vi. Truncation errors.

        vii. Algorithmic errors.

    c. Most values produced in floating-point arithmetic are subject to rounding errors.

    d. The size of the relative error in computer floating-point arithmetic is affected by the word length and method of rounding.

    e. In computer arithmetic care should be taken over:

        i. The order of operations performed.

        ii. Accumulated errors.

        iii. Choice of alternative formulae.

        iv. Ill conditioned problems.

POINTS TO NOTE

30.33 a. It is important to relate these topics to computer arithmetic. So in examination questions look for phrases suggesting this such as "working to three figures", which would suggest the rounding of intermediate stored results.

    b. Make use of these methods in you own programs, particularly your examination project. It will save you time and trouble and improve the quality of your work.

STUDENT SELF-TESTING QUESTIONS

1. a. Define the terms "Numerical Error", "Absolute Error", "Relative Error".

    b. State five sources of error.

2. Give the maximum value of

    i. the absolute error and

    ii. the relative error

for each of the following numbers. Assume they are rounded off to the number of digits specified.

    a. *80 (2S)*

    b. *0.125 (3S)*

    c. *350 (2S)*

    d. *6.25 (2D)*

3. a. State three causes of error in computer arithmetic.

    b. State the two main factors that affect the size of errors produced in computer arithmetic.

4. Assume that arithmetic is being done in 4-digit decimal floating-point arithmetic and that rounding off occurs where necessary what is the magnitude of the maximum relative error?

STUDENT SELF-TESTING QUESTIONS CONTINUED

5. Two systems store numbers in 16 bit words. The first system uses a fixed point representation with the point assumed to be after the tenth bit (from the left). The second system uses a normalised floating binary point representation with a ten bit mantissa and six bit exponent. Both systems store negative numbers and use two's complement notation.

Example: The floating point representation of 4 is

0100000000   000011

i. Compare the range of positive numbers in each system and examine the accuracy of the floating point representation of the largest number in the fixed point system. *(6 marks)*

ii. If in the fixed point system, two successive 16 bit memory locations contain the hexadecimal numbers 00DC and FD40, write down the denary equivalent of both numbers. *(4 marks)*

iii. In the floating point system write down the binary equivalent of the denary numbers $\frac{7}{32}$ and -24. *(4 marks)*

iv. Outline the main steps needed to multiply the two numbers in the floating point system. Include in your answer the steps required to normalise the result.

(6 marks)

(AEB)

QUESTIONS WITHOUT ANSWERS

8. Suggest a suitable procedure for evaluating $y = 2x^3 - 9x^2 + 12x - b$ for values of x between 0 and 3 so that accurate graphs based upon 30 points may be drawn for various values of b.

GLOSSARY CHECKLIST

Absolute error	30.4	Nesting	30.27
Absolute values	30.4	Numerical errors	30.2
Accumulated errors	30.25	Relative error	30.4
Algorithmic errors	30.25	Rounding down	30.10
Batch adding	30.28	Rounding errors	30.9
Computational errors	30.12,30.19	Rounding off	30.10
Conversion	30.8	Rounding up	30.10
Conversion errors	30.18	Significant digits	30.11
Data errors	30.6	Sources of error	30.5
Decimal places	30.11	Transcription errors	30.7
Floating-point error formula	30.23	Truncation	30.13
Ical values	30.4	Truncation errors	30.13
Ill conditioned	30.30	Truncation sequence	30.13
Maximum relative error	30.21	Truncation series	30.13
Mistake	30.2	Unbiased rounding	30.17

COMPUTER SYSTEMS ORGANISATION II

1. The next few chapters continue the subject of computer system organisation with more emphasis on the software. The program examples are given to illustrate methods rather than as a training in programming. In recent years most examinations have given less emphasis to low level programming and have concentrated more on the principles and practical implications.

2. Chapter 31 concentrates on machine language and consequently covers several aspects of machine operation.

3. Chapter 32 considers the use of low-level programming languages and uses programming examples for that purpose. After reading chapter 32 the reader may benefit from re-reading chapter 31.

4. Chapter 33 shows how various methods have been devised to overcome the difference in speeds between peripheral devices and processor so that the devices can operate at, or near, full speed with minimum sacrifice of processing time.

5. Chapter 34 examines the workings of the operating system.

31: Machine Language

INTRODUCTION

31.1 The purpose of this chapter is to demonstrate the various features of machine language. The chapter also explains how a computer can carry out instructions presented to it in machine language. It is assumed that you have by now acquired some programming skill, (eg, from chapters 15 – 19 and practical course work) and are ready to supplement that skill by taking a closer look at machine-language facilities. If you feel you still need more programming practise leave the detailed points from this chapter for a second reading.

31.2 A **machine language** is a (programming) language in which the instructions are in a form that allows the computer to perform them immediately, without any further translation being required.

31.3 Instructions in **machine language** are in the form of a **binary code**, also called **machine code**, and are called **machine instructions.**

31.4 Machine instructions are stored in the same way as data (chapter 6), and each instruction corresponds directly to a hardware facility on the machine for which it is written. The handling of instructions in the processor (chapter 13) will be discussed further in this chapter, and machine logic (chapter 26) is the instrument used.

31.5 The set of machine instructions that a computer can perform is called its **instruction set.** Any operation not provided by the hardware, and therefore not in the instruction set, can only be provided by using more than one instruction.

NB. This principle applies both at the microprogrammed level and at the machine level. In this chapter we are concerned with the machine level, not with microprogramming.

31.6 The size of the instruction set will affect all of the following items:

a. The cost of the machine: more hardware costs more money.

b. Speed and efficiency: if a large number of different instructions exist, then it is likely that a given task may be performed in fewer instructions than on a machine with a small instruction set.

c. Choice of word size and instruction format: a large instruction set implies that the function field of each instruction must have a larger number of bits. If the machine has a large word size it may be possible to fit each instruction into a single word, but in the case of most microcomputers and minicomputers instructions may each occupy several words. For example, in the case of the 8-bit Z80 microprocessor instructions may be 1, 2, 3 or 4 words long. In such cases an instruction fetch is a multiple fetch, one per word, and carries with it an obvious time penalty.

31.7 **Instruction format.** A machine instruction has several components. The **instruction format** is the size and arrangement of these components. Two major components are the **function code (opcode)**, which specifies the function or operation performed, and the **operand addresses**, which specifies the locations of the **operands** used. As was indicated in paragraph 6c, on a given machine there may be several instruction lengths and there may be an even greater variation in instruction formats. For example, on an IBM 370 there are 5 basic instruction formats, on the PDP 11 there are 13 and on the Z80 there are 26.

31.8 **Address format.** This is the part of the instruction format that deals with specifying the address of operands. Several quite different methods may be used. Their general features are given here and details of addressing will be given later. The main methods are:

a. **The three-address format.**
Each instruction specifies the address of two operands and gives a further address for the result of the operation, eg, addresses of two numbers and address for their sum. This method demands a long instruction in order to give the three addresses, and is therefore little used.

Example. | FUNCTION | ADDRESS | ADDRESS | ADDRESS |

b. **The two-address format.** Each instruction specifies the address of two operands. The result of an add operation would **replace** one of the two operands. It is an improvement over the three-address format.

Example. FUNCTION ADDRESS ADDRESS

c. **The one-and-a-half address format** (or one-address format). One operand is held in a special register or accumulator having first been fetched and placed there. The instruction specifies the address of the other operand, and the number of the accumulator, if there is more than one. The result is placed in the specified accumulator. This gives a further shortening of the instruction, since fewer bits are needed to specify accumulators than are needed to specify an operand address.

Examples. FUNCTION ADDRESS   Single-accumulator machine

or   FUNCTION AC ADDRESS   AC = Accumulator number.

d. **Between accumulator operations.** A one-and-a-half address format may be used to **fetch** or **load** operands into the accumulators from main store, but thereafter the instruction may just specify the two or three accumulators that are to be used for operands and results.

Example. FUNCTION AC AC   AC = Accumulator number.

NB. On small computers these instructions may be spread over several words. For example, a two-address format like the one shown in paragraph 8b would occupy three 16-bit words in a PDP-11.

TYPES OF INSTRUCTION

31.9 There are many ways of grouping or classifying the members of an instruction set and the choice of method will depend on the machine being described. The following headings often prove useful.

　a. Arithmetic and logic operations (instructions).

　b. Transfer of control or branch instruction.

　c. Load (fetch) and store instructions.

　d. Input/Output instructions.

　e. Memory reference instructions.

　f. Processor reference instructions.

31.10 **Arithmetic and logic operations (instructions).** These are instructions that use operations of the ALU. Typical examples are given here:

31.11 **Arithmetic operations.**

　a. Addition, subtraction, multiplication and division. The method will depend on the **address format**. Different operations will be required for fixed and floating numbers.(Details of arithmetic in chapters 28 and 29.)

　b. **Increment** and **decrement** operations, ie, increasing or decreasing the contents of an address or accumulator by 1.

　c. Negation and complementing, ie, producing ones or twos complements. (See logical operations.)

　d. **Arithmetic shifts,** ie, moving bits in registers either left or right in order to multiply or divide. Examples are given here in detail because of their practical importance.

31.12 **Examples of arithmetic shifts.**

　a. **Arithmetic shift one place left.** (Arithmetical meaning is preserved, twos complement convention.)

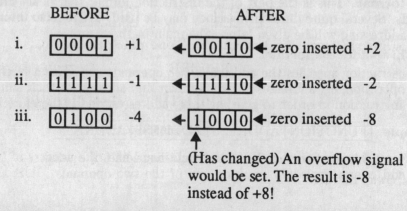

　　　　　　　BEFORE　　　　　　　　　　AFTER

　i.　0 0 0 1 +1　← 0 0 1 0 ← zero inserted +2

　ii.　1 1 1 1　-1　← 1 1 1 0 ← zero inserted -2

　iii.　0 1 0 0　-4　← 1 0 0 0 ← zero inserted -8

(Has changed) An overflow signal would be set. The result is -8 instead of +8!

Note. In multiple shifts, a further shift after an overflow would cause an arithmetic error signal to occur.

b. Arithmetic shift one place right. (Arithmetical meanings preserved twos complement convention.)

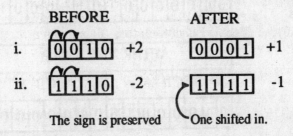

(This is called **"sign propagation"**.)

31.13 Logical operations.

a. Various Boolean operations, eg, AND, OR. They are usually performed between registers as in this example, where the AND operation is used to "mask out" one character in a register.

	ASCII 'A'	ASCII 'B'
FIRST 'X' REGISTER CONTAINING 2 CHARACTERS	0 1 0 0 0 0 0 1	0 1 0 0 0 0 1 0
SECOND 'Y' REGISTER CONTAINING A 'MASK'	0 0 0 0 0 0 0 0	1 1 1 1 1 1 1 1
RESULTS REGISTER CONTAINING X.Y (performed on each bit pair)	0 0 0 0 0 0 0 0	0 1 0 0 0 0 1 0

b. Negation, the Boolean NOT also performs ones complementation.

c. Rotation, also called logical shift, ie, moving bits left or right but replacing each bit at the opposite end of the register (this terminology is *not* universal).

Examples.

i. Logical shift (with a rotation) one place left. (A logical shift need not include a rotation.)

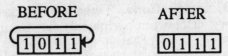

"1" removed on left is replaced on the right in the case of rotation.

ii. Logical shift (with a rotation) one place right.

"1" removed on right is replaced on left in the case of rotation.

iii. Logical shift (without a rotation) one place left.

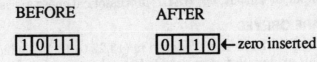

iv. Logical shift (without a rotation) one place right.

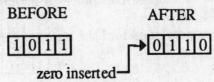

d. Swaps, ie, changing the left-hand and right-hand half of a word.

Examples. Swap halves.

BEFORE THE SWAP	
ASCII 'A'	ASCII 'B'
0 1 0 0 0 0 0 1	0 1 0 0 0 0 1 0

AFTER THE SWAP	
ASCII 'A'	ASCII 'B'
0 1 0 0 0 0 1 0	0 1 0 0 0 0 0 1

31.14 Transfer of control or branch instructions.

These are instructions that change the sequence in which instructions are obeyed. Their execution causes a "jump" to an instruction given elsewhere. The details follow shortly. First we list the two main types of these "jump" instructions.

  a. Unconditional transfer of control. The jump always occurs, for example,

    i. Jump to a specified address.

    ii. Skip the next instruction or skip a specified distance.

  b. Conditional transfer of control. The jump will only occur if the result of an operation has a particular value.

  Examples.

    i. Jump to a specified address if the accumulator contains zero.

    ii. Jump to a specified address if the accumulator contains a negative value.

    iii. Skip the next instruction if the accumulator contains zero.

    iv. Increment or decrement specified address, and skip next instruction if result is zero.
    (Details of how these jumps are achieved follow in paragraph 18.)

31.15 Load (fetch) and store instructions. These instructions cause the transfer of data between accumulators and memory, eg, load contents of specified address into a specified accumulator.

31.16 Input/Output (I/O) instructions. These instructions implement the transfer of data between peripherals and memory, or between peripherals and accumulators.

  Examples.

    i. Checking to see if a terminal typewriter has data ready for transfer.

    ii. Moving a character from a terminal typewriter into an accumulator.
    (Input and Output is dealt with later in chapter 33.)

31.17 a. Memory reference instructions. These are operations that require access to memory during their execution, hence they include **load and store instructions** and may also include some arithmetic, logic and control transfer instructions.

  b. Processor reference instructions. These are instructions that do not require memory and do not involve input or output, eg, HALT processor.

HOW INSTRUCTIONS ARE OBEYED

31.18 We must continue with the ideas introduced in (13.22 to 13.29), which you may wish to re-read before you continue. This explanation uses details from the processor diagram in appendix 2.2.

31.19 The diagram in Fig 31.1 is simplified in order to highlight the basic features. A more practical example was given in Fig. 26.1.

31.20 Remind yourself of the purpose of each of the registers (13.22) before you read on.

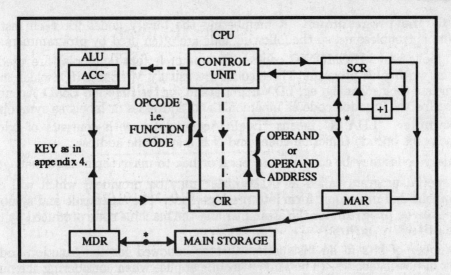

Fig. 31.1.

31.21 Further details of the fetch-execute cycle. (Follow these steps on Fig. 31.1.)

    a. Fetching the required instruction.

        i. The MAR is loaded with the address of the instruction to be performed. This address is copied from the SCR.

        ii. The controls of the SCR are then increased by 1 so it is ready to be referenced for the next fetch.

        iii. The fetch is completed by loading the instruction into the CIR via the MDR.

    b. *Executing* the instruction.

        i. The **opcode** or function part of the instruction is decoded by the control unit. What happens next depends on the type of instruction.

    Examples. Steps for instructions NOT requiring memory reference.

        i. The control unit sends command signals to the appropriate devices in the desired sequence until execution is completed.
        Steps for transfer of control instructions.

        ii. An unconditional transfer instruction causes the address held in the SCR to be overwritten by the address held in the right-hand half of the CIR, thereby ensuring that the desired instruction is obtained in the next fetch. A conditional transfer instruction will only lead to the SCR being overwritten if the specified condition is met. A special **status register,** not shown in Fig. 31.1, is altered by the ALU when specified conditions occur (eg, accumulator zero) and the control unit uses the contents of the status register to determine what control action to perform next.

    Steps for load and store instructions. (Requiring memory reference.)

        i. The appropriate operand address will be copied from the CIR into the MAR.

        ii. Data will then pass from the specified storage location into the accumulator via the MDR in the case of a load instruction (or the reverse direction in the case of a store).

    Steps for arithmetic requiring memory reference, eg, adding a number in main store to one in the accumulator.

        i. The appropriate operand address will be copied from the CIR into the MAR.

        ii. Data will then pass into the ALU from the specified storage location via the MDR. The ALU will receive the data, adding it to the contents of the accumulator, which may then be replaced by the result.

AN IMAGINARY MACHINE LANGUAGE

31.22 We are now going to consider the machine language for an imaginary computer. There is great variation between computer manufacturers in their design of machine codes. In order to give a balanced picture we will consider alternative examples in many cases. Familiarity with a real machine language should be obtained in your practical work if possible. It is very important that the reader realise that the imaginary computer described is much simpler than a real computer. To create a balanced view some more practical examples will be provided later in this chapter.

31.23 Aids to the programmer. Remembering the binary codes for each instruction, or just each function, is troublesome, so the following aids are often used by programmers.

   a. Symbolic and MNEMONIC codes. Groups of letters (symbols) are used by the programmer when writing his program. These codes are usually MNEMONIC, which means that their sound suggests their meaning, eg, LDA might stand for the function **LoaD** Accumulator. It is usual to describe the function code as mnemonic and addresses or labels as symbolic.

   Example. "LDA N" means "LoaD Accumulator with contents of address N". LDA is a mnemonic opcode (function code) and N is a symbolic address.

   b. Binary codes may be converted to octal or hex to make them more manageable.

   c. A special program called an **Assembler** may be provided, which will convert a program in symbolic and mnemonic form into machine code. The mnemonic and symbolic program is called the **source program** for the assembler and the machine code produced by the assembler is called the **object program**.

31.24 The number of bits in an instruction that are allowed for the function code will determine the number of possible codes. (The same principle applies when considering the number of bits required to represent a given number of characters.) If two bits were allowed then 4 function codes would be possible, ie, 00, 01, 10, 11. In general n bits allow 2^n function codes. However, the situation is more complicated than this in practice because of the variations that occur in instruction format within the same machine. For each format the same principle applies though.

31.25 For our imaginary computer we will take an example where in a fixed-(word) length instruction 4 bits are used to represent a possible 16 function codes. The codes, their functions and associated mnemonics are given on the next page.

31.26 Suppose that our imaginary computer has a fixed word length of 16 bits. The function code requires 4 bits so 12 bits remain for the operand addresses. If the machine had two accumulators we would require one bit, set to 0 or 1, to specify the accumulator. We will assume there is just one accumulator and hence it will not require **explicit** addressing. We will thus have the following arrangement:

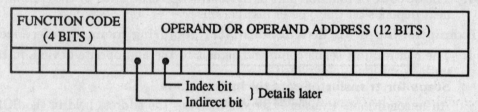

Note to the following diagram.

   a. In instructions where there is no memory reference, eg, I/O operations, the operand address bits may be used to extend the function options.

   b. It is in this respect of having just one instruction format that this imaginary computer is particularly simple compared with most real computers.

METHODS OF ADDRESSING

31.27 The location address ultimately determined by hardware is called the absolute address. Within the instruction various methods may be used. The main methods of addressing are:

   a. Direct addressing.

   b. Indirect addressing (also called deferred address).

   c. Indexed addressing.

   d. Modified addressing.

   e. Relative addressing.

   f. Page addressing.

   g. Immediate addressing.

   h. Symbolic addressing. (Not possible in machine language.)

Hardware determines the address type by decoding the operand part of the instruction in the SCR. It then produces the correct absolute address. The data path from CIR to MAR in Fig. 31.1 therefore gave a simplified view of what happens.

MACHINE CODE (BINARY CODE)	OCTAL EQUIVALENT	FUNCTION (OPERATION)	MNEMONIC
0000	00	Load Accumulator with contents of specified address	LDA
0001	01	STore contents of Accumulator in specified address	STA
0010	02	LoaD specified Number into accumulator	LDN
0011	03	ADD contents of specified address to accumulator contents	ADD
0100	04	SUBtract contents of specified address from accumulator contents	SUB
0101	05	ADd specified Number to contents of accumulator	ADN
0110	06	SUbtract specified Number from contents of accumulator	SUN
0111	07	perform a boolean AND on specified address and accumulator contents	AND
1000	10	perfotm a boolean OR on specified address and accumulator contents	OR
1001	11	Jump to specified address if Accumulator contents Zero	JAZ
1010	12	JumP Unconditionally to specified address	JPU
1011	13	Jump to specified address if Accumulator contents Greater than zero	JAG
1100	14	Jump to specified address if Accumulator contents Less than zero	JAL
1101	15	Jump to specified address if Accumulator contents Not zero	JAN
1110	16	perform specified Input / Output operation	IO
1111	17	STOP the program ie HALT the processor	STOP

31.28 Direct addressing is being used if the number given in the operand part of an instruction is the actual address of the operand (data) to be used.

Example.

FUNCTION CODE: LDA	ADDRESS $111_2 = 7_8$														
0	0	0	0	0	0	0	0	0	0	0	0	0	1	1	1

In this example the instruction would be to load the contents of Location 7 into the accumulator.

31.29 Direct addressing is simple, fast and effective but the number of locations addressable is limited. In the above example the 12 bits available allow just $2^{12} = 4096_{10}$ locations to be specified. This problem may be overcome by

a. Using longer words.

b. Using more than one word for the address by using the next location (called an **extended address**). This is common in microcomputers.

c. Using alternative methods. Since a. and b. are frequently impractical on the one hand because longer words prove wasteful and expensive and on the other because the method is slow and complicates the fetch-execute cycle.

31.30 Indirect addressing. When **indirect addressing** is used the address given in the address part of the instruction is NOT the address of the required operand. Instead the address part is the address of the location that contains the required address. An address is **either** direct **or** indirect.

Example.

FUNCTION CODE: LDA	ADDRESS OF LOCATION CONTAINING OPERAND ADDRESS														
0	0	0	0	*1	0	0	0	0	0	0	0	0	1	1	1

* This bit (the indirect bit) is set to "1" to signify indirect addressing or "0" for direct addressing.

CONTENTS OF LOCATION 7															
*0	0	0	0	0	0	0	0	0	0	0	0	1	0	0	1

a. **Note.**

   i. The data to be loaded is in location 9. It is **not obtained directly** because its address must **first** be found in location 7. Hence the term **indirect address** (two memory accesses will be necessary).

   ii. Almost **all** of location 7 may be used to specify the data address, so $2^{15} = 32768_{10}$ locations may be accessed, a considerable improvement.

b. Practical difficulties with this example arise because it is not possible to access locations greater than $2^{11} = 2048_{10}$ directly. One unavoidable drawback of indirect addressing is the need for two memory accesses instead of one.

c. Indirect addressing is sometimes called **deferred addressing**, and if the second address is yet a further indirect address then the address is called a **multi-level address**. (Note the * in location 7 shown in the diagram.)

31.31 Indexed addressing.

In this method the required address is obtained by **adding** the contents of the address part of the instruction to a number stored in a special register called the **index register** or **modifier register**.

Example.

FUNCTION CODE: LDA	INDIRECT BIT	INDEX BIT	REMAINDER OF OPERAND ADDRESS
0 0 0 0	0	1	0 0 0 0 0 0 0 1 1 1

THE CONTENTS OF THE INDEX REGISTER IS 9_{10}															
0	0	0	0	0	0	0	0	0	0	0	0	1	0	0	1

Index bit set to "1" to signify the use of the index register. DATA ADDRESS = 9 + 7 = 16.

Note.

a. The need to do an addition makes this method slower than direct addressing, but once the address is calculated it can be accessed in one step, ie, directly.

b. A further bit has been used in our example to indicate whether or not the index register is to be used. This further limits the range of the address given in the instruction.

c. The index address and indirect bits could both be set to one, thus allowing an **indirect indexed address** where the address given by address part + index register contents would be an indirect address.

d. No index register is shown in Fig. 31.1, which highlights the limitations of this imaginary computer. In some later examples we will take memory location zero to be the index register, which is not so unrealistic as it may first appear because it is not unknown for the first few locations in memory to be constructed and used as registers.

31.32 You can see from the previous examples that bits may be taken from the address part of the instruction in order to specify such things as the accumulators to be used or the type of addressing to be used. For a given machine the instruction format must be designed to allow for these different **modes of addressing** to be added in some way.

31.33 Other methods of addressing will now be described. It would be uncommon for all these methods to be used on any one machine, although all are in use on different machines, but on a given machine the mode of address would be specified by a suitable part of the instruction format.

31.34 Modified addressing.

If an instruction is altered or modified so that the same function is performed again but on an operand in a different address then a **modified address** has been used. Two basic methods are:

a. Using indexed addressing and changing the contents of the index register before the instruction is repeated.

   NB. A common use is to successively add one to the index register so as to access successive locations in memory.

b. Changing the address part of the instruction. This can be done by treating the instruction as an operand (data) and either adding or subtracting some number from it.

   NB. The use of this method is almost invariably a bad practice because it is a threat to program readability and reliability. In any case, it limits the ways in which the code can be reused.

31.35 Relative addressing.

a. The address part of the instruction is used to give a **displacement** from some **stated** address. In one sense an index address is a relative address since the address part of the instruction gives the location of the operand as so many places **past** the location **stated** in the index register.

b. A further example occurs when the address part of the instruction specifies an address relative to the instruction currently being performed. The address field requires one bit to specify this type of address. The remainder of the address field may be positive or negative. When the instruction is performed the hardware uses the value in the sequence control register + the displacement to generate the absolute address.

   Example. JPU (SCR)−2 ie, jump back two instructions.

31.36 Base address. The address to which the relative address is referred is frequently called the **base address.** Thus the **displacement** is added to the **base address.**

31.37 Page addressing. (Used where word length limits the size of the address field.) This is a special form of **relative addressing.** The main storage area is divided into units of equal size (512 locations say) and the units, called pages, are numbered 0, 1, 2, 3, etc. A register can be set to the value of a given page number and then until it is altered all addresses given in the address part of the instruction are added to the zeroth address for that page.

Usually the size of the address field in the instruction is such that it can only specify N different locations, where N is the size of the pages.

31.38 Immediate addressing. If instead of giving the location of the data in the address part of the instruction the address part itself is used as data, then immediate addressing is being used, ie, the address part is used as the operand. In paragraph 25 we saw functions LDN, ADN and SUN, which would be using immediate addressing. (The operand is an **immediate operand.**)

31.39 Symbolic addressing. Symbolic addressing is NOT possible in **machine code** but it is used by the programmer when he or she uses an alpha-numeric symbol to specify an address. The symbolic address must at some stage be translated into a **machine address.**

Example. (Program section adding two numbers and storing the result.)

$$\text{labels} \left\{ \begin{array}{ll} \text{A:} & 3 \\ \text{B:} & 5 \\ \text{C:} & 0 \end{array} \right\} \quad \text{Contents of these locations}$$

Instructions using symbolic addressing		
LDA	A	Load accumulator with contents of address labelled by A.
ADD	B	Add to accumulator the con tents of the address labelled by B.
STA	C	Store the sum in the address labelled by C.

FURTHER FEATURES OF THE MACHINE

31.40 The imaginary machine described earlier in this chapter, and used as a basis for simple examples, is too simple to serve as a basis for all the points requiring discussion here. The simplified machine shown in Fig. 31.2 will be used from now on.

31.41 Examine Fig. 31.2 and note the following points.

a. Many of the registers are the same as in Fig. 31.1.

b. Data is transferred in parallel and many transfers use the internal data bus.

c. The index register (31.31) is represented in the diagram. The ALU could be used to perform the arithmetic needed for indexed addressing.

d. Two registers met for the first time in Fig. 31.2.

    i. **A status register.**

    ii. **A stack pointer.**

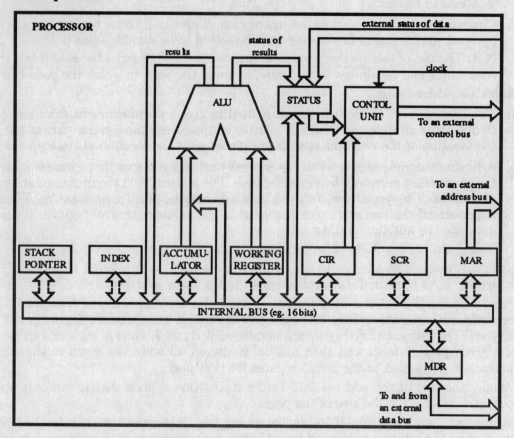

Fig. 31.2. A Simplified View of a Typical Processor.

31.42 **A status register** such as the one shown in Fig. 31.2 has its contents set by hardware devices such as the ALU and is used by the control unit. For example, one bit in the status register might be used to signify whether or not the last ALU result was zero. The control unit would examine this bit when it controlled a conditional branch instruction such as JAZ or JAN.

31.43 Other bits in the status register could be used to signify result states such as:

a. Negative result.

b. Positive result.

c. Overflow.

d. Parity error.

The larger and more powerful the processor, the longer and more comprehensive is the status register likely to be.

31.44 The status register may also hold data relating to the state of external devices, but discussion of the details is left until chapter 33.

31.45 **A stack pointer** holds an address of a location in memory into which data may be placed temporarily. The data is organised and accessed in a data structure known as a **stack**. Full details of what stacks are and how they may be manipulated will be given in chapter 39. For the time being just two basic stack operations need to be understood. These operations are normally called **"push"** and **"pop"**.

31.46 **Push.**

Fig. 31.3a shows a stack onto which the data values "15" and "12" have been placed in two separate push operations. 15 was "pushed" onto the stack first, then "12" was pushed on. A further push operation with the number 23 as operand would leave the stack as in Fig. 31.3b. Note how the stack pointer is changed by the push operation.

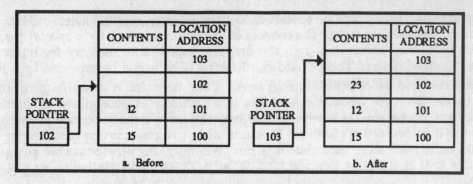

Fig. 31.3. Pushing "23" onto a Stack.

31.47 A **pop** operation is the reverse of a push operation, ie, the item is removed from the stack and the stack pointer is altered. Thus Fig. 31.3b shows the stack before a pop that removes "23" and Fig. 31.3a shows the stack after the pop operation.

31.48 Push and pop operations are often provided as machine instructions. Even some 8-bit microprocessors have this facility, eg, the Z80, 6502 and 6809.

31.49 In some machines special registers are provided within the processor to form a stack and may be used instead of memory.

31.50 The three main uses of stacks at machine level are:

a. Use in simple computations to hold intermediate results.

b. Use in handling subprogram calls.

c. Use in handling interrupts.

The last two of these three will be discussed in later chapters. An example of (a) would be a simple swap operation when two variables (a = 9 and b = 12 say) were to exchange values. A possible method would be:

i. push a's value onto the stack.

ii. copy b's value to a.

iii. pop the value off the stack into b.

The code for this could be something like this:

```
PUSH A
LDA B
STA A
POP B
```

LOADING AND STORING PROGRAMS IN MACHINE CODE

31.51 Nearly all modern computers have available programs called **loaders** or **loading routines**. A loader will take a program written in machine code and in some suitable input form such as disk, and input the instructions from the disk into their specified storage locations. The loader is often permanently in main memory. You may ask "How is the loader loaded?" We shall now answer this question.

31.52 **Manual communication.** Information about the processor may be displayed on a special panel called the **console**, which may often be used in conjunction with a typewriter called the **console typewriter**. The console panel will have lights to display the contents of various registers or addresses and switches by which those contents may be altered. On a 16-bit word machine there would probably be 2 rows of 16 lights, representing in one row the binary addresses, and in the other the contents of that address in binary. Underneath these lights there might be 16 switches used for selecting addresses or changing their contents.

31.53 By the manual use of these switches one could enter a whole program in machine code by setting the binary code for each instruction on the switches one at a time. On the early computers this was the only way! Today an engineer would use this method in two main situations, which are:

a. to "key in" a very simple loader by hand in order to load all other programs. This might be done when for some reason the loader was not in memory.

b. to make very minor alterations to programs already loaded.

31.54 Bootstraps. Bootstraps or bootstrap loaders are very simple loaders, which are **either** placed in memory manually by use of the console **or** placed in memory by a special piece of **hardware**, and which will place instructions into the first few locations in memory for input of instructions from some specified device. These "hardware" instructions would be provided by a ROM.

31.55 Absolute and relocatable programs. (The need for relocatable programs will be discussed in chapter 34.) An **absolute address** is an address as determined by hardware. An **absolute program** is one that is always loaded into the same fixed locations in main store for which the **absolute addresses** are known. A **relocatable program** is one that may be loaded into different locations in main store each time it is run. When writing a **relocatable program** it is common to assume that it starts at location zero, ie, all addresses are relative to an assumed base address at zero.

SUMMARY

31.56 a. Instructions in **machine language** can be performed without further translation.

b. The address format can be classified by the number of addresses specified, eg, one address format.

c. Types of instructions can be classified under the headings:

    i. Arithmetic and logic
    ii. Transfer of control
    iii. Load and store
    iv. Input/Output
    v. Memory reference

or more concisely

    i. Memory reference
    ii. Processor reference
    iii. Input/Output

d. Symbolic, mnemonic codes aid programming in machine code.

e. Methods of addressing possible are:

    i. Direct
    ii. Indirect (deferred) and multilevel
    iii. Indexed addressing
    iv. Address modification
    v. Relative
    vi. Page addressing
    vii. Immediate
    viii. Symbolic (not possible in machine language).

f. The absolute address is the address determined by hardware.

g. Status registers and stacks were introduced.

h. A program must be placed in main store before it is performed. This may be done by

    i. A loader program
    ii. Manual setting of switches
    iii. A hardware load.

i. A loaded program may be either absolute or relocatable.

POINTS TO NOTE

31.57 a. Once the instruction format is fixed there are limits set on the number of different instructions that can be coded and the number of locations directly addressable in a single instruction.

b. Indexed addressing and indirect addressing overcome the limitation to the range of addresses accessible by a single instruction at the cost of either extra arithmetic or further access.

c. The relative speeds of indirect addressing and index addressing depend entirely on the hardware of the particular machine on which they are used. Usually index addressing offers a greater flexibility.

d. Exam questions are often set on an imaginary machine instruction set, so be prepared to get familiar with an instruction set in a hurry.

e. When working through a machine-language program it often helps to tabulate successive contents of relevant locations.

f. Relocatability mentioned in this chapter is "static". Some machines can relocate programs while they are being executed, ie, they provide "dynamic relocatability". (Further discussion will occur in chapter 34.)

g. Specimen programs are given in the next chapter.

h. The reader is advised to get a working knowledge of at least one real machine, having first become familiar with the contents of this chapter and the next one.

STUDENT SELF-TESTING QUESTIONS

1. A small one-address computer has storage for 4096 18-bit words. Each machine instruction is one complete word and must be able to address directly any cell in the store. How many different machine-instruction operation codes can there be?

2. a. What purpose is served by the following registers:

   i.   program counter,
   ii. current instruction register,
   iii. status register,
   iv. memory address register,
   v.   memory buffer register.   *(5 marks)*

   By referring to these registers, explain the concept of *automatic sequence control* and describe the effect of an interrupt upon this.   *(7 marks)*

   b. Illustrate the action of the following instructions in the execute phase of the fetch-execute cycle:

   i. self-relative conditional jump,
   ii. unconditional immediate jump.   *(4 marks)*

   c. A particular machine has 16 general purpose registers. Suggest formats, including instruction length, for both register-to-register and storage-to-storage instructions.   *(4 marks)*

                                                                              (AEB 1987)

3. What is meant by an instruction format? Describe the following forms of addressing.
   a. Direct.
   b. Immediate.
   c. Indexed.
   d. Symbolic.

4. Distinguish between a logical shift instruction and an arithmetic shift instruction. Show what happens to the following bytes after
   a. a 2-bit arithmetic shift right.
   b. a 2-bit logical shift right.

      i. *00110110*
      ii. *11010111*

QUESTIONS WITHOUT ANSWERS

5. Repeat question 4 for 2-bit left shifts.
6. Investigate the word length and instruction formats of the computer you use.

GLOSSARY CHECKLIST

32: Low-level Languages

INTRODUCTION

32.1 This chapter is primarily concerned with low-level languages and how programs are written in low-level languages. Low-level languages programming requires some knowledge of machine-language and so some aspects of machine-language programming have been included in this chapter, rather than the previous chapter, in order to make the subject matter more coherent.

MACHINE-LANGUAGE PROGRAMMING

32.2 We will now consider three machine-language programs in order to illustrate programming features. These examples are based on the imaginary computer introduced in 31.22. We will use the instruction format 31.31, signed integer arithmetic using twos complement and the instruction set specified in 31.25.

32.3 In writing specimen programs the following notation will be used.

a. Machine instructions will be shown in octal as well as binary to show how octal coding aids the programmer.

For example, the instruction "Store contents of accumulator in Location 7" is

COMMENTS	FUNCTION CODE:LDA			INDIRECT BIT	INDEX BIT	REMAINDER OF OPERAND ADDRESS								
BINARY	0	0	0	0	0	0	0	0	0	0	0	0	1	1	1
OCTAL	0		0		0		0			0		0		7	

b. In writing MNEMONICS, the address notation will be as shown in the following instruction examples.

i. STA 7. Store accumulator contents in location 7. (Direct address.)

ii. STA @ 7. The @ indicates an indirect address. In this case store accumulator contents at the location specified in location 7.

iii. STA 5, X. The "X" indicates that the indeX register is to be used. In this case store accumulator in location given by (contents of index register) + 5.

c. Numerical values will be in OCTAL.

32.4 **Example 1.** A program to add two numbers stored in locations 5 and 6, and to place the result in location 7. (Look at the MNEMONICS **FIRST**.)

LOCATION OF INSTRUCTION (OCTAL)	MACHINE INSTRUCTION (OR DATA) (BINARY) Function Code	Operand or Operand Address	MACHINE INSTRUCTION (OR DATA) (Octal Coded)						MNEMONIC EQUIVALENT (Numerics octal)	
0	0000	00000000101	0	0	0	0	0	5	LDA	5
1	0011	00000000110	0	3	0	0	0	6	ADD	6
2	0001	00000000111	0	1	0	0	0	7	STA	7
3	1111	00000000000	1	7	0	0	0	0	STOP	
4	0000	00000000000	0	0	0	0	0	0		0
5	0000	00000000110	0	0	0	0	0	6		6
6	0000	00000001010	0	0	0	0	1	2		12
7	0000	00000000000	0	0	0	0	0	0		0

Note.

i. Simple direct addressing is being used here.

ii. Data and instructions are stored in **exactly the same way**, so data can be treated as an instruction or an instruction as data, eg, had the STOP instruction been omitted the data value

0 held in location 4 would be treated as the instruction LDA 0 and the processor would continue to obey each word of store as an instruction until a STOP code was met.

32.5 Example 2.

The same task is performed as in example 1 but different methods of addressing are used for illustration, although they are unnecessary.

LOCATION OF INSTRUCTION (OCTAL)	MACHINE INSTRUCTION (OR DATA) (BINARY) Function Code	MACHINE INSTRUCTION (OR DATA) (BINARY) Operand or Operand Address	MACHINE INSTRUCTION (OR DATA) (Octal Coded)	MNEMONIC EQUIVALENT (Numerics octal)
INDEX REGISTER	0 0	0 0 0 0 0 0 0 0 0 0 0 1 0 0	0 0 0 0 0 4	4
1	0 0 1	0 0 0 0 0 0 0 0 0 0 1 1 0	0 2 0 0 0 6	LDN 6
2	0 0 1 1 1	0 0 0 0 0 0 0 0 1 0 1	0 3 4 0 0 5	ADD @ 5
3	0 0 0 1 0	1 0 0 0 0 0 0 0 0 1 1	0 1 0 0 0 3	STA 3, X
4	1 1 1 1 1	0 0 0 0 0 0 0 0 0 0 0	1 7 0 0 0 0	STOP
5	0 0 0 0 0	0 0 0 0 0 0 0 0 1 1 0	0 0 0 0 0 6	6
6	0 0 0 0 0	0 0 0 0 0 0 1 0 1 0	0 0 0 0 1 2	12
7	0 0 0 0 0	0 0 0 0 0 0 0 0 0 0 0	0 0 0 0 0 0	0

Note.

i. LDN 6 results in the number 6 being loaded with the accumulator.

ii. ADD @ 5 results in the address of the data being found in location 5. That address 6 leads to the data 12_8. This results in the data 12_8 being added to the accumulator.

iii. STA 3, X results in the sum, 18, being stored in location 3 + contents of index register, ie, location 3 + 4 = 7.

32.6 Example 3. Extending the previous program.

a. The STOP instruction in location 4 could be replaced by an unconditional jump to the next instruction in location 10 (OCTAL) say. The appropriate instruction would be JPU 10. The binary and octal forms are:

BINARY	OCTAL
1 0 1 0 0 0 0 0 0 0 0 1 0 0 0 1	2 0 0 1 0

To terminate the program, eg, if the sum is 20_8, the following group of instructions would suffice. (Binary and octal codes are omitted for clarity.)

LOCATION	INSTRUCTION MNEMONIC	COMMENT
10	SUN 20	Test for 20_8 by subtracting 20_8 and
11	JAN 13	skipping the STOP if the result is non zero
12	STOP	Performs this STOP if sum 20_8
13	etc.	This instruction is obeyed if the sum is not 20_8

32.7 Final points on machine-language programming.

a. All the machine's operation codes (function codes) have to be memorised.

b. All memory addresses have to be assigned and a track kept of them (ie, we must give each variable an address and record our action).

c. Instructions have to be written in the sequence in which they are to be executed. Thus insertions or deletions entail the movement of all succeeding instructions, (eg, to insert code between locations 6 and 7).

d. Subsequent revision of a completed program would be so impractical as to almost require a complete rewrite.

e. The whole process is very time consuming and inefficient in terms of human effort.

LOW-LEVEL LANGUAGES

32.8 We saw the advantages of using MNEMONICS to describe machine-language instructions. It seems logical to write the program in this SYMBOLIC form and to get the machine to do the translation to machine language. This is what is done with **low-level languages.**

32.9 Definition. Low-level languages are **machine-orientated languages** in which each instruction corresponds to or resembles a machine instruction.

32.10 Common features of low-level languages.

    a. MNEMONIC codes are used in place of machine codes, eg, using LDA 5 in place of 00000000000001(

    b. Symbolic addresses are frequently used instead of actual machine addresses, eg, using LDA N where N stands for the address, which can be assigned a numerical value at a more convenient time.

32.11 The (symbolic) low-level language must be translated into machine language before use, because although easier for the programmer to work with it is not usable by the machine in symbolic/mnemonic form.

The translation is actually done by the computer by means of a special translating program.

32.12 Assembly language.

    a. Each computer manufacturer normally devises a low-level language that corresponds closely to the particular machine language used by that manufacturer. This language is called an ASSEMBLY LANGUAGE. The manufacturer provides a program called an ASSEMBLER or ASSEMBLER PROGRAM, which translates the ASSEMBLY LANGUAGE into MACHINE CODE.

    b. A program written in ASSEMBLY LANGUAGE is called the SOURCE PROGRAM. The translated program in MACHINE CODE is called the OBJECT PROGRAM.

(The features of assemblers will be left until Chapter 37.)

32.13 Pseudo-assembly languages. Assembly languages differ, since the features of each assembly language depend on the particular computer on which it is used. This makes computer courses and examinations difficult to standardise. To answer this problem several low-level assembly-like languages that are **machine independent** have been devised for educational purposes. They are **pseudo-assembly languages** since they do not fulfill the usual task of an assembly language, but are useful educationally.

Examples are:

    a. CESIL: Computer Education in Schools Instruction Language.

    b. City and Guilds 319 Mnemonic coded.

The mnemonic code used for examples in the previous chapter may also be regarded as a pseudo-assembly language.

ILLUSTRATIVE PROBLEMS IN ASSEMBLY LANGUAGE

32.14 The assembly language instruction format used here is based on the instruction format used in the earlier examples. Here are the details.

Instruction Format

	LABEL	:	FUNCTION CODE	OPERAND OR OPERAND ADDRESS
eg,	A	:	LDA	5

Note.

    a. The LABEL is **optional** and may be used either

        i. to give an instruction a symbolic address, or

        ii. to give a numerical value a symbolic address.

    b. The operand address can take these forms:

        i. a direct address or operand, eg, 5

        ii. a direct index address, eg, 5, X
            The address will be 5 + contents of index register.

        iii. indirect, indicated by an @ eg, @ 5 or @ 5, X.

        iv. up to three letters used as a symbolic address, eg, N.

c. Examples.

i. LDA 5   Load accumulator with contents of address 5.

ii. LDA N   Load the contents of (symbolic) address N into
the accumulator. Further down the
contents of N are specified
next to the label.

           N : 5

iii. LDA @ N   The symbolic address N holds the address
of the data to be loaded
into the accumulator.

iv. LDA 5, X   Load the contents of location 5 + (X)
where (X) means *contents*
of index register.

32.15 Specimen Problem 1. To add a set of numbers stored in successive locations starting at location 30_8 and terminated by a location containing zero. The program will be placed in location 10_8 to 25_8 inclusive and the data is organised as shown here:

LOCATION ADDRESS (OCTAL)	CONTENTS	
	pointer value (initialised to 30)	A **pointer** to the address of the next number to be added.
26		
27	total value	Value of the **total**.
30	15	Specimen
31	18	data with
32	14	sentinel value
33	0	zero.

32.16 The method is given in pseudocode in the following table. **All numbers are in octal.** The pointer contains the address of the next number to be added. Indirect addressing is used in the assembly program and this is indicated in pseudocode by the use of parentheses. Thus, for example, "(pointer)" means the data whose address is currently assigned to pointer.

PSEUDOCODE	ASSEMBLY LANGUAGE	COMMENTS
(* Take all variables to be non-negative integers. *) **Begin**	.START 10	A directive to the assembler to start the program storage at location 10
total : = 0	LDN 0 STA 27	Setting the contents of location 27 to zero ie. total : = 0
pointer : = 30	LDN 30 STA 26	Loading the number 30 into location 26 where it is to be used as an indirect address
number : = (pointer)	LDA @ 26	Loading the number whose address is in location 26
While number <>0	A: JAZ B	Checking for zero terminator (label used later)
total : = total + 1	ADD 27 STA 27	Adding number to total then store the new total
pointer : = pointer + 1	LDN 1 ADD26 STA 26	Increasing the address stored in location 26 by 1 so that next time it is used it refers to the next number to be added.
number : = (pointer)	LDA @ 26 JPU A	Same as before Jump to load next number.
endwhile **end**	B: STOP .END	STOP A directive to the assembler to end the translation.

32.17 Note the following points about this assembly language program.

a. A **while loop** has been constructed using a combination of conditional and non-conditional jump instructions.

b. The way the data is stored in memory from location 30 onwards is comparable with the way data is stored in an array and the pointer is comparable with the subscript of an array.

c. The use of a "directive".

32.18 Directives. .START and .END are *not* ASSEMBLY LANGUAGE instructions. They are DI-RECTIVES, ie, instructions to the ASSEMBLER requiring immediate execution and *not* requiring translation as part of the program.

32.19 Specimen Problem 2. The main purpose of this problem is to show how **if-then-else** may be implemented using an assembly language. Locations 3 and 4 hold integer values corresponding to the costs, in pence, of purchased goods. If the sum of these two values is no more than 100p then the additional postage and packing cost is 30p. If the sum is more than 100p then the additional postage and packing cost is 50p. The program is to calculate the total cost and store it in location 5.

32.20 The method is given in pseudocode in the following table. **All** numbers are in octal. Note the way in which the jump instructions are used to select the appropriate actions.

PSEUDOCODE	ASSEMBLY LANGUAGE		
begin		.START	10
total_cost := first_cost + second_cost		LDA	3
		ADD	4
		STA	5
if			
total_cost <= 100		LDN	100
		SUB	5
		JAL	G
then			
total_cost := total_cost + 30		LDN	30
		ADD	5
		STA	5
		JPU	E
else			
total_cost := total_cost + 50	G:	LDN	50
		ADD	5
		STA	5
endif			
end	E:	STOP	
		.END	

SUBROUTINES (SUBPROGRAMS)

32.21 A subprogram (16.62) written in a low-level language is usually called a subroutine. Subroutines were invented as an aid to efficiency, but have become even more important in high-level programming as a program-structuring feature. In the following paragraphs the low-level language features that support subprograms will be discussed.

32.22 A subroutine is a set of program instructions forming **part** of a program and used to perform a specific task. Used wisely the **same** subroutine may be used to do the same task at different stages in the main program without the need for rewriting it each time.

Figure 32.1 illustrates the basic principles.

32.23 In the simplest cases there will be no parameter passing and no hardware to handle the subroutine calls and returns. The former is often the case when a high-level language does not support full subprogram facilities. The latter is rare these days. Nevertheless it is convenient to start with the simplest case in order to introduce the ideas in easy stages.

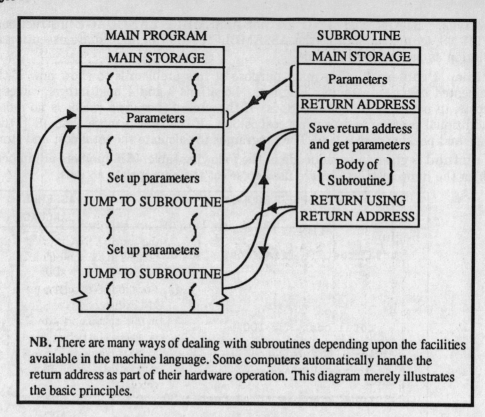

NB. There are many ways of dealing with subroutines depending upon the facilities available in the machine language. Some computers automatically handle the return address as part of their hardware operation. This diagram merely illustrates the basic principles.

Fig. 32.1. Handling Subroutines.

32.24 Subroutine Example 1.

At different places in a program a character must be input by a terminal typewriter and its code placed in the accumulator. Suppose that a subroutine is available for doing the task and that the subroutine starts at location 400. Show how the **same** subroutine may be used each time that it is needed.

Comments:

a. The last instruction in the subroutine will be an unconditional jump back to the appropriate location in the main program. This return address must be stored (saved) for use by the subroutine, prior to entering the subroutine.

b. There are two common ways of returning from subroutines when there is no explicit hardware facility provided. These are by using **either** indirect addressing **or** address modification.

32.25 Instructions for entering the subroutine.

LOCATION	MNEMONIC EQUIVALENT OF INSTRUCTION STORED IN LOCATION	COMMENTS
16	LDN 21	Load return address
17	STA 0	Store return address in location
20	JPU 400	Unconditional jump to subroutine.
21		1st instruction on return from subroutine.

Fig. 32.2.

To return from the subroutine if the return address is stored in location 0.

Last instruction in subroutine could use:

a. **Indirect addressing**, eg, JPU @ 0

b. **Address modification**, eg, JPU 0, X (assume location zero is used as the index register).

414

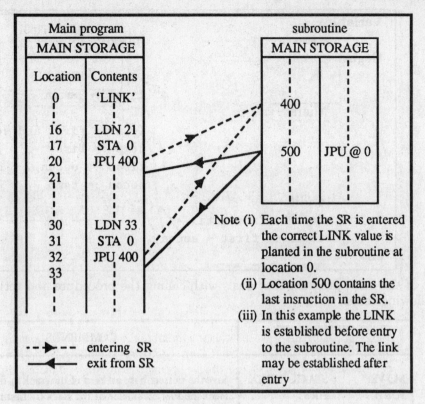

Fig. 32.3.

32.26 Subroutine Example 2. In this example we consider a case where hardware is provided for handling the subroutine calls and returns and we also deal with parameter passing.

32.27 For the purpose of this example we will assume a machine architecture like that shown in Fig. 31.2, in which a stack pointer is present. We will further assume the following extensions to our assembly language. These instructions are included in the language:

a. The **PUSH** and **POP** operations described in 31.46–31.47.

b. A **MOVE** instruction that takes the form MOVE A B where A is a register whose contents are moved to register B and where the accumulator, index register, stack pointer and sequence control register have the symbolic addresses ACC, INDEX, STACK and SCR respectively. For example, MOVE INDEX STACK moves the contents of the index register into the stack pointer.

c. A Jump To Subroutine instruction with mnemonic **JSR** where, for example, the instruction JSR B will cause the contents of the SCR to be pushed onto the stack, thereby saving the return address, and a jump equivalent to JPU B will be performed.

d. A Return From Subroutine instruction with mnemonic **RTN**, which pops the top of the stack into the SCR, where the contents of the top of the stack should be the return address for the subroutine previously placed there by means of a JSR instruction.

e. An instruction to increment the contents of a register with mnemonic **INC**. For example, INC ACC will add 1 to the contents of the accumulator.

In addition to these features we will assume that all labels and symbolic addresses may be up to 5 characters long. In other respects the language will be taken to be the same as that defined in 32.14. So, for example, LDA 5, INDEX is equivalent in meaning to LDA 5, X shown in 32.14 iv.

32.28 In this example a procedure called "order_and_add" is to take two integers place them in ascending order, and calculate their total. The procedure takes the following form. (**Note.** "Second" has been abbreviated to "secon" because assembly code names are typically short.)

Procedure order_and_add (**IN-OUT** first, secon : **integer OUT** total integer)

(* This procedure places first and secon in ascending order and calculates their total.*)

```
Variables
        temp :                          integer
Begin
        if
                                        first > secon
        then
                                        (* swap first and secon *)
                                        temp := first
                                        first := secon
                                        secon := temp
        endif
        (* calculate total *)
        total := first + secon
end
```

32.29 The part of the main program that deals with calling the procedure and returning from it is shown in the following table.

PART OF THE MAIN ASSEMBLY PROGRAM		COMMENTS
MOVE	STACK INDEX	Save the current base address of the stack in the index register.
PUSH	FIRST	Place the first parameter on the stack (ie first number).
PUSH	SECON	Place the second parameter on the stack (ie second number).
INC	STACK	Make space on the stack for the third parameter (ie total).
JSR	OAA	Jump to the subroutine which orders and adds.
POP	TOTAL	Remove the OUT parameters (total) from the stack.
POP	SECON	Remove the IN-OUT parameter (SECON) from the stack.
POP	FIRST	Remove the IN-OUT parameter (FIRST) from the stack.

32.30 The contents of the stack at critical stages in the execution of the program part just described are given in Fig. 32.4.

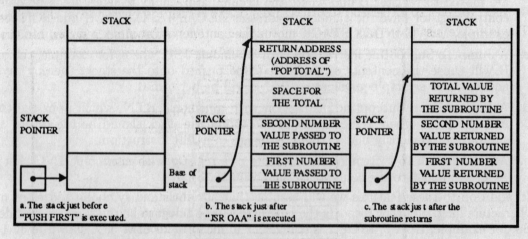

Fig. 32.4. Stack Contents for Subroutine Calls and Returns.

32.31 The subroutine is given in the following table.

ASSEMBLY SUBROUTINE		COMMENTS
PUSH	INDEX	Save the contents of these
PUSH	ACC	registers on the stack.
LDA	1,INDEX	Check whether first number is
SUB	0,INDEX	greater than second.
JAG	N	Do not swap if numbers are already in order.
PUSH	0,INDEX	Swap numbers if they
LDA	1,INDEX	are not in order.
STA	0,INDEX	See 31.50.
POP	1,INDEX	
N: LDA	0,INDEX	Add the two numbers
ADD	1,INDEX	and store the
STA	2,INDEX	total.
POP	ACC	Restore the register
POP	INDEX	values.
RTN		Return to the main program.

32.32 Note the following points about this example:

a. A local variable, corresponding to "TEMP" in the pseudocode, is created on the stack during subroutine execution.

b. The use of the stack base address, held in the index register, which makes it easier to locate variables even though the stack pointer changes.

c. The way the stack base address is used means that this subroutine could be called from within another subroutine, which had already placed items on the stack, and would work in exactly the same way as shown in this example.

32.33 OPEN and CLOSED subroutines. These are the two types of subroutine.

a. **OPEN** subroutines are part of the main program and are inserted into the program where required.

b. **CLOSED** subroutines are not part of the main program. They are **linked** to the main program by the entry and return procedures outlined in the last four paragraphs. The term **Link** is often used to refer to either the return address or the return instruction from the subroutine.

The example just given was a closed subroutine; an open subroutine is shown here in Fig. 32.5.

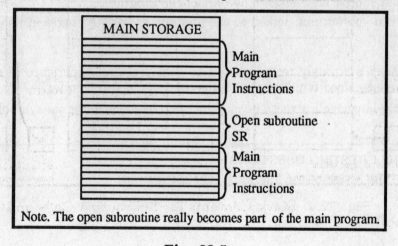

Note. The open subroutine really becomes part of the main program.

Fig. 32.5.

32.34 It should be noted that:

a. The subroutine has to be in main storage in order to be entered. It must either be loaded along with the main program (if not already in main store) or the main program will be halted while the subroutine is loaded. In the latter case the loading is done automatically by software provided for the purpose. Most frequently the subroutines would be available on disc in such cases.

b. The subroutines may even be written in a different language from the main program.

c. Closed subroutines save main storage space.

MACRO INSTRUCTIONS

32.35 Notice that low-level languages made program writing easier, but the programmer had still to write out **every** single instruction in source language. A macro instruction is a **single** instruction written as part of the source-program language which when assembled will generate **many** machine-code instructions. These "macros" (some written by the manufacturer, some by the user) are used as a library of open subroutines to perform common tasks such as input/output operations. The assembler does the job of inserting the instruction for the MACROS into the object program.

Example.

A macro to add 1 to the contents of location N.

MACRO INSTRUCTION written as ADD 1 (N)

ADD 1 (N) generates

$$
\begin{cases}
\left. \begin{array}{l} \text{S: 0} \\ \text{STA S} \end{array} \right\} \text{saves present accumulator contents} \\[2ex]
\left. \begin{array}{l} \text{LDN 1} \\ \text{ADD N} \\ \text{STA N} \end{array} \right\} \text{adds 1 to location N} \\[3ex]
\text{LDA S} \left. \right\} \text{replaces original accumulator contents.}
\end{cases}
$$

SUMMARY

32.36 a. Low-level languages are machine orientated, are easier for the programmer than machine language because of their symbolic and mnemonic forms, but require translation to machine code before they can be executed.

b. There is a one-to-one relationship between low-level language instructions and machine-language instructions, with the exception of macros.

c. It is possible to build the high-level program constructs such as control structures and data structures from low-level language instructions. One high-level instruction may take several low-level instructions to implement.

d. When a subroutine is called, parameters have to be set up prior to the call, the return address and contents of registers need to be saved for the return and within the subroutine local variables may be created. The exact mechanisms vary considerably from machine to machine.

e. The two types of subroutine are:
   i. Open subroutines: essentially part of the program.
   ii. Closed subroutines: linked to the program at various stages in its execution.

POINTS TO NOTE

32.37 a. The reader is strongly recommended to gain practical experience of a real assembly language having once gained familiarity with the contents of this chapter.

b. Assembly-language instructions may be referred to as "external symbolic machine instructions".

STUDENT SELF-TESTING QUESTIONS

1. Describe the action of the following instructions.
   a. SUN 7
   b. ADD @ 7
   c. ADD 7
   d. SUB 7,X
2. Distinguish between low-level languages and machine language.

STUDENT SELF-TEST QUESTIONS CONTINUED

3. Define the terms
   a. assembler program
   b. assembly language
   c. assembly process

4. Given that the ASCII value of "*" is 52_8 and that
   a. LDN 52
      IO 2

   will cause the output of a "*"

   b. LDA CR
      IO 2
      LDA LF
      IO 2

   will terminate the current line of output and prepare the printer for the next line.
   Write a program in assembly language to output a triangle of asterisks thus:

```
          *
        *   *
      *   *   *
    *   *   *   *
```

5. A particular computer has a 16 bit word length and supports two's complement integer arithmetic with the following instructions:

   ADD loc1, loc2   ..adds the contents of loc1 to the contents of loc2
   INC loc1   . . adds 1 to the contents of loc1
   ADC loc1   . . adds the contents of the carry register C to the contents
                    of loc1
   CMP loc1   . . one's complements the contents of loc1

   where loc1 and loc2 are the addresses of two locations in memory and C is a single bit carry register.
   Further with the first three instructions the carry register C is set to 1 if there is a "carry-out" otherwise C is set to 0.
   a. State the maximum and minimum values that can be stored in a single location. Show also the bit settings.   *(4 marks)*
   b. Show the sequence of instructions that will allow the contents of one location to be subtracted from another location.   *(3 marks)*
   c. State the maximum and minimum values that could be manipulated by using two consecutive locations ie, double length integer working. Show also the bit settings.   *(4 marks)*
   d. Show the sequence of instructions that will permit double length working for
      i. addition,
      ii. subtraction.   *(7 marks)*
   e. Show how your answer to part d.ii. may be set up as a macro instruction.

     (2 marks)

   (AEB)

QUESTIONS WITHOUT ANSWERS

6. Rewrite your answer to question 4 as a subroutine where the vertical height is passed as a parameter.

7. Write a subroutine that takes three IN parameter values, arranges them into ascending numerical sequence and returns them together with their total.

8. An 8 bit byte contains the ASCII code for one of the characters A through F, decimal 65 through 70 respectively. These characters may be considered to represent a hexadecimal digit. Show how the contents of this byte would be converted to the binary integer value represented by this code. Your answer should consist of a sequence of one address instructions.

(4 marks)

(AEB)

GLOSSARY CHECKLIST

33: The Input-Output Subsystem

INTRODUCTION

33.1 This chapter discusses the general methods of computer input and output (I/O for short). It first introduces terminology and I/O problems. It then develops a discussion of the methods of I/O and shows how the various problems are overcome. The main methods discussed include the use of buffers, multiplexors, data channels, and, perhaps the most important, interrupts.

33.2 An overall view of a **typical Input-Output** (I/O) system is provided by Fig. 33.1. Reference to this diagram may be made throughout this chapter, but we will first define some terminology to be used.

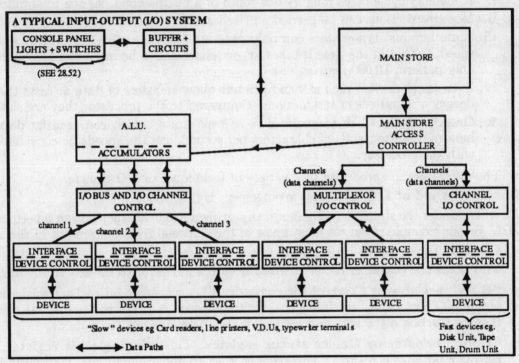

Fig. 33.1.

33.3 A **buffer** is a temporary storage area that holds data during different stages of input or output. A buffer may be one of the following types:

    a. Internal buffer area. This is an area of main store set aside to hold data awaiting output or data recently input but not yet processed.

    b. Buffer registers. These registers are located at various positions along the data path between the I/O devices and the processor. They hold characters or groups of characters in the process of being transferred.

33.4 A **channel** is a path along which I/O data signals flow. Control signals follow a similar path to regulate the data flow. The peripheral end of the channel may be called a **port.**

33.5 A **bus** (also known as a **highway**) is an item of hardware within the processor through which data signals pass from any one of a choice of sources to any one of a choice of destinations. On one side are connections to the channels for various devices including memory, on the other are connections to accumulators in the ALU.

33.6 An **Interface** is an item of hardware located on each channel adjacent to the processor. It converts control and data signals from the processor, which are in a **standard form,** to forms usable by the device connected to the interface. It also turns all peripheral input to **one standard form for the processor.**

The I/O control signals received by the interface from the processor are usually generated by I/O **control circuitry,** which itself is under the control of the **main control unit.**

33.7 On the device side of the interface further **device-control circuitry** is at work. Part of it may be an integral part of the interface, yet more is resident within the device itself. This **control circuitry** is capable of a large amount of **autonomous operation** but works in response to conditions established by the **I/O control circuitry.**

33.8 Reference to Fig 33.1 will show the many paths between devices and main store that are available and that some of these paths do not require the data to go via the accumulators in the ALU. The reasons for this and details of operation will come later in the chapter. For the moment it should be noted that Fig 33.1 is intended to emphasise the different possible data paths, but in practical terms the circuitry may be such that to external appearances all data pass through one rather elaborate bus.

33.9 **The problems of speed differences.**

    a. Communications between the processor and peripherals are fraught with problems caused by the differences in speeds between the two. To put this into context the following points may be considered.

        i. A memory cycle takes roughly one-tenth of a microsecond, ie, one ten-millionth of a second.

        ii. Most instructions can be carried out well within 1 microsecond.

        iii. Some terminal typewriters can only generate 100 characters per second when at maximum speed, so that in the time it takes for one character to be input the computer could comfortably perform 10,000 instructions.

        iv. Even faster devices such as band printers allow transfers of data at rates that correspond to dozens or hundreds of instructions. Compared to the processor they are slow.

        v. Only for devices like magnetic disk or tape units, which can transfer data at the rate of hundreds of thousands of characters per second, can the speeds be considered as compatible with the processor.

    b. The differences in speed lead to a variety of techniques of I/O transfer.

33.10 **Simple method of I/O** (a typical arrangement is described).

We will consider the simplest method of transferring a single character from a peripheral and use the VDU for our example. First we must know of three special registers present in the interface card.

    a. **Data buffer or Data buffer register.**

    This holds one character either received from the device or to be sent to the device.

    b. **"Busy" register or Control bit register.** This is a single bit register solely under the control of the I/O control, ie, not influenced by the device. It is set to 1 when the channel is opened, thereby starting a transfer, and set to 0 if the channel is not to be used.

    c. **"Done" register or Device status register.** This is a **single bit register** normally set to zero as a busy bit is set to 1. This register is set to one when a signal is received from the device, as it completes the transfer between itself and the data buffer register. A single bit register of this type is often called a FLAG.

This diagram summarises the arrangements (it is not intended to give a complete picture).

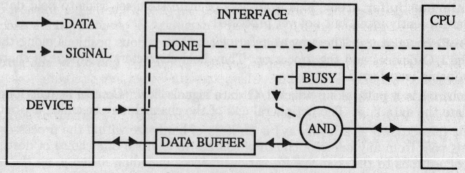

33.11 **Crude, inefficient method of I/O)** (because the partial autonomy of the device is not used).

The following annotated pseudocode shows the types of machine instructions used in the various stages of input.

    Notation   B :   Value of busy register

                      D :   Value of flag in done register

Begin

Start input on specified device $\Bigg\{$ The control circuitry will set B to 1 and send signals that will initiate the transfer of a character from the device to the data buffer register. It will also set D to zero. The peripheral then operates autonomously.

while D <> 1
endwhile $\Bigg\{$ Repeated checks to see if the device has set the device status register to 1, thereby indicating the completed transfer of data to the buffer.

$\Big\{$ This is a "listen loop". The processor would waste time repeating this loop thousands of times.

transfer data from
data buffer to accumulator $\Big\{$ A single machine instruction.

store contents of accumulator
in main storage $\Big\{$ A single machine instruction.
end

Note.

i. A similar procedure is adopted for output.

ii. This method is only sensible if the processor has nothing to do until it receives the data. Not the usual case in any reasonable system.

iii. Some "editing" of input data may be necessary before it is stored, eg, parity bits may be stripped off or one code form changed to another, eg, BCD to pure binary.

33.12 Simple I/O with other devices. In principle many devices can operate in the manner just described with slight variations. Some examples are:

a. **Document Readers.** Extra instructions are needed for non-read actions such as removing the document from the hopper. The device-status register is not just a single flag register as before, but holds codes giving information on such things as when the document is under the read station, when no documents are left, or when a document is jammed. Again each separate character is read in much the same way as described before.

b. **Line Printer.** The **data buffer** register will hold a number of characters corresponding to a section of a line or a whole line. Characters are loaded into this buffer one after another and once the register is full a single print action is started by a suitable instruction.

c. **Graph Plotter.** All drawing actions can be reduced to instructions such as:

   i. Raise or lower pen.
   ii. Move pen one unit across $\pm$ Y direction.
   iii. Move pen (or drum) one unit side to side in $\pm$ X direction.

The instruction operand contains a control code for the appropriate movement. The instruction starts the device action, which when terminated results in a flag being set.

Note. c.ii. and c.iii. may be combined to give 8 possible moves.

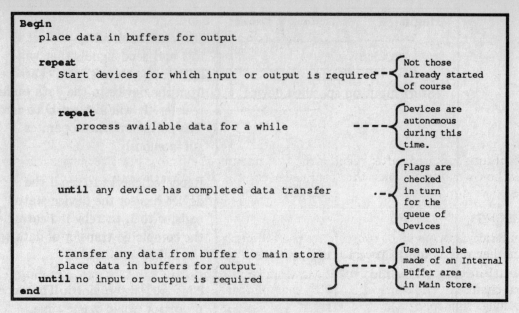

```
Begin
    place data in buffers for output

    repeat
        Start devices for which input or output is required

        repeat
            process available data for a while

        until any device has completed data transfer

        transfer any data from buffer to main store
        place data in buffers for output
    until no input or output is required
end
```

- Not those already started of course
- Devices are autonomous during this time.
- Flags are checked in turn for the queue of Devices
- Use would be made of an Internal Buffer area in Main Store.

Fig. 33.2.

33.13 Where the program needs to make use of **several devices** for input and output and has processing to do at the same time, the following technique may be adopted. The method makes slightly better use of the processor's time, but *"listening"* still forms part of the method.

BUFFERING

33.14 Buffering. The technique just described is a simple example of buffering. Buffering is the name given to the technique of transferring data into temporary storage prior to processing or output, thus enabling the simultaneous operation of devices. This can only be achieved because of the autonomous operation of peripherals, which leaves the processor **free for other work.**

33.15 Example. Suppose 2000 documents need to be input and the details on the document printed out on a line printer (one print line being used for each document read). The document reader operates at 1000 documents per minute and the printer at 500 lines per minute. The processing cycle and time required, would be as illustrated at Fig. 33.3.

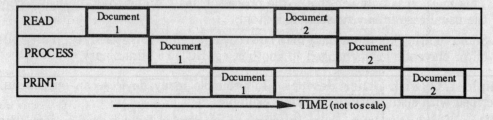

Fig. 33.3

Total time required:

$$\text{READ} = 2000 \times \frac{1}{1000} = \text{2 MINUTES}$$

$$\text{PROCESS} \quad \text{NEGLIGIBLE} \quad -$$

$$\text{PRINT} \quad 2000 \times \frac{1}{500} = \text{4 MINUTES}$$

$$\text{TOTAL} \quad \text{6 MINUTES}$$

33.16 It should be recognised that whilst a document is being processed both the document reader and printer are idle. Similarly, when a document is being read the processor and printer are idle, and when a line is being printed the processor and reader are idle.

33.17 Solution. Buffering is the name given to the technique of transferring data into temporary storage prior to *processing or output.* This enables the *simultaneous operation of devices* as illustrated at Fig. 33.4.

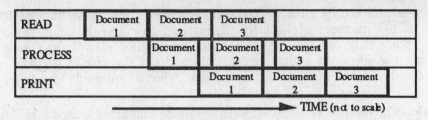

Fig. 33.4.

Total time required: after reading the first document all subsequent reading, processing and printing can be overlapped. Thus the total time required is a little over the speed of the slowest device, ie, just over 4 minutes.

MULTIPLEXING

33.18 Buffering is one way of overcoming the differences in speed of hardware devices and the processor. Another way is by the use of **multiplexors.**

33.19 Multiplexing. This involves the transmission of character codes from a number of devices along one channel. The hardware device that performs this task is called a **multiplexor.** (Alternative spelling: multiplexer.)

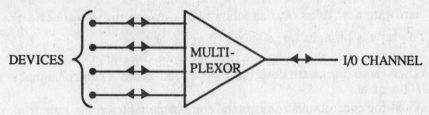

33.20 How it works. The multiplexor has its own buffer register used to receive characters from the various devices to which it is connected. These characters may be transmitted directly to a buffer area in main store as they arrive in the multiplexor buffer or they may be transmitted in a block at regular intervals. Either way a number of control signals are sent to and fro in order to identify the source of data so as to reorder it when received in main store (see Fig. 33.5). Multiplexors may act **synchronously** (ie, transfer data at a regular timed frequency) or **asynchronously** (ie, transfer data as it is ready). Devices 1, 2 and 3 are inputting the strings ABC, PQR and XYZ respectively.

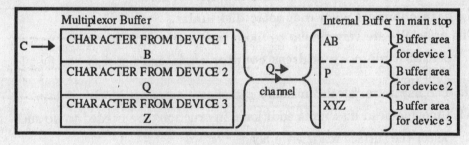

Fig. 33.5.

Note.

i.   B has been transmitted and is about to be replaced by C in the multiplexor buffer.

ii. Q has just been received in the multiplexor buffer and is being transmitted.

iii. Z has been transmitted.

iv. Synchronous operation would involve a regular scan and clearing of the buffer.

33.21 Communications multiplexors. Multiplexors are particularly useful in handling data from a number of terminals placed at positions remote from the central processor and connected by telephone links. **Communications multiplexors** are themselves remote from the central processor and transmit data from a number of terminals connected to them. They often provide simultaneous transmission of data from several devices. There are various practical possibilities.

DATA CHANNELS

33.22 You will see from Fig. 33.1 that the transfer of data between main store and devices such as disk or drum units is through a direct channel often called a **data channel.** Once the necessary conditions have been established by software, the transfers are entirely under the control of hardware. The data channel "steals" memory cycles from the instruction currently being performed in order to do the transfer. Since only one memory access can be handled at a time (through the main store-access controller), the access by a data channel slows down the rate of program memory accesses. Once started the device has autonomous operation. This technique is known as **DMA** (Direct Memory Access).

33.23 Example. The method is discussed with reference to magnetic tape and disk. We take the *magnetic tape case first.* You may wish to refresh your memory about the physical features of these units and the blocking of records (7.10 and 21.11) before you read on.

   a. Before the transfer can take place, machine instructions must be used to do the following:

      i. The tape is wound forward from the header label so as to bring the read /write heads over the IBG, which lies in front of the first block of records on the tape file. (When writing *all* previous blocks and gaps are overwritten.)

      ii. Data from the tape will be read into an internal buffer area (or data will be written from this area to the tape). The address of the first location in this buffer will be placed into a special **memory address counter register.**

      iii. The number of records or blocks to be read (or written) will be placed in another register.

      iv. The tape read instruction is then issued.

   b. The hardware now takes over as follows (ie, **autonomous operation**).

      i. The tape is brought up to speed (if necessary).

      ii. Magnetic coded marks on the tape indicate the start of the tape block to be read.

      iii. When these marks are detected by the read heads a control signal is issued by the tape drive I/O control.

      iv. When the control unit receives the control signal from the tape it automatically uses the next available memory cycle to transfer the first character between the tape block and the address specified in the memory address counter register.

      v. The memory address counter register is increased by one, and the counter of number of records transferred adjusted.

      vi. The hardware continues automatically to steal memory cycles (perhaps taking every other one) until the counter indicates that the transfer of all characters is complete).

      vii. A "done" flag is then set by the I/O control unit.

33.24 Using data channels with magnetic disk units.

   a. The principles are very similar to those used with magnetic tape:

      i. Setting **a memory address counter register** to specify the first location of the internal buffer area.

      ii. The hardware "steals" memory cycles as it transfers blocks of data.

   b. With moving-head disk units additional instructions are needed to do such things as:

      i. Select the surface read/write head.

      ii. Move the heads over the appropriate tracks.

   c. The unit detects data block positions by code marks on the disk. Timing tracks enable the I/O control to maintain accurate rotational speeds.

SYSTEM CONTROLS

33.25 The I/O methods described so far have been described in terms of a single program handling the data transfers. To fully appreciate our next method you need to know these points about the **operating system** that handles it. (Operating systems are described in detail in chapter 34.)

   a. An operating system is a suite of programs that takes control over the operation of the computer.

   b. A minimum operating system, and centre of a large one, is an "Executive" or "Supervisor" program, which controls and schedules the use of hardware.

   c. A program requiring to input or output data does so via the operating system in all but the simplest machines. The next method will be described in terms of such an arrangement.

INTERRUPTS

33.26 An **interrupt** is a break into the normal automatic sequential control, so that instead of fetching the next instruction as part of the fetch execute cycle the control unit fetches the first instruction of another program (the supervisor), or an instruction from another part of the same program. Details will be given in the next few paragraphs.

33.27 Use of interrupts in I/O. (Practical implementations vary; this example is simplified but typical.) For ease of explanation we start with a device that has *completed* a data transfer and therefore requires service.

   a. The device attempts an interrupt request by setting the "done" flag to "1". If the device's interrupt status is also "1" (ie, busy = 1) a "1" will also be loaded into a device status register, thus making an interrupt request.

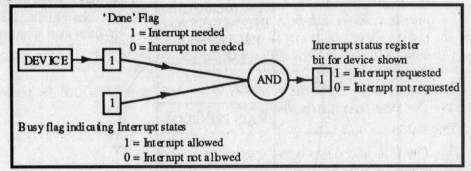

   b. Just prior to **fetching** the next instruction, during the normal sequence of instructions, a check is made automatically by the processor hardware to see if there are any **interrupt requests** (interrupt bit 1). If there are requests then there is a break in the normal sequence of instructions and the interrupt requests are dealt with. Control is then returned to the original interrupted program.

   c. The checks for interrupts are only done if the interrupt system (hardware) is activated, so instructions usually exist for turning the interrupt system on or off. (An interrupt ON/OFF flag is used.)

   d. Since more than one device may request an interrupt at any given time, a position of priority is assigned to each device, eg, by the position of the devices bit in the interrupt register.

   e. A program that wishes to output data can request an interrupt in a similar way to a device. One way is to use an instruction that sets a special interrupt bit to "1". The resultant interrupt causes an immediate exit from the program to the supervisor. On some systems the interrupt request is generated by the program attempting an I/O instruction. The hardware "traps" the instruction and causes an interrupt.

33.28 The role of the supervisor. After an interrupt the supervisor is entered as follows:

   a. One particular location is used to hold the address of the first instruction in the supervisor program, eg, location zero may be used; we will assume it is.

   b. An interrupt request causes the processor hardware to instigate an unconditional jump to the instruction whose address is specified in location zero. In this way the supervisory program is entered.

   Provision is made for the supervisor program to save the link in order to return to the main program, eg, the interrupt may place the contents of the SCR in a specified accumulator register.

   c. On being entered the supervisor has these tasks to do:

      i. The link for return to the main program must be saved.

      ii. The contents of all the accumulators must be saved so that they may be replaced before returning to the main program.

      iii. If an interrupt occurred during execution of a routine which was itself handling I/O from a device, it could cause the loss of data by that routine. In such cases the routine usually switches off the interrupt system until it has completed its task and then switches it on again. While the interrupt system is switched off no interrupt can take place (an interrupt ON/OFF flag 1 = ON O = OFF shows the interrupt system status).

      iv. If the interrupt system is left on while handling one interrupt, it is possible that yet another interrupt will occur. If this happens, then again steps b and c will be repeated. It is usual to store links and accumulator contents in LIFO stacks so that they can be obtained in the reverse order.

Note. A stack may be used for i. and ii. in a similar manner to that shown in 32.30.

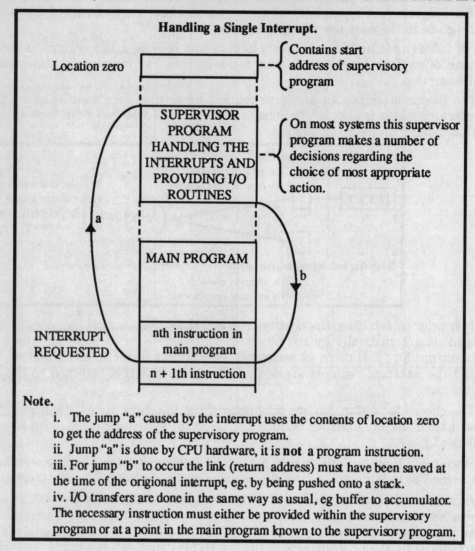

Handling a Single Interrupt.

Location zero — Contains start address of supervisory program

SUPERVISOR PROGRAM HANDLING THE INTERRUPTS AND PROVIDING I/O ROUTINES — On most systems this supervisor program makes a number of decisions regarding the choice of most appropriate action.

a

MAIN PROGRAM

b

INTERRUPT REQUESTED

nth instruction in main program

n + 1th instruction

Note.

i. The jump "a" caused by the interrupt uses the contents of location zero to get the address of the supervisory program.

ii. Jump "a" is done by CPU hardware, it is **not** a program instruction.

iii. For jump "b" to occur the link (return address) must have been saved at the time of the origional interrupt, eg. by being pushed onto a stack.

iv. I/O transfers are done in the same way as usual, eg buffer to accumulator. The necessary instruction must either be provided within the supervisory program or at a point in the main program known to the supervisory program.

Fig. 33.6.

33.29 Using interrupts for input and output provides two main advantages over the "look for flag/listen loop" method described earlier.

a. The interrupt occurs as soon as the device requires service, not when the program gets around to checking for the flag. The device can more easily be kept working at its maximum speed using interrupts.

b. It is essential with some devices that a check for the flag is made soon enough or data will have time to pass beneath the read/write heads or read stations. Interrupts allow these checks to be done as soon as possible before data is lost.

33.30 **Assigning priority.** (A more general discussion will follow later, chapter 34.) The I/O channels usually have a priority assigned to them and the positioning of the devices along the I/O bus will therefore affect their priority. There are usually ways of overriding these basic hardware priorities and we will consider them shortly. First we will consider the way device speed affects priority.

33.31 **Device speed.** Low-priority devices tend to wait a longer time for service (see device 3 in Fig. 33.7). A slow device if given low priority might eventually hold up all processing activity by not having input sufficient data. As a general rule therefore low-speed devices are given higher priority.

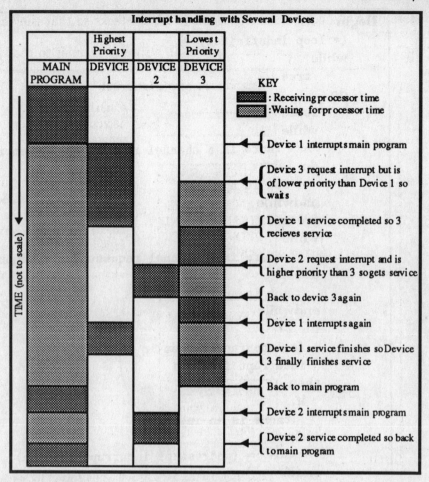

Fig. 33.7.

33.32 Masking out low-priority devices. The supervisor routine may need to prevent interrupts from low-priority devices while it handles I/O from a high-priority device. This can be done by a simple AND operation as shown here:

DEVICE	1	2	3	4	
INITIAL INTERRUPT STATUS	1	1	1	1	All devices requesting interrupts

MASK	1	0	0	0	

INTERRUPT STATUS AFTER AND WITH MASK	1	0	0	0	Only device 1 allowed to interrupt

Note. The same method can be used to change priority.

33.33 The fetch-execute cycle requires the following amendments to cater for DMA via data channels and interrupts.

429

```
Begin
    (* loop indefinitely *)
    while
        true
    do
        fetch
        while
            there is a channel request for a memory cycle
        do
            set it up
        endwhile
        execute
        while
            there is a channel request for a memory cycle
        do
            set it up
        endwhile
        if
          (* interrupt system is on *)
          interrupt flag = 1
        then
          if
            there is an interrupt
          then
            SCR := (address of interrupt routine)
          endif
        endif
    endwhile
end
```

SUMMARY

33.34 The main techniques are summarised in this table:

TECHNIQUE	DEVICE USED	PROCESSOR INVOLVEMENT	SOFTWARE/ HARDWARE ORIENTATION	COMMENTS	COMPLEXITY
"Listen loop" or program/ listen combined	Slow devices, eg, terminal typewriter	Total	S	Only used in single-program environment	Minimum
Autonomous peripheral transfer	Fast devices, eg, disk, tape	Minimal setting up and closing down hardware used	H	Processing speeds are affected because of stolen memory cycles during fetch-execute.	More complex hardware
Interrupts	Maximum advantage with slow devices Used in set up or close down autonomous peripherals	Processor free interrupts between some extra work handling interrupts	S/H	Necessary when handling more than one program	Extra hardware needed

POINTS TO NOTE

33.35 **a.** Take care to distinguish between the two types of buffer.

b. Note that when hardware "steals" memory cycles it does not change the normal sequence of instructions, it merely slows things down a little.

c. Although described separately within the chapter all the methods are usually in use on a given system.

d. It is unusual and not desirable to use some devices without an interrupt system. Most devices that are in constant motion during data transfer run more smoothly and give faster rates of transfer if operated using interrupts.

e. The use of interrupts extends beyond input and output, but the principle of working is the same. (Further discussion follows in chapter 34.)

f. The handling of data in internal buffers often involves the use of queues, stacks, strings and lists (chapter 39).

g. Buffering may be improved by **double buffering** in which one buffer is filled by the program as another is emptied by the device. The two swap over at a convenient stage (see 21.15).

STUDENT SELF-TESTING QUESTIONS

1. What are the problems of speed differences between the processor and its peripherals?
2. What is DMA? How does DMA work?

QUESTIONS WITHOUT ANSWERS

3. Suggest possible ways in which VDU I/O could be handled on a system in which multiple VDUs are in use.
4. What is meant by the following terms:
   a. channel
   b. port
   c. interface
   d. autonomous operation.

GLOSSARY CHECKLIST

Buffer	33.3	Highway	33.5
Buffering	33.14	Interface	33.6
Buffer registers	33.3	Internal buffer area	33.3
Bus	33.5	Interrupt requests	33.27
Channel	33.4	Interrupts	33.26
Communications multiplexors	33.21	Multiplexing	33.18
Data channels	33.22	Multiplexors	33.18
Double buffering	33.35	Port	33.4

34: Operating Systems

INTRODUCTION

34.1 The concept and basic purpose of an operating system was introduced in the previous chapter. This chapter explains the purposes, facilities and functions of operating systems and also describes various types of operating system.

WHY OPERATING SYSTEMS WERE ORIGINALLY DEVELOPED

34.2 Over many years the increased processing speed of the processor and its massive problem-solving capability brought about the need for more sophisticated modes of *operating* computers. *Problems* encountered on the early generations were:

a. **Set-up time.** Required as each job was put onto the machine and during which time the computer was completely *idle*. For example, changing tape reels on tape units, changing stationery on a printer, etc.

b. **Manual intervention.** This was necessary in order to investigate error conditions and to initiate corrective action. Again the machine would lie idle while this was being done.

c. **Imbalance between processor and peripherals.** This meant that the central processor was lying idle for "long" periods of time during the operations of peripheral units.

34.3 When analysed it can be seen that in a computer system composed of *many* units only a small part is "in action" performing a specific task at any one point in time. What is required is a "super controller" to ensure that the vast facilities are used to optimum advantage. It became clear that the job could only be undertaken by some form of *internally* stored program. This became known as an **operating system**.

DEFINITION

34.4 From what has just been stated, an operating system may be seen as a suite of programs that has taken over many of the functions once performed by human operators. The sophistication and speeds of modern computers is beyond the capability of human operators to control without the aid of an operating system. The role of the operating system is therefore one of resource management. The primary resources it manages are:

a. processors,

b. storage,

c. I/O devices,

d. data,

e. programs.

34.5 An **operating system** is a suite of programs that takes over the operation of the computer to the extent of being able to allow a number of programs to be run on the computer without human intervention by an operator.

BASIC ORGANISATION

34.6 It can be seen from what has been said so far that the operating system controls the way software uses hardware. This control ensures that the computer not only operates in the way intended by the user but does so in a systematic, reliable and efficient manner. This "view" of the operating system is shown in Fig. 34.1.

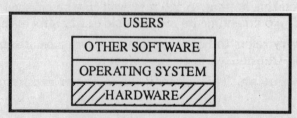

Fig. 34.1. The Operating System's place in the organisation of the overall system.

BASIC ORGANISATION

34.7 Part of the operating system remains in main storage permanently during the running of the computer. This part is called the EXECUTIVE (or SUPERVISOR or KERNEL) and as the name suggests is the "controlling" part of the operating system. It controls the running of all other programs. The remainder of the operating-system programs are stored on a direct-access storage device (preferably) from which any particular one will be "called" into main storage by the executive when required.

34.8 On small computers the operating system takes the form of a rudimentary control program normally called a **monitor**.

34.9 On many very small microcomputers the monitor is stored permanently in ROM and starts execution the moment the computer is turned on. A message is usually displayed on the VDU screen by the monitor to signify it is ready to accept commands, which the user may type in at a keyboard.

34.10 On most other modern computers the monitor or executive is not in main storage when the machine is switched on. The system must be "booted up". This often involves pressing special "boot buttons" or switches, which cause the hardware to load the monitor or executive into main storage from a predetermined position on a disk.

THE FUNCTIONS OF AN OPERATING SYSTEM

34.11 The functions may include:

a. The scheduling and loading of programs, or subprograms, in order to provide a continuous sequence of processing or to provide appropriate responses to events.

b. Control over hardware resources, eg, control over the selection and operation of devices used for input, output or storage.

c. Protecting hardware, software and data from improper use.

d. Calling into main storage of programs and subroutines as and when required.

e. Passing of control from one job (program) to another under a system of priority when more than one application program occupies main storage.

f. Provision of error correction routines.

g. Furnishing a complete record of all that happens during processing (usually in the form of a printed log).

h. Communication with the computer operator usually by means of the console typewriter. The operator communicates with the operating system by means of a JCL (Job Control Language), which is translated and executed by an interactive command interpreter.

METHODS OF OPERATION AND MODES OF ACCESS

34.12 Operating systems are often described in terms of the methods by which they *operate the system* and the modes of system access they provide. The common alternatives are introduced here. More detail will be given in the following paragraphs where necessary.

a. **Multiprocessing.** This is the name for the situation that occurs if two or more processors are present in a computer system and are sharing some or all of the same memory. In such cases two programs may be processed at the same instant. In the remainder of this discussion assume just one processor is used unless otherwise stated.

b. **Multiprogramming.** This occurs when more than one program in main storage is being processed **apparently** at the same time. This is accomplished by the programs taking turns at short bursts of processing time.

c. **Batch processing.** The job (program + data) is not processed until fully input. The jobs are entered and stored on a disk in a **batch queue** and then run one or more at a time under the control of the operating system. A job may wait in a batch queue for minutes or hours depending on the work load. No amendments are possible during processing.

d. **Remote job entry** refers to batch processing where jobs are entered at a terminal remote from the computer and transmitted in to the computer.

e. **Interactive computing.** This occurs if the computer and terminal user can communicate with each other.

433

    f. **Conversational mode.** This is interactive computer operation where the response to the user's message is immediate.

    g. **Multi-access.** This occurs if the computer allows interactive facilities to more than one user at a time.

    h. **Time-sharing.** Processor time is divided into small units called **time slices** and shared in turn between users to provide multi-access.

    i. **Real-time system.** A real-time system is a computer system that is capable of processing data so quickly that the results are available to influence the activity currently taking place. There is often a need for multiprocessing and a front-end processor in these systems.

CHOICE OF OPERATING SYSTEM

34.13 Choice of operating system. The applications for which a computer is needed largely determine the choice of hardware and accompanying software. The operating-system supplier will need to consider these factors:

    a. The hardware provision and basic design of the computer.

    b. The applications intended for the computer.

    c. The method of communication with the computer, eg, many or few peripherals.

    d. The method of operating the computer.

TYPES OF OPERATING SYSTEM

34.14 Single-program systems. The majority of small microcomputer-based systems have **monitors**, which allow a single user to operate the machine in an interactive conversational mode but normally only allow one user program to be in main storage and processed at a time, ie, there is no multiprogramming of user programs.

34.15 There are a number of well-established operating systems that fall into this category. Apart from those operating systems that are specific to particular manufacturer's machines there are some that are available on a wide variety of different machines. Examples: CP/M (Control Program for Microcomputers) produced by Digital Research and MSDOS produced by Microsoft.

34.16 Simple batch systems. These are systems that provide multiprogramming of batch programs but have few facilities for interaction or multi-access. Many commercial computer systems in use during the 1960s and early 1970s were of this type.

34.17 Multi-access and Time-sharing systems. The majority of operating systems fall into this category, but there is a wide range of complexity in such systems.

34.18 On the larger microcomputers and smaller minicomputers there are a number of operating systems that are available for use on a variety of machines produced by many different manufacturers including SUN, SEQUENT, UNISYS, PEC and even IBM. One such operating system that is gaining in popularity is UNIX, which was developed by Bell Laboratories in the USA.

34.19 On large minicomputers and mainframes, operating systems are normally specific to the particular machine and manufacturer.

34.20 Real-time systems. The operating system has to cater for the type of real-time system being used. The three types are given here in order of increasingly fast response time.

    a. A more complex multi-access time-sharing system where each user has a largely independent choice of system facilities, eg, each using a different language.

    b. Commercial real-time systems in which there is essentially one job, such as handling booking, and the multi-access user has a clerical rather than programming function. These systems often make use of extensive data bases.

    c. **Process control systems,** eg, a system to control the operation of a chemical-factory plant. Response to changes must be as fast as possible and reliability is essential. Real-time process control systems vary greatly in size. The big systems, such as the one just mentioned, are at one extreme. At the other extreme are the embedded Real-time control systems used in microprocessor-based instruments and monitoring devices, eg, the control system in a service station petrol pump.

OPERATING SYSTEM LANGUAGES

34.21 The three types of language to be considered here are:

    a. Command languages.

b. Job-control languages.

c. Languages in which to write operating-system software.

34.22 Command language. A programming language used for communications with the operating system is called a command language (see 11.7). Most statements (commands) in the language are directives requiring immediate execution and are handled by **command interpreters.** Some command languages provide no more than a set of single-line commands, which may be keyed in by a user, eg, individual commands to print, compile, load, execute, copy or delete a named file. Other command languages also provide control structures so that commands may be selected or repeated according to specified conditions. An example of the latter is the shell language on the UNIX operating system (34.18).

34.23 Job Control Language (JCL). This is a special command language that is used to identify jobs and state their requirements to the operating system. JCLs are of particular importance in batch processing. An example of a fictitious JCL now follows.

34.24 Example. The **JCL program** shown here is a user's fictitious JCL program. Assume that it is to be loaded by the operating system and then executed under the action of a JCL interpreter that forms part of the monitor.

A JCL program called ABC.JCL.

```
* USER 12345
* COPY XYZ.CBL (DISK 1) FROM XYZ.CBL (TAPE 1)
* COMPILE XYZ.CBL (DISK1)
* LOAD XYZ.OBJ (DISK 1)
* RUN
* ENDJOB
```

Notes.

i. The first JCL command identifies the user to the operating system. The operating system can check that the user's number, ie, 12345, is valid and then book charges to the user's account.

ii. The copy command causes the operating system to copy COBOL source program "XYZ.CBL" from a magnetic tape input device onto disk. The copy is given the same name.

iii. The third JCL command causes the program XYZ.CBL to be compiled. Assume that the "COBOL" compiler is to be used. The compiler produces an object program XYZ.OBJ which may be written to disk.

iv. The fourth JCL command causes the program XYZ.OBJ to be loaded into main storage either replacing the compiler or to some other part of main storage.

v. The fifth JCL command causes the program in main storage to be executed.

vi. The sixth JCL command indicates the end of the JCL program.

34.25 Languages in which to write operating system software vary considerably. It is common to find some parts of the operating system's software written in assembly language because of the machine-orientated nature of the software or for reasons of efficiency. However, in order to aid operating-system portability and improve system programmer productivity a number of higher-level languages are used. These are often variations on high-level languages or are special-purpose languages. For example, there are system programming languages based upon PL/1 such as PL/M, which was used in the creation of CP/M (34.15), and there are special-purpose languages such as BCPL, and "C", which is used on the UNIX system. "C" has gradually been adopted for a wide variety of purposes.

PROCESSES

34.26 A concept fundamental to the understanding of how an operating system works is that of a process.

34.27 A **process** may be thought of as the *execution of a program,* and clearly the process will be carried out by a processor. However, there is rather more to the idea of a process than that because it is seldom the case that there is just one program assigned to a given processor for execution.

34.28 At this point it may help to use a simple analogy. Let us compare a processor executing a program with a student reading a book borrowed from the library. It will help if we think of the *process* of "reading the book" as starting once the book is borrowed and ending when the book is returned. The student (processor) will have other things to do than just carry out the process of reading the book and so at any one time the book may be waiting for the reader to start or continue reading it, or have the student in the act of reading it. Whenever the student sets the book to one side in order to do something else it will be necessary for the student to remember the point reached in the text and to remember any facts needed in order to be able to read on later. This is very like the case when the processor executes a program. The process may be in a state where it is waiting for the processor to continue execution or it may be in the running state. If running is suspended it will be necessary to save details of the point reached in the program and the state of variables, registers, etc.

34.29 **Example.** Consider the execution of the JCL program given in paragraph 34.24. The whole job is a process and stages in the job involve other processes. The process begins when the system gets the job and identifies it and the user. The process ends with the system recording the final details of the user's use of the computer. The stages in the job are:

> **Begin**
>> Copy XYZ.CBL
>> Compile XYZ.CBL
>> Load XYZ.OBJ
>> Execute XYZ.OBJ
>
> **end**

34.30 Each of these four stages is a process. The first three processes involve executing system programs and the last one involves executing an applications program. The job process has its execution suspended each time it requires one of these processes to be created and run. Its execution resumes after each of these processes is completed until eventually the job process is completed. There are some complications to this situation, however. First, if an error arises during the execution of a process and is detected by the operating system then the process will be suspended. Should the error be one that the operating system cannot overcome (a " **fatal**" error), the process will be aborted (examples of such errors will be given later). Secondly, if multiprogramming is taking place, processes will be suspended and resumed as they take turns at using the processor. We will now pursue these ideas further by examining multiprogramming in batch.

MULTIPROGRAMMING IN BATCH

34.31 The operating system will try to optimise the use of hardware by jobs currently available to it using the following methods.

34.32 **Job priority.** It is also advantageous to assign a priority to the job before it is submitted, for example, by a command switch (11.8). The two factors influencing this are:

a. The relative proportion of I/O operation and processing.

  i. A job requiring a **large amount of I/O operation** will be given **high priority** because such a program will allow other programs more opportunity to use processor time.

  ii. A job requiring a large amount of processor time would be given **low priority** because if given high **priority** it would prevent I/O programs from obtaining the small amount of processor time they need.

b. A secondary factor is the urgency with which the program must respond to peripherals, since data can be lost if some devices such as magnetic tape units are not serviced in time.

Note The **priority** of a job is **not** the same as its **importance**.

34.33 a. Jobs requiring a large amount of peripheral time are called **peripheral bound** or **I/O bound**.

b. Jobs requiring a large amount of processing time and little I/O are called **processor bound**, or **CPU bound**.

34.34 **Scheduling.** There are two types of scheduling in a batch-operating system.

a. **Job schedule.** This system software routine works out a "priority index" for each job based on such factors as:

  i. Processor time required by the job.
  ii. I/O time required by the job.
  iii. Resources available on-line, eg, free memory and free I/O devices.
  iv. The deadline by which the job must be completed.

b. **Processor schedule.** This system software routine is entered frequently to decide "WHAT TO DO NEXT"'. It works out the hardware resources currently demanded by each job and checks what resources are available. It then gives processor time to the most appropriate job according to a **scheduling strategy** such as : "Process the highest, priority job that can use available resources". The job given processor time will run until

  i. It has ended,
    or
  ii. an interrupt occurs, eg, I/O request, operator break-in or run-time error,
    or
  iii. an interrupt is requested by the job, eg, for output.

34.35 Passing control from one job to another under a scheduling scheme. This transfer of control is handled by the executive as follows:

a. The cause of an interrupt may be:

  i. **External**, eg, an input device requesting service, or
  ii. **internal**, eg, a programming error that causes an exit from the compiler.

In either case control is transferred to the executive.

b. In the case of an external interrupt the executive might transfer control to a routine to handle data input, taking it from a **processor-bound** program.

c. In the case of an internal interrupt the executive might terminate the job and pass control to the most suitable program under the given scheduling scheme.

THE GENERAL WORK OF OPERATING SYSTEMS

34.36 Before examining examples of operating systems in more detail we will find it helpful at this stage to look through the general work common to most operating systems. The main headings are:-

a. I/O control
b. Interrupt handling
c. Error correction
d. Device allocation
e. File security and management
f. Log of events and operator communication
g. Loading programs and subroutines
h. Storage management

34.37 I/O control. This will consist of a set of programs for controlling the input from and output to the various devices. These programs form part of the executive and are entered via the executive when an interrupt occurs, eg, one such program might set up and read blocks from a tape.

34.38 Interrupt handling. This is one function of the executive. When an interrupt occurs, control is passed to the executive, which determines the cause of the interrupt and transfers control to the most appropriate program. Sources of interrupts are listed here.

a. **An interrupt caused by power failure.** This usually has highest priority. The executive saves vital information using the dying power supply so that it can be restarted when power is returned.

b. **Arithmetic or logic errors.** When the arithmetic and logic unit detects that an error has taken place it generates a signal that causes an interrupt, eg, overflow or underflow may cause an error signal, or output may be requested to a non-existent device. Control is transferred to the executive, which initiates the appropriate error routines. Control will be returned to the program once corrective action has been taken and error messages printed, or in the case of a fatal error that cannot be corrected the program will be suspended permanently.

c. **Hardware malfunction** (eg, parity errors) The I/O control for each device and its associated hardware normally takes care of parity checking. If a parity error is detected the executive is notified by an interrupt, and so on.

d. A clock, often called a real-time clock, can generate interrupts at regular time intervals by treating this clock as an input device. This facility provides the means by which **time-sharing** can take place.

e. I/O interrupts (33.26).

f. **External interrupts** caused by events such as the operator pressing an interrupt key in the console or caused by signals from other processes in a multiprocessor machine.

34.39 Provision of error-correction routines. Little can be done about errors in jobs that are the result of programming faults, apart from providing information as to the type of fault. The operating system should be able to handle errors that occur as part of the normal operating activity however. For example, if data is lost during transfer because of late service of an interrupt, a routine should be available to recover the data by setting up the read process again.

34.40 Allocation of devices. Several jobs may request the same output media. If more than one output device is available for that medium, then some programs will be allocated one device and other programs another device. If subsequently the queue for one device is longer than for another then reallocations are made. To do this track must be kept of the allocations made.

Example

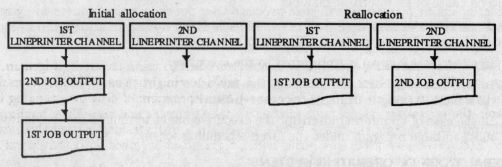

34.41 File security and management. This involves these main activities:

a. Preventing illegal access or amendments to user or system files.

b. "Dumping" the contents of files from time to time in case of future loss, eg, disk files may be transferred to tape and then stored off-line.

c. Keeping track of file descriptions and locations.

34.42 Furnishing a log of events.

a. Most of the information will be presented to the console typewriter and provided by a monitor program, which keeps track of job execution and hardware use. These may also alternatively be written to a tape file or disk file called the journal.

b. Information may also be furnished as part of the user's job output either as a result of errors or because of job-control requests. Further contributions to the console log come from communication with the operator.

34.43 Communication with the operator. This is usually via the console keyboard. Apart from the operator's job of loading and unloading peripherals mentioned earlier the operator also has the responsibility of dealing with errors missed by the operating system, and in the event of operating-system failure the operator must re-establish it. The operator can key in responses to prompts from the system and also key in commands available in the command language (paragraph 22). Routine activities include:

a. Operator activities such as:-

   i. Using the command language to load jobs or other software.

   ii. Using the command language to call in routines for tracing faults.

   iii. Using the command language to terminate a job, eg, in the case where a program starts printing out page after page of garbage.

b. System messages such as:

   i. Reporting the completed run of a job.

   ii. Reporting details of job usage, eg, time it ran and processor time used.

   iii. Reporting program suspension caused by error conditions such as lack of input data or device not connected.

   iv. Requests for operator action, eg, loading, unloading and connecting peripherals.

34.44 Loading programs and subroutines.

Main storage is not usually able to hold all the software that is being used so transfers between main storage and direct-access storage are frequently being made. The following transfers are handled:

a. Loading system software into main store as required, eg, a compiler.

b. Swapping applications programs or part of the programs between main storage and direct-access storage as part of the multiprogramming activity.

c. Bringing into main store and linking together the applications or systems subroutines to be used in conjunction with particular jobs.

STORAGE MANAGEMENT

34.45 The operating system may organise main storage into blocks of convenient size called **partitions**. It can then allocate storage space by partitions rather than by piecemeal allocation by individual locations.

a. In order to place jobs in whatever partition of main storage is available the programs must be **relocatable** (see 31.55). Their **absolute (hardware) address** is set by the executive when it adds the base address of the partition to the relative address of each instruction.

b. The executive may be able to change continually the allocation of programs by repeated reapplications of the process described in (a). This is called **dynamic allocation** of main storage.

34.46 Tasking, Multi-tasking and segmenting.

a. Today, the term **multi-tasking** is most often taken to mean the multiprogramming of *user programs*. On a single-user computer *without multi-tasking*, such as MSDOS, the multiprogramming is primitive in that there is typically a very limited number of programs running together. These are: the operating system, *one* interactive user program and *possibly* a **background** (ie, non-interactive) program running a printer queue. In a multi-tasking system there can be a number of interactive user programs being multiprogrammed together with the operating system and probably some background tasks too.

b. True multi-tasking is **pre-emptive** which means that if a process is interrupted it will not necessarily be resumed immediately after the interrupt has been serviced because other processes may have a higher priority. Modern general purpose minicomputers and mainframes have pre-emptive multi-tasking operating systems. In the case of **non pre-emptive multi-tasking** a single user process, if interrupted, will normally be resumed once the interrupt has been serviced and may therefore gain an unfair share of the processors time. It has the general appearance of multi-tasking to the user but provides a less smoothly balance performance between tasks. Non pre-emptive multi-tasking is sometimes called **pseudo multi-tasking**.. Example of non pre-emptive multi-tasking are Microsoft Windows 3 running under MSDOS and the Apple Macintosh MACOS version 6 Multifinder.

c. On some minicomputers and mainframes there are more sophisticated forms of multi-tasking. In such cases a job may be broken down into stages called **tasks**. It may be possible to treat these tasks as separate programs to the extent that they may be multiprogrammed with each other. This is called **tasking**.

d. A job may be divided up into convenient storage units called **segments**. (A segment may well correspond to a task.) These segments may be organised so that only those segments currently requiring processing are held in main storage. The rest are held on direct-access storage. This is known as **segmenting**. As each new segment is brought into main store it is said to **overlay** the segment it replaces. When segments of different programs are multiprogrammed the method is called **interleaving**. The term **multi-tasking** is also used for this, more advanced form of multiprogramming although it is probably safer to use the term **interleaving** to avoid ambiguity with the simpler forms of multi-tasking. *The reader should beware of the pitfalls of terminology in this area which is made worse by variations in the terminology used by different manufacturers.*

34.47 Virtual Storage.

A combination of segmenting and dynamic allocation of main storage can make it possible for the programmer to write a program (which can be broken into in segments) with little regard to the main storage available. The segments of the program will be brought into main storage from special files on direct-access storage and dynamically allocated a block of main storage (a **partition**). Such a storage management arrangement is known as **virtual storage** since main storage can be regarded as larger than its real size. The special files on direct access storage used to hold the programs, or segments of programs, not currently in physical memory are called **page files** or **swap files**. When a program, or program segment, is transferred between main storage and such a file it is said to be "paged" or "swapped" in or out of memory.

AN EXAMPLE OF MULTIPROGRAMMING

34.48 This example is intended to illustrate multiprogramming under a batch-operating system.

In this example we suppose that the main storage not occupied by system software has been **partitioned** into three areas, each being used for one job. The jobs considered in the example are:

a. Job A. Which is initially of highest priority during its input stage and is receiving data from a "slow" peripheral.

b. Job B. Which is also peripheral bound but assigned a lower priority than A and which is receiving data from a device that needs prompt servicing.

c. Job C. Which is processor bound and therefore given lowest priority.

d. Job D. Which is much the same as B but which is in the queue of jobs awaiting service and currently on backing store.

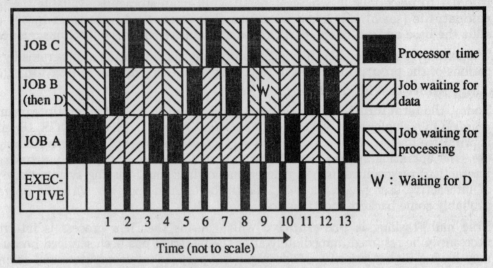

Fig. 34.2. Multiprogramming three programs.

Explanatory notes (see numbers on diagram).

1. A requests data. Executive uses I/O control then transfers control to B.

2. B requests data. Executive uses I/O control than transfers control to C.

3. Interrupt from A's peripheral. Input handled by executive and control passed to A.

4. Interrupt from B's peripheral. Input handled but control returned to A because of higher priority.

5. A requests data. Executive passes control to B.

6. As for 2.

7. Interrupt from B's peripheral. Executive handles input and hands control to B.

8. Internal interrupt caused by error in B. Operator informed. Loading of D started. Executive passes control to C.

9. As for 3.

10. Interrupt caused by completed load of D. Executive leaves control with A.

11. As for 1.

12. Interrupt from A's peripheral. Input stage of A now over so higher priority given to D and control passed back to D.

13. D requests data. Executive uses I/O control and transfers control to A.

34.49 Time-sharing operating systems. Time-sharing was defined in paragraph 12.h. Although time-sharing can occur as a method of multi-access to a single program it is often used as a strategy for multiprogramming. The smaller multi-access, multiprogramming systems may be restricted to one language at a given time, eg, multi-user BASIC. Larger systems allow multiprogramming in different languages.

The following facilities are usually made available by a time-sharing operating system.

a. The programmer is informed of errors in his source program or execution of his program immediately.

b. The programmer is able to make corrections to his source program on-line, ie, editing is possible.

c. Debugging (ie, removing the faults (bugs) from a program). This is done by the programmer being able to have variable values printed at various points in the execution and by amending values at the same time.

34.50 In time-sharing the division of processor time into "time-slices" is provided by a "real-time clock", which generates pulses at regular and frequent intervals. These pulses cause interrupts just as input devices do. Time slices are shared between the users in a way which gives each user a fair share of processor time and conversational facilities.

34.51 A typical time slice lasts less than one-hundredth of one second. At each pulse of the clock the user program currently being executed has its execution suspended. (The user will probably not be aware of this because time slices happen so frequently that within a second execution is likely to be resumed). Then the operating system checks the status of each user, in strict sequence, to see whether the user requires processor time. Some may not. For example, they may have paused during typing for some reason. Once the operating system finds a user requiring processor time, that user's program is allowed to continue execution for the duration of the time slice.

34.52 When the end of the sequence of users is reached, the operating system returns to the start of the sequence and repeats the sequence again. This is known as **polling** in a **round-robin.**

34.53 The operating system has greater demands made on it than in a batch multiprogramming system. For example:

   a. Process scheduling must take account of fair waiting time and time-slice length.

   b. Frequent interrupts demand more frequent transfers of control between programs and greater movement of programs or program segments between main storage and backing store.

   c. With frequent changes a single source statement under time-sharing may require all the control given to a whole-batch job.

34.54 **Real-time systems.** The systems described so far are **single-program systems,** ie, the use of one processor means that only one program is active at any one instant in time. Real-time systems often have more than one processor, a front-end processor with its own executive often being used. The front-end processor takes care of I/O control communications with peripherals and some aspects of scheduling. The main processor (processors) handles the time-shared multiprogramming required. The multiprogramming of system software is common on these systems. Details of real-time operating systems are beyond the scope of this book.

OFF-LINING AND SPOOLING

34.55 These are methods of getting around the I/O bottleneck and are used in various multiprogramming environments.

   a. **OFF-LINING.** A job that requires to output data, to a line printer for example, places the output data onto backing store instead, and is therefore able to complete processing quickly. Later, either

      i. the tape or disk is physically moved to a separate processor, which outputs the data onto a line printer, or

      ii. the tape drive or disk drive is reassigned to another front-end communications processor, which outputs the data to a line printer.

   b. **PSEUDO OFF-LINING .** This happens when the output data is transferred from backing storage onto the appropriate output device by the main processor at some later more convenient stage.

   c. **SPOOLING** (Simultaneous Peripheral Operation On Line). This uses the same principle as OFF-LINING. The term can refer to pseudo off-lining using disk. (Simultaneous operation is "apparently" possible because of the autonomous peripheral operation as data is placed onto the disk). Alternatively spooling can form part of a multiprocessing system. The program that transfers data from the disk to the output device is called a despooling program (see Fig. 34.3).

Job and data flow in OFF-LINING AND SPOOLING

SUMMARY

34.56 **a.** The operating system is a suite of programs that takes control over the operation of the computer.

   b. The operating system handles the flow of jobs through the systems. Its functions were listed in paragraph 11.

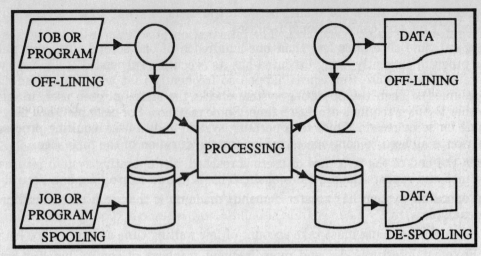

Fig. 34.3.

c. We considered features of operation and communication of:

    i. Multiprocessing.

    ii. Multiprogramming.

    iii. Batch processing.

    iv. Multi-access.

    v. Time-sharing.

    vi. Real time.

d. We considered systems that used:

    i. Single-program operation.

    ii. Batch operation.

    iii. Time-sharing operation.

    iv. Real-time operation.

e. These operating-system languages were discussed:

    i. Command languages.

    ii. Job Control Languages (JCLs).

    iii. Languages in which to write operating-system software.

f. The concept of a process was introduced.

g. The executive or supervisor program is the basic control program at the centre of the operating system. We have considered these executive functions:

    i. Handling interrupts, which may be internal or external.

    ii. Controlling peripherals.

    iii. Allocating peripherals to jobs.

    iv. Loading and memory management.

    v. Scheduling.

    vi. Responding to error conditions and preventing illegal actions.

    vii. Program suspension and restart during multiprogramming or under error conditions.

    viii. Communications with the operator.

    ix. Maintaining a log of events by the use of a monitor.

    x. Directing fault-tracing facilities.

h. To do the tasks listed the executive makes use of the various systems programs that make up the operating system.

i. The more advanced the system the greater is its use of techniques of memory management, multiprogramming, time-sharing methods, OFF-LINING, SPOOLING or communications handling.

POINTS TO NOTE

34.57 a. The terms foreground and background are sometimes used to distinguish between, in the first case, programs that make use of multi-access interactive activities and, in the second case, those running on the same system which are being handled in batch mode.

b. On very small computer systems the so called "operating system" is usually a subset of what we have discussed as the executive. The intervention of an operator may be very frequent in such cases.

c. Small-scale interactive time-sharing systems may be referred to as pseudo real-time systems.

d. Terminology is far from universal when it comes to naming what we have called the Executive. Other commonly used terms are **Kernel, Nucleus** and **Core**. Each operating system has its own version of an executive too, so what we are considering are typical cases.

e. **Multi-tasking** normally means the multiprogramming of user programs and can be pre-emptive or non pre-emptive.

f. In some situations a complete program may be formed from a number of components which can be executed as separate processes. Multiprogramming involving such units is called **interleaving** or **multi-tasking**. The program sub units may be executed as **"subprocesses"**.

STUDENT SELF-TESTING QUESTIONS

1. Explain why a machine should support privileged instructions (for example, those instructions to disable and enable interrupts). *(2 marks)*

2. a. Distinguish between **multiprogramming** and **multi-access**. Outline the methods by which each is achieved by an operating system and indicate the effects on the user. *(8)*

   b. Give **four** examples of **interrupts**. *(6)*

   c. Give **two** examples of **utilities** that are provided with a modern operating system and show how a programmer could take advantage of them. *(6)*

3. What is meant by "automatic sequence control"? *(2 marks)*

4. a. The system nucleus in an operating system consists of program modules which include the interrupt handler and the dispatcher. List the steps involved, including the functions of the interrupt handler and the dispatcher when an interrupt occurs, which will alter the status of the current process. *(8 marks)*

   b. Describe three of the main duties of a job scheduler in an operating system which supports multi-programming and multi-access. *(6 marks)*

   c. In such an environment it is possible for a situation to arise in which no process can continue because the resources each process requires is held by another, with the resources being unshareable.

      i. Give an example of one shareable resource and one unshareable resource. *(2 marks)*

      ii. Describe a strategy for resolving this difficulty. *(4 marks)*

QUESTIONS WITHOUT ANSWERS

5. An operating system carries out several functions that ensure the efficient operation of a computer system. Three such functions are

   i. optimising use of the processor,

   ii. memory management and

   iii. management of files and peripherals.

   Describe techniques that can be used to implement these functions. *16*

6. Explain the differences between the ways in which an unbuffered printer (eg, a teletypewriter) and a buffered printer (eg, a line printer) are driven from the central processing unit of a computer system.

QUESTIONS WITHOUT ANSWERS

7. a. Briefly describe four functions of an operating system that encourage efficient utilisation of the hardware.

b. On one particular multi-access computer, two versions of the operating system are available:

Version A allocates a fixed time period, 50 milliseconds, to each user terminal regardless of tasks in hand. At the end of the period, control is passed to the next terminal in sequence.

Version B allows a particular terminal's program to run until delayed waiting for an input or output transfer. When a delay occurs, control is passed to the next terminal in sequence.

i. Compare the effectiveness of versions A and B of the operating system when each manages the following combination of jobs:

Job 1. A slow teletypewriter interactively running a game of noughts and crosses.

Job 2. A visual display unit where a long mathematical calculation has been initiated and no further input-output activity is expected until the end of the computation.

Job 3. A teletypewriter printing a long list of names and addresses.

(8 marks)

ii. Suggest **two** methods of improving one of the above versions of the operating system.
(4 marks)

8. a. Explain what is meant by the term **multiprogramming** and describe briefly how it works and why it is useful.

b. Two programs that run in a multiprogramming system both direct output to a line printer during their execution.

There is only one line printer available.

Explain carefully how spooling makes it possible for the two programs to run concurrently. State the main reasons why such a system uses spooling.

GLOSSARY CHECKLIST

Background	34.46	Monitor	34.8
Batch processing	34.12	Multi-access	34.12
Command interpreters	34.22	Multiprocessing	34.12
Command languages	34.22	Multiprogramming	34.12
Conversational mode	34.12	Multi-tasking	34.46
CPU bound	34.33	Non pre-emptive multi-tasking	34.46
Executive	34.7	Off-lining	34.55
External interrupts	34.38	Operating system	34.4,34.5
Interactive computing	34.12	Overlay	34.46
Interleaving	34.46	Page files	34.47
Interrupt handling	34.38	Partition	34.47
I/O bound	34.33	Peripheral bound	34.33
Job control language (JCL)	34.23	Polling	34.52
Job priority	34.32	Pre-emptive	34.46
Job schedule	34.34	Process	34.27
Kernel	34.7	Process control systems	34.20

GLOSSARY CHECKLIST CONTINUED

SOFTWARE

1. The material in this Part is relevant to all examinations at which this text is aimed.
2. **Definition.** Software is the term used (in contrast to *hardware*) to describe *all* programs that are used in a particular computer installation. The term is often used to mean not only the programs themselves but their associated documentation.
3. There are numerous types of software, so chapter 35 is used to provide a classification of the different types and a description of each type.
4. Chapter 36 describes the features of high-level languages.
5. In Chapter 37 Translations are defined.

35: Software Types

INTRODUCTION

35.1 This chapter explains the difference between the various types of software and describes each type. It serves primarily as a summary with numerous cross references to more detailed coverage elsewhere in the text.

TYPES OF SOFTWARE

35.2 The two basic types of software are:

a. Systems software

b. Applications software.

35.3 **Systems Software.** The user of a computer has at his or her disposal a large amount of software provided by the manufacturer. Much of this software will be programs that contribute to the control and performance of the computer system. Such programs are given the collective name **systems software.** Any one of these programs is a **systems program.**

35.4 **Applications software.** Applications programs may be provided by the computer manufacturer or supplier, but in many cases the users produce their own applications programs, called **user programs** (eg, payroll programs, stock-control programs, etc). A single applications program is often called a **job.** especially when used for batch processing. Sometimes a job may be divided into smaller units called **tasks.** A job may comprise program + data. Most applications programs can only work if used in conjunction with the appropriate systems programs.

35.5 **Further subdivision.** A more detailed subdivision of 2a and 2b is as follows:

a. Operating systems and control programs
b. Translators
c. Utilities and service programs } Systems Software
d. Data Base Management Systems (DBMS)

e. User applications programs } Applications Software
f. Applications packages

35.6 The remainder of this chapter discusses software under headings that correspond to this classification.

OPERATING SYSTEMS AND CONTROL PROGRAMS

35.7 Computers are required to give efficient and reliable service without the need for continual intervention by the user. This requirement suggests that computers should monitor and control their own operation where possible. **Control programs** and **operating systems** are the means by which this is achieved. Such programs controls the way in which hardware is used. Details of operating systems were given in the previous chapter. The following description merely summarise the range of software from simple control programs to full operating systems.

35.8 Under many circumstances at least two programs are within main storage. One may be an applications program, the other will be a control program, which monitors, aids and controls the applications program.

35.9 On small computer systems, such as microcomputers, the control program may also accept commands typed in by the user. Such a control program is often called a **monitor.**

35.10 On larger computer systems it is common for only part of the monitor to remain in main storage. Other parts of the monitor are brought into memory when required, ie, there are "resident" and "transient" parts to the **monitor.**

35.11 The resident part of the monitor on large systems is often called the **Executive, Kernel** or **Supervisor program.**

35.12 The executive is one of a suite of control programs that are able to allow a number of applications programs to run concurrently and in sequence without the intervention of the user. Such a suite of control programs is called an operating system, but a more precise definition is now given.

35.13 An **operating system** is a suite of programs that takes over the operation of the computer to the extent of being able to allow a number of programs to be run on the computer without human intervention by an operator.

35.14 The reader should now be aware of what operating systems and control programs are, and how they relate to other software.

TRANSLATORS

35.15 These will be described in chapter 37.

UTILITIES AND SERVICE PROGRAMS

35.16 Utilities, also called service programs, are systems programs that provide a useful service to the user of the computer by providing facilities for performing common tasks of a routine nature.

35.17 Common types of utility programs are:
  a. Sort
  b. Editors
  c. File copying
  d. Dump
  e. File maintenance
  f. Tracing and debugging.

35.18 **Sort.** This is a program designed to arrange records into a predetermined sequence. A good example of the requirement for this service program is the need for sorting transaction files into the sequence of the master file before carrying out updating. Sorting is done by reference to a record key.

  a. **Parameters required.** It is a *generalised* program that must be *"specialised"* as it were, before use; this is accomplished by supplying the program with parameters that will be different for each application. Such parameters are:
    i.   Key – size and number (if more than one).
    ii. Record size (length).
    iii. Peripheral units available for the sorting process, ie, number of tape units, disk units, etc, that can be made available to the program.
    iv. Required sequence (ascending order of numeric or alphabetic keys, etc).

  b. **How accomplished.** Sorting methods will be discussed in chapter 40.

35.19 **Editors** are used at a terminal and provide facilities for the creation or amendment of programs. The editing may be done by the use of a series of commands or special edit keys on the keyboard. If, for example, a source program needs correction because it has failed to compile properly, an editor may be used to make the necessary changes. For further details see chapter 5.

35.20 **File copying** (also called media conversion). This is a program that simply copies data from one medium to another, eg, from disk to tape.

35.21 **Dump.** The term "Dump" means "copy the contents of main storage onto an output device". This program is useful when an error occurs during the running of application programs. The printed "picture" of main storage will contain information helpful to the programmer when trying to locate the error. It is also used in conjunction with a CHECKPOINT/RESTART program. This program stops at various intervals during the running of an applications program and dumps the contents of main storage. If required, the checkpoint/restart program can get the applications program back to the last checkpoint and restart it with the conditions exactly as they were at the time.

NB. "Dump" is sometimes used to mean "copy the contents of on-line storage onto an off-line medium", eg, dumping magnetic disk onto magnetic tape for back-up purposes.

35.22 **File maintenance.** A program designed to carry out the process of insertion/deletion of records in any files. It can also make amendments to the standing data contained in records. File maintenance may also include such tasks as the reorganisation of index sequential files on disk.

35.23 **Tracing and debugging.** Used in conjunction with the debugging and testing of application programs on the computer. Tracing involves dumping internal storage after obeying specified instructions so that the cycle of operations can be traced and errors located. Debugging is the term given to the process of locating and eliminating errors from a program.

NB. Well-written and tested programs will tend to be more reliable and will therefore require less debugging than badly written programs.

DATA BASE MANAGEMENT SYSTEMS (DBMSs)

35.24 These will be described in chapter 41.

USER APPLICATIONS PROGRAMS

35.25 User applications programs are programs written by the user in order to perform specific jobs for the user. Such programs are written in a variety of programming languages according to circumstances, but all should be written in a systematic way such as that indicated in the Parts on programming.

35.26 For many applications it is necessary to produce sets of programs that are used in conjunction with one another and that may also be used in conjunction with service programs such as sort utilities.

35.27 For some applications it may be necessary to compare available software or hardware before writing the applications software. For example, the user may wish to compare the performance of two different COBOL compilers. Such a comparison may be made using a benchmark.

35.28 **Benchmarks.** A benchmark is a standard program, or assembly of programs used to evaluate hardware or software. For example, a benchmark might be used to:

a. Compare the performance of two or more different computers on identical tasks.

b. Ascertain if the configuration provided by a manufacturer performs according to his claims.

c. Assess the comparative performance of two operating systems.

APPLICATION PACKAGES

35.29 These have already been introduced as a series of examples earlier in the text.

SUMMARY

35.30 a. Software falls into two main categories:

  i. Systems software
  ii. Applications software

b. A further subdivision of software is as follows:

  i. Operating system and control programs, which ensure efficient hardware use with a minimum of human intervention.
  ii. Translators, which translate from one language to another.
  iii. Utilities and service programs, which perform routine tasks for the user.
  iv. Database management systems, which maintain data bases.
  v. User applications programs, which are written by the user for a specific purpose.
  vi. Applications packages, which are purchased by the user for a particular application.

POINTS TO NOTE

35.31 a. Time spent in running systems software is really non-productive from an organisational standpoint.

b. The operating system (especially the executive part) can be regarded as a "program that controls programs".

STUDENT SELF-TESTING QUESTIONS

1. Distinguish between systems software and applications software and give further sub-classifications of each.
2. What is an editor and how might an editor be used?
3. When might the user of a computer consider using an applications package instead of writing programs from scratch?
   How would they be able to decide which package to use from among those available?

QUESTIONS WITHOUT ANSWERS

4. Find out about the various kinds of software available on the computer system that you use.

GLOSSARY CHECKLIST

36: High-level Languages

INTRODUCTION

36.1 This chapter explains why high-level languages have been developed. It describes both the general features of high-level languages and the particular features of a cross-section of high level languages in use today.

THE DEVELOPMENT OF HIGH-LEVEL LANGUAGES

36.2 The development of high-level languages was intended to overcome the main limitations of low-level languages, which are:

a. Program writing is a relatively time-consuming business for the programmer because the assembly process produces machine instructions on a ONE-for-ONE basis.

b. Low-level languages are **machine orientated,** each conforming to the instruction set of the machine on which they are used and therefore restricted to use on that machine.

36.3 High-level languages are intended to be machine independent and are **problem-orientated languages (POLs),** ie, they reflect the type of problem solved rather than the features of the machine. Source programs are written in statements akin to English, a great advance over mnemonics.

36.4 The first high-level language to be released was FORTRAN (FORmula TRANslation) in 1957. Over the next few years many other high-level languages appeared and established themselves. In fact, new high-level languages have been coming into existence ever since. Most, but not all, have disappeared into obscurity.

36.5 The machine independence of high-level languages means that in principle it should be possible to make the same high-level language run on different machines and then write programs in that language that are portable. Such portability has a number of advantages.

a. A user of a program can change to a newer or bigger computer without the need to rewrite programs.

b. Users of different computers may be able to share or exchange programs and thereby reduce costs.

c. An organisation producing software for sale can sell the same program to users of different computers without the need to rewrite the program for each type of computer. Again, this reduces costs.

36.6 In practice, there are a number of obstacles to such portability. Perhaps the most serious obstacles are those resulting from variations that occur between different versions of each language. Each different *dialect* is usually the deliberate creation of a computer manufacturer, who will try to attract new customers with a "better" product and who will then keep existing customers because their programs will no longer be portable to the computers of other manufacturers.

36.7 Despite these seemingly unavoidable variations, which have proliferated over time, the development of high-level languages has been accompanied by many successful moves to standardise high-level languages and the ways they are defined.

36.8 Standardisation is organised on an international basis. The international body is the **ISO** (International Standards Organisation). Member countries have their own representative bodies on the ISO committees. For example, in Britain the representative body is the BSI (British Standards Institution) and in the USA it is ANSI (American National Standards Institution). The standardisation of high-level languages has often been carried out in the USA. Subsequently the ANSI standard has become the ISO standard. Britain has produced some standards too, notably the standard for the language **Pascal.**

36.9 Every few years new versions of high-level languages appear in the form of new standards. For example, COBOL '68, COBOL '71 and COBOL '84 are versions of COBOL based on ANSI standards for those years.

GENERAL FEATURES OF HIGH-LEVEL LANGUAGES

36.10 a. They have an extensive vocabulary of words, symbols and sentences.

b. Programs are written in the language and whole statements are translated into **many** (sometimes hundreds) of machine instructions. This translation is often done by a special program called a **compiler**, which is described in chapter 37.

c. Libraries of macros and subroutines can be incorporated.

d. As they are **problem orientated** the programmer is able to work, at least to some extent, independently of the machine.

e. A set of rules must be obeyed when writing the source program (akin to rules of grammar in writing English if you like).

f. Instructions in high-level languages are usually called **statements**.

TYPES OF HIGH-LEVEL LANGUAGES

36.11 Types of High-level language. Five main types are:

a. Commercial languages.

b. Scientific languages.

c. Special-purpose languages.

d. Command languages for operating systems.

e. Multipurpose languages.

COMMERCIAL LANGUAGES

36.12 The most well known commercial language is COBOL (Common Business Oriented Language). It is the most widely used commercial and business language and the fact that something like 80% of all computer usage is of this type reflects its importance.

36.13 COBOL was devised by an independent committee called **CODASYL** (Committee on Data Systems Languages) in 1959. CODASYL intended that any program written in COBOL would be compiled and, within reason, run on any computer. This has not worked out in practice, however, for reasons discussed earlier in paragraphs 5 to 9.

36.14 There are many other high-level languages used for commercial computing, full **BASIC** and **UCSD-Pascal** are often used on small computers for example, but COBOL will be discussed further here because it is still the major commercial language.

FEATURES OF COBOL

36.15 The main features of COBOL and other business languages are:

a. Extensive file-handling facilities such as the naming, movement and processing of files, records, fields, etc.

b. Close resemblance to English in terms of incorporating common English terms in sentence-like forms and avoiding mathematical notation.

c. Suited to structuring and handling layouts of tabulated outputs, reports, special forms, etc.

36.16 Each COBOL program is written in what appears to be a stylised but mostly readable form of English. Every COBOL program consists of *four divisions*:

a. **Identification division.** This contains the title of the program for identification purposes. It may also contain the date on which the program was written and the name of the author.

b. **Environment division.** Specifies the particular configuration (hardware) on which the object program will be compiled and executed, eg, model of machine (IBM 4341), internal storage size needed for running the object program, peripheral units, etc.

c. **Data division.** All items of data to be used in writing the program are listed and identified. Names or labels are given for each *file* and any *records* or *fields* referred to later. Record/field *sizes* and *contents* (eg, whether alpha or numeric) are also specified. Working storage areas are defined.

d. **Procedure division.** Contains the program instructions necessary to solve the particular problem indicated in pseudocode. These are to be in the form of statements written in a type of English and which conform to the rules of the language. (COBOL language). The statements written must use the data labels as defined in divisions 2 and 3. The compiler will report any inconsistencies. Also used are RESERVED WORDS, which can only be used in a specific context because they convey a special meaning to the compiler. (Misuse of these words is reported by the compiler.)

36.17 COBOL examples are given here:

  a. Illustration of reserved words. "ADD TAX TO GRADPENS".
  ADD.... TO are reserved words indicating to the compiler that two items of data must be added together. "TAX" and "GRADPENS" are labels (identifiers) of two items of data defined in the data division.

  b. Examples of COBOL Statements. (The statements are in block capitals; explanatory notes in small letters.)

   i. Peripheral instructions. OPEN INPUT-PAY-FILE (prepares a file for processing). READ PAY-FILE AT END MOVE "EOF" TO FILE-STATE (reads a record from a file into memory). WRITE PAY-LINE AFTER ADVANCING ONE LINE (print after throwing paper up by one line).

   ii. Arithmetic instructions. MULTIPLY HOURS BY RATE GIVING BASICPAY. ADD BONUS TO BASIC PAY GIVING GROSSPAY. SUBTRACT INCTAX FROM GROSSPAY GIVING NETPAY.

   iii. Branch instructions. GO TO PENSION-RTN (unconditional branch). IF GROSS-PAY GREATER THAN 100 GO TO EXCEPTION-RTN (conditional branch).

   iv. Control structures (other than the unstructured forms just given).
   IF GROSS-PAY GREATER THAN 100 PERFORM HIGH-PAY ELSE PERFORM LOW-PAY (a **selection** between two paragraphs to be performed). PERFORM READ-FILE UNTIL END-OF-FILE (a simple loop structure) .

   v. Data-handling instruction. MOVE DEDUCTIONS TO DATAC (transfers a field to working store).

SCIENTIFIC LANGUAGES

36.18 The first scientific language was **FORTRAN** (paragraph 4). The first standard for FORTRAN was established in 1966, but that standard has since been replaced by the 1977 standard. FORTRAN is still widely used for engineering applications and scientific use.

36.19 An early competitor of FORTRAN was **ALGOL** (**ALG**orithmic Oriented Language). ALGOL was devised by a working group of IFIP (International Federation for Information Processing) in 1960 and the language definition was published in a report that year. The report was particularly significant in that for the first time the syntax of a language was defined formally, using a notation called BNF. BNF will be discussed in chapter 37.

36.20 Later forms of ALGOL, notably **ALGOL 68,** were so much more extensive that they are probably better regarded as different languages.

36.21 A third language that deserves an explicit mention here is **BASIC** (Beginners Allpurpose Symbolic Instruction Code). BASIC was created in 1964 by J. G. Kemeny and T. E. Kurtz at Dartmouth College, USA. The language was originally designed as a simplified version of FORTRAN for use in teaching programming.

36.22 Early versions of BASIC, and sadly many versions in use on small computers today, deserve strong criticism for features that encourage bad programming methods. However, some newer versions, such as the product "True BASIC" devised by T.E. Kurtz and based upon the latest ANSI standard, are very significantly better.

36.23 It is expected that the reader will use a language such as **BASIC** or **Pascal** as part of the practical coursework and will thereby gain experience of the features found in a scientific language. **Pascal** has many similarities with ALGOL.

36.24 General features of scientific languages are:

  a. Extensive arithmetic computational ability.
  b. Large library of inbuilt mathematical functions.
  c. Ability to handle mathematical expressions and procedures.
  d. Array-handling facilities.

SPECIAL-PURPOSE LANGUAGES

36.25 These are languages intended to be "tailor made" for a particular type of problem, eg, machine control, wages, simulation, control of experiments. Examples are:

  a. **C.S.L,** which is a simulation language.
  b. **Coral-66,** which is used for real-time applications such as process control, ie, the direct control of physical processes, eg, experiments.

c. **RTL/2**, also used for real-time application.

d. **Ada**. A relatively new language used for real-time and possibly general-purpose application. Ada will probably replace Coral-66.

e. **Modula** and **Modula-2**. This is a compact language, almost an extended form of **Pascal**. It allows object-orientated programming methods (as does Ada) and is suitable for real-time applications.

f. **SQL** (Structured Query Language) and **QBE** (Query By Example) are examples of database query languages. Further discussion will be given in chapters 41 and 42.

g. Some languages are special purpose in that they adopt radically different approaches to programming. Examples will be discussed later in the chapter. Such languages include **LISP** (a list-processing language), **SNOBOL** (a string-processing language) and **PROLOG** (Programmed Logic).

COMMAND LANGUAGES FOR OPERATING SYSTEMS

36.26 These are languages used to control the operation of the computer. The required facilities should be apparent to you having read chapter 34.

MULTIPURPOSE LANGUAGES

36.27 Example: International Business Machines (IBM) introduced the language PL/1, which it claimed can cope with business and scientific use. "Pascal" is a somewhat different example. It was originally intended as a language for teaching programming. It is now widely used for a variety of applications, particularly on small computers.

LANGUAGE FEATURES

36.28 Common features upon which comparisons between languages may be made are:

a. **Control structures.** Pascal and PL/1 are languages rich in control structures, eg, Pascal has WHILE, REPEAT... UNTIL and FOR loops. IF... THEN... ELSE and CASE statements and allows the nesting of control structures. Minimal BASICs have very limited control structures. Full ANSI BASIC competes favourably with Pascal and PL/1 in terms of control structures.

b. **Data structures and files.** Pascal and PL/1 provide a variety of data types and structures. Pascal allows more complex types of structures to be built from simpler ones. COBOL has a variety of basic data types, provides a wide variety of file types and also has facilities for dealing with databases. Again BASIC varies greatly according to the level of implementation.

c. **Computations.** FORTRAN, ALGOL, Pascal and BASIC provide facilities for mathematical expressions and functions. Computations in COBOL may be expressed in mathematical form but are more usually expressed in an English-like form (see para. 17b.ii).

d. **Procedures and Subprograms.** Pascal, FORTRAN and ALGOL have facilities for handling procedures and subprograms. Comparable features in minimal or small implementations of BASIC are almost **nonexistent**. COBOL has facilities that give a flexible combination of procedure calls and control structures.

36.29 There are many other features that could be discussed, eg, facilities to deal with controlling the format of data being input or output, but the reader should by now have some feel for the ways in which features may be compared.

OTHER FORMS OF HIGH-LEVEL LANGUAGE

36.30 The high-level languages so far described in this chapter may be described as **procedural languages** in that they provide facilities for the programmer to express procedures or algorithms. Procedural languages necessarily require a style of programming in which the programmer must express **how** computations are to be carried out, ie, what to do and in what order. This is known as an **imperative style** of programming and these languages are also known as **imperative languages.**

36.31 There are alternatives to imperative languages that employ an **assertional method** of programming, in which the programmer expresses (asserts) **what** is required in a calculation rather than how it is done.

36.32 The ideas of assertional programming are much simpler than they at first sound. For example, if you require the square root of the number "x" what you require is "y" such that $y^2 = x$ and this is easy to express compared with how to find y.

36.33 Clearly, sooner or later the "what" must be translated into a "how", and so we may regard assertional languages as being at a higher level than imperative high-level languages.

36.34 There are two basic approaches to assertional programming:

a. **Logic programming**, for which one popular language is **Prolog**.

b. **Functional programming**, for which one popular language is **LISP**.

36.35 The current state of computer science is such that, although the properties of assertional languages are seen to be of possibly great importance in the future, the current forms of assertional languages are too restricted and inefficient to deal with many practical problems currently handled by procedural languages.

PROLOG

36.36 PROLOG deals with "objects" and "relationships" between them. The three main ways in which it does so are: declaring facts, asking questions and defining rules. Facts about what people will eat may be expressed in PROLOG thus:

```
eats (fred, chips).
eats (john, fish).
eats (bruce, caviar).
.... etc....
```

Having keyed in these statements we may pose the question "will fred eat chips?" by keying in

```
? - eats (fred, chips).
```

PROLOG will respond with the answer "yes".

LISP

36.37 LISP was devised around 1960 at the Massachusetts Institute of Technology by J. McCarthy. This was some 10 years before the arrival of PROLOG. It also shows how long it is taking for functional languages to get established for general applications.

36.38 There are many versions of LISP. A typical LISP program operates upon items of data in *symbolic* form referred to as S-expressions (S for symbolic). The program is expressed in terms of procedures that operate upon S-expressions and that are called M-expressions (M for metalanguage).

36.39 Further discussion is not merited in a book at this level.

SUMMARY

36.40 a. The development of high-level languages was discussed, starting with the release of FORTRAN in 1957.

b. High-level languages are problem orientated, rather than machine orientated, and are intended to be largely machine independent.

c. Types of high-level languages are:

i. Commercial languages, eg, COBOL.

ii. Scientific languages, eg, FORTRAN.

iii. Special-purpose languages, eg, CSL, Ada, QUEL.

iv. Command languages for operating systems.

v. Multipurpose languages, eg, PL/1, full ANSI BASIC and increasingly "C".

POINTS TO NOTE

36.41 a. The choice of programming language in a particular situation may be severely restricted both by the availability of languages for the particular machine that is to be used and by the expertise of the staff whose responsibility it will be to write the programs.

b. High-level languages are altered as time goes by in order to respond to changes in technology or new knowledge about the subject.

c. One language of growing importance is "C" which was originally used primarily for systems programming for the operating system UNIX. It has been widely adopted, is the subject of an ANSI standard and is, in many respects, the most portable general-purpose language in use today.

STUDENT SELF-TESTING QUESTIONS

1. What are the advantages and disadvantages of high-level languages?
2. What advantages can be obtained from high-level language program portability? What are the practical obstacles to such portability?
3. Two friends have each purchased home microcomputers. The computers are of different makes but are both claimed to provide the BASIC language.

   The friends find that they are unable to use one anothers programs despite the fact that all programs are written in BASIC. Explain this state of affairs and suggest what could be done to help this particular problem and what measures can be taken in general to prevent such situations arising.

QUESTIONS WITHOUT ANSWERS

4. Critically describe the language(s) that you use as part of your practical coursework.
5. a. Name one general-purpose high-level language, and discuss its suitability for each of the following:

   i. scientific programming,

   ii. commercial programming. *(10 marks)*

   b. Give a typical sequence of assembly-language instructions that would execute a loop. *(5 marks)*

   c. State, with reasons, one application where an assembly language would be more suitable than a high-level language. *(5 marks)*

GLOSSARY CHECKLIST

Ada	36.25	ISO	36.8
ALGOL	36.19	LISP	36.37
ALGOL 68	36.20	Logic programming	36.34
ANSI	36.8	Machine oriented	36.2
Assertional method	36.31	Modula	36.25
BASIC	36.21	Modula-2	36.25
BSI	36.8	Pascal	36.14
C	36.41	Problem-orientated languages (POLs)	36.3
COBOL	36.12	Procedural languages	36.30
CODASYL	36.13	PROLOG	36.25,36.36
Coral-66	36.25	RTL/2	36.25
C.S.L	36.25	SNOBOL	36.25
FORTRAN	36.4	SQL	36.25
Functional programming	36.34	Statements	36.10
Imperative languages	36.30		

37: Translators

INTRODUCTION

37.1 This chapter deals with **translators**, how they are used, and how they work. A **translator** is a program that converts statements written in one language to statements in another language, eg, converting assembly language to machine code. The assembly-language program would be called the **source program** and the machine-code program would be called the **object program.**

37.2 Two other main topics applicable to translation and compiler writing have already been discussed in chapter 27 and therefore will not be discussed again here although some questions about them are included at the end of this chapter. They are:

  a. Language definition and description.

  b. Reverse Polish notation for handling expressions.

37.3 There are three types of translator:

  a. Assemblers.

  b. Compilers.

  c. Interpreters.

37.4 The meaning of the terminology is not completely universal, but generally accepted definitions are:

  a. **Assembler.** A program that translates assembly language into machine code. One machine instruction is generated for each source instruction. The resulting program can only be executed when the assembly process is completed, (see Fig. 37.1).

  b. **Compiler.** A program that translates a high-level language into a machine-orientated language, often the machine code. Many machine instructions are generated for each source statement. The resulting program can only be executed when compilation is completed (see Fig. 37.1).

  c. **Interpreter.** A program which translates and executes each source statement in logical sequence as the program is executed.

37.5 The assembler:

  a. Translates mnemonic operation codes into machine code, and symbolic addresses into machine addresses.

  b. Includes the necessary linkages for closed subroutines and inserts appropriate machine code for macros.

  c. Allocates areas of storage.

  d. Detects and indicates invalid source-language instructions.

  e. Produces the object program on tape or disk as required.

  f. Produces a printed listing of the source and object program with comments.

(Rather like the table in 32.4.) The listing may also include error codes if appropriate.

37.6 To illustrate the methods used we will make use of the imaginary assembly language introduced in 32.14 - 32.20. We must first look at the **directives** (32.18) in more detail.

37.7 A **directive** is used to control the assembly process, it is not assembled, but is obeyed by the assembler when it is encountered, eg, "END" indicates to the assembler that no more source code follows. The function code of a directive, eg, "END", is sometimes called a **pseudo-operation code** or **pseudo-opcode**. All pseudo-opcodes in these examples can be recognised by an initial full stop.

37.8 **Specimen program for assembly.** The program places the number 7 in the accumulator and subtracts the number whose address corresponds to the label N. The result is stored in the location labelled R. Capital letters are part of the program. Other entries are comments.

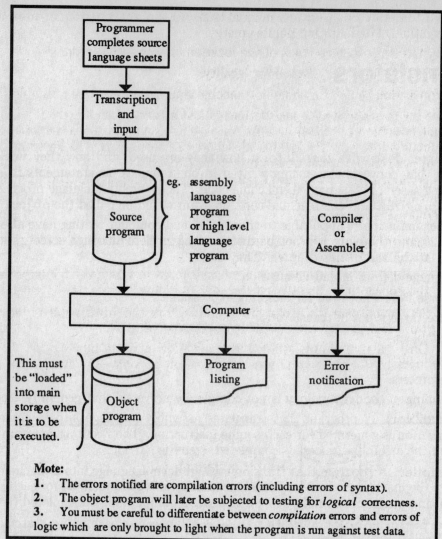

Mote:
1. The errors notified are compilation errors (including errors of syntax).
2. The object program will later be subjected to testing for *logical* correctness.
3. You must be careful to differentiate between *compilation* errors and errors of logic which are only brought to light when the program is run against test data.

Fig. 37.1. Using Assemblers or Compilers to Produce Object Programs.

OCTAL LOCATION WHEN STORED	COMMENTS	PROGRAM	COMMENTS (All numbers are in OCTAL)
–		.START 16	Directive to the assembler for program storage to start at location 16_8.
16_8		LDA 7	Load number with *literal* address 7_8 in the accumulator.
17_8	No labels	SUB N	Subtract from it the number with *symbolic* address N
20_8		STA R	Store the result into the location with *symbolic* address R
21_8		STOP	Stop program execution *(no operand)*
22_8	labels	N : 5	location will contain value 5_8
23_8		R : 0	location will contain value 0
–		.END	Directive to the assembler indicating end of source code.

37.9   Manual translation. Consider manual translation of this program in order to identify the problems of translation. The following points emerge:

a.   It is necessary to keep track of the location of each instruction.

b.   Instructions must be checked for legality.

c.   A conversion table of mnemonic/machine equivalents must be available (31.25).

d.   If we try to translate the instructions one at a time, when we reach "SUB N" we will find that it is not possible to proceed because we have not yet determined the location corresponding to the symbolic address N. By looking ahead we can see that N is at location 22_8 but this information is not yet reached when we are processing "SUB N".

37.10   Two-pass assembler. The problems of forward references described in 37.9d. are overcome by the use of a two-pass assembler, in which the source program is scanned twice as follows:

a.   On the first pass or scan

   i.   **symbol tables** are constructed in which each symbolic operand or label is entered together with its corresponding address.

   ii.   **pseudo-operation tables** are constructed in which the addresses are the entry points for the appropriate directives if they are to be interpreted on the second pass.

b.   On the second pass the tables are available, thus the directives may be executed and the object programs and listings are output to appropriate devices.

Note. Only on very simple systems is the source program input twice. It is normally either held in main memory for the second pass or placed on backing store and read from there for the second pass.

37.11   The two-pass assembly process may be summarised by these diagrams of one example.

a.   PASS 1

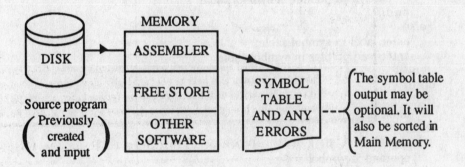

b.   PASS 2

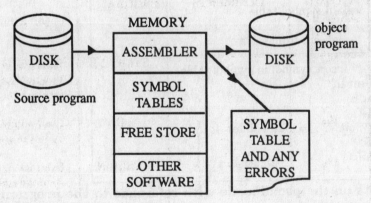

37.12   How the first pass works.

a.   A variable called the *load pointer* is used to keep track of the location of the instruction currently being examined and is incremented when necessary.

b.   opcodes are checked for legality and type.

c.   Labels are entered in the symbol tables and addresses in the pseudo-op table.

d.   Errors are entered in the error table.

Note. Labels and symbolic address operands may either be matched up as the first pass proceeds and checked at the end or they may be entered each time they are encountered and linked at the end of the first pass. The first method is used in the example that follows.

37.13 The main features of the first pass are outlined in the pseudocode on the following page.

```
MAIN FEATURES OF THE FIRST PASS
Begin
  Load pointer : = O
  while more source instructions need processing
    read next source instruction
    check legality and identify instruction type
    if
      instruction is a pseudo-op
    then
      translate
      enter start address of directive in the table
      execute pseudo-op if it is relevant to the 1st pass
    else
      if
        label present in instruction
      then
        seek in symbol table
        if
          label present in symbol table
        then
          if
            address present
          then
            the address is ambiguous so
            enter error in error table
          else
            enter load pointer in symbol table
          endif
        else
          enter label in symbol table
          enter load pointer in symbol table
        endif
      endif
      if
        operand present
      then
        if
          operand is symbolic
        then
          seek in symbol table
          if
            absent from table
          then
            insert symbol in symbol table
          endif
        endif
      endif
      load pointer : = load pointer + 1
    endif
  endwhile
end
```

37.14 Comments on the pseudocode with reference to the program in paragraph 37.8.

    a. The ".START" directive with pseudo op START will be translated and *executed*, thus setting "L" to the value 16_8.

    b. The instruction "LDA 7" has no label and a literal operand so the only action is the incrementing of "L" to 17_8.

c. i. "SUB N" has no label but does have the symbolic operand "N" so the "N" will be inserted in the symbol table as follows.

SYMBOL TABLE	
SYMBOL	(OCTAL) ADDRESS
N	

The address is not yet defined

    ii. "L" will be set to 20_8.

d. "STA R" will be treated in the same way as "SUB N" and "L" will be set to 21_8.

e. STOP has no label and no operand so the only action is to increment "L" by one to 22_8.

f. Label "N" will be found in the symbol table and the current location counter value $L = 22_8$ added. The same will happen with R to give this symbol table.

SYMBOL TABLE	
SYMBOL	(OCTAL) ADDRESS
N	22
R	23

g. The directive ".END" will be translated and executed, resulting in the output of a symbol table, and possibly error messages (none in this case). If no errors occur in pass 1 the ".END" directive starts pass 2.

h. If N : 5 had occurred before "SUB N", then both the symbol "N" and its address would have been entered at the same time.

i. Other pseudo-ops beside .START and .END might include macros to

    i. change the location counter "L"

    ii. reserve blocks of storage

    iii. evaluate expressions

    iv. make alterations to the symbol table.

j. **Conclusion.** The output for pass 1 is the table in f. and a corresponding table in memory.

37.15 The main features of the second pass, again in pseudocode, are shown on the next page.

37.16 The listed output from pass two for the program in (37.8) would look like this:

OCTAL LOCATION ADDRESS	OCTAL CONTENTS INSTRUCTION OR DATA	SOURCE PROGRAM
		.START 16
000016	000007	LDA 7
000017	040022	SUB N
000020	010023	STA R
000021	170000	STOP
000022	000005	N : 5
000023	000000	R : 0
		.END

37.17 Absolute or Relocatable. In the examples given here we are dealing with **absolute programs** (31.55), in which the absolute address of each instruction is determined, ie, given ".START 16" we can work out the machine address of each instruction. A **relocatable program** (31.55), in which instructions may occupy different instructions each time they are loaded, can be assembled assuming ".START 0". if it is to be loaded into memory starting at location 16 then all addresses will be increased by 16 when the program is loaded.

37.18 The assembler may add extra binary data to the front of the object program to tell the loader program where program storage starts. (Compare with .START 16.) Further data may be added to specify the **run-time start address**, ie, which instruction in the program should be executed first.

```
                MAIN FEATURES OF SECOND PASS
    Begin
            location counter := O
            while there are more instructions
              (*NB The directive ".END" terminates the pass*)
            read next source instruction
            while instruction is a pseudo-op
              if
                  relevant to second pass
              then
                  obtain start address from table and execute macro
              endif
              read next source instruction
            endwhile
            if
              function code
            then
              find binary value of function code (from table)
            else
  (*must be a constant*)
              find binary value of constant by calculation
            endif
            (*NB This is the first step in building a complete *)
            (* binary machine instruction *)
            obtain (binary) machine address from symbol table
            add to machine function code
            (*NB The remainder of the instruction is added.*)
            (* Immediate operands will be converted to binary form*)
            Output object instruction in required forms
            (*NB. i. The binary machine instruction will be output as an*)
            (* object program.*)
            (* ii. The machine instruction will be output on a listing*)
            (* octal or hex form beside its octal or hex address and *)
            (* mnemonic form. Error notes may be included*)
            location counter : = location counter + 1
      endwhile
    end
```

COMPILERS

37.19 The compiler:

a. Translates the source-program statements into machine code.

b. Includes linkage for closed subroutines.

c. Allocates areas of main storage.

d. Generates the object program on cards, tape or disc as required.

e. Produces a printed listing of the source and object programs when required.

f. Tabulates a list of errors found during compilation, eg, the use of "words" or statements not included in the language vocabulary; or violating the rules of syntax.

37.20 Although in outline a compiler appears to do much the same job as an assembler in fact it does far more, particularly in the translation of source statements and the linkage of subroutines.

37.21 Form of the object program. It is sometimes not practical for the compiler to complete the translation process because of the large amount of storage required. Instead the object program is stored as a table of macros with appropriate linkage entries, and the program is put together ("consolidated") when the program is loaded into main storage for execution. The program that performs these tasks is often called a linker loader.

STAGES OF COMPILATION

37.22 The compilation process may be broken down into stages just like the passes of an assembler. The compiler may have to translate instructions that are combined into simple sentences, each of which will require analysis as a whole in terms of words, grammar and logic but not semantics (meaning). The three major parts of the compilation process are

a. Lexical analysis

b. Syntactical analysis

c. Code generation.

37.23 Lexical analysis. This stage often includes such things as

a. Checking for valid "words", eg, valid data names or operator symbols, or detecting double decimal points in a single number.

b. Placing all input forms into the same form, eg, disk and tape may have different forms.

c. Coding **"reserved words"** (ie, words that have a special meaning to the compiler and that may not be used as data names), eg, in a printing instruction containing a reserved word "PRINT", the word print may be replaced by a single non-alphanumeric character code. Codes representing words and operators are called **tokens.**

d. Standardising formats and removing spaces so that a standardised format is presented to the next stage. As part of this standardised format the tokens may be replaced by pointers to **symbol tables.** A symbol table for programmer-defined identifiers would be created during lexical analysis and would contain details of attributes such as data types.

Pre-defined symbol names such as arithmetic operands would be held in permanent symbol tables within the compiler.

37.24 Syntactical analysis. This stage often includes such things as:

a. Checking statements for correct grammatical form. (Their meaning is not determined at this stage.) This process may go beyond grammatical analysis of individual statements however, eg, there may be checks to see that every **"if"** has a matching **"endif"** (this may be considered as a separate semantics stage).

b. Complex forms may be broken down into simpler equivalents and more manageable forms.

NB. The part of the compiler that performs this lexical and syntax analysis is called a parser. Further details of parsing will be covered later in the chapter.

37.25 Code generation. This stage often includes such things as:

a. Translating each statement into its equivalent form. This involves

   i. The use of tables as in the assembly process,

   ii. the setting up of various linkages,

   iii. fetch subroutines from the systems library.

Since many instructions are of a similar form, use is often made of skeleton subroutine linkages, which are modified to suit the particular case.

b. Optimisations where possible.

37.26 The code-generation phase is often subdivided into three distinct stages.

a. **Intermediate-code generation.** This intermediate code is obtained fairly directly from the parser. It has a simple form that is easy to optimise.

b. **Optimisation.** The intermediate code is transformed so as to make the program execute faster and need less storage space.

c. **Code generation.** The optimised code is finally used to produce the object code. The object code is usually in machine language but could be in higher level forms such as assembly language, or an "ideal" machine code, which is then interpreted.

37.27 The efficiency of the compiler will depend primarily on the way in which the various tables are constructed and accessed. Efficient use of storage, although relevant, is still largely in the hands of the programmer, since it is he who should make economies in his choice of variables, storage requirements, etc.

INTERPRETERS

37.28 Interpreters are more easily understood by comparing them with compilers.

37.29 Both compilers and interpreters are commonly used for the translation of high-level language programs, but they perform the translation in two completely different ways.

37.30 The **compiler** translates the whole of the high-level language source program into a machine-code object program prior to the object program being loaded into main memory and executed. Contrast this with the interpreter, which deals with the source program one instruction at a time, completely translating and executing each instruction before it goes on to the next. Interpreters seldom produce object code but call upon inbuilt routines instead. Some intermediate code is usually produced temporarily, however.

37.31 If a **compiler** is used, the same program need only be translated once. Thereafter, the object program can be loaded directly into main storage and executed.

37.32 If an **interpreter** is used, the source program will be translated every time the program is executed. Executions carried out in this way may be ten times slower than the execution of the equivalent object programs!

37.33 Despite their apparent inefficiency, interpreters are widely used, particularly for the programming language BASIC on small computers, because they are easier to use than compilers.

37.34 Uses.Interpreters are used for such things as:

a. Handling user commands in an interactive system.

b. Debugging programs as they run (ie, removing program faults).

c. Handling software produced for or by a different computer. In this case the interpreter may be essential if:

  i. Two dissimilar machines are to be connected together for operation, or
  ii. If software produced on an old model and not yet converted had to be run on a new one.

NB. **Interpretive routines** have many uses, eg, handling individual commands or directives.

37.35 Simulation and Emulation.

a. The procedure described in 37.33c.ii. is often referred to as simulation since the interpreter allows the new computer to simulate the behaviour of the old. Interpreters can also be used to simulate a new machine not yet provided but for which software is already written.

b. As was discussed in 26.47, sometimes it is possible to encode the microsteps that describe each instruction cycle in a special memory in the processor called a control store. In this way, the instruction set can be readily altered, and the technique is termed microprogramming. Microprogrammable computers can therefore be set up to obey the instruction set of any other computer, and this process is called **emulation**.

OTHER TRANSLATOR VARIATIONS

37.36 **Generators.**

These are programs that create programs to a given specification. For example the generator might be able to produce programs that print out the contents of the files on a choice of devices. The generator would be given data that specified such things as output device, type of file, name of file, format of output. The generator would then create the desired program.

37.37 **Compiler-Compilers.**

Compiler-compilers are generators that produce a compiler for a given language from a definition of the language. They are intended to save man-hours in compiler writing and speed up the production of compilers.

37.38 **Cross Compilers and Cross Assemblers.** Cross compilers and cross assemblers are translators that are used on one computer in order to produce object programs for use on a second computer. Usually the computer used for the translation is a minicomputer or mainframe and the object program is used on a microcomputer.

SUMMARY

37.39 a. The 3 types of translators are

  i. Assemblers
  ii. Compilers
  iii. Interpreters.

b. Assemblers can use two passes to translate assembly language into machine code. The first pass creates a symbol table and the second pass does the translation. On large machines the two passes can be handled in one, in which case the loader may handle forward references in the table.

c. Compilers translate high-level language programs to machine-orientated language in stages, the main ones being

  i. Lexical analysis

ii. Syntax analysis

iii. Code generation.

d. Interpreters are not efficient alternatives to assemblers and compilers, but have uses in debugging, simulation and, because they are easy to use, in small systems.

e. The relationship between level of language and type of translation needed is shown in this table.

LANGUAGE	TRANSLATOR	INSTRUCTIONS GENERATED	ORIENTATION
Machine	None	N/A	N/A
Low level (symbolic)	Assembler	1 for 1 (+ macros)	Machine
High level	Compiler	Many for 1 statement	Problem

POINTS TO NOTE

37.40 a. Translation to machine code is only the first step towards using a program. Before it is performed it must be **loaded into main storage**. Only then can the **execution phase** be started.

The emphasis in this chapter has been on techniques. You should however notice that the techniques apply to:

i. The assembly process.

ii. Compilation, both in terms of checking correct lexis and syntax and in the ordering of operations during code generation.

iii. Interpretive routines.

STUDENT SELF-TESTING QUESTIONS

1. Name three types of translator and distinguish between them.

2. Use the methods described in 37.10 – 37.15 to assemble this program and produce a listing.

```
        .START  200
D:      LDA     X
        JAZ     E
        SUB     1
        JAL     E
        STA     X
        LDA     Q
        ADN     1
        STA     Q
        JPU     D
E:      STOP
Q:      O
X:      60
        .END
```

What does this program do?

STUDENT SELF-TESTING QUESTIONS CONTINUED

3. a. In the context of the compilation of a source program into executable machine code, state what you understand by

    i. lexical analysis,

    ii. parsing,

    iii. code generation.

(6 marks)

  b. In a particular high-level programming language, only the first two characters of a variable identifier are significant. Thus, TIME and TITLE will be treated identically. What are the advantages and disadvantages of this feature of the language? *(2 marks)*

  c. A particular high-level language allows assembly code to be inserted at any point between high-level statements. What are the advantages of this feature of the language? *(4 marks)*

  d. A programmer uses an interactive loop executed 1000 times but containing no executable instructions other than those controlling the loop, in order to provide a pause while a particular complex diagram is held on the VDU screen. Explain why this technique may give satisfactory results when the program is interpreted, but may not when it has been compiled. *(3 marks)*

(London)

4. A conditional jump statement in a simple programming language contains one expression that has two single-letter operands separated by one of the operators =, ≠, AND, or OR. Write productions that will generate legal expressions. The complete statement consists of a 3-digit line number followed by "IF", followed by the expression just described, followed by "THEN", followed by another 3-digit line number. Write the remaining production needed to generate whole statements. The line number is in the range 100 to 999 inclusive.

QUESTIONS WITHOUT ANSWERS

10. Compare the use of compilers and interpreters for the translation of high-level languages.

11. a. Explain the relationship between an assembly language and the corresponding machine code, and describe the major features of an assembly language that make it easier to use than machine code. *(6)*

  b. Describe in broad outline how an assembler works. *(11)*

(Cambridge)

12. Programs written in a high-level programming language may be run on a particular computer using either a compiler or an interpreter. In each case the first part of the process is the same; as the program is entered a check is made for syntax errors, a symbol table is created, and the program is translated into Reverse Polish form. For the compiler the second part of the process is to translate the Reverse Polish form of the program into machine code, which can subsequently be loaded and run. For the interpreter the second part of the process consists of interpreting the Reverse Polish form of the program and executing it step by step.

  a. Explain what a symbol table is and how it is used.

  b. Describe, with the aid of examples, what Reverse Polish form is. Why is it often used in the translation of high-level programming languages?

  c. Comment on the differences between the compiler and the interpreter. What particular advantages and disadvantages does each method have? *(Cambridge)*

GLOSSARY CHECKLIST

APPLICATIONS IV

1. This fourth Part to deal specifically with applications is more general in nature. It deals with issues such as the criteria for using computers followed by a series of brief descriptions of various application areas.

2. The general topics are relevant to all examinations for which this text is aimed. Other material about specific applications is probably best checked for relevance by the reader against his or her own syllabus.

38: Applications Areas

INTRODUCTION

38.1 The purpose of this chapter is to focus attention on the areas where computers are employed. In doing so we will concentrate on the underlying principles rather than the details of the procedures themselves, many of which have been dealt with elsewhere in the manual. First of all, however, we will consider the criteria for using computers.

CRITERIA FOR USING COMPUTERS

38.2 The following are the criteria by which to judge an application's possible suitability to the use of computers:

a. **Volume.** The computer is particularly suited to handling large amounts of data.

b. **Accuracy.** The need for a high degree of accuracy is satisfied by the computer and its consistency can be relied upon.

c. **Repetitiveness.** Processing cycles that repeat themselves over and over again are ideally suited to computers. Once programmed the computer happily goes on and on automatically performing as many cycles as required.

d. **Complexity.** The computer can perform the most complex calculations. As long as the application can be programmed then the computer can provide the answers required.

e. **Speed.** Computers work at phenomenal speeds. This, combined with the ability to access records directly and from remote locations, enables them to respond very quickly to a given situation.

f. **Common data.** One item of input data can effect several different procedures. For example, a customer's order for a particular stock could involve production of an invoice, updating of the customer's record, updating the stock record, and initiating a re-order for the stock item. The many files involved can all be stored in one physical location and accessed together so that a decision is made in the light of all the information. Contrast a manual system where the item of data will go through many separate independent procedures.

38.3 It is usually the combination of two or more of the criteria listed that will indicate the suitability of an application to computer use. The criteria that have been described will be used by those who carry out the preliminary survey in order to judge the suitability of applications for computerisation.

38.4 Technological innovations over the last twenty years or so have not only increased the range of technically feasible applications, they have also reduced costs so that computers provide a cost-effective solution to a far wider range of problems than they did before.

38.5 If the general criteria for using a computer suggest that a particular application may be suitable for computerisation, then there are a number of questions that will require satisfactory answers before any decision to computerise is taken. The main questions will be:

a. Is the use of a computer for this application **technically feasible?** ie, can it be done with the computer technology currently available?

b. Would the use of a computer be **cost effective?** ie, would the computer pay for itself in terms of the benefits it would provide?

c. Would the use of a computer be **socially acceptable?** ie, would the impact of the computer on people's work, jobs or general lifestyle be acceptable?

MAIN AREAS OF APPLICATION

38.6 Two main areas of computer application may be identified:

a. **Commercial applications.** This covers the use of computers for clerical, administrative and business uses, in private and public organisations, ie, the emphasis is on data processing.

b. **Scientific, engineering and research applications.** This covers the use of computers for complex calculations, the design, analysis and control of physical systems, and the analysis of experimental data or results, ie, the emphasis is on scientific processing or **industrial computing**.

There are other minor areas that do not fall into either of the two main categories, eg, "personal computing," ie, computing done as a hobby. One could argue that it falls into either category.

38.7 Many organisations use computers for a variety of applications. For example, a manufacturer may use computers for data processing, scientific research and engineering development work.

38.8 Further benefits can be obtained by integrating different applications, eg, linking the payroll system to the labour- or production-control system.

MAIN COMMERCIAL APPLICATION AREAS

38.9 In general terms one can consider the commercial application areas under two headings:

 a. Routine administrative, or clerical.

 b. Management.

The earliest computers concentrated on the clerical applications such as payroll and order processing, but today there is an awareness of the power of the computer in many other areas, notably management information and office automation.

ROUTINE APPLICATIONS

38.10 Some of these you will have already met elsewhere in the manual:

38.11 a. **Payroll.** This was invariably one of the first applications to be put onto the computer by a user. It is a well-defined procedure sometimes involving complex piece-rate and bonus calculations. Much of the data could also be used for labour-cost control.

 b. **Order processing.** This can satisfy nearly all the criteria. Notice the data common to stock recording, sales ledger, and invoicing.

38.12 Although these and similar applications may be considered as routine tasks, a great deal of the data is of use in aiding planning and control. Also there is a definite link between production, purchasing, sales, etc, and the computer applications should reflect this link. For this reason the routine and the control applications would ideally be part of an *integrated* system.

38.13 Many organisations have taken the levels of computerisation of routine tasks to very advanced states, thereby increasing their efficiency and expanding their spheres of activity. The clearing banks are a notable example. They first computerised cheque clearing in the late 1950s. Now they have extended banking concepts with the aid of computers to create on-line cash dispensers and credit transfer facilities, which may lead to the distant goal of the "cashless society".

38.14 The price paid for such advances is total reliance on computer systems.

38.15 **Office automation.** Office automation involves the substantial use of computers, in conjunction with other electronic equipment, to automate the basic secretarial and clerical tasks of the office. It is the routine nature of a large amount of office work that makes office procedures a likely candidate for automation, and reduced equipment costs now make it cost effective.

38.16 *Basic* office automation consists of word processors (chapter 5) connected to one another and to a corporate computer by means of a local network.

38.17 Most office automation systems in use today go far beyond the function of providing word processing on networks. PCs or workstations are connected onto a network which provides access to a wide variety of software including:

 a. word processing software

 b. spreadsheet packages

 c. drawing packages

 d. database packages

 e. electronic mail facilities

 f. access to other systems via a network connection.

38.18 Also on the network there may be a number of file servers and print servers (4.54). As part of such an arrangement there is increasing use of a **client-server** arrangement. A special example of client-server was described in chapter 8 in connection with x-windows but that was rather unusual because of the location of server on the workstation. In most client-server arrangements an application program (the client) runs on a PC or workstation and communicates via the network connection with the server program which runs on another machine. The server machine is usually larger and more powerful and is often dedicated to the role of being a server. Servers may be dedicated to tasks such as:

 a. providing access to a printer

 b. providing access to electronic mail

    c. providing access to a database (details later in chapter 41)

    d. providing access to other systems

38.19 Servers are often **multi-threaded** which means that a number of application can be connected to the server and serviced by it at the same time.

MANAGEMENT

38.20 A company needs information on which to base decisions concerning the current operations and future plans. It requires this information to be timely and accurate.

Examples of the use of computers in the area of management control are now given.

    a. **Stock control.** The computer is able to process data quickly, making available information on stock levels, slow-moving items or trends in demand. A central computer can link together widely separated warehouses, thus treating them as one vast stock holding. Customer orders can be satisfied from an alternative warehouse should an item not be available in the local area. Used in this way the computer enables stock holdings to be kept to a minimum, thus releasing cash for other purposes.

    b. **Production control.** This is an extremely complex area especially in batch-production factories. Production must be able to respond quickly to changes in demand and other circumstances. To do so requires the provision of up-to-date information that is accurate and timely. On-line systems such as plastic badges help to get the data from the shop floor quickly enough to influence current events. Machine loading, materials control, batch-size calculation and machine utilisation are all things that a computer can make more efficient because of its ability to make complex calculations and sift vast amounts of data speedily and accurately. Sophisticated computerised control systems must be capable of assessing the effect on production of the continuing happenings that are the everyday lot of the production manager.

    c. **Labour control.** Much of the information used in the control of labour can be obtained from the payroll and personnel records applications. Ideally they will all be part of an integrated system. An analysis of labour hours into various categories such as idle time, sickness and absence, can aid forecasting future requirements. Departmental and sectional summaries help to highlight these problems on a wider basis. Actual performance is measured against budgeted performance. Daily reports for the shop-floor manager aid control of routine operations. Reports of a more general nature will aid overall manpower utilisation.

    d. **Network analysis.** This technique is used for the planning and control of large, complex projects. Examples are the building of a factory, the installation of new plant and the manufacture of an aircraft or ship. The model (which requires the careful preparation of large amounts of base data) shows each stage in the project and its dependence on other stages. For example, when new plant is being installed, it cannot be moved in until the site has been prepared, and this in turn cannot take place until the old machines have been removed. When the necessary data has been supplied, the program produces a plan that management can use. A great advantage of the technique is that the plan can be quickly modified by the program in the light of actual progress, and revised plans produced at short notice to allow for delays. The program also indicates the *critical path*, ie, the series of interdependent activities that will take longest to complete and that, if delayed, will hold up the whole project. Resources can then be concentrated on these activities.

    e. **Linear programming.** This technique is used to find the optimum solution (ie. that which maximises profits or minimises costs) from a large number of possible alternatives. Examples are the optimisation of product mix and the minimisation of transport costs. Again, a considerable amount of accurate base data has to be supplied to construct a model. The methods used are not dealt with in detail here; the key point to note is that the computer has the storage capacity and the speed to calculate and evaluate every feasible solution and thus to find the best one. The manager, if dependent on human resources, cannot possibly do this; the timing required to make the necessary calculations would be prohibitive. He would have to depend on his experience and perhaps instinct.

    f. **Financial modelling.** A model is constructed of the company's finances: its resources, its income and its expenditure. It is possible by using the model to *simulate* the effects of different policies. For example, the likely results of different investment policies can be forecast, and external factors such as the national growth rate and the trend in national incomes can be introduced to see what effects they will have. It is possible by a series of computer runs, with variations of the basic assumptions on each one, to obtain a forecast of the likely effects of alternative policies. The usefulness of the computer lies in its high speed, which enables it to simulate in a few hours events that will actually occur over many years. The technique is of great use to the manager in enabling the evaluation of the results of different decisions that can be made.

MORE ADVANCED PACKAGES

38.21 Rather more mathematically advanced than the spreadsheet packages are the integrated packages that aid in such things as financial planning or statistical analysis. One example of such a package is "TREND", supplied by Planalysis, which has facilities for model building, calculation, printing, graphical display and so on. These packages support the decision-making processes by taking away the routine calculations and manipulations, but do not go so far as recommending courses of action. For that, it is necessary to make use of a system having some characteristics that we normally associate with human intelligence. Such systems are already in use. They are called Expert Systems or Intelligent Knowledge-Based Systems (IKBSs).

A Toshiba T5200 DESKTOP Portable 386

Photograph supplied by courtesy of Toshiba

EXPERT SYSTEMS

38.22 An expert system is a specialised computer package that can perform the function of a human expert. Some of the first expert systems to gain widespread publicity were those used for medical diagnosis. A medical consultant, assisted by his staff, took part in a lengthy exercise in which both the knowledge base required and the decision-making procedures were transferred to the computer. Subsequently, the computer was able to ask the same questions and draw the same conclusions from the answers as the consultant so that a relatively junior doctor, aided by the computer, could be as expert as the consultant!

38.23 There are many possible applications for expert systems, for example, company law, investment, finance and personnel. Products are gradually appearing on the market.

38.24 Expert systems normally have the following features (a law expert system will be used to provide examples):

    a. An organised base of knowledge – often in the form of a database (eg, Acts of Parliament and case law.)

    b. A user interface able to support diagnostic or similar discussions with the user, (eg, to enable the user to pose legal problems or to check the legality of an intended action).

    c. A facility to hold details of the status of the current consultation, (eg, the user, in consulting the expert system, may have to go through a lengthy question and answer session and the system has to keep track of the state of the questioning).

    d. An inference engine, ie, software that can use the knowledge base and current status of the consultation to either formulate further questions for the user or draw conclusions about what actions to recommend to the user, (eg, a mechanism for formulating and sequencing appropriate questions about the user's legal problem).

    e. A knowledge acquisition system, ie, a facility to update the knowledge base. It is via the knowledge acquisition system that the human expert is able to endow the expert system with knowledge, (eg, a suitable system for entering the relevant facts about company law).

38.25 Although these basic components are bound to vary from one discipline to another (eg, the knowledge base for company law is very different from the knowledge base for personnel management) the basic structure is the same. Therefore, an established method for developing an expert system is to build the particular expert system required from a standard non-application-specific basic system called a shell. It is possible to purchase a complete expert system or merely a shell from which an expert system can be created.

38.26 The user of the expert system sits at a terminal, PC or workstation and takes part in a question and answer session in which data about the problem is typed in. At various stages during the session, or maybe just at the end, the system makes an assessment of the problem and recommends actions to be taken.

38.27 Expert system packages are not confined to large computers. Several are available on personal computers, eg, business information techniques and the "Parys" system, which is used as an aid in personnel management.

38.28 **Intelligent Knowledge-Based Systems (IKBS).** These systems have appeared on the market in the last few years. They are intended to provide an expert consultative service to management and are sometimes also called **"expert systems"**.

38.29 A typical system contains a large database containing details of a particular discipline, eg, company law or medical diagnosis. The system is also programmed with a decision-making strategy, which has been developed by careful consultation with people who are experts in the field. The third component is an interactive facility built into the system. The user sits at a terminal and takes part in a question and answer session in which data about the problem is typed in. At the end of the session the system makes an assessment of the problem and suggests actions to be taken.

38.30 Current systems are limited in scope, but can be very effective.

CHANGES IN THE SPREAD OF APPLICATIONS

38.31 Computers have been successfully applied to many new areas of work in the last few years. Notable examples are:

    a. Office automation (see paragraph 15).

    b. The use of microcomputer-based systems in small firms and offices.

    c. CAD/CAM (Computer-Aided Design/Computer-Aided Manufacture). (Details later.)

38.32 The advent of microcomputer-based systems has meant that applications such as payroll and stock control, which could only be economically computerised in organisations of some size, can now be usefully introduced into very small firms.

PARTICULAR APPLICATIONS AREAS

38.33 In this section a number of particular applications areas are described because of their importance and interest.

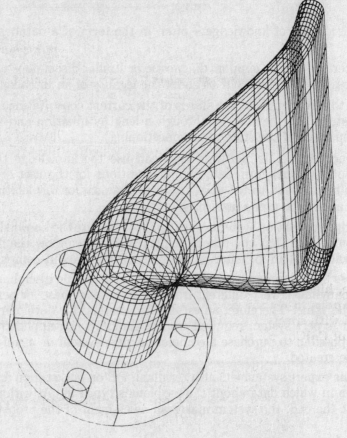

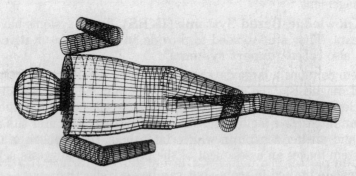

Two graph-plotter outputs produced by an applications package in CAD, called SPIDER, which uses a library of routines called BEZLIB. The package can be used to design complex surfaces such as those used for vehicle bodywork castings, etc.

(Courtesy J. Beasley. The Hatfield Polytechnic).

38.34 Applications exploiting the full computational power of computers. Many of these applications have a scientific bias. They include:

  a. Weather-forecasting systems. Reliable weather-forecasting demands vast computational powers. This is an area for the super-computers such as those described in 13.67-13.70.

  b. Mathematical and statistical analysis. This includes large calculations and the solution of mathematical problems. The applications requiring this include research in physics, chemistry, geology, archaeology, medicine, astronomy, etc. Some commercial problems also have a mathematical bias, eg, those that require mathematical analysis to determine the optimum use of resources.

  c. Design work Computers can be exploited as a design tool in engineering and other disciplines. **CAD** (Computer Aided Design) is growing in importance in electronic, electrical, mechanical and aeronautical engineering and in architecture. This application often also exploits **computer graphics.**

A large-scale, high-accuracy flatbed pen plotter from CalComp, which can use either ballpoint or liquid ink pens to plot at very high speeds (up to 42 ins/sec.) on standard drafting media or can be fitted with special tools for scribing or cutting strippable film. Photograph with caption by courtesy of CalComp Ltd.

The beltbed pen plotter is a unique CalComp design in which the drafting **medium**, in this case any size up to A00, is taped to a continuous belt of stable polyester film which moves up and down in the x axis while the pens move back and forth along the y. Photograph with caption courtesy of CalComp Ltd.

38.35 Medical applications. There are numerous applications of computers in medicine. Here are some examples:

a. Computers can be used as an aid to medical research by analysing data produced from experiments, eg, in the trial of drugs.

b. Computers can be used to aid diagnosis. The computer acts as a large bank of data about known medical conditions. Once the computer system has been set up by medical experts an ordinary doctor can be taken through a question and answer session by the computer until a correct diagnosis is made. This is an example of an IKBS (paragraph 19).

c. Computers can be used to hold details of dentists' or GPs' patients. Small computer systems have been used for this purpose in increasing numbers since the late 1970s.

d. Computerised children's health records for immunisation have been used by local health authorities for a number of years. These records are used by medical officers, health visitors, etc.

38.36 Education. Computers are not only used extensively as part of specialist study in computer science, they are also used as an extremely versatile way of aiding the understanding of a wide variety of other subjects. The computer can guide a user through a course of instruction at a VDU. The computer can provide instructions and ask questions of the user. This kind of activity is called **CAL** (Computer-Aided Learning) or CAI(Computer-Aided Instruction).

38.37 Computers are also used for a number of other applications in education, eg, the marking of multiple-choice examination papers and processing examination results for many examinations boards.

38.38 Manufacturing. Some aspects of computer use in manufacturing have already been covered, eg, stock and production control, and engineering design. The design, manufacturing and testing processes are all becoming increasingly computerised, hence the terms **CAD** (Computer-Aided Design), **CAM** (Computer-Aided Manufacture) and **CADMAT** (Computer-Aided Design Manufacture and Testing).

38.39 Robots. The word "robot" comes from a Czech word meaning "to labour" and first appeared in a play written by Karel Capek in 1920. For many years the term "robot" was associated with science fiction rather than science fact. That association is now changing. Even so, modern industrial robots do not resemble people (see Fig. 48.1).

38.40 The main difference between modern industrial robots and other automated machines is that a robot can be programmed to carry out a complex task and then be reprogrammed to carry out another complex task. Each complex task is a series of actions involving multiway mechanical manipulation.

38.41 The majority of robots in current use, eg, in car-assembly lines, are "blind" and lack a "sense of touch". The next generation of robots will probably be able to find and locate objects or detect their presence by touch and a light-sensing mechanism.

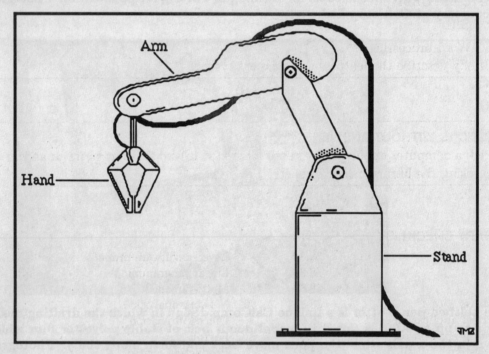

Fig. 48.1. An Industrial Robot.

CONCLUSION

38.42 Many of the procedures and techniques are possible without a computer, but it is the speed and accuracy with which the computer carries them out that makes it such an invaluable tool of management.

SUMMARY

38.43 a. The criteria for using a computer are, volume, accuracy, repetitiveness, complexity, speed, and the use of common data.

    b. Computers can be applied successfully to administrative tasks and to the production of management-control information.

    c. Expert systems are an advanced form of package.

POINTS TO NOTE

38.44 a. Not all applications have been dealt with - other applications will be dealt with elsewhere, eg, analog and hybrid computing is covered in chapter 50.

b. The term "applications package" has been used in this chapter as a very broad category for software. Even so, not all software products sold as "packages" would be called applications packages. For example, some database software is sold in very much the same way as applications packages but provides facilities "on top of" those provided by the standard systems software and can be used by applications software. Such packages are often referred to as **"layered software products"** because of their position between standard systems software, which they add to, and the applications software.

STUDENT SELF-TESTING QUESTIONS

1. Explain the terms:
   a. technical feasibility
   b. cost effectiveness
   c. social acceptability.
   in the context of computerisation of an application

2. Explain these terms:
   a. IKBS
   b. CAD/CAM
   c. CAL
   d. Word processing.

3. Briefly describe the features of an expert system.

QUESTIONS WITHOUT ANSWERS

3. Pick a computer application you are interested in and find out as much as you can about it by using the library, magazines, etc.

GLOSSARY CHECKLIST

CAD	38.34	Layered software product	38.44
CADMAT	38.38	Linear programming	38.20
CAM	38.38	Multi-threaded	38.19
Client-server	38.18	Network analysis	38.20
Commercial application	38.6	Office automation	38.15
Engineering application	38.6	Payroll	38.11
Expert system	38.22	Production control	38.20
Financial modelling	28.20	Research applications	38.6
IKBS	38.28	Robot	38.39
Industrial computing	38.6	Scientific application	38.6
Labour control	38.20	Stock control	38.20

PROGRAMMING II

1. This Part continues with the topics introduced in chapter 17, but also uses the methods described in programming Part I. The reader may find it useful to re-read chapter 17 before you continue. The study advice given in "PROGRAMMING I" applies here too.
2. Chapter 39 concentrates on details of further data structures and how to use them.
3. Chapter 40 covers other methods not necessarily related to data structures. It also examines sorting, including methods applicable to files.

39: Further Data Structures

INTRODUCTION

39.1 This chapter introduces data structure called STACKS and QUEUES and also shows further methods of using TREES. The problems associated with trying to find data elements quickly and easily are examined. That leads into a broadening of the discussion on ACCESS TABLES (7.36).

QUEUES

39.2 Consider this example. It is a common occurrence for a computer to create data for output at a speed that cannot be matched by the output device for which the data is intended. When this happens the data may be placed in a "buffer area" of main storage, where it takes its place in a **queue,** and waits its turn to be output. **Queues** have many uses, but remember this example as we now define a queue more precisely. The technical meaning of "queue" is not quite its everyday meaning.

39.3 **Features of a queue.** Data is added to the "end" of a queue but is removed from the "front". The term "FIFO" is used to describe queues because the First datum In is the First datum Out. Data in what we call a **queue** is *not* moved along like people in a cinema queue. Instead, each datum stays in its storage location until its turn comes, thereby reducing time spent in data movement. The use of pointers makes this possible.

39.4 **Example.**

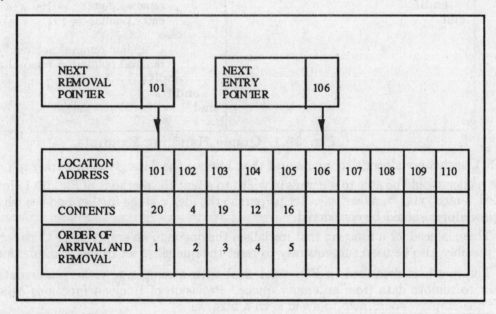

39.5 Overflow and Underflow.

   a. **Overflow** occurs when an attempt is made to add data to a queue when all available locations are occupied.

   b. **Underflow** occurs when an attempt is made to remove data from an empty queue.

39.6 **Example of queue handling.** Assume locations 101 to 110 are available to store a queue with each location storing just one number. Assume that two procedures called "place" and "fetch" are available as follows:

procedure place (**IN** pointer, number: **integer**)

(*This procedure places number in the memory location whose address value is pointer.*)

procedure fetch (**IN** pointer : **integer OUT** number : **integer**)

(* This procedure fetches number from the memory location whose address value is pointer. *)

The methods for entering and removing numbers from the queue are outlined in the pseudocode in Fig. 39.1. You should note that the Boolean variable called overflow is set to true if overflow is attempted. Assume that initially entry pointer = 101 and removal pointer = 100. In this example locations at the front of the queue are not reused once they become empty. Instead, the process is restarted once the whole queue is empty.

```
(* Entering a number *)              (* Removing a number *)
(* outline method *)                 (* outline method *)
variables                            variables
   entry_pointer,                       entry_pointer,
   removal_pointer,                     removal_pointer,
   number      :integer                 number      :integer
   overflow    :boolean                 underflow   :boolean
Begin                                Begin
   (* assume previous initialisation *)  (* assume previous initialisation *)
   if                                   if
      entry_pointer = 111                 removal_pointer = 100
   then                                 then
      overflow := true                    underflow := true
   else                                 else
      (* place number in location given   (* fetch number from location
         by entry_pointer *)                 given by removal_pointer *)
      call place(entry_pointer, number)   call fetch(removal_pointer, number)
      (* update pointers *)                if
      entry_pointer := entry_pointer + 1     (* queue is now empty *)
      if                                     removal_pointer = 110
         removal_pointer = 100               OR
      then                                   entry_pointer = removal_pointer +1
         removal_pointer := 101            then
      endif                                   (* reset queue for reuse *)
   endif                                      removal_pointer := 100
end                                           entry_pointer := 101
                                           else
                                              (* update removal_pointer *)
                                              removal_pointer := removal_pointer +1
                                           endif
                                        endif
                                     end
a.                                   b.
```

Fig. 39.1. Queue Handling Example.

NB. Use this pseudocode to create and then remove the data given in paragraph 4.

39.7 The reader should be able to see ways in which to adapt the methods of Fig. 39.1. into two procedures called "enter" and "remove" say. Let us pursue the idea a stage further and see what other functions or procedures should be considered.

a. There is need for a function that initialises the queue to an empty state. The same function could possibly also be used subsequently to reset the queue, so let us call the function "clear".

b. The methods described in Fig. 39.1 deal with attempts to either enter data to a full queue or to remove data from an empty queue. Provision of Boolean functions called "q-is-full" and "q-is-empty" would help to avoid such a mistake.

39.8 Some programming languages allow sets of functions and procedures associated with a data structure such as a queue to be grouped together into a single programming unit called a **module** or **package.**

39.9 The user of a queue module might have the following simple functions and procedures provided by the module:

a. **Procedure** clear. A parameterless procedure that sets the state of the queue to empty.

b. **function** q_is_empty: **boolean.** A parameterless function that returns **true** when the queue is empty and returns **false** otherwise.

c. **function** q_is_full: **boolean.** A parameterless function that returns **true** when the queue is full and returns **false** otherwise.

d. **Procedure** enter (I N number). This procedure places a number on the end of the queue. If the queue is full the procedure has no effect.

e. **Procedure** remove (**OUT** number). This procedure removes a number from the head of the queue and returns it. If the queue is empty, an undefined value is returned.

39.10 When entering and removing data these functions need to be used in conjunction with one another, eg,

a. To add a number

    if

        q_is_full

    then

        output ("queue is full")

    else

        enter (number)

    endif

b. To remove a number

    if

        q_is_empty

    then

        output ("no data in queue")

    else

        remove (number)

        output ("next value is", number)

    endif

39.11 **Note** the following points, which arise from these examples.

a. A data structure described in terms of the operations performed upon it, as the queue was in paragraph 9, may be called an **abstract data type.**

b. The functions in paragraph 9 do not pass either the stored form of the queue or its pointers because they are already contained within the module and are **global** to all functions and procedures within the package. They are local to the module, however, which is why this method of representing the handling of data structures is sometimes called **information hiding.**

NB. In functional decomposition these data items would be passed as parameters.

39.12 The use of abstract data types (information hiding) is important in advanced programming, but further discussion of such methods are beyond the scope of this text.

39.13 **Queue organisation in lists.** Queues may be stored in the form of lists (17.47). A list used to store a queue is called a **Push-up list.**

Example.

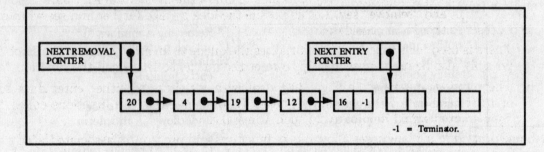

-1 = Terminator.

STACKS

39.14 **Stacks** are frequently used for temporary storage, but in a different way from queues. A **stack** differs from a queue in the method of data addition and removal. Data is added to the "top" of a stack and is also removed from the "top". The Last datum In is the First datum Out (LIFO). Compare this with a pack of cards on a table with cards either added to or removed from the top.

NB. Examples of stacks at machine level were given in 31.45 and 32.30.

39.15 a. Example.

Note. The stack provides the facility to retrace the steps of data insertion.

b. Example of use. One common application of stacks is for storing return addresses (link values) for closed subroutines (32.30). When entering a subroutine, the return address is placed on top of the stack. Should a second subroutine be entered from the first, then the return address will again be placed on the stack. When the time comes to return from the second subroutine to the first, the correct return address will be on top of the stack. The return address will be removed revealing the return address to the main program. The same method can be applied when many subroutines are "nested" in this manner and proves useful in other applications, which are discussed later.

39.16 Example of stack handling (we make the same assumptions made in paragraph 6, except that locations will be reused if they become vacant). The methods for entering and removing numbers from the stack are outlined in pseudocode in Fig. 39.2. You may remember from 31.46-31.47 that the operation of placing an item on a stack is sometimes called **"push"** and the operation of removing an item from a stack is sometimes called **"pop"**.

```
(* Entering a number *)              (* Removing a number *)
(* outline method *)                 (* outline method *)
variables                            variables
   entry_pointer,                       entry_pointer,
   removal_pointer,                     removal_pointer,
   number        :integer              number        :integer
   overflow      :boolean              underflow     :boolean
Begin                                Begin
   (* assume previous initialisation *)  (* assume previous initialisation *)
   if                                   if
      entry_pointer = 111                  removal_pointer = 100
   then                                 then
      overflow := true                     underflow := true
   else                                 else
      (* place number in location given    (* fetch number from location
         by entry_pointer *)                 given by removal_pointer *)
      call place(entry_pointer, number)    call fetch(removal_pointer, number)
      (* update pointers *)                (* update pointers *)
      removal_pointer := entry_pointer     entry_pointer = removal_pointer
      entry_pointer := entry_pointer + 1   removal_pointer := removal_pointer -1
   endif                                endif
end                                  end
a.                                   b.
```

Fig. 39.2. Stack Handling Example.

482

NB. Use this pseudocode to create and then remove the data given in paragraph 15.

39.17 As for the queue, the stack may also be described in terms of the operations that may be performed upon it. There are numerous ways in which this may be done. Typical functions are:

a. A **clear** procedure analogous to that described for the queue.

b. Functions called "stack-is-empty" and "stack-is-full", also analogous to those for the queue.

c. A **push** procedure, eg, **procedure** push (**IN** number), to insert numbers on to the top of a non-full stack.

d. A **pop** procedure. The pop procedure, which involves removing the top items from the stack, is sometimes split into two operations:

    i. **pop**, which merely deletes the top item from the stack, and

    ii. **top**, which returns the stack's top item to the calling program without deleting it from the stack.

39.18 Stack organisation in lists. Lists used to store stacks are called "push-down lists".

Example. (Note the use of "backward" pointers rather than "forward" pointers.)

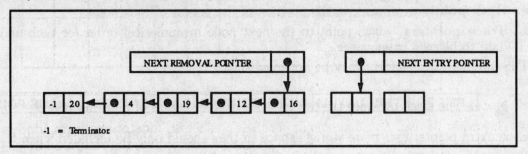

TREES CONTINUED

39.19 You may first wish to re-read (17.56-17.59) in which trees were introduced and constructed.

39.20 Deletions from a tree. We will use this tree as an example.

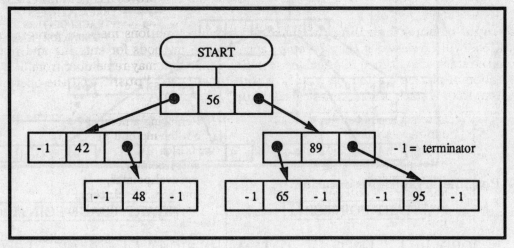

a. **Method.**

Case (i) **Deletion of a terminal node,** eg, 48. Replace the pointer to the node by a terminator.

Case (ii) **Deletions within the tree,** eg, 89. Change the rightmost node of the left-hand subtree below the node to be deleted. (If there is no left-hand subtree, change the first right-hand node below the node to be deleted.)

b. **Example** (48 has been deleted as in case (i) and 89 has been deleted as in case (ii)).

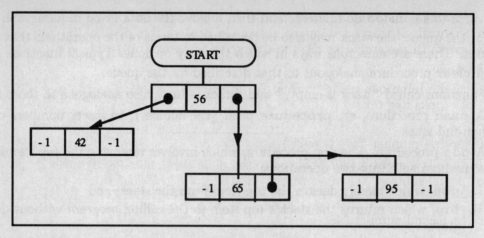

39.21 Other tree pointers.

These pointers are often used as part of the tree elements:

a. **Back pointers,** which give the position of the parent of each node.

b. **Trace pointers,** which point to the next node in numerical order for each node. This allows data to be read in sequence.

The complete tree element may be arranged thus:

| LEFT POINTER | DATUM | RIGHT POINTER | BACK POINTER | TRACE POINTER |

Each extra pointer uses more storage space so they should only be included when they are needed.

39.22 Example. (Pointers are arranged as just indicated.)

a. **Flowchart.**

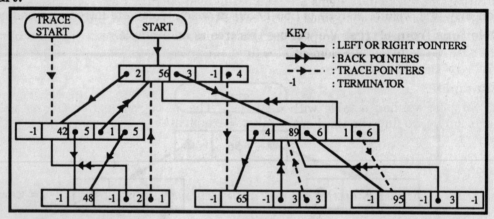

b. **Possible array representation.**

| START POINTER | 1 | | START TRACE POINTER | 2 |

ORDER OF ENTRY INTO THE TREE	LEFT POINTER	DATUM	RIGHT POINTER	BACK POINTER	TRACE POINTER
1	A(1,1) = 2	A(1,2) = 56	A(1,3) = 3	A(1,4) = -1	A(1,5) = 4
2	A(2,1) = -1	A(2,2) = 42	A(2,3) = 5	A(2,4) = 1	A(2,5) = 5
3	A(3,1) = 4	A(3,2) = 89	A(3,3) = 6	A(3,4) = 1	A(3,5) = 6
4	A(4,1) = -1	A(4,2) = 65	A(4,3) = -1	A(4,4) = 3	A(4,5) = 3
5	A(5,1) = -1	A(5,2) = 48	A(5,3) = -1	A(5,4) = 2	A(5,5) = 1
6	A(6,1) = -1	A(6,2) = 95	A(6,2) = -1	A(6,4) = 3	A(6,5) = -1

NB. If elements were of different data types, an array of records would be used.

39.23 Using stacks instead of trace pointers. This method can be used if trace pointers have not been provided. If traces are only occasionally needed, this may be the best way of providing trace facilities. In this example we use the tree given in paragraph 39.20.

Procedure.

a. Find the **leftmost node** placing old pointers on the stack as you go. When we reach "42" the stack looks like this:

1				

(The first number "42" is read.)

b. If there is a **right-hand pointer** to the node then enter the right-hand subtree and repeat step a. in the subtree. When we reach "48" the stack looks like this:

1	2			

(The second number "48" is read.)

c. If you reach a terminal node, remove the top pointer on the stack and use it. Continue with step b. Stack:

1	4			

(The fourth number "65" is read.)

When the stack is empty **and** there are no more right-hand subtrees the trace is completed. Try to use the method to complete the trace.

SEARCH AND ACCESS

39.24 Search time and search length (when accessing data). An important characteristic of a data structure is its search time. The **search time** is the **average time** taken to find a datum in the structure. It is often expressed in terms of the **search length**, which is the average number of elements examined in order to find a datum.

In situations where data items are required individually the data structure with the shortest **search length** will be preferable, since it will save processor time and thereby increase efficiency.

39.25 The linear search (the simplest and most common type of search). To perform a **linear search** the data is examined one element at a time in physical order until the required datum is found. (See 17.26 for the method.)

Example.

a. Suppose we had a table with 5 entries. The 5 possible search lengths are 1, 2, 3, 4, 5. For example, to find the third entry takes 3 examinations. The average search length will be

$$\frac{1+2+3+4+5}{5} = 3$$

b. For a table with N entries the average search length would be:

$$\frac{1+2+3+4+ \dots \dots + (N-1) + N}{N}$$

This sum can be simplified if we notice that writing the series backwards can add it twice easily:

Add columns

1	+	2	+	3	+	4 +... +	(N-1)	+	N
N	+	(N-1)	+	(N-2)	+	(N-3) +... +	2	+	1
(N+1)	+	(N+1)	+	(N+1)	+	(N+1) +... +	(N+1)	+	(N+1)

There are N terms.

So **twice** the sum $1 + 2 + 3 \dots \dots + N$ is $N(N+1)$

So average search length $= \dfrac{N(N+1)}{2N} = \dfrac{(N+1)}{2}$

A linear search can be performed on all the data structures described so far.

(Structures like trees are constructed so as to reduce search length.)

39.26 Search length for a binary tree. For a well-balanced tree the search length is approximately $\log_2 N$, where N is the number of elements in the tree (eg, if N = 32 the search length is 5, because $2^5 = 32$ or $\log_2 32 = 5$).

To justify the use of this formula we can see that:

If we had two (2^1) nodes we would find the datum after one examination.

If we had four (2^2) nodes we would find the datum after 2 examinations.

If we had eight (2^3) nodes we would find the datum after 3 examinations, etc.

39.27 Binary search. A sorted array can be searched in a way analogous to the method used for searching a binary tree, this is called a binary search. In a binary search the value in the middle of the array is examined to see if it is equal to the value being searched for. If the searched-for value is not equal to the middle value, then the process is repeated with either the first half of the array or the second half of the array according to whether the middle value is larger or smaller than the searched-for value. The process is repeated with smaller and smaller subdivisions of the array until either the value is found or there are no more subdivisions to make. A procedure for performing a binary search is given in Fig. 39.3. The method should be compared with that given for the linear search in fig. 17.8. Note that the function called int(x) returns the largest integer less than or equal to x.

NB. The binary search has a search length of $\log_2 N$.

39.28 Many attempts to reduce search times are based upon the use of tables such as the ACCESS TABLE (17.36). Various types of table used to improve the access by reducing search time are described in the following paragraphs.

TABLES AND THEIR USES

39.29 Keys. Accessing most tables described in this section involves using **keys.** A key is a data item that is associated with the data and that can be used to locate or identify other data. It may form part of the data to be located, or it may be quite separate. A subscript of an array may be thought of as a key of this second type.

39.30 To illustrate the various types of table we will take as an example data that are the telephone numbers of various people. You may think of the telephone number as the datum item to be accessed and the person's name as the key to that number assuming names are unique.

NAME (KEY)	TELEPHONE NUMBER (DATUM)
ALEX	3012
CHARLOTTE	7641
EMMA	5962
JAMES	4243
KATY	2126
LUCY	3562

39.31 LOOK-UP tables. (Types of access table used independently or in conjunction with other data structures.)

a. Suppose that each location in main memory can store 4 characters. The telephone number can be stored like this for example.

LOCATION ADDRESS	101	102	103	104	105	106
CONTENTS	3012	7641	5962	4243	2126	3562

b. Given a name, "CHARLOTTE" say, we may want to find the corresponding telephone number. The key "CHARLOTTE" is too long to fit into one location in this case, but using just the first four letters may do just as well, and that is what we use in this example (ie, CHAR).

c. This is the look-up table:

KEY	ADDRESS OF CORRESPONDING DATA
ALEX	0101
CHAR	0102
EMMA	0103
JAME	0104
KATY	0105
LUCY	0106

N.B. In this simplified example the 4-character data could occupy the space given to their 4-character addresses, thus removing the need for the look-up table! *In general the data may occupy several successive locations, the first of which is specified in the look-up table.*

```
Procedure search_array (IN    number_of_elements, search_value :  integer
                                search_array :  array [1..100] of integer
                        OUT subscript :  integer
                             found :  boolean
  (*  This procedure performs a binary search through the search_array for the
      search_value.  If it finds the search_value it returns found = true and the
      subscript of the found value.  Otherwise, it returns found = false and the
      subscript value last checked.
  *)
variables
    high,                    (* high and low designate the range of *)
    low: integer             (* subscripts still o be searched.  *)
    search_failed :  boolean
Begin
  (* initialise variables *)
  found := false
  search_failed := false
  high := number_of_elements
  low := 1
  repeat
    (* get a subscript mid way between low and high *)
    subscript := int (high + low)/2)
    if
      search_value = search_array(subscript)
    then
      found := true
    else
      if
        (* at last stage in search *)
        subscript = low
      then
        if
          search_value = search_array(high)
        then
          found := true
        else
          search_failed := true
        endif
      else (* still searching *)
        (* reduce range of search *)
        if
          search_value > search_array(low)
        then
          low := subscript
        else
          high := subscript
        endif
      endif
    until found OR search_failed
end
```

Fig. 39.3. A Procedure for Performing a Binary Sarch.

d. This is how the look-up table could be stored:

LOCATION ADDRESS	81	82	83	84	85	86	87	88	89	90	91	92
CONTENTS	ALEX	1011	CHAR	0102	EMMA	0103	JAME	0104	KATY	0105	LUCY	0106

487

e. To find the required datum we perform **a linear search** in the look-up table for the datum's key and thereby find the address of the datum.

39.32 DIRECT-ACCESS tables.

Any datum in the direct-access table can be accessed directly, ie, *without search*. This is achieved by using a *mapping function*, ie, a formula or procedure that is applied to each key to produce the location address of the corresponding datum.

39.33 Example.

a. **Mapping function.** Consider a simple example in which the first letter of each key is given a value corresponding to its position in the alphabet, ie, A = 1, B = 2, C = 3, etc. A possible mapping function is

LOCATION ADDRESS = 100 + KEY VALUE

For example, for "CHARLOTTE" the key value is "3" and the location address of the datum will be 100 + 3 = 103.

b. The data is stored and accessed as shown in this table. *Only the data is stored.*

KEY	FIRST LETTER OF KEY	KEY VALUE	LOCATION ADDRESS (=100 + KEY VALUE)	CONTENTS
ALEX	A	1	101	3012
	B	2	102	
CHARlotte	C	3	103	7642
	D	4	104	
EMMA	E	5	105	5962
	F	6	106	
	G	7	107	
	H	8	108	
	I	9	109	
JAMEs	J	10	110	4243
KATY	K	11	111	2126
LUCY	L	12	112	3562
	M	13	113	

Note

i. There is a waste of storage space; the price of direct access.

ii. This simple mapping function would not be suitable if two keys started with the same letter, so it is hardly practicable.

39.34 HASH tables. (These use methods very similar to those described in (22.34) on random files). The hash table is a compromise between the direct-access table technique and the need to reduce unused storage space. Hash table mapping functions are allowed to be ambiguous, ie, generate the same location address for two different keys. When this happens, and data is allocated to storage space that is already occupied, a procedure is used to find it alternative storage space within the table.

39.35 Example: The "open" hash table.

a. In this example

i. The datum's key is also stored with the datum, so that the datum may be identified when accessed.

ii. The mapping function is:

DATUM LOCATION ADDRESS = 100 + (2 x KEY VALUE)
KEY LOCATION ADDRESS = DATUM LOCATION ADDRESS − 1

eg, CHARLOTTE's datum will have the location address 100 + (2 x 3) = 106 and the key CHAR will have location address 106 − 1 = 105.

iii. If a datum is assigned a location that is already occupied, the datum will be placed in the next empty location instead. (This is the "open" hash method).

b. The hash table looks like this after seven entries:

KEY	FIRST LETTER OF KEY	KEY VALUE	DATUM		KEY	
			LOCATION ADDRESS [100 + 2 × (KEY VALUE)]	CONTENTS	LOCATION ADDRESS [DATUM ADDRESS −1]	CONTENTS
ALEX	A	1	102	3012	101	ALEX
BERNard	B	2	104	4251	103	BERN
CHARlotte	C	3	106	7641	105	CHAR
	D	4				
EMMA	E	5	110	5962	109	EMMA
	F	6				
	G	7				
	H	8				
	I	9				
JAMEs	J	10	120	4243	119	JAME
KATY	K	11	122	2126	121	KATY
LUCY	L	12	124	3562	123	LUCY
	M	13	126			

c. If we now try to add a datum "5482" with the key "ANN", it will be allocated location 102, which is occupied. The next available space is that normally used by "D" and so the datum "5482" will be placed in location 108 and its key "ANN" will be placed on location 107.

d. The table is **"circular"** if values not accommodated at its end are referred to the start of the table, (eg, refer "Z" to "A").

39.36 Other features of hash tables in brief. (A detailed understanding is not called for.)

a. Hash tables work most efficiently when the data is evenly spread out rather than clustered together. If clustering does occur then either the method of choosing the next available location must be changed, or a complete rehash must be made (ie, the table must be remade using a different mapping function.

b. An alternative to the **open hash** is the **closed hash**, in which instead of using adjacent locations in the table for surplus data a **pointer** is placed in the table indicating where the **"overflow"** data may be found.

c. The search length for a hash table is approximate.

$$\frac{2L - N}{2(L - N)}$$

where L is the length of the table and N is the number of entries. The proof of this formula is beyond the scope of this book.

39.37 The binary search in tables. When a direct-access table or hash table *have not been used* it is often possible to improve over a **linear search** by means of a **binary search**, provided the table is in some logical order.

SUMMARY

39.38 a. The data structures discussed in this chapter were:

  i. **Queues**, in which the first item added is the first item removed (FIFO).

  ii. **Stacks**, in which the last item added is the first item removed (LIFO).

  iii. **Look-up tables**, in which the address of a datum is found by a linear search for its key.

  iv. **Direct-access tables**, in which mapping functions are used on the key of a datum to give its location directly.

  v. **Hash tables**, in which mapping functions are also used but for which the location generated is not unique.

b. The **search length** for various structures was discussed:

  i. The **linear search** is a basic method that may be used in any data structure. Search length = $(N + 1)/2$.

  ii. The **binary search**, which can be used on tables in logical order, usually provides quicker than a linear search. Search length = $\log_2 N$.

  iii. If well balanced, the **binary tree** structure produces the same search length as a binary search.

  iv. A direct-access table provides access to the data without a search, ie, search length = 1.

  v. A hash table is almost as fast as a direct-access table when it only has a few entries, but otherwise still gives fast access.

Search length $\simeq (2L - N)/(2L - 2N)$

POINTS TO NOTE

39.39 a. If you are asked to compare data structures then consider these points:
   i. Method of access/storage.
   ii. Use and wastage of storage space.
   iii. Application. (Nature and use of data.)
   iv. Flexibility in handling variable data, overflow, etc.
  b. Try to gain practical experience in setting up and handling various data structures.
  c. **Double buffering** is an alternative to buffering. One **queue** is filled while the other is emptied.

STUDENT SELF-TESTING QUESTIONS

1. What advantages can a list have over simple strings or tables. Make reference to data storage within main store to illustrate your answer.

2. Name three types of table and compare their features.

3. a. Explain how a binary tree may be represented in a high level language which supports arrays. Illustrate your answer by showing how the following data may be stored as a binary tree for subsequent processing in alphabetic order. Assume the first data item is the root of the tree and the tree is created by entering the data at run time in the order given: Leeds, Bradford, Halifax, Huddersfield, Batley, Dewsbury, Wakefield, York, Wetherby, Hull, Malton, Scarborough. *(8 marks)*

   b. Describe **two** situations in which it would be advantageous for data to be stored in the form discussed in part (a) rather than as a structure in which the data is in a list where the data items are stored in the order of their run time input. Explain clearly the advantages of the tree structure. *(4 marks)*

   c. Use pseudo code, or flowcharts, to describe in detail how the structure described in part (a) can be traversed to output the data in ascending alphabetic order. *(8 marks)*
      (A.E.B.)

4. Assume that an array called "S" with 20 elements is to be used to hold the contents of a stack and write pseudocode for the functions outlined in paragraph 17.

QUESTIONS WITHOUT ANSWERS CONTINUED

5. A census organisation carried out a survey of income received by men and women in four regions of the United Kingdom. They collected the following information:
   Name
   Region (E = England, W = Wales, S = Scotland, N = N.Ireland)
   Sex   (M = Male, F = Female)
   Income (U = Upper, I = Intermediate, L = Lower)
   A sequence number (starting at 1) was associated with each name and this data was stored in a sequential file in sequence number order.
   The Region, Sex, and Income data was stored in a data structure of the following nature (only 12 names are used in this example):

   Region index (points to elements in the list rpointer)

attribute:	E	W	S	N
start:	12	11	4	10

   Sex index (points to elements in the list spointer)

attribute:	M	F
start:	12	11

   Income index (points to elements in the list ipointer)

attribute:	U	I	L
start:	10	12	8

5. *continued*

Sequence Number	Name	rpointer	spointer	ipointer
1	G. Dunne	−1	−1	−1
2	D. Bell	−1	1	1
3	A. Drew	1	2	2
4	V. Fleet	2	−1	3
5	R. Forster	−1	4	−1
6	R. Hawes	3	3	4
7	K. Girling	−1	5	−1
8	I. Glover	5	6	6
9	I. Lloyd	6	8	7
10	D. Miller	8	7	5
11	R. Powell	7	10	9
12	A. Hornby	9	9	11

Each index points to the start of a linked list with the given attribute. For example the income index points to entry 10 (D. Miller) as the start of the list of people in the upper income group. The income pointer for entry 10 shows entry 5 (R. Forster) as being next in the list. The income pointer for entry 5 is - 1, ie, there are no further entries with that particular attribute.

For reasons of efficiency successive elements in the linked lists are in reverse order of the order in the names file. The last element in each linked list is a negative pointer.

a. Using the above example determine:

   i. the number of females in the given list,

   ii. the number of males living in Wales,

   iii. the number of people living in England in the Intermediate income group,

   iv. the names of all the males living in England in the Lower income group. *(5 marks)*

b. Use pseudo-code or a flowchart to describe an algorithm to obtain a printout of all the names which possess three attributes to be specified at run time. *(13 marks)*

c. Suggest why the file of names is maintained independently of the linked lists. *(2 marks)*

      (AEB)

6. The diagram shows a representation of an English sentence stored in a computer. Part of the store is given in the diagram (with addresses 100 to 120) together with its contents. Some of the cells shown contain pointers to the beginning of words and some contain codes for letters themselves, so that A is coded as 1, B as 2, and C as 3, etc. Zeros are used as terminators.

   i. What sentence is stored here?

   ii. What is the purpose of the zero in cell 109?

   iii. What is the purpose of the zero in cell 104?

   iv. How is the ordering of the words achieved?

   v. Describe, using a flowchart or a set of written instructions, an algorithm which, when supplied with two of the word-pointers, may interchange them so that an alphabetic ordering of the words is achieved.

QUESTIONS WITHOUT ANSWERS CONTINUED

100	105
101	115
102	119
103	110
104	0
105	13
106	1
107	18
108	25
109	0
6. 110	12
111	11
112	13
113	2
114	0
115	8
116	1
117	4
118	0
119	1
120	0

(London Specimen Paper)

7. **a.** A list of N records is maintained in immediate access memory in sequential order of key field.

   i. Explain the sequential search method to find a record in the list and state what the average number of accesses will be.   *4*

   ii. Explain the binary search method to find a record in the list and state what the maximum number of accesses will be.   *4*

   b. Describe an efficient hashing algorithm to store a record in a randomly ordered list held in immediate-access memory, assuming that collisions can occur and that the record keys are randomly distributed. State why the algorithm is efficient.   *8 = 16*

   (JMB)

8. Show, by means of diagrams or otherwise, what constitutes the type of data structure called a stack.

   Explain how it is used and describe the operations that make use of it.   *(6)*

   (Cambridge)

QUESTIONS WITHOUT ANSWERS CONTINUED

9. A warehouse of tinned foodstuffs keeps records of the stock in a fully indexed direct-access file. A record is held containing data about each type and size of tinned foodstuff and the record key is a code consisting of five letters. The index is arranged as a hash table, with chains (linked lists) for index entries held in a table. A hashing algorithm applied to the record key identities has a table entry that points to the first item in a chain. The items in the chain consist of the record key, the number of the disk block that contains the record, and the chain link. The free space in the chain table is itself held as a chain. This structure is illustrated in the following diagram, which includes some example entries.

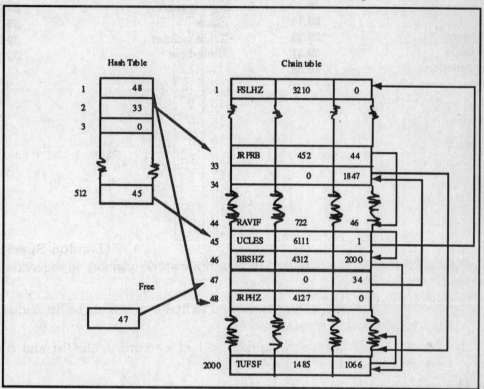

The example data shows only a single tinned foodstuff (record key JRPHZ) with a hash value of 1, many with a hash value of 2, none with a hash value of 3, and two with a hash value of 512.

Describe algorithms for the following operations:

a. accessing the record corresponding to a given record key;

b. inserting a new record and record key corresponding to a new variety of tinned foodstuff.

c. deleting a record and record key corresponding to a discontinued variety of tinned food-stuff.

In each case assume that the record key gives a hash value denoted by H. Your algorithms need not give details of any reorganisation of the records in the file made necessary or desirable by (b) or (c). **(Cambridge 1982)**

10. In the queue example in this chapter the queue was allocated addresses 101-110. When the next entry pointer became 111 the queue was declared to be full. However, there may have been space at the front end, eg, if the removal pointer was 105, then 101 to 104 were available to be used for new items. This leads to the idea of a circular buffer where after address 110 we would use 101. Write a pseudocode for the functions and procedures identified in paragraph 9 for the manipulation of a queue stored in this way in a "circular buffer".

GLOSSARY CHECKLIST

40: Further Methods

INTRODUCTION

40.1 This chapter briefly introduces further methods not included in chapter 39 because they are of general value.

SORTING

40.2 The two most common kinds of sorting are:

a. the sorting of files

b. the sorting of sets of data in main storage.

The latter is also used as a stage in file sorting so we start with file sorting.

40.3 The **number of records to be sorted in a file** and **limitations of main storage** do not normally allow the sorting to be done in one attempt, so the sort is usually split into two stages:

a. **String-generation phase.** Manageable groups of records from the unsorted file are read into main storage. These groups are sorted into sequence and written as sequenced groups or **strings** onto other output tapes/disks.

b. **String-merging phase** during which strings are read into main storage, **merged** into larger groups (records are in sequence within groups) and written out to disk or tape. The process is repeated until the whole file is in one sequence.

Each repetition of the string merging is called a **pass**.

40.4 **Internal sorting.** This is sorting within main storage and is the type of sorting done during the string-generation phase. Two basic types of methods are:

a. methods that swap whole records each time.

b. methods that swap keys and pointers.

The difference is illustrated by this diagram

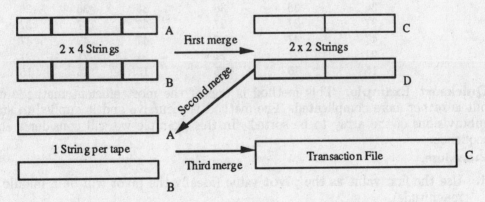

40.5 **Sort Examples.** A detailed example of sorting was given in 17.20. Some further methods are outlined here. The first two examples sort the data into descending sequence, which is less common than sorting into ascending sequence. The reader is invited to rework them as ascending sequences as an exercise.

a. **Sort Example 1.** This is just one of the many possible methods. Suppose that 10 numbers in an array are to be sorted. The following methods could be used.

Procedure.

i. Find largest number

ii. Swap it with 1st number

iii. Find next largest (ie, largest between 2nd and last)

iv. Swap with 2nd number

v. Find next largest (ie, largest between 3rd and last)

495

vi. Swap with 3rd number.

etc (see following).

Step 1		Step 2		Step 3		Step 4		Step 5	
10	←	53		53		53		53	
32		32	← swap	51		51		51	
51	swap	51	←	32	←	47		47	
24		24		24		24	←	43	
53	←	10		10		10	swap	10	←
43		43		43	swap	43	←	24	swap
36		36		36		36		36	←
37		37		37		37		37	
47		47		47	←	32		32	
21		21		21		21		21	
15		15		15		15		15	

b. Sort Example 2. (bubble sort)

The previous example shows a method that takes no account of the initial order of the data. The bubble sort is quicker if the data is partially sorted.

Procedure.

i. Work down from the top to find the first number out of sequence.

ii. Move the number up until its correct position is found moving other numbers down as you go. (The number rises like a bubble in liquid.)

iii. Repeat as long as necessary.

Step 1	Step 2	Step 3	Step 4	Step 5	etc.
10 ↓	32 ↓	51	51 ↓	53	53
32 ↑	10 ↑ ↓	32	32 ↑ ↓	51	51
51 raise 32 lower 10	51 ↑	10 ↓	24 ↑ ↓	32 ↓	43
24	24 raise 51 lower 10	24 ↑	10 ↑ ↓	24 ↑ ↓	32
53	53 and 32	53 raise 24 lower 10	53 ↓	10 ↑ ↓	24
43	43	43	43	43 ↑	10
36	36	36	36	36	36
37	37	37	37	37	37
47	47	47	47	47	47
21	21	21	21	21	21
15	15	15	15	15	15

c. Quicksort Example.

This method is one of the most efficient methods of internal sorting but is rather more complicated. The method is recursive and is applied to smaller and smaller subdivisions of the array to be sorted. In this example we will consider a sort into ascending sequence.

Procedure.

i. Use the first value as the **pivot** value (ideally the pivot will be a middle value in terms of magnitude).

ii. Permute the remaining values so that for a given subscript (the partition subscript) all values with this and lower subscripts are lower in value than the pivot and all values with higher subscripts are larger than or equal to the pivot. To permute the values perform a set of swaps in which successive high values in the lower part of the array are swapped with successive low values in the upper part.

iii. Swap the pivot value with the value at the partition subscript.

iv. Re-apply the procedure to the part of the array above the partition subscript and to the part below the partition subscript.

Step 1			Step 2			Step 3			Step 4		
36 ←	Pivot ←		21 ←	Pivot ←		10 ←	Pivot		10		10
15		|	15		|	15			15		15
37 ←		|	32 ←		←	21			21		21
10 |		|	10 ←			32 ←	Pivot ←		24		24
53 |	←	|	24			24		←|	32		32
21 |	|	←	36			36			36		36
51 |	|		51 ←	Pivot ←		37 ←	Pivot		37		37
24 |	←		53		|	47			47 ←	Pivot ←	43
43 |			43		|	43			43	←|	47
32 ←			37		←	51			51		51
47			47 ←			53			53		53

NB. The pivot is pointed to in those parts of the array in which sorting is incomplete.

STRING MERGING (NB. These are strings of records not character strings)

40.6 The merge sort This works as follows:

a. Sequenced strings are placed alternately on two magnetic tapes. (Disks could be used but the "classical" method uses tapes.) Call the tapes A and B.

b. The 1st string from A is merged with the 1st string from B and this new sequence string is written onto a third tape C. (If possible these strings are placed alternately on two tapes C and D.)

c. The process is repeated until just one string exists. This is the transaction file ready for use.

Note. The tape pairs AB and CD can be used alternately as input and output tapes as shown in this diagram.

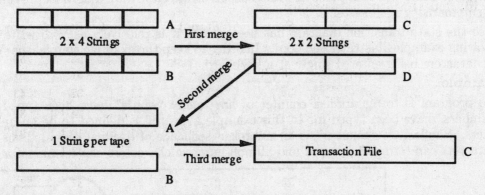

40.7 The procedure for merging the strings is given in the following pseudocode. The pseudocode shows the logic of merging one pair of strings rather than the practical details.

```
Begin
    if
            there is a record left in both string A and string B
    then
        if
    key of string A > key of string B
    then
            place the A record onto C
    else
            place the B record onto C
            endif
    endif
    place the remaining records onto C
end
```

40.8 Three-tape merge using the Fibonacci sequence.

The Fibonacci sequence starts, 1, 1, 2, 3, 5, 8, 13, 21... and successive terms are the sum of the previous two, eg, 21 = 8 + 13. Strings are distributed on two of the three tapes in proportion to two suitable successive terms in the Fibonacci sequence, eg, 8 strings would be distributed 5, 3. The following diagram outlines the method. (Details of tape copies and records are omitted for the sake of clarity.)

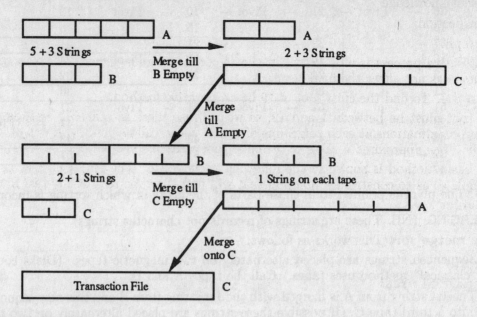

STATE TRANSITION DIAGRAMS

40.9 In many situations in which programs are used for control or monitoring a system it is useful to be able to identify the various states that the system can be in and to determine what actions or changes in state will take place as events occur. State transition diagrams provide a simple notation for summarising such systems.

Once the state transition diagram has been drawn it is relatively easy to write the program. The following example illustrates the point. In order to keep the example simple, the "events" correspond to characters being entered singly at a keyboard.

40.10 Example.

The program is to maintain a counter of how many "words" have been typed in and how many "numbers" have been typed in. In this example a "word" is defined to be an unbroken sequence of letters. Similarly, a "number" is an unbroken sequence of decimal digits. Thus all non-alphabetic characters can terminate a word and all non-numeric characters can terminate a number.

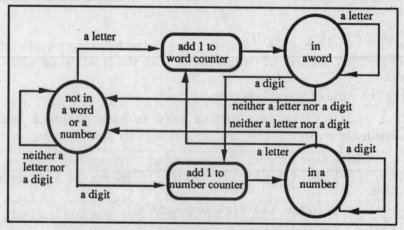

Fig. 40.1. A State Transition Diagram.

In Fig. 40.1 the states of the system are represented by circles. The inputs are labels on the arrowed lines. The round-cornered boxes are actions.

ITERATION

40.11 This topic is mainly of interest in numerical computing. In an **iterative process** for the solution of a problem, newer approximations are obtained from earlier ones by repeated application of some formula or procedure. We say that the result has been obtained by **iteration**.

40.12 Starting and stopping. To start an iterative process one or more first approximations are needed. These first approximations are called **starting values**. Starting values may be obtained by:

a. guessing

b. prior knowledge

c. inspection

d. graph.

An iterative process is stopped when the required accuracy is reached. Rounding of intermediate results does not affect the final accuracy.

40.13 Example. To find the cube root of 19 by an iterative method.

The root must be between 1 and 19, so we will use these as **starting values**. This method uses two approximations at each stage, one of which is low, called "low", and one of which is high, called "high". The approximate value of the cube root at each stage of iteration is called "approx".

The basic method is shown in the following pseudocode. The reader should be able to adapt this example so as to construct a function that will find the cube root of any real number.

variables

low,

high,

approx,

approxcubed : **real**

Begin

  (* initialise variables *)

  low   := 1

  high   := 19

  approx   := (low + high)/2

  approxcubed := approx ↑ 3

  while approxcubed <> 19

    if

      approxcubed > 19

    then

        high := approx

    else

        low := approx

    endif

      approx := (low +high)/2

  approxcubed := approx ↑ 3

  endwhile

  output("The cube of 19 is", approx)

end

The following table shows the first few steps using this pseudocode.

low	high	approx	approxcubed	Comment
1	19	10	1000	approx too high, replace high
1	10	5.5	166.375	approx still too high, replace high
1	5.5	3.25	34.33 (2D)	approx still too high, replace high
1	3.25	2.125	9.596 (3D)	approx too low, replace low
2.125	3.25	2.6875	19.41 (2D)	approx too high, replace high
		etc		

The cube root of 19 is 2.66840 correct to six figures.

Note The process could appear to go on for ever, but in practice there is a practical limit caused by the accuracy of the computer on which the program is run.

40.14 This simple example shows how relatively easy it can be to solve problems iteratively. It is therefore no surprise that iteration is a common technique.

SUMMARY

40.15 The chapter has outlined methods involving

    a. State transition diagrams.

    b. Iteration.

POINTS TO NOTE

40.16 Iteration is a term sometimes also used to mean looping.

STUDENT SELF-TESTING QUESTIONS

1. Explain the term **iterative process**.

2. Show the steps needed to look up Birmingham using a binary search on the following list:

> Aberdeen, Birmingham, Cambridge, Exeter, Manchester, Newcastle,
> Norwich, Oxford, Reading, Sheffield, Southampton, York

(2 marks)
(AEB)

3. When all syntax errors have been eliminated from a program other sorts of errors may remain. Explain the nature of such errors and suggest how they may be eliminated. *(5 marks)*

(AEB)

4. a. High level languages vary in the number and type of primitive (built-in) data structures they support. Describe one data structure which is desirable as a built-in feature for a commercial language and one which is desirable as a built-in feature for a scientific language. In each case give **one** example of a programming situation in which the data structure you have described would be particularly useful. *(6 marks)*

    b. i. State the main features of a recursive procedure from a programmer's point of view. *(2 marks)*

      ii. State **two** advantages for a programmer in using a high level language which supports recursion. *(2 marks)*

      iii. Give an example of an application in which the use of recursion is helpful to the programmer. *(2 marks)*

      iv. Describe briefly **one** disadvantage of the use of recursion. *(1 mark)*

    c. Some high level languages allow the programmer to pass *parameters* to subroutines and permit the use of *local variables* within a sub-routine.

      i. Explain the meaning of the terms in italics. *(2 marks)*

      ii. Explain why the italicised features are useful to the programmer. *(3 marks)*

      iii. Describe **two** mechanisms which a compiler might use to transmit parameters to subroutines. *(2 marks)*

(AEB)

QUESTIONS WITHOUT ANSWERS

5. In 23.10 you were invited to rework the sorting examples so that the results were in ascending order. If you have not yet done so do so now.

6. With reference to 23.13 show how a file of 21 sorted sequences of records can be split up and successively merged into one sorted file.

7. Draft out the pseudocode for the program specified in Fig. 40.1.

GLOSSARY CHECKLIST

DATABASES AND 4GLs

1. This part introduces databases, how they are organised and the languages used to access them. Databases both large and small are of growing importance and this is reflected in all the examinations at which this text is aimed.
2. Chapter 41 concentrates on database architecture and related matters.
3. Chapter 42 concentrates on database query languages and related products called 4GLs.

41: Database Architecture

INTRODUCTION

41.1 When organisations first began to use computers, they naturally adopted a piece-meal approach. One system at a time was studied, re-designed and transferred to the computer. This approach was necessitated by the difficulties experienced in using a new and powerful management tool. It had the drawback, however, of producing a number of separate systems, each with its own program suite, its own files, and its own inputs and outputs. The main criticisms of this approach are that:

a. The computer-based systems, being self-contained, do not represent the way in which the organisation really works, ie, as a complex set of interlocking and interdependent systems.

b. Systems communicate with each other outside the computer. This proliferates inputs and outputs and creates delays. For example, input of a customer order to an order processing system might create an output of an invoice. This in turn would have to be converted back into input for activating the sales accounting system. Similarly, if the order reduced stock levels to the re-order level (ie, the level at which they must be re-ordered so that ordered stock arrives before existing stock runs out) another output would be created, which would then have to be input to the production control and/or the purchasing system.

c. Information obtained from a series of separate files is less valuable because it does not give the complete picture. For example, the sales manager reviewing outstanding orders from customers has to get information about stocks from another file.

d. Data may be duplicated in two or more files, creating unnecessary maintenance and the risk of inconsistency.

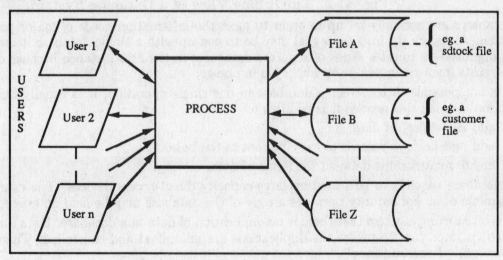

Fig. 41.1. An Integrated File System.

INTEGRATED FILE SYSTEMS

41.2 Integrated file systems represent an approach to solving the problems just described by conventional means. In an integrated file system the data is pooled into a set of inter-locking and interdependent files, which are accessible by a number of different users.

41.3 When a transaction enters an integrated file system *all* the appropriate files are updated. The features of an integrated system are shown in Fig. 41.1.

41.4 A large number of integrated file systems are in use today. Many of them have been tailor-made to meet the requirements of particular organisations.

41.5 Integrated file systems do not provide a satisfactory answer to all the criticisms mentioned in paragraph 41.1, however. They tend to suffer from the problems caused by *data duplication* (41.1d) and from the fact that the task of maintaining the data is shared between the programs that access and maintain the data and therefore lacks proper central control.

NB. The idea of integrating the *processing functions* will be returned to later in this chapter.

DATABASES

41.6 Databases represent a radically different approach to solving the problems discussed so far in this chapter.

41.7 **Database definition.** A database is a single organised collection of structured data, stored with a minimum of duplication of data items so as to provide a consistent and controlled pool of data. This data is common to all users of the system, but is independent of programs that use the data.

41.8 The independence of the database and programs using it means that one can be changed without changing the other.

41.9 The users of a database may find it convenient to imagine that they are using an integrated file system like the one shown in Fig. 41.1. In reality the database is organised as in Fig. 41.2. A more detailed description of the organisation is given later in this chapter.

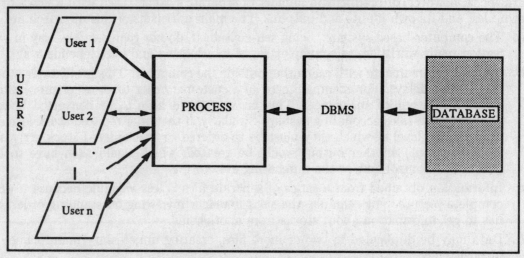

Fig. 41.2. An Outline View of a Database System.

41.10 Databases are normally set up in order to meet the information needs of major parts of an organisation. Although the long term goal may be to end up with a single database it is very common for an organisation to set a series of separate databases in the first instance because of the time, risks and costs involved in doing the whole job in one go.

41.11 It is not possible to construct a database in one single operation, it is usually built up section by section. During this process it is possible to:

a. add new "files" of data.

b. add new fields to records already present in the base,

c. create relationships between the items of data.

41.12 A database requires to be stored on large-capacity direct-access devices. The usual medium is the magnetic disk. For security purposes a copy of the database may be held on magnetic tape or disk.

41.13 It is often *wrongly stated* that there is no duplication of data in a database. Data may be duplicated, but it is important to realise the duplications are minimised and controlled. This is referred to as **"controlled redundancy"**.

41.14 Although, to the user, the database may appear as a collection of files, data in the database is organised in a more complex way than data in conventional files.

41.15 Databases may be classified according to the approaches taken to database organisation. The classes are:

a. Relational.

b. Network.

c. Hierarchical.

d. File inversions.

The last two are more basic, have a number of practical limitations, and do not merit further discussion here.

41.16 **Relational** databases use types of tables called **relations**. The terminology is initially confusing because of the use of the name "relation" for a table and because relations are not the same as relationships. However, relational databases were developed from mathematically sound ideas, have an elegant simplicity and are likely to be increasingly important in the future.

41.17 **Network databases** have been around in several forms for a number of years. In recent years the network approach has been developed by the work of CODASYL. Network databases are based upon ideas similar to those used for linked lists. The links are used to express relationships between different items of data.

41.18 When new sets of data are added, it is often found that some of the required data is already stored for other purposes.

41.19 The database is maintained by a "single input". This means that just as there is little duplication of data, there is also no duplication of inputs. One transaction will cause all the necessary changes to be made to the data.

41.20 As the base is expanded, or as user requirements change, the links or relations in the database can be changed and new relationships can be established.

41.21 The user is unaware of the structure of the database. The Database Management System (see paragraph 24) provides the user with the services needed and handles the technicalities of maintaining and using the data.

COMMUNICATING WITH THE DATABASE

41.22 Some databases have their own computer languages associated with them which allow the user to access and retrieve data at a terminal. Other databases are only accessible via languages such as C, COBOL, Pascal, BASIC, Ada or FORTRAN, to which extra facilities have been added for this purpose.

41.23 Data descriptions must be standardised. For this reason, a **Data Description Language (DDL)** is provided, which *must* be used to specify the data in the base. Similarly, a **Data Manipulation Language (DML)** is provided, which must be used to access the data. The function of these two languages may be compared to the declarations and processing statement in a conventional programming language. As indicated by the previous paragraph DDLs and DMLs may be either free-standing or embedded in another language. The combination of a DDL and a DDL is often referred to as a **Data Sublanguage DSL**. Probably the most common DSL in use today is **SQL (Structured Query Language)**. SQL will be discussed in the next chapter.

THE DATABASE MANAGEMENT SYSTEM (DBMS)

41.24 The database management system is a *complex software system* that constructs, expands and maintains the database. It also provides the controlled interface between the user and the data in the base.

41.25 The DBMS allocates storage to data. It maintains indices so that any required data can be retrieved, and so that separate items of data in the base can be cross-referenced. As mentioned above, the structure of a database is dynamic and can be changed as needed. In what follows for the sake of generality and simplicity operations are described in terms of records and files. However, the reader should not that the actual structure and organisation of the data is not merely in the form of simple files but in terms of such things as rows, tables or nodes according to the database's type (eg, Relational or Network).

41.26 The DBMS maintains the data in the base by:

a. adding new records,

b. deleting "dead" records,

c. amending records.

In addition to these functions (which are performed by any file-maintenance program) it can expand the base by adding new sets of records or new data to existing records.

41.27 The DBMS provides an interface with user programs. These may be written in a number of different programming languages. However, the programmer need not be familiar with the structure of the base because the data his or her program requires is retrieved by the DBMS.

41.28 The DBMS provides facilities for different types of file processing. It can:

a. Process a complete file (serially or sequentially),

b. Process required records (selective, sequential or random).

c. Retrieve individual records.

It can also, as has been explained above, retrieve related records or related data within records.

41.29 The DBMS also has the function of providing security for the data in the base. The main aspects of this are:

a. Protecting data against unauthorised access.

b. Safeguarding data against corruption.

c. Providing recovery and restart facilities after a hardware or software failure.

The DBMS keeps statistics of the use made of the data in the base. This allows redundant data to be removed. It also allows data that is frequently used to be kept in a readily accessible form so that time is saved.

41.30 Data dictionary. The DBMS makes use of descriptions of data items provided by the DDL. This "data about data" is called a **data dictionary**. Often the data dictionary is actually implemented as an additional database accessed by the DBMS.

41.31 Clearly, something so complex as a DBMS needs to be organised in a logical way. This logical organisation is achieved by having a number of distinct levels within the DBMS. At the top level, data is expressed in a form compatible with the view of individual users, (as applications files, say). At the middle level the data is expressed in global terms applicable to all applications. At the bottom level the data is expressed in forms that relate to the way the data is actually stored. The DBMS transforms data as it moves it from level to level.

DATABASE SYSTEM ARCHITECTURE

41.32 The growing importance of database systems in most office environments merits a more detailed discussion of how a modern database system is organised.

41.33 Fig 41.3 shows the organisation of a modern database system. The client application programs run by users are able to connect to a DBMS server. The DBMS server is normally a special program which is able to accept multiple connections from many client programs at the same time. It is therefore said to be **multi-threaded**.

41.34 The client program sends a request to the DBMS server using a DSL such as SQL. SQL will be used in this example but the ideas are completely general. The DBMS server treats the SQL statement as a request which it must translate and act upon. The client may request data to be defined, inserted, updated, deleted or retrieved depending upon the SQL statements issued to the server.

41.35 Once the DBMS server has translated the SQL statement it retrieves data from the database into a **Data Cache** where it can be access and manipulated more quickly and easily. The data will also be more readily available to any other client once it is in cache but the DBMS server has to manage any such multiple accesses to the data so that client programs do not interfere with each other's data.

41.36 A well know problem which has to be avoided is the **lost update** which occurs if two separate clients are allowed to update the same data value at the same time. Suppose that two clients "A" and "B" each wish to update an account balance by 100 and that the initial value of the account is 500. Suppose they follow the following sequence:

a. "A" take a copy of the balance of 500.

b. "B" takes a copy of the balance of 500.

c. "A" adds 100 to its copy of the balance and replaces the balance with 600.

d. "B" adds 100 to its copy of the balance and replaces the balance with 600.

e. the final balance is 600 *but it should be 700!*.

The DBMS server prevents the kind of problem from happening. The most common way is for it to use **locks**. When a lock is taken on data by a client it restricts what other clients may do. An alternative arrangement to the one above is as follows.

a. "A" requests a **write lock** on the data which is granted by the DBMS.

b. "B" requests a **write lock** on the data which is denied by the DBMS so "B" must wait.

c. "A" take a copy of the balance of 500.

d. "A" adds 100 to its copy of the balance and replaces the balance with 600.

e. "A" releases its lock so the DBMS now grants 'B" the lock it requested.

f. "B" takes a copy of the balance of 600.

g. "B" adds 100 to its copy of the balance and replaces the balance with 700.

h. "B" releases its lock.

i. the final balance is 700.

41.37 In the example given above a **write lock** was mention. A write lock is held by a single client to have exclusive access to data while it is being updated. An alternative kind of lock is the **read lock** which may be held by many clients wanting to read the same data. The client share access to the date but by holding read locks they prevent any other client from taking a write lock and changing the data while they are using it. Now back to the processing of the SQL statement.

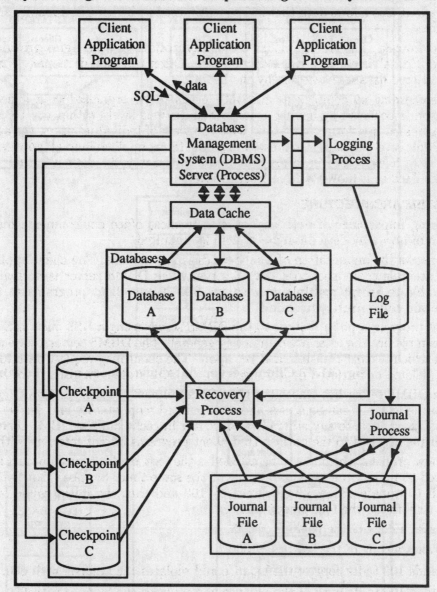

Fig. 41.3. The organisation of a Database System.

41.38 When data has been updated in cache it must be written back to the database. The changes may also be recorded in a log file from where they may copied into journal files. The reasons for this are to enable data to be recovered if the system should fail for any reason such as power failure. There is also the need to coverer the bad case of a database being lost because of a "disk crash".

41.39 Then **checkpoints** shown in Fig 42.3 are "snapshots" of the database before it was updated by clients and the **journal** hold details of the updates subsequently made. In the event of failure the **recovery process** can rebuild the database.

41.40 In subsequent diagrams the logging and recovery details are omitted for the sake of clarity.

41.41 Fig 41.3 shows a database system as it might be set up on a single machine such as a minicomputer or mainframe. It is also very common to set up database system to operate in client-server mode on a network. Fig 41.4 shows such an arrangement. There are three workstations acting a clients and there is one server machine, a minicomputer say. The **communications process** enable the clients and server to communicate with one another just as if they were on the same machine. Such an arrangement is not only very flexible it also makes very good use of processing resources because the load is spread between clients and their server in a cost effective way.

41.42 Fig 41.5 shows a further more advanced arrangement where the clients are accessing a **distributed database**. There are two databases, A and B, on different machines each accessible by their own DBMS servers. However, the clients have **distributed database servers** which enables them to access both "A" and "B" at the same times as if they were a single database. The combined database is said to be distributed.

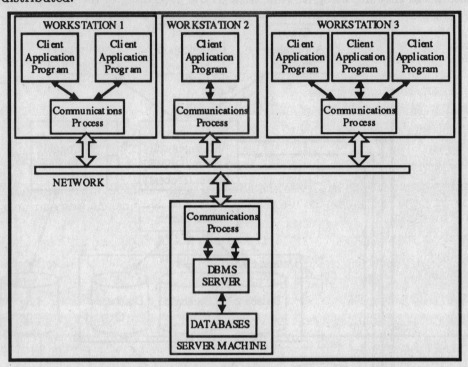

Fig. 41.4. Client-server database access on a network.

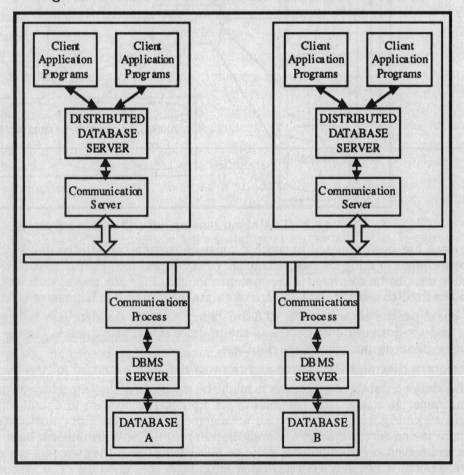

Fig. 41.5. A distributed Database System.

508

THE DATABASE ADMINISTRATOR (DBA)

41.43 The importance of a database is such that a special manager is often appointed, sometimes with a staff. His functions are described below.

The DBA must have a sound knowledge of the structure of the database and of the DBMS. The DBA must also be thoroughly conversant with the organisation, its systems, and the information needs of the managers.

41.44 The DBA is responsible for ensuring that:

a. The data in the database meets the information needs of the organisation.

b. That the facilities for retrieving data and for structuring reports are appropriate to the needs of the organisation.

41.45 The DBA is responsible for the following documentation:

a. The data dictionary.

b. Manuals for users describing the facilities the database offers and how to make use of these facilities.

41.46 Another function is to supervise the addition of new data. For this purpose, the DBA will have to liaise with the managers who use the data, and the systems analysts and programmers who develop the systems.

41.47 Security of the database is also the responsibility of the DBA and further, the requirements of privacy.

41.48 The DBA is also responsible for periodic appraisal of the data held in the base to ensure that it is complete, accurate and not duplicated.

EXAMPLES OF A DATABASE

41.49 There are at present few organisations who have a really comprehensive database. An example is given here of a database used by a major computer manufacturer.

41.50 The database comprises:

a. Records of customers who have purchased or who rented the manufacturer's computer equipment.

b. Records of the different items of equipment, ie, processors, peripherals and other devices.

c. Records of spare parts showing the location where they are stored and the quantity held.

d. Records of customer engineers responsible for maintenance and repairs.

41.51 The uses made of the database are too numerous to list completely, but a selection does give some idea of the facilities that a database can provide.

a. **Accounting.** Customers are billed for maintenance and rental charges. Any change in configuration automatically causes the customer charges to be amended (the "single input" principle).

b. **Spares.** The database is used to control stocks of spares. It can also be used to find the location of a spare part nearest to the installation that requires it.

c. **Modifications.** If a modification to a particular item of equipment is needed, all installations in which it is present can be quickly identified.

d. **Engineering services.** The database shows which customers are served by which engineer (an example of the "linking" or cross-referencing of records). Engineers can be allocated to cover absence or sickness or to assist at an installation that is in trouble. The records show which types of equipment the engineers are qualified to service.

ADVANTAGES OF A DATABASE

41.52 The following are the advantages of a database:

a. Information supplied to managers is more valuable because it is based on a comprehensive collection of data instead of files that contain only the data needed for one application.

b. As well as routine reports, it is possible to obtain ad hoc reports to meet particular requirements.

c. There is an obvious economic advantage in not duplicating data. In addition, errors due to discrepancies between two files are eliminated.

d. The amount of input preparation needed is minimised by the "single input" principle.

e. A great deal of programming time is saved because the DBMS handles the construction and processing of files and the retrieval of data.

f. The use of integrated systems is greatly facilitated.

INTEGRATED SYSTEMS

41.53 The database represents the integration of the data/information of an organisation. Associated with this concept is the integration of the systems that use the data. As has been seen, the development of separate systems increases the amount of external communication (inputs and outputs) between systems and is also likely to duplicate programming effort.

41.54 The concept is best illustrated by an example of three systems that are often integrated: order processing, sales accounting and stock control.

    a. The basic input to the system is that of a customer order.

    b. On input, the order is validated in the normal way. It is then

    c. checked against the customer record to ensure that the credit position is satisfactory, and

    d. checked against the stock file to ensure that the stock is available.

    e. After the order has passed these checks, the files are updated. The stock level is reduced by the amount ordered. An invoice is generated, and the customer record is updated.

    f. The documentation is distributed as necessary, eg, the invoice is sent to the customer and the copies for despatch procedures sent to the warehouse.

    g. If the supply of the order causes the stock level to fall below the re-order level, a report is printed indicating that replenishment of stock is necessary.

    h. Subsequently, the monthly statement for the customer would be produced.

41.55 This example obviously represents only a small part of the total activities of the company. Possible future development would be:

    a. In a manufacturing organisation, input of a customer order would generate the necessary works order. This would be the "input" to the production-scheduling system, which would in turn generate the bill of materials.

    b. The bill of materials would be "input" to the stock-control system. The necessary stocks would be allocated. If purchases were necessary, an input to the purchasing system would be generated.

    c. Subsequent receipt of the invoice from the supplier would cause another input to the purchase accounting system, resulting in checking of the invoice, notification of queries and eventual payment of the suppliers.

    d. The production scheduling system would allocate the necessary machines and labour using and updating plant and personnel files.

    e. At the due date, the production scheduling system would activate the production control system. Progress of the job through the factory would be controlled and actual inputs from the factory floor would be received to monitor progress.

    On completion of the order, the documentation would be produced and the customer file updated with details of the invoice.

41.56 It will be realised of course that a number of new files would have to be added to the database to make this possible - resource files of plant and labour, supplier file, work in progress, etc.

At the time of writing the above is somewhat *futuristic,* as very few organisations have constructed a *comprehensive* database and *fully* integrated their systems. A gradual approach, building up the database section by section and adding new systems one at a time is obviously desirable. There is really nothing difficult to understand in the concept; the approach is simply to move into the computer *all* the files, *all* the systems and *all* the communications between them, instead of using the computer for only the more straightforward work and linking the computer-based systems externally.

FILE-MANAGEMENT SYSTEMS

41.57 A number of software products have appeared on the market in recent years that appear to offer *some* of the features of databases on even the smaller computers. These products, some of which claim to be "database packages", are usually more correctly called "file-management systems".

41.58 Typical file-management systems usually have rudimentary DDLs and DMLs, which allow the user to set up and maintain a few files with a minimum of programming effort or skill. Facilities are often included that allow limited but extremely useful data retrieval functions such as sorting and selecting.

41.59 A file-management system may therefore be thought of rather loosely as a "computerised filing cabinet".

SUMMARY

41.60 **a.** The development of separate systems with their own files is simple but does not make the best use of resources. Integrated files, databases, and integrated systems are more difficult to install, but have many advantages.

b. A database is a comprehensive, consistent, controlled and coordinated collection of structured data items.

c. A **Database Management System (DBMS)** is a software system that constructs, maintains and processes a database.

d. Communication with the database is via the **Data Description Language (DDL)** and **Data Manipulation Language (DML)**.

e. The **data dictionary** holds "data about data" in the database.

f. Some of the more modern database systems may be set up using a client-server architecture which in some cases may enable distributed databases to be used.

g. Where there is concurrent access to a database the multi-threaded DBMS server must control access so as to prevent problems such as the lost update. One method is to use locks.

h. A **Database Administrator (DBA)** is the manager responsible for that database.

i. Integrated systems are a natural corollary to databases.

POINTS TO NOTE

41.61 **a.** Locks are commonly used to control concurrent access but they can also be problematical. For example, a client may hold a lock unnecessarily long causing other clients to wait too long. A further problem called **deadlock** can occur when two clients are each waiting for the other's lock and cannot finish their transaction and release their own lock until they get the other! The DBMS server must attempt to manage deadlock, for example by aborting one of the two deadlocked transactions.

b. Another term you may come across is "**data bank**". This has a slightly different meaning to "database". An organisation constructing a database will put into it only data that it expects to use - for obvious reasons of economy. A "data bank", on the other hand, is designed to contain any data that may be required - just as a librarian has to keep stocks of books, some of which may never be referred to. An example of a data bank is a file of legal cases; they all have to be there because enquiries cannot be predicted, but some may never be inspected.

c. The integrated system extends the database to include *all* information flows in a business and automates as many "decisions" as possible to produce a comprehensive management-information system.

d. The computer is being increasingly used as the centre of a *communications network*. Many organisations are replacing the traditional centralised methods of data collection with terminal devices linked to a central machine. The flows of data (inwards) and information (outwards) are greatly accelerated, and there is considerable improvement in communication and control.

e. Integrated file systems are integrated systems without the use of databases.

STUDENT SELF-TESTING QUESTIONS

1. Distinguish between a database and a file-management system.
2. Explain the terms:
   a. DDL.
   b. DML.
   c. DBMS.
   d. DBA.

GLOSSARY CHECKLIST

42: Query Languages and 4GLs

INTRODUCTION

42.1 In recent years there has been a major increase in the use of relational databases. The increase has been accompanied by a number of different products that aid the development of new systems. These new products are often described as being **"Fourth Generation Languages (4GLs)"** because they are considered to work at a higher level than normal high-level languages such as COBOL, Pascal and C. The latter are often, consequently, called 3GLs. The actual facilities provided by 4GLs vary considerably.

42.2 Many 4GLs make use of relational databases, which themselves have query languages (DDLs plus DMLs), which perform operations at a very high level. Some 4GLs are actually the combination of a database query language and other facilities. For this reason query languages and 4GLs are both discussed in this chapter.

QUERY LANGUAGE FEATURES

42.3 A query language normally comprises a DDL and a DML all rolled into one. The name **query language** is therefore something of a misnomer since query languages do much more than handle queries to the database.

42.4 Query languages have two basic modes of operation:

a. **Terminal monitor mode.** The user is able to use the query language at a terminal, in much the same way as a command-language interpreter is used. The idea is for the end-user to formulate ad hoc queries in order to obtain useful information from the database. The importance of such facilities is greatly overrated, however, because in practice a great deal more control and care must be taken when accessing most databases. Nevertheless, such facilities can be of great value to those developing queries to be run in the other mode.

b. **Embedded query languages.** The query-language statements are included within the code of programs written in some other programming language, eg, COBOL or C, and effectively becomes part of the program, hence the term "embedded query language".

42.5 In order to give more concrete illustrations of the features used, the following examples are all based upon what is undoubtedly one of the most widespread query languages, **SQL (Structured Query Language)**.

42.6 SQL is an international standard for database query languages and has been adopted by many computer manufacturers and database product suppliers, eg, IBM, Digital, INGRES, ORACLE, SYBASE and INFORMIX.

42.7 Tables. Data in a relational database is stored in tables (sometimes called "relations"). Each row in the table is broadly comparable to a single record in a file having simple records all of the same size. Another name for a row is a "tuple".

Example

A table called "CUSTOMER"

Account No.	Name	Address	Credit Limit	Credit
A13245	John Brown	39 Graveside Gardens	1000	25
A13495	Robert Peel	21 Police Station Rd	1000	120
A13554	Anna Seed	15 Sweetbriar Rd	1500	500
A13782	Mary Christmas	22 Pundit Close	1200	200
A14854	Anita Dresser	99 Avenue Rd	2000	750

Fig. 42.1. A Relational Database Table.

42.8 Each row should be uniquely identifiable by a suitable key. For a given table the key may be either a **simple key** consisting of the value in one column or a **composite key** consisting of multiple columns. In the example just given (Fig. 42.1) the account number acts as a simple key.

42.9 **To create a table** like the one given in Fig. 42.1 using SQL a statement such as the following could be used.

```
create  table customer
        (
        accountno       char(6)     not null unique,
        name            char(20)    not null,
        address         char(40)    not null,
        creditlimit     smallint,
        credit          smallint
        )
```

The meaning of the statement is to a large degree self-explanatory. The layout has been chosen for readability, with the definition of each column in the table set out on a separate line in the order in which it is to appear in the table. The line "accountno char(6) not null unique," states that the first column is to be called "accountno", it can be up to 6 characters long, it must not be "null" (ie, it must have a value and not be left blank) and its value must be unique. The line defining the last column "credit" merely defines the data type of "credit" to be a small integer (ie, low precision).

42.10 **To retrieve values from a table a SELECT statement is used.**

The following select statement retrieves rows from the table "customer" displaying just the three columns "accountno", "name" and "creditlimit". The expression after the word "where" defines what properties values in a row must have for the row to be selected. In this case the credit limit must be between 1000 and 2000.

```
select
        accountno, name, credit
from
        customer
where
        creditlimit > 1000
        and
        creditlimit < 2000
```

This data is retrieved.

accountno.	name	credit
A13554	Anna Seed	500
A13782	Mary Christmas	200

42.11 **To insert a row into a table an INSERT statement may be used.**

In this example a row is inserted in which three columns are assigned values and the other two left blank (ie, have the value null). **Note.** The single quotation mark is part of SQL syntax.

```
insert  into     customer
                 (accountno, name, address )
         values  ('A14900', 'Simon Simple', '1 Pyman Close')
```

After inserting this row into the table given in Fig. 42.1 the table would be as shown in Fig. 42.2.

Account No.	Name	Address	Credit Limit	Credit
A13245	John Brown	39 Graveside Gardens	1000	25
A13495	Robert Peel	21 Police Station Rd	1000	120
A13554	Anna Seed	15 Sweetbriar Rd	1500	500
A13782	Mary Christmas	22 Pundit Close	1200	200
A14854	Anita Dresser	99 Avenue Rd	2000	750
A14900	Simon Simple	1 Pyman Close		

Fig. 42.2. The Table Called Customer after an INSERT.

42.12 **To change values in one or more rows in a table an UPDATE statement may be used.**

In the following example the credit for account number A13245 (ie, John Brown's account) is increased by 30 to 55. The use of the "where clause" (ie, "where" followed by an expression) identifies just one row. Without the where clause the update would cause all rows to be updated. If no rows satisfied the where clause none would be updated.

```
update   customer
set
         credit = credit + 30
where
         accountno = 'A13245'
```

42.13 To remove one or more a rows from a table a DELETE statement may be used

In the following example "Anna Seed's" details are removed from the customer table.

```
delete
from     customer
where
         accountno = 'Anna Seed'
```

After these updates and deletes the customer table would look be as shown in Fig. 42.3.

Account No.	Name	Address	Credit Limit	Credit
A13245	John Brown	39 Graveside Gardens	1000	55
A13495	Robert Peel	21 Police Station Rd	1000	120
A13782	Mary Christmas	22 Pundit Close	1200	200
A14854	Anita Dresser	99 Avenue Rd	2000	750
A1490	Simon Simple	1 Pyman Close		

Fig. 42.3. The Customer Table After Further Changes.

42.14 Now suppose that there are two further tables called "ORDER" and ORDERLINE" as shown in Fig 42.4 and Fig 42.5. Note how there is a relationship between ORDER and CUSTOMER because the customer account number appears as a column in ORDER. A customer may make many orders each with a different order number key. Also note that each order may have many order lines and that order number is part of a composite key for ORDERLINE. The complete key for ORDERLINE is the combination of the order number and product number. A simple "data model" showing these these relationships is given in Fig 42.5.

Order No	Account No	Order Date
X300000	A13245	1-MAR-1993
X300001	A13782	1-MAR-1993
X300002	A14854	2-MAR-1993

Fig. 42.4. The Table called "ORDER".

Order No	Product No	Quantity Required
X300000	P20000	10
X300000	P25000	25
X300000	P24000	15
X300000	P20000	28
X300001	P21000	20
X300001	P23000	45
X300001	P24500	30
X300001	P25000	29
X300002	P25000	32
X300002	P25100	37
X300002	P24000	36
X300002	P23000	26

Fig. 42.4. The Table called "ORDERLINE".

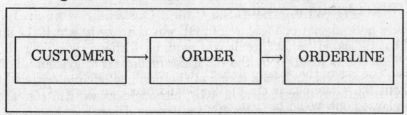

Fig. 42.5. A simplified data model showing the relationships between the tables.

42.15 By using the relationships between tables it is possible to retrieve cross referenced data from a number of tables. For example the following select statement performs what are called **join operations** across the three tables shown in Fig 42.5.

```
select
        c.accountno,
        c.name,
        o.orderno,
        o.orderdate,
        ol.prodno,
        ol.prodqty
from
        customer c,
        order o,
        orderline ol
where
        o.accountno = c.accountno
        and
        o.orderno = ol.orderno
        and
        orderdate = '1-MAR-1993'
```

42.16 First some points on the syntax of the SELECT. In the lines following "`from`" abbreviations for table names are defined which helps to simplify query writing. For example, "`customer c`" implies that "`c`" may be used as a shorthand for the name of the customer table. Also not the use of the **dot notation** for specifying columns in tables which is essentially the same as the dot notation used for records. For example, "`c.accountno` means the `accountno` column in the customer table. Now back to joins.

42.17 A first join in the query matches the order account number with the customer account number. This is expressed as "`o.accountno = c.accountno`. The second join matches the order's order number with the order line's order number. This is expressed as "`o.orderno = ol.orderno`".

42.18 Fig 42.6 shows the result of the above join.

Account No.	Name	Order No	Order Date	Product No	Quantity Required
A13245	John Brown	X300000	1-MAR-1993	P20000	10
A13245	John Brown	X300000	1-MAR-1993	P25000	25
A13245	John Brown	X300000	1-MAR-1993	P24000	15
A13245	John Brown	X300000	1-MAR-1993	P20000	28
A13782	Mary Christmas	X300001	1-MAR-1993	P21000	20
A13782	Mary Christmas	X300001	1-MAR-1993	P23000	45
A13782	Mary Christmas	X300001	1-MAR-1993	P24500	30
A13782	Mary Christmas	X300001	1-MAR-1993	P25000	29

Fig. 42.6. The result of SELECT with two joins.

42.19 That concludes the introductory examples of SQL, but it barely scratches the surface in terms of all the features and facilities of SQL. It would take a whole book to cover them all. One of the strengths of SQL, not drawn out fully from the from the examples, is its ability to manipulate data from several tables in a single statement as in the join example. Another example would be an insert statement which updated one table using values from another.

FOURTH GENERATION LANGUAGES (4GLs)

42.20 You may have noticed that one feature of SQL was the way in which the statements were expressed in a form that indicated "what" result was required without specifying "how" the result was to be obtained. That job is handled by the database management system. This very high level way of expressing processing requirements is one of the principal characteristics of a 4GL. For this reason SQL is itself sometimes described as a 4GL, although, as we will see, a 4GL normally has other important features too. However, some 4GLs use menu-driven user interfaces instead of a conventional "language".

42.21 4GLs may be regarded as the most modern form of **"applications generator"**, a type of software that has been in existence for many years.

Those who promote or sell 4GLs claim that they offer more productive and cost-effective alternatives to the high-level languages such as COBOL associated with the era of 3rd generation computers, hence the name "4GL". There is indeed some truth in these claims, although few current 4GLs are able to provide sufficient facilities to completely remove the need for 3GL in more than a narrow range of applications. Since there is such a variation in the features of products claiming to be 4GLs it is useful to define here those features that ought to be provided for the term 4GL to be used.

42.22 **Features of a 4GL.** A 4GL may be regarded as being a very high-level language that provides simple and powerful ways for the user to do such things as:

a. Define data.

b. Define what processing must be performed on the data.

c. Define layouts of reports or screen based forms, including the formats of printed or displayed data.

d. Define the processing operations to be carried out in the preparation of reports or in the user's interaction with screen-based forms.

e. Define input data and validation checks.

f. Select combinations of standard processing operations.

g. Handle user queries.

Depending upon the way in which the 4GL has been designed it may either be used by the end-user directly or used by a computer specialist to "build" an end-user system.

Thus the 4GL either works by tailoring a generalised piece of software to handle a particular application or by using a general set of software tools to construct a particular application system

42.23 It is useful to distinguish between the following:

a. **A 4GL** – as described above.

b. **A 4GL tool.** A 4GL tool is an item of software that works *either* in the same way as a full 4GL but has more limited purpose *or* forms part of a full 4GL.

For example, there are 4GL tools specially designed to handle the production of reports. Alternatively, SQL may be regarded as a 4GL tool.

c. **An applications generator.** Although a full 4GL is indeed an applications generator, the term applications generator tends to be more commonly used for simpler software products that provide flexible means of parameterising a general software package to deal with particular situations.

SUMMARY

42.24 a. A query language comprises a DDL and a DML all rolled into one.

b. Query languages may either be used in terminal monitor mode or as embedded languages.

c. SQL is the most widespread query language.

d. A 4GL may be regarded as an advanced form of applications generator.

POINTS TO NOTE

42.25 a. The term **DSL (Data Sub-Language)** is sometimes used to mean the combination of a DML and a DML but the term query language is more common.

b. 4GLs may be used to build **prototypes** of new systems either as a means of investigating what is required or as a first step towards developing the whole system.

STUDENT SELF-TESTING QUESTIONS

1. Explain the term "embedded query language".

2. What features would you expect a 4GL to have?

GLOSSARY CHECKLIST

APPLICATIONS V

1. This part continues the theme of the previous Part by providing a summary of Information Storage and Retrieval.

43: Information Storage and Retrieval

INTRODUCTION

43.1 This chapter serves as a summary of various aspects of information storage and retrieval covered in the text. It also fills in a few gaps so as to complete the picture.

43.2 As was pointed out in the very first chapter, a distinction is sometimes drawn between data and information. By using the description "information storage and retrieval" rather than "data storage and retrieval" the emphasis is firmly placed upon something meaningful to a user rather than upon the technicalities of storage. Nevertheless, packages used for information storage and retrieval are most commonly called "database packages". The term database is often used *very loosely* to describe any complete set of data being used for a particular application or by a particular organisation. The reader would be well advised to use the terms carefully in any examination or course work. This chapter aims to use a clear and consistent set of terms.

STORAGE

43.3 Ultimately information in its various forms (eg, text, numbers, images, sounds) is stored on backing storage in computer files of various types. In every case, software translates information from its meaningful form into suitable bytes as it stores it and translates it back again when it is retrieved. It is the different ways in which software provides mechanism for the user to handle such information which is of interest here.

43.4 The more meaning that has to be represented and stored the more complex the storage organisation and structures must be. This is reflected in the difference between text file editing and word processing. In the former the file structures are simple whereas in the later the files can be quite complex in order to hold all the information about fonts, formats etc, and only usable by the appropriate word processor. If search and access times are important then various indices may have to be added to the document for that purpose. Some specialist **text database** packages provide just such facilities. As documents are stored in these systems their contents are automatically indexed by the software. Subsequently, the user may be able to find every instance of selected words or phrases very quickly. This can be most valuable for specialist applications involving document research.

43.5 Some forms of data make far higher demands on storage space than others and it is only the arrival of lower priced storage devices with larger capacities, such as the CD-ROM in recent years that has made some data practically usable on a computer. The two most obvious examples are images and sounds which often require storage space measured in terms of megabytes. **Data compression** techniques are often used by the software so that when stored on disk the sound or image is held in a coded form which needs less space. The stored form is decompressed when it is retrieved.

43.6 Yet another factors affecting the situation is the need to give multiple users concurrent access to the same data. Aspects of this problem were discussed in chapter 41 in connection with the operation of a DBMS server.

43.7 The general conclusion that can be drawn from this is that the provision of suitable information and storage retrieval requires data to be structured, organised, stored and retrieved in an manner suited to the kind of data and to the information needs of the user.

TYPES OF SYSTEM

43.8 Here we are mainly concerned with systems primarily aimed at providing effective means of information storage and retrieval as opposed to many other system which store and retrieve data merely as a way of maintaining it on backing storage when not in use.

43.9 The most broad classification is the split between:

a. File based systems

b. Database systems.

43.10 **File based systems** use the standard file facilities provided by the operating system. The application or applications packages is then built using such facilities. This approach is relatively simple and effective and can be very efficient for specialist applications. This method is most commonly used for the following.

i. Record storage and retrieval takes place via a **File Management Package** which in a more advanced form may be called a **database package.** There are many such single-user packages available on home computer and PC. They vary enormously in terms of there facilities.

ii. **Report writer packages.** These are application packages which provide methods of generating reports from files produced by other programs such as payroll programs or stock control programs. They are commonly used on minicomputers and mainframes. Report writers normally provide a means for the users to specify the layout of reports to be generated from the data. They normally also provide some simple arithmetic. The term **report writer** comes from the fact that many of these packages are in effect interpreters for programs written in a report writer language.

iii. **Text retrieval systems.** These were mention earlier. They provide a fast and efficient way of searching documents stored as text files or document files.

43.11 **Database systems.** These were discussed in detail in earlier chapters. In contrast with file based systems the DBMS approach provides the controlled and coordinated means of managing the access to the database which is quite separate from the application program itself. This approach also lends itself to a client-server architecture and addresses the problems of controlling concurrent access.

43.12 Another classification of systems, which follows on from the previous point, is the simple one of classifying systems as either **single-user** or **multi-user.** The former are most common on PCs and the latter are the norm on minicomputers and mainframes.

43.13 Systems can also be classified according to the kind of specialist information they deal with. However, such classifications become blurred with time as packages become more generalised. Also, the steady rise in **multimedia** suggests that in the long run more and more packages will provide support for a variety of types of data.

USER ACCESS

43.14 In chapter 11 a variety of interfaces were introduced and some aspects of information storage and retrieval were illustrated by the examples. Usually, the data request as expressed by the user is translated by the application software into a form which the underlying software can interpret. For example, a client application may present a user with a menu option but the choices may be passed to the DBMS server in the form of SQL statements. Even so, there are some applications which allow end-users to request data from the database by typing SQL directly in what is normally called an **interactive terminal monitor.**

43.15 One much more sophisticated information storage and retrieval interface is that provided by **hyper-card,** a system first established on the Apple macintosh. The HCI is a direct manipulation GUI able to provide some multimedia facilities The reader is urged to gain practical experience of using such an interface.

43.16 Much more common and mundane are the **forms based systems.** These merit a brief description to illustrate a number of point.

FORMS INTERFACES

43.17 Many packages use a user interface which mimics paper based forms and is therefore called a forms interface. An example is provided by figures 43.1 and 43.2.

43.18 Fig. 43.1 shows a screen on which a "**form**" has been displayed. The screen contains text headers and boxes for data. Such information on forms is called "**trim**", to distinguish it from data. Along the bottom of the screen a series of options is displayed for the user to choose from. For example, if the user wants to print what is on the screen he or she must press a function key on the keyboard labelled "F3". Of course, this assumes that a suitable keyboard is available. The form shows a query typed in by the user, who wants to find out information about all students with surnames beginning with "J" who have passed (the pass mark is 40). You will notice that the line on the form just below the titles the contain "J*" in the "Surname" column and ">= 40" in the "Overall Marks" column. The "J*" means all names beginning with J and followed by any other letters. The symbol used to stand for any letters, as "*" is used in this case, is called a "**wild card**". The ">= 40" means all values greater than or equal to 40. When the user presses the function key for "SELECT" (key F1) the data which satisfies the query will be retrieved onto the form. The result of pressing key F1 is shown in Fig 43.2.

STUDENT MARKS ENQUIRIES FORM

Student Number	Initial	Surname	Overall Mark
		J*	>=40

SELECT (F1)   DISPLAY (F2)   PRINT (F3)   END (F4)

Fig. 43.1. A simple enquiry on a form.

STUDENT MARKS ENQUIRIES FORM

Student Number	Initial	Surname	Overall Mark
2104	N	Johnson	63.00
2105	G W	Jones	80.00

SELECT (F1)   DISPLAY (F2)   PRINT (F3)   END (F4)

Fig. 43.2. The result of the enquiry in Fig 43.1.

STUDENT SELF-TESTING QUESTIONS

1. Compare file based systems with database systems.

QUESTIONS WITHOUT ANSWERS

2. What is a "wild card" and how might it be used in data retrieval?

GLOSSARY CHECKLIST

SYSTEMS DEVELOPMENT

1. This Part covers the activities involved in developing a new computer system. Chapter 44 gives an overview of the whole process followed by a more detailed description of the various stages. It also explains what a methodology is.
2. Chapter 45 describes methods used in systems development.
3. In chapter 46 the final stages of the development are described.
4. Finally, in chapter 47 the Part ends with an examination of project management.
5. This Part gives an overview of common practice today rather than concentrating upon a single approach and should therefore give the necessary general background for examination purposes. Candidates may find that on the course which they study a particular methodology is taught in more depth. In such cases the material in this part is probably best read first and again later, after particular experience, for revision purposes.

44: Methodologies

INTRODUCTION

44.1 New computer systems frequently replace existing manual systems, and the new systems may themselves be replaced after some time. The process of replacing the old system by the new happens in a series of stages and the whole process is called the **"system life cycle"**.

44.2 This chapter provides an overview of the system life cycle. The individual stages in the life cycle are described in detail in subsequent chapters.

THE LIFE CYCLE IN OUTLINE

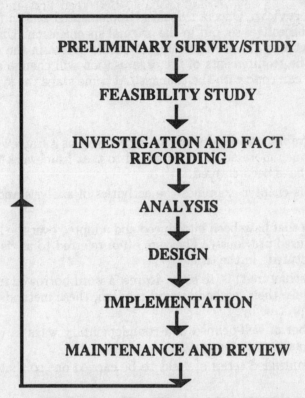

PRELIMINARY SURVEY/STUDY

↓

FEASIBILITY STUDY

↓

INVESTIGATION AND FACT RECORDING

↓

ANALYSIS

↓

DESIGN

↓

IMPLEMENTATION

↓

MAINTENANCE AND REVIEW

↓

Fig. 44.1. The System Life Cycle.

44.3 Fig. 44.1 shows the major stages in the system life cycle.

44.4 The start of a new system life cycle is normally the result of some **"trigger"** such as the perception of a business need, failures or limitations of the existing system causing dissatisfaction, or heightened awareness of modern developments. Whatever the reason it is management who will initiate the selection of a project for preliminary study or investigation.

44.5 **Preliminary survey/study.**

The purpose of this survey is to establish whether there is a need for a new system and if so to specify the objectives of the system.

44.6 **Feasibility study.** The purpose of the feasibility study is to investigate the project in sufficient depth to be able to provide information that either justifies the development of the new system or shows why the project should not continue.

44.7 The findings of the feasibility study are presented to management in the form of a report, which will make appropriate recommendations. If the report finds in favour of the project then senior management may decide to move to the next stage.

44.8 **Investigation and fact recording.** At this stage in the life cycle a detailed study is conducted. This study is far more detailed and comprehensive than the feasibility study. The purpose of this study is fully to understand the existing system and to identify the basic information requirements.

44.9 Analysis. Analysis of the full description of the existing system and of the objectives of the proposed system should lead to a **full specification of the user's requirements.** This **requirements specification** can be examined and approved before system design is embarked upon. In recent years greater emphasis has been placed upon this stage because of former expensive and frustrating experiences of designs that failed to meet requirements. The earlier in the system life cycle that a mistake is discovered the less costly it is to correct.

44.10 Design. The analysis may lead to a number of possible alternative designs. For example, different combinations of manual and computerised elements may be considered. Once one alternative has been selected the purpose of the design stage is to work from the requirements specification to produce a **system specification.** The system specification will be a detailed set of documents that provides details of all features of the system.

44.11 Implementation. Implementation involves following the details set out in the system specification. Two particularly important tasks are programming and staff training. It is worth observing in passing that the programming task has its own "life cycle" in the form of the various stages in programming, ie, analysis and design occur at many different levels.

44.12 Maintenance and review. Once a system is implemented and in full operation it is examined to see if it has met the objectives set out in the original specification. Unforeseen problems may need to be overcome and that may involve returning to earlier stages in the cycle to take corrective action. From time to time the requirements of the organisation will change and the system will have to be examined to see if it can cope with the changes. At some stage the system life cycle will be repeated again and yet again.

METHODOLOGIES

44.13 The preceding paragraphs presented the system life-cycle as a framework within which a new system can be developed. Much more needs to be added to that framework before all activities involved in such a development have been covered.

44.14 The remainder of this chapter examines the activities of analysis and design within the system life cycle.

44.15 Many of the methods that have been introduced and adopted over the last ten years or so are radically different from those used previously. They are often referred to as **"structured"** methods. Several have the word "structured" in the title.

Although the term "structured" is, to some degree, a word borrowed from the programming world by marketing staff to make their methods sound modern, these methods do indeed impose a structure on the development process by:

a. providing a number of well-defined and complementary ways in which to represent information about important aspects of the system;

b. providing a recommended series of tasks to be carried out so that the methods fit together as a whole;

c. lending themselves to some degree of automation and the corresponding controls that go with it.

44.16 Such a system of methods, with its orderly and integrated collection of various methods, tools and notations, is often called a **methodology** so as to distinguish it from *mere* method.

PROPRIETARY METHODOLOGIES

44.17 A considerable number of methodologies are in use today and, although many are described in specialist texts generally available to the public, they are mostly sold as products composed of manuals, specialist training, consultancy services and automated aids. Among the better known methodologies are:

a. Structured Analysis and Design by Yourdon.

b. Structured Systems Analysis by Gane and Sarson.

c. Information Engineering from James Martin.

d. Jackson Systems Development (JSD) by Michael Jackson.

e. SSADM, originally produced by LBMS for the CCTA.

44.18 It is *not* the purpose of this text to describe any one of these methodologies in any detail. A number of general points deserve mention though.

a. Each methodology has its own overall method within which the various activities fit.

b. All of the methods make use of **charting techniques** whereby particular properties of the system are represented diagrammatically using an appropriate convention.

c. The particular kinds of property chosen for representation give each methodology its "orientation". For example, several methods place considerable emphasis on analysing the data within the system so as to represent its essential properties as it is stored, accessed or moved around the system, (eg, SSADM, Yourdon, and Gane and Sarson.) Other methods place less emphasis on the data and greater emphasis on the processing activities and events that affect them (eg, JSD).

44.19 An introduction to some of the more commonly used techniques is presented in the next chapter.

REQUIREMENTS SPECIFICATION

44.20 An important aim of the analysis is to produce a **Requirements Specification.** The modern methods make it easier to produce a Requirements Specifications which present information in an implementation free form which is intelligible to the user. Not all the contents of the Requirements Specification may be intelligible to the user, however, because some parts of the requirement may be technical in nature and need to be expressed formally.

44.21 It should be clear by now that the Requirements Specification should present a clear, thorough and unambiguous description of WHAT the system is required to do and should NOT fall into the trap of ruling out possible design alternatives by specifying HOW the system should be designed and implemented. However, there are bound to be some limitations on the kinds of design which can be considered and some very specific and essential features about the design may be know right from the start. For example, there may be specific limitations on the budget available, the accommodation which can be used or the timescale in which events must happen. Also, it may be essential that the new system makes use of or is compatible with some existing equipment. Such information belongs in the Requirements Specification along with the implementation free descriptions which may be regarded as the "high level" features of the design.

44.22 A Systems Analyst, with sound business knowledge, will discuss the Requirements Specification with the users. This analyst, aided by the Requirements Specification, will have the important task of bridging the gap between the system's user and the technical designer.

44.23 At the end of these discussions the Requirements Specification should be in an accepted form, estimates for alternative designs should be prepared, and the decision to proceed with a particular design can be made.

44.24 **Conceptual Models.** Within the documentation of the Requirements Specification is a system definition also expressed in an implementation free way ie. free of the constraints of any particular design alternative. Such a system definition is called a "conceptual model", a term originally used in database design. Unfortunately, terminology is far from standard in this subject area and is made worse by the way in which those selling methodologies often use their own names for common methods for marketing purposes. "Conceptual models" are often described as high level **logical models**. The key feature to note is the *implementation free* form of representation. At a later stage in the development process a **physical model** will be produced. Further variants in terminology refer to **logical designs** and **physical designs**.

44.25 Don't be put off by the terminology because most high level ways of representing the analysis in an implementation free way use some combination of three very natural components:

a. a **data model** which defines the data requirements, probably in terms of entities, attributes and relationships, for example, an entity such as an order contains attributes such as quantities required and has a relationship with other entities such as customers).

b. a **process model** which defines the processing requirements in terms of events and operations, for example, the event of an order arriving gives rise to operations such as the update of stock data and production of invoices).

c. a **system model** which defines functional areas and their interrelationship (eg. one functional area may deal with the reception of an order and then pass it to another functional area which processes the order).

AREAS OF RESPONSIBILITY

44.26 Different types of staff are responsible for different stages in the life cycle. For example, the early stages will have significant involvement by senior management, the middle stages will be the responsibility of "systems analysts" and a stage such as implementation will give major responsibility to programmers.

44.27 In the remainder of this Part those activities that are primarily the responsibility of the system analyst will be discussed. The responsibility of programmers have already been discussed in earlier chapters.

44.28 It is during the design stage that the system developer is called upon to use his or her creative abilities. The implementation-free nature of the requirements specification means that *all* feasible alternative designs are open to consideration. By applying judgement, skill and knowledge an analyst can interpret the requirement specification to create one or more **system specifications (or system definitions)**. A system specification provides *detailed* documentation of the new system, ie, it gives the detail of a particular implementation, unlike the requirements specification, which is implementation free. A system specification requires acceptance by management just as the requirements specification does.

44.29 We now deal with the elements of design and the sequence in which they might be carried out. Design criteria are then dealt with and are followed by a description of a system specification.

DESIGN ELEMENTS

44.30 The design of a new system can be conveniently divided into the following elements:

    a. Outputs.

    b. Inputs.

    c. Files or database components.

    d. Procedures and programs.

44.31 **Outputs.** It is necessary to consider what is required from the system before deciding how to set about producing it. These requirements will have become clear as the project progressed. The analyst will need to consider form, types, volumes, and frequency of reports and documents. Choice of output media will also have to be made including when to use hard copy and when to use screen displays.

44.32 **Inputs.** Consideration of input will be influenced greatly by the needs of output, eg, the necessity for quick response from the system would determine the need for an on-line type of input. Consideration would be given to:

    a. Data collection methods and validation.

    b. Types of input media available.

    c. Volumes of input documents.

    d. Design of input layouts.

44.33 **Files and database components.** These elements are very much linked to input and output. Input is processed against the stored data to produce the necessary output. Considerations involved in designing files are:

    a. Storage media.

    b. Method of file organisation and access.

    c. File security.

    d. Record layouts.

44.34 **Procedures and programs.** Procedures are the steps that unify the whole process, that link everything together to produce the desired output. These will involve both computer and clerical procedures. They will start with the origination of the source document and end with the output document being distributed. The design of the computer programs will constitute a major task in itself.

44.35 Because of their importance in the design of a new procedure the aspects of form design and internal checks are dealt with in some detail below.

44.36 **Forms design.**

    a. **Introduction.** The design of forms and the design of procedures are very much linked. The completion of a form may be the first operation of a procedure (eg, compilation of an order form); a by-product of an operation within a procedure (eg, a receipt, as a by-product of posting to the cash book, in machine accounting); the end product of a procedure (eg, reports to management); or the form may be completed at various stages within a procedure (eg, invoice sets). Whether the requirements of the form dictate the procedure, or the steps in the procedure dictate the design of the form, is determined by individual circumstances. Very often, the justification for expensive machines brings in its wake the need for redesign of forms to fit the procedure.

    b. **Aim.** The aim is to keep forms to the minimum consistent with serving the needs of the system.

    c. **Features of design.**

i. **Sizes.** Standard-size forms should be used, as it is more economic to do so, and *handling, filing* and *copying* are simplified.

ii. **Types of paper.** The quality of paper used should be appropriate to requirements. Consideration should be given to such things as frequency of handling, storage needs, conditions under which forms are completed, and prestige requirements.

iii. **Identification.** There should be a brief, self-explanatory title; copies should be identified by different colours or bold symbols; serial numbering may be required for internal check purposes.

iv. **Common information.** If two forms are used in conjunction with each other, the common information should be in the same sequence and position.

v. **Vertical spacing.** There should be adequate space for each item of entry (eg, an invoice should have enough spaces to cover the normal number of items ordered). If a typewriter is being used in recording data on a form, consideration must be given to the normal vertical spacing requirements of the machine.

vi. **Columns.** The length of column headings should be tailored to the width required by the information to be entered in the column.

vii. **Pre-printing.** As much as possible of the common detail should be pre-printed, leaving only variable data to be entered.

viii. **Clarity.** There should be overall simplicity of instructions. Material of a similar nature should be grouped together. A logical sequence for completion should be followed and unambiguous wording should be used. The size of the print should make for ease of reading.

ix. **Miscellaneous.** There may be a requirement for perforation for subsequent bursting or pre-punched holes for subsequent filing.

x. **Multi-part sets** Where more than one document is to be raised at the same time, consideration should be given to the method employed in carrying the image through all copies, eg, carbon; no-carbon-required paper, carbon patches, etc.

44.37 Internal check.

a. **Definition.** The arrangement of procedures and systems, and the allocation of duties so that there is an automatic check on what is being done.

b. **Principle.** No one person should be placed in the position of having responsibility for all aspects of a business transaction. Thus the work flow is so arranged that the work of one person, or section, is independently checked by some other person or section.

c. **Purposes achieved.**

i. The possibility of fraud and error is reduced.

ii. The responsibility for errors is determined.

iii. Supervision is assisted (because of the built-in checks).

iv. The work of internal and external auditors is reduced.

d. **Examples of the operation of internal check.**

i. The serial numbering of forms.

ii. The requirements for two signatures on cheques.

iii. The use of control accounts.

DESIGN METHOD AND DESIGN SEQUENCE

44.38 Over the last ten years or so a number of design methods have become established, each with its own set of dedicated supporters.

44.39 The advocates of each of these methods naturally proclaim the advantages of their methods over the alternatives. Terms such as "structured", "hierarchical", "top-down", and others are used to label the different approaches to design.

44.40 What all these design methods have in common is a recognition that large problems, such as those found in design, can only be tackled effectively if they are broken down into smaller, more manageable, tasks in some systematic way. The same ideas were first put into practice with considerable success in program writing, where terms such as "structured" and "top-down" suffer less ambiguity.

44.41 Without going into unnecessary detail about any particular method it is still possible to identify the following design sequence:

a. The system is described at a logical level in terms of what it will do in the context of a particular design, ie, a combination of design elements will be put together in a way that can meet the requirements in general terms.

b. The "logical model" is refined in a series of steps in which successive detail is added. Some steps may be re-traced as the emerging design is evaluated. Considerations of physical details are postponed as long as possible, because, for example, it is senseless to design a report document before it is decided exactly what the report should contain.

c. Finally the physical detail is added to the logical detail so that the design shows not only *what* the system should do but also exactly *how* it should do it.

CRITERIA FOR DESIGN

44.42 Purpose. The purpose must be to meet the demands of the requirements specification and, for that matter, the objectives that were agreed at the beginning of the project. At one time, and still in some organisations, a requirements specification was not produced at the end of the analysis stage and so the system specification had to serve both purposes.

44.43 Some of the criteria outlined in the following paragraphs may be applied to the requirements specification. Where the criteria do apply it is a clear indication of the economic benefits of the requirements specification in catching errors earlier and saving inappropriate design effort and costs.

44.44 Economical. The costs and benefits of the new system should be compared with those of the existing system. This is not easy to do because of the difficulty of quantifying benefits such as "better or more" information. It is important, however, that the attempt be made.

44.45 Work flows. The best work flows must be attained. This includes methods of transmitting data to and from the computer, the number of runs required, file organisation, the requirements of internal check, and the link with clerical procedures.

44.46 Specialisation, simplification and standardisation. The benefits to be derived from the practice of the "three Ss" are well known. The analyst will have them in mind throughout the design stage.

44.47 Flexibility. Points to be considered here are:

a. **Integration of procedures.** Systems should be designed with possible integration of procedures in mind. This is particularly important as the centralised nature of computer processing makes possible the integration of many procedures carried out independently under conventional methods.

b. **Modularity of hardware.** It is important when choosing the hardware to ensure that it is capable of being expanded (units added) when the need arises.

c. **Peak periods/treatment of exceptions.** The system can be designed to cope with peak-period processing; an alternative arrangement is to use a bureau for the unusually high loads. Similarly, exceptional items (ie, those not recurring frequently) could be designed into the system, but it may be more convenient to have them dealt with separately by conventional methods.

44.48 Exception principle. The principle of exception should be incorporated in the design of the new system, so that only deviations from plan are reported for management's attention. In a stock-control system, for example, warnings would be given of slow-moving stocks. The analyst must ensure that only necessary output is produced.

44.49 Reliability. The reliability of all the hardware and software must be considered. The analyst must ensure that facilities required for the new system have a proven record of reliability. Maintenance requirements, the expected life of the hardware and the back-up facilities (in case of breakdown) must be considered.

44.50 Forms. Data must be presented to the computer in a machine-sensible form. The analyst must consider all the methods of input and try to reduce the steps necessary between origination of data and its input. If output from one run is used as the input to another, the ideal medium for the subsequent input should be used. When output is required in a humanly legible form, choice of method of presentation is important. Methods available are visual display, printed copy, graphical, etc, and the needs of the person receiving the output will determine which one is appropriate.

44.51 Existing system. Consideration must be given to the existing staff, procedures, equipment, forms, etc, in the design of any new system. For example, if old-fashioned equipment is currently being operated, the procedures already exist for transferring the source data into a machine-sensible form, although it may well not be incorporated into the design of a new computer system.

44.52 Continuous control. As the majority of steps are carried out automatically, there is an even greater need for care in internal check. Audit trails (ie, documentary records of various stages in processing that can be used to check that procedures have been carried out correctly) must be laid to the satisfaction of the auditors. Controls should be incorporated.

44.53 Time. The analyst must design the system to satisfy time requirements. Speeds of equipment, modes of access and processing methods must be considered. The length of the processing cycle is a most important consideration. The presentation of source data to the computer and the production of output documents will be subject to strict time constraints.

SYSTEMS SPECIFICATION (OR DEFINITION)

44.54 The systems specification is the detailed documentation of the proposed new system. It serves two main purposes.

 a. **Communication.** It serves as a means of communicating all that is required to be known to all interested parties; as follows:

  i. **Management** for final approval.

  ii. **Programmers** to enable them to write the programs necessary for implementation.

  iii. **Operating staff,** detailing all necessary operating procedures.

  iv. **Users,** as they will ultimately be responsible for running the new system. They must therefore be fully aware of the contents of the specification and their agreement is essential.

 b. **Record.** A permanent record of the system in detail is necessary for control. It will be used for evaluations, modification, and training purposes.

44.55 Different persons require to know only parts of the whole specification (eg, programmers need to know the functions required and the file layouts, but will not need to know the timings for data preparation or numbers of staff required, etc). The specification is also produced at different stages of design *in outline* for top management, *in detail* for lowest levels. The specification is sectionalised to enable only the appropriate parts to be sent to the interested parties.

44.56 Contents. The following are the main items to be found in a systems specification.

 a. **Preliminary information.** This comprises contents, lists, names of recipients of particular sections, names of those having authority to change files, programs, etc.

 b. **Objectives of the system.** A brief statement is given of the aims indicating the departments and the main procedures involved. The benefits arising from implementation are also stated.

 c. **Systems description.** This will detail all procedures both clerical and computer using flow charts where applicable.

 d. **Detailed specification of:**

  i. Input files
  ii. Output files } with specimen layouts
  iii. Master files

  iv. Source documents
  v. Output documents } with specimen copies of each document or screen
  vi. Screen layouts and dialog designs

 Supporting narrative would accompany each item. Methods of file organisation and modes of access are detailed.

 e. **Program specification.** This contains:

  i. Details of inputs, outputs and processes for each program run.

  ii. Test data and expected results.

  iii. Stop/start, file-checking and error-checking procedures.

  iv. Controls.

  v. Relationship between procedures and computer runs.

 f. **Implementation procedures.**

  i. Detailed timetable (using networks or other scientific aids).

  ii. Details of conversion procedures.

  iii. Change-over procedures, including systems testing.

 g. **Equipment.** All equipment including backup equipment and its maintenance arrangements.

h. **User-department instructions.** These relate to the input to the system (ie, times for forwarding source documents), the output from the system (ie, dealing with documents and control totals, etc).

SUMMARY

44.57 a. The system life cycle is the series of stages involved in replacing an old system with a new one.

b. The life-cycle stages are:

i. Preliminary survey/study - initiated by management.
ii. Feasibility study.
iii. Investigation and fact recording.
iv. Analysis.
v. Design.
vi. Implementation.
vii. Maintenance and review.

c. Some form of documentation accompanies all stages in the cycle. The following documentation is of particular importance:

i. Feasibility study report.
ii. User requirements specification.
iii. System specification.

d. The design stage is the creative stage in systems and analysis. All feasible design alternatives should be considered.

e. The systems analyst can use the requirement specification as the criteria against which to judge his or her designs.

f. The systems specification is important as a means of communication and a record of the detail design.

g. The idea of a **methodology** was introduced together with an explanation of what a structured method is.

POINTS TO NOTE

44.58 a. "System analysis" takes place at all stages in the life cycle, not just the analysis stage.

b. Terminology is not universal. For example a "systems specification" may also be called a "requirement specification". This is seldom a practical difficulty because the context normally prevents any ambiguity.

c. The terms *"specification"* and *"definition"* are used synonymously.

d. The systems specification acts as the *acceptance* of the design of the new system by all levels of management.

e. In reading this chapter on design, students should realise that much of the detail involved has been described under the appropriate headings, eg, data collection, computer files, etc.

STUDENT SELF-TESTING QUESTIONS
1. What is a "methodology"?
2. What is a system specification.
3. What is the purpose of a feasibility study?
4. What are the factors that govern choice of output media and device?
5. Describe the contents of a systems specification.

GLOSSARY CHECKLIST

45: Development Methods

INTRODUCTION

45.1 This chapter examines some methods which are commonly used in systems development.

BASIC PRINCIPLES

45.2 Although it is very important to be familiar with the latest methods, and to be able to use them properly, it must also be recognised that most methods become dated eventually. Therefore, it is important to recognise any basic principles that apply whatever the method. In fact, there must be dozens of principles that apply to the process of systems development. Here are some important ones expressed as a set of recommendations.

   a. Make sure you understand the problem.

   b. Fully identify the requirements and get them agreed by the client.

   c. Clearly document all work as you do it.

   d. Have all work checked to an agreed standard of quality at every stage.

   e. Be systematic.

   f. Be creative but make sure it works.

   g. Allow for future changes.

   h. Make sure that all users find the system usable.

   i. Break the problem down into manageable tasks and carry them out in a planned and methodical way.

   j. Make sure that the final system is all there, in full working order, and does what it's supposed to do, **before** you say it's ready.

DATA MODELS

45.3 A data model is a representation of the properties of the data within an existing or proposed system. The basic elements from which a model is made are called **modelling constructs** and the complete process of constructing a data model from scratch is called **data analysis**.

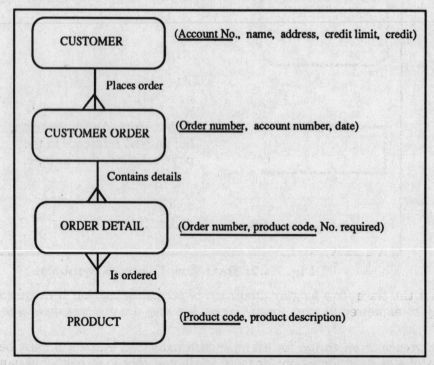

Fig. 44.1. An EAR Data Model of an Ordering System.

45.4   EAR Models. The EAR model is one of the most common and successful types of data model around. Its basic elements are called **Entities, Attributes** and **Relationships**, hence the name EAR model, or occasionally **ER model**.

45.5   The modelling constructs are as follows:

  a. Entity. An entity is any "thing" about which data can be stored. For example, if the system needs to store data about customers or products, then the model would have customer or product entities.

  Note. Although the definition is stated in terms of what must be stored, in fact it is retrieval of the data that is the fundamental requirement.

  b. Attributes. The attributes of an entity are those facts that need to be stored about the entity. For example, the attributes of a customer might include the account number, name, address and credit limit.

  c. Relationships. Relationships exist between various entities within a system. For example, there may be a relationship between the customer and an order.

45.6   For such a data model to be considered **valid** it must conform to a set of rules. A valid data model is one that is **fully normalised** and the process of converting an invalid model into a valid one is called **normalization**.

45.7   The aim of normalization is to ensure that each fact is only recorded in one place so that facts cannot be inconsistent and the performance of updates cannot produce anomalies by updating one copy of the fact but not another.

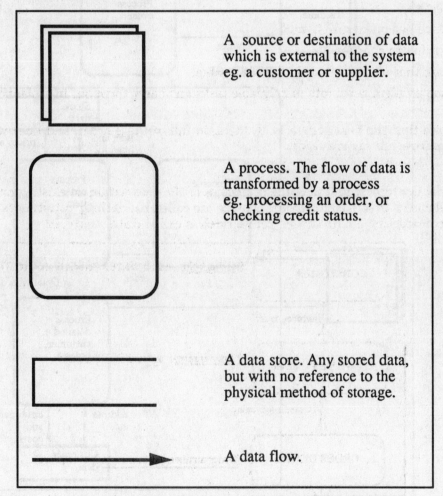

A source or destination of data which is external to the system eg. a customer or supplier.

A process. The flow of data is transformed by a process eg. processing an order, or checking credit status.

A data store. Any stored data, but with no reference to the physical method of storage.

A data flow.

Fig. 44.2. Data-flow Diagram Symbols.

45.8   This is not the place for a lengthy discussion of normalization, but here are some basic details. The rules may be expressed in more formal terms, but they are not considered suitable in a book at this level.

Each occurrence of an entity, for example each individual customer, must be uniquely identifiable by means of a key containing one or more attributes. The customer's full name or account number might serve as a key, for example. Other attributes (non-key attributes) may be regarded as facts about what the key stands for (eg, facts about the customer). So given the key other facts relating to the key can be obtained.

The process of normalization ensures that in each entity of the final model every non-key attribute is a fact about *the key, the whole key and nothing but the key.*

45.9 To round off this description of data models here (Fig. 44.1) is a diagram of a simple EAR model concerning customers making orders for products.

In the diagram:

a. Entities are represented by round-cornered boxes.

b. Attributes are listed beside the entities. For example, CUSTOMER entity has the attributes listed as

"Account No., name, address, credit limit, credit".

Keys are underlined. Note that the "order detail" entity has a **composite key**, ie, a key formed from more than one attribute. (It is assumed that each order number is unique and that each order can only be made by one customer.)

c. Relationships are represented by lines between entities. The "bird's feet" at the end of the arrows are used to show the **degree** of the relationship. In the example, **one** customer places **many orders**. The bird's foot shows the "many" end of the relationship.

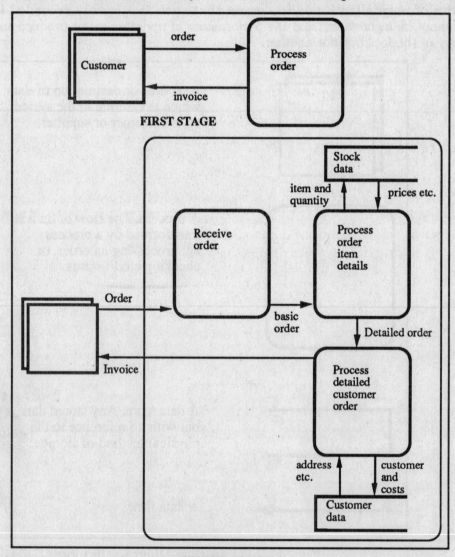

Fig. 44.3. A Data-flow Diagram of an Order Processing System.

DATA-FLOW DIAGRAMS (DFDs)

45.10 Data-flow diagrams provide an effective form in which to represent the movements of data through a system and the associated transformations of the data resulting from various processing actions taken upon it. The views they provide are free of unnecessary details and are therefore very useful in providing an overview of the system.

45.11 Diagrams 44.2 and 44.3 illustrate their use.

STATE TRANSITION DIAGRAMS

45.12 By way of a contrast to data models we will now consider state transition diagrams, which differ in form depending on where they are used. Originally, they were used mostly in programming, often at a relatively low level, but more recently they have been more widely used as higher levels of design.

45.13 The ideas are quite simple and effective. It is first necessary to identify **objects** within the system, which can each be in any one of a number of states depending upon the **events** taking place. An event gives rise to an **action**, or series of actions, which may cause a change of state. In the following simple example the operation of a simple object, a conveyor belt, is represented. The notation used is as follows.

a. Circles represent states that the system may be in.

b. Labelled arrowed lines from states signify events that give rise to actions.

c. Round-cornered boxes represent actions to be taken when events happen.

d. Arrowed lines from actions show a change to another state, or possibly a further action to be taken before a change in state.

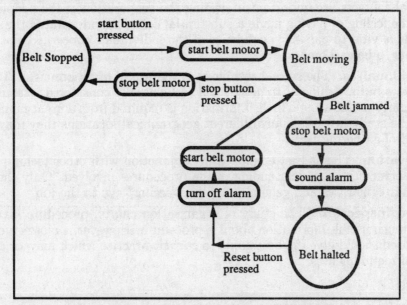

Fig. 44.4. A State Transition Diagram.

LEVELS OF MODELLING

45.14 The modelling process may take place at a number of different levels according to the stages in the life cycle. For example, the EAR data model, shown earlier, is called a **logical model** because it concentrates on **what** data is to be stored. A **physical model**, on the other hand, would provide detail on **how** the data was to be stored. For example, a physical model might be expected to detail the physical storage structures of files used to implement the system.

VALIDATION AND VERIFICATION

45.15 It was mentioned earlier that for a model to be **valid** it must observe certain rules. In addition, it is most important to **verify** that the model is a correct representation of the system being modelled.

TRADITIONAL METHODS

45.16 So far this chapter has concentrated on the modern methodologies and the more commonly used techniques associated with them. However, a number of traditional methods are still important and are often incorporated into the more successful modern methodologies. The remaining topics in this chapter concern these well established general methods.

TERMS OF REFERENCE

45.17 It is of the utmost importance that clear objectives are laid down by management for all projects. If analysts are allowed to set their own objectives, then these may not accord with the overall company objectives. Before the analyst begins his or her task, he or she should, therefore, confirm the terms of reference. The number of analysts required, and the length and breadth of the assignment will depend, to a great extent, upon the objectives set. For example, if the objective were "to reduce the turn-round time for orders from one week to a day" a completely new system would perhaps need to be designed requiring many analysts, taking a long time and having wide effects on the organisation. Conversely, the objective "to reduce the number of clerks in the accounts department" may require a straight transfer of existing manual procedures to a standard computer package and would therefore take shorter time and less organisational disruption. The terms of reference may well refer to the standards which must be used for the project. It is increasingly common for organisations to adopt standard methodologies which must be used for all their systems development projects.

FACT FINDING

45.18 It is essential to gather all the facts about a current system to ensure that all strengths and weaknesses are discovered. Thus, when a new system is designed as many of the weaknesses as possible are eliminated, whilst retaining the strengths.

45.19 There are four general techniques available, those used depending upon the particular circumstances:

a. **Interviewing.** This is probably the most widely used technique and the most productive. Interviewing is an art not readily acquired. During interviews facts about what is happening come to light, together with the opinions of the interviewee regarding weaknesses in the system. The personal contacts are important in getting the cooperation of the people involved, and in giving them the feeling of having made a substantial contribution towards the design of the new procedure. It is vital to gain the confidence of the individuals concerned at this stage in order for all the facts to be gathered.

b. **Questionnaires.** The second technique is the use of questionnaires. They save the time of the interviews but are difficult to design and are generally considered irksome to complete. They are particularly useful when a little information is required from a great number of people. Moreover, when the study involves many different geographical locations they may be the only practicable method of gathering facts.

c. **Observation.** This is best employed in conjunction with other techniques and carried out after the observer has an understanding of the procedures involved. Only then will he or she be able to spot irregularities and generally apply a "seeing" eye to the job.

d. **Record inspection.** The study of organisation charts, procedure manuals and statistics, can reveal much useful information about a procedure. However, a close study of the forms currently being used should give the best guide to current practice which may, or may not, accord with the original requirements.

FACT RECORDING

45.20 **Fact recording.** Unless the investigator has formulated a plan for the keeping of notes of the facts obtained during the fact finding stage, he or she will end up with a mass of notes on all areas, which will be difficult to examine.

45.21 A good practice is to sectionalise notes into areas of investigation (eg. by department or operation) or by type of information (eg. organisation charts, interviews, forms, etc). Use should be made of the standard forms of presenting information about the system. This is where the newer methodologies can have a great deal to offer. Dataflow diagrams can be used both to represent information about an existing system and to represent a proposed new system. EAR data models can often be drafted at the fact finding stage too. Later they can be amended and redrawn as the results are analysed. Some traditional charting techniques have their place too. Decision table and systems flowcharts are good examples of techniques which can capture the details of *how* the existing system works.

45.22 Note that at this stage no attempt is made at analysis or design since the existing system must be fully understood first.

ANALYSIS

45.23 At this point, the analyst has gathered all the facts which are relative to the objectives set and has grouped them into a form suitable for analysis. The analysis stage is an important intermediate stage between investigation and design. The analyst must examine all the facts he or she has gathered in order to make a proper assessment of the existing system. He or she must resist the temptation to include ideas in the new system which have not been fully worked out. The aim of this stage is to ensure that all feasible alternatives are considered. According to the methodology used, there are different ways of dealing with this issue. As we will see shortly, many approaches attempt to present the information in a way which avoids making implementation decisions at this stage.

45.24 The present system may be criticised against the following **Principles of Procedure**, after which the strengths and weaknesses of the system should be apparent:

a. **Purpose.** Are the purposes being satisfied? Are they still necessary? Could they be achieved in any other way?

b. **Economical.** Is it economical? Benefits should be related to the cost of producing them. Are there more economical methods.

c. **Work flow.** Are the work flows satisfactory?

d. **Specialisation/simplification/standardisation.** Are the three S's being practised? Is the work capable of being carried out by computer? Can the complex procedures be simplified? Are standard practices observed?

e. **Flexibility.** Is the system flexible? What will be the effect on the system of a big increase of decrease in the volumes to be processed?

f. **Exception principle.** Is the principle of exception being observed? Factors requiring actions should be highlighted and not submerged in a mass of routine detail.

g. **Reliability.** How reliable is the procedure? What provision is there for such events as staff sickness, machine breakdown? Could more up to date equipment be justified?

h. **Form.** Is the information being produced in the form best suited to the recipient? Is there a need for a hard copy?

i. **Existing system.** If a change is made, what equipment and other facilities currently being used could be incorporated in the new procedure?

j. **Continuous control.** What types of errors are occurring? Are the controls satisfactory? What other types of controls could be used?

k. **Time.** Is the information being produced in time for meaningful action to be taken?

PROTOTYPING

45.25 There are three activities which are sometimes described as of prototyping:

a. **Mock-ups.** A "Mock-up" of a proposed system or subsystem is produced for demonstration purpose at the early stages of a project so as to aid the users and designers to make decisions about what is required. Usually, the prototype has the appearance of the final system but lacks any real processing or storage capability.

b. **Trial Prototyping.** A simplified working model of a proposed system or subsystem is produced. It may serve the same purpose as a mock-up but because it has some of the capabilities of a real system it can provide the opportunity to try out ideas and to investigate specific points of interest. Such a prototype might be used to design an appropriate user interface for a new system. Alternatively, it might be a prototype of a method of processing. Normally the intention is to throw away such a prototype at the end of the prototyping exercise. The results of the prototyping are fed into a conventional design life-cycle.

c. **Rapid Prototyping.** This is an alternative to the conventional life-cycle. It is most frequently used for small scale system which are required urgently and which will have a limited life. A simplified version of the system is built and then reviewed. At this early stages this is like method (b). Following the review the prototype is extended and upgraded to become version 1 of the new system. It is normally incomplete at this stage but may have all of the essential features in a simplified form. After a review the prototype is further upgraded, and so on. The rapid results provided by this method give rise to its name. The merits of the method is the short term gains of having a working system early. However, in the long run such systems can be come costly and difficult to maintain and tend to be less reliable than systems built by more conventional methods.

45.26 Of the three methods just described both (a) and (b) can be easily incorporated into the development life-cycle and have therefore become very popular in recent years because of the way they aid the work done in analysis and design. All three methods commonly make use of 4GLs.

SUMMARY

45.27 a. Some commonly used methods were introduced:

i. Entity-Attribute-Relationship (EAR) data modelling.

ii. The use of data flow diagrams (DFDs).

iii. The use of state transition diagrams.

b. The terms of reference of an assignment must be clearly laid down.

c. Fact finding, recording, and examination, are necessary to discover the strengths and weaknesses of the area under investigation.

d. The analysis stage is important because of the need to ensure that:

 i. the requirements are fully understood and correctly specified.

 ii. all feasible design alternatives are contemplated.

 It is an important breathing space between investigation and design.

e. Prototyping methods were described.

POINTS TO NOTE

45.28 a. There is a tendency, in practice, for some analysts to neglect the analysis stage and to go ahead with the design of a new system based on a preconceived notion that he or she has held from the beginning. In this way the system produced may be neither what is required nor the most feasible alternative. The mandatory production of a Requirements Specification guards against such bad practices. Most of the modern methodologies contain within them mandatory stages and methods in the life-cycle to guard against this danger.

b. Methods of analysis have been developed greatly over recent years. It is not necessary for you to learn these methods but you should be aware of their importance in improving the quality and effectiveness of Systems Analysis.

c. Improvements to the analysis stage have an impact on the design stage. The designer starts from a much stronger position if he or she has a Requirement Specification.

STUDENT SELF-TESTING QUESTIONS

1. Describe the basic features of a data model.
2. What are the modelling constructs of a state transition diagram?
3. A stock *master file* stored in sequence order of a numeric key is updated by a transaction file using *sequential file access*. Transaction records, which represent additions and deletions to the stock levels, are collected into batches over a period of time and *validated* before being sorted into key order. Invalid data is corrected and entered into the next batch of transactions. The ordered transactions are used to update the master file. The update process produces a new master file and a file of all changes to records, for audit purposes.

 a. Explain the meaning of the terms given in italics. (3 marks)

 b. Why is the transaction file sorted prior to updating the master file?

 (2 marks)

 c. Draw a data flow diagram, or a systems flowchart, of the system described.

 (7 marks)

 d. Assume all files are stored on magnetic disc and the transactions update the master records by overwriting the old record with the new record. How might loss of data be avoided if the disc controller develops a fault which causes it to write corrupted data? Explain carefully the necessary security procedures.

 (5 marks)

 e. The audit file contains the before and after quantities in stock corresponding to each transaction and the monetary value of the transaction. What information is needed in the transaction and master files to derive the audit file information? (3 marks)

 (AEB)

QUESTIONS WITHOUT ANSWERS

5. What features might you expect to find in a "structured" method?

GLOSSARY CHECKLIST

46: Implementation and Support

INTRODUCTION

46.1 Implementation follows on from the detailed design stage. This involves the co-ordination of the efforts of the user department and the data-processing department in getting the new system into operation. A Coordinating Committee is sometimes formed for this purpose, having as its members the managers of the departments concerned and a representative from the computer department. The analyst responsible for the design of the new system will be an important member because of his thorough knowledge of the system.

46.2 Planning for the implementation will have begun early in the design stage. Details will have been stipulated in the systems specification.

They would cover the following:

a. Training of staff.

b. Programming.

c. System testing.

d. Master file conversion.

e. Changeover procedures.

f. Review and maintenance.

46.3 Whatever applications computers are used for it is important to ensure that they are used effectively and not abused. This chapter deals with the issues involved.

TRAINING OF STAFF

46.4 The amount of training required for various categories of personnel will depend upon the complexity of the system and the skills presently available. The systems analyst would be required to ensure that all persons involved with the new system were capable of making it an operational success. The following aids would be used, as appropriate:

a. **Handbooks.** These will be produced as part of, or as a development from, the systems specification.

b. **Courses.** Either full-time or part-time courses, often run by the computer manufacturers.

c. **Lectures.** General background knowledge, or knowledge of specific areas, could be covered by means of lectures.

PROGRAMMING

46.5 The programmer must design programs that conform to the requirements set out in the system specification. The stages in programming have already been discussed in earlier chapters.

46.6 The work of the programmer has already been discussed in chapter 18. Program implementation can pose problems of management in large computer departments where the programmers might specialise in certain areas of programming. These specialisms may be:

a. **Applications.** Applications programmers are the people who write the initial programs for each application.

b. **Maintenance.** Once the programs written by the applications programmer are operational they are handed over to a maintenance programmer, whose job it will be to carry out any amendments or improvements that may be necessary.

c. **Systems software.** This programmer will specialise in writing "non-application" programs, ie, systems software. These programs will supplement those supplied by the manufacturer.

46.7 In smaller installations, of course, a smaller team of programmers will have to turn their hands to any task that comes along.

SYSTEM TESTING

46.8 There is a need to ensure both that the individual programs have been written *correctly* and that the *system* as a whole will work, ie, the link between the programs in a suite. There must also be co-ordination with *clerical* procedures involved. To this end the systems analyst must provide the necessary test data as follows:

a. **Program testing.** The systems analyst will need to supply test data designed to ensure that all possible contingencies (as specified in the systems specification) have in fact been catered for by the programmer. *Expected results* of the test must be worked out beforehand for comparison purposes.

b. **Procedure testing.** The aim of procedure testing will be to ensure that the whole *system* fits together as planned. This will involve the clerical procedures that precede input; the actual machine processes themselves; and the output procedures that follow. Overall timings and the ability of staff to handle the anticipated volumes will be under scrutiny.

MASTER FILE CONVERSION

46.9 It is necessary to convert the existing master files into a magnetic form. The *stages* of file conversion will depend on the method currently used for keeping the files (eg, manually; in box files) but are likely to be:

a. Production of control totals by adding machine.

b. Transcription of all "standing" data (such as account number, address, etc), to a special input document designed for ease of data entry.

c. Insertion of all *new* data required onto input document, eg, account numbers where none were used previously.

d. Transcription of data from documents to magnetic media. This can be a major task in the case of a large manual system. Extra staff may need to be drafted in.

e. Verification of transcribed data.

f. Data is then used as input to a "file-creation run". A specially written computer program procedures the master records in the required format.

g. Printing out of files for comparison with old files.

h. Printing out of control totals for agreement with pre-lists.

i. At a date immediately prior to changeover, variable data is inserted in master files. (eg, *balance* on accounts).

CHANGEOVER PROCEDURES

46.10 There are two *basic* methods of changing over to a new system:

a. Parallel.

b. Direct.

46.11 Parallel.

The old and new systems are run concurrently, using the same inputs. The outputs are compared and reasons for differences resolved. Outputs from the old system continue to be distributed until the new system has proved satisfactory. At this point the old system is discontinued and the new one takes its place.

46.12 Direct.

The old system is discontinued altogether and the new system becomes operational immediately.

A variation of either of the two basic methods is the so-called "pilot" changeover.

A "pilot" changeover would involve the changing over of part of the system, either in *parallel* or *directly*.

46.13 The features of the various methods of changeover are:

a. **Parallel.**

i. It is a costly method because of the amount of duplication involved.

ii. This method would mean the employment of extra staff or overtime working for existing staff. This can create difficulties over the period of the changeover.

iii. It is only possible where the outputs from old and new systems are easy to reconcile, and where the systems are similar.

iv. Its use does give management the facility of fully testing the new system whilst still retaining the existing system.

b. **Direct.**

i. If the new system bears no resemblance to the old then a direct changeover is probably inevitable.

ii. There must be complete confidence in the new system's reliability and accuracy before the method is used.

c. **Pilot.**

i. Use of the variation of the two main methods is possible when part of the system can be treated as a separate entity, eg, a department or branch might be computerised before the undertaking as a whole.

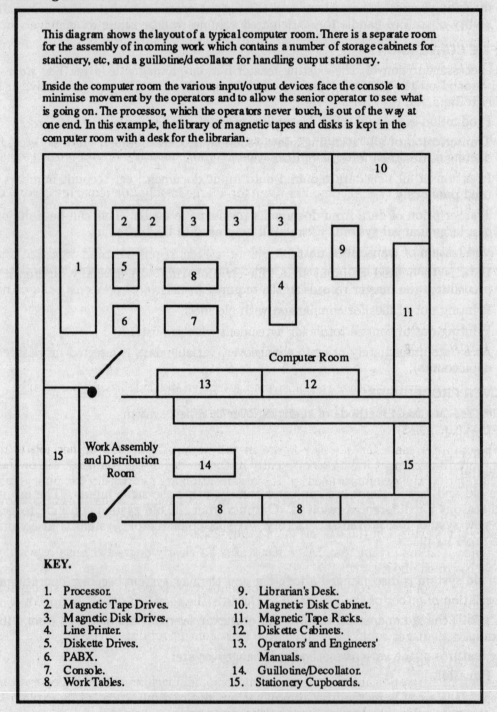

This diagram shows the layout of a typical computer room. There is a separate room for the assembly of incoming work which contains a number of storage cabinets for stationery, etc, and a guillotine/decollator for handling output stationery.

Inside the computer room the various input/output devices face the console to minimise movement by the operators and to allow the senior operator to see what is going on. The processor, which the operators never touch, is out of the way at one end. In this example, the library of magnetic tapes and disks is kept in the computer room with a desk for the librarian.

Computer Room

Work Assembly and Distribution Room

KEY.

1. Processor.
2. Magnetic Tape Drives.
3. Magnetic Disk Drives.
4. Line Printer.
5. Diskette Drives.
6. PABX.
7. Console.
8. Work Tables.
9. Librarian's Desk.
10. Magnetic Disk Cabinet.
11. Magnetic Tape Racks.
12. Diskette Cabinets.
13. Operators' and Engineers' Manuals.
14. Guillotine/Decollator.
15. Stationery Cupboards.

Fig. 46.1. Layout of a Computer Room.

REVIEW AND MAINTENANCE

46.14 Once the system has become operational it will need to be examined to see if it has met its objectives. For example, the costs and benefits will be compared with the estimates produced at the system's inception. This particular activity is often known as "post-audit".

46.15 The system will also need to be reviewed and maintained periodically for the following reasons:

a. To deal with unforeseen problems arising in operation, eg, programs may need to be modified to deal with unforeseen circumstances.

b. To confirm that the planned objectives are being met and to take action if they are not.

c. To ensure that the system is able to cope with the changing requirements of business.

46.16 The results of a systems review would be used in future systems-analysis assignments.

OPERATIONS AFTER IMPLEMENTATION

46.17 The day-to-day operations of the computer system rely upon a number of specialist staff including the following:

a. Operations manager. He or she is responsible to the computer manager for operation of the computer and ancillary equipment. Also under his control will be:

  i. Data-control section.
  ii. Data preparation.
  iii. Tape and disk library/ies.

b. Computer operator handles and operates the hardware in the computer room. He or she handles the input and output media (eg, placing tapes onto tape drives), communicates with the operating system and tries to keep the installation running smoothly by stepping in when things go wrong to correct them immediately.

c. The layout of a typical computer room for a large installation requiring several operators is shown in Fig. 46.1.

BASIS OF ORGANISATION

46.18 The development and operation of a computer system requires careful organisation of the individuals involved and those individuals need to be suitably trained in the correct practices to follow.

46.19 The nature of several types of specialist work have been covered previously and do not merit repeating here:

a. Systems analysis.

b. Programming.

c. Operating.

Details of the work of other specialist staff are given in the following paragraphs.

THE COMPUTER MANAGER (DP MANAGER IN COMMERCIAL ORGANISATIONS)

46.20 The computer manager is a key figure in the organisation. His or her job is to ensure that the computer department functions efficiently in the service of the company. He or she is responsible for ensuring that the computer needs of the organisation are met within the policy guidelines laid down.

46.21 He or she must be a good administrator as well as having a sound business knowledge. He or she must also have the knowledge and expertise necessary to enable him or her to control his or her teams of specialists in the various computing fields.

46.22 Status. It is important that his or her status be clearly defined especially with regard to his right of access to the board.

46.23 Ideally one would like someone who has previous experience of installing successful systems, and the appointment should be made very early on in the planning cycle to enable the company to get the benefit of his or her specialist knowledge and experience. If not recruited from outside, the potential computer manager could be found in the management services division.

DATA-CONTROL STAFF IN A DP DEPARTMENT

46.24 These staff are responsible for the co-ordination of all machine-processing operations and for ensuring a smooth flow of work through the operations department. In order to explain their work we will trace a particular job through from beginning to end.

46.25 a. **Source documents** accompanied by control totals are received from the clerical function (outside the department) and vetted visually.

b. **Control totals** are agreed and documents passed under this control to the data preparation section.

c. The data-preparation section prepares floppy disks or other media for source documents.

d. Source documents are returned to the clerical function and the floppy disks now represent the input for a particular run (job), eg, "invoice run".

e. **The job-assembly** section "make up" the run and prepare a run authorisation document. This will detail the various tapes/disks required and how the output is to be disposed of. This is then passed to the computer-room supervisor.

f. **Tape/disk library.** The librarian will provide all the tape reels and disk packs required for the particular job and will pass them to the computer room itself for the computer to process.

g. On completion of the computer run/s the tapes/disks, etc, go back to the library and all the documentation goes to the data control section.

46.26 **The control section** now scrutinises the control log to ensure all action has been taken correctly and to initiate any possible corrective action indicated. Control totals will be reconciled. These will now include totals of items rejected on the run/s, but all totals will need to be reconciled back to those compiled at the beginning of the job.

46.27 The output is dealt with; invoices, for example, will be despatched to customers and warehouses, etc.

46.28 All necessary information will be fed back to the user department, eg, copies of all output despatched, error lists, control totals.

DATA-PREPARATION STAFF

46.29 These staff are responsible for:

a. Preparing floppy disks from source documents or preparation by other means, eg, on-line data entry.

b. Operation of ancillary machines such as floppy disk units, paper bursters, etc.

TAPE/DISK LIBRARIAN

46.30 All tape reels and disk packs used in the installation are stored in a library adjacent to the computer room. The librarian issues tapes/disks to the computer room as per a run authorisation document from data control.

46.31 The librarian will maintain a register of all tapes and disks, noting the particular generations required for current use. Maximum security is observed and access is strictly limited.

COMPUTER SUPERVISOR

46.32 The computer room is under the day-to-day control of a supervisor. Only authorised personnel are allowed entry. It is essential that anyone who has participated in the writing of the programs is forbidden for security and audit reasons to interfere with the operational running of those programs.

THE CONTROL OF COMPUTING ACTIVITIES

46.33 The use of computers imposes certain disciplines on those who work with them. Work has to be carried out in a uniform and orderly manner in the most efficient way. Staff and equipment will be well regarded if work is completed quickly and with the minimum of error or interruption. Well-defined standards allow the control of these activities to happen naturally.

46.34 Factors that aid control are:

a. **Organisation,** ie, all staff should know what their duties are and where they fit in the general picture (see Systems Development Part introduction).

b. **Staff training.**

c. **Supervision and working to plans.**

d. **The use of documentation** to guide and assist work.

e. **Clear procedures** for individuals to follow.

DATA SECURITY

46.35 One important aspect of control is the control of data to prevent its loss, misuse or disclosure. This type of control is called "data security".

46.36 Data security is the protection of data. In some situations data security will be concerned with preventing the loss of data, eg, in the file security method used during updates. In other situations data security will be concerned with preventing the misuse or unwanted modification of data, eg, due to access by unauthorised persons. A third situation is the prevention of disclosure of data to unauthorised persons, eg, where the data is important to national security.

46.37 Various measures can be taken to ensure all three types of security. Here are some common methods.

a. The use of back-up copies of tapes or disks, eg, in conjunction with generations of files (Fig. 21.2).

b. Physical prevention, for example:

    i. Write permit rings and similar devices.

    ii. Restricting the access of personnel.

    iii. Keeping data under lock and key.

c. The use of passwords to prevent unauthorised use of computer terminals or unauthorised access to on-line files.

d. constant checks of security.

46.38 People often demand higher standards of security from computer systems than they demand from manual systems. The reader might consider which is most secure, a folder of printed documents or a floppy disk holding the same information. A floppy disk can easily be damaged by dust or scratches so that its data is lost. On the other hand, specialist equipment and software will be needed to read its data, thus the data is more secure from those not trained in its use.

Even so, there has been a growth in computer crime in recent years, including an increase in "hacking".

SUMMARY

46.39 a. Implementation is concerned with the coordinating and controlling of the activities necessary to put the new system into operation.

b. *Staff training, programming, testing, file conversion, changeover,* review and maintenance are the stages in implementation.

c. The systems analyst is needed at this stage because of his knowledge of the designed system and its implications.

d. Careful organisation is needed to ensure that computers are used effectively and properly.

e. The work of various specialist staff was described.

f. The control of specialist work was discussed.

g. Data security was defined and methods of data security were described.

POINTS TO NOTE

46.40 a. Note the difference between program testing and procedure testing.

b. The responsibility for program testing lies with the programmers, who will be required to provide evidence of testing.

c. The Part you are reading is entitled Systems Development because the term is generally used to describe the particular activities detailed in its chapters. In practical terms, however, the various stages will be undertaken as part of the system life cycle and a systems study carried out on instructions of top management.

d. The emphasis throughout this Part has been upon systems development as it applies to commercial computer applications. However, the same basic principles apply to industrial applications. The most significant differences between systems development for commercial applications and that for industrial applications are:

    i. The systems being computerised (automated) in industrial systems tend to involve physical processes and are therefore well defined compared with commercial systems, which often rely on human sense and unwritten rules, which may be ill-defined.

    ii. Many industrial systems involve the time-critical processing of data read from instruments and this places a different emphasis on the whole analysis and design process.

e. The more dependent people or organisations are upon computers the more important becomes the need for careful control and organisation of how the computer application systems are developed and the way they are operated.

STUDENT SELF-TESTING QUESTIONS

1. What are the features of the various methods of changeover?

2. If a manual system is scheduled for future computerisation, what steps could be taken to alter the existing documents and procedures in order to make master file conversion more straightforward? (Hint: Apply your knowledge of methods of data entry.)

3. Define the term "data security" and identify three types of data security.

GLOSSARY CHECKLIST

47: Project Management

INTRODUCTION

47.1 Good planning is a prerequisite of any business activity and computer systems development is no exception. This chapter deals with the planning and management of systems development projects by tracing the steps involved in the system life cycle.

47.2 The reader should recognise the fact that in this chapter we are primarily concerned with the management aspects of the system life cycle, whereas in earlier chapters the systems analysis aspects were considered.

47.3 In this chapter the assumption will be made that the company is not currently using a computer for the application concerned and that the size of the application is such as to make computerisation have a major impact on the organisation. It should be noted, however, that even for small applications, such as those requiring the use of a single microcomputer, the management task must still be done. Indeed, there is a particular danger when managing the development of many small systems that the development will end up happening in a piecemeal and fragmented way, which can subsequently create serious management problems.

PRELIMINARY SURVEY OR STUDY

47.4 There will come a time when the question of using a new computer system will arise. As a result, the board will decide to make an initial investigation into the possibility of using one. This will probably be carried out by one or two senior executives or consultants.

47.5 **Application areas.** More often than not a prima facie case can be made for a computer in a particular application area and it is this which will have prompted the board into carrying out the preliminary survey. There are likely to be other application areas to consider, in which case a long-term plan (including a list of priorities) will need to be drawn up.

47.6 **Outcome.** The preliminary study will determine whether or not to continue investigating the need for a computer. If so, SPECIFIC COMPUTER OBJECTIVES will be drawn up. It is important that the user should both agree to and sign the objectives to be met by the system.

STEERING COMMITTEE

47.7 When a project is established it is quite common also to establish a steering committee for the project. The purpose of this committee is to "keep the project on course" so that it meets its objectives. The membership of the committee comprises management members and senior project staff such as analysts, so that the committee can carry out monitoring, controlling and consultative functions.

FEASIBILITY STUDY

47.8 Assuming the project is given the go-ahead, a study team will be formed to carry out a study of the application area or areas. This study team will be under the direction of the steering committee.

47.9 **Purpose.** The purpose of a feasibility study is to provide information in order to justify the use of a computer on three grounds:

   a. Technical.

   b. Economic.

   c. Social.

47.10 **Study steps.** Steps in the study will depend on individual circumstances but generally will include the following:

   a. The study team must be aware of the precise objective of the study.

   b. Establish the requirements of the particular system being studied.

   c. Make a detailed examination of the system to determine how these requirements are met. This will include details of volumes, information flows, time-scales, etc.

   d. Note any improvements that can be made in the system as it stands as these may well be implemented at once.

e. Formulate the new design on the basis of the application of computer methods, considering various alternatives:

    i. Processing method (batch, on-line, real-time).

    ii. Choice of system (microcomputer, minicomputer, mainframe).

    iii. Centralised processing or distributed processing.

    iv. Methods of data entry, storage and output.

It must be stressed that the appropriate use of manual methods must not be overlooked.

f. Assess costs of possible new systems (staff, buildings, hardware, software, etc) over the life of the project.

g. Make comparisons with the present system.

h. Considerations of social factors, ie, effect on staff relations, etc.

i. Make recommendations to the Board in the form of a Feasibility Study Report.

47.11 Depth. A feasibility study will be carried out in enough depth to enable the Board to make a decision on whether or not to proceed with detailed investigation and analysis. The contents of the report naturally will vary according to circumstances, but the main points on which information should be given are as follows:

a. **Aims and objectives.** It is important the aims and objectives be clearly stated. These should have been agreed with the line managers. The areas involved in the study should be defined.

b. **Cost/benefit comparison.** The alternative solutions will be outlined indicating the benefits to be gained from each and the costs involved. Comparisons with present methods will be attempted. Benefits that may accrue are:

    i. More timely information.

    ii. Better customer relations.

    iii. Improved cash flow.

Costs to be considered are development costs, capital outlay and operating costs.

c. **Outline of proposed system.** This will include details of:

    i. Inputs.

    ii. Stored data.

    iii. Outputs.

    iv. Processing activities from a business user's viewpoint.

    v. Programs and software.

The amount of detail assembled under each heading would be sufficient to enable a choice to be made between alternative solutions (if more than one is included in the report) and for the effects on existing procedures to be gauged.

d. **Effects on organisation.** The effects of the introduction of new methods and procedures on the organisation, in terms of change in posts, redundancy and staff re-training, will be included.

e. **Schedule of requirements.** Details of capital equipment, including costs, must be listed.

f. **Implementation.** the plan for the implementation of the proposed system will include a time-table. Methods of changeover will be stated.

g. **Recommendations.** These will recommend a particular solution which could conceivably be the adoption of conventional methods rather than computer methods to solve the company's problems.

CONSIDERATION OF REPORT

47.12 The board will consider the report and will want answers to the following questions:

a. Do the recommendations meet the objectives?

b. Do they still fit overall company objectives? (Note on 12a and 12b - some studies take so long that the original circumstances could have changed. The study itself could have led to a change in objectives.)

c. What is the effect on company profits going to be?

d. What is the effect going to be on company organisation and staff?

e. What are the costs involved and can the capital be obtained?

f. What is the time-scale for implementation?

g. Does it look sufficiently into the future, ie, does the proposal allow for possible future expansion and modification?

47.13 Decision. The board may well ask for further information in certain areas. After the feasibility study report has been studied in detail a decision has to be taken whether or not to proceed.

DETAILED INVESTIGATION AND ANALYSIS

47.14 Assuming that a decision is taken to proceed further, this stage continues the process started with the initial survey and feasibility study. At the end of the investigation and analysis a requirements specification is produced.

47.15 The production of a requirement specification provides the basis for a go/no-go decision between the feasibility study report and the full system specification.

CONSIDERATION OF THE REQUIREMENTS SPECIFICATION

47.16 The board will expect this report to answer the questions brought forward from their earlier considerations of the feasibility study report. In addition, the all-important question "Does this specification give a full and accurate statement of the data-processing requirements?" must be satisfactorily answered.

47.17 Decision. Although the requirements specification is "implementation free" it contains sufficient detail for the main design alternative to be identified. The board can approve the specification and decide whether or not to proceed with one or more designs. A balance has to be struck between the danger of eliminating a design alternative too soon and the cost of producing multiple alternative designs. It is also important when approving the specification to be sure that there is a clear technical (and in the case of outside contract, legal) basis for determining whether or not the specification has been satisfied when the system has been implemented.

FACILITY SELECTION

47.18 The selection of one of the main design alternatives is effectively a selection of the kind of facilities to be used. For example, manufacturers and suppliers of particular products may be selected and asked to submit proposals that indicate how they can meet the requirements.

Alternatively an independent firm of consultants may be requested to handle the problem.

DESIGN

47.19 The design stage was described in chapter 44. The outcome of this stage is the ultimate in documentation of the new system, the systems specification. This will contain full details of all clerical and computer procedures involved.

47.20 In the case of complete one-off systems the design stage will involve all the activities described in chapter 45. However, in the case of many smaller systems, the design process may be largely a matter of matching what is available to what is required in order to find an acceptable match.

47.21 Each system specification is considered, along with any associated proposals from manufacturers or suppliers. After what may be a very long process one of the alternatives is selected and pursued.

47.22 It may well have been decided to use external consultants, in which case the following stages would not necessarily apply.

RESOURCE PLANNING

47.23 Whether the organisation is acquiring a small, medium or larger computer system a great deal of detailed planning and preparation now needs to be done in order that the installation of the machine and changeover to the computer-based system are achieved smoothly and efficiently.

47.24 Changing over to a system based on a microcomputer does not, however, have the same far-reaching effect on the organisation as that of a medium-sized machine. A medium-sized machine is assumed in the following paragraphs.

47.25 Network. The planning required up to the time of delivery of the machine and then on to the time the system is operational is normally so involved that it needs to be planned out using a chart that shows the "network" of related activities and events that must take place and their interdependencies. The time-scale may well be linked to the date of delivery of the computer, and this could be many months. If there are many applications to be computerised, a schedule of priorities will ensure that at least one is ready for the computer soon after it is installed. **Estimation** of the time taken to complete tasks, and hence their related costs, must be done most carefully if any reliance is to be placed upon the network. Estimation is never easy but is improved in the long run by keeping records of time taken to complete various categories of task.

47.26 Main resources. The main resources requiring management's attention will be:

    a. **Site.** This has to be chosen and prepared.

    b. **Building.** A new building is to be erected or an existing one modified.

    c. **Environment.** Requirements of the computer regarding humidity, dust control, etc, will need special attention.

    d. **Standby equipment.** Arrangements will need to be made for such equipment in the event of a failure of the company's computer. In extreme cases involving "mission-critical" systems this may involve the creation of an off-site standby system.

    e. **Staff. Selection and training.** The decision has to be made on whether or not to recruit from within the company. Apart from the particular specialists who cannot be found in the company, it is generally found more satisfactory to recruit from within. At least such people will have a good knowledge of the company. Staff required will include:

        i. Management (computer manager, etc).

        ii. Clerical.

        iii. Analysts and programmers – a few trained people recruited outside to help train company personnel.

        iv. Operators – own personnel probably already employed in company as machine operators of some kind.

    The manufacturer will often give assistance with training staff and also provide the temporary assistance of his own specialists.

    f. **Finance.** Necessary arrangements will need to be made to ensure that the appropriate finance is made available. Detailed budgets will be drawn up for each area and strict control exercised over performance in accordance with budget.

INSTALLATION OF COMPUTER

47.27 This will affect only a small number of people. The manufacturer's engineers will be responsible for installation of the machinery in conjunction with the computer manager or his representative. The machine is tested from an engineering point of view and handed over. The whole operation is usually accomplished in a matter of days.

47.28 Maintenance. Maintenance of the hardware and software will normally be the subject of an agreement and will ensure the machine is always in working order and spare parts available when required.

IMPLEMENTATION

47.29 This consists of:

    a. Training of staff.

    b. Programming.

    c. System testing.

    d. Master file conversion.

    e. Changeover procedures.

    f. Review (system evaluation) and maintenance.

    Many aspects of implementation have already been discussed in chapter 46. Some additional points, regarding planning, are made here.

47.30 Planning this, the final and critical stage, would have started very early in the planning of the project as a whole. Indeed, quite often this particular stage will have a network of its own. This is the time when the computer system is going to take over from the old system and it is a very worrying time for everybody. There will be disappointments, setbacks and frayed tempers. It is a time of upheaval in the company and the value of good planning will be seen clearly during this period.

PROGRAM WRITING AND TESTING.

47.31 Programmers will get on with the job of producing the computer programs from the systems specification. Individual procedures are programmed and compiled and then tested for logical correctness using "dummy" data. After being tested individually the programs are tested as a complete system.

47.32 Program testing. It is the programmer's responsibility to ensure that each individual program meets its specification. Suitable test data must be used at each stage in programming. It is important that the programs are also subjected to independent testing.

47.33 The independent test data should be designed by people other than the program writers. The analysts in conjunction with the user department should do this job. This will ensure that every eventuality is designed into the test data pack and thus the programs are subjected to the most rigorous examination. All these eventualities must be considered before the specification is given to the programmer. It must be stressed, however, that the final testing is no substitute for good work practices and methods of quality assurance (QA), ie, setting and enforcing standards of design, documentation, reliability, etc. All the evidence available shows that considerable benefits can be obtained from sound QA.

REVIEW (SYSTEM EVALUATION) AND MAINTENANCE

47.34 Once the implementation process is complete and the system is operational there is a tendency to heave a sigh of relief, but it is just as important to follow up implementation with an evaluation process to ensure the original objectives are being met. This system evaluation is sometimes called "post-audit".

47.35 It must be a properly mounted operation and its findings will be of help in future projects.

47.36 The need to keep abreast of new techniques is also important in order that the full benefits can be reaped.

47.37 In order that the new system continues to run efficiently it must be constantly monitored and maintained. This maintenance is bound to be necessary sooner or later and should be planned for.

SUMMARY

47.38 a. The need for planning is vital because of the far-reaching effects of the changes that computers bring about.

    b. The stages in planning are:

        i.   Preliminary study.
        ii.   Feasibility study.
        iii. Consideration of report.
        iv. Detailed investigation and analysis.
        v.   Consideration of requirements specification.
        vi. Facility selection.
        vii. Resource planning.
        viii. Installation of the computer.
        ix. Implementation.
        x.   Review (system evaluation) and maintenance.

    c. All possible alternatives should be explored in a feasibility study.

POINTS TO NOTE

47.39 a. The detail concerned with many of the points raised in this chapter has been covered in chapters 43–46.

    b. The various steps do not follow neatly one after the other as in the text but overlap each other to a great extent.

    c. A feasibility study may be more correctly termed a justification study.

    d. Computer planning should not be geared to one application but should be designed to accommodate future applications when they arise.

    e. Note the different stages that involve a SYSTEM STUDY.

        i. Initial study.
        ii. Feasibility study.
        iii. Detailed requirements study.
        iv. Detailed systems study.

    f. Each of these studies in e. above (or if you prefer, phases, in what will be a complete study in the end) will be conducted to the depth required to make a particular decision.

        i. **The initial study** will only be made to the depth required for a decision to be taken on whether or not a prima facie case for a computer can be established.

        ii. **The feasibility study** will be in greater depth because it must provide the information that determines whether or not the use of a computer is justified to solve the company's problems.

iii. **The detailed requirements study** will identify the precise data-processing requirement in an implementation-free way.

iv. **Detailed systems study.** Further detail will be required to identify the precise hardware requirements and then to produce a systems specification for approval.

g. You may need to make an assumption in an examination answer about the type of system the computer system is replacing, ie, manual, computerised, etc.

h. The term systems study can be applied to any of the four studies referred to in 47.39e so be careful in answering an examination question on systems studies to indicate the one you are talking about.

i. The chapter has covered the various aspects of a large-scale project, but the same principles and basic practical issues are present irrespective of project size.

STUDENT SELF-TESTING QUESTIONS

1. When acquiring an in-house computer system, which criteria are considered when deciding between the various manufacturers who have submitted tenders?
2. How do the contents of a feasibility study report differ from the systems specification?
3. What points would you include in the review of a newly implemented computer system?
4. Discuss the functions of the following personnel in a typical mainframe computer installation:
   a. project leader, *(5 marks)*
   b. project librarian, *(5 marks)*
   c. systems programmer, *(4 marks)*
   d. computer operator, *(3 marks)*
   e. data control clerk, *(3 marks)*

   (AEB)

GLOSSARY CHECKLIST

Feasibility study	47.8	Steering committee	47.7
Installation	47.29	System evaluation	47.34
Post audit	47.34	System review	47.34

APPLICATIONS VI

1. This Part brings together the areas studied so far by discussing specific application areas in which complete computer systems are used. It is relevant to all courses at which this text is aimed. However, the business or industrial bias of the reader's own course should influence the time spent on each of the two chapters.

48: Business Computing

INTRODUCTION

48.1 This chapter examines the use of computers of different sizes from small to large. The three main topics considered are:

a. microcomputers

b. minicomputers

c. large computer systems (including the use of mainframes).

48.2 The basic hardware features of microcomputers and minicomputers were described in chapter 13. This chapter considers the use of these computers and examines where they fit in the overall picture of computer applications.

MICROCOMPUTERS

48.3 Microprocessors are now to be found in a wide variety of devices from petrol pumps to wrist watches. Such devices are highly specialised and the computer systems within them are called embedded systems. In this chapter we are primarily concerned with general purpose computer systems rather than those just described.

48.4 The processing capability of the larger microcomputers is comparable to that of many mainframes of the 1960s. This fact should emphasise the major role that these small machines can play if properly utilised.

48.5 Until the early 1980s most microcomputers used for business purposes were 8-bit machines. During the 1980s 16-bit microcomputers took over from the 8-bit microcomputers and by far the most popular models were personal computers produced by IBM and those compatible with them, produced by other companies, eg, Compaq. Very powerful 32-bit microcomputers are now available which challenge the power of minicomputers. The following points apply to a typical microcomputer used as a personal computer in business.

48.6 **Software.** The system software available on these systems may be rather limited but this limitation is more than compensated for by the wide range of software packages available.

48.7 System software is usually made up of a simple operating system and a choice of programming common languages, eg, BASIC, PASCAL, C, CIS-COBOL (A portable version of COBOL produced by Microfocus) and assemblers.

The operating systems used on 8-bit microcomputers are limited but effective. Probably the most common is CP/M. On 16-bit personal computers the predominant "operating systems" are PCDOS, used on IBM PCs, and MSDOS, which is used on personal computers produced by other manufacturers who produce IBM PC-compatible products.

The more recent versions of PCDOS and MSDOS are broadly comparable in functionality to their minicomputer counterparts with **one big exception** – the PC operating systems are almost all single-user non multitasking systems. However, some of the newer machines, including the IBM PS/2 OS/2 and the Archimedes are multi-tasking machines.

Another point, worthy of mention, is the growing number of **"laptop"** computers in use. These are portable microcomputers which are so small that they can be used when on a person's lap without discomfort.

48.8 Software packages are available for an incredibly wide range of applications including:

a. payroll

b. stock control

c. order processing, invoicing and sales ledger

d. production control

e. job costing

f. information storage and retrieval

g. word processing

h. spreadsheets, etc.

48.9 A number of well-established software suppliers produce software packages that can be made to run on a wide variety of machines produced by different manufacturers, eg, on an 8-bit microcomputer Micropro's WORDSTAR package for word processing and Visicorp's VISICAL package for financial modelling are widely available. There are numerous "portable" software products on PCs too, eg, LOTUS 1-2-3, DBASE, Word Perfect, Framework, PC INGRES, EXCEL and GEMDRAW.

A Compaq laptop computer.
Photographs courtesy of Compaq Computer Ltd.

48.10 Dual-purpose.

Many microcomputers are able to meet a dual purpose:

a. They may be used as "stand-alone" machines, ie, working autonomously for a particular purpose.

b. They may be used as "intelligent terminals" within a distributed data-processing system.

This enables such machines to deal not only with data processing that is only of "local" interest, but also with corporate data processing.

48.11 Advantages of a microcomputer include:

a. A full configuration can cost less than £4,000, although it may cost much more.

b. Cheap software packages arising out of the large volume of sales.

c. Just plugs into the nearest mains socket.

d. User-friendly "menu-driven" programs mean that there is no need to employ specialist staff, the computer can be operated by general clerical staff provided they are properly trained.

e. Brings computing within the budget of even the very smallest organisations.

f. Allows a large organisation to implement distributed processing, with each department possessing its own independent processing facilities.

48.12 Disadvantages include:

a. A lack of a multi-tasking operating system in many cases.

b. Limited file store and memory capacity although this is *not* a problem on the more recent models.

c. Smaller systems often lack a choice of languages.

d. Purchased software other than standard packages is often of a poor quality.

e. Too often purchased by non-specialists who are too easily convinced by salesmen.

f. Can lead to several departments duplicating the same procedures.

NB. 16-bit microcomputers with hard disks overcome 9a, and 9b is a problem of home computers rather than small business machines such as PCs.

MINICOMPUTERS

48.13 The hardware of a typical minicomputer system was described in chapter 13.

48.14 Whereas the typical microcomputer is designed as a single-user system, the larger microcomputers and typical minicomputers are multi-user systems.

48.15 A user with an apparent need for multiple microcomputers at one particular location may be able to meet the same need with a single minicomputer.

48.16 **Software.** There is far more system software available on most minicomputers than there is on the typical microcomputer, but perhaps surprisingly there is not always such a good choice of applications software.

48.17 System software on minicomputers has been developed over many years and had its origins in the fast key-to-disk system. Some single-user systems are in use but the typical minicomputer has a time-sharing operating system plus some communications facilities. The latter reflect the fact that minicomputers frequently form part of a distributed system.

48.18 The choice of programming languages on minicomputers is usually better than that available on microcomputers and is very similar to that available on most main frames.

48.19 Software packages are available for use on most minicomputers, but they do not have the same importance that they have with microcomputers. The reasons are simply that the production of applications software for minicomputers has tended to take place using the same methods as those used for mainframe computers. That is, software is often written *by the user or for the user* in order to meet specific requirements rather than to meet the needs of some general market.

48.20 This situation is changing, however, as many packages first written for microcomputers have since been converted and extended to run on larger systems.

48.21 The applications dealt with by minicomputers include all those listed earlier under the heading of microcomputers but also include such things as:

a. Retailing, eg, point-of-sale systems.

b. Banking.

c. Life assurance.

d. Stock Exchange dealing, etc.

48.22 **Multi-purpose.** Minicomputers may be used for several different purposes.

a. As "stand-alone" machines (often multi-users).

b. As the central host computer in a small distributed system, eg, with a number of microcomputers acting as "intelligent terminals".

c. As the second tier in a larger-scale distributed system, eg, acting as a local host to a number of microcomputers but also connected to some central corporate mainframe.

48.23 Relative advantages and disadvantages of minicomputers compared with other computers.

   a. They are more expensive than a typical microcomputer but much less expensive than a mainframe.

   b. They have systems software that is broadly comparable to that found on mainframes but they do not always have the same wide choice of applications packages found on microcomputers.

   c. They have greater file storage and memory capacities than most microcomputers and can cope with all but the largest data-processing problems.

   d. Their multi-user and communications facilities make them well suited to the integration of local data-processing activities and the provision of distributed processing facilities.

GENERAL CONSIDERATIONS

48.24 System support. Generally speaking, smaller organisations buying micro- and minicomputers will not be able to economically justify the employment of the DP specialists required in mainframe installations. The supplier must therefore either be able to offer suitable applications packages or be willing to get more involved in program writing for the user. The latter is seldom an economic alternative in the case of microcomputers because the full development cost must be borne by the one user. The supplier will also be expected to provide considerable support for the user.

48.25 To understand the market situation, it is important to realise that many micros and minis are sold in what is called the OEM market, ie, Original Equipment Manufacturer. That is to say, they are sold not to the eventual user but to another manufacturer who incorporates them into a larger system. Many manufacturers of micros and minis are wholly or partly dependent on this type of business. It was the decision of some of them to provide peripherals and software and to sell direct to the end user that created the explosion in "mini" and now "micro" sales.

LARGE COMPUTER SYSTEMS

48.26 We now illustrate the use of large computer systems by providing a discussion of two applications:

   a. an airline booking system (a real-time system).

   b. a system used by a large corporate organisation.

48.27 The first application is specialised whereas the second application considers the typical general-purpose large system. Refer back to real-time systems before you continue (34.20).

APPLICATION 1

48.28 Airline booking system. Records of seat availability on all its planes will be kept by an airline on a central computer. The computer is linked via terminals to a world-wide system of agents. Each agent can gain access to the flight records and within seconds make a reservation in respect of a particular flight. This reservation is recorded *immediately* so that the next inquiry for that flight (following even microseconds after the previous reservation) finds that particular seat or seats reserved. Notice the computer records reflect an accurate picture of the airline's seating load at all times because there is no time lag worth mentioning. The computer would then output information for the production of the customer's ticket and flight instructions, of confirmation on the booking by the customer, (see Fig. 49.1).

48.29 Each booking is a separate transaction and is processed immediately, ie, not batched. This is therefore a *transaction-processing system.*

FEATURES OF REAL-TIME

48.30 Response time. The service given by a real-time processing system can be measured in terms of *response* time. This is the time taken by the system to respond to an input, eg, the time interval between the pressing of the last key by the operator of a VDU and the display of the required (updated) information.

48.31 "Traffic" pattern. An important feature of real-time is the "traffic" pattern, ie, the *volumes* of data being input, the *times* at which they are input, the *types* of input and the *places* at which they are input.

48.32 Reliability. Because real-time systems operate automatically an extremely high standard of system reliability is required.

   a. Program protection. Many programs will occupy main storage simultaneously and the integrity of each program must be protected.

   b. File security. Duplicate files will probably need to be kept and in addition their contents will be dumped at intervals. These measures will aid reconstruction should the need arise. (Note the duplicate database in Fig. 49.1.)

   c. Standby machinery. In the airline application two processors would be required, one of which is operational and the other a standby machine. In the event of failure the standby machine would automatically come into use. (Again refer to Fig. 49.1.)

   d. Security. Confidentiality of information held on magnetic storage is achieved by the use of special code numbers allowing access to certain files only by certain people.

HARDWARE, SOFTWARE CONSIDERATIONS

48.33 Implicit in the operation of real-time systems described are:

   a. A large main storage requirement to accommodate systems software and application programs. Also required will be an area to use as buffers for queuing of messages.

   b. Direct-access storage of large capacity as backing storage.

   c. A sophisticated operating system to handle the many different operations being handled simultaneously.

   d. A data communication system linking the many terminals with the processor.

COST

48.34 Real-time systems are usually specially designed for a particular application and are extremely costly. Cost will vary with the service one wishes the system to provide. The better the service (ie, the shorter the response time generally) then the more costly it becomes in terms of hardware and software, etc.

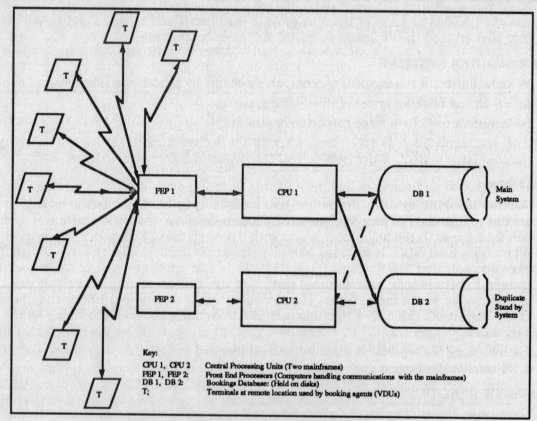

Fig. 49.1. A Real-time Airline Booking System.

APPLICATION 2

48.35 Systems used by large corporate organisations. Such systems are required to meet the diverse information needs within the organisations.

48.36 Depending upon the type of organisation any number of the following functions of the organisation may be supported by the computer system:

   a. Top-level management.

   b. Finance and accounting.

   c. Manufacturing.

   d. Marketing.

   e. Purchasing, stocking and distributing (ie, logistics).

f. Personnel.

g. Administration.

48.37 Levels of computer support vary from function to function but particularly distinctive levels are:

a. Automation of basic clerical procedures such as those found in ordering, invoicing, payroll production and bookings. Batch or transaction processing will be used as appropriate.

b. Office automation and communication to support the administrative functions, eg, by the use of word processors and electronic mail.

c. Automation of management-control operations such as the control of stock, production, materials, distribution, accounts and personnel.

d. Automated aids to strategic planning such as financial modelling, linear programming and other analysis methods.

FEATURES OF THESE SYSTEMS

48.38 In order to support the processing needs outlined in the previous two paragraphs these systems must be large, versatile, reliable and efficiently organised.

48.39 Specific features may include:

a. **Distributed facilities.** For example, there may be a mainframe computer at head office acting as host to smaller computers at divisional offices. A divisional office could deal with marketing or production say. A lower level of the distributed system might handle office automation by means of word processors linked to the main computers.

b. **Integrated files of databases.** The advantages of integrated file processing or databases can be exploited so that, for example, the receipt of orders may *automatically* give rise to the ordering of materials, the movement of stock, the scheduling of production, the control of production and the distribution of manufactured goods.

c. **Combinations of different processing methods.** Run-of-the-mill stock control and payroll production may take place by batch processing while enquiries, orders, bookings, etc are being handled by transaction processing. Additional processing loads, such as those used for financial modelling, will also be placed upon the system from time to time.

48.40 The hardware and software features of these systems have comparable complexity to those of the real-time systems mentioned earlier in the chapter. The principal differences are:

a. The distribution of processing, communications and data.

b. The use of many different types of software to support the varied processing needs.

SUMMARY

48.41 a. There is no difference in principle between a "micro" or "mini" and the larger computer.

b. Machines described as "micros" or "minis" vary widely in specification and price.

c. Essentially, the "micro" or "mini" is a smaller, cheaper, slower machine which is, however, acquiring an increasing degree of sophistication.

d. Although the typical microcomputer is noticeably different from the typical mini computer, the larger microcomputer and smaller minis are indistinguishable for most practical purposes. In answering examination questions, concentrate on typical features first and then mention any overlap.

e. "Micros" and "minis" play an important part in computer networks.

f. Software is usually supplied by the manufacturer as part of a complete system.

g. Applications cover a very wide range, and include all conventional accounting tasks.

h. The microcomputer is even smaller and cheaper than the "mini".

i. The two large-scale applications described in this chapter all use large amounts of hardware. The first system must have fast response times in order to satisfy the needs of the users. The second system must strike a balance between response and processing throughput. The airline booking system has essentially one large job to handle, but the other system has many different jobs to handle.

j. Real-time involves the processing of data as it arises, thus providing records that are permanently up to date.

k. Response time, traffic pattern and reliability are major features.

l. The hardware and software requirements are complex.

m. The system in a large corporate organisation will:

    i. Have distributed processing, communications and data.

    ii. Use many different types of software.

    iii. Exploit integrated files or databases.

    iv. Use a variety of processing methods.

POINTS TO NOTE

48.42 a. In the case of a transaction-processing system such as the one used by the airline the following points apply:

    i. The accurate assessment of response time and traffic pattern is very difficult but of vital importance, as errors can be very costly in terms of size of processor, sophistication of software and transmission line capacity. (Unlike batch processing, where overtime or an additional shift might be possible, real-time processing depends upon the system being able to cope at the time required.)

    ii. Because of the difficulties of accurate assessment, applications are normally implemented on a "pilot" basis (eg, with the airline reservations system – no pun intended – a few branch offices would have access initially).

    iii. The essence of a real-time system is that it should provide an up-to-date (real) picture of events as they occur. Therefore a retrieval system is generally associated with it. It is possibly for this reason that students give undue prominence in examination answers to this latter function, forgetting that they are dealing with a system of *processing* just as they were with batch systems.

b. Other areas where real-time applications of computers are applied are automated process control and production control.

c. Most large-scale organisations are now totally reliant upon systems like the one described in the second example in the chapter.

STUDENT SELF-TESTING QUESTIONS

1. What are the advantages and disadvantages of microcomputers for small commercial applications?

2. Name seven functions within a large organisation that could be supported by a computer system.

3. State the main factors that must be considered by a systems analyst before designing a system for implementation on a computer.

QUESTIONS WITHOUT ANSWERS

4. Describe a typical microcomputer and a typical minicomputer. Why is the distinction between a microcomputer and a minicomputer hard to make in some cases?

5. The widespread adoption of microcomputer systems by commerce and industry has led to a large increase in the use of general-application packages.

    a. What is an application package? (5 marks)

    b. Discuss the advantages and disadvantages for the user of general-application packages compared with user-produced software. (10 marks)

    c. Describe the documentation that you would expect to obtain with an application package. (5 marks)

(AEB)

QUESTIONS WITHOUT ANSWERS

6. Discuss the use of a computer system for airline bookings, including in your answer:

   a. the nature of the equipment at the point of sale and the way in which it is used;   (4,4)

   b. the equipment required to hold the files and process the transactions;   (6)

   c. why it is necessary that the software should ensure rapid response, and how it can be designed to prevent confusion when multiple demands are made on the same file;   (2,4)

   d. the effects of employing computers in this application and the reasons why they are not in general use in this way for other forms of transport.   (5)

                                                      (OLE)

GLOSSARY CHECKLIST

Business microcomputers	48.3	Laptop	48.7
Business minicomputers	48.13		

49: Industrial Computing

INTRODUCTION

49.1 In chapter 48 it was stated that the two main areas of computer application are:

a. Commercial applications

b. Scientific, engineering and research applications.

The vast majority of computer systems are used for commercial purposes, as is most probably evident to the reader from the material presented in previous chapters. The second area listed above includes within it a major area of computer usage which may be broadly termed **industrial computing**. Under this general heading we may put everything from the small embedded systems, now found in a wide variety of devices such as petrol pumps or washing machines, to large, complex systems found in manufacturing industry. A common feature of these systems is the use of computers to control or monitor individual machines, larger engineering systems and even whole industrial complexes.

49.2 There is a great variety in industrial computer systems mainly because a very high proportion of them are specially developed for particular purposes. Thus they are special purpose computers either by design or by the special development from general-purpose computers. This variety makes it harder to talk of typical examples. To overcome this problem this chapter covers two main topics. First it considers a simplified example of the use of computers in manufacturing. Then it considers the use of analog and hybrid computers, which are most widely used in industrial computing applications.

MANUFACTURING APPLICATIONS

49.3 Some general examples of the uses of computers in manufacturing were given in chapter 48. It should be clear that there are lots of different ways in which computers can be used in manufacturing. The **example** given here is intended to highlight a number of these ways.

49.4 A manufacturer of computer equipment has one factory production line dedicated to the manufacture of VDUs. The VDUs made on this line are all basically the same, but extra features can be added by placing additional components in the basic model. For example, the basic model only works in black and white, but an alternative screen and associated circuits can be included instead to make it a colour model.

49.5 Assembling a VDU is rather like making a kit or do-it-yourself product in that it starts with a tray full of components and proceeds in a series of ordered steps until the job is completed. The main difference is that several of the steps require specialist equipment and specially trained staff. Another difference in this case is that rather than have one person assemble a whole VDU, different people work on it at each stage.

49.6 The reader has probably noticed already that in this example the manufacturing process is not totally automated. The VDUs are not made by an army of robots! However, computers are used to control some of the equipment on the production line. Computers are used in other ways too.

49.7 The department responsible for the VDU production line receives orders for its VDUs from other parts of the company. There is a constant demand, so the production line runs every day, but each VDU is made to order. The department uses its own computer to deal with these orders and with the production line. The system works in the following way.

49.8 Orders are fed into the computer when they arrive. These orders specify exactly which models are required and how many of each. In the future the company hopes to have a computer network that allows these orders to be sent electronically.

49.9 The computer is able to determine which components are required for each VDU model from data it has in its files. It feeds these requirements through to an automated stockroom in which components held in boxes are removed from the shelves and placed on special trays. Each tray contains the components for one VDU.

The special device that removes the boxes from the shelves is controlled by computer. It is not actually a robot because it has no control over its own actions, but it has two metal arms, which clip onto handles on the boxes and it can move up and down and to and fro across the front of the boxes selecting those that it needs.

49.10 Trays from the automated stockroom are deposited on the front of the production line. Each tray has a label on it, which has been printed by the computer. The label specifies which model VDU is to be produced and contains lists of a number of things that must be checked and signed at various stages along the production line. These checks are used to make sure that the work done at each stage has been completed properly so that when the VDUs arrive at the end of the production line they are all undamaged and in proper working order. If at any stage a VDU is found to be faulty it is removed from the production line to be dealt with separately. We will not go into the details here.

49.11 The label on the tray also contains a bar-coded strip. As the tray completes each stage in assembly its code is read on a bar-code reader connected to the department's computer. This information enables the computer to keep track of the production process. This information is required by those in charge of the production line. They need to be able to use a computer terminal to gain up-to-date information of how work is progressing and they also need to be able to get the computer to print out reports containing tables and statistics about what production has taken place.

49.12 At some stage along the production line it is necessary to test the VDU electronically to see that each circuit has been properly fitted. To do this the VDU is connected up to the microcomputer, which can carry out a series of tests automatically. The computer not only indicates whether or not the partly assembled VDU has passed the test it also diagnoses the nature of any faults so that they can be corrected.

49.13 When the VDU arrives at the end of the production line it is turned on and run for a number of hours. During this test it is connected to another computer, which makes it perform in a variety of ways to test its functions. Some visual checks are done manually.

49.14 Finally, after the very last inspection, the VDU is placed in its box, onto which is stuck a label for its destination. This label has a bar-coded strip on it which is used in the automated warehouse prior to despatch.

49.15 The system in the warehouse assembles orders for despatch in a similar way to the system that assembles the tray of components. The individual boxes are loaded onto shelves as they come off the various production lines. The machine that does this looks rather like an unmanned fork-lift truck on rails and is controlled by computer. Once all boxes for an order have arrived in the warehouse the machine removes the required boxes from the shelves, where it placed them previously, and places them in the loading bay connected to the computer. Delivery notes are printed out for each order, which is deposited in the loading bay.

49.16 That concludes the description of the manufacturing system. The description was not complete in every detail but it should have given you an idea of how computers can be used in manufacturing. Some of the things mentioned, such as the automated warehouse, can be found in other applications, so some aspects of this example are quite general.

49.17 Notice how the computer was used for the following kinds of tasks:

    a. Maintaining and providing information, eg, about components and orders.

    b. Monitoring events, eg, what stage a VDU had reached.

    c. Controlling activities, eg, the production process.

    d. Controlling machinery, eg, the warehouse machine.

    e. Monitoring and testing, eg, testing VDU circuits.

49.18 The computer was able to give a number of benefits in the manufacturing processing. For example, it was able to keep such accurate information and tight control on the stock and production process that the amount of stock that needed to be held could be reduced, thus making savings. Also, it reduced labour costs because of the automation, it made savings because it was able to diagnose faults, and it helped to improve quality by aiding the monitoring and control process. Using a computer for things like the automated test equipment also meant that the equipment could continue to be used even if the design of the VDUs changes because the computer could be reprogrammed with new tests.

49.19 Of course the computer does not provide all the answers. Automation of production seldom pays off unless the numbers of things being manufactured are quite large and what is being produced is fairly standard. The computer can also create problems, particularly if automation leads to job losses. This point will be discussed in a later chapter. However, it should be noted that computers can do relatively few of the jobs that humans can do, only the repetitive and boring ones in fact, and therefore they pose little threat to jobs provided we have a society that finds appropriate ways of employing people. The computer industry is also a source of many jobs.

ANALOG AND HYBRID COMPUTERS

49.20 Analog and hybrid computers were defined in (1.8). This part of the chapter deals with their advantages, uses and limitations. It also deals with analog/digital conversion and a special application called "process control".

49.21 In order to keep the subject matter more manageable we start with a separate discussion of analog computers. It must be emphasised, however, that **the main use of analog computing devices is as components in hybrid computer systems in which the major functions of the system are carried out by digital devices.**

49.22 **Uses of analog computers.** The various elements of an analog computer have electronic properties, which makes their behaviour analogous to a variety of known physical phenomena. For example, the variation in output current with changing input voltage may be comparable to the variation in water flow in a given physical system when subjected to changing pressures.

In such a situation the analog computer could be used to study the physical systems by **simulating** it at less expense. Common areas of use are **simulation** of:

a. Mechanical systems, eg, the suspension system of a truck.

b. Hydraulic systems, eg, irrigation.

c. Aircraft and missile flight.

d. Chemical systems, eg, chemical production in a factory.

e. Electrical systems, eg, grid supply.

Many of these systems can be described in terms of differential equations and so analog computers are of general use in the mathematical modelling and solving of differential equations.

49.23 **Time scaling**

The time scales on which analog computers simulate phenomena can be adjusted to suit the applications. Examples:

a. Simulating the movement of a glacier would require a contracted time scale to speed up the simulation in order that observations could be made in reasonable time.

b. At the other extreme the movement of a camera shutter would need a dilated time scale to slow down the simulation.

49.24 **Real-time** operation is on a unit time scale, ie, on the same time scale as the simulated events. In many of the applications mentioned so far in this chapter an analog computer can work effectively in real time where a digital computer would be hopelessly slow. When working in real time an analog computer can continuously monitor the behaviour of the system it simulates, thereby giving the chance to immediately detect faults within the real system. The method can be extended to give a **feedback** system, ie, the output from the real system can be examined by the analog computer, which will "feed back" appropriate controls to correct system performance. One example is on-board missile flight control, another is an automated chemical process.

49.25 **Limitations.** The two main limitations of analog devices are:

a. It can take a considerable time to prepare the computer to do a task because many components have to be physically moved or reconnected, ie, the **set-up** time is long.

b. Very accurate numerical values are hard to obtain without prohibitive expense being incurred.

BASIC ELEMENTS

49.26 The basic elements used in analog computers are illustrated below. Their physical structure is beyond the scope of this book. (The scale is not part of the circuit but used to illustrate the action of the device.)

a. Summers (perform addition).

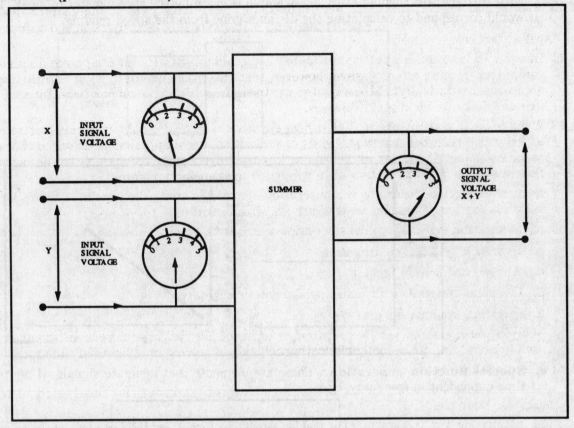

b. Multiplier (amplifies signals by a constant factor).

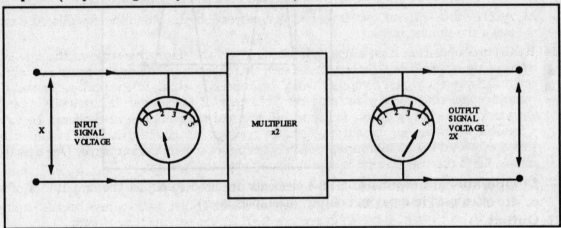

c. Potentiometer (corresponds to division or multiplication by a fraction).

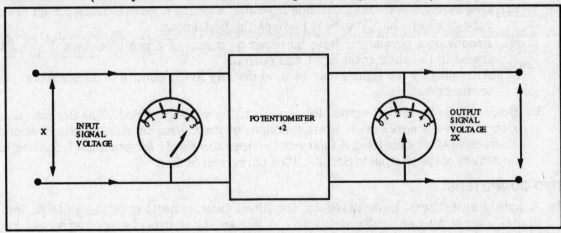

d. Integrator. Corresponds to the mathematical operation of integration. If you are unfamiliar with **integration** then an everyday example is given by the speedometer of a car. **Integration** would correspond to calculating the distance gone from the speed reading.

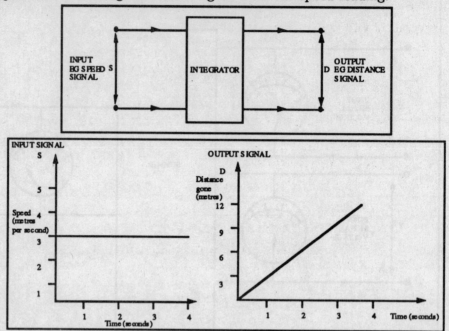

e. Special function generation. These are elements that generate signals whose magnitude is time dependent in some way, eg:

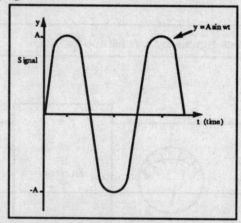

f. Operational amplifiers. These elements are used to adjust the amplitudes of signals. They are often used in input and output (examples later).

49.27 Output.

a. Two standard methods of output are:

i. Generating a trace on a cathode ray tube, which is a general name for an electronic display tube of which the TV tube is perhaps the best known.

ii. Producing a permanent trace on paper by means of a pen plotter: a device like those illustrated in the chapter on input and output.
Alternatively the signals may be used directly in the control of an operation of some process or machine.

b. Scaling. To be of use, output forms need to be suitably scaled. The horizontal axis is usually a time scale since most signals are functions of time. Real time is sometimes abandoned and an alternative time scale used if the events change too slowly for practical recording or satisfactory operation of the computer circuits. (See paragraph 50.23).

HYBRID COMPUTERS

49.28 A hybrid system can be achieved by the direct interconnection (using suitable interfacing) of a digital computer to an analog computer. A purpose-built hybrid computer would have the analog and digital elements combined within the same processor and would probably be built for a specific task. Most hybrid computers are of the former type with the analog components being mostly confined to peripherals with special purposes in instrumentation or the control and monitoring of physical devices.

49.29 Advantages.

a. The hybrid computer combines the analog advantage of continuous real-time response and immediate mathematical operation with digital advantages of storage capacity, easy programming and accuracy.

b. The digital computer can store an instruction repertoire for controlling the analog device, thus avoiding analog programming using a plug-in technique. The analog device can interrupt digital operation at the appropriate time when a response is needed, eg, when the process under control needs action.

c. The digital device can edit analog output or use it as a starting point to obtain a more accurate result.

ANALOG/DIGITAL CONVERSION

49.30 Any hybrid system requires units to convert analog output signals into digital representation, and units to convert digital codes into analog settings. A device that converts analog signals to digital codes is called a digitiser. The units' names are often abbreviated to D/A converter and A/D converter (digitiser).

NB. Digital computers may also use A/D and D/A conversion for some types of input and output, so these conversions are not just important for analog and hybrid computing.

49.31 Accuracy and Resolution. Accuracy indicates the closeness of the converted value to the true value, whilst resolution is the size of the steps between converted values, eg, a signal of 100mV or 100.5mV if the resolution was in units of 0.5 mV.

49.32 Input and output arrangements:

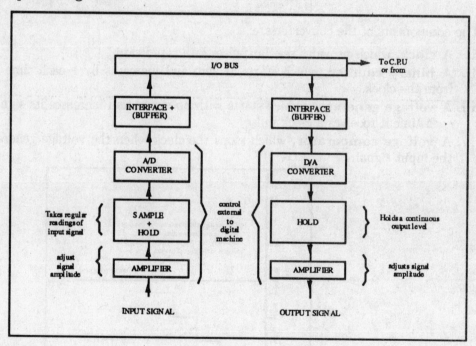

49.33 An Analog/digital converter (Digitiser). This process can be repeated rapidly to give frequent conversion readings.

a. Conversion Table.

Analog Signals (eg, Volts)	Binary Code
0 –	0 0 0
1 –	0 0 1
2 –	0 1 0
3 –	0 1 1
4 –	1 0 0
5 –	1 0 1
6 –	1 1 0
7 – 8	1 1 1

b. Main Features.

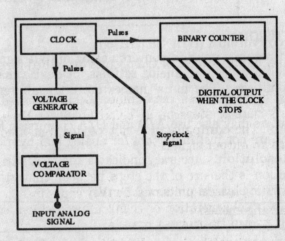

c. The components of the converter are:

i. **A clock,** which provides regular pulses at a rapid rate.

ii. **A binary counter,** which starts at zero and increases by 1 each time it receives a pulse from the clock.

iii. **A voltage generator,** which starts with no signal and increases its signal size by one unit each time it receives a clock pulse.

iv. **A voltage comparator,** which stops the clock when the voltage generator signal exceeds the input signal.

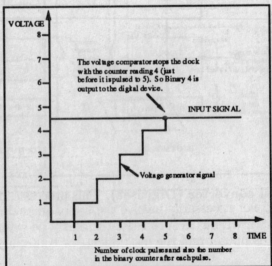

49.34 Optical method.

Example. The rotational speed of a shaft (perhaps on a disc drive) may be measured by coding zones on an optical disc using light and dark areas. A photo sensor is then used to read the code.

Gray's Code is normally used for coding the optical disc (7.26).

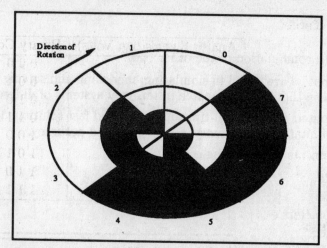

49.35 Digital/Analog conversion (D/A Conversion).

This can be achieved by the reverse of the process described for A/D conversion. The differences are these:

The binary counter is loaded with the number to be converted and is run backwards as the clock runs. The voltage generator steps up as before, but this time the process stops when the binary counter reaches zero. The **comparator** is not needed, but a hold circuit is needed to maintain the generator voltage as an output signal.

PROCESS CONTROL

49.36 a. The direct control of physical processes, be they experiments, machine operation or the large-scale plant used in electrical generation or chemical production, can be achieved by the use of hybrid systems. This is known as **process control.**

b. This application may exploit the combined features of hybrid machines.

c. If the digital processor forming part of a process-control system is also performing other processing tasks it is usual to give the analog input the highest priority in any interrupt system since immediacy of response may be vital.

d. Specialist high-level languages are available for these applications, eg, Ada and Coral-66.

49.37 Simplified example of a working arrangement.

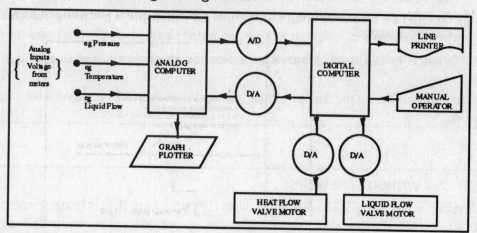

49.38 Process control need not necessarily involve the use of an analog or hybrid computer. In many cases digital computers are used, but in such cases there may be extensive use of D/A and A/D converters between the digital computer and the instruments or controls to which it is connected.

SUMMARY

49.39 a. Some of the uses of computers in manufacturing were illustrated by an example based upon a production line on which VDUs were made.

b. The computer is very well suited to monitoring and controlling mechanised processes in which the same or very similar tasks are done repeatedly many times and where the decision making necessary is easy to reduce to simple rules.

c. The three types of computer are:

i. Digital.

ii. Analog.

iii. Hybrid (a combination of the other two).

d. Analog computers are useful in simulating, modelling and solving problems concerned with physical phenomena that are describable in terms of systems of differential equations.

e. Analog computers provide real-time operation and fast solutions to some analytical problems but suffer from limitations in memory, set-up time and accuracy.

f. Standard elements in an analog computer are:

i. Summers.

ii. Multipliers.

iii. Potentiometers.

iv. Integrators.

v. Special-function generators.

g. Hybrid computers combine the features of analog and digital devices. They are often purpose built and interconnection of the analog and digital units requires A/D or D/A converters plus suitable interfacing.

POINTS TO NOTE

49.40 a. Most examinations are concerned with comparative features of analog and digital devices in relation to applications, and often require details of A/D, D/A conversion.

b. **Array processors** are extra-fast processing units which can perform high-precision arithmetic at speed by performing an array of "sequential" arithmetic operations in parallel. In the future they may be able to compete favourably with analog computers in many real-time applications.

STUDENT SELF-TESTING QUESTIONS

1. a. Describe, with numerical illustrations, each of the following codes, stating one advantage of each code:

   i. Excess-three code.

   ii. Gray's (or cyclic) Code.

   b. Explain how an analog computer represents and displays numerical information and state two advantages of using an analog computer to simulate physical problems.

   c. What is hybrid computing? Briefly describe an application of this form of computing.

   (AEB)

2. What is another name for an analog to digital converter? Explain how such a converter works.

QUESTIONS WITHOUT ANSWERS

3. A robot is required for the following task. Pick up a part that is lying at any place on a tray, but in the fixed orientation. Set it right way up and place it on an upright cone that is in a known place. The part has a socket in its base to fit the cone.

   a. Describe:

   i. the arm of the robot that would transfer the part and the way in which it would need to be linked to the computer controlling it;   (8)

   ii. the procedure by which the part could be collected, set upright and placed on the cone;   (6)

   iii. a convenient way of setting up or programming the robot to follow this procedure.

   b. What would be considered in order to decide whether to use such a robot?   (6)

   (OLE)

GLOSSARY CHECKLIST

COMPUTERS IN CONTEXT

1. In this Part we take a broader view of computers in terms of their general setting historically and in society.

2. Throughout the rest of this manual every effort has been made to present the reader with a modern view of computers. The reader's understanding will be increased by also seeing how computing took place in the past and why it changed to what it is today. For that reason an account of the evolution of computer systems is provided in the following chapter.

3. In chapter 51 we look at the role of computers in society and consider issues that affect individuals and the organisations in which individuals use computers.

4. Examination requirements vary considerably in this subject area, which is often taught and assessed by means other than written examination. Therefore, the reader is advised to check his or her syllabus.

50: The Evolution of Computer Systems

INTRODUCTION

50.1 Most modern computers are based upon general design principles that were established during the 1940s and that have not changed greatly since then. In striking contrast, changes in technology have revolutionised the ways in which computers are made.

50.2 In this chapter we consider not only those changes that led to the creation of the first true computers in the 1940s but we also consider the changes that have taken place since then.

THE ORIGINS

50.3 In looking for the origins of computers it is useful first to consider the origins of the methods of representing and storing data.

50.4 In ancient times herdsmen devised rudimentary methods of counting in which the number of pebbles, sticks or scratches on stone corresponded to the number of animals in their care. At a later date the use of those simple scratches led to the idea of using stylised pictures or symbols to represent objects, numbers and ultimately languages. Such representations provided a means of storing information for subsequent retrieval and use. The use of inventories and libraries exemplify two aspects of the use of such data.

50.5 Modern computers provide sophisticated ways of providing these long-established facilities.

THE DEVELOPMENT OF CALCULATING DEVICES

50.6 Simple calculating devices were already in use over two thousand years ago. A notable example of such a device is the **abacus**, which is a mechanised pebble counter in which beads are strung on wires or strings held in a frame (see Fig. 50.1.) The beads are slid along the wires when counting, adding, etc.

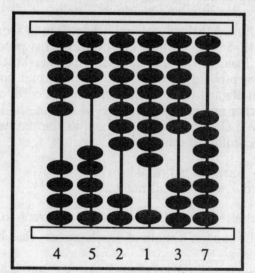

Fig. 50.1. A Simple Form of Abacus.

The abacus is still used today in parts of Asia.

50.7 The seventeenth century was the time for many significant developments:

    a. In 1614 **John Napier,** a Scottish mathematician, invented logarithms. Logarithms aid manual multiplication and division.

    b. In 1617 Napier devised a set of rods for use as multiplication aids. The rods were carved from bone and often called **"Napier's bones"**.

    c. In 1620 **William Oughtred,** an English parson, invented the **slide rule,** an **analog** calculating device that uses the principles of logarithms (Fig. 50.2).

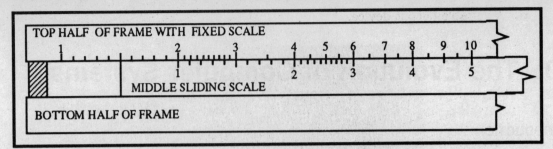

The middle scale has been positioned with the "1" against the "2" of the top scale so that multiples of 2 can be read off along the scale. Alternatively the scale shows divisions giving quotients of 2.

Fig. 50.2. A Section of a Simple Slide Rule.

d. In 1623 **Francis Bacon** made the first known use of binary codes for number representation.

e. In 1642 the French mathematician **Blaise Pascal** devised **the first true calculating machine**. It consisted of a series of six numbered dials and a ratchet "carry" mechanism. Addition and subtraction were straightforward, but multiplication and division were slow and laborious. Pascal's contribution to computing was given a mark of recognition in the late 1960s when Professor **Niklaus Wirth** of Zurich named his new programming language **"Pascal"**.

f. In 1671 the German mathematician **Gottfried von Leibniz** invented a calculating machine capable of true multiplication and division. The machine was a development of Pascal's idea. The new feature was a **shift mechanism**. Pascal had already devised a method of number complements for use in subtraction.

AUTOMATION

50.8　A major advance took place early in the nineteenth century through the brilliantly imaginative efforts of **Joseph Jacquard**, a French textile manufacturer. Between 1802 and 1804 Jacquard perfected a mechanical means of automatically controlling weaving looms to facilitate the production of woven cloth with complex patterns.

50.9　The machine, called "the Jacquard loom", was programmed by means of special punched cards, which stored information about the required patterns in the cloth. These punched cards were strung tightly together side by side in a long continuous strip.

They were automatically fed through a loom mechanism in sequence with the purpose of controlling the loom's weaving action. The pattern in woven cloth is produced by raising particular selections of warp thread (those fixed to the frame) each time the shuttle is passed across the frame. In the Jacquard loom each warp could be raised by an individual hook unless a sprung pin deflected the hook. If the sprung pin aligned with a hole in a punched card, one end of the pin would pass through the hole so that the other end of the pin failed to deflect the hook. Before each pass of the shuttle the next card was moved close to the pins. Then, as the mechanism operated, each warp was either raised or not raised according to the rule:

　　　Hole in card – warp thread raised.
　　　No hole in card – warp thread not raised.

50.10　The binary nature of the representation should be apparent to the reader.

50.11　Jacquard's loom was the start of a chain of developments that has lead to the robot-operated factory production lines of today.

50.12　The automation of calculations was attempted within a few years of Jacquard's invention by **Charles Babbage** a Professor of Mathematics at Cambridge University. In 1822 Babbage demonstrated a small working model of his **"difference engine"** to the Royal Society. The demonstration won government backing for Babbage, who wished to produce a larger machine able to generate reliable astronomical and mathematical tables containing values accurate to 20 decimal places. The machine was never completed because of mechanical difficulties. However, Babbage's researches led him to develop the concept of an **"analytic engine"**, essentially a general-purpose automatic calculator, which he designed in 1834. Its design owed much to Jacquard's invention and incorporated many features present in modern computers:

a. Data and program instructions fed in via a device using a suitable medium (punched cards).

b. Storage facilities for data and instructions.

c. A mechanised unit for calculation – a "mill".

d. A suitable output device.

An 80-column punched card on top of loom cards

of the same type as those used by Joseph Jacquard.

50.13 Lady Ada Lovelace, an amateur mathematician and friend of Babbage, produced supporting material for the analytic engine in the form of programs and explanatory documentation. It may be argued that Lady Lovelace was the first programmer. The programming language "ada" has been named after her.

50.14 Computer logic. An important theoretical development occurred between 1847 and 1854 as **George Boole,** an English logician, devised an algebraic system, now called "Boolean algebra", for representing and manipulating logical expressions. The full significance of these developments was not realised at the time.

50.15 Hermann Hollerith. Dr. Herman Hollerith was a census statistician at the US census bureau in the mid-1880s. At that time the bureau was still trying to count results from the 1880 census and saw little prospect of completing the count before the next census, which was scheduled for 1890. Hollerith proposed a mechanised solution to the problem that was based upon equipment handling punched cards. His idea was to "code" the data by representing it by punched-hole combinations on the cards. Some equipment was used to punch holes in the card. Other equipment was able to process the data by detecting holes in the cards. Electrical contacts brushed the cards and made contact through holes in the cards as the cards passed through the device. These devices were called **tabulators.** Tabulators were also used for the semi-automatic selection and sorting of cards.

50.16 The impact of Hollerith's methods was very striking. Whereas the census of 1880 on 50 million citizens had taken over 7 years to complete, the census of 1890 on 63 million citizens took only 3 years to complete.

50.17 These ideas were exploited further by the development of devices rather like difference engines fed with cards that could perform calculations like those designed by Babbage. Other developments continued in the commercial application of these machines.

50.18 Hollerith set up his own company, "The Computing Tabulating Recording Company", which later became the International Business Machine Corporation (IBM), which today is by far the largest computer manufacturer in the world.

THE DEVELOPMENT OF ELECTRICAL AND ELECTRONIC METHODS

50.19 Recording devices, valves and switching circuits. In 1900 **Valdemar Poulson** was developing recording devices that used media consisting of tapes and drums coated with thin films of magnetic material. These were the forerunners of a host of modern devices, including domestic audio-tape records, cassette recorders, video cassette recorders and, of particular interest, computer-data storage devices, including several versions also using magnetic tape. An even more significant technological advance took place in 1906 when **Lee de Forest** invented the **thermionic valve.** These resemble a squat cylindrical light bulb, glowing dimly, into which has been inserted a number of additional wires and metallic plates. Valves are able to amplify or switch electrical signals electronically, ie, without the movement of electrical or mechanical parts. Electronic switching is a vital feature within modern digital computers, and valves were the first devices to be employed for that purpose. Valves have since been superseded by newer and better alternatives.

50.20 The use of electronic switching circuits in computers is largely due to the fact that such circuits can be employed to perform logic and arithmetic. This fact was established in 1938 by **Claude Shannon**, an electrical engineer. Shannon showed how the hitherto theoretically Boolean algebra could be applied to practical problems of circuit design.

50.21 Another important theoretical step took place one year before Shannon's discovery, when in 1937 **Alan Turing,** a British mathematician, showed how *any* problem having a logical solution can be reduced to a solution based upon a small set of simple instructions. Modern computers are therefore able to solve very complex problems by the rapid application of a relatively small set of inbuilt operations.

50.22 **From electrical machines to electronic machines.**

a. **The Automatic Sequence-Controlled Calculator (ASCC)** – also called the **HARVARD MARK 1.**

The ASCC was a fully automatic electrically driven machine. Its development was started at Harvard University, USA, in 1937 by Professor **Howard Aiken** in conjunction with IBM.

Hollerith cards containing data or instructions were fed into the machine a few at a time and results were output onto punched cards or an electric typewriter. Aiken also developed punched paper tape as an input medium. The machine was completed in 1944. and was used until 1959.

b. **Early special-purpose electronic machines.**

i. During the Second World War electronic valve-based calculating machines called Z3 and Z4 were produced in Germany by **Konrad Zuse.** They are known to have been used for a time in 1941, and to have used stored programs to perform calculations, but they were later destroyed by Allied bombing.

ii. In Britain at the same time another valve-based machine called **COLOSSUS** was produced at the British Intelligence Establishment at Bletchley Park. **Alan Turing** was a member of staff on the project. The machine was used in 1943 to break a top-secret German code called ENIGMA.

c. **Electronic Numerical Integrator And Calculator (ENIAC).** This machine was developed by **J. Presper Eckert** and **John Mauchly** at Pennsylvania University and was completed by 1946. It was the electronic equivalent of the ASCC and contained some 18,000 valves. It could perform 5000 additions per second, and astonishing feat at the time, but consumed power at a rate of 150 kilowatts, which would be enough to heat a mansion, and needed to be water cooled.

50.23 **The Von Neumann Report.** In what is now a historic report **John Von Neumann** in 1946 set out a summary of the design requirements for the modern computer. The main points were:

a. Binary codes should be used for the representation of data and instructions in a way that would make no distinction between them, and allow them to be stored together and share the same storage space within the computer.

b. The computer should be able to process both data and instructions. This includes the modification of programs by programs.

These two principles contain within them the possibilities for the controlled modification and manipulation of data and instructions under one automatic process.

COMPUTER GENERATIONS WITH CHANGING TECHNOLOGY

50.24 **The first generation.** The "first-generation" computers were valve-based machines based upon Von Neumann's design principles. Starting with the first they included:

a. **Electronic Delay Storage Automatic Computer (EDSAC).**

This machine was built at Cambridge University by M.V. Wilkes and first ran in May 1949.

b. **Electronic Discrete Variable Automatic Computer (EDVAC).** This machine was built at Pennsylvania University, the home of ENIAC, and was completed in 1950.

c. **Automatic Computer Engine (ACE).** This was built at the National Physics Laboratory in 1951.

d. **Lyons Electronic Office (LEO).** This was the *first commercial computer* and it was produced in 1951 by **M.V. Wilkes.**

e. UNIVAC-1. This machine was produced by UNIVAC (Universal Accounting Company) in 1951. The company was set up by Eckert and Maunchly.

50.25 **The Transistor** was invented in 1948 by a team of scientists head by **William Shockley** at the Bell Laboratories in America. Transistors are made from materials called **semiconductors**, principally silicon (the main element in sand and rock), and germanium. A transistor is produced by "doping" layers of crystal with impurities that drastically alter the electrical properties of each layer.

50.26 Transistors are able to perform similar operations to valves, eg, amplification or switching, but they are simpler to manufacture, less prone to failure, cheaper, smaller, consume less power and have a longer life. They have replaced valves in all but a few specialist applications. Transistors and developments from them are often called **solid-state devices.**

50.27 Simple transistor circuits called **bistables** (two stable states) or **flip-flops** are of particular importance. They can be built to flip from one state to the other and back again in a clock-like fashion, or be built to hold either state until switched to the other by a single electrical pulse. These bistable states suggest the possibilities for using them for storing binary-coded data.

50.28 **The second generation.** "Second-generation" computers used transistors instead of valves. The use of transistors reduced size, manufacturing costs and running costs, and improved reliability and processing power. Early second-generation models were the IBM 7000 series and LEO mark 111. In 1962 Manchester University completed what was probably the best-known second-generation machine, the **ATLAS.** Atlas used **magnetic disk storage** and exploited the features of disk storage very well.

50.29 During the second generation manufacturers moved towards making computers of **modular construction.** A suitable combination of processing, storage, input and output units could be assembled from a range of possible modules in order to meet the particular needs of each customer.

50.30 Also at that time there were major advances in computer language away from codes directly usable by the machine (ie, machine language) and towards the "natural" languages of English and mathematics. The first of the **"high-level languages"** called **FORTRAN** (FORmula TRANslation) was released in 1957. Over the next few years many other new languages appeared. (See chapter 36.)

50.31 **Integrated circuits.** After the invention of the transistor it was realised that the properties of semiconductors would allow the production of entire electronic circuits within single crystals. The name **Integrated Circuit (IC)** was adopted for such units. The first IC was patented by **Harwick Johnson** of RCA in 1953, although the inventor is said to be **Jack Kilby** of the USA. Later developments resulted from:

a. The application of photo engraving to IC manufacture,

b. the use of layers of silicon oxide insulation in order to build up multiple layers of crystal circuitry.

The latter of these two methods is often referred to as **MOS technology (Metal-Oxide-Semiconduct**

50.32 **The third generation.** "Third-generation" computers using integrated circuits were first released onto the market in 1964. Two of the successful first series of third-generation computers were the IBM 360 series and the ICL 1900 series.

50.33 **LSI and VLSI** have been discussed in several earlier chapters and therefore do not require further detailed discussion here. One important LSI development that does deserve another mention here is the microprocessor. The first microprocessor was the model 4004 produced by the Intel Corporation in 1972.

THE PRESENT AND THE FUTURE

50.34 Technological advances continue to make an even greater number of applications cost effective to computerise. For example, office automation and home computing have increased dramatically over recent years.

50.35 Magnetic media costs have fallen relative to paper costs so that computerised filing systems are cheaper than conventional systems for many applications. Some predictions imply that magnetic media will be cheaper than paper for all but a few applications within eight years.

50.36 The developments in distributed systems and networks, together with advances in databases, have placed the computer systems of today into a position to play a far greater role within the organisations they serve. At the same time we see computers being successfully employed for many new applications all the time.

50.37 There are still many problems to be faced, however. Greater reliance on computers calls for greater reliability. More applications areas means the need for more software. The more widespread use of computers means the need for systems that are easy for almost anyone to use.

50.38 Although hardware costs have fallen, software development costs continue to rise. Modern methods of analysis, design and programming attempt to tackle the problem of software cost and produce systems that meet the user's requirements to a high standard of reliability.

50.39 Even more radical approaches to solving these problems are being taken, such as the design of new machine architecture and new types of programming languages.

50.40 Considerably more effort will need to be made in solving such problems as those of human/machine communication, the so called "Human-computer interface".

50.41 Clearly, computers have come a long way in the last fifty years and who can say what state of development they may be at in another fifty years? It is not inconceivable that the changes may be even greater than in the past. However, the really major questions concerning computers and the future are not technical ones but questions about how people, organisations and society at large will use them and regard them.

SUMMARY

50.42 a. This chapter has traced the origins of modern computers.

b. The work of a number of computer pioneers was described. Here is a checklist of names: John Napier, William Oughtred, Francis Bacon, Blaise Pascal, Niklaus Wirth, Gottfried von Leibnitz, Joseph Jacquard, Charles Babbage, Ada Lovelace, George Boole, Hermann Hollerith, Valdermar Poulson, Lee de Forest, Claude Shannon, Alan Turing, Howard Aiken, Konrad Zuse, J Presper Eckert, John Mauchly, John Von Neumann, M.V. Wilkes, William Shockley, Harwick Johnson and Jack Kilby.

c. Technical innovations, followed by advances in manufacturing methods, have made the use of computers in many situations not only technically feasible but also cost effective. The range of cost-effective applications is broadening all the time.

GLOSSARY CHECKLIST

Abacus	50.6	ENIAC	50.22
ACE	50.24	IC	50.31
Analytic engine	50.12	LEO	50.24
ASCC	50.22	MOS	50.31
ATLAS	50.28	Napier's bones	50.7
COLOSSUS	50.22	Solid state device	50.26
Difference engine	50.12	Tabulator	50.15
EDSAC	50.24	Thermionic valve	50.19
EDVAC	50.24	UNIVAC-1	50.24

51: Computers in Society

INTRODUCTION

51.1   The role of computers in society is a large subject to consider and this chapter merely highlights some important issues. Computers are just one example of automation although they have many special features. In a society that relies heavily on all forms of automation and on the automated handling of information, computers are bound to be very important. Issues related to jobs and privacy are particularly significant.

COMPUTERS IN INFORMATION TECHNOLOGY

51.2   It is generally recognised that we live in an industrial society in which the efficiency of production of wealth depends heavily on various kinds of automation. Computers are special in that they *automate many methods of processing information.* Computers are also playing an ever increasing role in many other forms of automation.

51.3   Computers, telecommunications equipment, and other technologies associated with automation, come under the general heading of **Information Technology (IT)**. Information technology is having an impact on individuals, organisations and society. Various aspects of this impact will be discussed in the remainder of this chapter. Particular reference will be made to computers, and some key issues, notably privacy and employment.

THE GENERAL BACKGROUND

51.4   Prior to industrialisation approximately 90% of the labour force was engaged in agriculture, ie, society was agrarian. Methods of communication were limited and a very small proportion of the labour force was involved with the processing, storage and retrieval of information, which in any case merely involved manual paper-based methods or word of mouth.

Industrialisation produced a major shift in the labour force, with the proportion involved in agriculture falling below 10% in the UK. With industrialisation came the beginning of information technology and the start of a series of IT developments, bringing us right up to the present day: telegraph, telephone, radio/TV, computers, micro-electronics, etc.

51.5   These new forms of IT, and other developments, produced new forms of work. The larger scale of organisations has given rise to large administrative structures in which there are large numbers of clerical workers and people with technical and managerial skills collectively known as "white-collar workers". Computerisation has mainly affected white-collar work so far.

51.6   In addition to changes in the type of work there has been an increase in the number of organisations involved in activities other than manufacture. Some such organisations, for example those in the power industries, contribute to manufacturing and provide a general service. As a result of this change only 25% of the labour force remained in organisations directly involved in the manufacture of goods. For a number of reasons, not particularly related to IT, that 25% has fallen to 20% in the last few years and levels of unemployment have risen.

51.7   The fact that so few remain in manufacture, although manufacturing continues to generate most wealth, has lead to society today being called the "post-industrial society".

51.8   Looking at the whole of the national and international community, and at the way organisations are run, highlights the fact that modern society is heavily dependent on the communication, processing and storage of information. It is claimed by some that we are moving towards an "information society" in which the majority of the labour force will be engaged in **Information Processing (IP)** and the use of **Information Technology (IT)**.

51.9   It is a mistake to imagine that technological innovation is what causes such changes. Such changes are the collective result of actions taken by those people able to control and influence the use and distribution of resources, within their own organisations, or within society at large. The uses of resources are determined by the goals that are being pursued. The next section looks at these issues.

ORGANISATIONS

51.10   The uses of computers in various kinds of organisations have been discussed in a number of earlier chapters. The term "organisation" was used fairly informally. However, it is possible to be more formal in defining what an organisation is and doing so highlights some significant points.

51.11 An **organisation** is a human group that has been deliberately constructed with the aim of seeking specific goals. An organisation will be reconstructed, from time to time, so that it can continue to seek its goals effectively.

51.12 The goals sought will depend on the organisation.

Examples.

a. The owners of commercial organisations may have profit as their goal with themselves as the main beneficiaries, eg, in private or public companies.

b. The goals of many organisations are to provide "services" to their clients or the general public, eg, medical services, schools and colleges.

c. Other organisations have the mutual benefit of their members as goals, eg, clubs or trade unions.

51.13 Any organisation needs to be controlled and coordinated and to be able to plan ahead. To do so it will need information and facilities to communicate.

51.14 In most organisations, and particularly in large ones, information technology can aid in the processing of information and thereby help the organisation to meet its goals. Whether or not an organisation uses such technology will depend on its evaluation of the technology in relation to its own goals.

EVALUATION OF INFORMATION SYSTEMS

51.15 There are many methods of evaluating new methods and technologies. In the area of computerisation the main methods are those used in systems development (chapters 44 – 47). A proposed computer system is evaluated in terms of how well it can meet objectives that will enable the organisation to meet goals such as optimum service or optimum use of resources.

51.16 The results of such evaluations determine whether organisations invest in computers. This in turn promotes or limits technological developments.

51.17 Large organisations such as government bodies or large corporations can have a major influence in this way. For example the US government attached a high importance to microelectronics and silicon chip technology because of the goals of providing national defence. That depended on having miniaturised electronic circuitry in rockets, aircraft, etc. The necessary research and development costs were provided from the defence budget.

COMPUTERISATION AND WORK

51.18 When computers are introduced into organisations because of the benefits they can provide, it usually affects the work of staff within the organisation. Some jobs are changed, some may be created and some may be lost. This creates a demand for training and retraining.

51.19 Any loss of jobs due to computerisation can give rise to alarm, particularly at a time of high unemployment. However, such job "losses" probably signify yet another shift in the work of the general labour force, as has happened many times in the past.

51.20 Only a very small proportion of the current level of unemployment is directly attributable to new technology. In certain particular applications jobs are likely to be lost, notably:

a. some office jobs, eg, caused by word processing.

b. Factory production, where industrial robots may replace production-line workers.

51.21 Whether these job losses will result in permanent unemployment is another matter. It depends on the process of redeployment of labour and labour retraining. It may help to consider an example at this stage.

51.22 In the USA in the early 1970s there were proposals to introduce bar-coded PoS equipment into supermarkets. This appeared to be an attractive proposition because a saving of $100 million could be achieved if such equipment was introduced into 5000 stores.

51.23 Initially there was alarm from the trade unions, who predicted 20% job losses by 1975, the date at which implementation was due to be completed.

51.24 These fears were unfounded for two reasons. First, the rate at which the new technology was introduced was much slower, which allowed staffing changes to be dealt with by redeployment and natural wastage. By 1979 only 803 stores had equipment installed. Very different from the predicted 5000 by 1975. The trade unions were also able to negotiate an automation deal with their employers. This protected their jobs. The store owners were still able to make large savings by the introduction of the equipment, and to redeploy staff in ventures that improved and extended company activities. (In Britain the banks have also used automation to allow them to redeploy staff in broader and better services.)

51.25 Since these early difficulties were overcome, the introduction of the equipment has continued smoothly in the USA and at an increasing rate. In Britain this kind of supermarket automation has happened more smoothly.

PRIVACY

51.26 Another consequence of higher levels of computerisation is the increase in the use of computer-based equipment to store large quantities of data about individuals. Some of this data is of a particularly personal or private nature and there is a natural concern that it should not be misused. There is also concern that individuals may have personal information stored about them without their knowledge or control, and that it may be hard or impossible to find out whether such information is accurate.

51.27 In 1975 a government white paper considered this issue and in 1976 a committee was set up chaired by Sir Norman Lindop. The idea was that systems dealing with records containing personal details should be controlled.

51.28 The Lindop report appeared about two years later and was well received. It established a number of principles, eg, that stored data should only be used for the purpose for which its use was originally authorised and intended. The report suggested that a **Data Protection Authority (DPA),** should be set up, which would enforce codes of conduct for different types of systems.

51.29 At about the same time, the Council of Europe set up a "Convention for the Protection of Individuals with regard to Automatic Processing of Personal Data". Each country signs twice, once to agree to legislate and the second time when it has legislated. Britain had only signed once by early 1984 and computer organisations such as the BCS (British Computer Society) and CSA (Computer Services Association) had expressed fears that delays could cost the UK dearly in terms of lost international contracts through failure to introduce legislation.

51.30 Such legislation is the primary responsibility of the Home Office, itself an important user of computer data banks of an unusual kind, eg, those concerned with police records like those held on the Police National Computer at Hendon (North London).

51.31 A further government white paper appeared early in 1982. It only covered some aspects of data protection. In April 1983 a Bill began its passage through Parliament, but ran into initial trouble over the issue of confidentiality. The Bill was lost when the general election was called. It was reintroduced in a slightly modified form, becoming an Act in 1984.

THE 1984 DATA PROTECTION ACT

51.32 The 1984 Data Protection Act was intended "to regulate the use of automatically processed information relating to individuals and the provision of services in respect of such information". What is immediately apparent is that the Act does not cover manual records. This fact is not only a disappointment to those concerned with freedom of information but may also be a discouragement to the use of computers for some applications.

51.33 The Act defines a number of terms including "data" (information in a processable form), "personal data" (data relating to identifiable living individuals) and "data subject" (the living individuals concerned).

51.34 The Act requires those using personal data to register with the **Data Protection Registrar**. The end of April 1986 was set as the deadline for initial registrations for existing users.

51.35 There are a number of general and specific exemptions. These exemptions are the subject of considerable controversy and practical difficulties. At the general level there are exemptions for a number of government departments for reasons stated to be related to national security and covering some aspects of criminal records, immigration, health and social security. More specifically, there are exemptions for work such as word processing, pensions, accounting and payroll. However, these exemptions are rather weak in that if the system under consideration carries out other tasks it may not be exempt. For example, if the payroll system is used for anything more than calculating and paying wages it will not be exempt.

51.36 An organisation may easily make a genuine mistake in interpreting these rules but will still be liable to criminal prosecution. Therefore, it is not surprising that many organisations have appointed an expert whose sole responsibility is to deal with matters concerned with the Act. The title for such a post is normally that of **data protection officer.**

51.37 In future, it will be important for all staff involved in data processing to have an awareness of what the Act covers so that they know when to consult a data protection officer for specific advice.

51.38 The main points covered by the Act that need to be borne in mind are:

    a. Data about individuals that is held for processing must have been obtained fairly for a specific lawful purpose.

    b. The data must only be used for the specific purpose and may only be disclosed in accordance with the specific purpose.

    c. Data must not be excessive for the purpose but merely adequate and relevant.

    d. Data must be accurate, up to date and kept no longer than necessary.

    e. The data must be protected and held securely against unauthorised access or loss but must be accessible to data subjects on request.

COMPUTER CRIME

51.39 Three aspects of computer crime are often reported in the media and deserve a mention here because of their social importance.

    a. Hacking and Computer fraud

    b. Computer viruses

    c. Copyright piracy

    d. Originally the term "hacker" meant a programmer who worked in an skillful but undisciplined way. More recently the name has become associated with individuals who make a hobby of making unauthorised access to computer systems, especially via dial-in lines or across computer networks. Although the individuals concerned often regard their activities as a game this anti-social behaviour often leads to loss and inconvenience to the individuals affected by the hackers. Legislation has now been passed in many countries, including the UK, to make hacking illegal in most cases. The methods used by hackers to bypass system security are often very similar to those used by individuals concerned in computer fraud. Those working with computer systems have a responsibility to make their own systems as safe and secure as possible.

    e. **A computer virus** is a piece of software which attaches itself to an another program on a system in order both to spread itself to other programs and to have some undesirable affect on the programs it becomes attached to. The parallels with the way in which a biological virus affects other organisms gave rise to the term "computer virus". Computer viruses usually infect system by being introduced via disks which have already been infected. When a virus infected program is run the virus, which has modified its host, is able to replicate itself. Some viruses are merely annoying, such as the one which causes a small dot to wander randomly on the screen. Others are downright nasty like those which cause data on disks to be corrupted or deleted. There are many virus detection packages on the market today.

    f. **Software Piracy** occurs when individuals use unauthorised copies of software. It is just like any other breach of copyright and the individuals or companies responsible can face stiff penalties.

THE FUTURE

51.40 The current rapid rate of computerisation and technical innovation has lead some people to talk of a "micro-electronics revolution". To others these changes are merely viewed as another phase in the process of automation that started with the industrial revolution. Either way it seems reasonable to expect change and yet more change in the future.

51.41 The "fifth-generation" super-computers may well be here by the end of the century if current research-and-development programmes keep to schedule. Who can say whether these computers will cause delight or dismay? The answers do not rest in the technology.

SUMMARY

51.42 a. The place of computers in information technology was discussed.

    b. The general background to the current state of computerisation in society was given.

    c. Organisations were defined and their role in computerisation was discussed.

    d. Computerisation and its impact on employment was discussed.

    e. Privacy and recent development in data protection were discussed.

    f. The future was considered briefly.

POINTS TO NOTE

51.43 a. Computerisation is not just a matter of technological innovation and development. It is a process that involves individuals, organisations and society in general.

GLOSSARY CHECKLIST

Revision Test Questions

1. What is understood by the terms high-level and low-level when applied to programming languages? Write down three major factors that influence the decision to write a program in a low-level language rather than a high-level language.

   Describe, with the aid of a flow diagram or its equivalent, how the number of binary ones in a computer word could be counted using an assembly language.

   (11)

   (Welsh)

2. Table A represents a dump in hexadecimal of part of the memory of a particular computer.

   Table A

address								
C800	0D67	C80A	15A6	0D68	00F0	C810	8C10	6932
C808	C81F	1329	0015	C804	C811	4349	5963	0000
C810	1234	C80E	2FFF	0000	0000	36BA	C8FF	0000

   a. For each of the following locations, convert the contents given in Table A from the form indicated to the desired interpretation:

      i.   location C803   encoded as a two's complement integer to interpret as a decimal number

      ii. Location C809   encoded as four 8421 weighted BCD digits to interpret as a four digit decimal number

      iii. location C80D   encoded as two ASCII characters, to interpret as two characters where hex 42 = character "A".

      (3 marks)

   b. Table B shows a set of assembler mnemonics, together with their effects, available on this computer.

      Table B

Function	Operand	Description
CLR	n	set the contents of location n to zero
STA	n	Stores the contents of the accumulator in location n
LDA	n	loads the accumulator with the contents of location n
SUB	n	subtracts the contents of location n from the accumulator assuming two's complement arithmetic
INC	n	increments the contents of location n
BEQ	n	branches to location n if the accumulator equals zero
BPL	n	branches to location n if the sign bit of the accumulator is not set
BR	n	unconditional branch to location n
RETURN		return from subroutine
@		appended to any instruction implies an indirect address

      An assembly language subroutine written using these mnemonics is shown below. This subroutine operates upon data indicated by the parameter passed in the 16-bit accumulator.

      i. Given that the subroutine is called with the accumulator containing the hex value "C800" and as a consequence operates upon the data shown in Table A, show the contents of the accumulator and the data locations MAX and TEMP after each iteration.

      (12 marks)

ii. Describe the function of this subroutine.   *(5 marks)*

```
START   CLR    MAX
LOOP    BEQ    EXIT
        STA    TEMP
        LDA    MAX
        SUB @  TEMP
        BPL    NEXT
        LDA @  TEMP
        STA    MAX
NEXT    INC    TEMP
        LDA @  TEMP
        BR     LOOP
EXIT    LDA    MAX
        RETURN
```

(AEB)

3. Suggest **two** reasons why it is often difficult to transfer data and programs from one type of computer to another.
(2 marks)

(AEB 1988)

4. Describe briefly what is meant by **three** of the following:

   i. multiprogramming

   ii. hybrid computation

   iii. virtual storage

   iv. optical character recognition

   v. interactive computing

(BSC)

5. In a multi-tasking operating system the dispatcher is responsible for selecting the most suitable process to run.

   a. Distinguish between a program and a process.   *(4 marks)*

   b. Explain the following three states a process may be in:

      i. running,

      ii. runnable,

      iii. unrunnable.   *(6 marks)*

   c. Describe **two** different methods a dispatcher could employ for selecting the most suitable process to run. *(6 marks)*

   d. State **two** circumstances in which the dispatcher is invoked.   *(4 marks)*

(AEB)

6. What is meant by batch process?

   Describe a typical example of the application of this technique that involves the sorting and sequencing of a transaction tape and the updating of a master file.

(AEB Specimen paper)

7. a. Four binary input signals are denoted by a, b, c, d where abc represents an octal integer and d is a control signal. An output signal x is required where $x = 1$ if d = 1 and abc represents 2, 3, 6 or 7, and $x = 1$ if d = 0 and abc represents 2 or 3, otherwise $x = 0$. Draw up a table to represent the above system of signals and sketch an equivalent logic diagram using AND, OR and NOT elements.   12

   b. What is an analog device? Briefly discuss, with the aid of an example, how such a device may be used in conjunction with a digital computer.   (8)

(AEB)

8. a. Explain the difference between an operand and an operand address as used with reference to an assembly language. State **four** ways in which the address part of a machine-level instruction may be used and give an example of each.   (6)

b. Describe one method of representing alphanumeric characters for storage in a fixed word length of 24 bits. State **two** machine-code operations that are desirable for the internal manipulation of such characters. (3)

c. Describe, with the aid of a diagram, **one** method of storing data items based on the principle of *last in-first out*. Draw flow diagrams to show how an item of data can be removed from the store you have described and how an item of data can be input, incorporating tests to examine whether the store is full or empty as necessary. (11)

(AEB)

9. a. Explain, with the aid of a block diagram, how the major functional units of a simple computer are interrelated with respect to the flow of information (ie, instructions and data) and the flow of control commands.

Note : *Use firm lines to show the information flow and dotted lines to show flow of control commands.* (7)

b. Draw a flow diagram to represent the basic process of the fetch-execute cycle in the control unit of a typical computer, naming and stating the functions of any special registers involved. Your diagram should show how the cycle takes account of jumps, address modification and indirect addressing.

Note: *You are not required to discuss or represent the electronic circuitry of the control unit.* (13)

(AEB)

10. Explain the functions of the following personnel in a computer installation and outline how their jobs interrelate.

a. Computer Manager, (4)

b. Systems Analyst, (6)

c. Programmer, (5)

d. Computer Operator. (5)

(AEB)

11. a. What is meant by *multiprocessing, networks, message switching* and *terminals*? (3, 3, 3, 3)

b. Backing storage for a network can be distributed, or concentrated at a point, or both. Discuss the advantages of these arrangements in relation to the type of work to be done. (8)

c. A network can be provided with intelligent terminals (terminals with processing power). Describe an application for this and explain why it would be an advantage. (5)

(OLE)

12. a. Explain the term *subroutine* and describe the purpose of subroutines. (3 marks)

b. How do *open* subroutines differ from closed subroutines? What advantage does the closed subroutine offer over the open variety? (5 marks)

c. A subroutine is stored from locations 1199 to 1250 inclusive. It will be called from location 499 and location 699 in the main program. Using these store locations:

i. explain the problem of subroutine linkage - the problem of organising return addresses when calling a subroutine from different points in the main program.

ii. describe **two** methods of solving the linkage problem. (8 marks)

d. The subroutine in (c) evaluates a result (R) given a parameter (X).
Explain:

i. how the value of parameter X might be passed from the main program to the subroutine.

ii. how the value of result R might be returned to the main program on completion of the subroutine. (4 marks)

(AEB)

13. i. Convert the following BASIC expression into a Reverse Polish form in which the variables appear in the same order as in the original expression.

$$A* (B + C) - (D/E)$$

(2 marks)

ii. Why is the Reverse Polish form of an expression such as this particularly convenient for processing during the execution of a program? (2 marks)

iii. Describe an algorithm, making use of a stack, that converts an expression such as that given in (i) into a Reverse Polish form. You should give a table indicating the priority of your operators. 6 marks

iv. Trace the algorithm you have given in (iii), using as input the expression in (i), by listing the contents of the stack, whenever these contents change. (5 marks)

(London)

14. a. The array T has numeric elements T (I) held in ascending order, when I ranges from 1 to 1000. Describe in either flowchart or pseudocode form a program to locate which, if any, element has the value N using the method known as binary search (binary chop). (10 marks)

b. Given below is a subset of the statements available in a particular assembly language. Write a program in this assembly language to load into the accumulator the element in Ith row and Jth column of an array A, which has 14 rows and 10 columns. Include a statement to allocate space to this array assuming that each array element occupies one storage location.

The assembly language subset:

```
FRED:  DEF   n        reserves n storage locations naming the first FRED
       LDA   var      load the contents of the location called var into
                      the accumulator
       LDA   (var)    load the address of var into the accumulator
       ADD   var      add the contents of var to the accumulator contents
       MUL   n        multiply the accumulator contents by the value n
       LD1   var      load into the accumulator the contents of the
                      location whose address is in var
       STA   var      store the accumulator contents in var
       SUB   n        subtract value n from the accumulator contents.
```
(10 marks)

(AEB)

15. A real-time system is to be introduced by a newspaper to enable reporters to prepare articles using a video screen and keyboard terminal. The reporters would collect information and rearrange the text over a number of days, and then produce a finished article of a specified size. Indicate what the objectives of such a system would be.

Discuss the main features of the software required for this task and indicate how this software might incorporate facilities for the inclusion of photographs. (15 marks)

(London)

16. A firm of consultants is brought in by a company to advise it on the present manual invoicing system. A systems analyst is seconded to the company to study the system and prepare a report.

State three ways in which he can obtain information about the system, and outline the factors that must be considered before any recommendation can be made. (12 marks)

Assuming a computerised system is proposed, describe the tasks that would be delegated to the programmers, and how the analyst would ensure that the program suite produced would satisfy the system requirement.

State how the new system could be brought into use, giving one advantage and one disadvantage of your method of changeover. (8 marks)

(AEB)

17. Answer any *three* of the following five questions.

a. Explain briefly what is meant by a protocol for a computer network, and explain why a protocol is necessary.

b. Explain briefly why a *systematic method of program* development is desirable, and describe one example of such a method.

c. Explain briefly the need for *recovery* procedures in an information-retrieval system and describe one example of such a procedure.

d. Explain briefly what is meant by a *feasibility study* system design and describe what might happen if such a study were not carried out.

e. Explain briefly what is meant by the *privacy* of data, and give examples of how privacy could be protected by legislation. (12 marks)

(London)

18. a. Write notes on **two** of the following:

b. Database management systems and their objectives. (10 marks)

c. Computers and privacy. (10 marks)

d. Distributed processing systems. (10 marks)

e. Structured program design techniques. (10 marks)

(AEB)

19. a. Magnetic tape remains an important form of backing store despite the faster access time of magnetic disk.

   i. Suggest, with reasons, one use in which tape is preferable to disk as a backing-store medium.

   ii. Discuss the factors that influence the time required to read a file from magnetic tape.

   iii. Describe methods of reducing the likelihood of errors when either writing to tape or reading from tape. (10 marks)

   b. A small microcomputer system is employed to collect and print meteorological information. Part of the system records wind direction as indicated by a weather vane.

   i. With a labelled diagram, show how wind direction might be sensed and converted to binary form. (Illustrate the principle of the device and ignore practical complexities such as weather-proofing.)

   ii. With an explanation, state the absolute accuracy of your design.

   iii. Discuss the factors that influence the frequency with which the wind direction should be monitored and the occasions when it should be printed by the computer. (10 marks)

(AEB)

20. a. With the aid of an example, explain the term *single-address instruction format* as applied to binary machine-code instructions. (4 marks)

   b. The assembly-language instructions for addition, ADN 27, ADD 27 and ADI 27 will be executed in different ways because of their different modes of addressing (*immediate*, *direct* and *indirect*, respectively).

   i. Distinguish between these three modes, showing the effect of the instruction in each case. (6 marks)

   ii. Explain how the processor would distinguish between each mode of addressing when executing the machine-code instructions. Relate the explanation to the individual instruction format and to the appropriate steps in the execution cycle. (10 marks)

(AEB)

21. a. Describe **two** methods of addressing immediate-access store. Explain why each of the methods is useful, and indicate any disadvantages. 8

   b. Most computers have backing store such as disks and/or magnetic tapes as well as immediate-access store. Give **two** advantages and **one** disadvantage of having both kinds of store in a system. 6

   c. Give **one** application for which backing store is essential, saying why. For this application describe why and when transfer occurs between the two stores. 6 = 20

(JMB)

22. A certain computer that has 16-bit words uses the following instruction format.

function code	mode	n
6	2	8

(number of bits)

The mode bits are interpreted as follows:

00 immediate - n is the operand, an 8-bit signed value (in twos complement notation):

01 direct – n is the word address of the operand;

10 indirect – the content of word address n is the word address of the operand;

11 indexed – n plus the content of the index register is the word address of the operand.

Describe the steps in the machine instruction fetch and execute cycle for this computer, using the instruction LOAD (load the accumulator with the operand value) for illustration. (Cambridge)

23. Explain what is meant by a recursive routine in a program and how a stack may be used in its implementation. To illustrate your answer, show what happens for the function call fib(4) where the function fib has a single non-negative integer parameter n and has the value fibval given by

    if n < 2 then fibval : = n
    else fibval : = fib(n-1) + fib(n-2)

590

Show the order in which the calls to the function are made, the order in which the returns are made, and the data that are stacked at each call. Use diagrams wherever possible in your answer. (Cambridge)

24. a. Explain the difference between the terms "privacy of information" and "security of information". 4

b. Briefly describe two developments in computing that might increase public concern about privacy of information. 6

c. Briefly discuss and justify two steps that might be taken by government to alleviate such public concern. 6 = 16

(JMB)

25.

This diagram is a very simplified illustration of a part of a computer. An active program initiates a read operation for a particular block from the disk; after a certain interval the read operation has been completed and the program may proceed to process the data that has been read.

Describe the activities that take place in the central processing unit, in the disk drive and in the interface between them during the disk read operation. (Cambridge)

26. A function PRN is available which takes a single integer value as its argument. The function uses a pseudo-random number generator in such a way that a series of calls PRN (J) will return a series of pseudo-random integers uniformly distributed over the range 0, 1, 2.....J.

A program is required to simulate the throwing of a die many times, until three consecutive sixes are thrown, to perform this task several times, and to print the average number of throws required to achieve three consecutive sixes.

Either write such a program, clearly annotated, in a programming language of your choice, or describe in detail an algorithm for such a program. (Cambridge)

27. a. i. With the aid of examples, distinguish between machine code and assembly language programs. *(4 marks)*

ii. In assembly language, what is meant by a directive? Give an example of a directive. *(2 marks)*

b. The central processing unit of a particular computer contains 8 general purpose registers of 8 bit word length labelled A, B...H. A simple assembly language is used, which allows the following instructions and predefined macros:

Function	Operands	Description
MOV	R1, R2	Move into register R1 the contents of register R2
LD	R, N	Load register R with the number N
ADD	R1, R2	Add to register R1 the contents of register R2 and set the carry flag if overflow
DEC	R	Decrement register R. If register R = 0 then zero flag is set
NEG	R	Negates register R
BN	Z, label	Branch to label if Zero flag is set
BN	NZ, label	Branch to label if Zero flag is not set
BN	C, label	Branch to label if Carry flag is set
BN	NC, label	Branch to label if Carry flag is not set

Registers can be paired together, eg, AB, CD... to form 16 bit single registers. For example, ADD GH, GH will add the contents of GH to itself with the carry flag set only if there is a carry from the G register, which is equivalent to shifting GH one place to the left.

All numbers are binary.

Macro TEST with parameter N is defined as

```
MACRO      TEST  N
           LD    G,N
           LD    H,0
           LD    C,0
           LD    E,1000
START:     ADD   GH,GH
           BN    NC,NOADD
           ADD   GH,CD
NOADD:     DEC   E
           BN    NZ,START
           MOV   CD,GH
ENDMACRO
```

i. If register D contains the binary number 00111011, list the contents of registers G and H at the end of each of the iterations when the macro is called by TEST 1011. *(10 marks)*

ii. Describe the function of this macro. *(2 marks)*

iii. If N is a negative number, stored in two's complement format, describe the additional steps which will be needed. *(2 marks)*

Appendix 1 : Answers to Questions

This appendix contains answers to student self-test questions set at the ends of chapters followed by an appendix with answers to revision test questions. The answers given either give references to chapters and paragraphs that provide the information required for the answer or they outline the points to be included in an answer. In the case of examination questions slightly more detail is given where necessary. Remember that in an examination you score marks for the number of relevant points you make not for the **number of pages you fill.**

Chapter 1

Answer 1. 1.2 and 1.5

Answer 2. 1.16 and Fig. 1.3

Answer 3. 1.19

Answer 4.

a. Monitor   b. Monitor screen   c. Printer Cable   d. Printer

e. Keyboard   f. Computer Cabinet   g. Floppy disk unit

Chapter 2

Answer 1.

a. Even

b.

CHARACTER	BINARY	OCTAL	CHARACTER	BINARY	OCTAL	CHARACTER	BINARY	OCTAL
0	001010	12	C	110011	63	0	100110	46
1	000001	01	D	110100	64	P	100111	47
2	000010	02	E	110101	65	Q	101000	50
3	000011	03	F	110110	66	R	101001	51
4	000100	04	G	110111	67	S	010010	22
5	000101	05	H	111000	70	T	010011	23
6	000110	06	I	111001	71	U	010100	24
7	000111	07	J	100001	41	V	010101	25
8	001000	10	K	100010	42	W	010110	26
9	001001	11	L	100011	43	X	010111	27
A	110001	61	M	100100	44	Y	011000	30
B	110010	62	N	100101	45	Z	011001	31

Answer 2. 2.9, 2.11 and 2.12.

The start and stop bits are needed in asynchronous transmission to inform the device that a transmission is about to take place. Data is sent at fixed intervals of time in synchronous transmission so there is no need to inform the receiver when transmission is to begin.

Answer 3.

a. Add a 0

b. Add a 1

Chapter 3

Answer 1.

a.

i.	26	ii.	32	iii.	37
iv.	46	v.	54	vi.	65
vii.	72	viii.	135	ix.	1357
x.	2655				

b.

i.	10 110	ii.	11 010	iii.	11 111
iv.	100 110	v.	101 100	vi.	110 101
vii.	111 010	viii.	1 011 101	ix.	1 011 101 111
x.	10 110 101 101				

c.

i.	16	ii.	1A	iii.	1F	iv.	26
v.	2C	vi.	35	vii.	3A	viii.	5D
ix.	2EF	x.	5AD				

Answer 2.

a.
i.	59	ii.	231	iii.	849
iv.	1260	v.	2011		

b.
i.	3B	ii.	E7	iii.	351
iv.	4EC	v.	7DB		

c.
i.	0011 1011	ii.	1110 0111
iii.	0011 0101 0001	iv.	0100 1110 1100
v.	0111 1101 1011		

Answer 3.

i.	106	ii.	239	iii.	712	iv.	839	v.	1754

Answer 4. 3352653 octal and DD5AB hex.

Chapter 4

Answer 1. 4.12

Answer 2. 4.26

Answer 3. 4.34

Answer 4. 4.45

Answer 5. Local Area Network, Long Haul Network, Interface Message Processor.

Answer 6. 4.47, a computer specialist

Answer 7. 4.74

Answer 8. 4.77

Chapter 5

Answer 1 5.4 b.i, A computer specialist.

Answer 2. 5.4 b.ii

Answer 3. 5.6

Chapter 6

Answer 1.

Note

R is 0101 0010 A is 0100 0001 M is 0100 1101

a. 8-bit microcomputer

01010010	R
01000001	A
01001101	M

b. 16-bit microcomputer

R	A
01010010	0100001
01001101	0000000

M

Chapter 7 *No questions.*

Chapter 8

Answer 1. 8.4d

Answer 2. 8.7, 8.21

Answer 3. 8.41

Answer 4. 8.14d

Chapter 9 *No questions*

Chapter 10

Answer 1. All stages - see 10.10.

Answer 2.

Human sensible - can be understood by a human.

Machine sensible - can be read by a machine. Examples MICR, OCR.

Answer 3.
INTRODUCTION

1. It must be noted that advantages and disadvantages are relative. Also in many cases a user will disregard certain disadvantages as being of no consequence or will be obliged to adopt a method despite its disadvantages. Finally, as has already been pointed out in the text, some methods will be better suited for certain applications than others.

MAGNETIC TAPE CASSETTE

2. **Possible Advantages.**
   a. Can be prepared as a by-product.
   b. Inexpensive
   c. Easily transportable.

3. **Possible disadvantages.**
   a. Slower input than $\frac{1}{2}$" tape.
   b. Smaller capacity of cassette.

KEY-TO-DISKETTE INCLUDING PREPARATION ON PCs

4. **Possible advantages.**
   a. Data is encoded directly onto the diskette.
   b. No other media handling involved.
   c. Error correction is easy.
   d. Diskettes are easily transportable.

5. **Possible disadvantages.**
   a. Diskette needs careful handling.

OCR

6. **Possible advantages.**
   a. No transcription is required, thus there are no errors in the data preparation stage.
   b. Characters are both human and machine sensible.
   c. Documents prepared in OC are suitable for use as turnaround documents.

7. **Possible disadvantages.**
   a. A high standard printing of optical characters is required.
   b. High document standards are needed to keep down error rejection.
   c. The cost of readers/scanners is relatively high, especially those used on line to the computer.

MICR

8. Advantages and disadvantages as for OCR, except that print tolerances are much stricter.
   Possible disadvantages.
   a. Very high degree of accuracy required in forming characters.

BAR CODED STRIPS AND SIMPLE MAGNETICALLY CODED STRIPS

9. **Possible advantages.**
   a. Data is captured at source.
   b. Data collection is done mainly by machine (handling excluded).
   c. Sales attendant's job is simplified as data is already recorded.

10. **Possible disadvantages.**
    a. There are limits to the amount of data that can be stored on the strip.

b. Problems arise if (in retailing) goods are marked down in price.

c. The strips have to be printed or stuck onto every single item sold singly.

PLASTIC BADGES

11. **Possible advantages.**

   a. Plastic badges are able to withstand much handling and are suitable for shop-floor systems and ordinary employees can operate the machines.

   b. The collection system is mechanised.

   c. The data-recording machines can be linked directly to the computer.

12. **Possible disadvantages.**

   a. Limited scope.

   b. The recording machines are operated by the workers themselves.

ON-LINE SYSTEMS

13. **Possible advantages.**

   a. Transcription can be eliminated.

   b. Speeds up entry of data to the computer and return of processed information.

   c. Cuts down delays in dealing with error rejections.

14. **Possible disadvantages.**

   a. Cost is considerable.

AUTHOR'S NOTE

There is a tendency for candidates in examinations to write down what they know about the subject of a question rather than answer the specific question. Beware of this danger!

To illustrate this point, suppose that rather than ask about the advantages and disadvantages of the methods and media for data collection the question had asked for a summary of these methods and asked what were the problems of data capture and their possible solution. The answer, although on the same subject matter, would need to be very different:

noindentA.

Data has to be presented to the computer in a form that is acceptable as input (so called machine-sensible form). This *capturing* of data can be accomplished in many ways, using different input media. A summary of the main methods and media is given below:

NO.	METHOD OF DATA CAPTURE	MEDIA USED
1	On-line (to computer)	Data transmission terminals, plastic badges, etc.
2	Character recognition	Source documents using OCR; MICR or OMR.
3	Key processing	Using computer-controlled data entry systems.
4	By-product	eg, cassette with cash registers.

noindentB.

BASIC PROBLEMS

a. **Accuracy and validity** of data when finally input to computer.

b. **Form of source data,** which in many cases means a clerically produced document and indifferent document standards.

c. **Cost** of machinery, operators and buildings, etc, which sometimes equals that of the computer system itself.

d. **Time.** Many of the methods outlined are cumbersome and very time consuming.

e. **Volumes of data.** Increasing volumes of data, indicating the need for more sophisticated methods of data capture.

f. **Movement of data** (in raw or transcribed form) to the central processing point present problems of packaging, delay, loss, etc.

g. **Control.** With so many stages involved with some methods the problem of controlling and coordinating the whole is far from easy.

noindentC.

DISCUSSION OF PROBLEMS AND SOLUTIONS (Methods referred to are those given in answer B.)

a. **Accuracy.** This problem is most acute with method 3, which requires *verification* to reduce errors made by operators. Even so errors will creep through and there is a necessity for a computer check of input. Limited *validity* checking can be carried out by the *computer*. Method 4 claims increased accuracy and certain validity checks can be done *off-line*.

b. **Form of source data.** On-line systems can do away with a source document, which is the ideal solution. Method 2 (character recognition) avoids the need for transcription, especially with the use of the "turn around" document. Method 4 (by-product) also enables the source data to be produced in a machine-sensible form. (example - cash registers equipped with cassettes which capture data as sale is entered), bar coded strips also obviate the need for manually scribed document.

c. **Cost.** Each method is going to cost a great deal, but computer-controlled data entry is probably more cost effective in large installations.

d. **Time.** Method 1 gets over this problem by capturing data at source and putting it directly into the computer. The methods that employ more machinery and fewer humans are likely to be more efficient in this respect.

e. **Volumes.** Similarly increased volumes point to the choice of on-line systems, character recognition, or computer-controlled data entry as appropriate.

f. **Movement.** The solution is the use of an on-line system or something approaching it.

g. **Control.** The methods that eliminate the most stages in data capture will be the answer. This points again to on-line systems and to a lesser degree character recognition, and computer-controlled data entry (and possibly by-product).

CONCLUSION

D. The capture of raw data for use within a computer system is a time-consuming and costly affair. The basic underlying problem is the interface of the slow human with the high-speed computer.

The ultimate solution must be to capture data at its point of origin in a machine-sensible form, thus eliminating the many stages involved at present in getting it into such a form.

However it is well to appreciate that very often cost and the *appropriateness* of a method of data capture to a particular application will be very important factors influencing choice.

Answer 4. Relative advantages.

VDU	Printer Terminal
No stationery costs	Produces permanent copies
Faster maximum speed	Not limited to length of
Quieter than most printers	screen when viewing
Very reliable: no moving parts	Nicer to read than a VDU
except the keyboard	screen
Parts of an output layout	
can be changed without	
redisplaying	
the whole screen	

Answer 5.

Appropriateness	–	the need for a hard copy. Multiple copies would prompt the use of an impact printer. A quiet environment would prompt the use of a non-impact printer, etc.
Cost	–	High speeds and extras raise the price.
Time	–	High-speed printers may be needed if there is little time to produce output.
Accuracy	–	Printer accuracy in positioning characters varies greatly. Impact line printers often produce slightly smudged and uneven lines of characters whereas daisywheel printers and good-quality matrix printers produce clear and accurate print.
Volume	–	Total volume of output in a given time is limited by printer speed.
Confidence	–	Well-proven printer types such as line and matrix printers tend to be favoured.

Answer 6.

Both verification and validation involve checking. Verification is the checking for transcription errors, validation is checking that data conforms to rules that apply to it.

Answer 7. 10.70

Answer 8.

a. i.   Data can be checked to ensure that each part of the date is valid, eg, if the month is given as a number it should be in the range 1...12.

   ii. The account holder's name can be cross-checked with the name assigned to the account number.

   iii. The account number can be checked for character type (numeric say), format and range. A check digit check may also be used.

   iv. Amounts in pounds should be numeric.

   v.   Signatures can be checked manually against a given copy.

   NB. One-day pattern recognition techniques may allow this check to be computerised.

b. eg,

```
┌─────────────────────────────────────────────────────────────┐
│                    BATCH CONTROL SLIP                         │
│                                        Date __ /__/__         │
│  Number of documents in this batch  [  ][  ]                  │
│                                           dd  mm  yy          │
│  Total of all amounts in this batch  [ ][ ][ ][ ]            │
│                                                               │
│  Total of all account numbers (hash total)  [ ][ ][ ][ ][ ][ ]│
│                                                               │
│  Sent by _____                                     │
│  Received by _____                                 │
└─────────────────────────────────────────────────────────────┘
```

c.

Field Number	Field Contents	Field Description
1	Account number	A 6-digit number, say.
2	Transaction type	"P" for payment "W" for withdrawals, say.
3	Date	A 6-digit number in the form YYMMDD*.
4	Account holder's name	Twenty character spaces, say.
5	Amount	A number between 0.00 and 999.99, say.

*eg, 3rd April, 1985, will have the form 850403

Chapter 11

Answer 1. 11.6

Answer 2. Via a HELP command 11.15.

Answer 3. 11.11, 11.12

Chapter 12

Answer 1. 12.17 – 12.22

Answer 2. 12.23

Answer 3. a. 12.5a b. 12.5 c. 12.15b

Chapter 13

Answer 1 13.41

Answer 2. 13.44 – 13.46

Answer 3.

i. 1.7		ii. 13.11		iii. 1.7	
iv. 6.21		v. 6.20		vi. 6.22	

Answer 4. 13.74

Answer 5.

The word "simultaneously" appears to imply that some kind of parallel multi-processor architecture is required and this may be the case (13.78 – 13.85). However, many multi-tasking systems can keep up with a number of digital instruments so other solutions could be acceptable.

Note. When answering a question such as this it is important to highlight the possible interpretations of the question and give reasons for the interpretation taken.

Answer 6.

LOCATION NO.	301			
CONTENTS	0000	1001	0111	0011

Answer 7.

a. 6.2 – 6.3, 7.1 – 7.2.

   Author's note. You should compare both features and uses of both.

b. **Access speed** is usually expressed in terms of the access time, ie, the time between the processor requesting data from a device and the time the processor receives it, eg, disk access time involves finding the track, waiting for a sector and reading the data into memory.

   Capacity. The amount of data a device can store is called its capacity and is usually measured in bytes or characters.

   Cost per bit. In order to obtain the cost per bit we need the cost of the device and to divide this by the capacity in bytes. Then we divide by 8 (8 bits/byte) to give the cost per bit.

   Generally speaking the cost per bit is greater for devices with high access speeds. These devices also tend to have lower capacities. At the other extreme devices with large capacities and low access speeds tend to have lower costs per bit, and so on.

c. Magnetic media are relatively cheap and can store data almost indefinitely if kept in controlled conditions. The read/write heads for such media can deal with data recorded at high densities but are expensive to produce. Therefore, the devices all adopt a method of moving the media under a limited number of read/write heads rather than having read/write heads for each section of the medium. High access speeds can therefore only be achieved by moving the medium quickly beneath the read/write heads or by increasing recording density. The high speeds and high precision required makes these devices liable to mechanical failure. Devices with no moving parts do not suffer from these problems.

Chapter 14

Answer 1.

a. 14.5		b. 14.25	c. 14.10		
d. 14.12 and 14.18 d		e. 14.10	f. 14.47		
g. 14.34		h. 14.48			

Answer 2. 14.10

Answer 3. 14.18

Answer 4. Acoustic coupler. 14.18

Answer 5. 14.22

Answer 6. 14.34

Answer 7. 14.38

Chapter 15
Answer 1.

a.

0000	0000	0111	1001
0	0	7	9

b. (See fig. 2.5 for codes).

0000	000111	001001
	7	9

c.

10110111	00111001
7	9

d. 0000   0000   0100   1111

    79

Answer 2. 15.2

Answer 3. 15.26 and 15.63

Answer 4.

a. The operands are of different types.

Suitable correction: either "15" < "26" or 15 < 26

b. Types are being mixed in this expression.

Possible correct: (5 < 10) OR (5 < 19) but this simplifies to 5 < 19.

Answer 5.

a. -384

b. True

c. True

Answer 6.

a. 49 + 51 = 100

b. "CAT"

c. "Z"

Chapter 16
Answer 1. 16.7 – 16.8

Answer 2. 16.22 – 16.23

Answer 3.

Key in an integer.

6

Key in another integer.

8.

The result is 7.

Answer 4.

```
Procedure discount (IN total_value :  real OUT discount :   real)
 Begin
    if
total_value > 100
then
        discount := Total_value / 10
    else
```

```
        if
            total_value > 20
        then
            discount := total_value/20
        else
            discount := 0
        endif
    endif
end
```

NB. This procedure could also be written as a function.

Answer 5. 16.69 and 16.74

Chapter 17

Answer 1. M(2,3), M(2,2), M(1,1), M(1,2), M(2,1), M(1,3)

Answer 2.

Answer 3. Outline solution:

```
function below_average (number_of_marks, mark, average_mark):   integer
   variables
       i :   integer
   Begin
       below_average := 0
       for i := 1 tonumber_of_marks
           if
               mark (i) <average_mark
           then
               below_average := below_average + 1
           endif
       endfor
   end
```

Answer 4. Outline solution:

a. procedure reverse_list (IN-OUT list :   array (1...N) of integer)
   variables
            bottom,
            top,
            temp :   integer
   Begin
       bottom   := 1
       top   := N

       while   bottom < top
       do
                temp := list (bottom)
                list (bottom) := list (top)
                    list (top) := temp
                    top := top - 1
                    bottom := bottom + 1
       endwhile
   end

b. As for (a) except "list" is a string, temp is a character and within the while loop the first three lines of code are:

```
        temp := list (bottom :  bottom)
        list (bottom :  bottom) := list (top :  top)
        list (top :  top) := temp
```

NB. N will be this list's string length.

Answer 5.

A two-dimensional array may be used. The array will have 100 rows, one for each stock item, and 20 columns, one for each location.

NB. Other possible solutions to this question could be based upon arrays of records.

Chapter 18.

Answer 1. 18.6 reasons 18.3-18.5

Answer 2. 18.7

Answer 3.

a. No! It is not user friendly. It is supposed to treat 999 as a sentinel but it treats 999 as data and produces a wrong value for t.

The program does not meet its specification.

b. (See a) The program is badly set out, data names lack meaning and comments are missing.

c.

```
program calculate_total
  variables
            number,
            total :  real
  Begin
        total := 0
        output ("Key in a data value or key in 999 to stop")
        input (number)
  while number <> 999
  do
            total := total + number
            Output ("Key in a data value or key in 999 to stop")
            input (number)
        endwhile
        output ("The total of all numbers input is ", total)
  end
```

NB. Comments are omitted here in order to save space.

Answer 4. 18.22

Answer 5. 18.23-18.27

Answer 6. Outline solution:

```
Program rectangle
constants
            star = ''*''
variables
            height,
            width,
            row,
            column : integer
begin
            (* get valid height *)
            repeat
                  output ("Key in rectangle height, NB at least 1")
                  input (height)
            until height >= 1
            (* get a valid width *)
            repeat
                  output ("Key in rectangle width NB at least 1")
                  input (width)
            until width >= 1
            for row := 1 to height
                  (* output a row of stars *)
                  for column := 1 to width
                        out(star)
                  endfor
                  (* generate a new line *)
                  output
            endfor
end
```

NB Assume "output" by itself generates a new line.

Chapter 19.

Answer 1. 19.17-19.18

Answer 2.

Conditions	Rules							
	1	2	3	4	5	6	7	8
age > 25	Y	Y	Y	Y	N	N	N	N
degree in computing	Y	Y	N	N	Y	Y	N	N
3 years programming experience	Y	N	Y	N	Y	N	Y	N
Actions								
Point 1 on salary scale						X	X	
Point 2 on salary scale		X	X		X			
Point 3 on salary scale	X							
Reject				X				X

Note Three conditions implies $2^3 = 8$ rules. Therefore the table is complete. The table can be reduced by one rule because rules 4 and 8 can be combined with a dash for age > 25.

Answer 3. Outline solution.

input layout

Key in Y or N in response to these questions.

Are you over 25 years old?

Have you a degree in computing?

Have you over three years' programming experience?

Output layout

Either You will be placed at point____on the salary scale or your application has been rejected.

```
Program salary
     variables
          age_response,
          degree_response,
          exper_response :  character
Begin
     (* prompt and get input-see layout *)
     if
          age_response = "Y"
     then
     if
          degree_response "Y"
     then
          if
               exper_response = "Y"
          then
               output ("You will be placed at point 3 on the salary scale")
          else
               output ("You will be placed at point 2 on the salary scale")
          endif
          else
          if
                    exper_response = "Y"
          then
               output
                    ("You will be placed at point 2 on the salary scale")
               else
               output ("Your application has been rejected")
                endif
          endif
     else
          if
               degree_response = "Y"
          then
               if
                    exper_response = "Y"
               then
                    output ("You will be placed at point 2 on the salary scale")
               else
                    output ("You will be placed at point 1 on the salary scale")
               endif
          else
               if
                    exper_response = "Y"
               then
                    output ("You will be placed at point 1 on the salary scale")
               else
                    output ("Your application has been rejected")
               endif
          endif
     endif
end
```

Chapter 20

Answer 1

Possible entities: members, accounts, transaction.

The member's entity might have attributes such as member's name, member's address, member's department, etc.

The account entity might have attributes such as account number, account holder, current balance, etc.

The transaction entity might have attributes such as account number, date, amount, type of transaction (credit or debit), etc.

Answer 2.

Key field 20.10.

a. May not be unique so not suitable.

b. Unique and usable but might be unnecessarily long.

c. Unique and usable. Specially designed for the job.

Answer 3.

hit rate 20.18

volatility 20.19

volatility is also used in connection with memory devices.

Chapter 21.

Answer 1. 21.6 – 21.8

Answer 2. 21.30

Answer 3.

a. Each record takes $\frac{250}{1600}$ inches plus $\frac{1}{2}$" for the IRG

Therefore, the file is 15,000 $\frac{(25+80)}{160}$ inches long

= 9843.75" = 820 feet

Time taken = $10 + \frac{250 \times 1000}{75 \times 1600} + 10 \times 15000$ ms

331250 ms = $5\frac{1}{2}$ minutes

With 5 records per block

Each block takes $\frac{250 \times 5}{1600} + \frac{1}{2}$" for the IBG

Therefore the file occupies 3000 $\left(\frac{125+80}{160} \right)$ inches

= 3843.75" = 320 feet

Time Taken $\left(10 + \frac{1250 \times 1000}{75 \times 1600} + 10 \right)$ 3000 ms

= 91250 ms = $1\frac{1}{2}$ minutes

Note the savings provided by blocking the records.

Double buffering (21.39) may reduce these times.

Answer 4.

The main types of storage are:

   (IAS)   Immediate-access storage   eg, RAM
   (DAS)   Direct-access storage   eg, disk
   (SAS)   Serial-access storage   eg, magnetic tape

The tasks that they are best suited to carry out are:

a. **Immediate access.** Because of its unique electronic properties giving extremely quick access to stored data this type of storage is used as the computer's main storage. Access to individual characters/bytes is completely independent of their position in store. It is in main storage that the programs are held during processing so that their instructions can be executed swiftly. Also the particular data currently being worked on is held in main storage. Ideally, IAS would be used for storage of all data because it is fast in operation. This is not practicable because of cost and volatility, and its use therefore is limited to main storage. Thus some alternative form must be found for storing the files and data which are not immediately required by the program.

b. **Direct access.** One such alternative is DAS. Storage capacity can vary from thousands to hundreds of millions of characters. DAS has the important facility of allowing direct access, that is, records can be accessed independently of each other. It is thus suitable for files being processed in a selective manner and also for storing programs, and systems software that are required to be called into main storage at any time during the running of an application program. It is an essential requirement for on-line processing or where file-interrogation facilities are needed.

c. **Serial access.** If bulky auxiliary storage is required and the need for random access is not present then the choice may well fall on SAS, the most common form of which is magnetic tape. It is also cheaper than main memory or disk. Because of its inherent serial nature, access to a record on tape is a function of its position on the tape.

Therefore every preceding record on a master file must be read (and written out onto the new tape) before the required record can be located. Nevertheless millions of characters can be stored very cheaply.

Answer 5.

a. 21,25 – 21.26

b. 21.27 – 21.28

Answer 6.

For the first part see 21.51 – 21.52.

a. **Flowchart. Note** that in recent years alternatives to flowcharts have also been accepted in the examinations.

There are many possible solutions to this problem. A reasonable solution might

i.   input the key, generate a block address and read hat block into an array.

ii. Scan the array looking at each record until either the record was found or the end of the block was reached.

iii. In performing this scan the key for each record must be selected. The record must be scanned until a "?" is reached, and if after a "?" a "/" occurs, then the end of the block has been reached. This suggests a nested loop structure for the scans.

b. The terminator / used in the question could be altered in an overflow situation to allow for a pointer to be provided. The pointer would have to provide the block address of the overflow records.

Procedure in obtaining record from overflow:

i.   Obtain block from overflow pointer.

ii. Read overflow block into string array.

iii. Repeat previously described search for record key.

Answer 7. See references for questions 4.

Answer 5. 22.11 – 22.22

Answer 9. 21.43

Answer 10.

a. If N is 1000 or more we may merely subtract 2500 from the key. If N is smaller, some rescaling will be needed too.

b. Each entry in the index will be a record consisting of a key and a record number. The index will itself have to be stored.

NB. These methods will be more complicated if, as is quite likely, the physical records and logical records differ in size. For example, in case (a) if there are 10 logical records per physical record, then the method may involve the formula

$$\text{address} - \text{INT} \left(\frac{\text{key} - 2500}{10} \right)$$

where the function int returns an integer value.

Chapter 22

Answer 1. 22.9

Answer 2. 22.11

Answer 3. 22.10

Answer 4. 22.25

Answer 5. 22.29 – 22.38

Chapter 23

Answer 1. 23.3 – 23.5

Answer 2. 23.9 – 23.13

The critical distinction is that real-time processing requires a response within a small enough time period to affect events in the "real world" as they happen.

Chapter 24.

Answer 1. 24.7

Chapter 25.

Answer 1.

i.   True   ii.   True   iii.   False

iv. True   v.   True

Answer 2.

A	B	C	D	(A.B) +(C.D)	(B+D).C	$(\overline{A}.\overline{D}) + B$	$\overline{B}.\overline{C}$
0	0	0	0	0	0	1	1
0	0	0	1	0	0	0	1
0	0	1	0	0	0	1	0
0	0	1	1	1	1	0	0
0	1	0	0	0	0	1	0
0	1	0	1	1	0	1	0
0	1	1	0	0	1	1	0
0	1	1	1	1	1	1	0
1	0	0	0	0	0	0	1
1	0	0	1	0	0	0	1
1	0	1	0	0	0	0	0
1	0	1	1	1	1	0	0
1	1	0	0	1	0	1	0
1	1	0	1	1	0	1	0
1	1	1	0	1	1	1	0
1	1	1	1	1	1	1	0

Answer 3.

   i. $\overline{B}$ ii. $B + \overline{A}$ iii. $A + \overline{B}.\overline{C} + D$

   iv. $X + Y + VW$ v. XY vi. $\overline{U.V.W.X}$.

Answer 4.

   i. $\overline{B}$ ii. $B + \overline{A}$

   iii. $X + Y + VW$ iv. $\overline{A}.\overline{B}. + AB\overline{C}$

Answer 5.

   i. $\overline{A.C}$.   ii. $B.\overline{D}$ iii. XY

Answer 6.

The dual is $(A.B.C) + (A.B.\overline{C}) + (A.\overline{B}.C.) + (\overline{A}.B.\overline{C}.)$

It simplifies to $(A.C + B\overline{C})$, which has the dual $(A + C).(B + \overline{C})$

Chapter 26

Answer 1.

   a) $\overline{a}$ $= \overline{a.a}$

   b) $\overline{a+b}$ $= \overline{a}.\overline{b}$ this uses AND, so the inverse of NAND
                             is required

              $= \overline{\overline{\overline{a}.\overline{b}}}$ $\overline{a}$ and $\overline{b}$ can be derived as above

              $= \overline{\overline{\overline{a.a}.\overline{b.b}}}$

              $= \overline{\overline{\overline{a.a}.\overline{b.b}}.\overline{\overline{a.a}.\overline{b.b}}}$

Answer 2.

Not ((not A) or (not B)) is $\overline{(\overline{A} + \overline{B})} = A.B$ (by De Morgan's rule), so the expression is simply A and B

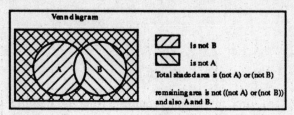

The whole of the left-hand circle is A.

The whole of the right-hand circle is B.

Generalised result $\overline{(\overline{A} + \overline{B} + \overline{C} + \overline{D} + ...)} = A.B.C.D$........

Table of values

N is the number represented in decimal

a	b	c	d	N	
0	0	0	0	0	
0	0	0	1	1	
0	0	1	0	2	
0	0	1	1	3	
0	1	0	0	4	reduces to a (by inspection)
0	1	0	1	5	
0	1	1	0	6	
0	1	1	1	7	
1	0	0	0	8	$a.\bar{b}.\bar{c}.\bar{d}$
1	0	0	1	9	$a.\bar{b}.\bar{c}.d$
1	0	1	0	10	
1	0	1	1	11	
1	1	0	0	12	
1	1	0	1	13	not allowed
1	1	1	0	14	
1	1	1	1	15	

Required function is

$$\bar{a} + a.\bar{b}.\bar{c}.\bar{d}. + a.\bar{b}.\bar{c}.d$$
$$= \bar{a} + a.\bar{b}.\bar{c}.(\bar{d} + d)$$
$$= \bar{a} + a.\bar{b}.\bar{c}$$

Answer 3.

Integrated circuits were the basis of third-generation machines in the form of SSI and, later, MSI. The first of these machines date from the 1960s.

Computers built since the mid-1970s, ie, fourth-generation computers, have been largely based on LSI, although some components may still be SSI or MSI. These computers include the microcomputers.

The fifth-generation computers will probably be based upon VLSI.

NB. Generation numbers are convenient labels to use for typical machines, but, like many systems of classification, are difficult to decide upon when applied to some specific examples.

Answer 4. 26.13 – 26.17

Answer 5. 26.27

Answer 6. 26.37

Answer 7. 26.40

i. combinational in basic form. (A full serial adder is sequential.)

ii. combinational.

iii. sequential.

iv. combinational.

Answer 8.

a.

A	B	C	D	E	F
0	0	0	0	0	0
0	0	0	1	0	1
0	0	1	0	0	1
0	0	1	1	0	1
0	1	0	0	0	0
0	1	0	1	0	1
0	1	1	0	0	1
0	1	1	1	0	1
1	0	0	0	0	0
1	0	0	1	0	0
1	0	1	0	0	1
1	0	1	1	0	1
1	1	0	1	1	0
1	1	0	0	1	0
1	1	1	0	1	1
1	1	1	1	1	1

NB A simplified version of this truth table could be given as an alternative answer.

b. $E = A.B.\overline{C}.\overline{D}. + A.B.\overline{C}.D. + A.B.C.\overline{D} + A.B.C.D.$
$F = \overline{A}.\overline{B}.\overline{C}.D + \overline{A}.\overline{B}.C.D. + \overline{A}.B.\overline{C}.D. + \overline{A}.B.C.D.$
$+ A.\overline{B}.C.\overline{D} + A.\overline{B}.C.D. + A.B.C.\overline{D}. + A.B.C.D.$

c. NBWith practice you may be able to omit (b) and write (c) directly from the truth table.
$E = A.B.$
$F = A.C + \overline{A}.D.$

d.

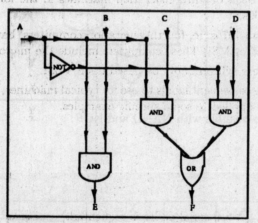

e. This implementation uses 5 gates. Implementations with NOR or NAND would use more gates.

Answer 9.

a.

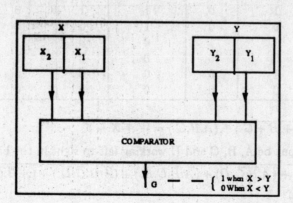

b.

X		Y		X > Y
X_2	X_1	Y_2	Y_1	G
0	0	0	0	0
0	1	0	0	1
1	0	0	0	1
1	1	0	0	1
0	0	0	1	0
0	1	0	1	0
1	0	0	1	1
1	1	0	1	1
0	0	1	0	0
0	1	1	0	0
1	0	1	0	0
1	1	1	0	1
0	0	1	1	0
0	1	1	1	0
1	0	1	1	0
1	1	1	1	0

c. $G = X_2 . \overline{Y}_2 + X_1, \overline{Y}_1 . (X_2 + \overline{Y}_2)$

d.

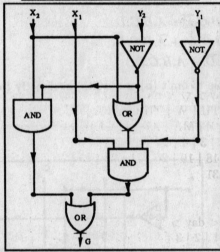

NB Alternative solutions are possible with NAND and NOR.

Answer 10.

a. 26.21

b.

A	B	C	$\overline{A+B}$	W = $\overline{A+B+C}$	$\overline{B+C}$	X = $\overline{A+\overline{B}+C}$	$\overline{C+A}$	Y = $\overline{B+\overline{C}+A}$	$\overline{A+B+\overline{C}}$
0	0	0	1	0	1	0	1	0	1
0	0	1	1	0	0	1	0	1	0
0	1	0	0	1	0	1	1	0	0
0	1	1	0	0	0	1	0	0	0
1	0	0	0	1	1	0	0	1	0
1	0	1	0	0	0	0	0	1	0
1	1	0	0	1	0	0	0	0	0
1	1	1	0	0	0	0	0	0	0

c. $(\overline{A.\overline{B}.\overline{C}}) + (A.B.C.) = (\overline{A+B+C}.) + (A.B.C.) = W + X + Y$

d. Let the four bits of the input be A, B, C and D working left to right in the bit pattern.

The output is $\overline{(A.B.C.D.)} + (\overline{A.B.\overline{C}.D}) + (\overline{A.B.C.\overline{D}.}) + (\overline{A.B.\overline{C}.\overline{D}.}) + (A.\overline{B.C.D.})$

which may be expressed as

$$\overline{(A+B+C+D) + \overline{(A+B+C+\overline{D})} + \overline{(A+B+\overline{C}+D)} + \overline{(A+\overline{B}+C+D)} + \overline{(\overline{A}+B+C+D)}}$$

Further simplifications may be derived from A.B + A.C + D.B. + D.C + B.C + A.D

610

Chapter 27

Answer 1. Each statement must have a single meaning.

Answer 2.

      a. 27.5   b. 27.5   c. 19.51 b.i   d. 19.51b.ii

Answer 3. Using the canonical parse:

a	+	b	*	c
\<var>	+	b	*	c
\<term>	+	b	*	c
\<exp>	+	b	*	c
\<exp>	+	\<var>	*	c
\<exp>	+	\<term>	*	c
	\<exp>		*	c
	\<exp>		*	\<var>
	\<exp>		*	\<term>

Parse fails here so we must backtrack to this expression:

\<exp>	+	\<term>	*	c
\<exp>	+	\<term>	*	\<var>
\<exp>	+		\<term>	
	\<exp>			

Thus, this is syntactically correct.

Answer 4.

\< date >	$\longrightarrow$	\< day > ▽ \< month > ▽ \< day number>
\< day >	$\longrightarrow$	M | TU | W | TH | F | SA | SU
\< month >	$\longrightarrow$	JA | F | MA | AP | MY | JU | JY | AU | S | O | N | D
\< day number >	$\longrightarrow$	1 | 2 | 3 | 4 | 5 | 6 | 7 | 8 | 9 | 10 | 11 | 12 | 13 | 14 | 15 | 16 | 17 | 18 | 19 | 20 | 21 | 22 | 23 | 24 | 25 | 26 | 27 | 28 | 29 | 30 | 31

Possible amendments

\< date >	$\longrightarrow$	\< day > ▽ \< month detail >
\<day number >	$\longrightarrow$	1 | 2 | 3 | 4 | 5 | 6 | 7 | 8 | 9 | 10 | 11 | 13 | 14 | 15 | 16 | 17 | 18 | 19 | 20 | 21 | 22 | 23 | 24 | 25 | 26 | 27 | 28 | 29

\< month detail >	$\longrightarrow$	\< jan > | \< feb > | \< mar > | \< apr > |..........etc
\< jan >	$\longrightarrow$	JA ▽ \<day number> JA ▽ 30 JA 31
\< feb >	$\longrightarrow$	F ▽ \< day number >
\< mar >	$\longrightarrow$	MA ▽ \< day number > | MA ▽ 30 | MA ▽ 31
etc		

Answer 5. (3, 2, 3, 2, 1, 3, 2, 3, 2, 1) Two back tracks are necessary.

Answer 6.

i. W X / Z Y * + Note. In table below the working is from *right to left*.

Symbol String	W	X	/	Z	Y	*	+
Rank Value	1	1	-1	1	1	-1	-1
Subtotal	1	0	-1	0	-1	-2	-1

The expression is "Well formed".

ii. a. AX CE + Y* =

    b. Y X B + W Z - / =

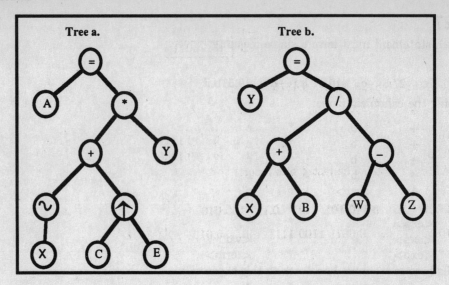

Answer 7.

$$3 \quad 4 \quad * \quad 5 \quad + \quad 1 \quad 6 \quad 3 \quad / \quad + \quad -$$

Paragraph 27.53 – the RPN expression is scanned left to right: whenever an operand is encountered it is placed on top of the stack, whenever an operator is encountered it acts on the top two items of the stack, removes them and returns the result of the operation to the top of the stack.

The diagram shows how the contents of the stack change as each term in the RPN expression is encountered:

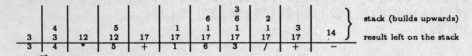

Scan the RPN expression one symbol at a time.

Chapter 28

Answer 1.

   a. 10110_2 b. 1011101_2 c. 110000_2 d. 110011_2

Answer 2.

   a. 102_8 b. 743_8

Answer 3.

   a. $120B_{16}$ b. $19ED_{16}$

Answer 4. Self-checking since the results are the same as for decimal.

Answer 5.

a. ones is 11101010, twos is 11101011

b. ones is 11011000, twos is 11011001

Answer 6.

$$
\begin{array}{rl}
7 & \textbf{0111} \quad \text{ADD} \\
-4 & 1100 \\
\hline
3 & \boxed{1}\ 0011 \\
\end{array}
$$

Answer 7.

    i. 0.75   ii. 0.8125   iii. 0.4375

    iv. 2.625   v. 5.375

Answer 8.

    i. 0.0101   ii. 0.1111

    iii. 110.0011   iv. 0.10001

    v. 0.00110011 Note. The last 4 bits recur.

Answer 9.

a. i. 0.011 110   ii. 0.110 101   iii. 0.111 100 010

b. i. 0.0010 1011   ii. 0.0011 1100 1111   iii. 0.0101 1011 1001

c.

    11 decimal is 1011

    3 decimal is 11   (twos complement is 1101)

```
Multiply    0 0 0 0 0
            0 0 0 0 0
          _____
              1 0 1 1
          _____
              1 0 1 1
            1 0 1 1 0
              1 0 1 1
          _____
          1 0 0 0 0 1   1011 × 11 = 100001
```

```
Divide.
          0 1 0 1 1
          1 0 1 0 0
        _____
          1 1 1 1 1   0
          0 1 1 0 0
        _____
          0 1 0 1 1
          1 0 1 1 0   shift
          1 0 1 0 0
        _____
          0 1 0 1 0   01
          1 0 1 0 0   shift
          1 0 1 0 0
        _____
          0 1 0 0 0   0 1 1.   (Result 3 remainder 2)
```

NB. The point is positioned thus 010.00.

Chapter 29

Answer 1.

a. Most positive $2^{11} - 1$, Least positive 1.

    Least negative -1, Most negative -2^{11}

b. Most positive $1 - \frac{1}{2}^{11}$, Least positive $\frac{1}{2}^{11}$

    Least negative $-\frac{1}{2}^{11}$, Most negative -1

Answer 2.

    i. 0.36×10^2 ii. 0.159×10^3 iii. -0.276×10^3

    iv. -0.56724×10^5 v. 0.37692×10^3 vi. 0.365×10^4

    vii. -0.498×10^2 viii. 0.9824×10^{-2} ix. -0.1562×10^{-3}

    x. -0.26×10^{-7}

Answer 3.

a. **Advantages of floating-point representation over fixed-point representation.**

    i. Wider range for given word length.

    ii. Automatic scaling.

    iii. Both fractional and integer representation.

iv. Convenience to programmer in handling range and scale.

b. **Disadvantages of floating-point representation with respect to fixed-point representation.**

   i.   Slower.

   ii. Extra expense if done by hardware because of hardware cost.

   iii. Loss of precision for given word length.

   iv. More troublesome conversion to other codes.

   v.   Less control over accuracy.

Answer 4.

a. The three possible methods are:

   i.   Twos complement method.

   ii. Ones complement method.

   iii. Explicit sign.

   They are given in the order in which arithmetic can be most efficiently performed and reverse order of simplicity of representation. The advantage of i. makes it the most common.

b. i.   +0.101 is + 0.625, decimal, +.5 octal, +.A hex.

   ii. Decimal −91 is −133 octal, 1011 011 binary, 5B hex.

   iii. +237 octal is + 010 011 111 binary , +9F hex and 159 decimal.

   iv. +E8 hex is + 1110 1000 binary + 350 Octal and + 232 decimal.

Answer 5.

a. $0111\ 1111_2$ 2, ie, $2^7 − 1$ or 127

b. Representations are normalised in order to keep numbers in a standard form, which allows control to be maintained over range, scale and accuracy.

   NB. The University of London University Entrance and Schools Examinations Council require this disclaimer be printed by all persons given permission to reproduce questions from their past examination papers:

   "The University of London University Entrance and Schools Examination Council accepts no responsibility whatsoever for the accuracy or methods of working in the answers given."

Answer 6.

a.

i.	0	1	0	1	0	0	0	0	0	0	1	1
ii.	1	0	1	1	0	0	0	0	0	0	1	1
iii.	0	1	0	0	0	0	0	0	0	0	0	0
iv.	1	0	0	0	0	0	0	0	1	1	1	1
v.	0	1	0	0	0	1	1	0	0	1	1	0
vi.	1	0	1	1	1	0	1	0	0	1	1	0
vii.	0	1	1	1	0	0	0	0	0	0	1	0
viii.	1	0	0	1	0	0	0	0	0	0	1	0
ix.	0	1	0	0	0	0	0	0	1	1	1	0
x.	1	0	0	0	0	0	0	0	1	1	0	1

b. i. $(1 − \frac{1}{2^7}) \times 2^7 = 127$

   ii. $\frac{1}{2} \times 2^{-8} = \frac{1}{2^9} = \frac{1}{512}$

   iii. $−(\frac{1}{2} − \frac{1}{2^7}) \times 2^8 = −\frac{1}{2^9} + \frac{1}{2^{15}}$

   iv. $−1 \times 2^7 = −128$

Chapter 30.

Answer 1.

a. 30.2, 30.4 a, 30.4 b

b. 30.5

Answer 2.

a. i. 0.5 ii. 0.00625

b. i. 0.0005 ii. 0.004

c. i. 5 ii. .0142857

d. i. 0.005 ii. 0.0008

Answer 3.

a. 30.5

b. Word length, method of rounding.

Answer 4. 0.0005

Answer 5.

i. For fixed point,

largest no	=	0111111111.111111
	=	+ 1023 + 63/64
	=	+ 1023.984375

For floating point,

largest no	=	0.111111111 011111
	=	$0.111111111 * 2^{31}$
	=	$+ 111111111 * 2^{22}$
	=	+ 1023 * 4*1024*1024
	=	+ 4,290,772,992

Smallest no	=	0000000000.000001
	=	+ 1/64
	=	$+ 2^{-6}$

Smallest no	=	0.100000000 100000
	=	$+ 0.1 * 2^{-32}$
	=	$+ 2^{-33}$

Zero can be represented as
0000000000.000000

Zero cannot be represented, as
it is not a normalised number,
unless treated as a special case.

Representing 1023.984375 in floating point,
= 0.111111111 001001 (rounded down) = 1023
or = 0.100000000 001010 (rounded up) = 1024.
In the second case, this is inaccurate by 1/64 or 0.015625.

ii.

00DC	=	0000000011011100
	=	11.0111
	=	+ 3.4375

FD40	=	1111110101000000, which is negative:
	=	− (0000001010111111 + 1), taking 2's complement,
	=	− (0000001011000000)
	=	− 11

iii.

7/32	=	$7 * 2^{-5}$
	=	$111 * 2^{-5}$
	=	$0.111 2^{-2}$
	=	0.111000000 111110

− 24	=	2's complement of + 24
+ 24	=	11000
	=	$0.11 * 2^{+5}$
	=	0.110000000 000101
− 24	=	1.010000000 000101

iv. Paragraph 29.28.

Chapter 31.

Answer 1.

Addressing 4096 cells requires the use of 12 bits. This leaves 6 bits to implement 64 distinct op.codes.

Answer 2.

a. i. Paragraph 13.50 – note: the Program Counter is another name for the Sequence Control Register (SCR).

    ii. Paragraph 13.46.

    iii. Paragraph 31.42.

    iv. Paragraph 13.46.

    v. Paragraph 13.46 – note: also known as the Memory Data Register.

Paragraph 31.21 gives details of the fetch-execute cycle. The effect of an interrupt on this is described in Paragraph 33.26.

b. A self-relative conditional jump instruction will have an address field which contains an address to jump to which is relative to the current contents of the SCR. If it is conditional, then it will only take effect if the condition (specified by the setting of a bit within the status register) is satisfied.

The execute phase will thus comprise:

check the appropriate bit in the status register

      – if a jump is not required then ignore this instruction and move to the next fetch.
      – if a jump is required then **add** the address field to the contents of the SCR and put the result back in to the SCR, then continue with the next fetch.

NOTE: the address field will be interpreted as a two's complement number, so that backward jumps will be accommodated. If 10 bits are allowed for the address field, this gives rise to a span of addresses from −512 to +511 locations relative to the current SCR contents (which will at that stage point to the next instruction).

An unconditional immediate jump instruction will have an address field which represents the absolute address which the program should jump to. In executing this instruction, the contents of the address field will be copied into the SCR - the next fetch will then take place from the new location.

c. Assume the registers are numbered - 4 bits will be required to identify each register, so at least 8 bits will be required for a simple register-to-register instruction which leaves the result in one of the registers (similar to two-address format - see paragraph 31.8). With a 16-bit processor, this would leave 8 bits for opcode and addressing modes.

ie.
opcode	address	R1	R2

Allowing 5 bits for the opcode and 3 bits for addressing modes this would give up to 32 different instructions with up to 8 different addressing modes.

It would be pointless to use two-address or three-address instructions in a machine with so many general purpose registers, so storage-to-storage instructions would be better in one-address format. The number of bits needed for the address field will depend on the amount of memory addressable. With a 20-bit (absolute) address, this will enable 1 Mbyte to be addressed, but the use of registers to modify the address field will reduce the number of bits needed in the address field - memory could thus be segmented into, say, 64k blocks, requiring 16 bits.

Four bits would still be needed to specify the particular modifying register, and a further 4 bits for the register containing the first operand, so with a 32 bit instruction this allows a similar range of instructions and address mode bits as described above.

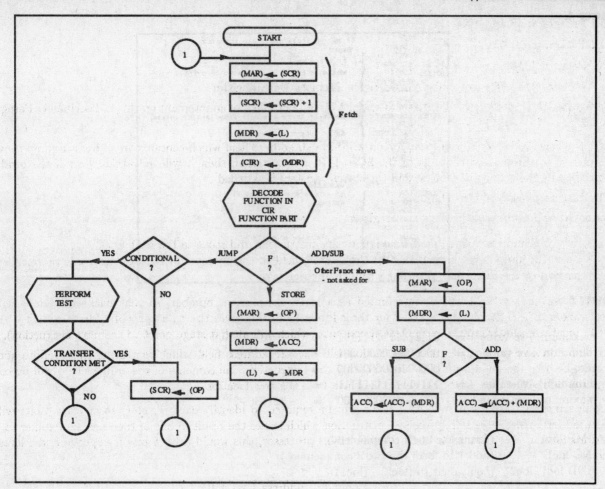

Answer 3.

31.7

   a.   31.28 - 31.29   b.   31.38

   c.   31.34   d.   31.39

Answer 4. 31.12–31.13.

a. i. 00001101 ii. 11110101

b. i. 00001101 ii. 00110101

Chapter 32

Answer 1.

a.	SUN 7	Subtracts 7 from the contents of the accumulators
b.	ADD @ 7	adds to the contents of the accumulator the data value stored in the location whose address is in location 7.
c.	ADD 7	adds to the contents of the accumulator the contents of location 7.
d.	SUB7, X	subtracts from the contents of the accumulator the contents of the location whose address is 7 plus the contents of the index register.

Answer 2. 32.8 – 32.9

Answer 3.

a. 32.12

b. 32.12

c. The process of translating an assembly-language program into machine code.

Answer 4.

```
            .START        (* NB. no_stars and i are integers.
        LDN 1         Begin
        STA NOST        no_stars := 1
OLOP:   LDN 4         while (* there is a line to be printed *)
        SUB NOST                 no_stars <= 4
        JAL FIN          do    (* print a line *)
        LDN 0
        STA 1          i := 0
ILOP:   LDA NOST       while (* there are more asterisks to output *)
        SUB 1                   i <= no_stars
        JAZ LINE         do (* output an asterisk *)
        LDA 52         out("*")
        IO  2
        LDA 1
        ADN 1          i:= i + 1
        STA 1
        JPU ILOP       endwhile
LINE:   LDA CR         (* generate a new line *)
        IO  2          output
        LDA LF
        IO  2
        LDA NOST
        ADN 1            no_stars := no_stars + 1
        STA NOST
        JPU OLOP       endwhile
FIN:    STOP           end
        .END
```

Answer 5.

a.

$$\text{maximum +ve value} = 0111111111111111 = +32767(2^{15} - 1)$$
$$\text{minimum +ve value} = 0000000000000001 = +1$$
$$\text{zero} = 0000000000000000 = 0$$
$$\text{minimum -ve value} = 1111111111111111 = -1$$
$$\text{maximum -ve value} = 1000000000000000 = -32768(-2^{15})$$

b.

```
CMP loc1        (forms the one's complement)
INC loc1        (add 1 to form the two's complement)
ADD loc1, loc2  (equivalent to (loc2) - (loc1))
```

c.

$$\text{most +ve value} = 0111111111111111 \; 1111111111111111$$
$$= +2,147,483,647 \qquad (+2^{31} - 1)$$

$$\text{most -ve value} = 1000000000000000 \; 0000000000000000$$
$$= -2,147,483,648 \qquad (-2^{31})$$

d. Assume two numbers, a and b, are stored in locations a_high, a_low and b_high, b_low respectively.

   i. ADD a_low, b_low
       ADC a_high
       ADD a_high, b_high

   ii. CMP a_high
       CMP a_low
       INC a_low
       ADC a_high
       ADD a_low, b_low
       ADC b_high
       ADD a_high, b_high

e. DEFINE MACRO double_subtract (a_low,a_high,b_low,b_high)

    .

    .

    .

END MACRO

double-subtract (10,11,15,16), for example, would substitute 10 for all references to a_low, 11 for a_high, 15 for b_low and 16 for b_high.

Chapter 33

Answer 1. 33.9

Answer 2. 33.22 – 33.23

Chapter 34

Answer 1.

A processor with a privileged instruction set has extra instructions which are available only when it is switched into a special mode (supervisory mode). These instructions are normally only available to the Executive of an operating system as it would be unwise to allow applications programs to have access to memory management facilities, access to interrupt mechanisms, etc. The operating system restores the processor to User mode (disabling the privileged instructions) when it passes control to other programs.

Answer 2.

a. 34.12, 34.31-34.35, 34.47-34.51

The effects on the user of multiprogramming are faster turnaround of jobs. Multi-access may enable alternative methods of use or even interaction with the program by the user.

b. i. Peripheral requires attention.

ii. End of time-slice.

iii. Hardware error/power failure.

iv. Program error, eg, overflow.
(See 34.36.)

(**Author's Note.** Software used for program development could be discussed here, eg, editors and compilers).

Answer 3.

This is another term to describe the fetch-execute cycle: the contents of the SCR are copied into the MAR and then incremented. The MAR is used to access a particular location, the contents of which are fetched.

The opcode part of the instruction is decoded and that operation executed (this may require further access to memory for direct or indirect operands). At the end of the execution phase, the cycle is repeated automatically until the equivalent of a STOP opcode is encountered.

Answer 4.

a. The first level interrupt handler determines the source of the interrupt and then initiates the necessary interrupt service routine (ISR). This handles the interrupt, which may cause a change in status of a process - eg, the interrupt may signal the end of a data transfer, in which case the process becomes "runnable". In this case, the ISR changes the status of the process and links that process into the processor queue at the appropriate place indicated by its priority. Alternatively, it may remove a process from the queue if its status changes to "unrunnable" by requesting a data transfer. The dispatcher is then entered, and this allocates the process at the head of the queue to a processor (this process may have been the one which was interrupted).

b. Introduction of new processes, assignment of priorities to processes, and implementing policies for allocation of resources. See Paragraph 34.34.

c. i. Shareable resources include processors, read-only files, and areas of memory protected against modification. Non-shareable resources include most peripherals, read-write files, and areas of memory allocated to a process and its data.

ii. This situation is known as deadlock and in its simplest form it will occur if process 1 is allocated resource A and later requires resource B, and process 2 is allocated resource B and later requests resource A.

The conditions which allow deadlock to occur are:

i. unshareable resources;

ii. process requesting new resources while holding an existing one;

iii. pre-emption does not occur;

iv. a circular chain of processes waiting for resources.

One way of dealing with the problem is to allow it to happen - if it occurs very irregularly (say, once every six months or so) then it is not worth the trouble of trying to do anything about it.

Another way is to try to ensure that the above conditions do not hold, and thus prevent it from happening - "Deadlock prevention".

A third strategy is to allow it to happen: to detect it and to try to recover from it. An example of this is to remove processes from the queue which are continually blocked for, say, one hour, and to try these processes later (useful for batch systems).

A fourth strategy is to take suitable anticipatory action by careful allocation of resources - so called "Deadlock avoidance".

Chapter 35

Answer 1. 35.3 – 35.5

Answer 2. 35.19. Also see chapter 5.

Answer 3. 35.25 – 35.27

Chapter 36

Answer 1.

The advantages and disadvantages of high-level languages are:

Advantages.

a. Program writing easier because of vocabulary, which is relatively simple to learn.

b. Program writing takes less time so programmers are utilised more efficiently.

c. Amendments during program writing are easily incorporated and subsequent revision is also easier.

d. Extensive use of macros and subroutines (both those of the manufacturer and the user) is permitted.

e. High-level languages are largely independent of the machine and orientated towards the problem.

f. Source programs may be understood by people other than the person who wrote them.

Disadvantages.

a. Require translation, unlike machine code. (This is not a too significant disadvantage since low-level symbolic languages have the same problem.)

b. A large number of rules must be adhered to.

c. The object programs tend to be less efficient in terms of storage utilisation and running time because of the general constraints of the language, which may conflict with the best method of solution.

Answer 2. 36.5 and 36.6

Answer 3.

Different manufacturers provide different dialects of BASIC.

The friends can attempt to solve their problem by attempting to define a common subset for each language, which they can both use to write programs.

In general there is a need for language standards. They could both have borne this point in mind when buying their computers in the first place.

Author's Note One of the most portable languages today is C. It has been implemented on a wide variety of machines but often the compilers used are in fact the same or carefully produced to be standard.

Chapter 37

Answer 1. 37.3 – 37.4

Answer 2.

```
Listing            .START
000200   000213   D:      LDA X
000201   010211           JAZ E
000202   040100           SUB 100
000203   140211           JAL E
000204   010213           STA X
000205   000212           LDA Q
000206   050001           ADN 1
000207   010212           STA Q
000210   120200           JPU D
000211   170000   E:      STOP
000212   000000   Q:      0
000213   000060   X:      60
                  .END
```

The program divides "X" by the number in location 100. The quotient is stored in Q and the number left in "X" is the remainder.

Answer 3.

a. (i), (ii) and (iii) 37.22 – 37.26

b. **Advantages.**

This restriction aids translation. In particular, it means that simple and compact symbol tables (37.23) can be used, which saves storage and improves the efficiency of the translation process.

Disadvantages.

The disadvantages are that when a programmer uses longer variable identifiers in order to improve program readability there is a chance that an ambiguity will arise. If the programmer tries to avoid that problem by keeping identifiers to two characters program readability suffers.

c. Advantages include the following:

i. It allows access to hardware facilities not directly accessible to the high-level language.

ii. It enables optimisation of critical sections of code.

iii. It allows extra functions and facilities to be incorporated into the language.

d. There are two probable reasons.

i. A good optimising compiler may detect that the loop is redundant and therefore miss it out of the object code.

ii. If the loop is translated into object code by the compiler its execution will be very much faster than when it is interpreted and therefore no longer satisfactory.

NB. The University of London University Entrance and Schools Examination Council require this disclaimer be printed by all persons given permission to reproduce questions from their past examination papers:

"The University of London University Entrance and Schools Examination Council accepts no responsibility whatsoever for the accuracy or method of working in the answers given."

Answer 4.

< expression >	$\longrightarrow$	< operand >< operator >< operand >
< operand >	$\longrightarrow$	|A|B|C|D|E|F|G|H|I|J|K|L|M|N|O| |P|Q|R|S|T|U|V|W|X|Y|Z|
< operator >	$\longrightarrow$	= | AND | OR
< statement >	$\longrightarrow$	< line number > IF < expression > THEN < line number >
< line number >	$\longrightarrow$	< digit >< symbol >< symbol >
< digit >	$\longrightarrow$	1 | 2 | 3 | 4 | 5 | 6 | 7 | 8 | 9
< symbol>	$\longrightarrow$	< digit > | < zero >
< zero >	$\longrightarrow$	0

Chapter 38

Answer 1. 38.5

Answer 2.

a. 38.21 and 38.28   b. 38.31

c. 38.36   d. 5.19

Answer 3. 38.24

Chapter 39

Answer 1.

Advantages of the list.

a. A more flexible method of storage, allowing deletion and insertion without moving existing data. This reduces the amount of data movement within store and hence saves time.

b. The size of a block of data may not be known before it is placed in store. With tables or strings a block of core might be set aside and then part of it might be left unused, thereby wasting storage. Enough storage might not be set aside and the table would have to be reorganised in a larger block. Using lists avoids these problems by placing data in the next available space.

c. Lists do not waste storage space by leaving gaps where deletions have occurred, as happens with tables and strings.

d. Using lists avoids rigid structures that can create difficulties when organising storage allocation.

e. When tables or strings have to be broken down into units of manageable size lists form an efficient method of connecting units.

Answer 2.

a. Look up table (39.31), slow access, saves space.

b. Direct-access table (39.32), fast access, can waste space.

c. Hash table (39.34) compromise between a. and b.

   The differences lie in the methods of storage and access and use of storage.

Answer 3.

a. Paragraph 17.56 and 39.22.

Entry order	Left Pointer	Datum	Right Pointer	Back Pointer	Trace Pointer
1	2	Leeds	7	0	11
2	5	Bradford	3	1	6
3	6	Halifax	4	2	4
4	0	Huddersfield	10	3	10
5	0	Batley	0	2	2
6	0	Dewsbury	0	3	3
7	11	Wakefield	8	1	9
8	9	York	0	7	0
9	0	Wetherby	0	8	8
10	0	Hull	0	4	1
11	0	Malton	12	7	12
12	0	Scarborough	0	11	7

Trace_start = 5

Zero used as terminator

b. With a tree structure the search time for an item is very fast - approaches binary search if tree is well balanced (Paragraph 39.27), whereas linear search would be required if list is in order of run-time input.

Also, there is no need for sorting or movement of data after it has been added to the tree structure, whereas this would be needed without a tree if the data had to be sequenced.

Examples of use could be quoted where ordering of data is required and/or where rapid searching is required, especially for large amounts of data.

c. Using the trace pointer array:

```
Begin

    pointer := trace_start
    Repeat
        output(datum(pointer))
        pointer := trace(pointer)
    until pointer = 0

end.
```

Answer 4.

```
Function stack is_empty (top :  integer) : boolean
```

```
      Begin
        if
            top = 0
        then
              stack_is_empty:  = true
        else
              stack_is_empty := false
        endif
        end
   function stack_is_full (top:  integer) :  Boolean
   Begin
        Stack_is_full := (top = 21)
   end
```

NB. This simplifies
to:
stack_is_empty := (top = 0)

Chapter 40

Answer 1. 40.11

Answer 2.

Number the items in the list for easy reference:

1. Aberdeen
2. Birmingham
3. Cambridge
4. Exeter
5. Manchester
6. Newcastle
7. Norwich
8. Oxford
9. Reading
10. Sheffield
11. Southampton
12. York

Start with two pointers hi (=12) and lo (=1)

Examine the element given by (lo + hi)DIV 2, ie, element 6 – Newcastle.

This comes after the element sought, so set hi to 5.

Examine the element given by (lo + hi)DIV 2, ie, element 3 – Cambridge.

This comes after the element sought, so set hi to 2.

Examine the element given by (lo + hi)DIV 2, ie, element 1 – Aberdeen.

This comes before the element sought, so set lo to 2.

Examine the element given by (lo + hi)DIV 2, ie, element 2 – Birmingham, which is the item sought.

Answer 3.

Run-time errors such as division by zero, overflow of numbers - can often be "trapped" by the program.

Data errors which lead to wrong answers being produced - validate input data.

Logical errors; the program does not produce the expected results - dry run or program trace.

Answer 4.

a. The record structure (Paragraph 17.37) for commercial languages, for use in most file-handling applications.

The 2-d array (Paragraph 17.17) for a scientific language, used for mathematical modelling of structures for stress, heat transfer calculations etc.

b. (Paragraph 18.67).

  i. A recursive routine is defined in terms of itself: it calls itself repeatedly, passing modified values as parameters which become local to that level of call. There must be some exit condition which is dependent on the parameters passed.

  ii. Routines are short and "elegant"; many data structures can be defined (and thus manipulated) recursively.

  iii. Traversing binary tree structures to obtain data in order.

  iv. Can use up a large amount of memory during run-time which is not in programmer control. Also they execute more slowly than the equivalent iterative routine (which do not require parameters to be passed).

c. i. Paragraph 17.12.

   ii. Chapter 18.

   iii. Paragraph 18.71.

Chapter 41.

Answer 1. 41.7 and 41.57

Answer 2.

    a.   41.23   b.   41.23

    c.   41.24–41.31   d.   41.43–41.48

Chapter 42

Answer 1. 42.4b

Answer 2. 42.22

Chapter 43.

Answer 1. (43.10 and 43.11)

Chapter 44

Answer 1. 44.16

Answer 2. 44.54

Answer 3. 44.6

Answer 4.

Basically the choice of output depends on its subsequent use, or the type of application.

CHOICE ACCORDING TO SUBSEQUENT USE

1. Output can be produced for use by humans or for use by machines:

   a. **Use by humans.** Output for use by humans must be in a form understood by humans so we have the following:

       i. **Printed output.** Either on pre-printed stationery or plain paper and in various formats.

       ii. **Visual display.** Output in the form of script or graphs, etc, displayed on a screen.

       iii. **Microfilm.** Output required for storage and subsequent reference.

   b. **Further use by machines.** Output for use by machines will be prepared in a machine-sensible form. The following are examples:

       i. **For subsequent re-input into computer.** Such output can be prepared on magnetic tape, disk, etc, as appropriate. For example, output that goes directly to another run as input.

       ii. **Output converted off-line to another medium.** Magnetic tape may be used for output from an updating run, which is subsequently printed as an off-line operation.

       iii. **Transmission of output.** Output to be transmitted over communication lines will need to be in a form acceptable to the transmission device.

CHOICE ACCORDING TO TYPE OF APPLICATION

2. Choice of output will vary with applications, one type of output being more appropriate to one application than another:

   a. **Batch processing.** Output will be on magnetic tape or disk if spooling techniques are used.

   b. **Real-time processing.** The use of data-communication devices is essential so that output can be transmitted immediately to the control point (a terminal).

   c. **Interrogation or enquiry.** A visual display or terminal is the choice where immediate response to enquiries for information held on master files is required. These can be located locally or at a remote point.

   d. **Turnaround document.** Used where output subsequently re-enters the computer system without there being any intermediate off-line coding process. To achieve this, output documents can be prepared in optical characters. Such documents can also be read by humans.

   Note. There is an obvious overlapping between 1 and 2.

Answer 5. 44.56

Chapter 45

Answer 1. 45.3 – 45.9

Answer 2. object, events and actions.

Answer 3.

a. Master file – Paragraph 20.9.

Sequential file access – Paragraph 21.28.

Validation – Paragraph 22.15.

b. It must be in the same sequence as the master file – Paragraph 21.5.

c. This would be very similar to Figure 22.10, with "Expanded orders" file replaced by an "Audit" file.

d. Regular back-up copies – Paragraph 21.43.

File control totals - Paragraph 22.45.

e. A master record needs to comprise the key, existing stock, and unit price. A transaction record should contain the key, quantity, and whether received or sold (Debit/Credit).

Chapter 46

Answer 1. 46.10 – 46.13

Answer 2.

The process of 46.9 can be made simpler if, well in advance, the manual documents are re-designed so that when the time for conversion comes they will be easy to transcribe. Better still, they will have been designed to exploit document-reading methods such as OMR or OCR.

Answer 3. 46.35

Chapter 47

Answer 1.

One of the difficulties in selecting the computer best suited to a company's needs is how to evaluate what each manufacturer has to offer. What a company must attempt to do is to match its objectives against the capabilities of the computer systems offered by the manufacturers. The following criteria are suggested, but it must be remembered that each user will place a different emphasis on the individual criterion.

a. Cost

b. Delivery time

c. Support –

i.   personnel supplied by manufacturers to aid user.

ii. education of user's staff.

d. Software supplied with system – cost and ease of implementation.

e. Reliability – the manufacturer to supply performance data.

f. Modularity – the ability to add to system later.

g. Conversion – the ease with which conversion from existing systems could be accomplished.

h. Experience – the manufacturer's experience with systems of the type that the company is installing.

Answer 2.

The contents of a systems specification are *included* in a feasibility report, to the level of detail required by management to enable them to make a decision between alternative ways of satisfying the objectives (eg, use of package vs own software). The feasibility *report*, apart from containing an *introduction, current situation statement,* etc, would also, therefore, include details of *alternatives*.

Answer 3.

The review of a computer system must not be regarded as a once-only task and ideally should be carried out periodically. The main question to be asked is "have the objectives been achieved"? This assumes that these were clearly defined in the first place. Thus, if the objective was "to reduce stock levels by 10%" or "to produce invoices one day earlier", the reviewer must judge the effectiveness of the new system against the achievement of these objectives. Some of the detailed areas that would occupy the attention of the reviewer are:

a. Costs – are these in line with budgeted costs?

b. Staff – with regard to retraining, redeployment and morale. Are staff happy with the new system?

c. Are any parts of the "old" system that should have been dispensed with still in use?

d. Standards of input and output.

e. Feedback from the company's customers.

Answer 4.

a. The project leader acts as a team leader, normally working for a project manager, and taking technical responsibilies.

b. The project librarian normally works for the project leader with responsibilities for all documentation including specifications, design documents and source code together with any software release or change control information.

c. A systems programmer is normally a technical specialist in some aspect of programming system operation rather than being an "applications programmer". As such a systems programmer is likely to do operating system related programming rather than be assign to an application specific project.

d. A computer operator performs routine housekeeping task on the computer as well as making sure that the schedule of batch jobs and online activities runs as required. The work frequently involves loading and unloading tape drive and disk drives plus constantly attending to the various printed outputs produced by the machine. Additionally the operator will be expected to monitor the operation of the machine and to report any problems to the appropriate support staff.

e. A data control clerk supervises the arrival and correct use of data arriving and leaving the computer room. The task is very dependent upon the methods of data entry used for batch processing. For example, if OCR documents are received for processing on a regular basis they will need specific handling.

Chapter 48.

Answer 1. Advantages 48.11, disadvantages 48.12.

Answer 2 48.36

Answer 3.

    Main factors considered.

a. Terms of reference must be laid down and objectives set.

b. Investigation and fact finding. The present system must be studied in terms of:

    i. Costs.

    ii. Staffing.

    iii. Equipment.

    iv. Procedures.

    v. Controls.

    vi. Data handled, volume, variety.

    vii. Data collection.

c. Analysis of facts with reference to the objectives laid down in the terms of reference and using principles of procedure.

Chapter 50

Answer 1.

a. i. 28.23

    ii. 28.37

b. Numerical information (values) are represented by physical quantities such as voltages and current magnitudes. These values are represented by generating a trace in a cathode ray tube or producing a graphical plot on paper.

    Advantages (two from the following).

    i. Cheaper than using the real thing.

    ii. Faster results than with a digital machine in some cases.

    iii. Suitable time scaling gives information earlier than with the real system.

    iv. No extra material costs.

    v. Safer in some cases.

c. (49.28). Application 49.30 and 50.38.

Answer 2. Digitiser. 49.30 – 49.34

Appendix 2 : Revision Test Answers

Answer 1. High-level language 36.3. Low-level language 32.8.

Factors in the choice of low-level languages:

i.   Efficiency in use of time or storage.

ii. The problem is specific to the hardware and not suited to high-level programming.

iii. The required facility is not available in the high-level languages provided for the system.

There are many possible solutions to the last part of this question. This method performs an AND operation between the word and a 1 in each bit position and counts the 1st to be encountered. The mask is shifted along after each test.

Outline method:

```
Begin
        Store zero in total
        Store 1 in mask
        Store wordlength in length
        Store 1 in position.
        While
            position <= length
        do
                load mask
                AND with word
                ADD 1 to total if result is not zero
                Load mask shift left one place and store
                ADD 1 to position
        endwhile
end
```

Answer 2.

a. i.   C803 contains QD68 = 0000110101101000 = +3432

    ii. C809 contains 1329 = 1329

    iii. C80D contains 4349 = B and H

b.

		Accum.	MAX	TEMP
		C800		
CLR	MAX	C800	0000	
BEQ	EXIT			
STA	TEMP			C800
LDA	MAX	0000		
SUB@	TEMP	F299		
BPL	NEXT			
LDA@	TEMP	0D67		
STA	MAX		0D67	
INC	TEMP			C801
LDA@	TEMP	C80A		
BR	LOOP			
BEQ	EXIT			
STA	TEMP			C80A
LDA	MAX	0D67		
SUB@	TEMP	0D52		
BPL	NEXT			
INC	TEMP			C80B
LDA@	TEMP	C804		
BR	LOOP			
BEQ	EXIT			
STA	TEMP			C804
LDA	MAX	0D67		
SUB@	TEMP	0C77		
etc				C805
		C810		C810
		0D67		
		FB33		
		1234	1234	C811
		C80E		C80E
		1234		
		B8D1		
		5963	5963	C80F
		0000		
		5963		

Locn	Contents	
C800	0D67	← *START*
C801	C80A	→ (i)
C802		
C803		
C804	00F0	← (iii)
C805	C810	→ (ii)
C806		
C807		
C808		
C809		
C80A	0015	← (i)
C80B	C804	→ (iii)
C80C		
C80D		
C80E	5963	← (iv)
C80F	0000	*TERMINATOR*
C810	1234	← (ii)
C811	C80E	→ (iv)
C812		
etc		

c. The subroutine accesses a linked list structure — the structure is held as a datum and pointer occupying consecutive locations in memory, as shown in the diagram. The subroutine is entered with the accumulator containing a pointer to the start of the list and it follows the pointers until a terminator of zero is met. The subroutine finds the largest value in the data items: this is returned in the accumulator upon exit from the routine.

Answer 3.

Different processors have different instruction codes, format and word lengths (8, 16, 32 bits).

Character data can be in ASCII or EBCDIC (or other) code, with odd or even parity, but no set standard for numerical data.

Storage and transmission media may use different and incompatible formats for blocks of data.

Methods of data transfer may be very different from one system to another.

Transmission and reception rates must be synchronised.

Answer 4.

i. 34.12b

ii. 1.11c

iii. 34.47

iv. 10.29

v. 34.12e

Answer 5.

a. Paragraph 34.27.

   i. A process which is described as running is one which is currently being executed on a processor within a computer system.

   ii. A runnable process is one which could be executed if a processor were allocated to it, ie, it is awaiting its turn in a processor queue.

   iii. An unrunnable process is one which would not be able to be executed, even if a processor were allocated to it. A common reason for this status occurring is when a process is waiting for the completion of a peripheral transfer.

   Paragraph 34.48 shows that these states constantly change with time.

b. The dispatcher is also known as the low-level scheduler and its role in the nucleus of an operating system is to allocate processors to the various processes. For simplicity, the dispatcher is entered whenever an interrupt has been serviced, as that interrupt service routine (Paragraph 33.27) may have changed the status of a process; eg, from unrunnable to runnable.

   In operation it will decide if a switch of processes is necessary as a result of the interrupt: if no switch is needed then the interrupted process will be resumed, but if a switch is necessary the dispatcher will save the working registers of the interrupted process, restore the registers of the process which is chosen to replace it, and transfer control to this new process - Paragraph 34.35.

   One way of determining the most suitable process to be run is by "round-robin" scheduling (Paragraph 34.52), whereby each process is assigned a time interval or "quantum": a process will run for its quantum or until it requests peripheral transfer, and the dispatcher merely has to choose the next process in a circular queue of processes. This is an old and widely used method, and is simple to implement and fair: however, response time can be slow in an interactive environment with many processes.

   An alternative method is to allocate priorities (Paragraph 34.32) to each process. Priority scheduling allows the runnable process with the highest priority to run, but to prevent one process from monopolising a processor, the priority may be changed dynamically at the end of a quantum (ie, if a process runs for its complete quantum without being interrupted, its priority would be reduced, eventually allowing a process with a higher priority to be run).

   More sophisticated operating systems may maintain more than one priority queue by putting runnable processes into different classes based on such criteria as maximum run-time allocation, maximum waiting time, or resource required. The scheduling method here would be to choose the highest priority queue but to adopt round-robin scheduling of this queue. Lower priority processes may be given longer quanta, but will be allowed to run less frequently.

c. The dispatcher is invoked automatically following an interrupt: this could be caused by a process requesting peripheral transfer, in which case the status of the process may change and thus the process would be removed from or added to the processor queue.

   Another source of interrupt is the real time clock which generates signals at preset intervals. If a process has run continually for its allotted quantum, it may have its priority changed.

   (The interrupt service routine would be responsible for changing the status of a process and adding/removing it from the queue as well as for changing the priority of a process, so that the dispatcher could allocate processors efficiently.)

Answer 6.

22.25 – 22.28

Answer 7.

a.

d	2_2 c	2_1 b	2_0 a	x
0	0	0	0	0
0	0	0	1	0
0	0	1	0	1
0	0	1	1	1
0	1	0	0	0
0	1	0	1	0
0	1	1	0	0
0	1	1	1	0
1	0	0	0	0
1	0	0	1	0
1	0	1	0	1
1	0	1	1	1
1	1	0	0	0
1	1	0	1	0
1	1	1	0	1
1	1	1	1	1

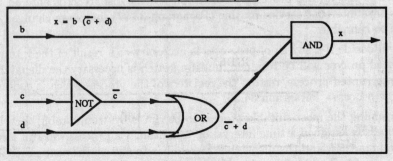

b. 1.8, 49.30 – 49.34

Answer 8.

a. 31.7 and four ways: (31.7 – 31.9).

b. Answers could include

    i. Using four 6-bit character codes, eg, 6-bit BCD

    ii. Using three 8-bit bytes, eg, ASCII with parity

1st	2nd	3rd	4th
6-bit code	6-bit code	6-bit code	6-bit code

Manipulation: Mask, shifts, swaps (31.13).

c. (39.14 – 39.17)

Answer 9. 1.16 – 1.19

Answer 10.

a. 51.4

b. 18.23

c. 18.26 and 46.5

d. 46.16

NB. Answers to the remaining questions are given in the supplement for teachers and lecturers, except where the publication of answers is not permitted by the examining board concerned.

Appendix 3 : Details omitted from the text for the sake of clarity

Appendix 3.1 : The Operation of the Processor

1. The diagram shown here provides a simplified summary of the operation of the processor in conjunction with memory and I/O devices.

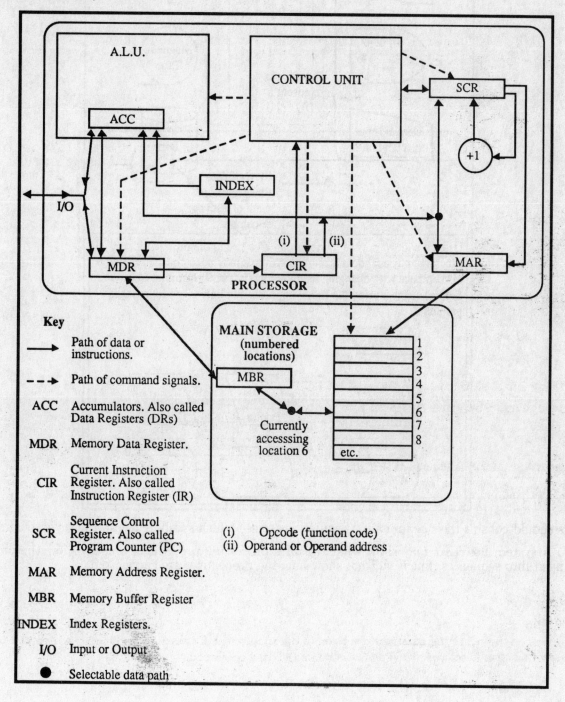

Key

→   Path of data or instructions.

- - →   Path of command signals.

ACC   Accumulators. Also called Data Registers (DRs)

MDR   Memory Data Register.

CIR   Current Instruction Register. Also called Instruction Register (IR)

SCR   Sequence Control Register. Also called Program Counter (PC)

MAR   Memory Address Register.

MBR   Memory Buffer Register

INDEX   Index Registers.

I/O   Input or Output

●   Selectable data path

(i)   Opcode (function code)
(ii)   Operand or Operand address

Appendix 3.2 Flowcharts

1. SYSTEMS FLOWCHART SYMBOLS.

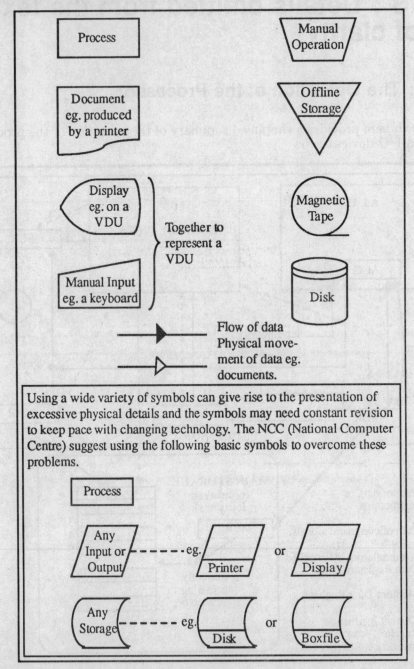

(Readers should consult their examination regulations to see which symbols to use their own examination.)

NB. A system flowchart may show what the data-processing procedures are, and how the procedures are arranged into sequences, but it will *not* show how the procedures are carried out.

2. PROGRAM FLOWCHART SYMBOLS.

The reader is recommended to use pseudocode rather than flowcharts when presenting algorithms because they tend to lead to a better "structured" solution. For situations where flowcharts are required the following common symbol convention may prove useful.

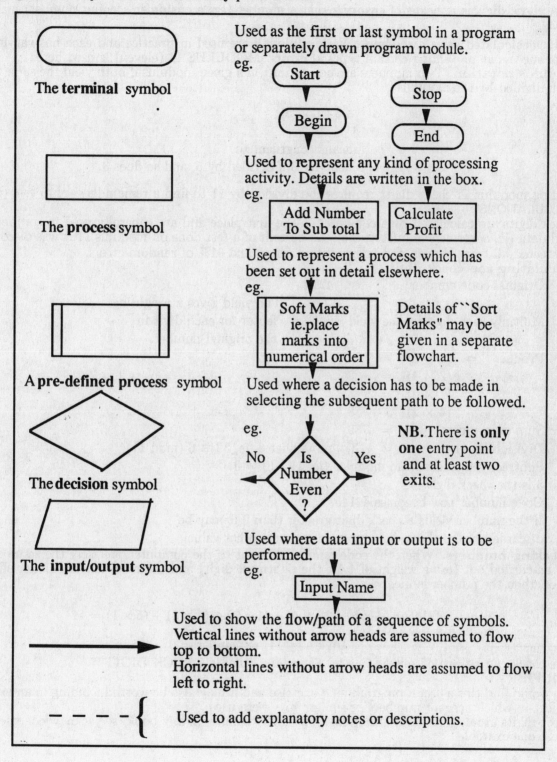

Appendix 3.3 : Modulo Numbers and Check Digits

INTRODUCTION

1. a. A check digit is a means of ensuring that a number (eg, a customer account number) maintains its validity.

   b. It is calculated using a modulus. Various moduli are used in practice and each has varying degrees of success at preventing certain types of errors. MODULUS 11 (eleven) is used here.

2. **Modulus notation.** Two numbers are **congruent** in a given modulus if both yield the same remainder when divided by the modulus

$$eg, \quad 8 \equiv 3 \ (mod \ 5)$$
$$\uparrow$$
$$means \ congruent \ to$$

   ie, 8 has remainder 3 if divided by 5, and so does 3.

3. Finding modulus 11 check digits requires the division by 11 to find a remainder, eg, $15 \equiv 4 \ (mod \ 11)$.

CALCULATIONS

4. Check digits are calculated by a computer in the first place and are generally used in conjunction with fixed data (ie, customers' numbers, etc). As a result of a test done on modulus 11 it was discovered that it detected all transcription and transposition errors and 91% of random errors.

5. **Calculating the check digit.**

   a. Original code number   4214

   b. Multiply each digit by the yield   5432 $\left\{ \begin{array}{l} \text{The yield gives a weighting} \\ \text{factor for each digit in} \\ \text{the original number.} \end{array} \right.$

   c. Product   = (4×5) =   20
                  (2×4) =   8
                  (1×3) =   3
                  (4×2) =   8

   d. Sum of products   =   39

   e. Division by 11   =   3,   remainder 6, ie, $39 \equiv 6 \ (mod \ 11)$

   f. Subtract remainder from modulus (ie, $11 - 6$) = 5

   g. 5 is the check digit.

   h. Code number now becomes 42145.

   i. If the number yields a check digit greater than 9 it may be discarded or the check digit replaced by some other value.

6. **Checking numbers.** When the code number is input to the computer precisely the same calculation can be carried out (using weight of 1 for the rightmost digit) and the resultant remainder should be 0. If not, then the number is incorrect.

$$42145 = (4 \times 5) + (2 \times 4) + (1 \times 3) + (4 \times 2) + (5 \times 1) = 44$$

Divide by 11; remainder = 0

7. This check can be carried out off-line by a machine called a CHECK DIGIT VERIFIER.

8. You would find this a useful programming exercise and it may also be worth including in an examination project in which account numbers or similar keys were used.

9. Check digits are used in many situations. The ISBN number in any book (see acknowledgement page ii) is just one example.

Appendix 3.4 : ASCII Control Characters

Binary Code	Decimal Value	Character Name	Description
0000 0000	0	NUL	All zeroes
0000 0001	1	SOH	Start of heading
0000 0010	2	STX	Start of text
0000 0011	3	ETX	End of text
0000 0100	4	EOT	End of transmission
0000 0101	5	ENQ	End of enquiry
0000 0110	6	ACK	Acknowledgment
0000 0111	7	BEL	Bell or an attention signal
0000 1000	8	BS	Back space
0000 1001	9	HT	Horizontal tabulation
0000 1010	10	LF	Line feed
0000 1011	11	VT	Vertical tabulation
0000 1100	12	FF	Form feed
0000 1101	13	CR	Carriage return
0000 1110	14	SO	Shift out
0000 1111	16	SI	Shift in
0001 0000	16	DLE	Data link escape
0001 0001	17	DC1	Device control 1
0001 0010	18	DC2	Device control 2
0001 0011	19	DC3	Device control 3
0001 0100	20	DC4	Device control 4
0001 0101	21	NAK	Negative acknowledgment
0001 0110	22	SYN	Synchronous or idle
0001 0111	23	ETB	End of transmission block
0001 1000	24	CAN	Cancel - error in data
0001 1001	25	EM	End of medium
0001 1010	26	SUB	Start of special sequence
0001 1011	27	ESC	Escape
0001 1100	28	FS	Information file separator
0001 1101	29	GS	Information group separator
0001 1110	30	RS	Information record separator
0001 1111	31	US	Information unit separator
0111 1111	127	DEL	Delete

Appendix 3 : Details omitted from the text for the sake of clarity

Appendix 3.5 : The Floating-point error formula

1. **The floating-point error formula.** This formula is used to find the maximum error in the result of a floating-point arithmetic operation. The general method is summarised by the formula:

$$R(x \ o \ y) = (xoy)(1 \pm \in) \quad \text{(See paragraph 4)}$$

where "o" represents one of the operations $+, -, \times$ or $\div$.
$\in$ is the **maximum relative error** for the given method of representation and $R(x \ o \ y)$ represents the worst result of the operation x o y.

2. **Examples.** (We continue with 3-digit decimal representations with $\in = 0.005$ as in 21a.)
   a. Consider the sum $195 + 23.4 = 218.4$ We take "o" as $+$, $x = 195$, $y = 23.4$ and $\in = 0.005$ substituting in the formula gives

$$R \ (195 + 23.4) = (195 + 23.4) \ (1 \pm 0.005)$$
$$\text{(We use the calculated value} = 218 \ (1 \pm 0.005)$$
$$\text{on the right-hand side)} = 218 \pm 1.09$$

   This tells us our *3-figure result* will have a maximum error of ± 1.09. The actual error is only 0.4 since the correct *result to 4 figures* is 218.4

   b. Consider $195 \times 23.4 = 4563 = 4560$ (3S)
   We take "o" as $\times$, x = 195, y = 23.4 and $\in = 0.005$
   substituting in the formula gives

$$R(195 \times 23.40) = (195 \times 23.4)(1 \pm 0.005)$$
$$\text{(We use the calculated value} = 4560(1 \pm 0.005)$$
$$\text{on the right-hand side)} = 4560 \pm 22.8$$

   This tells us our 3-figure result will have a maximum error of ± 22.8.

3. The main use of the floating-point error formula is in algebraic rather than numerical problems like those just demonstrated. Before working through an algebraic example we will deal with a problem to which the formula can be applied.

4. Equivalent algebraic formulae may not give results to the same accuracy because of the effects of rounding errors.
   Example. Consider the well-known relation $a^2 - b^2 = (a - b)(a + b)$
   If "a" is close to "b" then the right-hand side may give a more accurate value than the left.
   Take a = 3.17 and b = 2.95 and assume that *all intermediate results are rounded off to three figures.* This rounding corresponds to restoring the floating-point result at each stage of computer arithmetic. You may check the true result 1.3464 by performing the calculation to full accuracy, but we will use 3-figure accuracy.
   Using $a^2 - b^2$
   we have:
   $3.17^2 - 2.95^2 = 10.0 - 8.70 = 1.3$ (2S)
   Using (a − b) (a + b) we have:-
   $(3.17 - 2.95)(3.17 + 2.95) = 0.22 \times 6.12 = 1.35$ (3S)
   We see that the second method is superior and in this case it gives the true rounded value.
   Note: The advantage of using (a − b) (a + b) only occurs when a $\simeq$ b (try it with a = 31.7) and particularly if a − b is of the same **order of magnitude as** $\in$, ie, when (a − b) $\simeq \in$.

5. **A proof using the floating-point error formula.** We assume that the floating-point arithmetic in a particular computer is such that the result of each individual arithmetic operation has a relative error $\leq \in$ in magnitude. It is reasonable to also assume that errors of the order of $\in^2$ may be neglected. We can show that when "a" is approximately equal to "b" then (a − b) (a + b) is preferable to $a^2 - b^2$
   Proof using $R(x \ o \ y) = (x \ o \ y) \ (1 \pm \in)$
   a. Consider $a^2 - b^2$

$$\text{First Stage.} \quad R(a^2) = a^2(1 \pm \in) = a^2 \pm a^2 \in$$
$$R(b^2) = b^2(1 \pm \in) = b^2 \pm b^2 \in$$

   Second Stage.
$$R[(a^2 \pm a^2 \in) - (b^2 \pm b^2 \in)] = [(a^2 \pm a^2 \in) - (b^2 \pm b^2 \in)][1 \pm \in]$$
$$= a^2 - b^2 + 2(\pm a^2 \pm b^2) \in + (\pm a^2 \pm b^2) \in^2$$
$$\simeq a^2 - b^2 + 2(\pm a^2 \pm b^2) \in \quad \text{(i)}$$
$$(\in^2 \text{ terms ignored})$$

636

b. Consider $(a - b)(a + b)$

First Stage.
$$R(a - b) \qquad = (a - b)(1 \pm \epsilon) = a - b \pm (a - b) \epsilon$$
$$R(a + b) \qquad = (a + b)(1 + \epsilon) = a + b \pm (a + b) \epsilon$$

Second Stage.
$$R([(a - b) = (1 \pm \epsilon)] \quad [(a + b)(1 \pm \epsilon)] \quad = (a - b)(a + b)(1 \pm \epsilon)^3$$
$$\simeq (a^2 - b^2) \pm 3(a^2 - b^2) \qquad \text{(ii)}$$
$$\text{(ignoring terms in } \epsilon^2 \text{ and } \epsilon^3)$$

The magnitudes of the maximum errors in (i) and (ii) are $|2(a^2 + b^2)|$ and $|3(a^2 - b^2)|$ respectively. The second of these errors will be the smaller one if $a \simeq b$.

NB. The floating-point error formula is not intended for use in numerical computations. It is for use in establishing *error limits* for given algebraic expressions that are to be evaluated on a floating-point machine. For many numerical calculations the formulae may give maximum errors higher than those attainable in practice.

Appendix 4 : Course-work Projects and Study

Course Work.

Most of the examinations for which this book is a preparation require students to undertake a considerable amount of practical programming work throughout the course and include a project as part of the final examination.

Approaching Course work.

You may find the following ideas useful.

a. Try to relate your practical work to the theory you have covered so far (ie, turn principle into practice).
b. You can often build on earlier work or experience so look for:

   i. A pattern in a problem.
   ii. Similarities and differences between the present problem and those done earlier. (This helps you to build up a set of general programming skills.)

c. Keep your work in a suitable folder and in sufficient order that you can understand it later, eg, keep a diary or log.

Projects.

(If possible choose *real* problems with *real* data.)

a. Plan ahead and keep to deadlines as you prepare it.
b. It is easier to develop a project that has been clearly defined in terms of objectives at each stage and an overall aim.
c. Don't get sidetracked into trivial work that may make your program look nice when you should be tackling programming problems. The examiner will not be fooled by pages of printout that hide a lack of substance in the work.
d. The examiner has to be able to understand your project when he reads it. He can only mark what you give him, and may miss some of what you have submitted if it is not clearly presented.
e. The required contents of a project are usually specified for each examination. Make sure you include every section. In particular, projects should make sense to possible other users.

Other Study.

1. Visits to installations near your home can give you an insight into current practice.
2. Reading occasional articles in weekly computer magazines can give you details of modern ideas and developments and sometimes provide case studies, which act as a framework for examination answers.

INDEX

The format of the references is
chapter number . paragraph number.